# Laptops All-in-One Desk Reference For Dummies®

Cheat Sheet

## Keeping Your Laptop Safer

Book X reveals all you need to know to keep your laptop as safe as possible.

- ✔ Set up a firewall.
- ✔ Install an antivirus program.
- ✔ Install antispam and antispyware programs.
- ✔ Add an integrated security suite.
- ✔ Maintain your system.
- ✔ Lock the hardware.
- ✔ Create and use a strong password.
- ✔ Encrypt your disks.

## Nine Things to Pack in Your Laptop Bag

- ✔ Flash memory key: To store critical information off the hard drive.
- ✔ Recordable CD/DVD: To make backups of files on the road.
- ✔ Identification card: List your phone and e-mail and promise a reward.
- ✔ Mini-flashlight: Ever try to find something on the floor of an airplane?
- ✔ Ethernet cable: To connect to a wired network.
- ✔ Phone cord: For emergency use of the dial-up modem.
- ✔ Windows: A copy of the Windows install disk for emergency restarts.
- ✔ Reference: *Laptops For Dummies Quick Reference.*
- ✔ Bottle of pain reliever: Life on the road isn't all peaches and cream.

## Laptop Support Web Sites

Acer at http://global.acer.com/support

Compaq at www.compaq.com/support

Hewlett Packard at http://welcome.hp.com/country/us/en/support.html

IBM/Lenovo at www.lenovo.com/us/en

Toshiba at www.techsupport.toshiba.com

Windows Update at http://windowsupdate.microsoft.com

*For Dummies: Bestselling Book Series for Beginners*

# Laptops All-in-One Desk Reference For Dummies®

Cheat Sheet

## Most Useful Windows XP/Vista Keyboard Shortcuts

| Shortcut | Function |
| --- | --- |
| Ctrl + C | Copy |
| Ctrl + X | Cut |
| Ctrl + V | Paste |
| Ctrl + Z | Undo |
| Ctrl + A | Select all |
| Alt + Tab | Switch between open items |
| Alt + Esc | Cycle through items in the order opened |
| F5 | Update the active window |
| ⊞ | Display or hide the Start menu |
| ⊞ + Break | Display the System Properties dialog box |
| ⊞ + M | Minimize all of the windows |
| ⊞ + Shift + M | Restore the minimized windows |

## Taking It Easy On Your Battery

- ✔ If you're not using a device, turn it off.
- ✔ Avoid unnecessarily using the hard drive.
- ✔ Don't play a music CD while you work.
- ✔ Don't use external devices that draw power from the laptop battery.
- ✔ Stay away from high heat.
- ✔ Make sure the cooling vents aren't blocked.
- ✔ Turn down the light.
- ✔ Reduce the load on your microprocessor by not multitasking.
- ✔ Be aware of the varying demands of different software.
- ✔ Understand the difference between Hibernate and Standby (or Suspend).

## For Dummies: Bestselling Book Series for Beginners

# Laptops
## ALL-IN-ONE DESK REFERENCE
### FOR
# DUMMIES®

# Laptops
## ALL-IN-ONE DESK REFERENCE
### FOR
# DUMMIES®

by Corey Sandler

WILEY

Wiley Publishing, Inc.

**Laptops All-in-One Desk Reference For Dummies®**

Published by
**Wiley Publishing, Inc.**
111 River Street
Hoboken, NJ 07030-5774

www.wiley.com

Copyright © 2008 by Wiley Publishing, Inc., Indianapolis, Indiana

Published by Wiley Publishing, Inc., Indianapolis, Indiana

Published simultaneously in Canada

For general information on our other products and services, please contact our Customer Care Department within the U.S. at 800-762-2974, outside the U.S. at 317-572-3993, or fax 317-572-4002.

For technical support, please visit www.wiley.com/techsupport.

Wiley also publishes its books in a variety of electronic formats. Some content that appears in print may not be available in electronic books.

Library of Congress Control Number: 2008925788

ISBN: 978-0-470-14092-5

Manufactured in the United States of America

10  9  8  7  6  5  4  3  2  1

WILEY

# About the Author

Okay, I'll admit it: I've got a strange biography. I've been a writer all my life. My first semi-pro job was sports editor of my high school newspaper. (Go Commodores!) After college I was a political reporter for daily newspapers in Ohio and New York (I covered four national nominating conventions and two Presidential campaigns) and a correspondent for The Associated Press. And then, in 1983, I gave in to my inner geek and became the first Executive Editor of *PC Magazine*, back in the days when most people asked, "What is a PC?"

These days I keep my feet planted in four arenas; that's not an easy thing to do if you think about it. I write books about computers, history, sports, and travel. All told, I've written nearly 150 books and they've been translated into more than a dozen languages.

For all of my professional life I've been a road warrior. I started out with a notebook and a roll of dimes in my pocket. But by the early 1980s, I was one of the first users of a portable computer. That first machine was the size of a suitcase and each owner required an extension cord, an AC outlet, and a chiropractor. A few years later, though, I had one of the first battery-powered laptops, and in more than two decades I've almost never strayed more than an hour from home without one.

In fact, it's the laptop and the ability to connect to the world with or without wires that allow me to live far away from the real world: My wife Janice and I live at the end of a lane up from the beach on Nantucket Island, 30 miles out to sea from Cape Cod in Massachusetts.

# Dedication

To our one-time laptops William and Tessa, out of college (hooray!) and ready to strut their stuff.

## Publisher's Acknowledgments

We're proud of this book; please send us your comments through our online registration form located at www.dummies.com/register/.

Some of the people who helped bring this book to market include the following:

### Acquisitions, Editorial, and Media Development

**Project Editor:** Tonya Maddox Cupp

**Executive Editor:** Greg Croy

**Technical Editor:** Mark Chambers

**Editorial Manager:** Jodi Jensen

**Media Project Supervisor:** Laura Moss-Hollister

**Media Development Specialist:** Angela Denny

**Editorial Assistant:** Amanda Foxworth

**Sr. Editorial Assistant:** Cherie Case

**Cartoons:** Rich Tennant
(www.the5thwave.com)

### Composition Services

**Project Coordinator:** Patrick Redmond

**Layout and Graphics:** Reuben W. Davis, Stephanie D. Jumper, Ronald Terry, Christine Williams

**Proofreaders:** Laura Albert, Christine Sabooni

**Indexer:** Slivoskey Indexing Services

---

### Publishing and Editorial for Technology Dummies

**Richard Swadley,** Vice President and Executive Group Publisher

**Andy Cummings,** Vice President and Publisher

**Mary Bednarek,** Executive Acquisitions Director

**Mary C. Corder,** Editorial Director

### Publishing for Consumer Dummies

**Diane Graves Steele,** Vice President and Publisher

**Joyce Pepple,** Acquisitions Director

### Composition Services

**Gerry Fahey,** Vice President of Production Services

**Debbie Stailey,** Director of Composition Services

# Contents at a Glance

# Table of Contents

# Introduction

Your basic, truly wondrous laptop computer — a device that can take your dictation of the Great American Novel, balance your checkbook, sing you a song, show you a movie, and allow you to communicate with practically anyone in the world similarly equipped — weighs about six pounds.

Most wondrous of all, most new laptop computers don't come with a full instruction manual. (Not that those delivered with older machines were all that good.) From the very moment of the first personal computer's birth, it's always been a fact that the hardware was great, the software was amazing, and the manuals were awful. (The fact that they called the impenetrable prose "documentation" should have been a hint.)

It was for that very reason that the entire computer book–publishing industry, including the *For Dummies* series, was born. We professional writers thank the engineers every time we produce another book that translates Geekspeak to terms the rest of us can understand.

In *Laptops All-In-One Desk Reference For Dummies* you find news you can use. It's not my goal to teach you how to make your own laptop computer from a pile of sand and iron filings, and you're not going to learn how to write a software program to manage the countdown sequence of the space shuttle.

This easy-to-use, truly impressive all-in-one book weighs a shade under three pounds. It contains just about everything you need to know to select, set up, start up, and fix up a laptop computer.

## About This Book

Each of the ten mini-books deals with a particular subject. One more thing you do not need, then: A week's worth of uninterrupted time to plow through several hundred pages in sequence, from start to end — this book is a reference tool which can be read front to back, back to front, middle to the outsides, or with a direct dive into the page that matters most to you. Check out our handy and quite dandy index.

## How to Use This Book

If you've read one *For Dummies* book . . . well, you've not used them all, but you have some idea of how each author tries to present particular types of information and instructions in a particular way. You can call them conventions, or styles or things-that-are-always-shown-in-the-same-way. Here are a few of them.

### Technical terms

The first time that a new technical term is used in a particular mini-book or an extended section of the book, you'll see it marked in *italics* just like this. This should help you quickly scan a page if you're looking for laptop features and thingies like *USB port* or *webcams*.

### Web sites

Whenever I can, I'll refer you to Internet web sites that have information or utilities of other nifty things. You'll recognize them by either of two sets of letters: www.dummies.com is the most common form, indicating it is located on the World Wide Web.

http://microsoft.com may be a company that does its own thing, without regard to convention, or it may actually be a location on the Internet but not officially on the Web. I know this sounds like a distinction without a difference . . . and it probably is. Just recognize that the http:// part indicates that this is an Internet address.

Oh, and one more thing: I've tried as best I could to avoid ending a sentence with a Web address but sometimes it will happen. Ignore the period that may have been appended by the typesetter; it is not part of the address. The same thing goes for addresses that span two lines of the book; enter the whole address and ignore any hyphenations that may have snuck into the name.

## What You Absolutely Need

One of the beauties of a laptop is that all the basics are in one box: the computer, its memory, the microprocessor, a screen, and a built-in mouse or other pointing devices.

So, you need one of those.

You need an operating system, which manages the hardware and interprets the demands of the software. This book concentrates on the two most popular modern versions: Windows XP and Windows Vista.

And you need to have some nifty software. Again, I concentrate on the most common options here: Microsoft Word for word processing, Microsoft Excel for spreadsheets, Outlook Express for e-mail, and Microsoft PowerPoint for presentations.

At one time it seemed to make a difference to the marketing department to call basic machines *laptop computers* and the smallest devices *notebooks*. Even further back, a class of machines called *portable computers* was just barely moveable from one place to another. Today, at least for your purposes in this book, I make no distinction between laptops and slightly smaller notebooks.

If you use a different brand or type of office program, fear not. The basic concepts are the same, and this book helps you get a handle on them all.

## What You'll Probably Also Want

It's not essential that you have an Internet connection for your laptop, but I'm not going to lie to you, either: You'll want one. Here's why:

✦ An Internet link allows you to easily register, update, and fix problems with your operating system and its software.

✦ Having access to the Internet allows you to *download* (that means bring from somewhere else to your machine) today's newspaper, tomorrow's airline reservations, and all the music and video and *stuff* that's out there on the World Wide Web. You can't Google or perform any other kind of nifty search for information you never knew you needed without a connection to the Internet.

✦ A link to the Internet is required to send and receive e-mail, instant messages (IMs), and (did you know you could do this?) use your laptop as your own personal telephone system.

## What You May Want

Many laptop users have everything they need in the box as delivered from the manufacturer. They learn to use the slightly cramped keyboard and the downsized pointing device and can keep their files and programs within the available space on the built-in hard drive.

That's a worthy goal — especially for those who travel a great deal with a laptop. Simplicity is a virtue, and it also helps prevent backaches, shoulder strains, and lost objects.

But other users might need or want to replicate their desktop wherever they are. Here are some of the things you may want to add:

✦ An external mouse or other pointing device that offers more control or comfort than the built-in unit on a laptop

✦ An external hard drive to add a huge extra block of storage space

+ An external CD or DVD drive or writer to upgrade your laptop's facilities

+ A video camera (often called a *webcam*) that can send an image of your face along with your words

+ A media reader to allow direct upload (or download) of images or music to or from a digital camera or digital music device

+ A set of more-robust speakers to give some oomph to the movie or music you play

+ An external monitor for use as a second display or an LCD projector to put a presentation up on a silver screen

+ An extra battery that sits beneath or alongside the laptop to solve the problem of a very, very long airplane flight or travel in places where electrical outlets are few and far between

## What You Don't Need

You don't need these things to be qualified to read this book:

+ Prior experience on the job

+ Parental guidance

+ An advanced degree in computer science (or an unadvanced degree, for that matter)

## Icons Used in This Book

Special icons in this book draw your attention to diamonds mixed in amongst the pearls of wisdom. One icon even rings your chimes to warn you of danger.

Stop! Here there be dragons. Well, not really dragons, but dangers and pit-falls and problems that you don't want to run into.

This icon suggests that you fail to forget, decline to overlook, and do not lose recall of something important. Okay, these are things you should remember.

This good stuff will save you time, make it easier to do your work, and other-wise improve your quality of life.

Into each life a little bit of complexity must fall, especially when it comes to high technology. I promise to be gentle, and concentrate on clearing the air instead of fogging your mind.

# How This Book Is Organized

The smart people at Dummies world headquarters call this particular version of their best-selling series an *All-In-One Desk Reference,* which I abbreviated in my planning as AIO-DR and pronounced "Yeow, doctor." But don't let its size and heft scare you; the beauty of the Yeow scheme is that it is broken up into bite-size pieces.

The covers hold 10 mini books, each dealing with a particular subject. You can go directly to any one of them (the index or table of contents will help) or you can read from front to back or back to front.

Here are the books, and what they contain.

## Book I: Choosing the Best Laptop

You explore the nature of a laptop and then read the important difference between a need and a want. Then I take you a guided tour of a modern laptop and introduce you to the essentials of microprocessors, memory, and operating systems. And then I discuss laptop triage: When something goes wrong, is it worth fixing or is it time to exercise your credit card?

## Book II: Setting Up Your Laptop

Are you licensed to operate a computer? I tell you what you need to know about choosing, using, and upgrading the Windows operating system. And I discuss the framework used by Windows to keep all of your letters and numbers from bumping into each other: files, folders, windows, and more.

## Book III: Running Basic Windows Operations

What exactly can you do with this thing called an operating system? You start with the built-in application, utilities, and other facilities of Windows.

## Book IV: Using Common Applications

Here you find the news you can use about the most common software installed on laptops. I concentrate on the most current version of Microsoft Office, including Word, Excel, and PowerPoint. But fear not: The same principles apply to older versions, as well as to competitive products from other companies.

## Book V: Playing with Multimedia

Man and woman do not live by work alone; sometimes we get to steal a few moments to play, or listen to music, or watch a movie. Here I discuss all sorts of media, including using your laptop to broadcast your own video and audio.

## Book VI: Managing Your Power Supply

Footloose and fancy free, your laptop can carry its own source of power with it to the beach (watch out for sand in the keyboard), on an airplane (beware the flight attendant with the pitcher of coffee), and anywhere else you'd care to take it (don't let it out of your sight). In this book I discuss how to manage your batteries and AC power supplies.

## Book VII: Upgrading Your Laptop

Within the bounds of reason and the laws of physics, your laptop can be more tomorrow than it is today. Here I tell you how you can add memory, increase the size of the hard disk drive, and work with almost any kind of external computing device.

## Book VIII: Networking and Linking to the Internet

Your laptop is a marvelous device all by itself, but why limit yourself in that way? Explore networking to other computers with wires and in all manners of wireless communication. I tell you what you need to know about the Internet, e-mail, and how to use your laptop as a telephone. Really.

## Book IX: Protecting Your Laptop

Be careful out there. The world isn't a perfect place. In this mini-book I discuss ways to lock down your hardware, hold on to your personal and financial information, and protect you and your machine from the scourge of computer viruses, spam, spyware, and other, ugly perversions of modern technology.

## Book X: Troubleshooting Common Problems

Alas, sooner or later something will go bump in the night or boom on your screen. But not all hardware or software injuries are fatal; I show you ways to diagnose problems, make repairs, and get back out on the road where you belong.

# Book I

# Choosing the Best Laptop

# Contents at a Glance

# Chapter 1: Knowing What You Want, Getting What You Need

## In This Chapter

✓ Comparing needs and wants

✓ Knowing when the price is right

✓ Deciding whether you're an off-the-shelf or custom-fit person

*I* know what you want: a screaming-fast laptop with a gigantic hard disk; a zippy, high-resolution DVD drive; a sparkling widescreen display the size of an opened phone book; a pair of speakers with a deep bass subwoofer; and a full-sized, no-compromise keyboard.

Oh, and you want the whole thing to weigh three pounds, fit into a tiny carry-on bag, and be constructed out of bulletproof titanium.

And the cost: You could get a desktop system with all of these qualities — and more — for about $1,000. So you want to spend that much — or less — for a small box to take with you on an airplane, a commuter train, or from one room in your house to another.

## Figuring Out What You Really Need

Before I gently introduce you to the economics of laptops, allow me to raise a different question: What do you really need?

You *need* transportation to get from home to the supermarket and back, a distance of 3.2 miles with a local speed limit of 30 miles per hour, a task that could be accomplished in a 1989 Yugo GVX with a 55-horsepower hamster cage of an engine, 0-to-45 miles an hour eventually, and a big badonkadonk hatchback with plenty of room for groceries.

You *want* a 640-horsepower Lamborghini Murciélago capable of going from standstill to 60 miles per hour in 3.4 seconds. You may have room for a bag of chips and a six-pack buckled into the passenger seat.

In city traffic, both cars get you to Super Bag & Stuff in exactly the same amount of time. One might cost you a few thousand dollars and the other a few hundred thousand dollars. The Yugo can handle dents and scratches and other indignities without anyone noticing; you'll probably want to hire an armed guard and bring a set of portable guardrails (in a separate truck) to protect the Lamborghini from evildoers.

Obviously, in this extreme example I present a situation where the user needs a basic machine, not an overpriced headache. But my bigger point is this: There is no benefit to going to extremes for features that you will not use, or that bring problems with them.

Now consider a different scenario, and this time I stick to computers instead of cars. You want to travel with a portable version of the multimedia megastar that you use at work or home; you truly need to edit digital photos, and to capture and edit digital video from a camcorder or TV tuner. And you require a device that is sturdy enough to pass through airport screening several times a week but light enough for you to avoid a visit to the chiropractor at the end of every trip.

In this situation, money invested in speed, capacity, and construction pays off in true utility. And so, with great pride and apprehension I present the first of Sandler's rules for laptop users:

✦ **Differentiate between your needs and your wants, and get a laptop that comes closest to your requirements instead of your wishes.** Buy a laptop that meets your needs, and spend the extra bucks taking it places.

And following close behind, Sandler's second rule for laptop users:

✦ **Whatever you buy today will immediately be outdated.** Rapid obsolescence doesn't matter because the realistic useful life for a laptop (or a desktop computer) is about 3.5 years. Capabilities go up month by month while prices remain stable or decline over time. I bet you had little understanding of how you would use a laptop three years ago; your laptop needs three years from now will be different from today's.

That doesn't necessarily mean that your laptop will fall apart like a one-horse shay after four years; a well-built machine may last for many years. However, the pace of hardware and software advancements usually makes today's hot new product look very old and stale after a few dozen moons have passed.

Now: Define the difference between your needs and your wants. You can get what you want, but not without some compromises and challenges.

You might want to sit down and ask yourself some questions. (Be sure to do this in a private place or people will think you're acting a bit odd, or odder than usual.)

✦ Is *fast* good enough or do I need *super-duper turbocharged faster than fast?* (The latest and greatest microprocessors are marvelously zippy, but most laptop users may never tax them to the fullest; word processors and web browsers work just fine with a CPU a step or two below the fastest processors on the market. The only tax here is the price you pay if you buy more speed than you need.)

✦ Do I need a super-sized screen or will a more standard screen suffice? (A big screen looks great and is easier to read, but the laptop will be larger, heavier, and a few hundred dollars more expensive.)

✦ How many hours of battery life do I really need? (If the longest time you anticipate being between wall outlets is two hours, don't pay for a larger-capacity battery. More power adds weight and cost.)

✦ Am I willing to pay a big premium to get less, or can I handle an extra pound in my traveling case? (When it comes to size and weight, less costs more.)

A super-powered laptop computer is going to be relatively big and heavy. A super-lightweight, ultra-small laptop will amaze you with its size and heft, but not with its screen size, durability, and special features. And both the super-power and super-lightweight machines cost significantly more than a middle-of-the-road machine.

Just one example of the highest of tech and the lowest of weight: Toshiba's Portege R500 series includes a model with *solid state storage* (a set of lightweight memory chips that retain data even when the power is turned off, instead of a hard disk drive) and a superb but relatively small (12-inch diagonal) display. Because there is no disk drive (no CD or DVD drive, either), the laptop's battery can be smaller because of lower demand. The bottom line: a fast machine that weighs 1.72 pounds, and a price that is more than double that of a middle-of-the-market laptop.

## Squeezing the Goods into Your Lap (top)

In computers, smaller is more expensive than larger, and extra poundage costs less than a well-made lightweight. The reason for this is something engineers call *integration.* You can think of it as the cost of shrinking something big and complex down to something tiny and even more complicated. It's kind of the opposite of the economics of housing: It's all about the real estate, but in the case of laptops (there's a pun in there), the smaller the plot, the more valuable it is.

# Evolution

The first personal computers (like the original IBM PC that I still have stuffed deep in a closet of my office) were the size of a suitcase — and not the kind that could fit in an airplane's overhead bin. The *motherboard,* which held the computer's microprocessor brain, its *random access memory (RAM),* and other supporting chips was more than a foot square and even at that size it was not large enough to hold all of the computer's electronics.

On the original personal computer, book-sized circuit boards rose from individual slots at right angles from the motherboard. These boards were called *adapters;* despite the name, they added essential features to the computer. One adapter allowed the computer to display characters or graphics on a monitor; another added audio; and yet another adapted the computer for work with a printer or an external modem. (And just for the record, my first IBM PC — the one that launched me on what has been a 25-year career as a technology writer — cost nearly $5,000 for a system that is less capable than one of today's iPod music and video players or a cell phone with a built-in calculator.)

Everything in a laptop is squeezed down and packed tightly. Single chips now do the work that used to be performed by dozens of circuits, and new microprocessor families can do their amazing calculations and manipulations while sipping very shallowly from the cup of electrons in the rechargeable battery that makes a laptop truly portable.

Today's *liquid crystal diode (LCD)* displays have advanced from primitive low-resolution monochrome (single color, like white-on-black or green-on-black) to screens that can display millions of different shades at resolutions meeting or exceeding anything you're likely to find on a desktop.

Then the engineers have to figure out ways to protect the delicate innards from damage while the notebook is on the move. They do this in a number of ways including reinforced plastic cases, super-strong (and expensive) metal cases, internal bracing, cushioning and shock absorbers, and other technologies. Among the highest-tech features: a built-in sensor that detects an impending (or actual) tumble and retracts the read-write heads and shuts off the vulnerable hard disk drive before impact.

Most quality notebooks are designed to survive falling off a desktop to the floor at least once; in my experience, a more common field test is a tumble from the exit chute of an airport X-ray machine. I'd suggest you do your research in reviews and specifications and not conduct your own tests, though. In this instance the best protection is a sturdy work surface and a tight grip on your laptop at the airport.

And there's one more element — you can call it a *factor,* as in the engineering term *form factor.* That's a fancy word for the laptop's shape, dimensions, and weight. The fanciest trick performed by computer designers is packing 30 pounds of computer, monitor, and accessories into a 5-pound box roughly the size of a, well, notebook.

If you're buying apples, you generally pay by the pound. If you're buying shelter, a mansion will always cost more than a trailer. But when it comes to laptops, the economics are upside down. If you're comparing laptops with equal speed and capabilities, a two-pound laptop almost always costs more than a five-pound model. (The rare exception: special industrialized or militarized laptops intended for use in very dirty or rough environments. These are built like armored tanks.)

Designers reduce weight in several ways:

✦ Using exotic construction materials like titanium or machined aluminum for the cases and some internal structural components

✦ Making smaller, lighter motherboards based on continually tighter integration of processors, chipsets, and other components

✦ Removing unnecessary appendages such as dial-up modems and floppy disk drives

✦ Using new lightweight technologies for rechargeable batteries

✦ Bucking the trend toward supersize widescreen LCDs, and instead using smaller and lighter displays

# Approaching a Laptop Purchase

Henry Ford made it so easy for buyers of his Model T, offering it in any color customers wanted as long as they wanted black. Actually, that was only partly true; there was a period when buyers could get off-black, shiny black, and even a few shades of very dark green that were not quite black. But you get the idea: He built his company on its ability to mass produce millions of copies of the basic model at a low price.

The idea was appealing, at least at the start. Buyers had very few decisions to make because there were very few variations. And the nearly identical fleet made it easy for owners and mechanics to make repairs or swap components.

The first laptop computers were offered in a somewhat similar manufacturing and marketing environment. First of all, users were not meant to open the boxes. And secondly, the machines were offered in just a few basic configurations. Buyers looked for a model based around a particular processor, with a specific amount of RAM, and a particular size of hard drive.

Today, though, laptops own nearly half of the personal computer market share. And though many retail and online stores sell "take-it-or-leave-it" prepackaged laptops, you can also custom configure many models by direct order from a factory or reseller. And designs now offer a wide range of sockets, ports, bays, and openings for upgrades for currently used machines.

How do you know which purchase route to take?

## Buying a package

A preconfigured package may have a number of advantages to offer you:

✦ **You want it now.** Models are usually available in stores or from online sellers for immediate purchase. What you see is what you get, and you can get it now (or within a couple days if it is shipped to you).

✦ **You want it cheaper.** Some preconfigured models are less expensive than comparable systems that are custom ordered from a manufacturer. The reason? Like Henry Ford, computer makers can maximize their profit by making a whole bunch of identical models; the cost of components goes down, as does marketing, support, and maintenance.

✦ **You want it without much thought.** Would you be happiest picking a model off the shelf at an electronics store or from an online listing? It can free you from having to make decisions.

## Configuring your own

You may want full control over as many components of your machine as possible. Why customize?

✦ **You're choosy about what you want.** You can get pretty close to the exact components that you need, and exclude some that you don't want. As one example, if you work with a lot of graphics, you may want to order a machine with an extra-large hard disk drive (500MB on the road, no problem) and a customized graphics adapter within the case.

Although some preconfigured machines represent great bargains because they are part of a large assembly line run (the Model T theory), you may also find terrific bargains on a configure-yourself machine if the manufacturer wants to put on a sale or if the company is clearing out particular components.

✦ **You want the latest and greatest.** Any preconfigured machine you see on the shelves or online was put together months ago. A machine you custom order may offer some components that are brand new to the market, and come with the latest software versions and updated drivers.

When customizing, you choose a base model from companies like Dell, Hewlett-Packard, Lenovo, Toshiba, and others, and then configure internal components such as the following:

✦ Microprocessor type and speed, within the range of chips supported by the particular motherboard used in each model.

✦ Type, amount, and speed of RAM.

✦ Hard disk drive size and speed, along with extra options such as encryption and automated backup systems.

✦ Choice of an operating system. As this book goes to press Microsoft Windows was offered in at least three Windows XP versions and four consumer versions and a few more specialized editions of Windows Vista. Some users may want to use an alternate operating system, and many manufacturers will assist you in meeting that specification.

✦ Resolution (an LCD screen draws characters and images with millions of tiny dots; the more dots that are packed per square inch generally translates to the sharpness of the screen and/or the amount of information that can be shown) of the display, along with some special features such as an antiglare surface or a high brightness level.

✦ Choice between an *integrated* (built-in) graphics controller that uses some of the system RAM to construct images, or a separate graphics card plugged into the internal electronics of the system and equipped with its own RAM and specialized processor.

✦ Selection of a CD or DVD drive, with options including writing recordable discs and using the latest technology, called BluRay, to play high-resolution movies (which is, for most of us — at least right now — a want and not a need).

✦ Options to add various speeds and designs for WiFi wireless communication for Internet and e-mail, and Bluetooth for managing cordless mice and information interchange with music players and other devices.

✦ Selection between basic or upgraded audio circuitry, basic or high-fidelity internal speakers, and basic or specialized sound synthesis and playback software.

✦ Choosing between the standard battery or a more capacious (and usually heavier) battery that offers extended life between recharges.

## Plugging into a custom machine

The third option for buying a laptop is to find a preconfigured package that is as close as you can get to your needs . . . and then customize the rest yourself. Depending on the machine's design, you might add some parts for installation within compartments on the case. And then there is the amazing and evolving world of external attachments.

First, consider the components that you can install into compartments on many modern laptops:

✦ RAM. Nearly every current laptop has a small panel on the underside of the machine that you can open to expose one or two sockets that hold memory modules. In Book VII I discuss the process of adding memory. . . and the unhappy fact that sometimes you have to remove perfectly good memory to install new and larger modules.

✦ WiFi or Bluetooth communications. Some laptop designs let you install a new wireless communication module or update an existing one by opening another compartment or slot on the bottom or side of the case, or by installing a new device into a PC Card or ExpressCard slot.

✦ Batteries. Laptop batteries are meant to be easily changed, usually with the unlatching of a catch or two on the bottom. In most situations you can replace an old battery with a new power source of the same design; you may be able to upgrade to a battery that holds more power, allowing for longer time between recharges.

✦ CD, DVD, floppy disk drive, and other devices. Some laptops have bays that allow easy plug-and-play installation. This sort of swap usually requires use of a customized part sold by the laptop manufacturer, but there are also some third-party manufacturers that sell adapters to allow you to use off-the-shelf drives.

Now consider the things you can do with plugs and cables. Modern laptops now come equipped with at least two and sometimes four or more all-purpose *ports* that can connect to external devices. The most common modern port is called the *Universal Serial Bus (USB);* coming into increasing use is a newer design called *External Serial ATA (eSATA).*

I define and discuss both of these important superhighways to your computer's motherboard in the next chapter. For the moment, allow me to offer the following: They are both extremely flexible and very fast. You need an extra hard drive? Insert the cable in one of the ports. An external mouse? Plug one in.

# Chapter 2: Touring a Modern Laptop

## In This Chapter

✔ Going inside the box

✔ Seeing ports of call

✔ Knowing what goes where

*L*ittle boxes on the store shelf. Little boxes made of ticky-tacky. And they all look the same.

Okay, all of you who weren't alive during the 1960s — or were but don't remember them: There was this song by Malvina Reynolds that lampooned the dull, look-alike suburbs that were being constructed at the time. The song goes on, "There's a green one and a pink one, and a blue one and a yellow one," and don't you know, they all look just the same.

So what does this have to do with laptop computers? To begin, they all are basically little boxes of roughly the same dimensions. And interestingly, nearly all are mostly black or silver.

## Flipping Your Lid

Unlike a desktop PC, the interior of a laptop computer isn't intended to be examined by mere users. Opening a case is a difficult task often requiring specialized tools. Reassembling the case is even more difficult because the internal parts are so tiny and so tightly integrated. (And nearly every laptop computer manufacturer promises to void your warranty if they determine you've poked around in places where you're not authorized to go.)

But on behalf of you, the reader, I have broken the secret bonds of laptops many times; my toolkit includes weapons such as Torx drivers, tiny jeweler's pliers, and other implements of miniaturized exploration. My report is thus: A laptop's interior is a dark and cramped place. But in the end, its guts are not all that different from an ordinary PC — that is, if you think of a desktop computer that has been run over several times by a steamroller. Think thin.

To be precise about it, a laptop is actually made up of a pair of containers:

✦ A top box that contains the screen and its supporting electronics

✦ A bottom box that holds the motherboard, memory, disk drives, pointing device, keyboard, and one or more batteries

There's a hinge that connects the two boxes and a set of ribbon cables that bring power and information from the bottom to the top.

If you consider the common desktop PC, you'll realize that it is basically a two-dimensional object — at least as far as users are concerned. The box has six surfaces, but only two are for devices and connectors. There's a front, which has a power switch, one or more CD or DVD drives and sometimes a floppy disk drive; most modern machines also offer one or two USB ports on the front for quick attachment of music players or card readers for digital or video cameras. And then there is the back of the PC, which is usually a thicket of ports and connectors: more USB ports, inputs and outputs for the audio system, and a connector for the plug that brings AC power from the wall. That's it: nothing on the top, nothing on the bottom, nothing on the sides.

But a laptop computer, compressed into two small boxes, has no space to spare. Across the pair of boxes are 12 surfaces, and 8 on a typical laptop are for one purpose or another.

## Saving Your Box Top

Start your tour with the upper section and work your way down and around. At the very top of the upper box is a latch or other device that keeps the two halves together. When you release the latch, the laptop opens like a clamshell (which was one of the original industry names for this type of design — a clamshell computer).

The top half of the clamshell holds the display and its associated electronics. Typical screen sizes (measured on the diagonal) range from about 10 inches for the lightest and smallest models to 17 inches for multimedia spectaculars.

Unless you're planning to build your own LCD some day, here's what you need to know: An LCD works by sending tiny amounts of electrical current to tiny spots of a compound called *liquid crystal*. In most designs, a dot becomes dark when energized and goes clear when the power is taken away. Tiny color filters sit in front of each dot, and combinations of dots produce various hues. In most designs, a lamp — often a version of a fluorescent tube — provides backlighting that shines through the dots to present an image onscreen.

A screen needs only a small amount of space around its edges to connect a grid of tiny wires that provide power to individual picture elements *(pixels)* on the screen. This allows for more viewable real estate than on an old-style *cathode-ray tube (CRT)* monitor, which required a frame of at least an inch.

LCDs are thin, perhaps one-quarter of an inch thick or less, and the screen itself is fragile and could easily be scratched or cut. Manufacturers place a protective surface across the front of the screen to guard against scratches and damage. Some models include a special filter to deflect glare and some add a privacy screen that reduces the angle of view. You probably want to see your television screen from almost anywhere in your living room; when it comes to your laptop, you might want not want the stranger sitting alongside you on an airplane to have a clear view of your screen.

In addition to the frame that surrounds the display, some manufacturers add a sturdy plastic or metal *roll cage* to guard against damage to the display as the result of a fall or other insults it might suffer. Even with the cage, putting a heavy object on top of your laptop is not a good idea — it's not a bullet-proof shield. And one other issue: For many of us, the biggest threat our laptop computer faces is the sudden recline of the seat in front of us on an airplane.

What's the best seat on an airplane for a road warrior with a laptop computer? Well, First Class isn't bad, but if you're back with the common folk in Economy, try to get a seat in an exit row. On most airplanes that row is wider and the seat in front of you doesn't recline. If you're in a regular row, consider politely asking the person seated in front of you to give you advance warning before reclining the seat. If that doesn't work, wedge your knee against the seat.

On some of the latest machines, the clamshell's upper half is also home to a tiny lens and digital Webcam for video or photos; one or two audio microphones may be nearby. At the bottom of the upper half are the hinges and hidden within them (or in the gap between the two pieces) is the ribbon cable carrying power and electronic information.

Although the ribbon cable connecting the upper and lower halves of a laptop computer is generally well engineered and protected, *do not* bend the display too far back or to spread it too quickly. It is possible — trust me, I've done it — to disable an otherwise perfectly good laptop by opening it so wide that the cable becomes disconnected from its internal connection. It can cost a few hundred dollars to have a technician open the case and plug the cable back in.

# Getting to the Bottom of the Box

Let me define the surfaces for the bottom box: top, bottom, back, and four sides.

The top of the bottom box — the upper flat surface — is home to most of a laptop's built-in user-input devices. What is a *user-input device?* It's anything that allows you — the user — to directly instruct the computer; I'm talking about the keyboard, the touchpad or other mouse equivalent, and special-purpose buttons and switches. (WiFi and other wireless communication ports and connectors to external components aren't user-input devices.)

The bottom of the bottom box holds several access covers. These compartments most commonly hold slots for RAM, allowing the user to add more memory without the need to have a technician open the case. On some models, other compartments are available for enhancement or replacement of WiFi transceivers.

Many laptop owners dream of the day when they can upgrade their graphics adapter through an externally accessible compartment; such a design may be offered some day. Until then, only a handful of laptops let you change the graphics adapter, and the process requires opening the case, not just a compartment. If you need high-speed graphics, shop for a laptop with that capability right from the start.

The sides of the bottom box are typically for quickly, temporarily attaching plug-in devices. You may also find a volume control for audio systems on the side; other designs place the volume control on the front or on top, near the keyboard.

One some models, the bottom back is primarily for attaching devices when the laptop is in repose on a desk. These attachments begin with the power connector for the AC adapter and typically include a monitor's video output and modem and Ethernet cable connectors. Many of the latest machines have cleared the back bottom of all connectors. This serves important purposes: It lessens the chances of damage to the connectors and allows a more robust hinge between the LCD and the bottom box, which protects the internal electrical cabling and creates a more substantial frame.

Throughout much of this book I use a Toshiba Satellite P205 as an example of a modern laptop. (See Figure 2-1.) This fully equipped model includes a brilliant 17-inch widescreen LCD, a 200GB hard drive, WiFi and wired Internet access, and a CD/DVD player and recorder. The built-in pointing device is a large touchpad, located slightly left of center below the spacebar.

On modern machines, the AC adapter, external video port, and several sets of USB ports are located on one or another of the sides of the bottom box.

**Figure 2-1:**
Toshiba
Satellite
P205.

## Top of the bottom box

The most common user-input devices are described in this section, starting
with the biggest and most obvious. (Have you guessed what that is?)

### Keyboards

Modern laptops (except for super-small, super-lightweight models) offer a
keyboard almost as large as those attached to a desktop computer. (A typical desktop keyboard devotes about 11 inches to its core components — the
alphanumeric keys for letters and numbers, plus a set of *F* (or *function* or *Fn*)
keys, and shift keys including Alt, Ctrl, and Windows-specific keys).

Not for the germophobic: In most homes or offices, what are the two dirtiest,
most germ-laden places? One is the door handle out of your bathroom, and
the other is . . . your computer keyboard. Think about it: Everything that's
on your fingers gets transferred to the keys, and things only get worse if you
eat at your desk. Don't put your keyboard into the dishwasher, but do use a
clean rag or gauze dampened with an antiseptic cleaner once a week or so.
You can also use prepackaged keyboard wipes or similar products intended
to clean up after baby.

On smaller notebook computers, the keyboard doesn't include separate
numeric keys. And you also generally find smaller keytops and — this
matters more to some users than to others — a significantly shorter *travel
distance,* which is one of a number of technical terms used by manufacturers
to measure how far the key has to be pushed before it makes electrical contact with the tiny switch that lies beneath. What you have here is a matter
of physics. (Remember the idea of cramming ten pounds of stuff into a
five-pound box?) Keys on a desktop keyboard can be elevated a quarter-inch
or more and use a fairly robust spring (or a rubber-like dome that serves the
same purpose) to provide feedback to your fingers as you type. But on a

laptop, everything is shrunken, and a bit of protective space must cushion the top of the keys and the front of the LCD when the clamshell is closed. And so on a laptop, the keys barely rise above the surface and the travel distance is greatly reduced.

However, a new class of widescreen laptops have arrived, and they're equipped with super-sized LCD screens. On the demonstration model Toshiba Satellite P205, the oversized LCD within the top box leaves plenty of room on the bottom box for a slightly more spread-out keyboard that includes a numerical keypad. (See Figure 2-2.) As a bonus, these larger laptops also often have enough space to permit a decent set of speakers.

**Figure 2-2:**
The wide keyboard on the Toshiba Satellite P205 model includes a nearly full-sized keyboard with a separate numeric keypad, as well as a complete set of function keys.

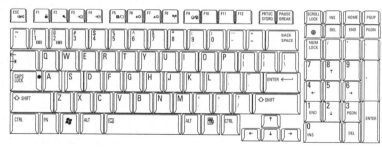

*Courtesy of Toshiba America, Inc.*

Some laptop users have no problem at all with the smaller, more tightly spaced, and very "touchy" keys. Others, with large hands and a tendency to punch the keys rather heavily (like me), often find that typing speed and accuracy on a laptop are noticeably less than on a desktop keyboard. Over time, though, you can get used to almost anything, it seems.

### Function and other special-purpose keys

Computer designers have incorporated a full set of Control (Ctrl) commands, and then added Alternate (or Alt) characters that don't show on the keyboard but that you can print. Today these special characters are usually easier to find by choosing a special symbols font, but the old Alt shift characters are still there, deep down in all current versions of Windows.

# A Royal pain

Way back in the dinosaur era of computerdom, keyboards weren't much different than a typewriter's. As I type these words, I realize that some of you may have never used a typewriter; they were amazing devices, combining efficient user input with a built-in printer. What they lacked, of course, was what makes computers so attractive: intelligence, storage, and the ability to delete, insert, move, and otherwise manipulate text.

The first computer keyboards merged the basic functions of a typewriter with the specialized characters that had been inserted into teletype and similar machines. One of the first new keys was Escape, which was basically a way to wave your hand in the machine's face and say "Stop" when things started to go awry, as they often did. Then came the idea of adding extra levels of shift. Pressing a Shift key typed a capital letter instead of a lowercase character.

The first new level of shift was Control (or Ctrl), which added a whole new set of symbols

intended to give direct instructions to the computer. For example, a Ctrl + M key combination was a carriage return. (What, you may ask, is a *carriage return?* Most typewriters were designed to have the paper move from right to left as characters were pounded onto them; at the end of a line or a paragraph, the carriage — which included a roller to advance the paper up or down — was returned all the way to the right so you could begin typing the next line.)

PCs also picked up special-purpose keys that are part and parcel of how the computer has gone past the typewriter. We've got Insert and Delete (or Ins and Del) to add or remove characters. To quickly move to the top or bottom or beginning or end of a line or a page or a selection, you've got Home, End, Page Up (PgUp), and Page Down (PgDn). To capture an image on the screen, you've got Print Screen (PrtSc or PrtScr on some laptops). And since the arrival of Windows 98, many keyboards have also sported a Windows key that brings up the operating system's Start menu with just one push.

Start by pressing the NumLock key (another form of Shift) and use the numeric keypad. Press and hold Alt while picking a number of as many as four digits. For example, if you've got a yen to use the Japanese currency symbol, type Alt + 157 and you see ¥. If you're wondering how to show you've still got some cents, try Alt + 155 and receive ¢. Happy? Try Alt + 1 for ☺. The Euro symbol (€), which may be of some real value to users, is found in the latest set of additions to the codes, at Alt + 0128.

But all of this is just prelude to what is (thus far) the ultimate in hardware expansion of the keyboard: the function, or Fn, keys. Designers at first added ten keys; modern keyboards offer an even dozen. You can assign function keys to a particular purpose within a program; for instance, F1 usually calls forth an application's Help screen. F12 often invokes the Save As command.

On a laptop, though, function keys are often assigned all sorts of special functions that exist outside the operating system and applications running under it. In Table 2-1, you can see the special assignments (called Hot Keys by Toshiba) given nine of the function keys on the Toshiba Satellite P205 laptop.

| Table 2-1 | Toshiba Hot Keys |
|---|---|
| *Key* | *Function* |
| F1 🔒 | Activates the Security Lock. The screen clears and the user login screen appears. You must log back in to use the computer. |
| F2 🔍 | Displays available power options. Pressing the key cycles through options. |
| F3 → | Puts the laptop in Sleep or Standby mode. |
| F4 → | Puts the laptop in Hibernation mode. |
| F5 💻 ○ | Toggles among sending video output to the built-in LCD, an external monitor, or both. |
| F6 ▼☼ | Decreases the LCD screen brightness each time you touch it. You can see the brightness level as a number or as a position on a slider onscreen. |
| F6 ▲☼ | Increases the LCD brightness each time you touch it. You can see the brightness level as a number or as a position on a slider onscreen. |
| F8 📶 | Enables or disables installed wireless facilities, including WiFi a Bluetooth. |
| F9 ⊡/⊞ | Enables or disables the touchpad or other built-in pointing device. |

*Images courtesy Toshiba America, Inc.*

You can keep an external keyboard on your desktop and plug it into your portable computer as a substitute for the built-in facilities when you're off the road. You can attach external keyboards to USB ports or to a PS/2 connector if the laptop maker provides one.

### Touchpads, pointers, and mini-mice

Techie-types like to rhapsodize over the latest *GUI,* which they pronounce *gooey.* It may sound like a sticky candy, but they're talking about a *graphical user interface,* better known as one or another form of Windows.

At the heart of a GUI is the ability to electronically reach onto the screen and move or manipulate text, images, icons, buttons, and other elements.

This works because the computer maps every viewable piece of the screen, and the computer can detect actions performed at particular locations.

The means to use a GUI is an onscreen cursor that you can move from place to place by a pointing device; a set of buttons that you can click to indicate a selection or initiate an action. On a desktop computer, the most common type of pointing device is a mouse which is moved around on a mouse pad or on the desk itself to cause a similar movement on the screen. The second most common desktop pointing device is a *trackball* which remains stationary but translates the manipulation of its large ball into movement on the screen.

With a laptop, of course, the emphasis is placed on squeezing everything into a very small space, and that doesn't allow room for a standard mouse and mouse pad. Instead, the common designs for pointing devices on a laptop include the following:

✦ **Pointing stick.** This little pencil-eraser-sized nub is embedded into the keyboard (often in the triangle in the midst of the G, H, and B keys). It functions something like a joystick: Pushing it up moves the onscreen cursor toward the top of the screen. A bit of intelligence in the computer can tell the difference between a small push and a determined shove, translating that into small or large movements.

On IBM and Lenovo laptops, the pointing stick is often called a TrackPoint; on some Dell machines a similar mechanism is called a TrackStick. The pointing stick works in conjunction with a pair of mouse-click buttons in front of the spacebar.

✦ **Touchpad.** This common replacement for a mouse on a laptop is an electrically sensitive rectangle of several square inches usually mounted just below the spacebar. These devices work by sensing changes in the very low power electrical charge on the pad caused by a finger movement. Moving the finger to the right causes the onscreen cursor to move in that direction; as with a pointing stick, the computer senses the difference between a slow move which is translated as a small movement onscreen and a quick sweep, which moves the cursor a greater distance.

Some touchpads add a second sensor beneath the tiny pad that detects a finger tap. The pad can be programmed to interpret a single tap as calling for highlighting of a word or option, and a double tap to mean "execute" a command. In any case, touchpads are accompanied by a pair of buttons that are the equivalent of a left or right mouse button.

Got sweaty fingers? Some touchpads don't properly respond if your fingers are wet, sweaty, or inside a glove. Nothing personal, but they need the touch. If you have problems using a touchpad, consider adding a clip-on trackball as an alternative.

✦ **Touchpad with a pointing stick.** Some laptops offer double for your money, letting you to choose whichever device works best for you all the time or for a particular assignment.

✦ **Clip-on trackball.** If you're averse to the built-in touchpad or pointing stick, you can easily attach a clip-on trackball; it connects to the laptop through a USB port and attaches to the side of the machine. Make sure the attaching mechanism doesn't damage your laptop case and be very careful not to close the clamshell with the attached trackball in place — you could end up damaging the LCD.

✦ **External mouse.** If you've got the space, perhaps when your laptop is being used on a desktop in a motel or in the office of a client, you can attach any standard external mouse to a USB port and use it. You can also purchase a mini-sized mouse, about the size of a matchbook.

### Power switches

Unless you've got one of those very rare foot-pedal-powered laptops with a windvane turbo assist, you're going to need electrical power to energize the microprocessor, its memory, storage, and other devices. Since I'm talking about things you will likely find on the *top* of the bottom box, let me start with the all-important power switch.

On most modern laptops, the on/off button is located somewhere on the top side; proper design puts it in an upper corner where you are unlikely to accidentally hit it while typing or making other adjustments. The switch is thus also protected against accidental pushes when you close the clamshell. A generally bad design: putting the on/off switch on the side of the laptop where it could accidentally be touched.

A common design for the on/off switch is a circle partly split by a vertical line. (See the left of Figure 2-3.) Another version uses an off-center arrow within a circle. (See the right of Figure 2-3.) One possible explanation for the less-than-obvious symbolisms: they combine the ancient computer markings of 0 for off and 1 for on, an extension of binary mathematics.

Other designers may be more obvious: a switch clearly marked with an On label. On one of my fancy new laptops, the button glows neon blue when the machine is powered up and changes to a mellow green or strident yellow, respectively, when the computer is in Standby or Hibernation mode.

**Figure 2-3:**
Two
versions of
an icon for
a laptop
power
switch.

*Courtesy of Toshiba America, Inc.*

One more thing: Modern laptops make multiple use of their on/off switch. For example, pressing and holding it for a second while the machine is off may turn on the power; pressing and releasing it quickly while the machine is running may put the system into hibernation. And you may also be able to initiate an automated orderly shutdown of a running machine by pressing and holding the button down until it changes color. When all else fails, consult your instruction manual for details.

## Multimedia controls

The distinctions between a portable music device, a battery-powered DVD player, a digital recorder, and a laptop computer have nearly vanished. Today, nearly all capable laptops include a CD or DVD player and either a sound card (better) or sound card-equivalent software (not quite so good).

I discuss sound card hardware and software in Book V. Here I focus on buttons and controls on the top surface of the bottom box of a laptop, and quite a few are found.

The most basic of controls is for volume, and here you find several possible designs and locations:

✦ A Shift-Function Key control on the keyboard. For example, on some machines you may be asked to press and hold the Ctrl key and then tap F9 to reduce the volume or F10 to increase the volume.

✦ A toggle switch built into the top side of the bottom box. Hinged at the middle, you lower the volume by pressing the left side of the rectangular button and raise the noise level by pressing the right side.

✦ A rotary dial that raises the volume when rolled in one direction and reduces it when turned the other way. On most machines that use this design, the rotary dial is on one of the two thin sides; the Toshiba Satellite P205 moves the dial to the front edge of the lower box.

✦ An instant mute button or a function key that serves the same instant-off purpose. On the P205 model and some other machines, the Function-Esc key combination turns off the sound; depending on your machine's design, the mute may turn off only the sound system's output to the laptop's built-in speakers, or may also disable headphones or external speakers attached to the computer. See Figure 2-4.

**Figure 2-4:**
A
multipurpose
Escape key
with audio
mute
functions.

*Courtesy of Toshiba America, Inc.*

The next level of multimedia controls is your basic CD player; the controls are sometimes alongside the keyboard, while other machines place a set of tiny buttons along the very front edge of the bottom box — more or less below where your wrists rest while typing.

On some laptops, including Toshiba models, you may find a button that truly blurs the line between sophisticated laptop computer and basic CD music player: a Music CD button that activates a simple media player in the computer, allowing you to play music CDs without turning on the rest of the machine. So if you're cruising at 29,000 feet and too tired to do any more work on your spreadsheet, you can play the latest Dixie Chicks CD for hours while your computer gently sleeps.

Other multimedia CD buttons include your basic play, pause, next track, previous track, and stop. Most of the icons came from DVD players, which adapted them from VCRs, which took them from tape recorders.

## *Indicator lights*

If you're of a certain age — or are a fan of old science fiction movies and TV shows — your mind's eye will have an image of blinking lights and indicators. (One of the more animated computers was the robot on *Lost in Space*, famous for his to-the-point warnings for the intrepid young hero: "Danger, Will Robinson! Danger!")

You'll likely find these indicator lights on most modern laptops:

✦ **Hard disk drive indicator.** A fluttering lamp, usually marked by an icon that looks like a stack of tiny dishes, tells you when your computer is reading from or writing to its internal hard disk drive. (See Figure 2-5.) Think of your laptop's hard disk drive as a can of data and you can relate to the simple icon used by most designers; sometimes the can is shown stacked, a representation of the multiple platters that exist within many cans of data, err, hard disk drives.

This is more than mere entertainment: It tells you that your computer is alive and at work, even if nothing is happening on the screen. Don't turn off the power to a computer that is reading or writing to the hard drive; doing so could corrupt data or damage essential Windows registry and other files required for startup.

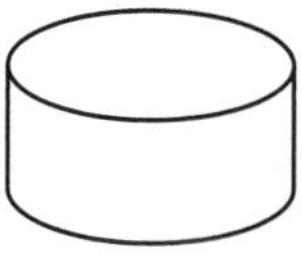

**Figure 2-5:**
A typical
icon
representing
a laptop's
hard disk
drive.

*Courtesy of Toshiba America, Inc.*

✦ **Power status indicators.** Depending on your model, you may have little green or red (or other color, I guess) lights that tell you such important things as: Is the power on? Is the laptop receiving AC power from the wall? Is the laptop receiving power from its rechargeable battery? Designers often use a small pictogram of an electrical plug to indicate that the laptop is receiving power from an AC wall outlet — through an adapter that converts the current to DC, to be precise. (See Figure 2-6.)

**Figure 2-6:**
One designer's icon represents a laptop receiving AC power from a wall outlet.

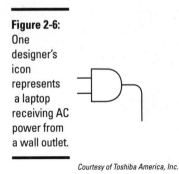

*Courtesy of Toshiba America, Inc.*

Some machines include a bit of extra information, like changing colors on a lamp that tells you whether the battery is fully charged, half depleted, or in dire need of a few hours plugged into an AC outlet. On my most modern Toshiba machine, the respective colors for these three conditions are soothing green, anxious amber, and urgent flashing red. (You can see an example of a battery icon in Figure 2-7.)

**Figure 2-7:**
A version of the symbol for a battery is used by laptop makers to indicate that the machine is running on its own battery-stored energy.

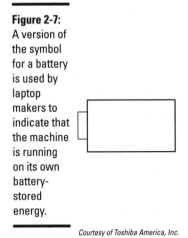

*Courtesy of Toshiba America, Inc.*

## Bottom of the bottom box

The underside of the laptop is a place that you can't access while you're using the machine — unless you're in zero gravity. For that reason, it houses compartments and access hatches meant to be accessed on rare occasions and not while the machine is powered up.

The modern Toshiba Satellite P205 offers four ports of access; see Figure 2-8. The rechargeable battery is located in a large pocket. To release it, unlock it on the left and then release the latch on the right. The system's two user-accessible RAM module slots are beneath a cover near the middle of the machine. The large bay in the bottom of Figure 2-8 is for this particular system's WiFi adapter; it has room for other electronics in future designs. The bay to the left holds this model's tiny 200GB hard disk drive.

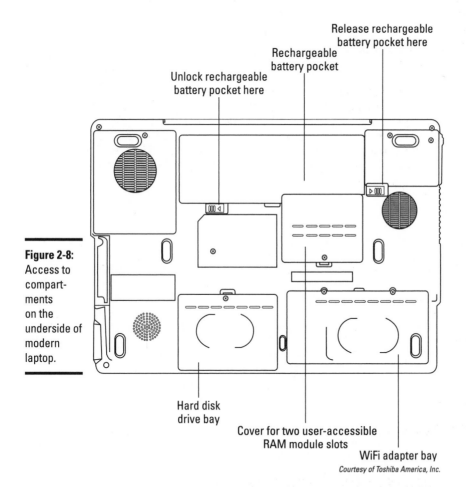

Release rechargeable
battery pocket here

Rechargeable
battery pocket

Unlock rechargeable
battery pocket here

**Figure 2-8:**
Access to
compart-
ments
on the
underside of
modern
laptop.

Hard disk
drive bay

Cover for two user-accessible
RAM module slots

WiFi adapter bay

*Courtesy of Toshiba America, Inc.*

These common ports of entry are on the bottom of a laptop:

✦ **Access to RAM modules.** Most modern laptops offer two tiny sockets to hold memory, usually provided on a tiny SODIMM module not much larger than a postage stamp.

Your machine may have come with one or both of the memory sockets already populated with memory. Unfortunately, sometimes you must remove one or both perfectly good memory modules if you need to upgrade the amount of RAM in your system. If you do end up with superfluous RAM, consider donating the modules to a school or a program that redistributes high-tech devices to those in need, including inner-city students and third-world nations. Or, if you must, there's always eBay.

Try to anticipate your memory needs at the time you purchase your system. You can take one of two strategies here: Order the system from the manufacturer with a full load of memory installed (at least 1GB, although Windows Vista works much better with 2GB), or order the system with the absolute minimum memory and plan on removing the insufficient RAM and replacing it with larger modules you purchase on your own. Depending on market conditions, sometimes doing it yourself is less expensive and sometimes it's a better deal to accept the manufacturer's package deal.

✦ **Rechargeable battery.** On many laptops the battery is held in place by a latch, and sometimes an additional sliding lock-like device. On some laptops, access to the battery may be from the side.

While you're looking at the bottom of the bottom box, note the various stickers placed there by the manufacturer. You will likely find the model number for the laptop itself, along with a serial number for your specific unit. You may also find the product key for your Windows operating system. Other details may include information about the wireless LAN in your system.

Take the time to record all the important numbers you find. You may need to recite them to a support technician one day when you call in for help . . . and you might need them to file a missing laptop report. You can use the ancient technology they call "handwritten notes on paper." Or you can go modern and use a digital camera to take close-up photos of the stickers. However: Don't store the only copy of that photo on the laptop and don't keep your handwritten notes in the laptop case. If the laptop stops working or goes missing, the picture or the notes won't help you at all.

While you're looking at the bottom of the bottom box, note the little rubber feet or nubs that hold the laptop a fraction of an inch above the desk. I tend to lose at least one of these every six months or so. To replace a small nub, try carefully gluing on a pencil eraser; to replace a larger rubber standoff, you may have to carve your own standoff from a larger eraser or other soft but sturdy object.

## Sides of the bottom box

On one side of the laptop computer you usually find the access to the built-in CD or DVD player or recorder. Some laptops also have a bay designed to hold an ultra-miniaturized hard disk drive; you can easily replace or upgrade these drives, although you have to use a drive that includes matching connectors and guide rails. (The *connectors* bring together the laptop's and drive's data and power lines; the *guide rails* allow the drive to slide into place securely.)

Upgrade parts for laptops are sometimes particular to a manufacturer. For example, the rails and connector location for a slide-in hard disk drive for a Toshiba machine may be similar to but incompatible with those intended for a Lenovo laptop. A number of third-party resellers offer upgrade and replacement parts. The more popular your laptop brand, the more likely a reseller offers a line of parts for it.

On the other side of the bottom box you may find as many as a dozen small connectors for various temporary assignments. Here's the set from one Toshiba model:

✦ **Volume control dial.** Rotating the dial one direction or the other raises or lowers the volume. Your laptop also includes volume controls that are part of Windows as well as any specialized audio software, including Sound Blaster and similar programs.

If your sound system makes no sound, even if the volume dial is all the way to its maximum, see if audio has been turned all the way down (or muted completely) in onscreen Windows control panels or by other software components on your system.

✦ **WiFi power switch.** You must have a way to turn off the WiFi transmitter and receiver on a wireless system. Why? Because some places frown on unauthorized or unwanted radio signals: airplanes in flight, hospitals, the front lobby of the Central Intelligence Agency . . . that sort of place. A second reason: The WiFi subsystem uses electrical power any time it is switched on, and you've no reason to deplete the storage in your battery when you don't need WiFi.

Some laptops place the WiFi on/off switch on the top of the bottom box, up near the function keys. The WiFi switch and some of its controls are marked by a symbol that shows waves radiating out from an antenna; see Figure 2-9. Laptops use internal wiring rather than external antenna.

**Figure 2-9:**
A version
of a WiFi
symbol used
on modern
laptops.

*Courtesy of Toshiba America, Inc.*

In addition to the hardware on/off switch for the WiFi system, most laptops include wireless control software provided by the wireless system manufacturer; this software may have a feature to enable or disable the transmitter. Shutting off the WiFi system at the software level makes it impossible to use the wireless facilities but might not end the hardware's draw on the battery. Use the on/off switch instead.

✦ **Audio input.** Depending on the design and capabilities (and any extra sound adapter software you ordered as an option), your machine may have one or more audio input jacks. Most common is a microphone input, used — you guessed this, right? — for recording directly from a microphone. Many laptops use an icon of an old-style microphone to indicate this input; see Figure 2-10. A line input port is another type, used to record from an amplified source such as a tape recorder, digital recorder, or home stereo system.

**Figure 2-10:**
Many
laptops use
a drawing of
an antique
microphone
as the
symbol for
microphone
input.

*Courtesy of Toshiba America, Inc.*

✦ **Audio output.** Again, you may see one or more output plugs for use with headphones or as an output for use with another electronic device such as a home theater system or a tape recorder. One of the simpler icons on many laptops looks like an earmuff for a housefly: a tiny set of headphones; see Figure 2-11.

**Figure 2-11:** The audio output port, often a set of headphones, can provide a low-power signal to an amplifier for use with external speakers or a stereo system.

*Courtesy of Toshiba America, Inc.*

✦ **USB 2.0 port.** This near-miraculous piece of technology when it was introduced is still pretty nifty: The Universal Serial Bus is capable of two-way communication with almost any type of external device. You want to add a mouse? Plug it into the USB port. Need an external hard disk drive? Get one that attaches to a USB port.

One commonly used icon for a USB port is meant to indicate its multi-purpose functions; the signal can go directly to a device or to a hub that splits into multiple paths. See Figure 2-12. Depending on your laptop design, you may find only one or two USB ports on the side of the box, with another two on the back. The versatile (and comparatively large) Toshiba Satellite P205 series offers a pair of USB ports on each side of the box.

**Figure 2-12:** One version of an icon for the USB.

The first version of the USB standard was quite appropriately called USB 1.0, which was quickly replaced by USB 1.1. As this book goes to press, the much-faster USB 2.0 is state-of-the-art, and that's what you want to buy. Anything slower is just a waste of good electrons. If you have an old machine that offers USB 1.1, shop for an adapter that plugs into a PC Card or Express Card slot and delivers much-improved USB 2.0 functionality.

✦ **iLink, i.Link, FireWire, or IEEE 1394 port.** Introduced at about the same time as USB, this other near-miraculous piece of technology (under whichever name you choose to call it) is primarily used by digital video cameras. This technology was originally Apple's FireWire; Sony was behind a miniaturized version mostly used in connection with video cameras and other home entertainment devices.

Don't feel badly if your laptop doesn't have one of these ports; if you need one, you can add one . . . with an adapter that plugs into a USB port. The iLink icon is a stylized lowercase *i;* the icon for FireWire is a stylized *Y.* If your laptop has one of these ports, you can more easily spot it based on its shape rather than looking for a particular icon; the miniature port looks like a smaller version of a USB rectangle, with a U-shaped indent in the top. It's like a dented pizza box.

✦ **eSATA port.** This miraculous piece of technology arrived on PCs in 2007 and laptops in 2008. This port is an extension of the high-speed internal bus that connects hard disk drives, CD or DVD drives, and other such high-demand storage devices. The original ATA standard was a *parallel technology,* meaning that eight or more wires were required to send a signal to represent a single computer word; the advanced SATA converted that to *serial technology,* with one bit of information moving behind the other and requiring just two wires. Then eSATA brought SATA outside the box to an external port. SATA and eSATA have icons, but you're just as likely to see the letters themselves on the case near the port.

✦ **PC Card slot.** Another way to add functions to a laptop is through the use of a credit card–sized circuit board. WiFi cards and broadband cellular modems are among devices you can use in this plug-and-play slot. This older technology is rapidly being replaced by external USB devices, but is still useful for upgrades or as a workaround for certain failed components. Cards have three possible thicknesses: Type I, Type II, and (the least-common) Type III. Most modern laptops with PC Card slots are intended for Type II cards.

✦ **ExpressCard slot.** The latest incarnation of a plug-and-play upgrade slot for laptops is the ExpressCard, which is a higher-speed, more versatile, and smaller version of the PC Card. Two card sizes are in use today: the

ExpressCard/54, which is the same width as a PC Card at 54mm or 2.125 inches (although its depth is shorter and its connector is smaller), and the ExpressCard/34, which is not much bigger than a stick of gum at 34mm wide, about 1.3 inches. See Figure 2-13.

As with PC Cards, an ExpressCard slot is a good way to add an internal upgrade or workaround to a laptop computer; devices designed to this specification include eSATA adapters, advanced WiFi cards, and broadband cellular modems.

**Figure 2-13:** Business card or matchbook-sized devices plug into small ExpressCard slots on many modern laptops.

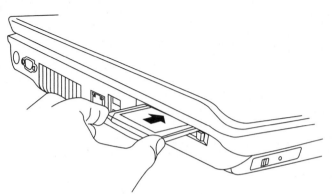

*Courtesy of Toshiba America, Inc.*

A *workaround* is a way to deal with a broken or outdated element of your laptop without having to replace it or repair it. For example, your laptop may have been delivered with a relatively slow and outmoded 802.11a WiFi system, and you want to use more modern 802.11n communication. (Don't worry about the alphabet jungle; I'll define 802 *dot whatever* in Book VIII, Chapter 2.) A workaround is like this: Disable the built-in WiFi system through Windows or other control software, and install an upgrade in the PC Card or ExpressCard slot.

✦ **Media card reader.** Some laptops offer a tiny slot capable of accepting one or more types of flash memory as used in audio players, digital cameras, and other devices. The problem here is that these media come in so many different forms, among them CompactFlash, SmartMedia, Secure Digital, Micro Secure Digital, XD, Memory Stick, and others. And each requires its own particular size of slot and internal connectors.

If your laptop doesn't have a direct read slot like the one shown in Figure 2-14, you can add an external card reader that attaches to a USB port or use an appropriate cable to connect the camera or player to a USB or iLink port on the computer.

**Figure 2-14:**
Many laptops can directly accept one or more types of flash memory like the ones used in digital cameras and music players.

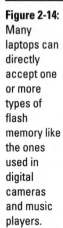

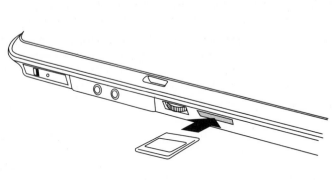

*Courtesy of Toshiba America, Inc.*

## Back of the bottom box

On most laptops, the back side of the bottom box is for devices that you use for a while — for example, devices that you leave behind on the desktop when you travel.

If you're buying a larger laptop, like the Toshiba Satellite P205 machine I use as an example of a current machine, you may find that the back of the laptop is clean and empty; the large 17-inch LCD screen allows for extra room on the sides of the laptop for ports and connectors. The advantages of this design include protection against breaking off parts attached at the rear. The disadvantages of a larger screen include shortened battery life, extra weight, and a very tight squeeze on an airliner's tray table.

You can expect these sorts of ports on the back of the bottom box on some models:

✦ **Power connector.** The business end of the AC adapter connects to most laptops on the back plane of the bottom box. One end of the adapter plugs into a wall current and the other end delivers DC voltage to the computer.

Be cautious where the power connector protrudes from the back. If the laptop tumbles or tilts too far back, if the power block falls from the table, or if a frozen block of blue ice drops from a jet flying 30,000 feet over your head, the connector can snap off. According to one service company I consulted, this repair is expensive and one of the most common causes of laptop damage.

✦ **RGB monitor output.** This 15-pin female port mates with a 15-pin male cable that can connect to an external video monitor, an analog LCD display, or an LCD projector. The most advanced of current laptop models (and many coming machines, I expect) add a digital video output for use with external LCDs that receive that sort of signal.

✦ **S-video output.** This alternate form of video output isn't common. For most uses and users, the RGB output offers superior performance; if you've absolutely got to use an S-video output to send a video signal from your laptop to a particular device . . . well, here's your connector.

✦ **RJ-11 modem port.** If your laptop has a built-in dial-up modem, the cable connects here. Most users would rather undergo root canal surgery without Novocain, but if you find yourself in a situation where you can't possibly connect at high speed over a wired or wireless broadband connection, this may be the route you must take. I suggest you accept the Novocain for the dentistry . . . or for the sssllllooowwww dial-up connection.

✦ **RJ-45 Ethernet LAN port.** The connection for a high-speed wired Ethernet looks confusingly like the one for an ordinary telephone wire for a slow dial-up modem; the difference is that the Ethernet port (and its associated cable) is about 25 percent larger. It's impossible to squeeze an Ethernet cable into a modem port, but a truly determined user might be able to force a telephone connector into an opening expecting an Ethernet cable. You have been warned!

✦ **USB ports.** Some modern laptops offer several more USB ports on the back side of the bottom box. They function just like the ones on the sides.

# Chapter 3: Microprocessors, Memory, and Operating Systems

## In This Chapter

✔ Meeting the mother of all boards

✔ Delving into a bit of binary

✔ Deciding whether to get the latest operating system

**Y**ou can see the external hardware — the screen, the keyboard, the ports — and you know the software's name and capabilities. But these things that you can see and touch are mere slaves to three essential masters: the CPU, the memory, and the operating system.

The *central processing unit (CPU),* also known as the *microprocessor,* is the engine. The bigger, faster, and more efficient it is, the more powerful the computer; think in terms of horsepower under the hood.

The *memory* (also called *random access memory* or *RAM*) is the brain, the place where work gets done. Too little memory means the microprocessor either has to make notes on "scratch paper" (by writing things to the considerably slower hard disk drive) or that the memory is simply overloaded and likely to throw a temper tantrum, start a petition drive, or otherwise diss you in public.

And the *operating system:* It's the boss of the hardware. Facing one direction, it tells the microprocessor where to go and helps manage the huge block of memory. Looking the other way, it maintains an index of all data and programs stored on the hard disk drive, and it receives requests from the software for the use of the display, the disk drive, and anything else attached.

The executive team actually has a fourth member, and it's one that most buyers never see: the *motherboard,* which holds everything together and paves the pathways between them with streets of gold. Or copper. Or tin and other conductive metals.

Truth: Some motherboards actually use industrial-quality gold plating on some of the electrical contacts. Gold is an excellent conductor and doesn't rust over time. At one time nearly all motherboards used the magic metal — a little bit can go a long way, but today you're only likely to find real gold used in machines intended for use in extreme humidity or on mission-critical devices. Laptops and desktops tend to reach the end of their useable life after three to five years, well before rusting should become an issue.

# Feeling the Need for Speed

The more work you expect your laptop to perform in a short period of time, the more horsepower you need under the hood.

Today's modern laptops deliver higher and higher *resolutions* (details) on their screens, millions of colors (hundreds of thousands of hues at various intensities of brightness), high-fidelity audio and high-definition video, and run an operating system with a *graphical user interface* (also known as a *GUI,* and pronounced *gooey*) that lets you interact with the machine by pointing at almost anything on the screen and clicking a mouse.

All this wonderful stuff requires the creation, recording, management, and movement from place to place of billions of 0s and 1s per second. The following principal components deliver the horsepower.

## Macromanaging the microprocessor

Today, nearly all laptops use a CPU designed and built by Intel or AMD. The CPU is where the numbers are crunched, received in one form and converted to another; sent out as a command to another piece of equipment or software, or transmitted to a storage device.

In general, faster is better than slower. Once you're past a certain point, though — say a speed of 1 GHz or more — other factors come into play. The CPU has to be matched with a fast *bus* (a superhighway of wires) that can move data around the machine quickly, and it has to work with memory that can keep up with its demands. Otherwise you'll be doing the equivalent of trying to load and unload ten pounds of data with a five-pound bucket; it won't all fit at once and you're going to quickly develop a huge backlog at each end of the process.

Laptops use the same sort of processors that desktop machines use, and sometimes identical models. Because laptops run on batteries and because heat buildup within a closed little box can lead to problems, designers generally use modified CPU designs that use less power, can switch features on/off, or can adjust their speed (and thus power draw and heat generation) as needed.

TECHNICAL STUFF

# Bringing binary to the CPU

Imagine a building with, oh, 150 million or so on/off switches plus wires that run between them and amongst them. Each switch's on or off position can be set, read, or changed as fast as two or three billion times *per second*. And even with all of that activity, this building only consumes perhaps 30 or so watts of power. And then imagine that this building is smaller than a postage stamp and about as thick as a slice of pepperoni.

There. You've got a sense of the size of the microprocessor, the brute force miracle that makes computers possible. Why do I say it is a "brute force" device? Because, in the end, modern computers are very dumb but very, very, very fast.

If you spot me in an airport waiting for The Grace L. Ferguson Airline (and Stormdoor Company) to patch together an airplane to get me home within two or three days of my scheduled arrival time, buy me a drink and I'll explain how binary math works.

In the meantime, for your purposes here, you need to know that a computer knows only two numbers: 0 and 1. And it only knows how to add.

How does a computer subtract 12 from 15? It converts the numbers to something called a *two's complement* and then adds them together. And how does your laptop multiply 7,345 times 15,237? Well, obviously: It adds 7,345 to 7,345

again and again — 15,236 times, to be precise. Like I said, very dumb but very fast. Buy me that drink and we can discuss the elegance and simplicity of the world of binary math.

What does your laptop do with all of those 0s and 1s? In a word, it makes words out of them. Each of those 0s or 1s is called a *bit* and in computerese, a 0 means none, no, or off while a 1 means one, yes, or on.

Depending on where it sits within a computer word, it can indicate (from right to left, not left to right as most of us humans count) either a 0 or a 1 or any other even number. (It only takes a single 1 to convert an even number to an odd number, right? And if the first bit is set at 1, the seventh bit to the left is also set at 1, and all the other bits are 0s, that means this particular word means one 1 and one 64.) You and I might call that 65, but to the computer, 01000001 could mean the number 65. Or, it could mean the alphabetic character *A*. It could also indicate a very dark and dull shade of blue if that is the value assigned to the blue component of an RGB (Red-Green-Blue) computer color chart. Or it might mean to place your Ultimate Alien Life Form at a spot onscreen that the computer's memory represents as location number 65.

Okay, so maybe you only have to buy me a small drink since I've already spilled some of the details. But that's the general idea of how a computer does the voodoo that it do so well.

Figure 3-1 shows an advanced laptop CPU. One of the most advanced CPUs for laptops, as this book goes to press, the Intel Core 2 Extreme Mobile Processor contains a pair of *cores,* or processors, each packing 291 million transistors into less than one square inch. The processor runs at a speed of 2.6 GHz and can slow the speed (and power use) when not needed.

Intel's current families of laptop CPUs also include, in order of most to least powerful:

✦ Intel Centrino Duo, which is based on the Intel Core 2 Duo used in desktops; a quad-core version of the processor is expected in 2008, based on four-processor CPUs offered for desktops.

✦ Intel Centrino, which is a variation of the Intel Pentium 4.

✦ Intel Celeron, which is at the low end of the company's product line today.

**Figure 3-1:**
Hidden within a plastic cover and mounted on the motherboard encased within the shell of your laptop is its micro-processor.

AMD's families of laptop CPUs includes

✦ AMD Turion 64 X2 Dual-Core processor; as with Intel, a quad-core version is due.

✦ Mobile AMD Athlon is a mid-level processor.

✦ Mobile AMD Sempron is another mid-level processor.

You'll have a hard time finding processors made by companies other than Intel or AMD on current mainstream laptops. Like it or not, Intel CPUs are the standard and AMD is the only major manufacturer whose processors are essentially completely compatible with operating systems and software designed for Intel-based systems. If you're offered an alternative, make certain it supports whatever operating system you choose to use.

## Taking a walk down memory lane

If the microprocessor is the engine, RAM is the factory floor. Although memory chips are tiny, about the size of a fingernail, they contain a huge amount of real estate within.

Think of a memory chip as a very large chalkboard divided into millions or billions of tiny cells. Each cell has an address, like a house on a street. An index keeps track of which particular bits of information (0s and 1s) are placed where.

While I'm writing these words on my computer, they are resident in a section of RAM as individual characters; at the same time, the microprocessor works with the graphics processor to create the information that allows the LCD screen to display a picture of all the characters (using specific fonts and styles) as well as icons, menus, and an onscreen cursor and pointer.

On some systems, the graphics processor has its own block of memory used for onscreen image construction; this is generally the fastest way to generate an image, especially for high-speed games or complex digital pictures. Other laptops allocate a portion of main system memory to the graphics processor; this saves a small amount of money but may be the slowest and least flexible arrangement. In the middle: systems that give the graphics processor its own memory but let it borrow some system memory when needed.

## Bossing your machine: The operating system

And I bet you thought you were in charge, huh?

You've got all this great hardware: the microprocessor and its associated chipsets that deliver graphics, audio, storage device management (like hard disks and CD or DVD drives), the memory, the keyboard, and dozens of other things that install into bays or slots. And you've got all of this great software to handle word processing and other office tasks (spreadsheets and databases among them); e-mail and instant messaging software keep you in touch whenever, wherever, and however you want; and high-tech power tools to edit digital images, video, and audio.

But who's the boss? In the simplest of terms, think of the operating system as a great big box of rules and regulations that sits in the middle of your laptop's computing universe. Above it are software applications, the keyboard and mouse, and you. Below it are all of the pieces of hardware that do the actual work.

## Driving my "carmputer"

Drivers are the key to the way Microsoft Windows works with so many hundreds of thousands of available pieces of hardware and software. Think of them as customized interpreters. When you connect a fancy new scanner to your laptop, its manufacturer also provides (either on a disk or online) a device driver that describes all of its particular capabilities (for the edification of the operating system). In this way, a hardware maker can add custom features (or limitations) to the basic commands. Similarly, a piece of software can teach Windows new tricks by supplying a software driver. In Book III I explain how you can make sure your system has the latest drivers and show you how to update — or retreat to a previous version if problems arise.

In theory, the operating system could be built into your laptop's hardware. Or, your software could be designed to directly control the hardware. But for most of us, that isn't a good solution. Here's why: Not all hardware is the same, and you can install nearly an infinite number of combinations of devices. And, although one company's digital photo editor may be very similar to another, each is written differently and wants to interact with the hardware on its own terms.

Here, then, are the main jobs assigned to the operating system.

### Managing the hardware

When a piece of software asks for data conversion, for image display, or submission of product over the Internet, it sends out a series of commands. The operating system receives the orders (with the helpful assistance of a device driver; see the handy and quite dandy Technical Stuff note) and translates the command into something that the hardware can understand.

### Managing the software

When a company (more precisely, a squadron of programmers) writes a piece of software, it has no idea what kinds of hardware is installed on customers' machines. They can make general assumptions and publish requirements, but they can't possibly take into account every type of microprocessor, chipset, hard disk drive, graphics adapter . . . or any other type of part. What they can do, though, is specify a particular operating system, and let the operating system read the software and device drivers and make everything hunky-dory in Computerland.

Am I saying that modern operating systems eliminate all conflicts and confusion between and among various combinations of hardware and software? Yes, and they can establish world peace, end hunger, and reverse global warming. Well, actually, no, they can't. But a well-written operating system in combination with properly constructed device drivers and software drivers and competently designed hardware can work together pretty well, and each new generation of these components smoothes the rough edges.

In other words, Windows Vista and Windows XP, and software and hardware designed for either, aren't perfect, but they're a lot better than what users had to deal with. And you can hope for ongoing improvement. And that other stuff too: peace, food, and an environmentally sound planet.

### Managing stored data

Where's your passport? Where are your car keys? The receipt and UPC code for your two-year-old printer that needs repair? And don't just say, "They're on my desk." Your computer must find every last bit of information you've ever stored since the beginning of time (or at least from the beginning of its time in your home or office). And it needs to find it almost instantly. And then remember where it returned the data after editing.

The operating system is boss of the files index, including data (words, images, music, and numbers included), software, drivers, settings, and the thousands of operating system files themselves. The computer's filing system uses *NTFS,* which stands for *New Technology File System.*

The machine that currently serves as my assistant has a 200GB hard drive, and when on my desk (the computer, not me) I plug it into not one, but two external backup drives. (I'm a belt-and-suspenders kind of guy; I make backups of my backups.) The last time I paid attention to the numbers crawling across the screen of my computer as my antivirus scanner did its work, there were nearly 1 million files spread across the three drives.

Just to make things even more complex when it comes to tracking what data is placed where: Sooner or later nearly every file ends up broken into many smaller pieces stored — not necessarily in sequential order — all over the surfaces of a hard disk. I discuss fragmentation in Book III. For now, here's what you need to know: Fragmentation happens, and eventually wastes space and slows down your computer. The cure, quite naturally, is called *defragmentation,* and I show you how to use a software utility.

### Putting on a pretty face

Many a user cares all about looks. With all of the hard work that goes on beneath the surface — the hardware, the software, the drivers, the data, and the operating system — the most important thing is the GUI appearance onscreen. The image on the display has to be attractive, orderly, and easy to use.

With a GUI like Windows, the screen is alive. You can highlight a word and pick it up and move it elsewhere. You can drag an icon from one place to another. You can click a button and make your laptop sing "Cheekah Bow Wow" by the Vengaboys.

For much of your interaction with a laptop, you don't have to type in a command, issue a verbal order ("Open the pod bay doors, Hal"), or even create your own list of possible actions. All you need to do is point and click at an option suggested by the operating system or a piece of software, or use the mouse to pull down more options and choose one of them.

## Running with the Biggest Operating System Dogs

Some people (guilty, your honor) need . . . or at least want . . . to always have the latest and greatest technology. How can you look yourself in the mirror knowing that the guy in the next cubicle is running Vista Premium and you're stuck with XP Home? Well, yes, he's a dork, and you're much more productive, and handsome, and due for a raise. But he's got a newer operating system.

As this book goes to press, the most current version of Microsoft's operating system is Windows Vista in its various versions. Nearly all new systems delivered from now on are likely to use Vista. However, millions of machines are already in use that happily employ one or another earlier operating system from Microsoft. At the end of 2007, nearly 80 percent of desktop and laptop machines used Windows XP and just over 5 percent used an Apple operating system. The remaining machines use either an antique version of Windows (including Windows 98, Windows NT, or Window ME) or one of the alternative operating systems, including Linux.

Why hang on to an outdated version of Windows? Two reasons:

✦ Inertia. It takes a few hours and a bit of money and sometimes some gnashing of teeth and wailing to upgrade from an older operating system to a new one. If your system is working properly with Windows XP and you can run all of the software and hardware you need, it isn't illogical to stay with what you've got for as long as you can.

✦ Incompatibility. Many older machines are simply incapable of running operating systems that weren't available at the time they were introduced. Each successive version of Windows is more demanding on the system hardware — upgrading may require a faster processor or more memory or a more capable graphics card.

And you may find out that not all of your existing hardware or software will run properly with a new operating system, or you may have to purchase a software upgrade to bring them screaming and kicking into the new age.

# Chapter 4: Doing It Yourself versus Calling in the Cavalry

## In This Chapter

✔ **Fixing your own laptop**

✔ **Calling in the experts**

✔ **Sending in the special forces**

A laptop computer's essential nature is its construction from a pair of relatively small, densely packed, and (most notably for this chapter) tightly sealed boxes. By comparison, most desktop PCs are easily opened, and anyone with a bit of nerve can remove the covers and examine the innards, make changes to internal cards or drives, or even perform major surgery to replace a motherboard, fan, or power supply. (I used to say, "anyone with a bit of nerve and a screwdriver," but the most modern of PCs no longer require the use of tools for many repair jobs.)

But very few owners ever see the inside of their laptops. You can read the specifications and run software utilities that reveal the manufacturer, brand, and speed of the microprocessor, but you'll never see it. You know the machine has a graphics controller and a sound card or subsystem because you can see images and hear music or tones, but again, they're out of your sight.

And you can enjoy the sharp and colorful images shown on the LCD screen. But it's not even close to easy for the average user to repair or replace that display if it fails, grows dim, changes color, or is snapped in half when the 6-year-old zooms the airline chair back the same way he does when he plays around on grandpa's lounge chair.

## Daring to Fix Your Own Laptop

Can you fix your laptop? Ah, a perfectly simple question that requires an uncertain, qualified, and equivocal answer: yes, no, or maybe. Oh, and it depends on the situation.

Although modern laptops are generally quite sturdy and reliable, savvy users always act as if the next time they try to bring the machine to life, it will play dead. Or the lights may flash and the screen may light up, but instead of a friendly (or at least familiar) Windows desktop, you'll see an uncharming, barely comprehensible fatal error message: Your hard disk drive can't be found (it's there — you can see it — but the computer can't) or your system files or file allocation table have been corrupted.

If the computer hardware is functioning properly, you *can* fix most problems with software, operating systems, and settings. In the worst possible case, you can reinstall the operating system, software, and data (if you've made backups of the data to an external device or to removable media like a CD or DVD).

## Hard times for hard drives

If the hard drive has suffered a hardware failure, on most modern laptops you can remove it from an externally accessible bay or pocket built into the side or bottom of the closed lower box. With this sort of design you can easily install a replacement drive purchased from the laptop manufacturer; depending on the popularity of your machine, you may find a replacement at a third-party retailer and web site.

Any time you replace a laptop's primary internal drive, you need to install the operating system, software applications, and any backups you have of data files. Be sure to keep your Windows and application installation disks in a safe place, and get in the habit of making regular backups of your essential data files on a removal media like a CD, DVD, or external drive.

Your hard drive or another component of your laptop will die one day. Maybe today, maybe years from now. The proper preparation: clean living, good thoughts, and a full set of backup CDs or DVDs of your data files as well as the system discs provided by the laptop manufacturer when you bought it.

## Seedy CDs and dud DVDs

On certain laptop models, the CD or DVD drive installs in a bay that you can access with the removal of a few tiny screws or the withdrawal of a latch. This allows easy substitution — within a range of devices approved and supported by the laptop's maker — of a replacement optical drive of the same specifications or an upgraded model.

Devices such as CD or DVD drives must be accompanied by the proper device driver; this snippet of software must match the operating system as well as the particular hardware in your machine.

## Feeling powerless at a time of need

If your machine doesn't power up, several possible causes may be to blame. Three points of failure can be fixed from outside the box, and one cannot. Here are the possibilities.

### AC adapter problems

The adapter plugs into wall current at one end and the computer at the other; in between is a sealed box that converts 100 to 240 volts of alternating current (depending on the laptop design) to about 15 to 20 volts of direct current. If the adapter (or the cord that plugs into wall current, or the cord that goes from the adapter to the laptop) is working improperly, the computer won't receive power and its battery won't recharge. The good news is that you can purchase a replacement adapter from most manufacturers or from third-party sources.

Here are the possible points of failure when it comes to power sources:

✦ All things electronic have a finite life; they will eventually fail. They may receive *dirty power* that stresses components. They heat up and cool down each time you use them. Internal parts may corrode. With luck, your adapter won't reach its moment of mortality before the laptop itself retires.

✦ The converter in the sealed box could become fried from a power surge coming in from the AC line.

✦ The cable from the converter to the laptop could come out of the machine. (This one's easy: Reattach the plug.)

✦ The detachable plug from the wall to the converter could become dislodged at its point of connection to the converter. (You know what to do here, right? Lodge it.)

✦ The detachable plug could break or the cable itself could become cut or shorted out. (Stop. Don't attempt to use an electrical device with obvious damage, especially on the AC side of the adapter. If you're lucky you can purchase a replacement cable.)

✦ The cable from the converter to the laptop could come out of the machine.

### Failing batteries

Batteries can fail, or over time can lose their ability to hold a charge. You can usually determine if a bad battery causes the problem by removing it from its bay (on the bottom or side of the laptop) and running the machine from the AC adapter only. If the batteryless machine runs properly when connected to the adapter, the battery has most likely kicked the bucket, shuffled off its mortal coil, and otherwise become defunct.

You can further test this hypothesis by substituting a known-good battery from another machine of the same model. You may be able to borrow a coworker's battery or take the laptop a cooperative retailer's repair counter.

On the other hand, if a batteryless machine doesn't run when connected to the AC adapter, either the adapter or the laptop's internal electronics have failed. Again, if you can borrow a known-good adapter, use it to see if the problem is caused by the cords or converter or if the issue lies deeper within the laptop itself.

### Failing electrical system

The electrical system inside the case of your laptop can fail, which is almost always bad news. Here are the usual suspects:

+ Physical damage to the connector. The little hole and attachment point on most laptops is one of the most vulnerable places. While most everything else on a laptop is carefully packaged within a closed case, anywhere a plug attaches from the outside world, the chance of serious damage is there. If the laptop falls even a short distance with something plugged into a port or other opening, there's a good chance that the connector could snap off or be damaged. The connector from the AC adapter could break, or the internal connection could be bent or broken. (Replacing an AC adapter is easy and relatively inexpensive; repairing a broken internal connector on the laptop itself usually requires a visit to the repair shop and doesn't come cheap.)

+ Damage to the internal connector and its associated electronics because of a surge or spark that penetrates the box. The adapter itself protects against most of these problems because it converts the AC to low-voltage DC. However, a high-voltage static electricity spark that jumps from your fingers on a cold, dry day can damage a laptop or other electronic device.

+ A cooked motherboard damaged by overheating. If a component malfunctions or if the internal cooling fan goes on the fritz, the laptop's circuitry or individual chips could fail. Sorry, but this one's got to go back to its maker for retooling.

### Lacking power

The most embarrassing but not-all-that-uncommon reason a laptop isn't receiving power from the AC adapter or battery is that the wall outlet isn't delivering the juice. Check to see that it is live by plugging a radio or a lamp into the outlet. And don't use an outlet controlled by a wall switch; these outlets are for floor lamps, not electrical devices that need a continuous flow.

I recommend that any expensive electronic device . . . or any inexpensive electronic device that you connect to an expensive one . . . use a surge protector between the plug and the wall. Although in theory the converter in a laptop's AC adapter may absorb some level of power surge, a major hit could fry the adapter and in very rare situations even pass along high-voltage AC or DC to the laptop. A basic surge protector: about $10. A typical laptop: about $1,000. You do the math.

## Senator, I Do Not Recall That Incident

Modern versions of computer memory are generally quite robust. And RAM modules are tested pretty thoroughly by manufacturers before shipping. That said, if a stick of memory goes bad, it usually happens within the first weeks of use. After then, they just sit there and remember things for as long as they receive electrical power.

However, if a memory module isn't properly installed in its slot, or if the laptop takes a major tumble, a block of memory could come out of its connector. Open the cover to the RAM (located on the bottom of most laptops) and ensure that the one or two modules installed in slots are properly seated.

One other possibility: If the memory seems to work some of the time but not all, you may have corroded contacts on the connector that holds the RAM module. If you open the hatch to the memory and an ounce of water trickles onto the desktop, you might have a real problem. All seriousness aside, the corrosion is usually obvious when you inspect the modules.

You can try carefully cleaning the modules with a fresh pencil eraser, being very careful not to leave crumbs of rubber on the memory or in the slot where it mounts. You can also purchase a special liquid cleaner at an electronics supply store; *don't* use a general-purpose solvent, which could make the situation worse by removing some of the conductive metal on the module.

## Drive, He Said

Some are hardware people and some are software people. Rarely does one designer work on both essential elements of a modern computer. Sometimes (most of the time, actually) the hardware comes out first and then the software people scramble to come up with an operating system or a piece of programming that best uses the hardware.

Occasionally a new operating system or a new application is a step or two ahead of the available hardware; it can't provide full functions until the chips catch up. Either way, hardware and software improvements are like a constant game of electronic leapfrogging.

In a perfect world, any new piece of hardware would come with device drivers that make it work without flaw with the latest operating systems and programming. And any new program would be delivered with software drivers that instantly translate its commands so that any hardware can immediately act upon them. Sorry to have to break the bad news, but this is not a perfect world. Instead, what we have is a situation where you have to put in a bit of work to make sure that your drivers are up to date.

Most major manufacturers of hardware and software issue driver updates to deal with significant changes like a new operating system introduction (the arrival of Windows Vista brought forth a parking lot full of device drivers for hardware, while the arrival of a new class of microprocessors demanded adjustments to software drivers for many programs).

Locate the Update button (part of many software applications); give it a try anytime your machine is connected to the Internet and you've got nothing else to do. In most situations, this should keep your programs up to date.

Cheap, Brand-X hardware can sometimes cost you more in the long run than a device from a company that is likely to stay in business for the lifetime of your laptop and its components. I've got a closet full of once-nifty devices sold by companies that took the money and ran, without maintaining an online or telephone support department and without offering necessary driver updates.

And visit the web sites of the manufacturers of any hardware you add to your laptop (either as a component in an internal bay, or as external device attached to a USB, eSATA, or other connection). Check for updates specific to your configuration; if you're running Windows XP, you don't need to update a driver written for Windows Vista, for example.

## Calling the Experts to Your Aid

For the vast majority of users, if you determine there is a problem that lies within the sealed case it is time to Stop and Do No Further Harm. If your LCD is cracked, your motherboard is fried, a connector is broken off, or a fan is no longer fanning, it's time to reach out and touch someone who has the tools . . . and the skills . . . and (if the machine is still under warranty) the permission to open the hood.

I'm old enough to remember the days when the TV repairman would come to the house to fix a Philco on the fritz. In fact, you could even run down to the neighborhood drugstore or hardware store and test the tubes yourself. More to the point, I can also remember a time when you could call up your personal computer's manufacturer and talk to a real human who offered knowledgeable repairs advice.

Alas, today you'll find it nearly impossible to speak with a real human being about problems with your laptop, at least at first. Instead, you have to navigate through a thicket of maddening automated telephone systems, online chat support, e-mail Q-and-A, and often useless lists of frequently asked questions that have nothing to do with your particular problem.

## Passing the buck

When it comes to customer support today, the basic philosophy of most laptop manufacturers is this: "Don't Ask Him, Don't Ask Me. Ask That Fellow Behind the Tree." The support line offered by many laptop manufacturers goes to great lengths to screen out calls they really don't want to deal with (or don't have to, according to the terms of the warranty).

First of all, most laptop makers refuse to assist you if they determine (or believe) that your problem is caused by any hardware or software you've added to the machine if they didn't supply it or specifically include in your warranty. Secondly, you may find yourself between a hard and a soft place if you run into a problem with the operating system, even if it was supplied by the laptop manufacturer with the machine.

One of the biggest problems with calling a hardware maker about a problem with the operating system is that many times their preferred solution is to have you reformat your hard disk drive and reinstall Windows and all of your software applications. That may well solve problems related to corrupted registries, missing files, and bad device drivers, but you will lose any data files you've not backed up to other media. In some cases this is the equivalent of using a sledgehammer to install a pin; it works, but it may also cause a great deal of damage.

Start with Microsoft, the maker of Windows of all flavors; in general, that company doesn't offer free support to users who receive their operating system preinstalled on your laptop by the hardware maker. That's because Microsoft sells manufacturers deeply discounted licenses allowing Windows installation on thousands or millions of machines at a time; you get a great deal on the cost of the operating system but Microsoft doesn't want to have to devote resources to supporting your system.

Now move on to the laptop maker: Although most offer some level of assistance with problems related to the operating system, they cut off support if they believe you've modified the supplied software or hardware. "Not our problem," they'll tell you.

And then there is a third line in the silicon: If the company suspects or determines that you or anyone else has opened the covers of the laptop without permission, they're quite likely to put their hands in their pockets, turn their back, and otherwise get all huffy about your serious transgression.

Lest you think there's no harm in just opening up your laptop by yourself to have a look-see, you should be aware that most makers include seals and other indicators that tip them off to unauthorized access. Nearly every laptop warranty declares itself null and void if the box has been worked on by someone *not* on the official list of repair people with secret decoder rings and special tools.

## Buying factory warranty services

If you are the semi-proud owner of a name-brand laptop from one of the major makers — including Acer, Apple, Compaq, Dell, Gateway, HP, Lenovo, Toshiba, and a few others — your first call should probably be to the manufacturer. It's time to begin the warranty dance.

I'm not meaning to exclude any particular other manufacturer from this list. Some less-known companies have fine machines on the market, and you may also find some generic machines imported by retailers from Asian sources (where nearly all laptops originate) and labeled Cougar or Rabbit or Orange or some other name spinoff. But before you buy a Ferguson 5151, make an effort to find out not only what kind of warranty is promised but what sort of resources stand behind that promise.

Nearly every laptop comes with at least a one-year limited warranty. At various times, some manufacturers have tried to cut corners (and prices) by offering warranties as short as 90 days. As this book goes to press, the minimum coverage period has generally crept back up to a year, although some makers offer a very short period of support on certain "bargain" machines.

Whatever the length of support provided at the time of purchase, though, you usually can buy a longer limited warranty: two, three, or four years. And the warranties come in different colors or levels or fancy names.

### Basic, standard, and limited warranties

Like it says, a limited warranty isn't complete, total, and without strings. Here, let me grab a copy of a "One Year Standard Limited Warranty" from one of the biggest laptop manufacturers. Got it: 15 pages of "disclaimers and limitation of remedy."

The following is a true example of the terms of a limited warranty, but please don't assume that the limitations here are exactly the same as the limitations that come with your particular brand and model of laptop. You're going to have to read the fine print yourself. I recommend preparing with a strong light and a stiff drink.

The warranty starts on the date of purchase, which may or may not be the day you receive a machine or first put it into use. And this particular warranty applies only to customers in the United States and its territories, Latin America, and the Caribbean; those fine folk in Canada and Europe and Asia have their own small print to peruse.

The company promises — in its sole discretion (that means, whether it's your preference or not) — to either restore a machine to its original factory specifications or replace it with a product at least equivalent to the one you bought. Any parts used by the company in repairs may be new, or they may be reconditioned parts equal to or superior to original equipment.

Here's one of my favorite sections: "Customer must read and follow all set-up and usage instructions in the user guides and manuals." First of all, if those manuals were any good (and you know they're not), there'd be no need for books like the one you're reading now. And in any case, this is part of the gigantic loophole they carve for themselves: It's not our fault, it's yours.

The data on your machine is your responsibility, not the manufacturer's. If the laptop (or its hard drive) dies a premature death, the company will replace or repair the machine, but if you don't have a backup copy of the data, that's your problem.

As for the work the machine does: The product isn't for assignments like life support, nuclear facilities, or commercial transportation, and therefore the company isn't responsible if you set up a nuclear-powered self-propelled heart monitoring system. Got that, Mr. Burns?

What isn't covered? Any service made necessary because of accident (fire, power failure, power surge and the like), misuse, abuse, neglect, or improper maintenance. Also, any cosmetic damage including scratches, dents, and faded keyboard keycaps.

Phew! It's hard to find things that are covered. Basically, it comes down to this: If a part breaks all by itself they'll fix it. If they can figure out a way to blame you, me, or the guy behind the tree, they're off the hook.

### Extended warranties

Most manufacturers allow you to purchase extra years of warranty coverage. In general, you must buy the extended warranty while the original warranty is still in effect; for example, if your machine comes with a one-year limited warranty, you must buy an extension within that first year.

If you buy an extended warranty, be aware that sometimes you can more cheaply get a three-year warranty with the original purchase instead of adding two years on later. Check to see if the manufacturer offers any special incentives or rebates.

## Going to a third-party warranty

Nearly all "generic" laptop makers — companies that sell machines that retailers and web sites rebrand — don't offer repair and maintenance services of their own. Instead, they offer contracts from national companies, or a chain of retail stores may provide warranty services on its own.

You may be offered a third-party warranty in another instance. Some retailers may offer an extended warranty for a brand-name laptop computer. These contracts kick in after the initial coverage period from the manufacturer but you must purchase while that original warranty is in effect.

I don't mean to paint all third-party warranty companies with the same brush; your local store may have demonstrated its trustworthiness. But hey, you're buying this book because you're looking for the voice of experience. An expert who knows what he's talking about. Someone who's been down the road. I guess that's me.

Be very cautious if you choose to consider third-party warranties. Some of these companies are more like insurance companies; they bank your money and hope that you don't make a claim. If you do have a problem — and if it fits their definition of a covered repair — they may hire an area repair company to do the work. Is that local company good at what it does, and will it use first-quality parts? I don't know; do you?

And you also run the risk that the warranty company (or the retailer who resold it to you) may not be in business a few years down the road. In theory, these policies are supposed to be backed up with some kind of financial bond, but that may not be much help to you if you need quick service.

# Explaining Repairs

Okay, so your LCD has stopped amazing you with 16-million colors spread across 17 inches of screen and instead you see a small flickering box of sickly shades of green. The machine is 6 months old and still under warranty. You never dropped the laptop, didn't take it out in a lightning storm, and carefully avoided using it as the countdown controller for the space shuttle liftoff. You're covered.

Now, how do you get the screen fixed?

You call the service telephone number and manage to convince the support department that your LCD really is dead and that the problem is theirs and not yours. Depending on the manufacturer and, increasingly, depending on the level of purchased protection, your laptop may be repaired three ways:

✦ **On site.** The manufacturer sends a technician to your office or home and the repair is done while you wait. You don't have to worry about shipping your machine, and the sensitive data on the hard drive is, in theory, safe from unauthorized eyes.

Some companies promise next-day service, and even — at the highest-priced contract level — same-day service. This is all theoretical, though; read the fine print and you'll discover that some companies don't promise to provide on-site service everywhere. (For example, only a handful of companies promise such service to my extremely rural location and in that situation, next-day becomes several days.)

✦ **Depot service.** You have to package up your laptop (that's why you held on to the special box and the foam cushioning that it arrived in, right?) and ship it to a service center. Depending on the plan, the cost of shipping to the depot may be your expense, or the company may send a prepaid label for use with FedEx or UPS or another carrier. Turnaround time may also vary from a day to a week or more.

I'm not accusing technicians of prying into your personal affairs, but any sensitive material on your hard drive is out of your control while it's at the depot.

One way to guard private information, including banking and financial statements, is to password-protect individual files or entire folders. You can do this with built-in Windows XP or Windows Vista facilities; you can also purchase third-party encryption programs. Just don't forget the password . . . and don't write it on a sticky note attached to the bottom of the laptop, either.

✦ **Carry-in service.** Many major laptop makers have regional service centers where you can personally deliver your machine. That doesn't mean you can take a seat in the waiting room while the laptop is immediately repaired; however, if the repair is something simple like swapping a failed battery for a good one, you may be able to take care of business in one trip. It's likely, though, that a maker might have a center on the West Coast and another on the East Coast; if it's not an easy drive, you're back to depot service.

# Calling in the Special Forces

The good news: Laptop prices have gone down as capabilities have gone up. The bad news: Among the ways laptop makers have sought to save money is by reducing (or eliminating) much of their product support services.

Years ago, laptop makers would maintain well-trained support departments available to spend hours on the telephone helping a user get past a hardware or software problem. The best of the companies offered these services almost without limitation; if you had one of their machines, you could call in with a question. Today, though, you're more likely to find severely limited support options. You may be allowed to make free requests for support only for the first few months after you receive a machine, or you may be allowed to make a specified number of calls.

And nearly all laptop makers have outsourced their support services. I've spent quality time with quite a few generally polite and sometimes helpful young men and women in India, the Philippines, Costa Rica, and other places.

Some laptop makers have also switched over to an online chat system for dealing with problems. Although this can result in quick and direct answers — in writing — it can also be rather frustrating. To begin with, if your laptop doesn't work or doesn't connect to the Internet, you can't use it to chat. (If you have another computer, you can use that one to communicate.) A second problem with chat lines is that the representative you're communicating with is usually dealing with more than one customer at a time, rotating from one to another like a chess master who takes on a room full of players by running from table to table. Sometimes it seems as if the chat expert is extremely dense; more likely, he's got too many problems on his plate.

And yet another option: online programs that allow a support department to reach into your computer over the Internet to run diagnostics or to change to settings or configurations. It's a great idea when it works, but they can fix relatively few problems — mostly operating system issues — this way.

If limited or impersonal service seems inadequate to you, well, for a few dollars more you can upgrade to a personal consultant or get priority in the waiting line. Some typical special support services follow:

✦ **Unlimited Support.** Subscribers receive a special phone number and ID code that permits them to dial in for assistance on either a specified type of problem (hardware, for example) or for support on any possible problem, including difficulties with the operating system and installed software.

✦ **Support Bundles.** Some companies sell a "bundle" of a specified number of support incidents. When the block of cries for help is exhausted, subscribers can purchase more access. (Most plans works so each problem is treated as an incident; if one call doesn't solve the problem, additional calls to the support line are treated as part of the same incident.)

✦ **Per-incident Support.** Some hardware and software companies (including Microsoft for Windows operating systems) sells access to an expert on a per-call basis. It's kind of like a computer game of Truth or Dare. For a fee, you get to ask a question about a single problem, error code, or incident. And the expert is supposed to stay with you, telephonically or by chat line, until the problem is solved.

✦ **Setup Services.** Some retailers and online sellers dispatch a technician to your home or office to set up or configure your new system. It's a pricey option, but for those users who are completely clueless — and I submit that doesn't include anyone smart enough to buy this book — it may be worthwhile. Note that this sort of service is bound by geography; if you live way out in the boondocks or on a sandy island (or both, like me), you will likely find that you're out of the local coverage area for personal service.

✦ **Rent Your Own Geek.** In many communities you will find knowledgeable computer experts — sometimes, dare I say, a mere kid — who comes to your home or office to fix a problem. You have to determine for yourself if you trust a person to enter your home or workplace, and once again, remember to safeguard any personal or financial information on your computer from unauthorized eyes.

## *Expanded or deluxe warranties*

As prices for laptops have declined over the years, manufacturers have looked to find ways to add value to their products; that's a fancy way to say that they're on the hunt for ways to create additional streams of income beyond the cost of the hardware itself. One way to do that is to sell "expanded" or "deluxe" warranties, which are less-limited versions of the standard protection.

Before you buy an expanded warranty, take to time to determine the specific differences between a standard, limited warranty and any extra-price "platinum" or "gold" or "deluxe" plans. What's covered under the premium plan that isn't protected by the regular warranty?

You may find these features in a deluxe plan:

✦ Accident protection. A standard warranty doesn't cover damage caused by a crash to the floor or a spill on the keyboard; some expanded coverages pick up (or clean up) the pieces.

✦ Priority repairs. A standard plan may say that machines will be repaired or replaced within ten days or two weeks; an expanded plan may offer two- or three-day service, or even send you a replacement unit by overnight express if the company determines that your machine is beyond repair.

✦ On-site repairs. Some plans promise to send a repair technician to your home or office within a specified amount of time; confirm that your location is within the normal coverage area. (I know for a fact that my home and office is on the far side of nowhere and I cannot expect on-site repair no matter what some salesperson says.)

✦ Special support lines. For the extra money you pay, you might be granted access to real live human beings who answer questions and assist in troubleshooting. Or you may be granted priority access, which means you can jump to the head of the line, leapfrogging over people who've been listening to recorded "Thank you for your patience; your call is important to us" announcements for three hours.

## Refurbished, remanufactured, or open box

Some people seek to save money by purchasing a laptop from a source that sells machines that are a bit less than brand new:

✦ **Refurbished.** What happens when someone purchases a laptop and then decides it's to too heavy, too slow, or too hungry when it comes to battery power? Most retail and online outlets offer a period during which you can return the laptop for a full refund (or sometimes for the purchase price minus a restocking fee).

If the seller is honest . . . and most, but not all, are . . . they won't resell this machine as if it were new. Instead, they'll refurbish it. This usually includes electronically wiping the hard disk clean, reinstalling the operating system and applications, checking to see that all the parts are in the box, and running basic tests on the hardware. And then they sell it at a discount.

✦ **Remanufactured.** What happens when someone buys a laptop and returns it because it's defective in some way? The fault may be minor, such as a broken key cap or a failed indicator light. Or the problem may be more significant, such as an inoperative or faulty hard disk drive or DVD drive.

Instead of throwing away the machine, the retailer (or the original manufacturer) may repair the laptop to bring it up to full specs. A bad hard drive can be replaced with a good one, for example. Again, though, the seller should notify the buyer that this machine has been electronically reborn.

✦ **Open box.** When you visit your neighborhood big-box computer store, you see row after row of laptop out for display. For days, weeks, or months, every other passing customer punches at a key or flicks at the screen.

Eventually, the model reaches the end of its shelf life and in this situation a scrupulous dealer offers the machine for sale as an open-box item. If it has any cosmetic marks that don't effect the operation of the laptop itself, it might be marketed as a scratch-and-dent special.

Should you buy any of these machines? In a word, maybe. The first thing I'd determine is the type of warranty offered by the seller. Is it the full year or two offered with a new machine, or is it a more limited 90-day or 30-day what-you-see-is-what-you-get policy?

Speaking for myself, I wouldn't purchase an open-box machine unless it came with a full warranty and then only, if the price were significantly less than a new machine. I say this for the same reason I don't recommend purchasing a used car from a rental fleet; I know how the cars have been driven. How do you know whether an open-box laptop has ever tumbled to the floor or had a lollipop inserted into the CD slot?

The decisions on refurbished or remanufactured machines are a bit harder to make. Again, I would consider buying one only if it had a full warranty and a deep discount. But at least you have reason to expect that the machine has been checked out; in fact, some remanufactured machines may have been subjected to more rigorous testing than those right off the assembly line.

The bottom line is this: The price of a current laptop is so comparatively low that I prefer to take my chances on a sealed box instead of paying for the privilege of spending time with a partner with an uncertain past.

## Accident and theft insurance

A laptop computer is fairly expensive, and is, by its very nature, portable. That means laptops are a prime target for thieves. Laptops are snatched in airports, hotels, Internet cafes, and from homes and offices. And laptops can suffer expensive damage that isn't covered in a limited warranty: a fall to the floor, a drink spilled on the keyboard, or a cracked or fractured LCD.

I talk about laptop locks and software-based laptop recovery systems in Book IX, Chapter 2.

But your friendly laptop manufacturer may have a solution for you . . . for a few dollars (actually, a few hundred dollars) more. Accident and theft insurance is now offered as an expansion of the standard warranty or as a separate but related product.

Most companies require that the term for the insurance match the number of years the machine is covered under warranty. In other words, you can only buy three years of theft and accident coverage if you've also purchased three years of warranty. In addition to bringing in more money to the computer maker, this offers the manufacturer some protection against unscrupulous users who might be less than honest in their claims.

Be sure to read carefully the terms of any insurance to understand what's covered. Determine if the company will replace a laptop that can't be repaired, and see if your data has any coverage value — there usually isn't.

Finally, check with the insurance company that covers your home or office to see if your laptop is protected already. If it is, find out if your policy provides replacement of a stolen machine (that's good) or merely a check for its depreciated value (not very good).

# Book II

# Setting Up Your Laptop

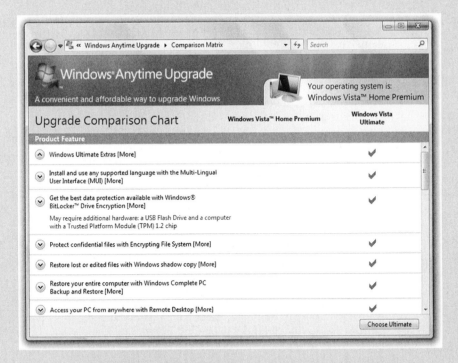

To automatically scan your laptop, go to the Windows Vista
Upgrade Advisor on the Microsoft web site.

# Contents at a Glance

# Chapter 1: Installing or Upgrading an Operating System

## In This Chapter

- ✔ Clearing up Windows
- ✔ Upgrading to Windows XP
- ✔ Upgrading to Windows Vista
- ✔ Gradually updating Windows

*O*nce upon a time there was DOS, the Disk Operating System that was the internal geek-in-charge of the first IBM PC. DOS (pronounced *dahss*) was amazing for what it was: a way for a personal computer user to directly instruct a machine to do something.

But it was hardly what you might consider user friendly. Trust me, I was there at its birth, as one of the first editors of *PC Magazine.* Hold on for a second while I get up from the keyboard and dig out one of the old manuals from the deepest recesses of my library.

Okay, I'm back. Sorry for the delay; the dust was an inch thick and the manual (an impressive hardcover binder that came with its own slipcover box) was heavy. And I fell asleep for just a moment as I reacquainted myself with a few of the commands that used to occupy so much of my time.

## Clearing Up Windows

Nearly every laptop user (and most everyone else) understands the basic idea of Windows: The program is a view (a window) into your computer that you can touch, manipulate, and change with an electronic hand. That hand can be the cursor you move around the screen via mouse or touchpad; on some machines the cursor can move by other means, including the human finger (think of your bank's ATM for an example) or spoken commands.

But more importantly, Windows is a *graphical user interface (GUI).* Unlike the dark days of DOS, modern users are working with what amounts to a live screen. You can click an icon to open a file or start a program; you can pull down a menu from a piece of software and initiate a command by clicking the one you want; and you can reach in and change text or even draw a picture using a mouse to move an onscreen tool.

And Windows also makes possible the amazing world of the Internet. The very nature of Microsoft's Internet Explorer (as well as other Web browsers such as Mozilla Firefox and other capable but less-popular competitors) is based on the Windows GUI.

# The dark days of DOS

When you turned on your machine, the floppy disk drive (which could hold the entire operating system) booted the system. When the code was loaded you were given the following exciting and self-explanatory greeting:

```
A:
```

That's right. The machine was telling you that it was ready to rock and roll, with all of its attention focused on drive A of your machine. Right away any youngsters are in alien territory: many people are completely unfamiliar with the concept of a drive with that name. On a modern laptop or desktop, hard disk drives begin with the letter designation C and go deeper into the alphabet from there.

The A disk, of course, is the first floppy disk. Or it was, anyhow; very few modern laptops come with a floppy drive today.

But pretend. Under DOS, if you wanted to know what data or programs were stored on the A disk, all you had to do was type:

```
A: DIR
```

and press the Enter key. The floppy disk drive spun for a few moments; the monitor displayed a list of files on the top level of the disk, and also told you the names of any subdirectories placed at a lower logical level. Say you'd created a subdirectory called DUMMIES. (The command to create that would have been MKDIR \DUMMIES.) To drill down a level to that group of files, you'd type

```
A: CHDIR \DUMMIES
```

as in Change Directory, and then press the Enter key. Then you could ask for a directory of the files.

And now, one last simple command: Rename a file. Using the verb REN (for rename), you'd type the name of the file you wanted to work on and then the new name for that file. Like this:

```
A: REN OLDNAME.TXT NEWNAME.DOC
```

That's the drill, folks. Users had to learn a completely new language, a very specific and unforgiving grammatical syntax, and keep track of where they were, how the machine was organized, and what was it that they had wanted to do in the first place.

If the days of DOS (which ran from about 1981 until about 1990) had a single bright side, it was this: Installation was a snap. You received a master copy of the operating system (along with that big binder of instructions) and you could format as many floppy disks with the system tracks as needed to boot your computer to life.

A few years into the history of the personal computer came the first hard disk drives, and the process was similar: Format the drive with the system tracks and you were off and running. DOS had no copy protection, and though the license pleaded otherwise, there were entire offices, dorms, and small towns that shared the same copy of the operating system. That's just a fact.

The dark side of DOS? You've just seen it. It was a command-driven operating system. You had to type commands to make something happen, and the more sophisticated the user (or the command), the more complex and lengthier the instructions.

And the command structure carried over to the software programs that operated under DOS, too. One of the more popular word processors of the time was WordStar, and everything came from the keyboard, too. Ctrl + KP meant print, Ctrl + KS meant save and resume, and Ctrl + PB meant begin (or end) a block of boldface.

The software required the operating system to run, but there was very little, if any, consistency between programs. Commands were different with each piece of software. Menus — if they were used at all — were not the same. And nearly every program had its own file format. There was a whole subindustry in conversion software that made it possible to exchange certain types of data files between programs.

And, in the end, the biggest deficit in DOS was the fact that it relied on characters and commands. To give credit where credit is due, it was the designers at Xerox's Palo Alto Research Center who developed the first usable *graphical user interface (GUI)* and the engineers at Apple who brought it to market. Once the Apple Macintosh was introduced, it was obviously the way to go for personal computers, and by 1985 Microsoft brought out the first version of Windows.

**Book II
Chapter 1**

**Installing or Upgrading an Operating System**

# Keeping the Windows Update Closed

Over the past 20 years or so, you could call your PC's GUI Windows (from versions 1.0 through 3.11, with more than a few minor numbers along the way), Windows 95, Windows for Workgroups, Windows CE, Windows ME, Windows NT, Windows 98, Windows 98 Special Edition, Windows 2000, Windows XP, and Windows Vista. Heck, you could even call it Bob. (Yes, Microsoft once tried to put a cute, human face on its GUI; Bob was a bust.)

Today is a moment of transition. In early 2008, Windows XP holds sway on more than 75 percent of all personal computers, while the newer Windows Vista is beginning to take over the market for the newest, highest-powered machines. Meanwhile, about 5 percent of machines still in productive use run one of Microsoft's older operating systems.

Microsoft will support Windows XP for the next few years, but eventually Windows Vista will be the chosen one . . . until the next great new thing is offered.

Why doesn't everyone immediately install and use the latest and greatest version of Windows? You might not for one of these four good reasons:

✦ Because you can't. Windows Vista's advanced features require the most powerful microprocessors, large amounts of RAM, and the most sophisticated graphics adapters. Most machines designed or manufactured before 2007 may be unable to run Vista or may offer only mediocre performance when they do.

✦ Because of other software. Not every piece of software written for earlier versions of Windows works properly with Windows Vista. Some manufacturers may offer updates (for free, or for a fee) or provide new drivers to registered owners. But some users may not want to risk adding problems to software that functions properly.

✦ Because of hardware problems. Some older hardware may require new device drivers to run with Windows Vista. Again, some users may not want to risk losing the use of hardware that works fine with an older operating system.

✦ Because you don't need to. Windows Vista is flashy and smooth and offers some exciting new geegaws and advanced security features. But if your existing operating system and all of its installed software and hardware is functioning properly, you may make the distinction between a need and want. Sometimes the wisest decision is: If it ain't broke, don't fix it.

## Windows XP

Microsoft offered five major editions of Windows XP. The vast majority of machines ran the Home version, even in offices, which aren't usually homes:

✦ Windows XP Home Edition. Smoother and more dependable than earlier versions of Windows, it offers improved digital media management for photos, video, and music.

✦ Windows XP Professional Edition. Intended for power users, it includes all the functions of Windows XP Home plus additional security, privacy, and recovery features. Added components include the Remote Desktop, which allows you to access your computer from another Windows PC and built-in file encryption and access control.

✦ Windows XP Tablet PC Edition. An adaptation of Windows XP Home intended for use with laptops and special monitors that include touch screens and voice recognition.

✦ Windows XP Media Center Edition. An enhanced version of Windows XP Home that adds an integrated set of controls for use with TV tuners and other multimedia devices.

✦ Windows XP Professional x64 Edition. A supercharged version of Windows XP Professional intended for use with microprocessors and software applications that can make use of 64-bit computer words (instead of the more common 32-bit designs).

News you can use: A machine, operating system, and software that can move around 64-bit words can (in theory) calculate and manipulate at twice the speed of 32-bit computers. But other things can choke the speed: the capability of the bus that interconnects components, the capabilities of the memory and the hard drive, and the nature of the work being done.

## Windows Vista

Microsoft also offered five versions of Windows Vista when it was introduced in 2007. (Actually, to be precise, it also announced plans to offer a simplified, lower-cost Starter version that is expected in developing nations and to educational and charitable organizations taking computers to places where they haven't been seen before.)

As with Windows XP, the most common version is likely to be Vista Home Premium; that version and the three preceding it offer the strictly cosmetic but very pretty Aero graphics scheme. All five consumer and business versions can support as much as 4GB of RAM in 32-bit versions:

- ✦ Windows Vista Home Basic. The new look and new "engine" of Vista is here, without the Aero appearance and also missing the Media Center, Windows Movie Maker, and Windows DVD Maker. Also absent: advanced rights management, scheduled backup, and drive encryption.

- ✦ Windows Vista Home Premium. This version and all others beyond Home Basic include the Aero desktop experience. To the features of Basic, it adds the Media Center, Movie Maker, DVD Maker, and scheduled backups.

- ✦ Windows Vista Business. This entry-level version is for business users; it lacks the media, movie, and DVD features but adds remote desktop, rights management, and other advanced features.

- ✦ Windows Vista Ultimate. The kitchen-sink version, it includes the Media Center, Movie Maker, DVD Maker, and every other advanced technical and security feature.

- ✦ Windows Vista Enterprise. Sold as a multi-unit license to large organizations (enterprises), it includes all of the features of Vista Business plus BitLocker drive encryption and a few other advanced features. No multimedia, though.

**Book II
Chapter 1**

**Installing or
Upgrading an
Operating System**

# Seeing the Windows Experience

Are you experienced? Have you ever been experienced? Have you ever heard Jimi Hendrix's guitar wail? You should be able to answer "Yes" to all three questions at some time in your life. And if you've got a laptop running Windows Vista, you should also find out your Windows Experience Index.

As already noted, rarely in the history of personal computing have new hardware and software capabilities been in sync. Often, new hardware — including microprocessors and chipsets — tantalize with their potential for years before software catches up. With the release of Windows Vista in 2007, it was the other way around: Some of the features and the look-and-feel of the operating system only work with the latest, most advanced hardware. That's not to say that Windows Vista can't be installed and used on a machine slightly behind the curve, but some of the bells will be muted and a few whistles won't sound quite right.

The Windows Experience Index is a component of Windows Vista. While not really a tool, it's more of a snapshot assessment of your machine's power and capabilities. But the Index is very valuable if you need to understand how well your laptop will work with Vista, or whether a new piece of software will perform adequately if you install it. See Figure 1-1.

The Index number is automatically calculated by the operating system when you first install it, and you can check the number through the Control Panel. If you later install more memory or adjust the hardware, you can go back and see if the system has determined that your work was of any value. Later, if you suspect your machine is operating beneath its original speed, check the Index to see if it has changed.

When you first receive your new laptop, or immediately after you upgrade your operating system, check the Windows Experience Index via the Control Panel and write down the results somewhere where you can find it again; I usually place notes about hardware and software installation in the original box the machine came in.

## Rating your Experience

The bottom line of the Experience Index is the *base score*. For reasons that must have made sense to someone in marketing, the lowest possible score is 1.0 and not 0. The highest possible score — at the time Windows Vista was first introduced — was 5.9. Microsoft says that it expects to raise the ceiling when new and improved hardware is available.

**Figure 1-1:**
The
Windows
Experience
score for a
zippy
Toshiba
Satellite
P205 lands
right in the
middle, at
3.1, because
of a merely
adequate
graphics
system.

**Book II
Chapter 1**

Installing or
Upgrading an
Operating System

The base score is set at the lowest of a series of subscores. The Index rates the following components:

✦ Random Access Memory (RAM); operations per second

✦ Microprocessor (CPU); calculations per second

✦ Hard disk; data transfer rate for the primary disk

✦ General graphics performance

✦ 3D graphics capability

The base score won't be higher than the lowest subscore; it isn't an average. If the microprocessor is your laptop's weakest link, with a score of 2.8, that's as high as the base score will go. (And since upgrading a microprocessor within a laptop is nearly impossible — or ridiculously cost-ineffective — that's the end of the story.)

Let me put that another way: When I'm talking about scores for the microprocessor, the chipset, and the graphics adapter, the best way to have and hold a laptop with a high Index score is to buy one with the number you want in the first place. Desktop machine owners have much more flexibility when it comes to upgrading things like the graphics adapter and sometimes the microprocessor itself.

On the other hand, if the amount of RAM or the hard disk drive's speed or capacity is holding back your Vista Experience, you may be able to boost the score a few tenths of a point. (Even if it doesn't, more RAM generally improves your laptop's performance, and upgraded hard disk drives are like closets in your house: It's nice to have more space to hold your stuff.)

As the market for Windows Vista software begins to mature, expect to see new applications labeled with Windows Experience ratings as part of their requirements. You may find that a graphics-intensive program lists a score of 3.0 or higher as a necessity for the full experience.

## Going inside the numbers

Windows Vista installs and runs on almost any current laptop. But not all machines can deliver advanced features. Table 1-1 roughly compares base scores.

| Table 1-1 | Windows Vista Experience Numbers |
|---|---|
| *Number* | *Translation* |
| 1.0 – 2.9 | Good enough for the office. Enough power to perform most general computing assignments, including office applications and basic Internet browsing. Don't expect experience Windows Aero or advanced multimedia functions. |
| 3.0 – 3.9 | Got game? Say hello to Windows Aero, and many of the other new Windows Vista features. This is the middle of the road, though; not all advanced features perform at a satisfactory level. For example, there might not be enough power to display Windows Vista at high resolution on multiple monitors or you might be able to display digital TV but not high-definition TV. |
| 4.0 – 5.9+ | Do you want it all? A machine with a base score in this range should deliver all the new Windows Vista features, including Windows Aero and multimedia experiences such as multiplayer and 3D gaming, recording and playback of high-definition TV, and be ready for new features that are added later. |

As this book goes to press, most current consumer-grade laptops are going to be in the range of 3.0 – 3.9. They are limited by the graphics card or built-in graphics facilities of their motherboards. You can expect a boost in the Experience in years to come. If high-end graphics are your highest priority, shop for a laptop that includes an advanced graphics adapter.

## Checking your machine's scores

The Windows Experience is less an *experience* and more like a *viewing*. You can see your computer's score by going to the Control Panel and clicking the Performance Information and Tools icon. Then read the report.

An example of the subscores for a Toshiba Satellite P205, shown in Figure 1-2, shows very high scores for its Intel Core 2 Duo microprocessor, its fast hard disk drive, and the installed RAM. But the fact that the machine relies on the built-in graphics chipset — standard fare for many laptops — drops the base score to mere ordinary.

The score is automatically calculated when Windows Vista is first installed on your machine; it isn't dynamic — it doesn't go up or down as you use your machine or add software. But if you have recently changed — such as adding RAM or installing an improved hard disk drive — you can instruct Windows Vista to recalculate the score to reflect changes. (Remember, though, that the final score will never be higher than the lowest subscore.)

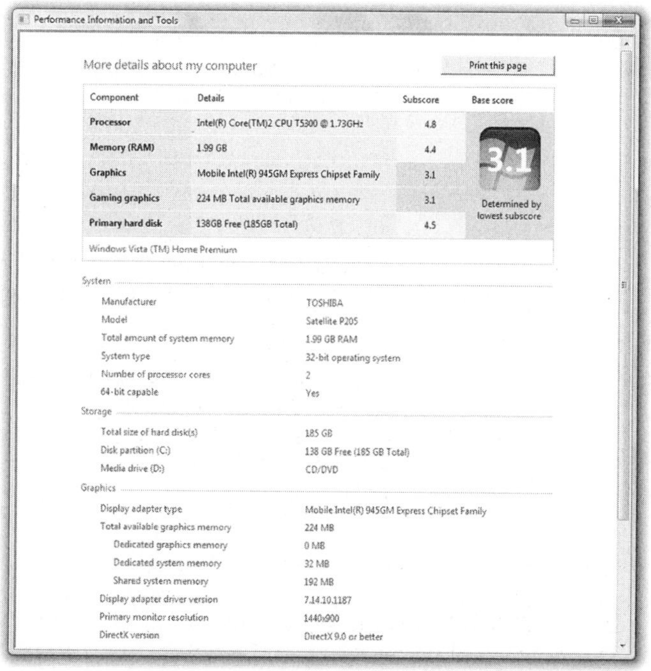

**Figure 1-2:**
An examination of the subscores that lie beneath the base score for the Windows Experience helps pinpoint a machine's weakest link.

Performance Information and Tools

More details about my computer                    Print this page

| Component | Details | Subscore | Base score |
|-----------|---------|----------|------------|
| Processor | Intel(R) Core(TM)2 CPU T5300 @ 1.73GHz: | 4.8 | |
| Memory (RAM) | 1.99 GB | 4.4 | |
| Graphics | Mobile Intel(R) 945GM Express Chipset Family | 3.1 | **3.1** |
| Gaming graphics | 224 MB Total available graphics memory | 3.1 | Determined by lowest subscore |
| Primary hard disk | 138GB Free (185GB Total) | 4.5 | |

Windows Vista (TM) Home Premium

System
| | |
|---|---|
| Manufacturer | TOSHIBA |
| Model | Satellite P205 |
| Total amount of system memory | 1.99 GB RAM |
| System type | 32-bit operating system |
| Number of processor cores | 2 |
| 64-bit capable | Yes |

Storage
| | |
|---|---|
| Total size of hard disk(s) | 185 GB |
| Disk partition (C:) | 138 GB Free (185 GB Total) |
| Media drive (D:) | CD/DVD |

Graphics
| | |
|---|---|
| Display adapter type | Mobile Intel(R) 945GM Express Chipset Family |
| Total available graphics memory | 224 MB |
| Dedicated graphics memory | 0 MB |
| Dedicated system memory | 32 MB |
| Shared system memory | 192 MB |
| Display adapter driver version | 7.14.10.1187 |
| Primary monitor resolution | 1440x900 |
| DirectX version | DirectX 9.0 or better |

# Upgrading to Windows XP

Say you've decided to upgrade to Windows XP from one of its relatively young cousins (Windows 98, Windows Millennium Edition [Me], or Windows 2000 Professional). I discuss the process for Windows Vista later in this chapter.

Before you buy a new version of the operating system, and certainly before you even think about starting to install it, determine the following:

✦ **Does your laptop meet at least the minimum hardware requirements for Windows XP?** An Intel Pentium or Celeron, or an AMD K6, Athlon, or Duron microprocessor or a compatible CPU, running at least 233 MHz (with 300 MHz a more realistic speed), at least 128MB of RAM (although I suggest 512MB or 1GB as the least amount of memory), and a video adapter capable of at least SVGA resolution.

You can visit one of two Microsoft web sites to see if your existing machine should work with XP. Try www.microsoft.com/windowsxp/ home/upgrading/checkcompat.mspx to learn about XP Home Edition compatibility. To see if XP Professional stands a chance, visit www. microsoft.com/windowsxp/pro/upgrading/checkcompat.mspx.

✦ **Can you reasonably expect that your major software pieces — purchased for use with an earlier operating system — will work properly with Windows XP?**

✦ **Will your installed internal and external hardware devices work properly with Windows XP?** In general, you want to use a device driver that's been updated to match your operating system; sometimes a more modern OS works with a driver from the previous generation, but I wouldn't bet the family supply of blank CD-Rs on it.

The Microsoft Windows XP Hardware Compatibility List (HCL) is available at www.microsoft.com/whdc/hcl/default.mspx.

## Hoping to upgrade your OS

You can change the operating system on your laptop two ways. One is to *upgrade* the existing system. The other is to perform a *clean install*. Okay, there's a third way, too: Buy a new laptop with the operating system installed and donate your old one to a school, a charity, or one of your kids. You'll have to migrate your old software to the new one (if you can), or buy new programs. Does this make sense? Some of you are nodding in agreement and the rest . . . well, you were smart enough to buy and read this book, so you're smart enough to make an informed decision about whether upgrading is worth the time, effort, and expense.

The advantage of keeping your existing hardware and upgrading the operating system is that you may be able to keep your current software, utilities, and data and merely replace the operating system. Take the time to consult the web sites and support desks for your software to see if they offer necessary updates for newer operating systems.

If you're going to have to pay for new software, include that cost in the total price of upgrading. Is the purchase of a new operating system plus new software plus time and effort justified?

The disadvantages of upgrading: Any viruses, corrupt files, file system damage, or other problems with the underlying logical structure on the hard drive may (or may not) be solved by the upgrade and could come back to haunt you.

Even though an upgrade theoretically allows you to hold on to your existing data and software, make sure you have a full set of data backups (on CDs, DVDs, or an external hard disk drive) just in case of a problem. You should also gather all your software program discs so you can reinstall them if necessary.

Never attempt to upgrade a laptop that is experiencing problems with its existing operating system. That's just begging for new headaches. Get the old OS running properly, or abandon the thought of an upgrade. Keep the system you've got or go for a clean install.

Microsoft only permits upgrades to Windows XP from certain versions of older operating systems. You can't upgrade from Windows 3.1 or Windows 95 or anything older than those systems, or from any evaluation versions of Microsoft operating systems. Windows NT 3.51 is also incompatible with an upgrade.

Your laptop must be running Windows 98, Windows 98/SE, or Windows Me in order to upgrade to Windows XP Home Edition. To go to Windows XP Professional, you can come from those three earlier operating systems plus Windows NT 4.0, Windows 2000 Professional, and Windows XP Home.

## Safety first: The upgrade rules

If you're like me, you're very cautious when it comes to the essentials of life. (My father calls this a "belt-and-suspenders" strategy.) Microsoft offers the Windows XP Upgrade Advisor for download to create an audit of your computer's current status and a report of any known incompatibilities between hardware and software.

I suggest you do this extra step after you've investigated your machine. After you determine that it meets (or even better, easily exceeds) the hardware requirements and after you closely look at the running software (and checked with the programs' makers to ensure they certified that it runs under

**Book II
Chapter 1**

**Installing or
Upgrading an
Operating System**

Windows XP), then you can run Microsoft's tool. It's a belt-and-suspenders approach, but I'd rather you thank me for the trouble you avoid than blame me for the disaster you find.

Here, then, are **Sandler's Five Rules for Operating System Upgrade Safety.** I'm talking here about Windows XP, although the same principles apply to the newer Windows Vista:

+ **Rule 1:** Before you do anything else, perform your own assessment of your laptop's hardware and software.

+ **Rule 2:** Check with the manufacturer your laptop and any devices you've added on your own to determine if they support an upgrade to Windows XP.

+ **Rule 3:** Determine from the laptop maker if the BIOS needs to be updated. (I explain more in the following section.)

+ **Rule 4:** Do the same with your software makers. Apply all available updates to programs, and consider the cost effectiveness of paying for any required upgrades to software necessary to run under a new operating system.

+ **Rule 5:** Run the XP Upgrade Advisor. If it gives you (your laptop, actually) a clean bill of health, cautiously proceed with an upgrade to Windows XP. On the other hand, if Microsoft notes any compatibility issues with hardware or software, stop. Do not pass go. Do not attempt to upgrade.

If you resolve all the compatibility issues uncovered by Microsoft's tool, you can proceed. If you can't satisfy the tool (a scary thought), I recommend either not attempting an upgrade or seeking professional assistance from Microsoft or the maker of your laptop.

Some computer retailers or repair shops evaluate your machine for a fee or for free; they do so with the hope (or expectation) you'll buy software or hardware from them in return.

## Updating your laptop's BIOS

Depending on your laptop's age, it may be necessary to upgrade your machine's BIOS chip. A computer's *Basic Input-Output System (BIOS)* code is exactly what it sounds like: the lowest level set of instructions used to bring an inert box of silicon, metal, and plastic to life and, once running, to manage the essentials of things like interpreting keystrokes from the keyboard, clicks from the mouse, and getting the computer otherwise able to deal with the operating system, the microprocessor, and you.

Your laptop manufacturer can tell you if it has any available and necessary BIOS updates. (A good manufacturer should have been in touch with you on their own to advise an upgrade, but. . . .) Follow carefully the instructions to download the BIOS update from the Internet and to flash the chip in your laptop. (*Flashing* has nothing to do with sudden exposure of skin to an unsuspecting passerby; it means to send an electrical signal to a special kind of rewritable non-volatile memory to save new code where once there was old.)

Flashing your BIOS with the wrong update, or performing the process incorrectly, can make your machine unable to go on with life; you may damage the BIOS or even the motherboard itself. If you have the tiniest doubt about the process, consult with your laptop maker . . . or don't fix something that isn't broken.

Make sure your laptop is plugged into an AC adapter and has a fully charged battery before attempting to perform a BIOS flash operation; this belt-and-suspenders protects against a power failure or low battery power that could leave you with a crippled machine.

## Running the Windows XP Upgrade Advisor

To run the Microsoft tool, click on "Download the Upgrade Advisor" from this web site: www.microsoft.com/windowsxp/home/upgrading/advisor.mspx.

The advisor will generate a report that describes any "blocking issues" (think of them as headaches, stomachaches, and other reasons you might want to reconsider upgrading to Windows XP). You can see the opening screen in Figure 1-3.

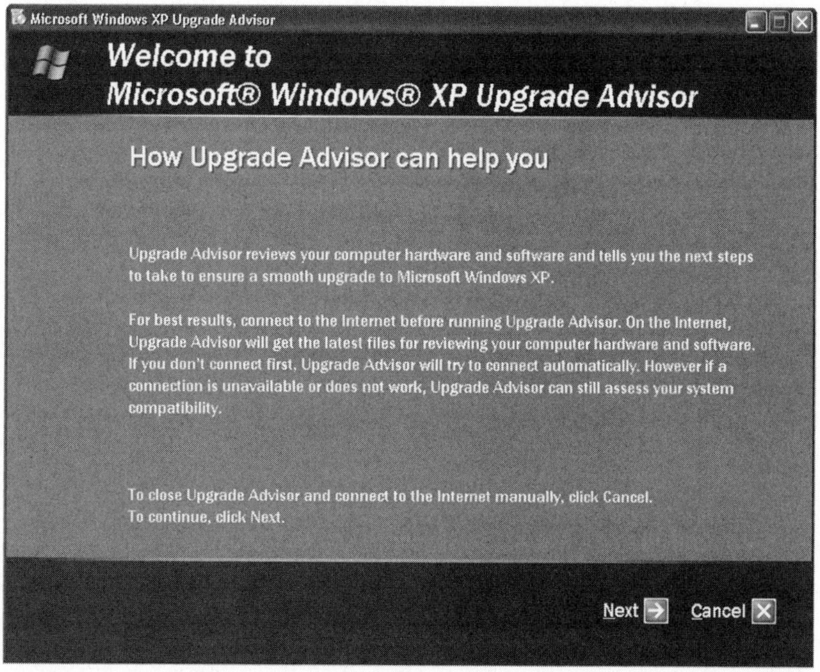

**Book II
Chapter 1**

**Installing or Upgrading an Operating System**

Figure 1-3:
Microsoft's
Windows
XP Upgrade
Advisor, a
free utility,
examines
your
machine to
see if
installed
hardware
and
software
are upgrade
candidates.

**Microsoft Windows XP Upgrade Advisor**

### Welcome to Microsoft® Windows® XP Upgrade Advisor

#### How Upgrade Advisor can help you

Upgrade Advisor reviews your computer hardware and software and tells you the next steps to take to ensure a smooth upgrade to Microsoft Windows XP.

For best results, connect to the Internet before running Upgrade Advisor. On the Internet, Upgrade Advisor will get the latest files for reviewing your computer hardware and software. If you don't connect first, Upgrade Advisor will try to connect automatically. However if a connection is unavailable or does not work, Upgrade Advisor can still assess your system compatibility.

To close Upgrade Advisor and connect to the Internet manually, click Cancel.
To continue, click Next.

Next ▶    Cancel ✖

## Taking final steps before upgrading

You're really going to do this? Here's the preflight checklist:

1. **Make sure the laptop is running from the AC adapter and not its internal batteries.**

   You don't want to run out of juice in the middle of an upgrade.

2. **Turn off any built-in power management settings on your machine.**

   You don't want the LCD shutting off or the hard disk drive spinning down during periods of inactivity. This is one situation where you want all power, all the time.

3. **Run a full antivirus scan on your files.**

4. **Empty the Recycle Bin.**

5. **Run a full drive defragmentation.**

6. **If you have a hard disk maintenance program, scan the disk for errors.**

   Otherwise, use the built-in Windows error-checking facilities accessible by going to My Computer ➪ Properties ➪ Error-Checking.

7. **Disconnect your machine from the Internet (unplug an Ethernet cable or shut off a WiFi link).**

   You need to reconnect later on in the process to register the operating system and download updates, but you don't want anything to interfere with the early steps of the upgrade.

8. **Disable any antivirus programs on your machine.**

   Don't worry — it's safe to do this now that you're disconnected from the Internet. You should re-enable the antivirus once the installation is complete.

9. **Start the upgrade and go watch a ball game.**

   Come back every ten minutes or so to see if you're needed to fill in a name, password, or make option selections. The whole upgrading process should take a few hours; enjoy the ball game.

# Installing Windows XP

The safest way to install a new operating system is to make a clean install onto a new hard disk drive or onto an existing hard disk drive that is reformatted and completely wiped clean of any vestiges of the old.

The downside: All your existing data files, settings, configurations, and program files are scrubbed away to make that clean slate. (Make backups of your data and settings on CDs or DVDs or on an external disk drive or other media.

Software applications can always be reinstalled; you did keep the original discs along with license keys and instruction manuals, right?)

## Making a clean installation of Windows XP

The same advance planning applies as that I recommend for an upgrade: Make sure your laptop more than meets the minimum requirements for Windows XP before you take the first step toward clearing the hard disk drive and installing the new operating system.

Once you install the OS, install your software applications and test them out. The final step is to load your data back onto the drive; putting the data on after the software is installed gives you the chance to clean up any problems related to inconsistent data storage you might have under your previous operating system.

## Installing XP as a second operating system

You *can* have it both ways: running both Windows XP and an earlier operating system on the same hard disk drive. You just can't do both at the same time. It's called *dual booting,* and it works like this: As the machine starts, it pauses and asks whether you feel like a Windows XP kind of kid or whether you're in a retro mood and want to load an oldie from the spinning platter.

Why would you want this option?

✦ Some users need to hold on to and use older software that just won't work under a newer operating system, and this is one way to go back from the future.

✦ Some users are very, very cautious (belts, suspenders, and safety pins) and like to have both the old and new available at least while they test a new operating system.

To install Windows XP to a new folder (also known as a *parallel installation*), you have to start up the machine from a boot disc supplied by Microsoft — not from the hard disk of an already functioning machine. Any of the following can start the machine:

✦ Microsoft Windows 98 or 98SE startup disk

✦ Microsoft Windows Millennium Edition startup disk

✦ Windows XP boot discs (created by the user from within the operating system as an emergency way to start the computer)

✦ Windows XP CD-ROM installation disc

**Book II
Chapter 1**

**Installing or
Upgrading an
Operating System**

To start your machine from a CD you must instruct the Setup screen of your laptop to boot from the CD or DVD drive if it finds a disc there. Consult the your machine's instruction manual for details on displaying the setup screen before the system boots.

### Performing a parallel installation

Setting your machine up with more than one operating system available begins as if you were making a regular installation. However, this is where you start these steps:

*1.* **Press the F8 key at the EULA screen.**

This screen contains Microsoft's bestselling, enthralling piece of popular literature known as the *End-User License Agreement* (known to friends as *EULA*).

*2.* **Select the partition where you want to install Windows XP and then press Enter.**

*3.* **Select the Leave the Current File System Intact (No Changes) option and press Enter to continue.**

*4.* **Press Esc to install to a different folder.**

The Setup program should detect the presence of another operating system and prompt you to enter a name for the new folder after the back-slash. A good and obvious and safe choice would be \WINXP. (If no other operating systems are detected, the Setup program automatically creates a folder called \WINDOWS, but if no other OS is detected and you know there is one . . . well, you've got a problem and should contact Microsoft for support for your newly purchased legal copy of Windows XP.)

*5.* **Follow the more-or-less straightforward instructions to install the second operating system.**

## Seeing to a Windows Vista Upgrade

With each successive improvement in speed and capability for operating systems, the demands upon computer hardware become greater and greater. And just to make things interesting, the two sides of the equation — hardware and software — almost never advance evenly.

Most of the time, the hardware gets way out in front of the software. For example, Intel and AMD are constantly pushing microprocessor design boundaries. The latest, greatest thing is *multicore* CPUs which give the computer two, or four, and eventually even more separate workspaces in the same chip. It will probably take several years before software, and the operating system itself, can make full use of the hardware's advanced features . . .

and by then there will almost certainly be new chips with new capabilities waiting to be used.

## Upgrading editions of Windows Vista

Sometimes the version of Windows Vista that comes preinstalled on your laptop computer may turn out to be less of an "experience" than you desire. Or your needs for advanced features may change over time.

Not to worry; Microsoft has made it easy to change (for a fee) the version of Windows Vista on your machine. Upgrading editions (from Vista Home to Vista Home Premium, for example) is a relatively simple process — much less daunting than changing operating system versions (from Windows XP to Windows Vista, for example).

In many cases, the installation or backup DVD for Windows Vista actually contains the code for all the available consumer editions. To go from one edition to another you'll need to purchase a software *key* to unlock the software. Some users may need to download the new edition over the Internet. See Figure 1-4.

**Book II
Chapter 1**

**Installing or
Upgrading an
Operating System**

**Figure 1-4:**
The
Windows
Anytime
Upgrade is
available
through the
Control
Panel of a
machine
running
Vista.

## Sizing up computer words

One of the elements of hardware evolution has been the increase in the size of the computer "word" that can be operated upon by the CPU and other components. What's in a word? A *word* is the unit of data manipulated by the computer, a particular number of individual *bits* that are grouped together.

Let me try an analogy that isn't about cars. A hungry alligator can open its jaws wide and quickly snap off a large chunk of, well, just about anything. A tiny piranha can do the same, but only with little nibbles. If they're both eating at the same speed — matching bite for bite — then the alligator is guaranteed to win. (What a natural contestant for a hot dog–eating contest, don't you think?)

Some situations — in the computer world as well as in the Amazon River — have even the small mouth (or small-word computer) taking much smaller bites but operating at a much faster speed than the big mouth. But for most of us, it's true that most modern laptops have both a big mouth and a fast mouth at the same time.

A computer microprocessor's design is linked to its word size. The *registers* (storage locations within the CPU) are usually word sized. The amount of data moved between the CPU and the computer's memory, or out of the computer to another device, is usually one word at a time. And software is designed to describe colors, characters, sounds, and other information with words.

The PC world arrived in the 32-bit age (words from 0 through 4,294,967,295) with the introduction of Intel's Pentium CPUs. Today most processors use that design. Just a handful of consumer-grade machines use 64-bit processors, paired with 64-bit versions of Windows XP or Windows Vista, but the future surely lies in that alligator's mouth. Many current programs for use with a 32-bit version of Windows work under a 64-bit operating system, although they may run slower or not play well with other applications. A handful of laptops are now on the market using AMD Turion 64 processors, with Intel equivalents in the pipeline.

## Speeding to a graphic processor

All versions of Microsoft Windows (as well as competitive systems including Apple Macintosh operating systems and Unix and Linux variants) are GUIs. And as GUIs they depend heavily on the speed and power of your laptop's graphics adapter and any specialized or shared graphics memory.

With each successive Windows version, the need for graphics adapter speed has increased. Windows XP was very demanding, and Windows Vista is very, very demanding.

## Take a bit

The original mass-market PCs, mostly built using the Intel 8088 processor, limited to words made up of 8 bits, were very limited in the number of colors and type of graphics they could display. Then came 16-bit systems, which ruled the universe for more than a decade. Today most PCs are capable of working with 32-bit words, and the cutting edge for consumer-grade machines are systems that know what to do with a 64-bit word when they see one.

An 8-bit word can represent a value from 0 to 255; more than one word must be connected to another for values higher than that, although each is evaluated and processed separately. A 16-bit word can represent a number from 0 to 65,535. Among 16-bit processors, the most commonly used was Intel's 80286.

Before you buy a new laptop on which to run Windows Vista, and especially before you consider upgrading an older model to run Vista, make sure the graphics adapter is up to the task. Here is one place where laptops present a challenge not faced by desktop owners: In nearly all laptop designs, you can't replace or upgrade the built-in graphics adapter.

If you're buying a new laptop, make sure it is certified for use with Vista (if that's your intended operating system). If you're hoping to install Vista on an older machine, check with the laptop manufacturer for advice.

Although Windows Vista is "certified" to run on a fairly wide range of graphics adapters, you may find that some older, slower pieces of hardware, or those with insufficient amounts of dedicated or shared graphics memory, may be unable to deliver all of the Vista features. The first feature to go may be the advanced Desktop Experience Microsoft calls Aero.

### Verifying your machine's capabilities

Microsoft, which is, after all, in the business of selling you its operating system, offers several tools that can help you determine if an existing machine's hardware is compatible with Windows Vista. To run an automated scan of your laptop, go to the Windows Vista Upgrade Advisor on the Microsoft web site. See Figure 1-5.

The direct route to that Web page is www.microsoft.com/windows/products/windowsvista/buyorupgrade/upgradeadvisor.mspx. Or you can go to www.microsoft.com and search for Upgrade Advisor.

**Book II**
**Chapter 1**

Installing or
Upgrading an
Operating System

**Figure 1-5:**
The good news in Microsoft's report is that my computer can run Windows Vista if I upgrade. The bad news comes in Devices and Programs, where the utility tells me of some incompatibilities.

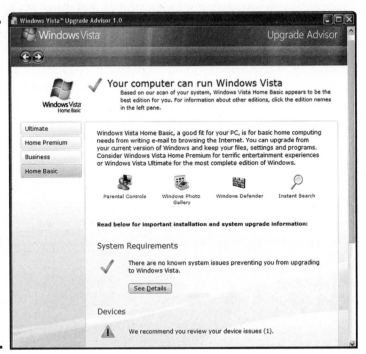

To read about the system requirements for Windows Vista, go to the System Requirements page on the Microsoft web site. To head there directly, enter the following into your Internet browser: www.microsoft.com/windows/products/windowsvista/editions/systemrequirements.mspx. Or you can go to www.microsoft.com and search for Windows Vista system requirements.

Once you've run the report, study its results carefully. The Microsoft utility that examined my laptop found a problem with a nifty little piece of hardware I plug into a USB port, which lets me work with an antique special-purpose printer that insists on an old-fashioned serial port. It also reported several utilities that needed to be replaced or updated if I chose to update to Vista. See Figure 1-6.

You can fix some incompatibilities by obtaining updated device drivers; others may require buying new software or hardware. If so, you need to decide if upgrading is worth the cost in time, effort, and expenditure.

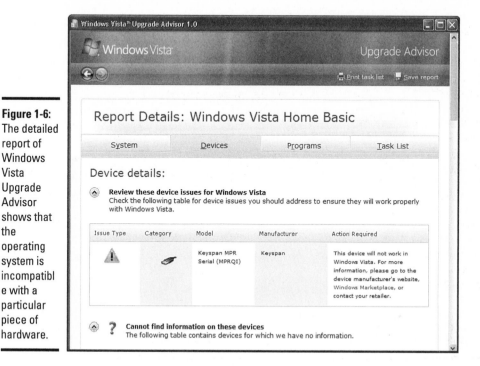

**Book II**
**Chapter 1**

Installing or
Upgrading an
Operating System

**Figure 1-6:**
The detailed report of Windows Vista Upgrade Advisor shows that the operating system is incompatible with a particular piece of hardware.

# Installing Windows Vista

A classic cartoon is regularly used in business, design, and other training classes. (I know, because I use it all the time when I consult.) You don't even need to see the pictures; the words alone tell the story.

Ready?

Fire!

Aim.

Yup, the point is that people who plunge into a project without preparation — and that includes installing or upgrading an operating system — are just asking for a headache that can range in intensity from mild annoyance to a complete failure of all personal and business systems. Stop, look, listen, and think before you act, and you save yourself a lot of time and effort.

## Doing first things first

In the spirit of aiming before you fire, take these logical steps:

1. **Plug your laptop into an AC outlet.**

   You're going to use a lot of power over a period that could extend to several hours, and you don't want your battery to run out of juice in the middle of an installation — that could be disastrous to the process.

   Even better, allow your laptop's battery to receive a full charge overnight before attempting an installation. If you do that, you should have a few hours of battery time to complete the installation or interrupt it at a proper moment in case the AC power fails.

2. **Update your antivirus program.**

   Make sure you have the latest version of your antivirus utility — and that the utility is compatible with Windows Vista. If your protective software isn't intended to work with Vista, uninstall it.

3. **Connect to the Internet.**

   Make sure your system is properly configured and able to get online. If you can do this using the original operating system, Windows Vista can pick up the information it needs to access the Internet without your help. And as installation begins, Windows Vista can automatically go online and download drivers, updates to the operating system, and other elements it may need.

4. **Scan your system.**

   Conduct a full system scan for viruses, spyware, and other nasties. You don't want to install a new operating system on top of old problems.

5. **Update your system BIOS.**

   If your machine was built before the release of Windows Vista, it may require a BIOS update to work with the latest operating system. See "Updating your laptop's BIOS," earlier in this chapter, for advice. And be careful.

6. **Back up your data files.**

   Make copies of any word processing, spreadsheets, databases, music, photos, videos, settings, and any other data you don't want to lose. (You should be doing this on a regular basis anyway, just in case your hard disk drive were to fail. But before you install a new operating system, prepare for the possibility that data may be accidentally lost.)

7. **Disable your antivirus program.**

   This allows the operating system to install and configure itself without tripping on elements of the antivirus program intended to prevent changes to Windows. (Do, though, remember to re-enable the antivirus program once Windows is up and running again.)

## Gathering the essentials

Let me go over the ingredients necessary for this Windows Vista pie:

✦ A Vista-compatible laptop computer. That means it meets all the requirements for processor speed, amount of memory, hard disk storage space,
and a DVD drive to hold the installation disc.

✦ The Windows installation DVD. With Windows Vista, Microsoft began
shipping its operating systems on DVD media. This allows the entire
system to fit on one disc; in fact, Microsoft includes all four of the most
common versions of the OS on the disc. The box you buy includes a key
number that unlocks whichever version you purchased.

If your laptop has a CD drive but not a DVD drive, you can contact
Microsoft and order (for an additional fee) a replacement set of discs in
CD format.

✦ Your product key. You'll find this code number on the disc holder inside
the box you purchase. On a laptop that comes delivered with Windows
Vista installed, the product key should be found on a label attached to
the bottom of the machine.

✦ Your computer name if it is connected to a wired or wireless network in
your home or office. You'll need to instruct Windows on how to find and
work with your machine as part of the installation.

If you don't know your computer name, here's how to find it on an existing
network:

*1.* **Start your laptop.**

*2.* **Click Start.**

*3.* **Right-click My Computer.**

*4.* **Click Properties.**

You find the computer name displayed on the most logically labeled
Computer Name tab.

# Oops, 1 Did 1t Again: Vista Installation Problems

Installing Windows Vista on a properly functioning laptop is pretty much of
an automatic process. Follow the instructions on the package or on the DVD
itself; on many machines you need to reboot the computer with the DVD in
the drawer.

If you're attempting a *full recovery of an existing installation* (resetting the
machine to the condition it was in when you received it from the manufacturer), you may be asked to power up the computer while holding down the

**Book II**
**Chapter 1**

**Installing or
Upgrading an
Operating System**

C key, releasing it when the name of the laptop manufacturer appears on the screen. Several hardware makers configure their restoration discs this way; you may find slightly different instructions with your machine.

You may encounter some other problems.

### Missing product key

If you obtain a copy of Windows Vista as a demo from Microsoft or a retail store . . . or borrow someone else's copy . . . you can probably install it on a Vista-capable laptop. However, you must purchase a new product key *and* activate the OS within 30 days. If you don't, the machine won't explode . . . but the operating system will stop working.

### Problem copying files

If the installation process starts but doesn't finish properly, several possible reasons exist, including

✦ The Windows installation disc is scratched, dirty, or otherwise defective. You can try cleaning the disc with a slightly wet, soft cloth. (Use only water.) Gently clean the disc by rotating the cloth around the platter as if you were moving around a clock face; don't move in from the outer edge or out from the center hole. Allow the disc to dry completely before attempting to use it. If the problem continues, you can get a replacement from Microsoft. Go to www.microsoft.com and search for Replace Lost, Broken, or Missing Software.

✦ Your CD or DVD drive isn't working properly. Try playing an audio music CD or using another disc you know to be in good shape. If they won't load properly, the drive hardware is malfunctioning.

✦ You're using the wrong drive. If your laptop has more than one CD or DVD drive, make sure you're using the proper one. Try installing the Windows disc in the other drive. You might try disabling one of the drives from within Windows so that the system only thinks there is one in the machine.

✦ You have a virus in your computer. You should have dealt with this problem by running an antivirus scan before you attempted the installation; if you didn't, do it now.

### Blue (or black) screen of death

If installation comes to a stop and your laptop screen sits there with an exceedingly dull and uninformative blue or black screen, the first thing you should do is . . . wait. A lot of work may be going on behind the scenes.

Take the dog for a walk. Watch a few innings of a Red Sox game. Talk to your significant other about the depth of your feelings. Or just sit and wait for about ten minutes. Keep an eye on the hard disk drive activity light found on most laptops. If you see it flicker from time to time, the process is probably still going on even though the screen is still blank.

If you've waited ten minutes and nothing at all seems to be happening, you may have a failed installation. Shut down the laptop and remove the Windows installation disc. Try to bring it back to life. If you can't get to the previous version of Windows, follow these steps:

*1.* **Uninstall any antivirus program.**

*2.* **Restart the computer.**

*3.* **Try installing the new operating system.**

Book II
Chapter 1

Installing or
Upgrading an
Operating System

If you successfully install the new operating system, or if you go back to the previous version, don't forget to reinstall the antivirus program.

If you still can't install the new operating system, you may have incompatible hardware in your laptop. Check again at the Microsoft web site to confirm your machine and all its parts are compatible.

If your computer is supposed to be compatible and you've tried the preceding steps, contact your computer manufacturer or retailer for assistance.

## Error message mid-installation

Okay, this one should be pretty obvious: If you receive an error message, read it carefully. If you're lucky (not always the case, alas) it just might tell you what you need to do to fix the problem.

Otherwise, take these steps:

*1.* **Make complete notes on the error message.**

*2.* **If you can get online, go to www.microsoft.com and search for information about the error.**

*3.* **Make a call depending on your installation type:**

- If you're installing new, call Microsoft.

- If you're restoring, call your laptop manufacturer.

## Losing power mid-installation

Always perform an installation with your laptop plugged into an AC outlet and with a fully charged battery in place. This belt-and-suspenders approach should protect you in case the power goes out.

If your machine does shut down in the middle of installation, Windows attempts to go to the previous operating system the next time you try to start it up (although some features may not work or may not offer full function).

If you have to start over, your best bet is to perform a clean installation. Start over from the beginning and reformat your drive and install Windows again. (You do have your data files backed up and your software programs available for reinstallation, right? Good for you.)

### Failed program or piece of hardware

You absolutely, positively checked your hardware and software for compatibility before attempting installation of a new operating system. Sometimes even those who follow all the rules run into problems.

*1.* **Reinstall the program or device.**

Windows Vista may recognize it's missing the latest hardware or software driver and go online to find it. If not, proceed to Step 2.

*2.* **If you can, visit the hardware or software's manufacturer web site and look for a solution posted there.**

*3.* **Call the program or device's manufacturer.**

## Uninstalling Windows Vista

What do you do if you go through the entire process of installing Windows Vista and you find that

Your machine can't handle the pressure?

or

Your software or peripheral hardware won't work properly with it and can't be updated?

or

You just plain don't like what you see in Vista?

First you scream, then you read the next sentence of this book: You can't uninstall Windows Vista.

Wait! Don't panic.

You can reformat the hard disk, erasing Windows Vista in the process, and then reinstall the previous operating system. You do have the original installation disc or discs from the earlier OS, right? If you don't, *now* is the time to panic.

Reformatting the hard disk also takes away all your software applications, as well as any data stored on the drive. That's why you made backups of all your data and gathered all your software installation discs in the first place. Right?

# Activating and Registrating

All sorts of people have all sorts of beefs with Microsoft about one thing or another and I sometimes agree with them some of the time. But here's where I differ: I firmly believe that users should pay for the right to use someone else's intellectual property.

As much as I would love to dispense my pearls of wisdom and offer solutions drawn from my decades of experience as a computer writer, editor, and consultant for free, I can't do that. This book is my work product, and it is offered for sale and its success feeds the mouths of my family, the staff of the publisher, and your friendly neighborhood bookstore. The same goes for software, in my opinion. We all need to pay our share, or else the market will offer no innovation.

Enough preaching to the grumbling choir. Here's the news: Microsoft now requires all users to *activate* their software. It's intended to keep users from installing and using software for which they don't possess a proper license or attempting to use illegally copied software.

That license may come when you purchase software or an operating system through a retail store or web site. Or the license may come along with the laptop as part of the package supplied by the manufacturer.

Beginning with Windows Vista (and other current application software such as Office 2007) you're required to activate your product within 30 days of installation; if you don't accomplish activation, the operating system or software is partially or fully disabled.

If your laptop can get online, you get activate your Windows Vista software that way as part of the installation. An alternate way to activate Microsoft software is to do so by telephone. Consult the instructions that come with the product.

Microsoft promises that the information collected as part of the activation process is used only for the stated purpose — to validate the software — and not to contact you or sell your name to advertisers.

## Reinstalling Windows on the same computer

You can reinstall Windows on the same computer as many times as necessary. The activation process pairs the Windows product key with information Microsoft gathers about your laptop's hardware; if you significantly change the system's hardware (such as adding a new hard drive or more memory), you may be asked to activate Windows again.

Reformatting a hard disk drive erases your activation status. But, of course, you would have to reinstall Windows anyway.

When all else fails — which could mean your operating system is hopelessly corrupted or you've installed a new internal hard disk drive — you may have to recover the original Windows installation. Nearly all laptop manufacturers supply a disc with all that you need, along with in-your-face warnings about the fact that all data files and settings on your drive are about to go to bit heaven. Stop, read, and think before pressing Yes or OK or What the Heck.

In Figure 1-7 you can see an example of a not-subtle warning that Toshiba includes in its reinstallation process; if you miss this little detail, you're moving way too fast for this life.

**Figure 1-7:**
Reinstalling Windows from a recovery disc restores your machine to the way it came from the factory; that means all added programs, utilities, and files are wiped out. You've been warned!

Be sure to follow all instructions displayed on the recovery disc. Reinstalling Windows from a recovery disc can take an hour or more, depending on your machine's complexity and component speed. Don't interrupt the process; doing so may cause file corruption. Always power the laptop from an AC adapter so you avoid running out of battery power mid-recovery. See Figure 1-8. Another possible cause of the need for reactivation: a virus that corrupts your hard disk drive.

## Checking your Windows activation status

You know your copy of Windows has been properly activated if it keeps working 31 days after you installed it. But if you want to assure yourself that you and your machine are in good standing with Microsoft, check your status this way:

*1.* **Click the Start button, then click Control Panel ➪ System and Maintenance ➪ System.**

*2.* **View your activation status under Windows Activation.**

You can also change your product key by clicking Change Product Key.

## Obtaining a new product key

If you lose the product key number that came with your copy of Windows, or if you try to activate Windows with an invalid key, you have to purchase a new code from Microsoft. You find information about how to do this on the Microsoft web site.

**Book II
Chapter 1**

Installing or
Upgrading an
Operating System

**Figure 1-8:**
Are you paying attention? Never interrupt the process of recovering an operating system or installing a new one.

TOSHIBA

**Applying Final Configuration**

*Please wait...*
*This may take several minutes.*
*System will reboot upon completion.*

DO NOT INTERRUPT

TOSHIBA

### Registering your software

Activation is required because it benefits Microsoft. Registration, which is mostly to the benefit of you the user, isn't required . . . but you really should register. When you register your software and provide information such as your street or e-mail address, you are eligible for certain levels of product support, tools and tips, and updates.

## Updating Windows Over Time

It's always in your best interests to keep your Windows operating system completely up to date. Like it or not, you need to obtain and install the latest patches for newly discovered flaws or security vulnerabilities. This is especially important if you use your machine in regular or permanent connection to the Internet. That group now includes most users, and is an example of the two-edged sword that is the World Wide Web: Evildoers are constantly dispatching viruses, malware, and other electronic nuisances.

Think of viruses and malware as burglars sneaking up your street at all times of day and night looking for unlocked doors. Microsoft and other companies are constantly looking for ways to bar the doors, and miscreants are staying up late trying to pick the locks. It's like an unfunny version of the carnival game Whac-a-Mole, but it's a game we must all master. I discuss antivirus and other security software in Book IX.

You have two ways to keep your Microsoft Windows installation updated, and they're interlinked. It all begins with turning on Automatic Updating.

### Automatic updating

If you want to be assured of having your machine kept up-to-date *any time it's connected to the Internet,* instruct Windows to look for and install new updates automatically. The settings for this free Windows feature are here:

*1.* **Click the Start button and click Control Panel.**

*2.* **Click Windows Update; then choose Change Settings.**

*3.* **Choose among the options given.**

Under Windows Vista, you have two main choices, helpfully labeled with a green check mark in a shield or a menacing red X. See Figure 1-9.

- Do you want the system to automatically check for, download, and install updates on a schedule you set?

- Do you want updates downloaded but not installed until you approve?

- Would you like a list of available updates?

The options are discussed further in the following sections.

### Install updates automatically (recommended)

If you select this option, your machine seeks out and finds critical updates, downloads them to your machine, and installs them. You can pick a particular time every day for this to happen, or limit the process to a specific day of the week.

For most users, handing this task to Microsoft and crossing it off your list of things to worry about is best; you might want to select a time of day least likely to interrupt your work — early in the day, late in the day, or during lunch hour, for example. I usually break for a midday precisely at noon (I start earlier than most people) and so I use that time setting for my machine. Certain types of updates require your computer to reboot, and I'm perfectly happy to have all of the toing-and-froing go on while I'm chowing down on a turkey bacon, lettuce, and tomato sandwich on sourdough bread.

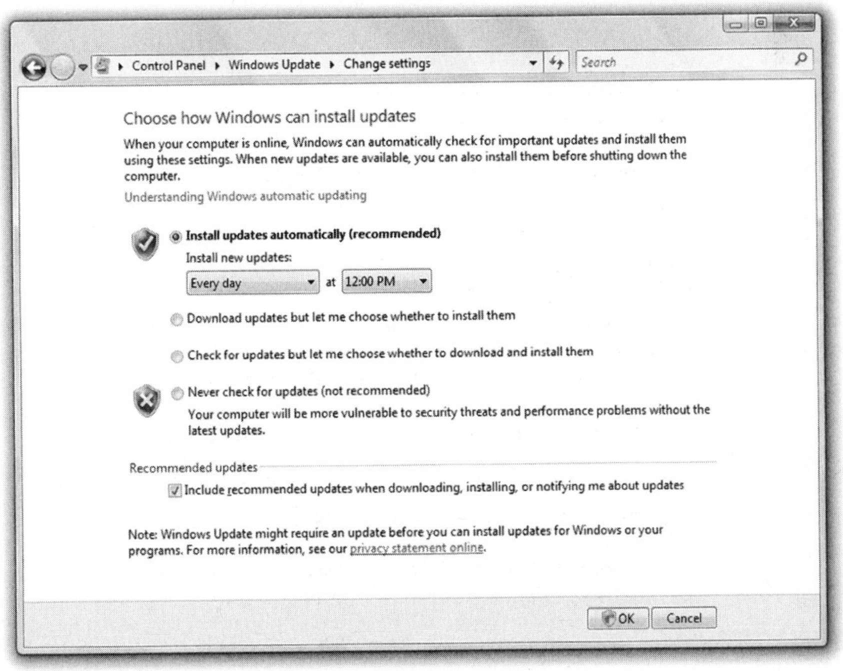

**Book II
Chapter 1**

**Installing or
Upgrading an
Operating System**

**Figure 1-9:**
In the Change Settings menu, you can instruct Windows on how you want to handle updates as they're available.

About once or twice in each operating system's life cycle, Microsoft usually offers a major package of updates and revisions called a *Service Pack (SP)*. An SP can be about as close to a completely new version of Windows as you can get. Most cautious users — and that includes me — usually put off installing a Service Pack for a few weeks after its release to the public. Call me crazy or call me very cautious, but I prefer to allow other people to try it out and look for any major incompatibilities.

### Download updates but let me choose whether to install them

Your system will communicate with the mothership at Microsoft, and suggested downloads are sent to your machine. But you are asked whether you really, really want to have any or all of them installed on your machine. See Figure 1-10.

The latest important Windows updates (plus a few optional ones) are automatically applied during the middle of the night (or the next time you turn on the machine after choosing this setting). You also have the option to install updates immediately.

**Figure 1-10:**
If you have updates for Windows Vista downloaded to your machine but not immediately installed, you can review proposed changes before they're applied at the specified time.

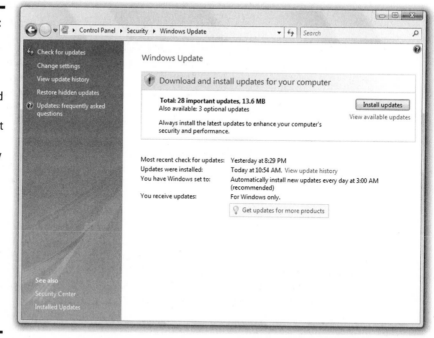

Why might you choose this option?

✦ Because you are very, very cautious about accepting Microsoft's opinion on what to install in your machine. Every once in a while, a Microsoft update introduces problems to a group of computers that might have a particularly unusual combination of hardware and software. Some users prefer to wait a day or so after Microsoft's delivery of an update before actually installing it; in the meantime they can watch the Internet chat pages and computer sites for reports of problems. Or,

✦ Because you may want total control over the timing of any patch installations. You can choose the moment that's best for you: when no critical operations are occurring, when nothing is downloading, or when an automatic or manual reboot (if one is required) won't cause disruption.

### Check for updates but let me choose whether to download and install them.

This approach is the most conservative. Your machine communicates with Microsoft, but all you receive is a list of recommended updates. If you choose to download and install any or all, you can instruct the system to do so.

If you choose the option shown in Figure 1-11, you can examine proposed changes to your system one by one and check off those you want installed. Click any suggested update to learn more about its details, including whether it's an optional update or a critical one, and whether it's intended to fix a problem with hardware or software that you don't have, need, or want.

### Never check for updates (not recommended)

This option is pretty extreme; until you re-enable the update feature, your machine's vulnerable to any new threats or newly discovered problems with Windows.

The only good reason to turn off the check for updates is if you're in the middle of trying to repair a problem with Windows or with an application that causes OS difficulties. It is generally the best practice to isolate your system from any changes while you're trying to make repairs; you can either turn off the update option or disconnect your machine from the Internet if access isn't required while you're making repairs.

Many third-party programs and utilities offer regular updates to their products. These updates may last for the product's life (generally until a new version is released) or a specific period of time; products like antivirus programs typically come with a one-year subscription to updates. Make sure you register your software properly and check regularly with its maker to keep programs current.

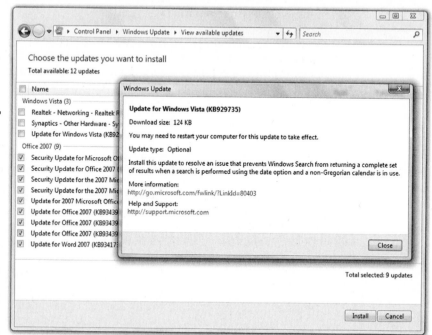

**Figure 1-11:** Microsoft is offering a repair for a relatively obscure problem: search errors for users who aren't using the Gregorian calendar.

## Microsoft Update

The latest wrinkle in support is the Microsoft Update web site, which works in conjunction with Automatic Update to keep not just Windows, but also many other programs, current. It adds automated updates for most of the components of Microsoft Office, Microsoft Exchange Server, and Microsoft SQL Server.

If you turn on Automatic Updates, your computer maintains scheduled contact with this page. If you want to go to Microsoft Update on your own, you can zoom there in one of two ways:

✦ **Click the Windows button, then click All Programs ➪ Windows Update.**

or

✦ **Open your Internet browser and go to www.update.microsoft.com.**

As this book goes to press, the Microsoft Update site supports Windows XP and Windows Vista, as well as current versions of Microsoft Office applications. If your machine is running relatively antiquated programs from Microsoft, including Office 2000 and older software, visit the Office Update web site at http://office.microsoft.com/en-us/downloads.

If you go to the Microsoft Update page on your own (as opposed to Automatic Update) you're offered two options:

✦ **Express (recommended).** The site looks for all high-priority updates for the programs installed on your machine and presents you with a list. You can click a single button to install all of them; some updates, though, must be installed in a particular sequence and may require rebooting between various items on your list.

✦ **Custom.** The site prepares a list of high-priority and optional updates. Use the pointer to tick the check box for individual items (or the entire list) and install them with one click; as with the Express option, you may have to install certain priority updates individually with a reboot between items.

**Book II
Chapter 1**

In the list of optional material, you can select Don't Show Me This Update Again. If you do, the list of options is reduced. If you want to restore a "hidden update," Microsoft has you recovered. On the web site, click Restore Hidden Updates, and that's exactly what it does.

If you hide a high-priority update, the system regularly reminds you that your system is missing a critical update. And if you later accept an update that requires a component you chose not to install, the web site brings the earlier update back to the list.

*Optional updates* are, well, optional. They may address minor issues that might not apply to your system or to the tasks you perform, or they may add some functions to your computer that you may not need or want. Read the optional updates' descriptions and make your own decision whether to bring them to your machine.

To read more about the nature of each update, click its name in the list. To read about system requirements and support information, click the Details link in the description.

Some updates, generally those that add new functions, may require you to accept one of Microsoft's highly entertaining and informative EULAs (pronounced *YOO-lah* by those in the know). The End User License Agreement protects Microsoft's patents and rights; it's a take-it-or-leave-it proposition for you the end user.

And certain updates require you to shut down any running applications (be sure to save any open data files first) and then reboot the system so Windows loads with all changes applied. If you've given Windows permission to download and install updates on its own, you may return from a trip to the refrigerator to find that your system has rebooted by itself. See Figure 1-12.

**Figure 1-12:**
Some updates require a reboot. If you download and automatic- ally install updates, your system may have shut down and restarted. You did save all your work before you left, right?

## Opening the door to Update

If you're very strict about your computer's security level, you may need to manually unlock the door to let Microsoft Update keep your operating system updated. To add this facility to your list of trusted web sites, open Internet Explorer and do the following:

*1.* **Click Tools ⇨ Internet Options.**

*2.* **Choose the Security tab, then click Trusted Sites ⇨ Sites.**

*3.* **Type** www.update.microsoft.com/microsoftupdate **in the space labeled Add this Web Site to the Zone.**

*4.* **Click Add ⇨ OK.**

# Losing Support

Microsoft's support for older versions of Windows only goes so far. Eventually the engineers move on to newer challenges, and you're left to fly through the air without a safety net.

Here's the official word from Microsoft: When you buy a product, the company promises to offer a *minimum* of five years of support for most operating systems and office applications, and three years of support for products released in annual versions (such as Microsoft Money, Streets & Trips, and the like).

Here's what Microsoft means by support: During the "mainstream" support period, the company maintains a team of engineers to patch any security breaches and repair any newly discovered problems or incompatibilities. The repairs are automatically delivered and installed on your machine if you use Automatic Update, and are available for manual installation from the Microsoft web site if not.

Keep these points in mind:

+ The support period begins with the product release. If you're the very last person to buy an operating system that a newer edition has replaced, the period of support is shortened. However, that five-year period has also proven to be a rolling deadline; when the release of Windows Vista was delayed, Microsoft extended its support for several of its older operating systems.

+ Once the active support period ends Microsoft maintains web sites with previously released patches and updates, as well as its Knowledge Base of repairs for known problems.

---

## Today's specials

As this book goes to press, Microsoft is only offering active support for three operating systems:

✔ Windows Vista: in all its various flavors.

✔ Windows XP: in all editions, but only for operating systems that have been updated with Service Pack 2; if you haven't installed SP2, that major update is available from Microsoft.

✔ Windows Server 2003: for operating systems updated with Service Pack 1.

✔ Windows 2000: for operating systems updated to Service Pack 4.

That means users still getting useful work out of laptops running Windows 98SE, Windows Me, and earlier operating system can rummage through Microsoft's online closet for old patches and repair tips, but won't receive new updates. And Windows 2000 is shuffling off toward retirement.

**Book II
Chapter 1**

**Installing or
Upgrading an
Operating System**

It isn't a perfect system, but it works pretty well for most users. If you have a machine and an operating system that work properly, and you don't need each and every new hardware and software advancement, you've no need to change your operating system.

And, in fact, many users see no point in making a radical change like going from Windows XP to Windows Vista; the newest operating system requires hardware capabilities that weren't offered when XP was introduced. And as we have already explored, most laptops have only limited areas in which their hardware can be upgraded.

More to the point: Although modern laptops are generally very well put together, their useful life is probably somewhere in the range of three to six years. Even if the hardware is in near-perfect shape after that period of time, you're eventually going to grow weary of lugging around an obsolete model. If you catch yourself casting envious glances at the machine in the aisle seat of row 24, or across the coffee shop at the table with the Dulce de Leche Latte, it's only a matter of time.

Microsoft warns (and it may well be correct) that users who continue working with retired operating systems are at risk of security breaches. However, it's also true that the bad guys move on: If someone is going to sit down and write a virus, he's more likely to attack the latest operating system — not one being used by fewer and fewer people every day.

# Chapter 2: Painting Flames on the Operating System: Customizing

## In This Chapter

✔ Choosing the Windows that match your decorum

✔ Picking a peck of pretty pixels

✔ Pointing with pride

*I*t's called Microsoft Windows, but for most accomplished users the goal is to make it your very own: My Windows, My Computer, My Colors, My Fonts, and My Sounds.

Microsoft does a pretty good job of building a soft machine that you can customize, adapt, rearrange, and decorate in nearly infinite versions. Just beneath the surface of Windows XP and Windows Vista (as well as older versions of the operating system) lies a full set of tools that give you the Power of Self-Configuration.

For your own convenience, and just because you can: Go forth and customize. I show you how.

In this chapter and throughout this book I use Windows Vista as the sample operating system; the basic concepts of customization are the same for all Windows versions. Where needed, I point out Vista-only facilities.

## Making New Screen Resolutions

Your laptop's screen is a *tabula rasa,* which is a highfalutin way of saying it's a blank tablet. Within the laws of physics, you can draw shapes (including letters and numbers) of any size.

It comes down to the screen resolution. Pardon me for a brief excursion into the land of technicalities; in computer terms *resolution* is determined by how many *picture elements* (or *pixels* or *dots*) your screen displays across its width and down its length. The more dots it has, the finer the level of detail; however, some of the details may be so small that they're hard for you to see.

If you want to get real, think of resolution in terms of this page, the one in the book in front of you. You can't change the width and length of the piece of paper; the same is true of your laptop's screen. However, the fine design team who put this book together could have used very large letters to make it big enough to read from across the room. The problem is, though, that only a few words would fit on each line. Or they could have chosen to save a forest full of trees by using eensy-teensy characters that allowed a few thousand words on the page. The problem with that? You might not be able to read these pearls of wisdom.

Getting back to computers, there's one other issue involved: A high-resolution display, one that uses millions of dots, requires a great deal more processing power and a lot more memory. And laptops have one additional issue: LCD screens are less flexible in their ability to work at various resolutions. LCDs generally have one *native* resolution, and any other selection is created through some fancy electronic footwork, which may or may not yield the best possible picture.

The base resolution for what is now an old-fashioned *cathode ray tube (CRT)* monitor on a desktop computer was 640 × 480 dots (a total of 307,200 pixels), although most users worked at higher resolutions, typically 1,024 × 768 (more than double the number of pixels, at 786,432). Today, most LCDs start at 1,280 × 800, and many can go much higher. And LCDs are now offered in widescreen versions that allow you more real estate to work with.

Our example of a current laptop, the Toshiba Satellite P205, has a native resolution of 1,440 × 900 (1,296,000 pixels). If you go to the Control Panel and select the icon for this particular machine's built-in graphics adapter (an Intel Graphics Media Accelerator Driver for Mobile), you find that you can downgrade the resolution to 1,280 × 800 or 1,024 × 768 (as well as several intermediary steps). A multimedia or gaming superstar may offer a native resolution of 1,920 × 1,200 on a widescreen version that allows you more real estate.

Going away from a laptop's native resolution usually results in a muddy and unappealing image onscreen — very different from the crisp image you see when you accept the default setting.

## Picking a pretty palette

One setting you can change on your laptop LCD is the number of colors used to construct images. The standard setting for most laptops is 32 bit, which allows for use of colors from a palette of 16,777,216 hues and intensities; in most systems, 32-bit color actually uses 24 bits to define the color and an additional 8 bits of information for other arcane details like transparency and texturing. You might pick up a few milliseconds of speed if you choose to downshift the color setting to 16 bits. Me, I leave this setting the way it came from the factory.

## Displaying the graphics control screen

Most laptops have two (sometimes complementary, sometimes superfluous) control panels to adjust screen resolution. Every version of Microsoft Windows includes a Display Settings window as part of the Control Panel, and this usually lets you change screen resolution and number of colors. An Advanced Settings tab may open the door to more technical adjustments.

The second set of controls is provided by the manufacturer of the graphics adapter or the chipset built into your laptop's motherboard. You may find that this window offers additional features; at the very least it's customized to the particular hardware in your machine.

To work with the generic graphics control window, click the Start button and choose the Control Panel. For an example, see Figure 2-1.

If you're running Windows Vista, follow these steps:

*1.* **Click Appearance and Personalization ⇨ Personalization ⇨ Display Settings.**

*2.* **Under Resolution, click the slider and move it to a setting of your choice.**

   For an LCD screen, the default is usually the highest resolution.

If your machine is using Windows XP, follow these steps:

*1.* **Go to the Control Panel.**

*2.* **Click Display Properties and choose the Settings tab.**

**Book II
Chapter 2**

Painting Flames
on the Operating
System: Customizing

**Figure 2-1:**
The standard set of controls offered by Windows allows you to select resolution and high or medium levels of colors, as well as other settings.

**3. Adjust the Screen Resolution slider.**

To work with the customized control panel provided by the graphics adapter or chipset maker, look for an icon in the Control Panel that has the manufacturer's name. It may be Intel or ATI for chipsets, or you may see the name of a graphics card like Radeon or nVidia. Sometimes graphics adapters makers place an icon in the taskbar's notification area; clicking opens a utility that allows you to adjust settings. See Figure 2-2.

**Figure 2-2:** The LCD Display Settings panel offered by many graphics adapter or chipset makers offers specific and more detailed choices than the generic controls that ship with Windows.

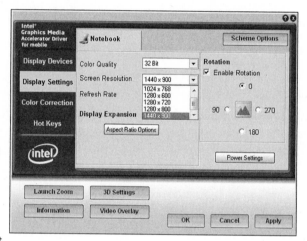

## Clarifying your view with ClearType

Microsoft offers a special technology that enhances the way text looks on an LCD screen; this special form of magic essentially manages to make something out of nothing. When you enable ClearType on an LCD screen, the system can use the individual vertical color stripes that make up each pixel on the screen.

It all comes down to adding an almost-invisible extra bit of thickness or thinness to letters onscreen, making use of fragments of pixels. ClearType almost always improves the appearance of text, especially on fonts with serifs. *Serifs* are the little lines like the shoulder pads on the letter T or the extra horizontal marks on a V; serif fonts also have varying thicknesses of certain parts of letters. The top half circles of the letter C may be thinner than the main part of the letter. Serif fonts are vestiges of old type styles, and we continue to use them because they're usually easier to read than *sans serifs* (without serifs) typefaces, which are considered more modern. In the book you're reading, the main text uses a serif font while the captions are in sans serifs style.

Do you have any reason not to enable ClearType on your laptop? Not as far as I'm concerned, although that's just my opinion; turn it on and see if text seems sharper and easier to read. If it looks worse to *your* eyes, turn it off.

 ClearType is for use with flat-screen LCDs like that on your laptop. It generally doesn't offer any noticeable improvement when used with a standard CRT monitor, although you can experiment with it turned on. And it has nothing to do with the appearance of type when you send a file to a printer.

To enable use of ClearType on your LCD, follow one of the following sets of instructions based on your OS.

For Windows Vista systems:

*1.* **Click the Start button.**

*2.* **Click Control Panel ➪ Personalization ➪ Click Window Color and Appearance ➪ Open Classic Appearance Properties.**

*3.* **Click the Effects tab.**

*4.* **Make sure this option ha a check mark: Use the Following Method to Smooth Edges of Screen Fonts.**

*5.* **Choose ClearType.**

See Figure 2-3.

**Book II
Chapter 2**

**Painting Flames on the Operating System: Customizing**

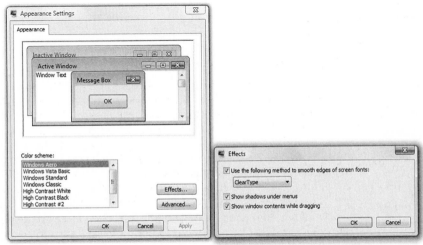

**Figure 2-3:** Enabling ClearType adds a small but noticeable improvement in the quality of characters displayed on an LCD.

For Windows XP systems:

1. **Go to the Control Panel and then click the Display icon.**

2. **Choose the Appearance tab and then click the Effects button.**

3. **Look for the dialog that asks: Use the Following Method to Smooth Edges of Screen Fonts.**

4. **Make sure the check mark alongside is enabled and then choose ClearType.**

Once you install ClearType on your machine, you may be able to kick it up a notch by going to the Microsoft typography web site and following the instructions for tuning the technology to match your particular combination of graphics adapter and LCD.

## Themes Like New or Old Times

Both Windows XP and Windows Vista presented significant changes — some say improvements — over previous versions. Windows XP made a number of major changes compared to Windows 98, while Windows Vista buffed and polished Windows XP.

But what may seem new and refreshing to some users is unfamiliar and uncomfortable to another. And so Microsoft offers users the option to go back to the past — at least in appearance — by selecting the Windows Classic theme, which presents an updated but recognizable version of the Windows 98 Control Panel, settings windows, and other features. You gain all the advantages of the improved engine without having to deal with a new appearance.

For Windows Vista users to select a theme, follow these steps:

1. **Click the Start button and click Control Panel ⇨ Appearance and Personalization ⇨ Personalization ⇨ Theme.**

2. **Under Theme, select the design you want and then click OK.**

Each person who has an account on the computer can choose his or her own theme.

For Windows XP users to select a theme, follow these steps:

1. **Go to the Control Panel.**

2. **Click Display and choose the Themes tab.**

3. **From the Theme drop-down menu, choose one of the available designs.**

Most laptop manufacturers offer their own themes, usually centered around an obnoxious display of their company name or logo. You may also find themes offered as freeware or for sale; never download or use software or settings from a web site you don't trust.

You can start with someone else's theme and modify it to your preferences. Or you can create your own theme, with its own desktop background, color selection for windows, and assigned system sounds.

Make your changes by following these steps:

*1.* **Go to the Control Panel.**

*2.* **Click Display and choose the Appearance tab.**

*3.* **Click the Advanced button and select options.**

*4.* **Return to the Themes tab.**

*5.* **Click Save As.**

*6.* **Enter a name for your custom theme.**

*7.* **Click Save.**

## Securing a Screen Saver

Every screen deserves to be safe; it's your responsibility as a laptop owner. I'm not talking about protection from ridiculous Nigerian lottery scams that come in by e-mail or the bizarre cow-tipping fetish web sites you visit when no one is watching.

No, I mean your screen should be protected against the serious scourge of *burn-in.* That's what happens when a program displays the same icon or image in the same place for a long time. The danger is that the display will become permanently etched with that particular symbol.

You should note that burn-in is much more of a danger to what is now considered the old-fashioned CRT that desktop computers used. LCDs used on laptops (and increasingly, with desktops) are more resistant to burn-in. However, you can cause a problem to LCDs if you display an unchanging, unmoving image for an extended period. I consider 24 to 48 hours or more to be worthy of concern.

Many LCDs are self-repairing; if an image is burned in, try solving the problem by turning off and rebooting. Sometimes it may require several on/off cycles before the liquid crystals return to their original condition.

How to protect against burn-in? The simplest solution is to enable a screen saver that comes on after a preset period of time and replaces the unchanging image with either a blank screen or moving image. Another advantage to using a screen saver: It keeps others from seeing the data on your screen . . . unless they lean in and press a character on the keyboard to clear the saver. (Some screen savers can be set up to require a password before they go away and the data returns.)

Many laptop owners enjoy setting up their machine to display unusual images. For a while, flying toasters were all the rage. Today, many users allow the laptop or OS maker to use the space for floating advertisements.

Now here's the bad news: A screen saver uses power to generate and move the image. It also requires power to illuminate the backlight, an essential element of an LCD. If your laptop is plugged into an AC electrical source, that's not an issue (except for your electrical bill and your personal contribution to global warming). However, if you're traveling, a full-color image of a waltzing cow is going to shorten the time you can run your machine off the battery. It might be a few minutes, but sometimes every minute counts.

On my laptops, I set up the screen saver to simply blank the screen to black, which results in a small draw on battery power. I can tell that laptop is still powered up by the little lighted battery icon on the front edge.

Never use a screen saver sent to you by someone you don't know, or download one from a source you cannot be certain is legitimate. A screen saver is a piece of active code and could easily be designed to include a virus or other malicious programming.

## Changing your screen saver

To set or change a screen saver, perform one of the following sets of instructions.

Follow these steps on a Windows Vista system:

*1.* **Click the Start button.**

*2.* **Click Control Panel ⇨ Appearance and Personalization ⇨ Personalization ⇨ Screen Saver.**

See Figure 2-4.

On a Windows XP system, go to Control Panel ⇨ Display ⇨ Screen Saver tab.

Under either operating system, look through the available images (including Blank) in the drop-down list and select one. You can see a preview of the design, and select the period of time of inactivity before the screen saver takes over the screen. Some of the screensavers also offer user-configurable settings.

**Figure 2-4:**
Windows offers a variety of screen savers, from the demure to the flashy. You can set the time period before the screen saver becomes active and make other adjustments.

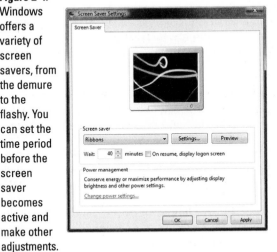

## Creating your own screen saver

Notwithstanding my recommendation to use a blank screen when you're running on batteries, you can create your own screen saver using pictures or videos.

Follow these instructions if you're on a Windows Vista machine:

*1.* **Click Control Panel.**

*2.* **Click the Personalization icon.**

*3.* **Click Screen Savers ⇨ Photos.**

This creates a slideshow from all images in the Photos folder.

Follow these instructions if you're on Windows XP:

*1.* **Click Control Panel.**

*2.* **Double-click Display.**

*3.* **Choose the Screen Saver tab.**

The Screen saver drop-down menu appears.

**4. Choose My Pictures Slideshow.**

This option automatically cycles through images it finds in the My Pictures folder. (Make sure you're okay with displaying anything that's there; if you have a picture that is much too personal for this use — and you know what I mean, right? — move it out of that folder to keep it off your screen.)

### Deleting a screen saver

The basic screen savers provided by Microsoft as part of Windows are yours to keep whether you like them or not; you can't remove them. However, if you've added a screen saver on your own and you want to be rid of it, that's easy to do.

Under Windows Vista, follow these instructions:

*1.* **Click the Start button.**

*2.* **Click the Control Panel.**

*3.* **Choose Programs ➪ Programs and Features.**

*4.* **Highlight the screen saver you want to remove.**

*5.* **Click Uninstall.**

For Windows XP users, follow these instructions:

*1.* **Go to the Control Panel.**

*2.* **Click Add or Remove Programs.**

*3.* **Highlight the screen saver you want to remove.**

*4.* **Click Uninstall.**

# Customizing the Tiny Picture on Your User Account

Windows users can add the ultimate in personalization to the little picture next to your user account (as well as on screens or menus that list your user name, including the Welcome Screen and Start menu). You can choose any of the generic images supplied with the operating system, or you can use a photo or drawing of your own.

If you want to use your own art, save it to your machine as a GIF, JPG, or BMP image format. The picture is going to be very small onscreen, so you can save space by saving it at a small size — about 1 × 1 inch — and at a screen resolution of 72 dpi.

On a Windows Vista machine, follow these steps:

*1.* **Click the Start button.**

*2.* **Click Control Panel ⇨ User Accounts (called User Accounts and Family Safety in certain editions of the operating system).**

A list of available user account changes appears.

*3.* **Click Change Your Picture.**

*4.* **Perform one of these steps:**

- Select the picture from the supplied images.
- Click Browse for more pictures and locate the image you want to use.

On a machine using Windows XP, follow these steps:

*1.* **Open the Control Panel and click User Accounts.**

*2.* **Choose an account to modify.**

*3.* **Click Change My Picture.**

*4.* **Perform one of these steps:**

- Select the picture from the supplied images.
- Click Browse for more pictures and locate the image you want to use.

Book II
Chapter 2

Painting Flames
on the Operating
System: Customizing

# *Hanging Wallpaper on the Desktop*

Some people — starting with me — like a simple black background behind the icons on the desktop. (I prefer simple elegance without distraction; whatever the male equivalent of a little black dress with pearls is, that would be my choice in fashion.) But then there are those who like plaid and madras and spinning bowties with LEDs. I suspect these same people like to dress up their desktop with pictures of their children or their pets or their significant others.

To meet this pressing need, Microsoft allows you to change the desktop background. It's actually called *wallpaper,* and you can choose one of the backgrounds provided with Windows, use a digital photo of your own, or use a solid background color.

To change the background, follow the set of instructions that match your OS.

On a Windows Vista machine:

*1.* **Click the Start Button ⇨ Control Panel ⇨ Appearance and Personalization ⇨Personalization ⇨ Desktop Background.**

**2. Choose the picture or color you want for wallpaper.**

If you want to use an image of your own, use the Browse function to locate the file on your computer. Double-click the image you want to use.

On a Windows XP system:

**1. Go to the Control Panel and click the Display icon.**

**2. Select the Desktop tab and choose an image.**

Otherwise, use the Browse function to locate the file on your computer. Double-click the image you want to use.

**3. Decide whether to**

- Have the picture fit the entire screen (an option that may result in distorting the picture)

- Center the image on the screen

Another way to make wallpaper out of any image stored on your computer, or nearly any image you're currently viewing, is to right-click the picture and then click Set as Desktop Background.

# Seeking Sidebars, Gadgets, and Doodads

Okay, there's nothing officially called a *doodad* (or a *geegaw* or a *thingamabob*), but Windows Vista offers a growing variety of things called *Sidebars* and *Gadgets*. What are they? Why, they're high-tech doodads.

A *Sidebar* adds new levels of active miniprograms and utilities being constantly updated from within your computer or from a source out there somewhere on the Internet. For an example, see Figure 2-5.

Your first assignment is to decide whether to use the Sidebar at all. Then decide whether to display it, hide it, and keep it on top of other windows. Finally, you can add or remove gadgets in the Sidebar; you can even detach individual gadgets from the Sidebar and place them on the desktop as items of their own.

## Opening and closing a Sidebar

Follow these steps to open Windows Sidebar:

**1. Click the Start button.**

**2. Click Programs ⇨ Accessories ⇨ Windows Sidebar.**

**Figure 2-5:**
In my Windows Vista Sidebar I monitor the weather in three places of interest to me, watch the fluctuations in the exchange rate for Danish krone, keep tabs on the stock market, and more.

Or, you can follow these steps:

*1.* **Click the Start button.**

*2.* **Enter** sidebar **in the Start Search window below All Programs.**

*3.* **Press Enter.**

   To close, right-click the Sidebar icon in the taskbar's notification area and then click Close Sidebar.

Exiting Sidebar closes the applications and gadgets and also removes the Sidebar icon from the taskbar's notification area. To get out, right-click the Sidebar icon and click Exit.

## Hiding and seeking with Sidebar

If the information the Sidebar shows is of paramount importance, you can have Vista display it on top of other windows. If you make that choice, any programs you open and maximize are automatically butted up against the Sidebar on the left or right side of the screen but not displayed over the top. (This works especially well on a widescreen laptop LCD; you can run your word processor or Internet browser at nearly full size, and keep an eye on sports scores, temperatures, exchange rates, or whatever gadgets you installed in the Sidebar.)

To make this setting:

1. **Right-click the Sidebar or the Sidebar icon in the taskbar's notification area.**
2. **Select Windows Sidebar Properties**
3. **Click to add a check mark to Sidebar Is Always on Top of Other Windows.**

   See Figure 2-6.

From the same properties screen you can instruct the system to always start Sidebar when Vista is loaded. You can also choose whether Sidebar is displayed on the left or right side of the screen.

And if you have a second monitor attached to your laptop, you can instruct the system whether to display Sidebar on one or the other display.

**Figure 2-6:** Sidebar properties in Windows Vista include placement and gadget display.

## Adding a gadget

You can add any installed gadget to your Sidebar. You can even add multiple copies of the same gadget. (Why? Perhaps you need to be constantly up-to-the-second on the time of day in Longyearbyen, Norway, as well as Papeete, Tahiti.)

1. **To add an installed gadget, right-click Sidebar and click Add Gadgets.**

   You see a display of the Gadget Gallery. See Figure 2-7.

2. **Double-click the doodad you want to use.**

To download a new gadget to your machine, consult Microsoft's official site at http://gallery.live.com.

**Figure 2-7:**
The Gadget Gallery shows gadgets that come standard with Windows Vista, as well as those you've added on your own.

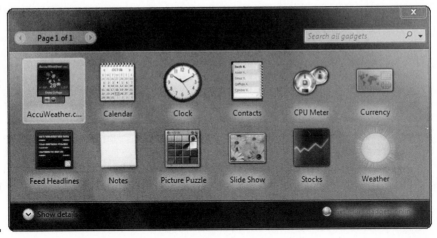

You may also find other gadgets offered for free or for sale at other web sites. Be very cautious about accepting one of these bits of active code from any supplier you don't know and trust; an evildoer could easily embed a virus in one.

## Detaching a gadget

You can fiddle with gadgets quite a bit. To release a gadget from the Sidebar and place it somewhere else on your desktop, follow along:

1. **Right-click the gadget and choose Detach from Sidebar.**

2. **Click and drag the gadget to the location you prefer.**

   To reattach the gadget, right-click it and then choose Attach to Sidebar.

To search for gadgets installed on your computer, locate the plus sign (+) at the top of the Sidebar and click it to open the Gadget Gallery. If you've installed just a few dozen or so, you see all their icons displayed; if you have more than can be shown at once, you can move from page to page by clicking the arrows at the upper-left corner of the Gallery. You can jump directly to a gadget if you know some or all of its name; enter it in the Search All Gadgets box.

# Mousing Around

At the heart of the concept of a GUI is the ability to reach in and move things around on the screen. Now, I'm assuming you realize that the "things" you're moving around aren't real — they're just two-dimensional pictures constructed out of illuminated dots. And you're not "reaching in" and touching anything; instead, you're using the computer's power and the operating system's intelligence to identify and act upon these virtual objects as if they were three dimensional.

All this is related to the creation of a bitmap, something like a gigantic checkerboard that allows the system to give an address to every part of the screen. The address is constructed from the intersection of numbered vertical columns and horizontal rows.

A computer *bitmap* is essentially an electronic version of Cartesian coordinates. Allow me to save you a trip back to your dusty old high school geometry textbooks. French mathematician René Descartes conceived of a system that allowed the determination of any point on a plane based on X (the horizontal axis) and Y (vertical axis) coordinates. In eighth grade, when you drew a chart of average temperatures across a week or month, you were using a form of Cartesian coordinates.

As you move your mouse, pointing stick, or any other similar device from location to location, the operating system maps its location by its column and row coordinates and makes note of what lies beneath — a button you can push, a check box that you can check, or part of an alphanumeric character or a picture.

Enough technobabble. The great thing about modern laptops is that you don't have to know about things like bitmaps, virtual objects, hot spots on the screen, or even how a touchpad or mouse works. (You don't need to know how an engine works in order to drive a car, but you do need to master the controls: the gas pedal, the steering wheel, and the brakes being most important.)

## Configuring your pointer

Mouse Properties sounds like a real estate directory for rodents. It's not, of course: It's the screen (or set of screens and advanced settings) that allows you to customize the way your laptop's pointing device responds to your touch and implements your commands.

Because laptops are essentially an all-in-one-box solution, nearly all models come with their pointing device installed. You may have a touchpad, a pointing stick, or some other variant.

New systems, delivered with Windows preinstalled, have the proper device driver in place. If you update your version of Windows (from Windows XP to Windows Vista, for example), the operating system automatically detects the installed device and locates a device driver for it (or asks you to provide it from a resource disc or from the Internet).

An example of a Mouse Properties screen for a built-in touchpad can be seen in Figure 2-8. The Synaptics Touchpad is used in laptops from many major makers including Toshiba, as well as Acer, Dell, Gateway, HP, and Lenovo. Most control panels let you choose the button actions (favoring lefties or righties, for example) and adjust how fast your double-clicking finger needs to be.

Many control panels for pointing devices let you customize the pointer itself. You can adjust the acceleration — how quickly the pointer travels in relation to your movement on the touchpad. One nice feature that works well with most applications and many web sites is a Snap To function, which automatically moves the pointer to whatever onscreen button is marked as default or most important in a dialog box. (This is often the OK or Next button, but in some instances programmers try to prevent accidents by setting the Cancel button as default.) See Figure 2-9.

**Figure 2-8:**
A Buttons tab for a Synaptics Touchpad in a Toshiba Satellite laptop.

**Figure 2-9:**
The Pointer Options dialog box of Mouse Properties usually offers valuable customization tools. Try them all and keep the ones that fit your work habits.

## Advanced mousing

Some manufacturers allow even greater customization of your mousing experience. Look for an Advanced button on one of the settings dialog boxes. For example, in Figure 2-10 you can see the highly customizable features of the Synaptics Touchpad installed in the Toshiba Satellite P205 laptop.

Another situation where you may find highly specialized controls is on a laptop where you choose to add an external pointing device such as a clip-on mini-mouse, an external full-size mouse, or a drawing tablet. These devices come with their own device drivers and install their own set of utilities in the Windows Control Panel, the Windows taskbar, or both.

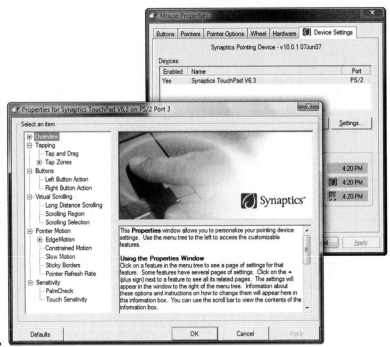

**Figure 2-10:** Advanced pointing device controls include adjustments to sensitivity of the touchpad and the use of "tap zones" to issue commands.

# Chapter 3: Transferring Settings, E-mail, and Documents

## In This Chapter

✔ Making your new machine act like your old one

✔ Transferring files and settings with the Windows Vista wizard

✔ Going back from the future with Windows XP

*I*nertia is a powerful thing. I'm not just talking about how nice it is to just sit there in your chair and not have to stand up until lunch. I'm also talking about how wonderful it is to have your laptop finally set up exactly the way you want it, with Internet and e-mail working properly, and all your preferences in place; when someone offers you a brand-spanking-new high-resolution widescreen multicore machine, the thought of having to redo all of those settings is *almost* enough to make you say, "No, thank you."

Almost enough.

Instead, know how to use the Windows Vista advanced features (and the almost-as-advanced similar facilities of Windows XP) to automatically transfer much of the personality of one machine to another.

## Giving Your Laptop a Personality Transplant

Microsoft has made it pretty easy to bring the look and feel and technical settings of one machine to another. If you're moving information from a laptop running Windows Vista to another machine running Windows Vista, you can make a near-identical clone. If you're changing from Windows XP (or an earlier, less-capable operating system) to Windows Vista, you get as much as the older OS can offer, but you have to configure the newer O/S on your own.

You can copy these items:

✦ User accounts

✦ Folders and files (including music, pictures, and video)

✦ Program settings

✦ Internet settings

✦ Internet favorites

✦ E-mail settings

✦ E-mail contacts and address books

✦ E-mail messages

What *can't* you transfer? In a word, software. Okay, a few more words: And the operating system.

Software and the operating system can't be automatically transferred by Windows for two pretty good reasons:

✦ It's dangerous. You could end up moving a corrupted or outdated version of programming to an otherwise unsullied machine. And your new machine may be organized differently than the old machine (different labels for hard disk drives, different folder names, a different file attribute system).

Some third-party software programs (not from Microsoft) promise to move software from one machine to another. I've even seen them work. But I can't guarantee 100 percent success with them, especially as software makers move to sophisticated validation schemes for their offerings.

✦ It's unseemly. The license for your software or operating system may not allow transfer to a different machine without the manufacturer's permission. Like it or not, software makers are becoming more insistent on treating their work as if it were a physical object; you can move it from one place to another (with permission) but you can't clone it so it exists in two places at the same time.

Some software makers offer multiple-machine licenses that permit installation of their products on two or more machines. That's a pretty good deal for a laptop if you want to have the same program on your laptop as you have on your desk.

## Using Windows Easy Transfer

Microsoft lays it on the line with the name of their utility in Windows Vista. Easy Transfer is supposed to be an automated tool that does all the heavy lifting of bits and bytes and transfers them to a new machine. And to a great degree, what they say is what you get.

Access to the transfer program is one of the choices on the Welcome Center screen that insists on popping up every time you start Windows Vista . . . until you uncheck the little box at the bottom of the screen to tell it not to do it again.

The other way to find the transfer utility is this:

*1.* **Choose Start ⇨ Control Panel.**

*2.* **Open the System and Maintenance folder.**

Choose the System folder if you're using Classics Menu.

*3.* **Choose Getting Started with Windows.**

The Windows Welcome Center is resurrected.

## *Revving up your transfer*

Before you can proceed with a transfer, you must shut down all running programs (except for Windows and — in most cases — your antivirus program). If you forget to do this, the program reminds you in midstream and waits for you to clear the decks.

You should always run an up-to-date antivirus program on all of your machines. I recommend conducting a full system scan of your old machine before you begin transferring files and settings to a new one; otherwise, viruses and spyware will happily hitch a ride over to your new machine.

Windows Easy Transfer works if you're seeking to move files and settings from a computer running Windows XP or Windows Vista to another machine running Windows Vista. If your old computer is running Windows 2000, you can transfer files but not settings. See Figure 3-1.

**Figure 3-1:**
The process for using Windows Easy Transfer is spelled out step-by-step on successive screens.

One exception: Windows XP Starter, a version of that operating system intended for use in third-world nations and certain other developing markets, doesn't work with Windows Easy Transfer. If you somehow have a copy of that limited operating system, you have to manually copy files you want to transfer and move them using a CD, DVD, flash disk drive, or other media.

If your source machine is running a version of Windows older than Windows 2000 (including Windows Me, Windows 98, or Windows 95), you should be able to purchase a third-party transfer program at a computer retailer.

Your first choice when using Windows Easy Transfer is between the following:

✦ Start a new transfer. You can select files and settings to move to a new system.

✦ Continue a transfer in progress. This allows you to resume a transfer where you've already made your selections.

The program asks if the machine where you're working is your new computer (the *destination* for the transferred files and settings) or your old computer (the *source*). The recommended procedure calls for starting the process on the new machine.

### Getting from here to there: Means of moving

You have three ways to move settings and data from one machine to another.

✦ **Easy Transfer cable.** Easy Transfer cable is the Microsoft moniker for a specialized USB cable that connects two machines; it differs from a regular USB cable because it has a large A connector at each end, instead of the typical large A computer end and small B device end.

Start Windows Easy Transfer on the new (destination) laptop and plug in the cable only when you're instructed to do so. You may need to use the Windows Vista installation disc on your old (source) computer to install the Easy Transfer utility there; the onscreen instructions walk you through the process.

✦ **Direct transfer over a network.** You must properly configure both source and destination computers and connect them to the same wired or wireless network. Start Windows Easy Transfer on your new (destination) computer. To transfer the files from the source computer, you're directed to obtain a key from the program on the new machine and then enter that key on the old (source) machine. The key serves as a password to protect files and settings moving over a shared network.

✦ **Removable media.** Copy files to a USB flash drive, a CD or DVD, or an external hard disk drive and then bring the media from the source to the destination for transfer. See Figure 3-2. As part of the process, Windows Easy Transfer estimates how much space is needed on a removable medium.

- A standard DVD can hold about 4.7GB of data.

- A dual-layer DVD can hold about 8.4GB.

- A CD has smaller capacity, usually between 600 and 800MB.

- Flash memory devices are now available in sizes up to 16GB (and you'll probably see them go much higher).

Another option is to copy the files you want to transfer to an external hard disk drive and then bring that drive from the source to the destination computer. The utility can split the files into as many groups as necessary, spreading data across more than one CD or DVD, or allowing you to use a flash drive as many times as needed to move all the files and settings.

**Figure 3-2:**
A flash memory drive is an easy way to transfer settings from one machine to another. This avoids setting up a wired or WiFi network connection between machines before settings have been moved.

### Feeling choosy about files to transfer

Sometimes you want to bring over everything from your old computer, and sometimes you want to have a nearly fresh start. Windows Easy Transfer offers three options.

✦ **All user accounts, files, and settings.** This choice is recommended if you want to essentially clone one machine to another (except for the operating system and software applications). All users need to create a new password the first time they log on to their account on the new computer.

If you've already created user accounts on the new computer, you can match the new accounts to the source accounts. (The new account names can be the same, or you can make changes in the process of matching settings from one machine to another.)

You must have administrative privileges on both machines to use the All User Accounts option. Administrative privileges are used mostly in large office settings where the computer department seeks to maintain consistency (and control) over all machines.

If you haven't yet created user accounts on the new computer, you can establish them as part of the transfer process. And again, they can be the same user accounts as existed on the source machine, or you can create new ones and match the data as you wish.

✦ **My user account, files, and settings only.** If you will be the only user of your new laptop, or if you do not intend to set it up with separate accounts for other occasional users, you can choose to transfer only the information that is associated with your personal user account on the source computer. You need to create a new password the first time you log on to the new computer.

✦ **Advanced options.** If you want to get choosy, transferring some user accounts but not others, or certain folders or program settings but not all, then come here. (See Figure 3-3.) This is called advanced because, well, it's not for newbies. If you're not certain which files or folders you need, or the nature of settings files, consult the Help section for each program (and Windows) for assistance.

## Revealing the secret beauty of a settings transfer

If you really want to be a cautious and very smart computer user, you can use Windows Easy Transfer (or the similar File and Settings Transfer Wizard of Windows XP) to make backup copies of your settings and configurations — and even your files.

Pretend you're setting up a new computer and gather all the files from the source machine onto a removable medium such as an external hard drive, DVD, or flash memory key. Then put the medium on the shelf and leave it there. In case of disaster, you can reconstruct all your essential settings and the files — as of the date you made the copy — for reinstallation on any machine.

## Windows XP Files and Settings Transfer Wizard

If your new machine is running Windows XP, you have a utility called the Files and Settings Transfer Wizard (that performs similarly to the Windows Vista Easy File Transfer utility). The wizard isn't magical (a bit less polished than the latest and greatest) but still allows most users to migrate their settings and files from one machine to another.

If your new (destination) machine is running Windows Vista, use the Easy File Transfer program that comes with that operating system. The installation disc for Vista includes a utility that you're asked to load onto your older machine to automate the process.

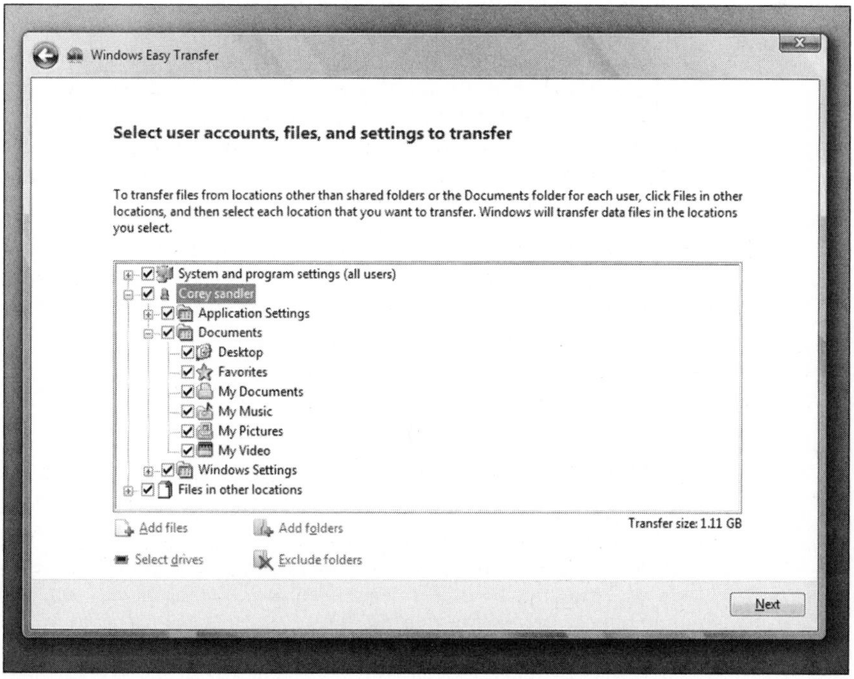

**Book II
Chapter 3**

Transferring
Settings, E-mail,
and Documents

**Figure 3-3:**
The advanced options of Windows Easy Transfer let you choose specific types of programs and settings.

Windows Easy Transfer

**Select user accounts, files, and settings to transfer**

To transfer files from locations other than shared folders or the Documents folder for each user, click Files in other locations, and then select each location that you want to transfer. Windows will transfer data files in the locations you select.

- System and program settings (all users)
- Corey sandler
  - Application Settings
  - Documents
    - Desktop
    - Favorites
    - My Documents
    - My Music
    - My Pictures
    - My Video
  - Windows Settings
- Files in other locations

Transfer size: 1.11 GB

Add files    Add folders

Select drives    Exclude folders

Next

The file wizard works with any operating system from Windows XP back in time through Windows Me, Windows 98, and Windows 95. You can transfer data from machine to machine over a

+ Network cable

+ PC-to-PC USB cable

+ Special form of serial cable called a *null modem* that can be purchased at computer stores; some software utilities designed for file transfer include this cable

 Note that most modern machines no longer offer serial ports. You can, though, purchase converters that make a USB port act like a standard serial connection, or that add a USB connector to a standard serial cable. In some designs and applications, these serial conversions operate much slower than either standard serial or newer USB ports.

To run the wizard, follow these easy steps:

*1.* **Connect the two machines by cable.**

*2.* **Click Start ⇨All Programs ⇨Accessories ⇨ System Tools ⇨Files and Settings Transfer Wizard.**

Unlike the design of the Windows Vista utility, under Windows XP you can start the transfer process at either end — the source or the destination. You need either your original Windows XP installation disc or to create a transfer floppy diskette (blast from the past) or use a flash memory key or other portable medium.

## Exporting Outlook Express or Windows Mail Contacts

If you run your life by e-mail (guilty as charged, dear reader) maintaining schedules, receipts, and confirmations in the folders of your mail client, you may want to spend the time every week or so backing up your address books and mail.

For most Windows XP users (as well as those people using outdated but recent versions of the operating system including Windows Me, Windows 98, and Windows 95) the most common e-mail client is Outlook Express, which is provided free as part of Windows. You may also choose to use a third-party e-mail client such as Eudora. Another option is Microsoft Outlook, which is a full-featured e-mail, calendar, and contact-management software package sold as part of various Microsoft Office packages. For simplicity's sake, I recommend Outlook Express.

With the introduction of Windows Vista, Microsoft differentiated between Outlook and its basic Outlook Express. Within Vista, the free e-mail client is called Windows Mail; that program is a slightly more polished version of Outlook Express.

As you explore in Book VIII, two common mail protocols in use on personal computers have an important difference.

## POP3

POP3, the current version of an older *Post Office Protocol (POP)* that dates back to the early days of PCs, downloads copies of all mail from wherever the messages are located and places them in a folder on your computer.

That's good, in a way, because you'll know you have a copy. But that's bad if your hard disk drive or the computer itself dies. And it isn't all that great for laptop users if you download e-mail onto your desktop machine and then hit the road without copies. And if you pick up mail while on the road, you may need to export copies to your desktop from the laptop.

## IMAP

*Internet Message Access Protocol* (*IMAP* or sometimes referred to as *IMAP4*) works differently than POP3. E-mail that comes into your Internet service provider's server stays there, on that server. Each time you sign on to look at your mail, a copy of the header (the subject, sender, date, time, and other information) is sent to your computer. To read a message's details, you instruct your e-mail client to download the message; however, your desktop and laptop keep no copy unless you instruct your computer to store it in a local folder.

Why is IMAP a better way?

✦ It adds a layer of protection against viruses and spyware; you can look at the e-mail headers sent your way and delete them from the server before they download to your laptop. (And most e-mail or Internet providers also scan messages at their end, identifying most viruses and other would-be intrusions; depending on your instructions to the provider, the nasty bits may be removed from the message, the entire message may be discarded, or the message may be marked as Spam or Virus to warn you of its content before you touch it.)

✦ Of particular value to laptop users is that any messages you receive while you're traveling also show up on your desktop when you return home. (That is, unless you move the message to a local folder on your laptop.)

Book II
Chapter 3

Transferring
Settings, E-mail,
and Documents

If you're given a choice when setting up your e-mail client (most commonly Outlook Express on Windows XP, or Windows Mail on Windows Vista) I recommend choosing IMAP. If you're not given a choice, contact the Internet provider and ask them to assist you in establishing an IMAP account.

# Exporting Address Books or Business Cards

For some users, even more important than the mail itself is the address book associated with an e-mail program. Here's where you store (or allow the computer to automatically store) the names, e-mail addresses, and other information about the people with whom you correspond.

Moving a contacts list with you is valuable when you move from machine to machine. You might also want to donate your list to a coworker or family member; make sure you think that gift all the way through before going ahead, though.

The process is simple.

1. *Export* **the address book (the term used in Outlook Express) or contact list (as is called in Microsoft Mail) to a file and store it on your computer.**

2. **Move a copy to the new machine.**

   Do so over a network or by copying it to a removable media such as a CD, DVD, external hard drive, or flash memory key.

3. *Import* **the file into the destination e-mail program.**

Windows Mail and Outlook Express support *exporting* the following types of address books:

✦ Microsoft Exchange Personal Address Book

✦ Text File (Comma Separated Values)

Windows Mail and Outlook Express support *importing* the following types of address books:

✦ Eudora Pro or Light Address Book (through v3.0)

✦ LDIF - LDAP Data Interchange Format

✦ Microsoft Exchange Personal Address Book

✦ Microsoft Internet Mail for Windows 3.1 Address Book

✦ Netscape Address Book (v2 or v3)

✦ Netscape Communicator Address Book (v4)

✦ Text File (comma-separated values)

✦ Business Card (vCard)

## Exporting and importing with Outlook Express

From within Outlook Express you can export address book data for use with another installation of the same program or to the full-featured Outlook program. The file you create can also be converted for use by Microsoft Mail and by many third-party e-mail programs.

*1.* **Choose Tools ➪ Address Book.**

*2.* **Choose File ➪ Export.**

To export an address book, follow these steps:

*1.* **Click the address book you want to export.**

*2.* **Click Export.**

*3.* **Follow the instructions on the wizard.**

*4.* **Store the file in the location of your choice.**

To export a business card, follow these steps:

*1.* **Click the desired .vcf file.**

*2.* **Click Save.**

Importing works the same, only backwards:

*1.* **Open Outlook Express.**

*2.* **Choose the Tools menu and click Address Book.**

*3.* **From the File menu, point to Import.**

*4.* **Browse to the location of the file you want to use.**

## Exporting and importing with Windows Mail

To export or import with Windows Mail, you have two choices (and one minor name change). With this program, the address book is called contacts.

To export, do one of the following:

*1.* **Choose File ➪ Export ➪ Windows Contacts.**

or

*2.* **Choose Tools ⇨ Windows Contacts ⇨ Export.**

To import, you have two choices:

*1.* **Choose File ⇨ Import ⇨ Windows Contacts.**

or

*2.* **Choose Tools ⇨ Windows Contacts ⇨ Import.**

## Exporting saved mail and mail folders

Exporting individual mail items or entire mail folders is similar to exporting an address book or contacts list. However, if you have a POP3 account, the mail itself resides on your laptop. If you have an IMAP account, the mail is somewhere out there in cyberspace.

To export messages from Outlook Express or from Windows Mail, do this:

*1.* **Click File ⇨ Export ⇨ Messages.**

*2.* **Perform the step based on your program:**

- **In Outlook Express:** Click OK to accept the following: This will export messages from Outlook Express Mail to Microsoft Outlook or Microsoft Exchange.

- **In Microsoft Mail:** Select the format you want to export mail to: Microsoft Exchange or Microsoft Windows Mail.

*3.* **Select a folder to hold the exported messages.**

# Chapter 4: Managing Files, Folders, Extensions

---

## In This Chapter

✔ Filing your tax forms . . . and everything else

✔ Uncovering hidden filename extensions

✔ Putting files into folders and moving them about

*I*'m a pretty organized guy; some might call me slightly obsessive. Within the bounds of reason, I try to have a place for everything, and everything in its place. That doesn't mean from time to time I don't build up a foot-high pile of papers on my desktop, but when the mountain threatens to topple over I stop production for a while to put things right.

I sort the papers by subject and then prioritize them. I have boxes that hold folders for things that need to be done immediately, things that need to be done later, records of tasks already accomplished, and ideas and notes for future projects. And I also maintain a lifetime collection of receipts, tax forms, and banking and investments records.

New stuff goes into new folders. Items that are continuations of earlier efforts are added to existing folders, and I place the folders between labeled dividers in one of four filing cabinets in my office. And at least once a year, I throw away anything that has sat around so long that I no longer remember why I kept it in the first place.

Now, I don't want to name names, but there's a woman I know very well whose idea of organization is to build those piles higher and higher until eventually she has to move to a different desk. Happily, she hasn't lost me in more than a quarter century of marriage, but over time she has misplaced just about everything else for at least some period of time.

## Opening an Electronic Filing Cabinet

Apparently the early designers of operating systems saw the world somewhat in the way I do, because from the start the metaphor for organizing massive amounts of information on a computer was a set of filing cabinets filled with folders.

The original PC *operating system (OS)* was envisioned as a tree with a thick root at the bottom, a substantial trunk, and then increasingly thinner and more distant branches. The base was (surprise) called the *root directory,* and the first level of subdirectory could branch off into an almost infinite number of subdirectories.

With the arrival of Windows, the same concept was envisioned by someone who must have seen my wife's desk. The *graphical user interface,* our friend the *GUI,* asks you to think of the opening screen (after all of the advertisements and advisories have come and gone) as the *desktop.* You can put just about anything you want on that desktop, but sooner or later it's going to get crowded, making it very difficult to find particular items.

Windows designers want you to think of their electronic desktop as sitting atop a set of broad and deep file cabinets. Back to the original computer metaphor: The desktop is the big sunflower and beneath it the folders and subfolders are the ever-narrowing roots.

And, with many modern computers and laptops containing more than one physical hard drive, or more than one *logical drives* (a physical drive identified to the OS as if it were two or more separate drives), you have wonderful options for a very sophisticated organizational scheme for your documents, media, and software.

That is, if you bother to use the tools at your disposal. Let me try to help.

# Rocking the Files

A file is a document, a picture, a song, a discrete piece of programming, or a stored setting or configuration. If you think that sounds like a very broad definition, well, you're right; in computer terms, a *file* is any stored block of information that has a name or number that the system is responsible for tracking.

A document created in Microsoft Word is a file. So, too, is a downloaded song from iTunes. And all of the thousands of identifiable sets of programming that make up software applications and the operating systems.

The Toshiba Satellite P205 that I am using as an example of a current machine has a capacious 200GB hard drive within its case, a piece of electronic real estate that was unimaginable for a laptop a few years ago. But today it needs that much space for the super-sized Windows Vista OS, as well as the many advanced purposes for which I use it, including capturing, editing, and playing back digital music, video, and photos. That one machine can easily build up 500,000 or more files of various sizes on it.

Can you imagine if all of those files were lumped into a big pile, kind of like the stack of papers on my wife's desk? The stack would be very, very tall. It would be difficult to find a particular file; once you retrieved a file it would be hard to remember where to replace it (assuming you had some kind of scheme in mind), and there would always be the possibility of a catastrophic collapse for any number of reasons: a gust of wind, a pounce of cat, or a discouraging word.

The solution is the big O, and I don't mean origami or that other thing (Oprah). I mean Organization.

## *Naming your files*

You can call your file Joe, or you can call it Al, or you can call it just about anything else that makes sense to you.

But remember a few important rules:

+ **Files are identified by three components.** The most important part is the filename, which is in the middle of the mix. The file location appears before the filename. And after the filename (although you may not notice this unless you go out of your way to look it up) is something called a filename extension (explained later in this chapter).

+ **Don't give two files the same name and filename extension . . . if they're in the same location.** If you did that, the computer wouldn't know which one you wanted, right? That statement has several "ifs," though. You can use the same filename for files with differing filename extensions. And you can have exactly duplicate names and extensions if the identical files are placed in differing (sub)folders or on a different drive inside or outside the laptop.

+ **Don't use certain characters as part of the filename.** Why? Because the computer wants those just for itself, usually as part of the location. Actually, this mostly irrelevant holdover comes from the days of DOS, but the banned characters are still part of modern Windows.

   The dirty near-dozen do-not-use-in-your-filename characters follow:

   / \ = + [ ] < > : ; " .

   The system uses the period to indicate the place where the filename ends and the extension begins.

+ **You can use a space or an underscore in your filename.** These placeholders are one way to give meaning names to files. For example, you could use filenames like these:

   My plans to rule the world

   My_Plans_To_Rule_The World

✦ **You can use CAPITAL letters or lowercase letters.** This also helps make sense of filenames. However, although the system records the name aNyHoW you want, you can't have two same filenames that differ only in capitalization. For example, the system allows you to save your files under either but not both of these names:

My Great American Novel

my great american novel

✦ **Keep it brief.** The filename can't be longer than 255 characters, including spaces, and applies if you're using a modern OS that employs the NTFS *file allocation table (FAT)* system. Some OS versions older than Windows Vista and some applications like WordPad don't like filenames longer than 127 characters. And if your machine uses a hard drive that is indexed using the old FAT system, you might be all the way back to what used to be called 8.3 filenames: eight characters in the name and two or three characters in the filename extension.

## Decoding hidden filename extensions

If filenames on current operating systems can be so long and descriptive, why do they also need an extension? It sounds like screen doors on a submarine, or training wheels on a tricycle, or political debates for and against the Department of Redundancy Department.

By default, Windows hides the filename extension when you look at a list. It does this, I suppose, because the wizards behind the curtains at Microsoft don't want to confuse poor users with more information than they really need. (Ha! If I had a dollar for every time a user became confused by a Microsoft decision . . . well, I'd have almost as many dollars as Bill Gates, I suppose.) You can usually get by without seeing the filename extension because the OS converts that extension into a recognizable icon, and because Windows automatically matches up most common file types with the appropriate program.

The filename extension identifies the *type* of file, not its name. You should know this for two important reasons:

✦ Literally thousands of different file types are in use on laptops, and personal computers and some are structured quite differently from another for good reason. For example, a file that contains the description of an image or a song may need to be laid out very differently from a spreadsheet or a word-processing document or a program. Sometimes the difference between file formats is a matter of finding the most efficient way to store a particular type of data; sometimes the various file formats are unusual just because one programmer insists on it.

✦ One of the virtues of Windows is that it maintains *associations* between filename extensions and the programs they work with. This little trick is pretty handy: Click a file with an extension .DOC and Windows automatically opens Microsoft Word with that document displayed, for example. The same works with spreadsheet files, which should open your spreadsheet program, and digital images files, which should bring your image editor to life.

As noted, known filename extensions come in the thousands. Table 4-1 lists some of the more common ones and the programs they're ordinarily associated with.

| Table 4-1 | Common Filename Extensions | |
|---|---|---|
| *Extension* | *Commonly Associated With* | *Function* |
| AI | Adobe Illustrator | Vector graphics file |
| AVI | Windows Media Player and compatible software | Audio Video Interleave for video files |
| BMP | Most image editors | Bitmap image file |
| DLL | Microsoft Windows | Dynamic Link Library of shared fonts, icons, and definitions |
| DOC | Microsoft Word | Document |
| DOCX | Microsoft Word | Office 7 document file |
| EPS | Encapsulated Postscript | Printer image file |
| JPG or JPEG | Most image editors | JPEG File Interchange Program (compressed image) |
| MP3 | Audio players or editors | MPEG music file (compressed) |
| MPEG | Video players or editors | Motion image file (compressed) |
| PDF | Adobe Reader and compatible graphics-editing programs | Portable Document File |
| PSD | Adobe Photoshop | Native image format |
| TIF or TIFF | Most image editors | Tag Image File Format (uncompressed image) |
| TXT | Word processors and simple text editors | Simple text file |
| ZIP | Windows or Unzip/Zip utilities | Compressed file |

When you install many programs, you're given the option of making that application the default association for a particular filename extension. For example, if you have more than one digital image-editing program on your computer (I have four on my laptop), you can assign the most sophisticated to automatically open with a complex TIFF file, the quickest and simplest to the most basic GIF file, and a specialized program to work with RAW files produced by a particular brand of digital camera.

The bidirectional nature of Windows means that even if a particular filename extension is associated with a particular program that doesn't mean you can't open and use that file by loading a capable program and then opening a file from a selection box.

If a program has somehow added the wrong extension to a filename, you can change it by following the same instructions I give later on in this chapter for changing the filename itself. Just add a period and the extension you want, as in .TIF for a TIFF image file. Note that changing a filename extension doesn't change the format of the file itself, but in certain rare situations, changing an extension solves a problem that's preventing you from opening a file with a particular program.

## Exposing those hidden filename extensions

To its credit, those same Microsoft engineers who tried to make things simple by hiding filename extensions also let you see them if you must. The process is easy, but be careful: You don't want to click the wrong box and make the Windows gods unhappy.

Here's how to instruct Windows to show filename extensions in all folders and other places that use the Windows Explorer system. These instructions apply to Windows XP; the process for Windows Vista is similar.

*1.* **Click Start ➪ My Documents (or double-click any folder).**

This opens Windows Explorer, the system that displays files and folders.

*2.* **Choose Tools ➪ Folder Options ➪ View tab.**

You get into the super-secret hidden area of Advanced Settings.

*3.* **Locate the Files and Folders section, and then find the Hidden Files and Folders section.**

*4.* **Click the Hide Extensions for Known File Types check box.**

*5.* **Click OK.**

While you're in the neighborhood, if you really want to be master of your Windows file and folder universe, you can also click the nearby button that says Show Hidden Files and Folders. Doing this instructs Windows to display the usually hidden system folders and files scattered here, there, and everywhere on your hard disk drive.

Showing hidden files is interesting to some users because, well, they love this sort of stuff. For most users, it's a bit overwhelming and not of much use.

One time you'll find it valuable to see hidden files and folders is if you get error messages complaining that Windows can't find a particular file. You can search for the file using the Windows built-in Search facility or you can conduct a folder-by-folder manual hunt — if you've turned on the display of hidden files and folders, that is.

## Changing a filename association

Suppose somehow your computer thinks it can open and edit a graphics file in a word processor? If you went down this road, you'd mostly likely see a screen full of 0s and 1s or other symbols and characters that are anything but words to be processed.

Or, suppose you have several graphics programs on your laptop. Say you have one or another of the utilities supplied with Windows (Windows Paint and Windows Photo Gallery) and you've also added a photo editor that came with your digital camera as well as one of the advanced tools from Adobe such as Adobe Elements, Adobe Photoshop Album, or the professional's tool, Adobe Photoshop. Which one should automatically open if you double-click a TIFF file? Many programs let you set them as the default application for particular filename extensions. You might choose, for example, to have all photos open in Photoshop.

Check the help screens for your program to see if you can assign filename associations. The other way to accomplish the same thing is to make an adjustment to the settings of Windows itself. Slightly different steps allow you to accomplish this in current versions.

### Changing filename associations in Windows Vista

Follow these steps to change the association in Vista:

1. **Click the Start button, and then click Default Programs.**

   You see a window that allows you to Choose the Programs That Windows Uses by Default.

2. **Click Associate a File Type or Protocol with a Program.**

   See Figure 4-1.

The system displays the Set Associations window. The three columns show all the filename extensions Windows Vista is aware of; the list is updated over the Internet from the mothership in Microsoft and includes both common and obscure. (In most cases you also see the little icon assigned to the filename extension.)

**3. Click a filename to highlight it.**

You can see a description of the file type that uses the extension and the current default association for the extension. In some cases the extension doesn't have an association, or it may be marked as an unknown application.

**4. Click the Change Program button.**

You see a window with the unusually simple title of Open With. See Figure 4-2.

**5. Select the program you want to set as the default for this extension.**

**6. Click OK.**

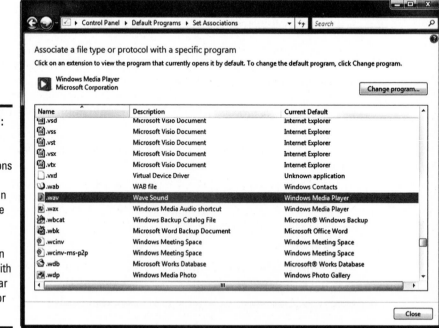

**Figure 4-1:** The Vista Set Associations window displays an impressive list of file types you can assign to open with a particular program or utility.

**Figure 4-2:**
The Open
With
window of
Vista will
make
suggestions
of the most
likely
programs to
associate
with a file
type. You
can also
browse for
others that
may be
installed on
your
computer.

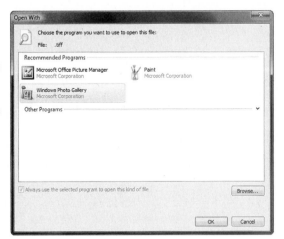

## Changing filename associations in Windows XP

To change or set filename associations (also called *Registered file types*) in Windows XP, follow these steps:

**1. Open either the My Computer or the Windows Explorer folder.**

Windows Explorer isn't the same as Internet Explorer. You can find either, but My Computer is usually right there on the taskbar as well as the Start menu. See Figure 4-3.

**2. Click Tools ⇨ Folder Options ⇨ File Types tab.**

**3. In the list of Registered File Types, click a file type you want to assign to a program or one that needs to be reassigned.**

**4. Click Change.**

The Open With dialog opens.

**5. Select the program you want to use and then click OK.**

The Folder Options dialog opens.

**6. Click OK.**

**Figure 4-3:** The Windows XP registered file type system uses different terms but accomplishes the same tasks as the filename association window of Windows Vista.

# Putting Everything in Its Place: Making and Using Folders

She's got this huge pile on her desk. When it comes to the files on her computer . . . she wants to keep them on the Windows desktop, too: all 500,000 of them. Oh, the trials and tribulations of a modern high-tech marriage.

The solution is to use folders and subfolders and sub-subfolders. Figure 4-4 shows just one example of how you could organize your system. In this particular design, all files are kept inside folders and subfolders within a top-level folder (think of it as the file cabinet) called My Documents, which is one of the folders Windows automatically creates for you. One level down from My Documents are two major folders, one called Business Files and the other Personal Files. They hold, respectively, business files or personal files . . . but you figured that out already, right?

Another level down, the business and personal files branch off again. On the business side, to folders dedicated to letters, financial matters, and (since my particular line of work involves publishing) manuscripts. On the personal side, folders are set up to hold private letters, financial documents, and digital audio and video.

There's no right and wrong way to organize your computer, and you can make the structure as simple or complex as you like. All that matters is that it makes sense to you . . . and that it gets the big pile of files off your desktop.

**Figure 4-4:**
An organizational scheme for files for a user who stores both business and personal data on a single laptop.

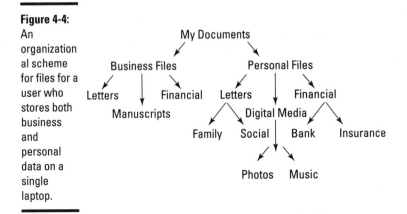

# Exploring Pre-Assigned Folders: The Big Three

The programmers at Microsoft really, really want you to get organized, too. That's why they instructed Windows to create at least a basic structure to hold your files. You can use their scheme, adapt it more to your liking, or create your own.

And many software applications install one or more special folders to hold files created with their program. Again, you don't have to use their suggested locations, but if you choose to store files somewhere other than the default location, make sure you keep track of where you place them.

These three top-level basic folders are automatically created by Windows XP.

## My Computer

Windows also sets up subfolders called Shared Documents (for files you identify as ones you want available to others on a network) and *Insert Your Name Here's* Documents. (It's not really called Insert Your Name Here; the computer creates a subfolder for each user account and places that person's name on the folder.)

If your laptop has only one user account, then this folder is just for you. If you allow the kids (why, oh why?) to use your laptop, be sure to set up a user account for them. Not only will it help keep any files they create separate from your own, but it also permits you to create different themes and settings for each user. That is, unless you want to come to the board room with your annual financial planning presentation and let the CEO see that your laptop's desktop has a huge, pulsing picture of SpongeBob SquarePants.

My Computer (on Windows XP systems) or Computer (on Windows Vista machines) also includes icons that represent storage devices such as the hard disk drives and any attached external devices. If you burrow down into the list of devices, you gain access to the folders they hold.

## My Documents

You can customize to add subfolders galore to this general top-level folder. Windows automatically creates subfolders including My Music, My Videos, and My Pictures. (And I bet you can guess the intended contents of each of those subfolders.) If these folder names make sense to you, leave them unchanged; many programs automatically dispatch files to those folders, even if you prefer to keep them somewhere else.

On my system, I add subfolders to distinguish between files I declare In Progress, Completed Assignments, and Archives. Once I finish a particular job and ship it to a publisher or a client, I move it from In Progress to Completed Assignments where it sits happily for a few weeks or months or even years until I'm certain that I don't need to do anything more with it. Then I move it to Archives where it just sits.

The advantage of a three-stage process like mine? Organization and tracking. I can easily find projects that I need to finish, and then I can readily find older projects if I need to change them or recycle parts for other purposes. And finally, I can easily copy Archives files to DVD or to one of my several external hard disk drives for deep, deep storage. (Trust me, you never know when some situation will arise where you find that you need to look at a file you created ten years ago. Go to the archives . . . .)

## My Network Places

Okay, this one isn't really a folder. At least, it isn't one located on your laptop. This listing is any location on a *local area network (LAN)* available to you. Permission can be granted to read files only, or to write new or modified files to that location. (Network places can connected by Ethernet wires, available on a WiFi wireless network, or even locations available somewhere out there on the Internet.)

Windows Vista has a similar but not quite identical set of folders. The most current OS automatically creates the same group of folders for each user. The top level folder is the User Account folder, and is named . . . for the user. Thus, there is a folder called Corey and within that folder the OS creates these subfolders:

+ **Contacts.** Any time you use the Windows Vista Mail program, the e-mail address and other details of anyone you correspond with are added to an address book here. Certain other applications, from Microsoft or other software companies, may also use this folder to hold information, settings, and other details of your electronic correspondence.

The creatively named Mail is a replacement for Outlook Express, which was part of most earlier versions of Windows.

✦ **Desktop.** Although your laptop's desktop looks as if it is one big spread-out place, actually all of its documents, shortcuts, and subfolders live within this top-level folder.

✦ **Documents.** This is where your (say it along with me) *documents* are supposed to go. You can (and should) create all sorts of subfolders within this folder to help you organize your stuff.

Because each user account has its own Documents folder within Windows Vista, you can keep others from viewing, changing, copying, or deleting your documents. All you need to do is to apply a password to your user account.

**Book II
Chapter 4**

**Managing Files,
Folders,
Extensions**

✦ **Downloads.** The default location for files brought to your laptop from the Internet is here, which makes them easy to find and manage. However, some web sites may insist on placing their downloads on the desktop or elsewhere on your computer; in addition, you may be able to Save As and place a download somewhere that is especially pleasing or logical to you.

✦ **Favorites.** Here Internet Explorer (the browser that helps you find, display, and interact with web sites) can store places you've visited and to which you hope to return. The favorites are listed on a menu within Internet Explorer, but stored here. (And because Windows allows you to open a file with a program, or a program with a file, you can go directly to a favorite site by double-clicking an icon or filename listed in this folder.)

✦ **Links.** One of the sorta-kinda new features of Windows Vista is the Navigation Pane on the left side of folders. It displays a list of your most frequently used folders and items. The upper part of the pane lists links to folders you use often; the lower half allows you to pop open the contents of those folders to display them in a branching tree format. (The broadest folder is atop the tree, and the various folders and subfolders beneath it spread out like thinner and more distant roots.)

✦ **Music.** Any digital tracks copied from CDs using the Windows Media Player are ordinarily stored here, in a folder after the CD's title (if the maker of the CD labeled the disc properly). Some other audio programs — music players as well as editors — may also use this folder to store tracks.

✦ **Pictures.** Are you getting the picture here, yet? Yup, this folder is the official place to store digital images from your digital camera, a scanner, screen captures from a web site, or from your own computer. Many digital editing programs seek out this folder for image placement unless you instruct them otherwise. On my machine, I add several layers of subfolders to divide the thousands of digital photos. I've got a folder called

Europe, for example, and below that are individual folders for countries, and one layer down the folders are identified by month and date.

✦ **Saved Games.** You're much too busy to waste time on games; there's work to be done. Spreadsheets, word processing, e-mail, Minesweeper, Spider Solitaire, FreeCell. Those last three aren't games, boss: They're mental exercises to keep me sharp and creative. So when you do play one of the games offered by Windows Vista, the OS stores any saved in-progress sessions as well as high scores and settings here. And some other games you install on your own may use this folder to store saved sessions. Or so I'm told.

✦ **Searches.** If you use the facilities within Windows Vista to search the files within your laptop, the saved results of that inquiry are stored here. Certain other third-party search utilities may also use this folder.

✦ **Videos.** Downloaded videos from the Internet or from a camcorder are ordinarily placed here. You can add subfolders to manage different types of files: for example family, travel, and "none of your business."

Many software programs insist on placing files you create in the folders that made sense to the programmers. However, in most programs you can change the default location for files. Check the Options menu from within the program.

Another way to manually instruct a program to place a file in a particular place is to use the Save As command. Save As is a command with its roots all the way back to the early days of computing, which explains its somewhat less-than-obvious name. When you tell the computer to Save As, you're going around any automatic settings for the program. In the instance of a word-processing program, you can

✦ Save the file under a name other than one the program automatically generates.

✦ Save an additional copy of the file under a new name.

✦ Save an original version of the file in a folder other than the default. This includes folders on your machine or, if your laptop is connected over a LAN, on another machine. (You must be granted permission to access to folders on networked computers.)

✦ Save a copy in a folder other than the default.

✦ Save the file in a format other than the program's standard.

You can explore some of these options in more detail in Book IV about office software.

# Digging into a Folder

It's all done with a flick of the finger: point to a folder and double-click it to open it and examine its contents. Do the same to open a subfolder. Or, if you'd prefer a slightly less aggressive method, point to a folder and give a gentle touch to the right mouse button. Then select Open from the menu that appears.

Want yet another way to get to a file? Every Windows program ties into the operating system's file index through the Open command. Most work like this: If you open the program and then seek to open a file, the Open command takes you to whichever folder has been identified as the default "look here first" folder. You can browse from there to any other folder on the machine. And you can change the default folder from within the program by going to its Options menu.

If you click Open from within most Windows programs *after* saving or opening a file, the folder you see is where the most recently used file is located. Again, you can navigate from that location to anywhere else on the machine.

## Seeing what you see

When you open a folder you see a list of files as well as any subfolders placed within. That's about all I can tell you in general terms, because Windows allows you a tremendous amount of display customization.

To begin with, you can show the contents of a folder as follows:

+ **List.** This is the simplest and is just what promises: a list of files and sub-folders. You see the filenames and folder names, accompanied by whatever icon or symbol you or the program associate with it.

+ **Details.** The same list, but this time presented with a great deal more information — as customized by you. For example, in addition to file-names and folder names, you can see the size of individual files (indicated in KB, meaning thousands of bytes). Other available information includes Type (such as File Folder, Microsoft Office Word file, Microsoft MapPoint map, or Adobe Acrobat Document), Date Created, Date Modified, Date Accessed, and much more.

In Windows Vista you can add *Tags* to files to describe a file's contents. Tags are particularly useful with digital image, music, or video files. You can add a few words to describe a digital camera picture (for example NEIL, LAMPSHADE, NEW YEAR). Years later, when you want to find that picture of Uncle Neil with the lampshade on his head you can search for any of those words and come up with a list of images that fit the bill.

✦ **Icons.** Since you're working in a gooey GUI, it is appropriate that software designers stick symbols alongside the words that name a file or a folder; I'm talking about icons. The *icons* are automatically applied to files because of the filename extension. Any software maker who plays by the official Windows rules can instruct the OS to display a custom icon for certain file types. That's why you see a small picture of a printed sheet of paper with a W to indicate a Microsoft Word file, or a musical note for an MP3 audio file.

You can also personally select a little icon for folders (for example, a tiny camera to indicate pictures, a miniature projection screen to hold PowerPoint presentations, a small group of miniature people to tell you that family matters are within). Icons also identify programs (or desktop shortcuts that lead to their location on your disk), and clicking them can launch the program.

✦ **Tiles.** If you know exactly what you're looking for (and have customized the heck out of your personal folders), you can look at a folder's contents as tiles: just the icons (a bit larger than in the regular view). Click any one of them to open the subfolder. (And just to be nice, if you hover your mouse over a tiled icon, a little screen tells you the nature and size of the folder or the file, and in the case of the file you learn the date it was last modified.)

✦ **Thumbnails.** And now for the really big show. (This would have been Ed Sullivan's favorite; if you don't know who he was, ask the nearest geezer.) Instruct the system to show you a folder's contents as *thumbnails,* which are really big icons. Plus, any images — digital photographs, scans, PDFs — appear as small versions of themselves. Switching to thumbnail view is a great way to quickly examine your photos. Open a folder's thumbnail by clicking it; clicking a file's thumbnail opens the file within the software program with which it's associated.

## Giving your folder a makeover

To select any of the available viewing options within an open folder, click the View menu and then use your mouse to select one of the available options: Thumbnails, Tiles, Icons, List, or Details. That's all there is to it.

Now, if you want to customize a particular folder's appearance, the process is also simple, but requires a few extra steps. If you're running Windows XP (Windows Vista is similar enough that you can figure it out from these instructions), here's how to assign an interesting, eye-catching, or meaningful icon to a folder:

*1.* **Click the current icon for a folder to highlight it, then right-click the folder.**

**2. Select Properties.**

The Properties dialog appears.

**3. Click the Customize tab.**

**4. Under Folder Icons, click Change Icon.**

Wow, that's a lot of icons to choose from. Windows comes supplied with several dozen little pictures, and some programs add their own to the system. You can also download or purchase icons from designers; if you download one from the Internet make sure you're dealing with a reputable source to avoid viruses.

**5. Select the icon you want and click OK.**

Back at the Properties page you see some other options, including the kind offer to use this folder type as a template for other folders. You can experiment here or (as I do) individually assign icons as I need them.

**6. Choose steps based on your decision:**

- Click Apply to assign the icon if you want to stay on the Properties page and do other things.

- Click OK to assign the icon and close the dialog.

## Renaming your folder or file

As you're probably beginning to figure out by now, you can usually accomplish a particular task under Windows two or three different ways. The OS designers tried to anticipate different types of users and different types of situations.

Here, then, are three ways to change the name of a file or a folder:

- ✦ Click the current icon for a folder or a file to highlight it. Click a second time on the box containing the filename to highlight characters. Type in a new name and press the Enter key to accept it.

- ✦ Click the icon for a folder or file to highlight. Then right-click. From the menu that appears, chose Rename and give it a new name.

- ✦ Click the icon for a folder or file to highlight. Then right-click. From the menu that appears, chose Properties. In the upper part of the box you see a box with the current filename; click in the box and change the name.

You can also change a filename from within a program by using the Save As command and inserting a different name; if you take this route, you end up with a copy of the file. You can keep both, or you can go in and delete one or the other version.

## Moving on up

Sometimes you put something in the wrong place. Or the darned machine goes and stores a file or makes a folder somewhere other than where you want it.

Before you change the machine, try moving the file or folder. And yes, you have multiple ways to do this:

✦ Open the folder where you want to move the file or subfolder. Then locate the folder or file you want to move. With both windows open (source and destination), click and drag the file you want to move. When the icon is where you want it, release the button. It's there!

✦ Locate the folder that holds the file or subfolder you want to move and highlight the item you want. On the left side of the folder is a set of File and Folder Tasks and, wouldn't you know it, one that offers Move This File. You're shown a complete listing of top-level folders where you can move the item.

# Being Wary of the Metadata

In case you thought your personal work on your computer was personal, consider this: The system tracks when a file is first created, most recently modified, and most recently looked at *(accessed),* even if nothing was changed. The program records the user who created the file as well as anyone else who made comments on the file, and the comments themselves are tracked. It also records the total amount of time spent with a particular file open and the number of times it was worked on. This information is called *metadata* (info about info, you know) and is silently inserted into your file every time you open, save, or close it.

Does metadata sound like something that might become of interest to an attorney in a lawsuit, or a detective, or a government agency? "You claim you never sent a stock tip to your friends and relatives before March 1? How, then, can you explain the following . . .?"

With the advent of Office 2007, Microsoft took a partial step back from edge of Big Brotherdom. It's called the Document Inspector, and you can scrub your files of any metadata you'd rather not share through the Prepare menu. Here's the drill:

*1.* **Click Microsoft Office Button ➪Prepare ➪Inspect Document.**

The Document Inspector dialog opens.

2. **Select the check boxes to instruct the program what to look for.**

3. **Click Inspect and review the results**

4. **Click Remove All to scrub the file.**

5. **Save the file either as an original or as a copy.**

I say Document Inspector is a partial step back because it helps you create a "clean" file that you can e-mail or otherwise send to another user. This process doesn't necessarily remove all the information that may be contained in the original file on your hard disk, any backups you have made, and any earlier versions that might be scattered about anywhere else.

**Book II
Chapter 4**

**Managing Files, Folders, Extensions**

# Book III

# Running Basic Windows Operations

"I hate when you bring 'Office' with you on camping trips."

# Contents at a Glance

# Chapter 1: Opening Windows

## In This Chapter

✔ **What you see is what you want**

✔ **Becoming a pop icon master**

✔ **Taming the taskbar**

✔ **Out to launch**

*O*nce upon a time, life was simple. In my first "real" job, I showed up for work to face an inbox on one side of the desk and two outboxes on the other. In between was an empty patch of desk. On the floor was a black rubber trash can.

My assignment was to take the top piece of paper from the inbox, examine it to see that all questions had been answered properly, add up the numbers (using a mechanical adding machine the size of a sewing machine), and deface it with my rubber stamp that said "Approved." Sometimes I had to use a different stamp; this one put a large red "Disapproved" mark on the page. Next step: Move the paper to the proper outbox: winners, losers, and the occasional trash.

Once or twice a day, someone from the mailroom would come by pushing a rumbling old cart. All of the approved papers would go in one large container and the disapproved into another; and then the clerk would refill my inbox with a stack of new forms. At night, the janitor would take away the trash; sometimes I imagined the garbage was being recycled into the inbox of the next desk to mine.

My job was very clearly defined. One paper at a time. Every question was either correct or incorrect. Everything progressed in one direction, from inbox to outbox. Garbage went in the trash can. And the computer? That would be me.

Today even the most basic of jobs bears almost no resemblance to my old job. First of all, regardless of what you think of your own native intelligence, when it comes down to it you're a computer operator. And though you may have lots of pieces of paper spread around your work area, most of the real labor takes place on that computer's screen. The cable or wireless connection is your inbox and outbox. And your desktop is virtual, a box of glowing dots.

## Deconstructing Windows

Even though it usually stands upright facing you, the work surface of Windows is called the *desktop.* Here you choose programs, open files, move folders, and otherwise perform your work. It's been like that ever since the dawn of Windows time, even though the desktop has become fancier and more sophisticated with each new version of the operating system.

Windows is designed so you can get where you want to go in any number of ways. For example, you can click a program and then open a file from within the application, or you can locate a file in a folder (or on the desktop) and double-click it to open the file within the program that created it. The same sort of wonderfully loosey-goosey logic applies to most Windows configuration controls; you can go to the central collection in the Control Panel or make adjustments from several other places within the operating system.

Now consider two appendages to the desktop. Think of them as electronic versions of remote controls: the Start menu and the taskbar.

The Start menu is one of several doorways that gives you access to your installed programs:

+ You can click any program to open it and create a file or load one you've saved to your hard disk. You can also jump directly to a selection of commonly used major folders that hold documents, pictures, music, or other specific types of files. See Figure 1-1.

+ You can hop to the Computer folder (called My Computer in earlier versions of Windows). From there you can burrow your way down to any internal hard disk, any folder on any disk, or any other attached storage device (including external hard disks, flash memory keys, and memory located within attached devices such as music players and digital cameras).

+ A one-click connection to the Network folder lists any other computers and linked devices (such as printers) that are part of a wired or wireless network.

+ From the Start menu you can also gain quick access to the most important customization and adjustment tool of Windows: the Control Panel.

Now consider the *taskbar,* which is a customizable list of programs and files you're currently working on. (With the arrival of Windows Vista — and only on those machines that have the horsepower to show off advanced features — hovering your cursor on one of the taskbar items displays a thumbnail image of what's going on in each program.) You can set up the taskbar to display all the time or only when you take the cursor down to its location. And you can anchor it at the bottom of the screen or along the sides of the desktop.

**Figure 1-1:**
The opening
screen of
the Start
menu under
Windows
Vista.

And then — only in Windows Vista — you have the sidebar, which you can equip with your own selection of gadgets. Do you need to know the temperature in Whapmagoostui at all times? Do you need to know — right now — the current currency conversion between Icelandic Krona and Estonian Krooni? How about live feeds of traffic on I-5 in Seattle? I discuss gadgets in Chapter II, Book 3.

# Uncovering Your Desktop

Whether it's upright or laid flat, the desktop is the metaphorical surface that presents your work. You can place things on the desktop (individual files or folders that contain many files) and you can place *shortcuts* to commands (icons that, when clicked, start a program or initiate an Internet connection, for example).

You can assign colors and styles to the desktop, use a drawing or a photograph as the background, and enable automated features such as screen savers. You can arrange the location of the files, folders, and shortcuts as well as the taskbar. Want a peek at my desktop? See Figure 1-2.

Shortcut arrows

**Figure 1-2:**
A Windows desktop personalized with a photo from my travel collection.

In my office, the top of my desk is sometimes invisible; it gets covered with books and mail and sheaves of paper covered with notes that seemed very important at the time I placed them there. A similar situation occurs with a Windows desktop. It's there, although most of the time you have it completely covered with your Internet browser, a word processor, or something really important like Spider Solitaire.

You can restore your view of the desktop three ways:

✦ The fastest, all-in-one zippy solution is to bring the onscreen cursor to your taskbar (usually at the bottom of the screen) and find the little icon called Show Desktop. If you don't recognize the icons by their design, just hover the cursor over them for a moment; the name appears. Clicking Show Desktop nearly instantly minimizes all open programs and folders and displays your desktop.

✦ The slower way to accomplish the same thing is to minimize each open program, file, or folder. To minimize something that's open on the Windows desktop, click the – symbol in the upper-right corner of the program, file, or folder.

✦ Close any open programs, files, or folders by either clicking the X symbol in the upper-right corner or clicking Close.

You can quickly restore minimized items by clicking their icon in the taskbar.

# Working with Desktop Icons

You've got this desktop. What do you do with it?

Just about the same things you do with a horizontal plank of walnut. You open up folders, you spread out files, and you apply intelligence to your work.

But the nice thing is how the computer can help you keep a neat workplace. All your folders and all the files within them represent the real thing; you can move them around, organize them almost any way that makes sense to you, and put them away in a secure place.

The Windows desktop is populated with *icons,* which are tiny, usually meaningful, pictures or symbols. A folder with a digital camera icon most likely means photos are contained within; the commonly used Microsoft Word uses a stylized *W.*

Windows comes equipped with a large supply of icons that it automatically applies to many popular programs and file types. Your laptop maker may have added some other icons for utilities and special features, and many applications you install on your computer come along with their own icons.

Here's the first and most important thing to know about an icon: Icons aren't just pictures. They represent an active zone on your desktop. Double-clicking a desktop icon starts a program or opens the folder represents. And if the icon marks the presence of a file, double-clicking it opens the document within the program with which it's *associated.*

## Adding, removing, and moving

On the desktop itself you see *icons,* the small pictures that represent an item, program, or action. The standard set of desktop icons usually includes the Recycle Bin (to hold files that you've "deleted," although that is an imprecise term; I explain how the recycle bin works in Book III, Chapter 3).

Depending on choices made by you, your machine manufacturer, and the maker of software you install on your laptop, your desktop may come festooned with other items. Typical icons include shortcuts to commonly used programs such as your word processor, a Web browser like Internet Explorer, and an e-mail client such as Outlook Express.

Icons that represent programs also are usually *shortcuts.* The shortcuts are linked to the location of the program itself. You can create shortcuts to folders or files. Once again, the shortcut *isn't* the item itself, but a pointer to its location. Shortcuts look similar to other icons, with the addition of an arrow.

See Figure 1-1 earlier in this chapter, which points out a couple of shortcut arrows. The arrow tells you that the program's located elsewhere, but that you can still get there from here.

Some users like a clean and simple desktop; call it the "cluttered-desk-is-the-sign-of-a-cluttered-mind" mentality. Others choose to fill up the desktop with icons for all their current assignments and essential programs. There is no right or wrong methodology. Whatever works for you is fine. I do, though, recommend devoting ten minutes or so every few days to cleaning up your desktop.

### Giving a desktop icon the boot

To clear an icon off your desktop, follow along:

*1.* **Use your cursor to highlight the icon.**

*2.* **Right-click with your pointing device.**

*3.* **Click Delete.**

Windows Vista users have another way to add or remove common (not custom) desktop icons:

*1.* **Right-click anywhere on an empty area of the desktop, and then click Personalize.**

*2.* **In the Personalization window's left pane, click Change Desktop Icons.**

*3.* **Click next to the common desktop icons you want to appear or delete.**

Selecting or deselecting the icon makes it appear or disappear, respectively.

*4.* **Click OK.**

You can add or remove these common desktop icons with this method:

Computer (or My Computer)

Network (or My Network)

Recycle Bin

Control Panel

Internet Explorer

Personal folders set up to hold your documents

An alternate way to remove any icon from the desktop is to right-click it and then choose Delete from the menu that appears.

### Adding a shortcut to the desktop

Follow these steps to leave a shortcut:

*1.* **Locate the item.**

The item you want to shortcut can be a file, a folder, or a program. You may find the item in the list of programs accessible from the Start button, or by burrowing through the folders on your hard drive using the My Computer (Windows XP) or Computer (Vista) or My Documents (Windows XP) or Documents (Vista) mega-folder.

*2.* **Use your cursor to highlight the item, then right-click with your pointing device.**

*3.* **Click Send To ➪ click Desktop (Create Shortcut).**

You can remove shortcuts from your desktop by dragging them to the Recycle Bin or by highlighting them and pressing the Delete key. If you delete a shortcut you remove only the *pointer* to a program or piece of data, not the item itself. You can still start the same program other ways: from the taskbar, from the Start button, from the folder on your hard drive, or by double-clicking a file created using the program and set up to be associated with it.

### Putting icons where you want them

If you allow Windows to do its own thing, it stacks icons in columns that build out from the left side of the desktop. You can, however, change that and move icons around yourself.

Do this to tell Windows to automatically arrange icons on the desktop:

*1.* **Right-click an empty area of the desktop.**

*2.* **Click View ➪ Auto Arrange.**

To turn off that instruction, deselect the Auto Arrange check box.

Windows tries to keep your desktop as neat as possible, placing icons along the columns and rows of a grid; the lines exist only in the computer's internal map of the screen — you can't see them. If you want a more free-form arrangement or want icons closer together, turn off this feature.

To turn on or off the icon grid, do these things:

*1.* **Right-click an empty area of the desktop.**

*2.* **Click View ➪ Align to Grid.**

If a check mark is already there, clicking Align to Grid turns off the grid (and removes the check mark); if the box is empty, clicking turns on the grid.

**Book III
Chapter 1**

**Opening Windows**

### Selecting multiple icons

You have two ways to move or delete multiple icons in one step.

To highlight a group of icons next to each other (in the same column or row, or in adjacent columns and rows), follow these steps:

1. **Click an empty area of the desktop near one of the corners of the icon group.**

2. **Keep pressing the left button and drag the mouse to draw a box around all the icons you want to act upon.**

3. **Release the mouse button.**

4. **Click in the box of icons and drag them where you want them.**

   That could be another location on the desktop, to another folder, or to the Recycle Bin.

To select more than one icon when they're not next to each other, do this:

1. **Click the first icon and release the mouse button.**

2. **Press the Ctrl key while clicking other icons you want to add to your group.**

3. **Release the Ctrl key and then click once more with the left mouse button.**

4. **Hold the mouse button and drag the icons where you want them.**

   You can move them to another spot on the desktop, to another folder, or to the Recycle Bin.

## Hiding desktop icons

If you want to temporarily clear your desktop of all icons without actually deleting them, follow along:

1. **Right-click an empty area of the desktop.**

2. **Click View ⇨ Show Desktop Icons.**

   This clears the check mark from that option. To reverse this operation, click Show Desktop Icons.

3. **Highlight the file or folder you want to move.**

4. **Press and hold the left mouse button and drag the item from its current location to the desktop.**

5. **Release the button to place it on the desktop.**

I can think of two very good reasons you might want to temporarily clear the desktop of icons. One is to present a blank background if you're capturing a picture of a program or file displayed on the desktop using Print Screen. Another reason: to keep prying eyes from seeing the icons on your desktop.

### Moving icons about on the desktop

It's your desktop, and you can allow it to get as messy as you'd like. But by default, Windows is going to try to make some sort of order from your chaos. The standard arrangement is for icons to be stacked along the left side of the desktop. You can rearrange icons by clicking and dragging them to a new location anywhere on the desktop (except for the hot zones occupied by the taskbar and the sidebar).

You can also instruct Windows to automatically perform housekeeping on your desktop. If you're running Windows Vista, follow these steps:

**1. Right-click an empty place on the desktop.**

**2. Click View ⇨ Auto Arrange.**

Your icons are neatly stacked along the left side of the desktop and locked into place. To unlock them, click Auto Arrange again and clear the check mark next to that instruction.

Note that Windows uses a built-in, invisible grid to align items on the desktop. If you want to be less rigid, or if you want to move items closer together, click View and deselect Align to Grid.

The process is similar under Windows XP, although different terms are used:

**1. Right-click an empty place on the desktop.**

**2. From the menu, select Arrange Icons By ⇨ Auto Arrange.**

This places orders and locks items; to unlock them, repeat the process and deselect Auto Arrange.

### Bringing the desktop to the front

Once you start running programs or opening folders, the desktop can be quite hard to find. It's still there, but like your real desktop it's completely covered with stuff.

To quickly see the whole desktop without closing or manually minimizing your open programs or windows, click the Show Desktop button on the taskbar. To *maximize* (make full screen) all the programs or windows, click the Show Desktop button once again.

**Book III
Chapter 1**

**Opening Windows**

# Exploring the Taskbar

A narrow ribbon of information is usually located at the bottom of the Windows desktop. The ribbon is called the *taskbar,* and among its multiple purposes is to show you which programs are running and allow you to switch between them with a mouse click.

The taskbar is one of the most flexible Windows tools. You can place it just about anywhere on the screen, make it appear and disappear on command, and decide whether it takes precedence over work in progress or hides out of the way until you need to use it.

You also can drag the taskbar to the top of the screen or to the left or right sides. Right-click the taskbar and click Lock to hold it in place.

## Managing the taskbar display

Right-click anywhere in the taskbar and then click Properties to display the controls for how the taskbar is managed.

Click the check box to turn on or shut off any of these options:

+ **Lock the Taskbar.** Prevents inadvertent or unwanted changes to settings.

+ **Auto-hide the Taskbar.** The taskbar appears any time you bring the onscreen pointer to it, and hides when you're working elsewhere onscreen.

+ **Keep the Taskbar on Top of Other Windows.** This ensures the taskbar is always visible, even when you're running a program in a maximized (full-screen) window.

+ **Group Similar Taskbar Buttons.** All items opened with the same program are grouped into one button on the taskbar.

+ **Show Quick Launch.** The Quick Launch bar makes it easy to point and click your way to any open program.

## The taskbar, left to right

The taskbar is made up of four sections:

+ **On the left:** The Start button is at the left end (when it's at the bottom or top of the desktop) or at its top (when it's along one or the other side). As part of Windows Vista, Start has been reduced to a colorful gumball of an icon containing a stylized version of the red-green-blue-and-yellow Windows flag; in Windows XP a less flashy flag sits alongside the very obvious label "start." The XP version looks something like this: ˘.

✦ **To the right of the left:** The Quick Launch Toolbar holds icons that let you load and run a program with one click.

✦ **The middle:** This area lists open programs and documents, permitting you to quickly switch between them with a click of the mouse. (Under Windows Vista, machines powerful enough to deliver a Windows Experience that includes Aero graphics display a thumbnail version of what you see onscreen if you maximize that program.)

✦ **The right:** The notification area, appropriately enough, notifies you of things you might want to know. These include a clock as well as icons that convey the status of running programs (mostly utilities). For example, look here to see if your antivirus program is enabled or to check if new mail has arrived in your inbox.

An example of a slightly crowded Windows Vista taskbar is shown in Figure 1-3. At far left is the Start button, which opens the door to installed programs, the Control Panel, and other important elements. In the Quick Launch area are icons that include Internet Explorer, AOL, Adobe Photoshop Album, Microsoft PowerPoint Viewer, and others. The middle shows that Internet Explorer and McAfee Security are running and folders for some of my lectures and pictures are open on the desktop. The notification area at right has utilities including a wireless network manager, a control panel for the laptop touchpad, and the volume control for the built-in audio system. Just to the left of the notification area is a Google search bar, an optional utility that investigates the contents of your computer as well as the Internet.

**Figure 1-3:**
A taskbar
with icons
and actions
left, right,
and center.

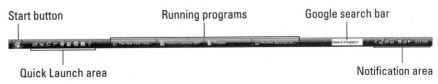

Start button                    Running programs          Google search bar

Quick Launch area                                    Notification area

One of the beauties of Windows is that it allows you to have many programs and utilities open and running, each in its own little space; otherwise, I suppose, the operating system would have had to have been named Window. Saying that all these programs are running *at the same time,* though, isn't quite accurate; instead the microprocessor has a case of electronic attention deficit. It very quickly rotates its attention from one running application to another, parceling out bits of time and energy as needed to keep each current. It all happens so quickly that we slow humans don't notice the tiny gaps.

## Adding a toolbar to the taskbar

Windows Vista and earlier versions come equipped with a set of standard toolbars, including Quick Launch and several others. As you enable certain utilities (such as Windows Media Player) you may add the toolbar to the available selection. Certain third-party applications may insinuate themselves into the list as part of their installation process.

You can, though, make your own choices here. It's more than just a question of your right to keep your life (and your taskbar) simple . . . or less complex than it might otherwise be.

To adjust the list of enabled taskbars:

*1.* **Right-click an empty area of the taskbar and choose Toolbars.**

*2.* **Click any item in the list to add it to the taskbar.**

If you click an item that already has a check mark, you remove it from the taskbar.

## Feeling smart with the Start button

The Start button sounds very important, but some users hardly ever go there. Once again, this is an example of Microsoft's Department of Redundancy Department. Everything on the Start menu can also be found at least one place elsewhere and sometimes in four or five other places; whatever works best for you is fine and dandy. Figure 1-1 shows you a Windows Vista Start menu; the equivalent menu from Windows XP is shown in Figure 1-4.

### Pinning it to the left

Clicking the Start button opens up the Start menu, which seems logical enough. There you find a display that makes it easy to choose from the usual suspects. Here's what that means: In the upper-left corner of the menu is a space where you can *pin* the program or application you want there. This space is separated from the other icons by a thin, horizontal line.

Some users put their most commonly used programs there, like a word processor or e-mail client; other users prefer to pin their most obscure applications here — the ones they have a hard time finding elsewhere.

To pin a program to this critical Start button corner, follow these steps:

*1.* **Find the program icon anywhere on the computer.**

The icon may be on the desktop, in a folder, or in the list of All Programs that branches off the Start menu.

*2.* **Highlight the icon with your cursor.**

**Book III**
**Chapter 1**

**Figure 1-4:**
A Windows
XP Start
menu.

**Opening Windows**

### 3. Right-click and choose Pin to Start Menu.

> To unpin a program and free up space in the corner, highlight it where you find it on the Start menu and then right-click to bring up the submenu. Click Remove from This List.

Below the horizontal line on the left side of the Start menus is space for other programs; the more items you pin, the less room you have for other icons. In whatever space is left, Windows automatically places the most recently used programs. If you have four programs pinned above the line, you may have room for six or seven temporary listings below.

A nice little feature here: If you hover your cursor over an icon on the left side of the Start menu, a little window pops up and describes what the program does. (A handful of software companies don't take advantage of this little bonus, although I'm sure overwhelming demand from satisfied users will force them to add a line of code in their next versions.) For example, if you hover over Windows Sidebar (a component added to Windows Vista) you can read the following: "Displays personalized slideshows, news feeds, and other customized information on the desktop."

Use the left panel of the Start menu in whatever manner makes the most sense to you. You might want to pin ten programs there so you always know where to find them. Or you might want to have no programs pinned and instead know that you can always go to the Start menu to find the applications you most recently used.

At the bottom of the list of pinned or most recently used programs is the key that unlocks the door to the grand list of installed applications and utilities on your machine. For such an important key, it bears such a simple name: All Programs.

Click All Programs and the Start menu blossoms into a full list, as you can see in Figure 1-5. You may be amused, amazed, or disturbed by the number of items that end up on the list over the lifetime of your laptop. But you'll also appreciate knowing that the list is there.

Click any icon to open that program; some icons have a caret or arrow to the right or left of its listing (depending on where the icon is in the list). Clicking that icon opens a submenu of associated programs. For example, the submenu may include an uninstall command or direct access to a utility for the main program.

**Figure 1-5:**
Click All Programs to expand the Start menu into a listing of all installed applications. Some icons hold a submenu of utilities and settings.

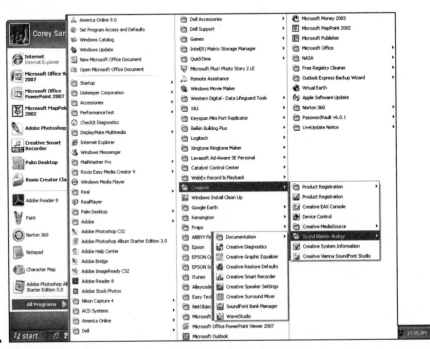

Windows Vista has an added element at the Start menu's bottom-left pane. Enter a bit of relevant text into the box marked Start Search and then click the magnifier glass icon. This leads you to a continually updated index of virtually everything on your computer. (You can install a similar function to Windows XP, although it won't appear on the Start menu.)

For example, if you type *PowerPoint* (or *powerpoint,* or just *power*) into the search box, the operating system would very quickly come back with a list of all programs and utilities that include the phrase in their title, all files that were created with any of those programs, all files that contain the word, and all e-mails or e-mail headers stored on your machine that include the phrase.

### Sticking it to the right

Move over to the right side of the Start menu. Here you find one-click access to the main folders for documents, pictures, and music. You can also jump to windows that open to a view of the contents of your hard disk drive as well as network-connected devices in the Computer and Network windows (My Computer and My Network Places under Windows XP). You also have access to the personal folder, which bears the name of the person who's currently logged onto Windows; on my laptop, that is me, and that is why I see a Corey Sandler folder as a Documents folder.

A Recent Items element appears in the Start menu's right pane. Clicking Recent Items opens a list of files you have opened recently; the listing is updated every time you open something else, with oldest files going away first. Near the bottom of the pane is a quick jump to the Windows Control Panel and to Windows Help and Support.

As with elements on the left side of the pane, hovering your cursor over one of the items here should produce a pop-up window that describes the wondrous things that lie beneath the simple names.

And finally, just to make things interesting for the very literally minded, Start is also the doorway to Stop. By clicking the icon, you have access to the Windows shut down, log off, restart, sleep, and hibernate commands. The icons branch off the bottom-right corner of the Start menu.

### Going out to launch

The taskbar area immediately next to the Start button holds the Quick Launch toolbar. You can't order fast food here; rather, you can *launch* (some might prefer to say *start*) any of a selected group of programs with a single click.

Your laptop may have come with one or more programs already listed in this area. And some programs you add on your own may insinuate themselves into place here, with or without your permission.

By default, Windows XP and Vista installations have a Show Desktop button, which does exactly what it promises — and in the process minimizes all open programs (but doesn't close or save open files). Vista adds a second button, Switch Between Windows, which similarly does what you think it would do. (Under Windows Vista, if your laptop has enough power to display Aero graphics, Switch Between Windows displays a nifty onscreen image of all open programs floating in space in an electronic effect Microsoft calls Windows Flip 3D. It's just for show, but a nice effect.)

Windows XP and Vista users can switch between windows by pressing the Alt + Tab keyboard combination. Press the Alt key and tap Tab to switch between open programs. It's like playing a game of musical chairs: whichever program is shown when you let go of both keys is maximized.

Follow these steps to add a program to the Quick Launch area:

1. **Click the Start button.**

2. **Highlight the program in the Start menu.**

3. **Right-click with your pointing device.**

4. **Click Add to Quick Launch.**

   To accomplish the same thing, find the program on your desktop or in any window, highlight it, and then drag it into the Quick Launch section.

To remove an icon from the Quick Launch toolbar, follow these steps:

1. **Highlight the icon with the cursor.**

2. **Right-click the pointing device.**

3. **Click Delete.**

You can resize the Quick Launch toolbar:

1. **Right-click an empty area of the taskbar.**

   A submenu appears.

2. **If there is a check mark next to Lock the Taskbar, clear the check mark.**

3. **Click the toolbar sizing handle and move it to expand or contract the space.**

   The *sizing handle* appears when you hover on the toolbar's border and is a double-headed arrow.

## Making the most of the middle

The taskbar is designed to display all open programs or files, but if you run multiple programs, sooner or later you're going to run out of real estate. The taskbar first shrinks the display section for each program and squeezes a few more across. Eventually, though, it uses one or both of a pair of space-saving techniques.

Assume you're running Microsoft Word, for example, and have three separate files open for editing. When the taskbar has no more space, it stacks all three icons under a single program name. Clicking the button shows you the names of each open file, and you can then choose one to jump to. Windows does this for any group of similar items: multiple images open for editing under Paint or another graphics program, for example.

To close all the items in a group, right-click the group's taskbar button, and then click Close Group.

The other way the taskbar deals with too many demands on too little space? It expands vertically into a hidden space. I'm not talking about magic here; instead, the operating system adds a set of arrows (**»**) at one end of the taskbar to indicate that you can display more items. Click the arrows to open a display.

## Keeping track of your windows

Any time you open a program, folder, or a document, Windows adds a button and icon to the taskbar. You can quickly see what programs are running and which folders are open. Every open program, utility, or process eats up somewhere between a tiny bit and a significant amount of your machine's processing power. It also demands a chunk of available RAM. Add to that the very large demands of Windows itself.

The good news is that modern laptops have very powerful processors and a lot of memory; the not-so-good news is that sooner or later your machine is in danger of slowing down because too much is going on for it to handle gracefully. If you're not using a program that demands a lot of resources (graphics editors and games are among the biggest hogs on the lot), close it down.

Each button shows the icon and the name of open programs. As you open more programs, the amount of space devoted to each is automatically reduced and the program name may be cut off from view; to read the full name, hover your onscreen pointer over each button.

Any active programs appear indented, as if they were pushed in. To switch from one program to another — changing it to active — merely click its button. Conversely, when a program is active, clicking its taskbar button makes it inactive and minimizes its window. Minimizing a program or folder doesn't close it or delete its contents or insult its sense of pride in any way; it merely removes it from the desktop and drops it down to the taskbar.

### Windows Vista Aero preview

One of the interesting bells and whistles of Windows Vista — available only in Premium versions of the operating system and only if your laptop has sufficient graphics horsepower and available memory to display the specialty Windows Aero features — is the *taskbar preview,* also known as a *thumbnail.*

If your laptop meets the necessary "ifs," when your onscreen pointer hovers above a taskbar button, a miniature picture appears of what lies beneath. If it's a word processor, you get a tiny view of any open document. If you have a graphics editor running, you can check in on the image. And the neatest of all: If one of your windows has a video or animation running, you can sneak peeks at it in the thumbnail view. See Figure 1-6.

**Figure 1-6:**
A thumbnail
of an
Internet
page on a
Windows
Vista
taskbar.

### Windows Vista Aero 3D desktop tiles

Windows Vista Home Premium, Business, and Ultimate editions users get a special treat — again, only if your system is robust enough to display Aero graphics. It's called Windows Flip and Windows Flip 3D, and they're as cool as a snow cone in an ice storm . . . in a technogeeky kind of way.

Windows Flip lets you flip through images of all your open windows and folders. And Windows Flip 3D, well, it does the same thing only in something that is about as close to 3D as you can currently hope for on a 2D display.

Windows Flip is a Windows Vista update of a similar but much less flashy way to move among open programs and folders: Press Alt and tap the Tab key. Let go of the Alt key to switch to whichever window is highlighted within the box. See Figure 1-7 for a view of the Windows XP version. The arrival of Windows Aero technology allows live thumbnails instead of icons.

And the most advanced version, Windows Flip 3D, shows not only thumbnails but live processes such as streaming video. On an Aero-capable machine, press and hold the Start key and then tap Tab to move through open windows. See Figure 1-8.

**Figure 1-7:**
In Windows XP, press Alt and tap Tab until your desired destination appears in the onscreen box.

BOOK03-01 Chapter 1 Opening Windows

Book III
Chapter 1

Opening Windows

**Figure 1-8:**
Windows Flip 3D shows all open windows; you can flip through to select the one you want in front.

## Notifying your intentions

Look to the notification area for messages of support, notices of threat, and the time of day. This section of the taskbar delivers important status updates, regularly updated by your essential utilities.

When you hover your cursor over an icon in the notification area, you see the name of the utility it represents and (in some designs) a quick report: Your antivirus program is enabled, you have new mail in your inbox, a WiFi signal has been detected, or your toast is burning. (The toast monitor isn't available in all areas and is subject to federal restrictions on air quality, gluten content, and your willingness to let this one slide by.)

Double-clicking an icon in the notification area usually opens the utility or a report generated by it. For example, the antivirus program may report on the status of all of its components or it may open the entire application so you can run scans or change settings.

Some items in the notification area are there just to alert you to something. For example, if you plug a device into a USB port on your laptop, a message may pop up to tell you that your system has recognized and is ready to use the device, or that it has detected a new device and needs to configure itself to accept it.

If you (or the laptop computer) don't use a particular item in the notification area for a while, the system automatically stops displaying its icon. The utility is still there and still available; it's just hidden until you use it next. If you want to see all possible icons, click the Show Hidden Icons button, a small left-facing chevron like this: ◄ .

# Chapter 2: Using Built-in Windows Applications and Gadgets

## In This Chapter

✓ Gadgets, widgets, and doodads

✓ Editing text without a word processor

✓ Painting a picture

✓ Getting those nice, bright colors, without Kodachrome

*W*indows, in any of its versions, isn't intended as a program all by itself; it's an operating system that constructs the framework for applications to run. Most users start out with Windows and install a word processor, a graphics program, a spreadsheet — just about whatever you want to use your computer for.

That said, from the very beginning, Microsoft has included a set of simple software as part of its operating systems. No one would confuse the basic functionality of WordPad — the "free" text editor included with Windows — with the amazing set of features in the extra-cost Microsoft Word program. The same applies if you compare the included Paint utility to the spectacular facilities of Adobe Photoshop.

However, you could write an entire book using WordPad and you could draw a picture in Paint. It wouldn't be quite as easy, and most users eventually find they need the extra power and features available only with products sold separately.

On the other hand, sometimes the mini programs included with Windows are so quick and nimble that they offer advantages over gigantic multipurpose programs. One quick example: The easiest way to store a copy of a screen capture (a picture of something that appears on your screen) is to press the Print Screen button on your keyboard, paste the image into Paint, and save it as a file.

## Inspecting Your Gadgets

*Gadgets* were amongst the bells and whistles that arrived with Windows Vista. You can add these mini programs to your desktop for highly specialized functions. Earlier in this book I cite the example of keeping a continuous eye on weather in a remote location; parents like me who have children living away from home understand the appeal. You could also track

✦ An airline flight

✦ A stock

✦ The price of a doodad in an online auction

For the record, Apple introduced the concept of Gadgets — they call them *widgets* — a few years before Microsoft proved the adage that imitation is the sincerest form of flattery.

You can turn on or off the display of Gadgets at any time, and customize them with selections from one supplied with Vista or added from other sources. A sample of some of the Gadgets on my system are shown in Figure 2-1.

The Gadgets generally reside in a newly staked-out area of the desktop that is called the *Sidebar*. As you no doubt guessed, that means a vertical strip that parks at one side of the screen; the standard position is at the right side, although you can put it on the left. You can detach Gadgets, though, from the Sidebar and allow them to free-float.

**Figure 2-1:**
A set of Windows Vista Gadgets tracking weather, currency exchange, the stock market, and today's calendar.

The base set of Gadgets that comes with Windows Vista offers a bit of

✦ Weather

✦ News

✦ A photo viewer

✦ Web clips

✦ A to-do box

✦ A calendar

✦ A desktop search box

As the operating system matures, Microsoft will likely add to the standard kit through updates.

You can change the order of Gadgets within the Sidebar by grabbing hold of its handle by clicking it with the onscreen pointer and dragging it to a new location.

Some Gadgets include a + to indicate that you can expand them with a *fly-out* that provides additional information or customization. For example, a stock ticker may fly out with more details of averages or specific trades. Other fancy features include a weather Gadget, such as one based around AccuWeather.com, that warns of severe weather. (As I'm writing these words, that particular Gadget on my laptop is warning me of high winds tonight; time to go out and tie down the garbage cans.)

You can't adjust the width of the Sidebar; Windows sets that. Depending on your laptop LCD's width and aspect ratio, it usually spreads about an inch off the right or left border of the screen.

## Configuring the Sidebar

The key to adjusting the Sidebar's appearance and operation is the Sidebar Properties window; you can get to it with these steps:

*1.* **Click the Start button.**

*2.* **Type** Sidebar Properties **into the search panel.**

Another way to the same window: Click the Sidebar Properties icon in the Control Panel.

The properties window includes a direct link to a set of help screens; click How Do I Customize Windows Sidebar? for answers to frequently asked questions, as well as a few you might not have thought to ask yet.

**Book III
Chapter 2**

Using Built-in
Windows
Applications
and Gadgets

### Closing and exiting the Sidebar

Closing the Sidebar is equivalent to minimizing a program; the various Gadgets are still active and continue to occupy slices of your computer's processing time and memory. However, the Sidebar disappears from view.

*1.* **Right-click the Sidebar.**

*2.* **Click Close Sidebar.**

Do this to open Sidebar again:

*1.* **Right-click the Sidebar icon in the notification area of the taskbar.**

*2.* **Click Open.**

Exiting Sidebar closes the utility and all its Gadgets. It also removes the Sidebar icon from the taskbar.

*1.* **Right-click the Sidebar icon in the notification area of the taskbar.**

*2.* **Click Exit.**

### Keeping the Sidebar and Gadgets on top of other windows

If you want to keep an eye on the various Gadgets in your Sidebar while working on other things — that is, of course, the purpose of Windows —configure it so it permanently occupies one side of your screen even when other programs are maximized.

Running applications expand up the outside vertical border of Sidebar.

To keep the Sidebar on top, follow along:

*1.* **Choose Start ⇨ Control Panel Open Windows Sidebar Properties.**

Or press Start and type Sidebar Properties into the search panel.

*2.* **Select the Sidebar Is Always on Top of Other Windows check box.**

A check mark appears there.

*3.* **Click Apply.**

To change this setting, click again to remove the check mark.

You can also toggle the Sidebar between being topmost or lower down by pressing ⊞ + spacebar.

A permanently displayed Sidebar works especially well if your laptop has a widescreen LCD.

### Adding or removing a Gadget

To add a Gadget to the Sidebar, you have to first install the Gadget on your computer — either as one of the default mini programs that ships with Windows Vista or added from another source. An example of a gallery of installed Gadgets is shown in Figure 2-2.

To add an installed Gadget, follow along:

*1.* **Right-click the Sidebar.**

*2.* **Click Add Gadgets.**

The gallery of available Gadgets appears.

*3.* **Double-click a Gadget.**

You can add two or more of the same Gadget to the Sidebar. (You might want to check on weather in two places at the same time, for example.) Just add the Gadget multiple times.

It appears on the Sidebar.

Remove an element from the Sidebar this way:

*1.* **Right-click the Gadget.**

*2.* **Click Close Gadget.**

**Book III
Chapter 2**

**Using Built-in
Windows
Applications
and Gadgets**

**Figure 2-2:**
To set up your Gadget display, choose from the set of installed mini programs.

### Putting a Gadget elsewhere on the desktop

You might prefer to detach a Gadget and place it as a free-floating item on the desktop:

1. **Right-click the Gadget.**

2. **Click Detach from Sidebar.**

3. **Drag the item where you want it to be.**

To return a detached Gadget to the Sidebar, do this:

1. **Right-click the Gadget.**

2. **Choose Attach to Sidebar.**

### Changing individual options for a Gadget

Certain Gadgets allow you to change their own settings. For example, a weather report may offer you the choice of displaying temperatures in Celsius or Fahrenheit; a stock ticker may permit you to choose particular indexes or individual equities to track.

To change a Gadget's options, do this:

1. **Right-click the Gadget.**

2. **Click Options.**

   If you don't see that choice, you can't personalize the Gadget this way.

## Getting more Gadgets

Microsoft has opened up the code for Gadgets, and you can expect all sorts of offerings from amateurs and professionals. It used to be that the difference between those two was that the former worked for free, but that isn't always the case today. Some amateurs offer their work as *shareware,* seeking contributions from users; some professionals offer free products *(freeware)* that promote their web sites or other products they're selling.

Microsoft has established Live Gallery and stocked it with some intriguing Gadgets. You can visit it at http://gallery.live.com. See Figure 2-3.

One thing is certain: You must be very cautious accepting and running any Gadget that comes from a source you don't know and trust. It's very easy for someone to insert a virus into a Gadget. Your antivirus program should be able to detect such nastiness, but why take the chance?

**Figure 2-3:** Additional Gadgets are offered for download from various sites, including Microsoft's own Live Gallery.

# *Sweating the Small Stuff: Text Editors*

What's in a word? Or in Word? Or WordPad?

Oh, and let's throw in Notepad while we're at it.

Well, they're all text editors, allowing you to create documents that you can read, edit, print, and give to others in electronic form. A *text editor* is a basic manipulator and storage mechanism for characters, words, and symbols. All the way over at the other end of the spectrum is a *word processor,* which does the same thing but adds a dizzying array of special features to allow you to format, design, research, and otherwise automate the process of preparing a document. (Just about the only feature missing from a word processor is the one I really would love to see: a button that says "Press here to have the computer finish this chapter for me.")

In theory, I could have written this entire book using WordPad or the even more fundamental Notepad. It would have been a slog, but it could have been done.

Wrap your mind around this for a moment: All word processors are text editors, but not all text editors are word processors.

I can think of all sorts of analogies to explain the difference between a text editor and a word processor: You could

+ Dig a swimming pool with a spoon or a backhoe.
+ Get from Boston to San Francisco on foot or by jumbo jet.
+ Cook a six-course meal using a wood fire and one tin plate or on a grand stainless-steel restaurant stove with eight burners, a griddle, an oven, and a built-in electronic sous-chef in the drawer.

But if you're already familiar with the capabilities of a computer when it comes to managing documents, displaying fonts and pictures, and its modern direct connection to the World Wide Web (the "old" name for the Internet), then here's one more somewhat self-referential set of analogies: a text editor is like a pencil with an eraser. With that tool you can write, you can make changes, and you can draw stick figures. It's very easy to use (Have you ever studied the instruction manual for a pencil?) and cheap.

A word processor? Well, it's got those same pencil and eraser features. But it also adds some fantastic power tools. If William Shakespeare had access to Microsoft Word, he might have written 100 plays instead of a mere 38. (And he could have cleaned up his spelling and grammar and maybe annotated his work with references to contemporary culture and classical texts.)

Here are some of the features of a typical word processor:

+ Fonts, sizes, styles (normal, bold, italic, and the like), and colors
+ Management and application of styles to chapter and section heads as well as blocks of text
+ Advanced layout of text including columns, embedded art, headers and footnotes
+ Spelling and grammar checkers
+ Dictionaries and thesauruses
+ Indexing and tables of content generators
+ Mail-merge and form-letter functions

You can easily use Microsoft Word as an example of a word processor because, well, almost everyone uses it. Microsoft Office (which includes Microsoft Word) owns about 75 percent of the market. Would-be competitors, which include Corel's WordPerfect Office and Apple's iWork, are quite capable products . . . and they essentially mimic or duplicate Word's features, as well as its look and feel.

Word processors have three important disadvantages:

+ **In most cases they're not free.** You have to pay for the right to use the program either as a component of the package that comes with your laptop or as a product you install on your machine. That said, free or shareware word processors are showing their faces.

Among the more intriguing word-processing freebies: Google Docs from the people at Google (you guessed that, right?), which allows you to use a word processor and a spreadsheet that reside on a computer somewhere out there on the Internet. You can save your files in a free account at Google, or store them on your local hard disk drive. And you can share files from one machine to another because Google Docs can store files in the Microsoft Word format, as well as other formats including RTF, PDF, and Open Office (a shareware product). Google will eventually seek to make money through the sale of ads, which may or may not bother you. On the plus side, you won't have to install a word processor on your laptop or bother to keep it updated if you use their application over the Internet.

+ **They're complex.** Over the years, word processors have added more and more features; some call it *bloatware*. The fact is that most people, including professional writers who spend nearly every waking moment of the day in front of a keyboard, use only a tiny fraction of the available features of a word processor.

The good news is that Microsoft (yes, the company with the overwhelming market share) has begun to rethink the way in which it offers all of those tools. You will now find context-sensitive menus that pop up with the click of the right mouse button, and the most current versions of Microsoft Office (beginning with the 2007 edition) also present a changing selection of commands at the top of the screen; the computer attempts to anticipate your needs based on the sort of work you're doing. All the functions are there, but they're not all waving their hands for attention at the same time.

+ **Files tend toward large.** Because word processors include all sorts of information about things like formatting and styles and multiple versions of a file or changes proposed by other users or accepted by the original author, a simple document can be quite large. Again, Microsoft has begun to address this with the latest versions of its Office suite. But in any case, a word-processing file will, by definition, be larger than a text-editing file, even if they contain the exact same number of characters.

Book III
Chapter 2

Using Built-in
Windows
Applications
and Gadgets

## Notepad

It's better than a typewriter. And it's almost as easy to use as a pencil and paper. You can type, move, print, store, and transmit characters to other users. You can't, though, get fancy.

It served a purpose — and for some users still does —where all you want is the information. Just the characters, ma'am. (See Figure 2-4.)

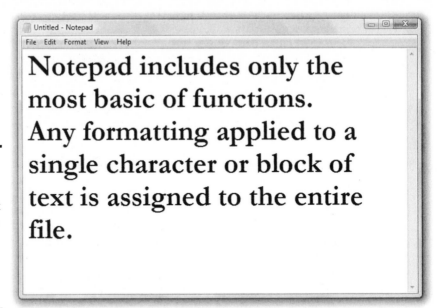

**Figure 2-4:** Notepad is the most basic of text processors, supplied with all current versions of Windows.

Notepad works very well in writing programs, creating notations for online calendars, or for those people who can appreciate the fact that a Notepad file of several hundred words can demand only a few hundred bytes within a container of 4KB; an equivalent WordPad file requires twice as many bytes, while the functional minimum size for a Microsoft Word file — even one made up of a single character — will be a minimum of 12KB and often larger. Notepad saves its files as a plain text document, helpfully labeled with a *.txt filename extension.

Does size really matter any more? Yes and no. Today's hard disk drives are so large, with prices dropping by the minute. The difference in overhead between a single Notepad file and a single Word file isn't going to make any noticeable difference. However, if you think about the contents of your computer in its totality, a few thousand bytes saved here and there will quickly add up to megabytes and gigabytes. Less is more; your machine will run more efficiently, and you'll help save the planet. (Think of the volts you will set free.)

### Opening Notepad

You can open Notepad several ways:

   ✦ Click the Windows Button ➪ All Programs ➪ Accessories ➪ Notepad.

✦ Click a shortcut to Notepad that you created on the Desktop, or that you pinned to the Windows Start menu. If you've recently used Notepad, a temporary shortcut already exists on the Start menu. Book III, Chapter 1 tells you how to create a desktop shortcut.

✦ Double-click the file created with Notepad. If your computer has been instructed to associate the file type TXT with Notepad, it opens that program. If you have another text editor (or a word processor like Microsoft Word), the file may instead open in that program. See Book II, Chapter 4 if you'd like to change an association.

### Jumping to a line

Actually, you can trace text editors one step back on the evolutionary path. The very first computers processed programs and accepted data one line at a time; data coming in or out was presented on numbered lines of a specified length. The first crude tools for working with the data were called *line editors*.

Buried deep within Notepad are some of the vestiges of a line editor. The program keeps track of information as if each line were a separate entity. And therefore, even though the document you're working on may not have numbers on each line, you can jump to a particular line if you calculate its position in the document.

**Book III
Chapter 2**

**Using Built-in Windows Applications and Gadgets**

## Take a note

Notepad is a holdover from the very early days of computing, back when machines dealt only with characters and not pictures. Quick lesson: Early computers assigned a number (called an *ASCII code,* if you must know) to each of the characters on the keyboard as well as a number of special purpose symbols.

So, an uppercase *A* was noted with the decimal value of 65. Computer video cards knew that when they saw a 65, they were to look up in an index a predefined picture of an *A*. Computer printers worked in much the same way, converting a string of numbers into a command to print an *A*. Early computer printers were basically electric typewriters that accepted a string of numerical commands; you might be able to change the font by switching the type ball or other mechanism to produce a character.

Today, though, Windows is a GUI. And as a graphical user interface, the image you see on screen or in hard copy from a printer is no longer (as far as you're concerned) based on numerical codes but instead on a map of dots in the computer's memory; to draw an *A*, the computer does the equivalent of blacking in the proper spots on a grid. And that grid can be manipulated: converted to boldface or italics or colorized almost without limit.

Jump to a specific line in a document this way:

1. **Choose Edit ⇨ Go To.**

2. **In the Line Number box, enter the number you want.**

   For example, to go directly to the ninth line of the document, type 9.

3. **Click OK.**

   The deed is done.

### Setting font style and size

Think of Notepad as a box of characters with a simple set of instructions on the label. You can assign any font available on your computer, choose a style such as italics or boldface, and pick a size. (See Figure 2-5.) So far, that sounds sort of like the way a word processor works.

But here's the difference: Whatever font, size, and style settings you make apply to all the text in the Notepad document. No menu bar offers quick choices for fonts; make settings by clicking Format ⇨ Font. From there you see the list of available fonts and styles.

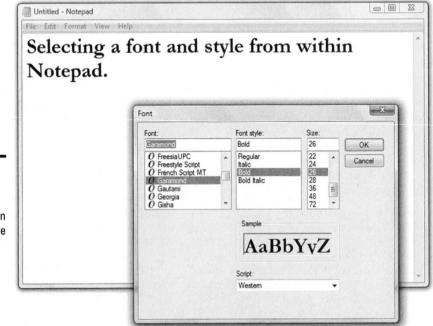

**Figure 2-5:**
Choices of
fonts and
styles within
Notepad are
applied to
the entire
file, not to
individual
characters
or words.

### Special functions

Notepad includes basic cut-and-paste facilities. As with other text editors, the process works much the same way:

*1.* **Select text.**

*2.* **Click the Edit menu.**

*3.* **Choose based on your needs:**

- **Cut.** To remove the text and place it in memory for insertion elsewhere.

- **Copy.** To leave the text where it is but store a copy in memory for use elsewhere.

- **Paste.** To put text from memory into a document.

To back out of a cut-and-paste operation, click Edit ➪ Undo.

Or, you can use keyboard commands to accomplish the same tasks:

✦ Ctrl + X to cut text.

✦ Ctrl + C to copy text.

✦ Ctrl + V to paste text.

✦ Ctrl + Z to undo the cuts, copies, and pastings.

Other available functions include Search and Replace, available from the Edit menu.

And, as with WordPad, Microsoft programmers have blurred the distinction between text editor and word processor a little bit by adding *headers* (lines of text at the top of every page) or *footers* (text at the bottom of printed pages).

To create a header or footer, follow along:

*1.* **Click File ➪ Page Setup.**

Both a Header and a Footer box appear. Default settings place the file-name at the top of the page and a page number at the bottom.

*2.* **Enter text.**

You can use just the text you enter or use it with special characters that tell the system to insert specific information. The codes in the following table are some of the most common within headers and footers.

**Book III
Chapter 2**

Using Built-in
Windows
Applications
and Gadgets

| Insert the date (from the computer calendar) | &d |
| Insert the time (from the computer clock) | &t |
| Insert the name of the file | &f |
| Insert the page number | &p |
| Align the header or footer flush left or flush right | &l or &r |
| Center the header or footer | &c |

# WordPad

You want free text editing that comes pretty close to offering the basic functionality of a word processor? Every owner of a laptop running current versions of Windows can find a copy of Microsoft's almost-ready-for-prime-time text editor, WordPad.

Not all that long ago in the history of personal computing, WordPad would've been considered a pretty capable word processor. Now it sits somewhere between a simple text editor and one of the big boys.

WordPad documents can

+ Include complex formatting and graphics.

+ Link to or embed objects such as pictures or other documents.

+ Save your files. Files can be saved in RTF (Rich Text Format) and later imported and converted for use within most other word processors, including Microsoft Word. And you can use WordPad to open most Word files, but you can't re-save them in Word's DOC or DOCX formats.

+ Let you reopen and edit files.

+ Print.

WordPad is more advanced than Notepad, but what does it lack? In two words: bells and whistles. It has no spell checker, thesaurus, or grammar utility. You've got to jump through a lot of hoops to work with images (as objects created in other programs and brought in). And you can't create tables.

Truth be told, though, WordPad is perfectly adequate for note taking and even preparing simple documents.

## Opening WordPad

WordPad is included in the standard set of accessories installed with Windows. You can open it in several ways:

+ Click the Windows Button ➪ All Programs ➪ Accessories ➪ WordPad.

✦ Click a shortcut to WordPad on the Desktop, or on the Windows Start menu. If you recently used WordPad, a temporary shortcut is already on the Start menu. Book III, Chapter 1 tells you how to create a desktop shortcut.

✦ Double-click the file created with WordPad. If your computer has been instructed to "associate" the file type (RTF, TXT, or Unicode) with WordPad it will open that program. If you have another text editor (or a word processor like Microsoft Word) the file may instead open in that program. See Book II, Chapter 4 if you'd like to change an association.

### Creating a document in WordPad

To open a new document, do one of these things:

✦ Click the new blank document icon on the toolbar.

✦ Click File ➪ New.

From the list of document types, choose from these types.

✦ **Rich Text Document.** This simple text file that includes codes for formatting and styles that can be used or converted by most other text editors and word processors. If you were to read an RTF file in a text editor, you might see a line like this:

```
This sentence includes a {\b bold} word, enclosed within
     curly brackets and indicated with a \b.
```

Onscreen in a word processor or printed out, the sentence looks like this:

```
This sentence includes a [BOLD]bold[UNBOLD] word, enclosed
     within curly brackets and indicated with a \b.
```

✦ **Text Document.** In theory, a plain text file is just what it sounds like; plain text, unadorned with any formatting or fonts. The original idea was that files would be like typewritten text, without any emphasis or formatting other than paragraph marks and spaces; over the years, though, some simple formatting and choice of fonts has been allowed. The letters, though, are all simple Roman characters. Plain text files are perfectly adequate for composing messages that you'll cut and paste into an e-mail program or are used just as notes.

✦ **Unicode Text Document.** This file type is for use with nearly any language, not just the Roman characters of English. WordPad stores these files using a format called UTF-16, which many other programs can use. Unicode files allow simple formatting, including choice of fonts and emphasis including boldface, italic, and underlining.

Book III
Chapter 2

Using Built-in
Windows
Applications
and Gadgets

Which file format should you use? For most people, the best choice is RTF. A Rich Text Format file should be readable by almost any other text editor or word processor.

Click View ➪ Options to instruct WordPad whether the words you write should

✦ Wrap at the end of the displayed window

✦ Wrap at the end of the ruler on the page

✦ Not wrap at all

Most users find it much easier to work with a file that wraps the text to the ruler or the displayed window. For certain technical uses, including writing a program or preparing code for a web site, you may need to turn off wrapping so that the file that is created is a pure text file. To read a file like this, scroll all the way to the right until you reach the end of a sentence (or the entire file).

The settings you make for word wrapping affect only how the text appears on the screen and in the raw file itself. If you printed from within WordPad or another text editor or word processor, it would automatically format the lines of characters to fit on the printed page.

### Opening an existing WordPad document

To open a file previously created and saved using WordPad, or to open a file created in another program but stored as an RTF, TXT, or Unicode file, do this:

*1.* **Click File Menu ➪ Open.**

*2.* **Click the file you want to work with.**

*3.* **Click Open.**

### Saving a WordPad document

When you're ready to put away a file you created, follow these steps:

*1.* **Click File ➪ Save.**

*2.* **Enter a filename in the highlighted space.**

*3.* **If you want to change the file type, click the Save as Type arrow.**

The file-type options appear.

Even though you were asked the type of file you want to create when you began working on the file, you can save the document in a different format.

You can enable the Automatically Save All Files as a Particular Type By Default check box.

**4.** **Ensure the name in the filename area is what you want.**

If you want a different name than one it had before, change the entry under filename before saving.

**5.** **Click OK.**

### Printing a WordPad document

WordPad integrates with the settings you made for printers on your laptop. If Windows knows of a printer and you properly installed its driver, you can create a hard copy of a file created in WordPad:

**1.** **Click File ➪ Print.**

**2.** **Go to the General tab.**

**3.** **Select the printer you want to use.**

You can add a printer if the one you want to use doesn't show up.

**4.** **Choose the range of pages to print:**

- **All**
- **Pages (ranging anywhere within the document)**
- **Current Page**
- **Just the highlighted block of text**

To see what your document will look like when you print it, click File ➪ Print Preview. Click Close to return to the document.

**5.** **Click OK.**

### Finding and replacing words

Why does a text editor include a relatively sophisticated function like find and replace? Just like car manufacturers, programmers can't keep their hands off their work; with each new version of WordPad (and as of the release of Windows Vista, there've been six major and many minor revisions), they pack more and more into the box.

Anyhow, WordPad has a basic search-and-replace function. To find a word or a particular group of characters in the file, do this:

**1.** **Click Edit ➪ Find.**

**2.** **Type the characters you're looking for in the Find What box.**

**3.** **Click Find Next.**

To move past the first "find" and continue searching, click Find Next or press F3. You can keep doing this until you reach the end of the file.

To replace specific characters or words, do this:

*1.* **Click Edit ⇨ Replace.**

*2.* **Type the characters you want to locate in the Find What box.**

*3.* **In the Replace With box, type in the text you want to insert in its place.**

*4.* **Click Find Next.**

*5.* **When the text you want to replace appears, click Replace.**

To replace all instances of the searched-for characters, click Replace All.

### Embedding or linking objects in WordPad

*Embedded objects* (including images and other files) in a WordPad document become part of the file.

✦ The good news is that if you give or send someone a copy of the file, the embedded material will accompany it.

✦ The possibly bad news is that if you change the original object after embedding it in a file, that change isn't reflected in the WordPad document. That is, unless you remove the original embedded object and replace it with the changed one.

An object also can look as if it's part of your file if you *link* to it. When you link an object, the object remains in its original location but a reference to it is created in the WordPad file.

✦ If you change an object that's linked to a WordPad file, the changes appear in the document when you view it onscreen or printed out.

✦ However, if you give or send someone a WordPad file that includes a link, you have to send along a copy of the original object (or embed the final version of the object in your document).

To embed or link an object, follow the following path:

*1.* **Click Insert ⇨ Object ⇨ Create from File.**

*2.* **Type the path and filename in the File Box.**

Or click Browse and find the file you want to embed or link.

*3.* **To link to an object, click the Link check box.**

If you want to embed the object, make sure the Link check box is cleared.

You can also embed an object by creating or opening it in its original program and using the Copy ⇨ Paste command. Similarly, you can link an object by choosing Copy ⇨ Paste Special.

### Formatting text

WordPad allows basic formatting, including font sizes and emphasis including italics, boldface, and underlines.

The simplified menu bar at the top of the document is one of two pathways to assigning formatting; you can find pull-down menus for font, size, and text encoding. If you don't know what text encoding is, that's because you're so . . . Roman. No, I don't mean you're of Italian heritage (not that there's anything wrong with that).

The English language, along with most other forms of written communication, uses a character set based on Roman (sometimes called *Latin*) letters. In the world of Microsoft, Roman is sometimes called *Western,* which is a bit less precise. The other options for encoding offered by WordPad are Arabic, Baltic, Central European, Cyrillic, Greek, Hebrew, Turkish, and Vietnamese. Why no Japanese or Chinese or other such languages? Well . . . there are ways to construct characters in those languages but they're based on adaptations of the Roman keyboard.

Until and unless you instruct your computer (actually, your operating system) that you'll be working with a non-Roman character set, WordPad always puts you back in the Western World.

Surprisingly, WordPad's paragraph-alignment function is actually a bit easier to use than the similar facility in some word processors:

*1.* **Click anywhere in the paragraph you want to align.**

You don't need to highlight all the text in the paragraph.

*2.* **Click Format ⇨ Paragraph.**

See Figure 2-6.

*3.* **Click one of the options in the Alignment section:**

- Left
- Right
- Center

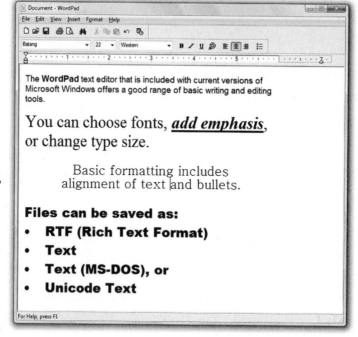

**Figure 2-6:**
WordPad includes the basics of most word processing; think of it as bells but no whistles.

Similarly, to indent a paragraph, follow along:

*1.* **Click anywhere in the block of text.**

*2.* **Click Format ⇨ Paragraph.**

*3.* **Enter a measurement in the Indentation section.**

The measurement should be in inches for the amount of space you want to the left or right (or both sides) of the paragraph. You can also choose an indent for just the first line.

To set or remove tab stops in paragraphs, follow along:

*1.* **Select the paragraphs you want to work on.**

*2.* **Click Format ⇨ Tabs.**

*3.* **Type a number in the Tab Stop box.**

The measurement can be in inches or decimal fractions of an inch.

*4.* **Click Set.**

A new tab stop is created.

To delete a tab stop, do this:

1. **Select the paragraphs you want to work on.**
2. **Click Format ⇨ Tabs.**
3. **Click a tab stop it in the list.**
4. **Click Clear.**

   To clear all tab stops in the selected paragraph, click Clear All.

Another way to set tab stops is to click where on the ruler you want them. To delete tab stops, click the marker for the tab and hold the mouse button down as you drag it off the ruler. On the ruler, a tab stop looks like an egg timer.

# Manipulating Images

I don't know much about art, but I know what I like. On my not-too-short list of masterpieces is an astounding photograph of Pablo Picasso taken way back in the prehistoric era. The summer of 1949, to be precise. In the photo by Gjon Mili, Picasso sketches a phantasmagoric centaur in the air using a flashlight. This was 40 years before PhotoShop existed as a noun, a verb, or a computer program. But the concept remains the same: drawing with light.

The big guys:

✦ **Adobe PhotoShop.** The Bigfoot of the image industry. It's by far the most popular power tool for photo editing and for painting with light (think of your onscreen cursor as Picasso's flashlight).

✦ **Picasa** by Google (free).

✦ **Paint Shop Pro Photo** by Corel.

A number of basic programs are included with the purchase of a digital camera.

If you're going to get serious about using a digital camera, creating your own artwork, or capturing images of the screens you see (or the contents of Web pages), you need to add a capable image-editing program. But the wizards of Microsoft will get you started with a pair of basic tools included with current versions of Windows:

✦ Paint

✦ Windows Photo Gallery (part of Windows Vista)

Book III
Chapter 2

Using Built-in
Windows
Applications
and Gadgets

## Paint

Pure and simple, Paint allows you to open most existing digital images and

+ Convert to another format
+ Change size
+ Make simple resolution adjustments
+ Draw on a picture (just like — well, almost like — Picasso)

On the painting side, the program offers a small set of tools including

+ Paint brushes
+ Pencils
+ Airbrushes
+ Erasers
+ Text

You can create your own masterpiece from scratch, or draw a mustache on a photograph of the Mona Lisa.

### Opening Paint

Paint is in the standard set of accessories installed with Windows. You can open it in either of these two ways:

+ Click Windows Button ➪ All Programs ➪ Accessories ➪ Paint.
+ Click a shortcut to Paint that you have created on the Desktop, or that you have pinned to the Start menu of Windows. If you recently used Paint, a temporary shortcut already exists on the Start menu.

To open an existing image stored on your laptop or on an attached networked device, click File ➪ Open. You can do this in one step by pressing Ctrl + O.

By default, the program looks for images in the Pictures folder that is set up with the installation of Windows. But you can navigate to other folders by clicking one of the Favorite Links shown on the left side of the Open screen.

Paint works with most common current file formats:

+ **BMP.** Bitmap files stored with a .bmp or .dib filename extension.
+ **JPG.** JPEG compressed images with a filename extension of .jpg, .jpeg, .jpe, or .jfif.
+ **GIF.** GIF compressed images with a .gif filename extension.

✦ **TIFF.** Uncompressed TIFF files with a filename extension of .TIF or .TIFF.

✦ **PNG.** PNG files with a .png filename extension.

✦ **ICO.** Icon files stored with a .ico filename extension.

## Working with images in Paint

You have several options when it comes to working with images. Work on one

✦ Uploaded from a digital camera

✦ Taken by pressing the Print Screen key

✦ Captured from an online source

If you have an image on your computer, start work this way:

*1.* **Open Paint.**

*2.* **Go to the image file from the Open window.**

*3.* **Double-click the image's icon.**

It opens in the editor. Windows makes it easy to find images by offering a small thumbnail version of the picture. See Figure 2-7.

**Book III
Chapter 2**

Using Built-in
Windows
Applications
and Gadgets

**Figure 2-7:**
From within
Paint, you
can open
stored
images of
the proper
file type for
manip-
ulation.

If you open Paint without loading an existing file, you can begin work with the paint tools immediately and then choose a storage format when you're ready to save your work.

You can use any of the standard file formats for your masterpiece, but generally it's good practice to at least temporarily save your work in a high-resolution, uncompressed format like TIFF; once you complete your work, save the file in a smaller format like JPG or GIF.

*1.* **Press the Print Screen key.**

A copy of the memory's image of the screen is captured. This step is just temporary.

*2.* **Press Print Screen again.**

The first image is replaced with a later version.

You can hold onto the contents of a Print Screen command by pasting the memory contents into an image editor, and Paint does just fine for that purpose.

*3.* **Open Paint.**

*4.* **Click the blank canvas.**

*5.* **Do one of the following:**

- **Press Ctrl + V.**

- **Click Edit ⇨ Paste.**

Unless the web site developer has blocked your ability to do so, you have a third way to capture an image from what you see onscreen:

*1.* **Go to a web site.**

*2.* **Right-click a picture.**

*3.* **Choose Save Picture As.**

*4.* **Choose JPEG.**

This way you get obtain a high-quality copy.

*5.* **Select a filename.**

*6.* **Choose a location for storage.**

Now you can open that file from within Paint (or other image editors) and edit it.

You can use Print Screen to grab an image of work you created on your own laptop or capture a picture of a web site. Similarly, you can use Save As to copy an image you find on a web site or in certain other displays. Remember, though, many images on web sites or in programs are copyrighted; get permission from the owner if you intend to use someone else's intellectual property in a work of your own.

Once you have the image within Paint, you can do the following, among other things:

✦ Crop

✦ Resize

✦ Flip (rotating it as if you were turning over a transparent piece of paper)

✦ Invert the colors from positive to negative; see Figure 2-8

The final, crucial, step is to save your image in a form that lets you use it or retrieve and edit it in a more-capable image editor. I suggest always saving a copy in TIFF format, which creates an uncompressed version of what you see onscreen. When you're ready to use your work for other purposes, you can save a second copy as a

✦ JPEG for e-mailing to someone else for further editing

✦ GIF for display on a web page or as a small image on your laptop

Book III
Chapter 2

Using Built-in
Windows
Applications
and Gadgets

**Figure 2-8:**
A photo from my personal collection, open for basic editing in Paint.

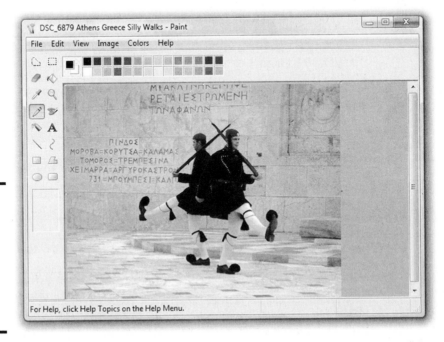

While space on a hard disk drive *is* a precious commodity, a number of alternatives are available if you want to keep images at their highest possible quality.

✦ External drive

✦ Flash memory key

✦ Burn them to a CD or DVD disc

Once an image is reduced in quality (by cutting its resolution or number of colors or by compressing it using a lossy technology such as JPEG or GIF), it can never be fully restored.

### Painting with Paint

Enough about photography; break out the paintbrush. Again, Paint offers all the basics of an illustration program, and I'm convinced that our friend Pablo Picasso could use it to create an amazing work of art.

It comes with a paintbrush, which is a good place to start. And there's an electronic pencil and a computer-assisted airbrush. The icon for the airbrush looks more like a can of spray paint, and that may be a very good metaphor for this program's capabilities: as a free basic tool, this program is not to be confused with a full-featured program like Adobe Illustrator or Corel Draw which allow an almost limitless number of adjustments to the width, hardness (an electronic equivalent of the stiffness or contour of the brush, including the amount of "paint" it applies), and other such refinements.

You can undo any action you take — drawing a line, brushing a stroke, filling with color, or erasing a portion of an image — by clicking Edit ➪ Undo. Alternatively, you can click Ctrl + Z. To *redo* something you've undone (aren't computer's wonderful?), choose Edit ➪ Redo or click Ctrl + Y.

Table 2-1 has the essential tools available to artists like you and me.

| Table 2-1 | Paint Tools |
|---|---|
| *Tool* | *How to use it* |
| Select | Drag the tool to select any square or rectangular portion of the image. |
| Free-Form Select | Reach into an image to draw a line of any shape to select a portion of the picture. |
| Eraser | You've got this one figured out, right? Choose the eraser (a pop-up menu shows four sizes) to overwrite any portion of the image with the background color. |

| Tool | How to use it |
|------|---------------|
| Fill With Color | If you selected an area of the image, fill the inside of that shape with whatever color you chose from the palette. If you selected nothing, this tool fills the entire image with the chosen color. |
| Pick Color | Click this tool and choose a color from the palette; you can assign the color as the foreground or background color of the image. See Figure 2-9. |
| Magnifier | Zoom in on a portion of the image; you can click directly on the picture or use the slider that appears on the toolbar. |
| Pencil or Brush | Draw straight lines or curves with an electronic pencil or paintbrush. You can draw in color by selecting a color from the palette; to draw using the background color, press and hold the right mouse button as you move the onscreen pointer. |
| Airbrush | Sprays paint in the color of your choice. The program includes three spray patterns, from a small and tight cluster to a larger and more diffuse design. Choose a color from the palette or use the background color by right-clicking as you drag the pointer onscreen. |
| Text | Put your words into the image by clicking the A icon; you're offered a background style and a color palette. Click inside the picture and enter text from the keyboard. You can move or resize the text box; change the font, size, and formatting up until the moment you click another tool and click outside of the text box in the picture; after that the text is assigned and can't be edited. |
| Line tools (including Line and Curve) | Insert exactly what's promised. Choose a color and then drag the pointer; to draw a straight line or a curve using the background color, press and hold the right mouse button while you drag the pointer. The Curve tool adds an extra wrinkle: Start with a straight line and then click where you want the arc. Drag the pointer to adjust the curve. |
| Rectangle and Rounded Rectangle | Draw closed boxes with square or rounded corners. Drag the pointer diagonally from one corner up or down to create a box; to make a square hold the Shift button while dragging the pointer. You can choose color from the palette or press and hold the right mouse button to use the background color. |

*(continued)*

**Book III
Chapter 2**

**Using Built-in
Windows
Applications
and Gadgets**

**Table 2-1** *(continued)*

| Tool | How to use it |
|------|---------------|
| Ellipse | Draw a perfect circle or an elongated ellipse. Click in the image to set a starting point and then drag the pointer to expand it; to draw a circle, hold down the Shift button while moving the pointer. |
| Polygon | Make a shape with any number of sides, from triangle to dodecagon (a 12-sided shape) and beyond. Pick a color, drag the pointer to create a straight line, and then click each point where you want to add a side. When done, double-click to turn off the tool. To create sides with 45- or 90-degree angles, hold down the Shift key while making sides. |

The Color Palette comes with 24 colors plus black and white. However, you aren't limited to those colors; double-click the palette to expand the choices to 48.

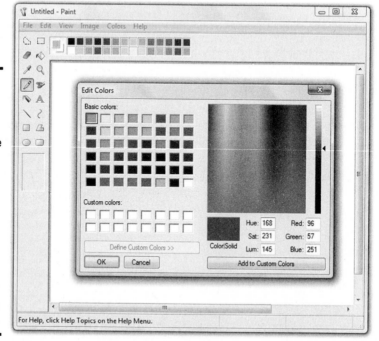

**Figure 2-9:**
You can work with the basic colors of the Paint palette. Create custom colors by moving an onscreen selector or manually entering color or hue information.

And you can go further, defining your own colors:

*1.* **Choose the Define Custom Colors menu.**

*2.* **Click into a set of colors.**

*3.* **Choose an approximate shade.**

*4.* **Use the slider to adjust its appearance.**

Or type values into the Red, Green, and Blue boxes; in this way you can

- Look up a color value in a reference book.

- Specify to a colleague that the particular shade of blue you want to use is created using 96, 57, and 251 in RGB values.

## Windows Photo Gallery

Digital photography is one of those modern technologies that has zoomed from Flash Gordon sci-fi to products so common and simple that even a college-educated adult can be taught to use them. See Figure 2-10. (In fact, the once-booming industry of film-based photography has dried up; you have to go out of your way to find a laboratory to develop film and make prints.)

The advantages of a digital camera are immediately evident to anyone who uses one.

✦ The cameras are microcomputers all by themselves.

✦ They can focus by themselves, choose the proper exposure, and otherwise capture what you see.

✦ The images are available immediately — starting on the screen that most cameras have, and continuing when you upload the digital files to a computer.

✦ When the images are loaded onto your laptop, you can use its much more powerful processor with advanced image-editing software to adjust

- Exposure

- Brightness

- Contrast

- Color intensity

- Picture size

✦ You can perform other tricks that go way beyond the antique world of film:

- Sharpen the pixels that make up the image.

- Change colors to hues not seen in the real world.

- Ship them from one computer to another (or to a cell phone or a personal data assistant or to a television screen) over the Internet nearly instantly.

✦ The cost of taking a picture is close to zero. You never have to buy film or pay for its processing; if you choose to keep your images in electronic form you don't even need to pay for prints.

As a professional photographer, I add one more wrinkle to that equation: I used to keep a casual running calculation of the cost of each picture I snapped. But now that I work entirely in the digital world, I have no hesitation shooting a few dozen versions of the same photo. I can try overexposure, underexposure, a different focus, a different lens. When I'm done for the day, I can look at 150 images and find the one or two that I want to keep. All I've spent is a few penny's worth of battery power.

What's the hard part?

✦ Sorting through hundreds or thousands of images to separate the printable wheat from the digital chaff

✦ Editing your images to improve color, brightness, contrast, and composition

✦ Organizing your images and finding them when you need them

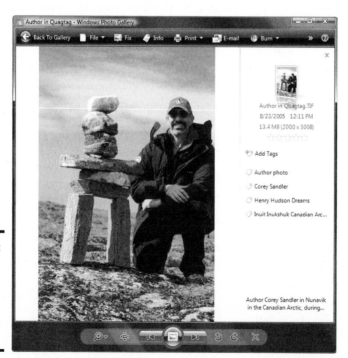

**Figure 2-10:**
Windows
Photo
Gallery
delivers
basic photo
editing.

### A free solution in Windows Vista

Windows Photo Gallery is offered as one of the "free" components delivered with Windows Vista. (You can download and use another version of the program, called Windows Live Photo Gallery, with Windows XP or Windows Vista.)

This program offers many of the basic photo-editing tools that are part of entry-level programs like Adobe Elements:

+ **Auto adjust.** A computer-directed set of adjustments to brightness, contrast, and exposure. This setting works with most images that are already close to how you'd like them to appear.

+ **Adjust exposure.** Manual sliders to increase or decrease brightness, contrast, or both.

+ **Adjust color.** Manual sliders to set color temperature, tint, or saturation. Color *temperature* is the warmth or coolness of the overall appearance of colors; think of the difference between the light from an incandescent bulb and a fluorescent; or the change in the feel of colors between midday and sunset. Adjusting the saturation is like adding more color to the electronic paint set.

   Setting color saturation all the way off effectively creates a black-and-white or grayscale image.

+ **Fix red eye.** This isn't a cure for disease; rather, it can, in many cases, remove the bright red spots that appear in human eyes when an electronic flash reflects back to the camera.

You can crop an image to remove Uncle Ned, or change its shape to fit a monitor or a picture frame.

The primary purpose of Windows Photo Gallery is to prepare your images — in a basic way — for these types of things:

+ Displaying in an onscreen slideshow

+ E-mailing to friends and family

+ Sending to a service bureau for prints

+ Burning a CD or DVD with copies of your pictures

The video DVD feature of Windows Photo Gallery is available only in Windows Vista Home Premium or Windows Vista Ultimate versions of the operating system.

**Book III
Chapter 2**

**Using Built-in Windows Applications and Gadgets**

Downsides:

✦ One feature that's absent from Windows Photo Gallery is the ability to change file formats (from JPG to TIFF, for example). (Despite this, the program can open and work with images of either type, as well as BMP and PNG formats.)

✦ You can't adjust the image resolution or its printable size. For these sorts of functions — very important to some users — you need to purchase a graphics-editing program.

 Now the good news: Windows Photo Gallery can function as the equivalent of a graphics database. If you assign *tags* to your images, you can use the program to search for all photos that meet a particular criteria. For example, you could create the following tags: family, travel, Europe, cruises, and "the time Janice got seasick."

After applying tags, you can search for any one particular image or an entire group that shares the same tags. A picture of Janice, seasick on a cruise in Europe, would probably turn up in a search for any of the tags I identified earlier; a search just for tags of Europe should turn up the same picture, as well as other images taken on land having nothing to do with cruises (or Janice).

The search function doesn't require that images be kept in any particular folder; the program searches all hard discs and other storage media installed within or attached to your laptop.

### An evolving version of Photo Gallery

In late 2007, Microsoft introduced Windows Live Photo Gallery, a free upgrade or replacement to Windows Photo Gallery that adds functions and can be installed within Windows XP as well as Windows Vista. See Figure 2-11.

Among its enhancements is the ability to convert a limited number of file formats from one type to another: JPG to TIFF, for example. It also adds a new file format, WMPHOTO (with a filename extension of WDP) for use with new features related to the world of Windows Live.

A new feature is Publish, which allows use of your images with Windows Live Spaces and other services (such as Flickr) that establish and maintain social networking or image and video sharing sites on the Internet.

## Who Knows Where the Time Goes?

Back in the olden days, many of us kept our calendars on the wall; some of us even had secretaries who kept our schedule in a leather-bound desktop book. Ah, life was simpler then.

**Figure 2-11:**
Windows
Live Photo
Gallery
extends
image
management
features
onto the
Internet.

Today, most of us live lives scheduled down to the minute, and we have to keep track where the time goes all by ourselves. The calendars are off the wall and in our pockets on personal data assistants and advanced cell phones, and on our laptops.

As part of Windows Vista, Microsoft introduced Windows Calendar. This tool includes a full set of tools for recording your appointments, issuing invitations to other meeting participants, and reminding us to get it in gear when we need to run down the hall or out to the airport. It can also maintain a personal to-do list; hold on while I make a note to set one up.

You can set up a personal or business calendar so you can coordinate your entries with other family members or coworkers. With permission, you can check someone else's calendar — or they can check yours — to set up meetings or travel.

For example, all the members of a family could have their own calendar running under Windows Vista on a single machine. Mom or Dad could check in to find out the kids' little league and ballet lesson schedules; the kids could find out what time the 'rents are due home so that they can clean up the evidence.

**Book III
Chapter 2**

**Using Built-in
Windows
Applications
and Gadgets**

In an office, a set of Windows Calendars could be shared amongst members of a specific workgroup or department, or the calendars could be kept private from each other but allow a supervisor to find out what's going on and when people can meet. The manager can reach in and place a claim on a time slot for all the members of the department.

The Calendar system can — and should be — protected by a strong password that you give only to those you want to have access. And if someone leaves your workgroup, change the password immediately.

As part of Microsoft's introduction of its Windows Live online facilities, you can *publish* the calendar online. This serves two purposes:

✦ It allows you to consult your schedule from your laptop (or from any other Internet-capable device) as you travel.

✦ It allows you to give permission to others to consult or even change your calendar from afar.

You can store it on a server at your office or at your Internet service provider; consult your technical support desk for advice on how to do this. Or you can use a public network (Microsoft would like users to use its Windows Live site) for this purpose.

Windows Calendar data is stored in the iCalendar format, which a number of other applications also use. This means you can interchange calendars even if someone else is using different programs to develop them.

# Chapter 3: Windows Maintenance Utilities

## In This Chapter

✓ Keeping your laptop's mind and body clean and neat

✓ Healing what's broken

✓ Dealing with device driver demons

✓ Recycling, defragging, and other healthy habits

*A*re you the sort of person who buys a new car and then keeps it like a museum piece for the rest of its life, vacuuming out every donut crumb, checking the air pressure in the tires weekly, and changing the oil every 2,999 miles before proceeding one inch farther down the road? Or do you let the pizza boxes pile up in the back seat, let the air slowly leak out of the tires, and allow the engine oil to turn to sludge?

If you're the first type of owner, your car is going to last longer, operate more efficiently, and hold on to its value for a much longer period of time. If you're not, your car will slow down day by day and one morning refuse to start at all.

It's pretty much the same thing with laptop computers. Not the part about the engine oil and the air in the tires: The stuff about the importance of keeping everything in tip-top mechanical condition and how if you don't one day, the machine won't go.

Keep in mind three very important concepts about personal computers:

✦ Every time you use your laptop — saving a file, deleting a file, installing a program, making a change to a setting, or connecting to the Internet — you leave the machine in a different condition than it was before you started. Files are moved from place to place on the hard disk drive, they become fragmented (more about this later), and miscellaneous pieces of temporary files are scattered about hither and thon (think of them as donut crumbs).

✦ Microsoft regularly issues updates, security patches, and repairs to current versions of Windows. One way or another they're acknowledgments of the fact that the operating system was less than perfect when first released and (more disturbingly) has been the subject of malicious attacks by hackers ever since. Those are the facts, and I'm not intending to join the small chorus of Microsoft-maligners. The world isn't perfect, and some of its occupants are unpleasant folk.

✦ The makers of other programs and utilities regularly update or repair their products. Based on the settings you establish for products you install within your operating system, these new bits of code are either automatically sent to your laptop over the Internet and installed or you receive notification that updates are available.

In general, you should configure your antivirus and other security utilities so that they're automatically updated; this helps your system fight off the latest viruses and other malware floating out there on the Internet and in e-mail. As far as other programs, you can make your own decisions regarding updates.

## Maintaining Windows and Applications

We have this imperfect world with imperfect operating systems and nasty people trying to cause you and your machine trouble. And we have a machine that, if left unattended, will not-so-gradually lose its new-computer smell and begin to slow down and eventually resemble a box of bricks.

What can you do to keep your computer's operating system and software in tip-top condition?

Happily, Microsoft and most other software makers do a pretty good job of keeping their products up to date. But as a user you have to make sure your machine is properly configured to accept updates, and you need to be vigilant about seeking them out and managing them. I discuss methods for Microsoft updates in Book II.

The most efficient way to maintain your software is to register your software with the maker and establish an Internet connection to their support system.

Although in theory you may be able to have updates and patches sent to you by postal mail on disc, that avenue is rapidly closing; today, most manufacturers assume that all users have a connection to the Internet that can be used to maintain software.

As an example, Adobe offers occasional updates to its powerhouse products such as Adobe Creative Suite or individual elements like Adobe Photoshop. Since this is a mature (though still improving) product, the updates are usually less focused on fixing bugs and more on adding compatibility with new file formats or integrating with features added by Microsoft to its operating system. See Figure 3-1.

**Figure 3-1:**
The Adobe Updater checks for recommend ation modifications to your installed software once a month.

Nearly every laptop now on the market includes an Ethernet port for a wired connection to the Internet, or a WiFi adapter for wireless communication. Most offer both. If you don't have Internet service at your home or office, a public library or school may offer free service or you can rent time at an Internet café. The software for Internet connection is built into Microsoft Windows.

I've always marveled about how veterinarians (and pediatricians) make their initial diagnosis of health problems with their patients. After all, neither puppies nor newborns can tell the doctor, "I've got a pain in my right ear." The vets and the baby docs both have to start out with external observations (poking, prodding, and magnifying scopes). If that does not provide a definitive answer, then there are blood tests, X-rays, and even invasive exploratory surgery.

Enough with the blood and guts stuff. Computers are not humans, nor the other way around; one of the ways in which machines are in some ways superior to animals is that in many instances they are capable of giving themselves a checkup and sometimes even healing themselves.

Modern laptops equipped with current versions of Windows include a wide range of tools that report on their hardware and software configuration, their vital signs, and can often warn about impending problems.

One huge hole in the ability of a computer to report on its own condition: It must be able to start up and run at least the lowest level of its built-in "boot" hardware or go a bit further to load the basics of the operating system. If the hardware can't start, we're no better off at initial diagnosis than a veterinarian trying to figure out what is wrong with a listless lizard.

**Book III
Chapter 3**

**Windows
Maintenance
Utilities**

## *Taking Inventory*

Before you poke around, run any diagnostics, or take a blood test, examine your laptop's installed hardware and software. You have several ways to do this, including a straightforward utility called System Information. (See Figure 3-2 for an example of a report.)

To check System Information, follow along:

*1.* **Click the Start button in Windows Vista.**

On Windows XP, choose Start ➪ All Programs ➪ Accessories ➪ System Tools ➪ System Information.

*2.* **Type** System Information **into the Start menu's search bar.**

You may find a number of versions of the utility.

*3.* **Click the System Information supplied as part of Windows.**

If you subscribe to AOL, you may also see an AOL System Information utility, which is also a quite capable examiner of your laptop, although it focuses more on the operating system, firewall, antivirus, and connectivity components of your machine — things of importance to an AOL connection — than it does on hardware.

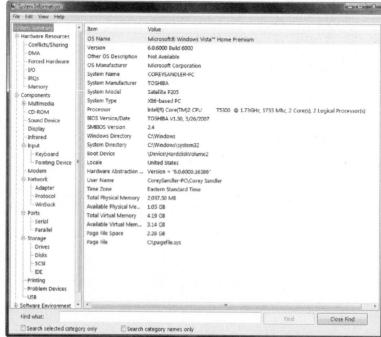

**Figure 3-2:** A Windows System Information screen shows details of the operating system, processor, and memory installed on a Toshiba Satellite P205 laptop.

Many laptop manufacturers add their own versions of a system information report. These reports often serve multiple purposes:

✦ Details of your system for you to examine

✦ A consistent report that can be examined over the Internet by support technicians for the maker of your machine

✦ A bit of advertising for Windows operating system upgrades or hardware accessories

On most current laptops running Windows Vista, manufacturer's system information screen can be found here: Click Start ➪ Control Panel System and Maintenance ➪ System. An example of Toshiba's screen is shown in Figure 3-3.

**Figure 3-3:** Toshiba's information screen includes the system's Windows Experience Index, its processor specs, memory, network configuration, and phone or online access to support technicians.

## Device Manager: Poking under the hood

Once you have a sense of what you've got, the next important utility in Windows is the Device Manager, which is boss of what lies beneath. This window, reachable through the Windows Control Panel (as well as other routes), displays all of the identifiable hardware components of your machine organized by function. See Figure 3-4.

Jump to the dessert before the main course: When you open up Device Manager, the first thing you should look for is one of the following:

✦ A yellow question mark (a possible problem)

✦ A red exclamation mark (there be dragons here)

These warning icons appear alongside a category or an individual component; double-click the item to learn why your laptop is concerned about its health.

**Figure 3-4:**
A Device Manager window for a modern laptop. Clicking a + symbol opens a category to display multiple items in that section.

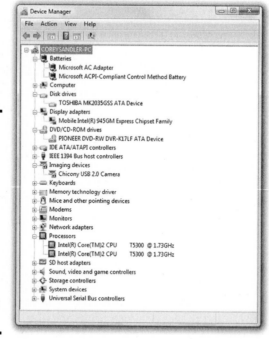

If problems are reported, they usually fall into one of these three areas:

✦ A non-responding or failed piece of hardware

✦ A conflict between two or more devices seeking to use the same resources (interrupts, DMA channels, or memory addresses)

✦ A problem with an installed device driver

Before you accept the laptop's report that a piece of hardware has failed, try

✦ **Rebooting the machine.** Sometimes errors of this sort happen only after a particularly unusual combination of commands, keystrokes, or software events.

✦ **Removing the cables.** That is, if the problematic device is external to your laptop — a hard disk drive or a camera attached to a USB port, for example. If the machine functions properly without them, test the external device on a different machine.

Resource sharing used to be a major headache on PCs, but with modern operating systems (including Windows 98, Windows 2000, Windows XP, and Windows Vista) all the heavy thinking is handled by the machine.

I suggest you attempt to manually change resource settings *only* if you're instructed to do so by a support technician for your laptop or the maker of an add-on device.

You must be logged on as an administrator or as a member of the Administrators group to complete procedures by using Device Manager. That is usually not a problem for laptop users, but if your computer is set up by a corporate or institutional computer department, you may need to seek their assistance or obtain an Administrator sign-on.

*1.* **Open Device Manager.**

*2.* **Double-click any device in the list.**

Its properties are shown. See Figure 3-5.

*3.* **Go to the General Tab.**

*4.* **Look for the Device Status.**

"This device is working properly" is a good sign, at least as far as the particular piece of hardware's relationship to the operating system is concerned; its device driver is proper and its use of system resources is acceptable to the system. What the device status screen doesn't tell you is if there is any physical damage to an external device. (If you want an automobile analogy, the status report is saying the engine and transmission are functioning properly, but isn't providing information on whether the tires are flat.)

Assuming you don't see red (or yellow), you can proceed to examine in depth the configuration of your machine and change settings.

Under Windows XP, do this:

*1.* **Right-click My Computer.**

*2.* **Select Properties.**

*3.* **Select the Hardware tab.**

*4.* **Click the Device Manager button.**

Under Windows Vista, do this:

*1.* **Open the Start menu.**

*2.* **Right-click Computer.**

*3.* **Select Manage.**

*4.* **Click Device Manager.**

This option is in the left-hand tree.

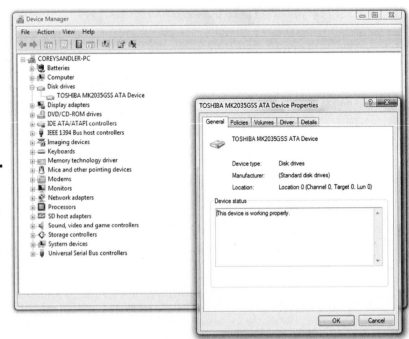

**Figure 3-5:**
On the General Tab of Device Properties, good or bad news is reported in the Device Status window.

## *Dealing with device drivers*

For many users, the most valuable use of Device Manager is the ability to

+ Identify the device drivers in use for each component

+ Install updated drivers

+ Roll back to an earlier version of the driver if the new code causes problems

The doorway to the controls for device drivers is here:

*1.* **Open Device Manager.**

*2.* **Choose the Device Properties window.**

*3.* **Select the Driver tab.**

There you can see any specific piece of hardware listed in the Device Manager. See Figure 3-6.

Take notes on what you've done and keep copies of the original and replacement device drivers to allow reversing your steps. (If you have an external flash memory key, this is a good place to temporarily store a copy.)

Tread carefully if you make any changes to the device drivers in Device Manager. Be certain of these things:

+ You're matching the proper device driver with your particular make and model of device

+ It's appropriate for the version of Windows you're using (In most cases, a Windows Vista device driver won't work under Windows XP; going the other direction may work, may not, or may provide only partial functionality.)

**Book III
Chapter 3**

**Windows
Maintenance
Utilities**

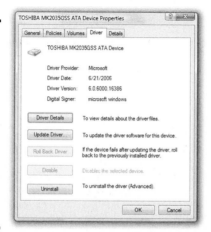

**Figure 3-6:**
The Driver tab of Device Properties allows you to inspect, disable, uninstall, update, or roll back a device driver.

Be very wary about accepting a device driver from a source you don't know and trust — and that includes "free" driver sites on the Internet. A corrupted device driver can cause many problems for your system, and an infected one can introduce nasty viruses. Your best bet is to accept assistance only from the maker of your machine, its major components, or significant software.

### Removing and reinstalling a device driver

If the Device Manager indicates you have a problem with a piece of hardware, a corrupted or outdated device driver may be the cause. A first step to attempting a repair is to remove the existing driver and reinstall it.

The most direct way to uninstall a driver is from the Properties window for a particular device:

*1.* **Open the Device Manager.**

*2.* **Locate the device you want to work on.**

It may be flagged with a yellow question mark or a red exclamation point.

*3.* **Click the Driver tab.**

*4.* **Click Uninstall.**

You're asked if you really, truly want to remove the driver. Stop and think.

*5.* **Click OK.**

*6.* **Restart the computer.**

Windows should automatically notice that it has a device without a driver and reinstall its copy from the original Windows installation files or from elsewhere on your hard disk. In certain circumstances — usually for particularly obscure devices — Windows may ask you to provide the driver from a CD or DVD supplied by the maker of the hardware or ask you to download it from a web site.

Once you uninstall a driver, the device with which it's associated stops working until you reinstall its driver. Be aware that if you remove the driver for the pointing device, you'll have to restart without use of the mouse; try Alt + F4 to shut down the system. If you uninstall the keyboard driver, you need to use the mouse to shut down.

### Upgrading a device driver

Sometimes the solution to a hardware problem is to upgrade to a later (presumably improved) version of the device driver. The maker of the hardware

✦ May have issued a newer version to fix a bug or incompatibility with other hardware

✦ May have issued an update to deal with a new version of the operating system

✦ May be enhancing the capabilities of its older hardware just because, well, they should

Your first effort should be to try the automated facilities of the Hardware Update Wizard. (See Figure 3-7 to see the Windows XP version of this tool.)

You'll get to the Hardware Update Wizard with these steps:

*1.* **Go to the Properties.**

Do so for whatever hardware you need to update.

*2.* **Go to the Driver tab.**

Refer back to Figure 3-6.

*3.* **Click the Update button.**

**Figure 3-7:**
The Windows XP version of the Hardware Update Wizard checks for newer versions of device drivers installed in your machine.

If Windows Update doesn't show you a newer version of the driver, conduct your own search:

✦ Visit the web site for the manufacturer of your laptop.

✦ Check the web site for the specific component (an external pointing device or an external hard disk drive).

You might be advised of the availability of an updated device driver through an automated update utility installed on your machine. Read the instructions you find accompanying the details of the update. Make absolutely certain the update applies to your specific hardware as well as the version of the operating system you're running.

Some manufacturers will instruct you to download the device driver to your laptop and then click on its icon for an automated installation of the new piece of code. That's the simplest and usually the best solution.

Occasionally you will find the device driver just sitting out there on a web site or on a CD or DVD disc. Follow the instructions provided by the maker of the hardware; you may be instructed to save a copy of the new device driver to your desktop and to then install the new piece of code from the Drivers tab.

Under Windows Vista, if you click the Update button you see a simpler but more sophisticated wizard that asks the very appropriate question: "How do you want to search for driver software?" Your choices are:

✦ Search automatically on your computer and on the Internet for the latest device driver software for your device.

✦ Browse your computer for driver software. (This is an easy way to install a device driver downloaded to your desktop.)

### Rolling back a device driver

What do you do if your hardware — which had been functioning properly before you meddled with it — suddenly stops performing properly after you have installed a new device driver? Why, go back to the past, of course.

The trick here is to roll back the driver, which has nothing to do with turning a used car's odometer backwards; instead, it amounts to uninstalling the new driver and replacing it with the one that had been in place before.

Do this to roll back a device driver:

*1.* **Open the Device Manager.**

*2.* **Right-click the device you want to work on.**

3. **Click Properties.**

4. **Click the Driver tab.**

5. **Click Roll Back Driver.**

6. **Accept your decision.**

    The driver rolls back.

7. **Click Close.**

8. **Restart your computer.**

# Checking Your Hard Disk for Errors

An automated hard disk error-checking utility isn't going to balance your bank account, convert the faulty logic in your term paper to Pulitzer-level insight, or correct your personality so you will meet the person of your dreams.

Here's what the built-in utilities of Windows Vista and Windows XP do:

✦ Examine the structure of your hard disk drive to make sure everything is properly indexed and that any problems with filenames, file attribute tables, security descriptors, and anything else related to the proper storage and retrieval of files is identified and fixed

✦ Look for one particular category of hardware problem on the disk itself: bad sectors

## CHKDSK

The error-checking utility is a modernized version of one of the oldest elements of MS-DOS, the original operating system for PCs. From the dawn of PC time — before Windows was a twinkling in Bill Gates' eyes — there has been a utility called CHKDSK (pronounced *check-disk*) that gives disk drives a physical and mental examination. (See Figure 3-8 for the Windows Vista Premium version of hard disk tools, which includes data backup; the Windows XP version offers a nearly identical toolbox.)

CHKDSK is one of the few utilities that still exists outside the operating system. There are two important reasons for this:

✦ Microsoft has (properly) chosen to maintain, as much as possible, downward compatibility between the latest and greatest and the oldest and least.

✦ As a matter of engineering it pretty much needs to do its work without interference from any other computer tasks.

**Figure 3-8:**
In My
Computer or
Computer,
right-click
the listing
for your
hard disk to
display its
Properties
window;
choose the
Tools tab to
conduct
error
checking or
defrag-
mentation.

If you think about it, it would be rather difficult to check the organization and the physical attributes of your hard disk while it was operating — kind of like trying to gauge the depth and quality of the water in a shallow pond at the same time as a speedboat passes by. There are just too many moving parts and the mere presence of the boat (or the activities of Windows) changes the environment too much for the test to get an accurate reading.

Instead, if you ask the system to check your hard disk for errors from within Windows, it asks that you schedule the test for the next time the computer is rebooted. And then the full test is run from outside Windows; although MS-DOS no longer exists like it did when it was the operating system for early PCs, there is a functional equivalent that underlies even the most current of GUIs, Windows Vista.

Be aware that the larger your hard disk drive and the more files recorded on it, the longer the CHKDSK process can take. On my Toshiba Satellite P205 test machine, a test (with the repair function turned on) required more than two hours to complete, and I couldn't use the laptop for any other purpose during that time. If you need to use your laptop, consider scheduling a test, rebooting your machine at the end of the day, and leaving it running all night.

## Selecting a testing level

Do you want a relatively quick checkup, or do you want your computer doctor to perform a detailed diagnosis and test and then reach in and per-form any necessary surgery? The checkup is the least disruptive, but nothing gets fixed: All you get is a report. If the tests show nothing is wrong, you'll have saved a great deal of time.

Depending on which version of Windows you have, you may be offered the option to merely scan your system for problems. All current versions go on to allow automatic fixes of file systems errors and bad sectors. Use the pointer to turn on the check box next to your choice:

✦ **Scan.** If you select no options, the system will examine the hard disk for logical and certain physical problems and give you a report.

✦ **Automatically fix file system errors.** The utility will examine all of the files, folders, and indexes on the disk and repair most basic problems it finds.

✦ **Scan for and attempt recovery of bad sectors.** The utility will check out the magnetic markings on the surface of the disk that demark sectors in search of any corrupted, incorrect, or damaged indicators. If possible, the utility will repair the sector marking. If the portion of the disk itself is damaged, the utility may be able to place an electronic fence around the sector so that the system does not attempt to place new information there.

✦ To check for and repair both file errors and bad sectors, select the check box next to both available options.

If you choose to run error checking, remember my explanation about how the system can't examine itself while the drive is in use. As you can see in Figure 3-9, you're asked if you want the machine to give itself a checkup the next time you turn it on — and before it loads Windows.

A *sector* is a slide of one of the circular tracks on a magnetic disk or optical disc. Each sector is intended to hold a particular amount of data. Under Windows, most sectors hold 512 bytes on a magnetic medium.

# Managing Your Disk Drives

Be good to your hard disks . . . and they won't die an early death. With mechanical devices — basically anything with a motor or a moving part — failure is only a question of *when,* not *if.*

It starts before you even take possession of your laptop. Brand-name laptops generally use better-quality components.

One way to measure the manufacturer's intentions is to look at the length of the warranty. A new machine with a 90-day warranty would scare me; the way I figure it, a company hopes to never have to pay for repairs. A longer warranty is one indication that they believe their machine—including its built-in hard disk drive—will stand a medium-to-long test of time.

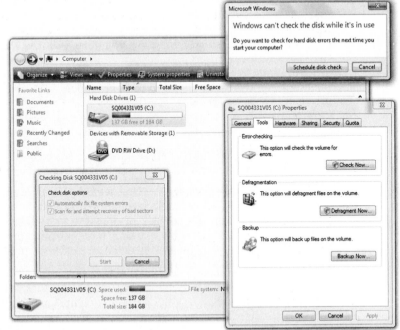

**Figure 3-9:**
You can
schedule an
error-
checking
session to
run the next
time you
start your
machine.

If you purchase a no-name or store-brand laptop, find out the maker of the hard disk drive within. There aren't that many backwoods disk-drive suppliers for current machines, but be wary if you don't recognize the name of the manufacturer.

Once the laptop is in your possession, you have several ways to find out the maker of the hard disk drive, and each of them is also the pathway to proper maintenance. Here's how to learn about your drive:

*1.* **Click My Computer.**

*2.* **Highlight the drive you want to investigate.**

*3.* **Right-click the drive label.**

*4.* **Choose Properties.**

Back in Figure 3-5 you see the properties information about the Toshiba-brand hard drive in this book's sample Toshiba Satellite P205 laptop; that's not a surprise since that company is one of the pioneers of the laptop industry and its drives are among the most reliable.

The Computer (under Windows Vista) or My Computer (Windows XP) screen shows you the automatically generated name for the hard drive in your laptop as well as the drive letter assigned to it.

Avoid reassigning the drive letter for the first disk drive in your machine; the laptop seeks out this device to boot the system and it's where Windows and many other programs expect to reside. It's possible to give it a different drive letter, but the potential for headache is more than I am willing to willingly accept.

5. **Get a quick measurement of the total capacity of the drive.**

6. **See how much of that space is still available for storage.**

   See Figure 3-10.

7. **Go to the General tab.**

8. **See the file system that is in use.**

Modern machines almost all use NTFS, while antiques (and certain external devices) may be based on the less-capable, sometimes incompatible FAT32 or FAT technology.

If you subdivided your physical hard disk so it includes one or more *logical* drives, each of them is shown separately. The logical drives are treated as if they were separate pieces of plastic, metal, and motors.

The capacity report on the hard disk drive shown in Figure 3-10 gives a great example of creative computing mathematics. The capacity is listed as 198,475,509,760 bytes, which is more or less the raw number of recordable computer words; alongside is a figure of 184GB, which is an estimate of its actual usable space when overhead and other factors are included. If you add up the numbers listed for used space and free space, you come up with yet another number, 184.7GB, which tells you how much your particular blend of data actually occupies on the disk. And the specifications for the laptop when you shop for it at the store? The hard drive's size is rounded up by the marketing department to an even 200GB.

Why subdivide a large hard disk with logical drives? It's all a matter of personal organizational tendencies; I like to put things into separate boxes.

If I have two drives in a laptop or desktop machine

✦ I usually reserve the C drive for the operating system, programs, and my current data files.

✦ On the second drive I usually make two logical disks:

   • One to hold backup copies of current data files

   • One as repository for my back pages, archives of older work

And then I make backups of both current and archival material onto an external hard drive and onto DVDs.

**Figure 3-10:**
The General tab of the Properties report for the internal hard drive is a reality check: you can see the total capacity of the drive as well as the amount of space that is in use. Note the Disk Cleanup button near the pie chart.

By the way, the first drive in a system is marked as location 0 and the second at location 1. (A third drive, if one is present, would be at location 2, and so on.)

Computer designers still hold on to bits and pieces (oops, a geekish pun) of the binary system in labels and other elements of the machines they design. Since binary math starts with 0, so does the numbering of the various connectors and pins inside your computer. So your first hard disk drive is to the computer drive 0, and to Windows drive C, and to you whatever you choose to call it.

## Keeping a clean drive

In the world of computers, it's not the content that matters so much as its orderliness on the disk. And then there's the matter of taking out the trash.

Let's talk trash first. There's an awful lot of it on any laptop computer that has been in use for a while.

✦ **Web junk.** If you use the Internet, web pages are constantly sending you images, icons, and other stuff to display on your screen; many of those elements are written to your hard disk as *temporary* files so they can be more quickly shown if you return to a particular page. In theory, those temporary files are supposed to be deleted when you close your browser; in practice, well, not all are.

+ **Updated garbage.** Then there are programs and drivers and updates that are downloaded to your machine to keep it up to date; if you're running a proper security or antivirus program, these are only accepted with your permission. Again, the installation packages for these files are supposed to be removed once the programs they deliver are put in place; not all are.

+ **Refuse refusal.** There is real trash, too, although on a computer things thrown away sometimes hang around for a long time before they go away. Say you press the Delete key to remove a file you no longer need. You'd think that meant the file was physically erased from the magnetic surface of your disk, but that's not the case.

First of all, for simplicity and speed, when you "delete" a file, all that actually happens is that its name is removed from the directory of available files that is maintained by the computer. It's even simpler than that: The first character of its name is changed from a standard alphanumeric symbol to one of the characters that the computer has reserved for its own purpose. The file is still there, only the system ignores it when you look at a directory of files.

For most users, this is a good thing; I'd say, on average, I accidentally delete a file about once a year. And, also on average, every few months I change my mind about a file I deleted and wish I could get it back.

Windows, as well as third-party add-on utilities, offers you a way to "undelete" a file from the Recycle Bin. (Cute name, don't you think? In early operating systems it was called the trash basket, but now it has a more ecofriendly name and it also hints at the fact that the stuff it holds may be pulled back out and put to use again.) A stylized icon for the Recycle Bin is shown in Figure 3-11.

Files stay in the recycle bin for hours, days, weeks, or even months until one of the following events occurs:

+ Right-click the recycle bin icon on the desktop and select Open. Once the contents of the bin are displayed onscreen, right-click a specific file and choose Delete, which gets rid of that specific file.

+ Right-click the recycle bin icon on the desktop and select Empty Recycle Bin, which dumps all files.

✦ Your recycle bin becomes so clogged up with deleted files that it automatically starts throwing away the least recently deleted files to make room for fresher garbage. (If you right-click the recycle bin icon and choose Properties, you can set the maximum amount of space you want to allow the bin to set aside. The more space you devote to it, the longer it takes before files are removed from the bin.)

Oh, and even if you do delete a file from the recycle bin, it *still* doesn't mean it is gone forever. It is only unavailable to ordinary users once the system actually writes new data over the location it once called home. That may happen immediately, or it may take quite a while.

**Figure 3-11:**
The Recycle Bin icon fills up with images of crumpled paper as you send files its way. When you empty the bin, the trash disappears to the accompaniment of a neat little sound of rustling paper.

Recycle Bin

### Retrieving erased files

As long as a file is still listed as being in the recycle bin, you can remove it from the can and return it to its prior location.

One word of warning: If you've deleted a file — or if a program has automatically deleted an older version of a file and resaved a current copy under the same name — be careful not to overwrite a newer version with an older one.

If you find yourself in that situation, before you recover a file from the recycle bin, rename the newer version by adding a date, number, or some other indication that it varies from the older file. A recycle bin stuffed with deleted files is shown in Figure 3-12.

To restore a file, do this:

*1.* **Double-click the Recycle Bin icon on the desktop.**

*2.* **Right-click an individual file.**

*3.* **Click Restore.**

Or, you can restore all the files in the recycle bin by clicking the Restore All Items button.

### Unerasing erased files

You can purchase third-party utilities that can "unerase" files that have been removed from the recycle bin but not overwritten. This is a bit of a last-ditch rescue effort, and you may find that not all the file is available to you (because the file had been fragmented).

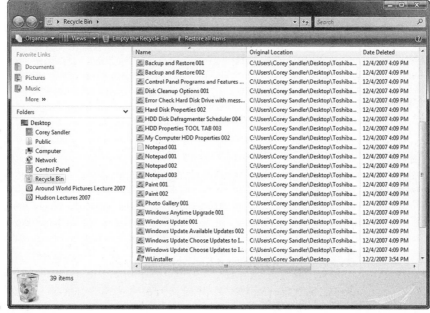

**Figure 3-12:** You can undelete an individual file, restore all deleted files, or empty the trash from the Recycle Bin screen.

One more thing: Law enforcement and spy agencies and some computer techies may be able to recover some or all files that have been deleted, removed from the recycle bin, and written over. They use super-sensitive scanning tools that can sometimes see the magnetic shadows of erased 0s and 1s on the disk.

Finally, there are fragments. I discuss how files get fragmented and how to defragment them in the next section; here, though, I'm talking about discarded partial files that once were part of a larger file or that have been left behind as files were revised or updated. You can also end up with fragments when a file is deleted and its space returned to available inventory on the disk; the computer may overwrite the first, third, and fifth piece of the file because they're closest to each other or to the location of the read-write head, leaving the second and fourth piece of the file as orphaned fragments.

### Adjusting recycle bin settings

Windows includes a number of options that allow you to customize the way the recycle bin works. One of the most important: setting the maximize amount of space devoted to the bin.

If you're not in the habit of regularly clearing your computer's Recycle Bin, or if you have a lot of extra space, consider setting up a large amount of space for its use.

Think of the size of the electronic bin as being roughly equivalent to the size of the real trash can beneath your desk. The larger the bin, the less often it has to be emptied. In the case of the computer's recycle bin, when the can reaches capacity, it starts permanent deletion of items from the bottom. In business inventory management this is referred to as *FIFO, first-in first-out.* In other words, the files that have been in the bin the longest are disposed of before more recent additions. Very large files aren't sent to the recycle bin, since they would otherwise displace a great many smaller files.

Other options — not ones I necessarily recommend — include these:

✦ Turning off the sometimes annoying message that asks if you really, really want to delete a file. It's supposed to make you stop and think, and it just might save you from heartache one day.

✦ Instruct the system to bypass the recycle bin and just remove files from your hard drive when you delete them. Again, I'd rather have the protective net of the bin.

To change the Recycle Bin settings, do this:

*1.* **Right-click the bin's icon on the desktop.**

*2.* **Click Properties.**

*3.* **Click the General tab.**

*4.* **Select from the available customization options.**

## *Your hard disk's fragmented mind*

A *fragmented file* is split into two or more pieces that aren't next to each other on your hard disk drive. In fact, files are commonly split up so the beginning is somewhere in the middle and the end comes before the middle.

Why do files become fragmented, and why should you care? In the spirit of fragmentation, I answer the second question first.

You should care because a disk that has files split up and spread hither and yon around its platters will operate less efficiently than one where everything is neat and orderly.

Here's how files get fragmented: Consider that fact that not every file is the same length. You may write a short note to yourself — a shopping list, or a to-do list, for example. Or you might just not have all that much to say on a particular subject. But depending on the size of your hard disk drive and the filing system it uses, your hard disk drive will have a minimum size for the block of space it allocates for a file; say it's 64KB.

If your file is only 1KB in length, it will sit within a 64KB section like the last remaining truffle in a beautifully packaged 64-pound box of chocolates. And if your file happens to be 65KB, it occupies one complete 64KB section plus 1KB in an otherwise empty container.

When you start a file the operating system opens a section of the disk for it and fills it up, but when it reaches the end of the first segment the next available space may or may not be directly next door. The next block of 0s and 1s may be all the way across the disk, on the other side of the same platter, or even on a different platter within the hard drive.

Then consider what happens the next time you open that file to do some editing or add more material. While the original file might have occupied a pair of contiguous segments, other work you have begun, copied, or edited may have since filled in segments all around it.

## Defragmentation mechanics

For years I've made a nearly handsome living describing how computers are very dumb but very fast. By that I mean that they accomplish their wondrous feats not so much by innate intelligence but instead by brute force and blazing speed. (To multiply 7,845 by 12,687 the machine adds 7,845 to itself 12,687 times.)

The same applies when it comes to defragmenting a hard disk. There is no magical algorithm or instant solution. Instead, defragging works like this: The machine locates a block of unused space on the hard disk. The bigger the space, the faster the defragmentation process will proceed.

Under control of the microprocessor, the system picks up the scattered pieces of files one by one and copies them from their former location to the unused space. As the files are rewritten they are compacted and made contiguous to each other. Once all the pieces of a file have been moved to a new location, the former location is cleared.

As large, contiguous blocks of space are opened near the beginning of the disk, the rewritten files are copied again and moved to the most efficient location available.

The process repeats itself over and over until the disk is as close as possible to this: a clean group of contiguous data and program files at the logical start of the disk, a block of clean, available workspace for the temporary needs of the microprocessor, and a block of open space for new files and for the creation of new fragments as old files are edited.

If just a few files are fragmented in this way, it's no big deal. Or if the particular set of files that are fragmented are ones that you use a great deal, it becomes more of a problem. And fragmentation can become a real detriment to computing if you regularly deal with very large files: digital photographs, streaming video, and music are good examples.

But one thing is certain: Left to its own, every computer will eventually slow down and lose available storage space because of fragmentation. It's designed right into the operating system.

### Defragger rock

The bad news is that the larger your disk, as well as the more files it holds, the longer it takes for defragmentation to be done; in some situations the process can take several hours. The good news: you don't have to do it yourself.

First of all, Microsoft Windows includes a capable defragmentation utility that you can invoke from the Tools tab of the Properties page for each of your hard disk drives.

*1.* **Click Computer (or My Computer).**

*2.* **Highlight the drive you want to work on.**

*3.* **Click Properties.**

*4.* **Select the Tools tab.**

*5.* **Click Defragment Now.**

See Figure 3-13.

**Figure 3-13:**
A defragmentation session is under way in Windows Vista. Microsoft's tool is capable but provides almost no information about its progress or results.

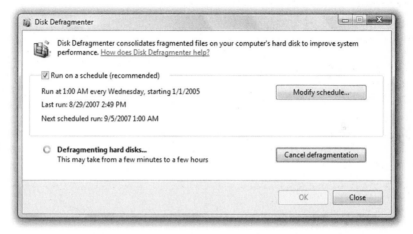

And if you want to go a few steps beyond the basic service included in Windows, you can buy one of several very sophisticated utilities that will generally

✦ Do the job faster

✦ May speed up your computer (using special algorithms that place the most frequently used programs in the places where the disk drive can find them fastest)

✦ Display a nifty color-coded chart that shows you before and after representations of a messy disk and a cleaned-up beauty

The most advanced utilities keep your hard disk drive defragmented *on the fly.* Here's what that means: Their utility will come to life and move files around any time it notices that your machine is not being tasked with other more immediate assignment. So if you get up to go to a meeting or out to lunch, the defragmentation program will churn away while you're gone and then shut off the moment you return your fingers to the keyboard or mouse.

TIP

Among the best third-party defraggers:

✦ Diskeeper Professional from Diskeeper Corporation at
   www.diskeeper.com

✦ Norton 360 from Symantec Corporation at www.symantec.com

Both of these products are intended to work in the background, essentially keeping your disk at or near full efficiency at all times. See Figure 3-14.

Some defragmentation programs are within products such as Norton SystemWorks, System Mechanic, and other maintenance-utility suites. These products generally are to work on a scheduled basis; you might instruct them to defragment your machine every Monday night beginning at 5 p.m., leaving your computer on for the night.

Most third-party defraggers also paint a picture of the condition of your hard disk drive before, during, and after they do their work. A seriously fragmented hard drive shows a report that looks like the aftermath of an explosion at a jellybean factory; afterwards you should see solid blocks of color denoting contiguous files and sections of memory set aside for use by the operating system for temporary storage. See Figure 3-15.

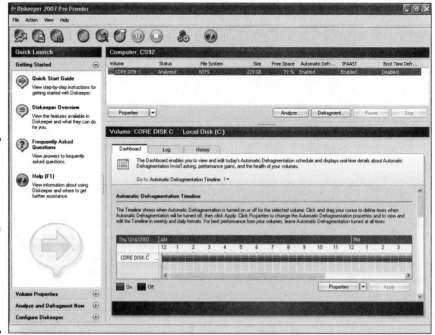

**Figure 3-14:**
The main control panel for Diskeeper allows setup of automatic defragmentation; the utility runs in the background.

Here's a three-in-one tip for defraggers.

✦ If you're going to use a scheduled defragmentation utility (as opposed to a background defragger), you will get better and faster results if you turn off the connection to the Internet while it is running; otherwise, new e-mail and other automatic activities that bring files to your computer slow down the process (sometimes to the point where the utility determines it has to start all over again).

✦ Don't let your drives get so fully packed that a defragger has no room to rearrange files. In most cases, you shouldn't fill up a drive to more than 85 percent of its capacity; that means leaving at least 15 percent available to the utility. Delete junk or move some files to external storage if you need to open up space.

✦ Help save the planet while running a scheduled defragmentation by turning off your monitor. It isn't needed for the process; you'll know the job is done when the hard disk activity light stops flashing.

**Figure 3-15:**
A post-operative report from Diskeeper shows how nearly all files have been reordered into contiguous sectors. The striped section is a portion of the drive claimed by the operating system for some of its work.

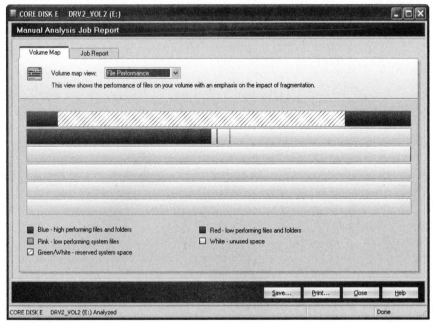

### Cleaning up before defragging

Before you defragment your disk using a manual program, clear away the dead wood:

+ Cut down temporary files. There's no purpose in defragmenting files you don't want to keep.

+ Empty the recycle bin. If you're certain you won't need any of the files residing in the recycle bin, throw those away before defragging, too.

Windows includes a small utility called Disk Cleanup. You'll find it on the General Tab of the Properties for your hard disk; look for the Disk Cleanup button like the one previously shown in Figure 3-10.

You'll be able to clean up just your files, or those of all users on the computer. On a laptop, the most common setup is to have a single user account. After the utility calculates the amount of space you can clean up, it will offer you a report on what unnecessary files it found. Click the check box alongside the types of files you want to clear off the disk.

For most users, it is best to accept only the recommended disk cleanup options. If you choose to go further, read and consider the descriptions of each before proceeding.

A sample report is shown in Figure 3-16; here I have selected deletion of 11.7MB of downloaded program files, temporary Internet files, and thumbnails that can be safely deleted. An additional 107MB of files occupy the recycle bin. For a deeper level of cleanup, I could choose to delete hibernation files, although that would disable that function on the laptop.

**Figure 3-16:**
Most people should accept only the recommended disk cleanup options.

Among the options for cleanup is removal of superfluous System Restore and Shadow Copies. If you click this option, all restore points except for the most recently recorded one are removed.

In theory, this should be acceptable if your machine is working properly; I don't like the idea, though. I'd rather find other ways to clear up space on my disk and keep a full library of restore points just in case there's a problem I haven't run into yet. Some editions of Windows Vista also store previous versions of files and backup images of system files created with Windows Complete PC Backup; these are called Shadow Copies. Again, I would rather hold onto these just in case.

### Opening up space other ways

On a desktop machine, running out of available space on the original hard disk drive is a relatively minor problem. You can replace the original boot drive with one of larger capacity (and transfer over the contents of the first drive). You can add a second internal disk drive. Or you can plug in an almost limitless number of external drives that can be hidden away under the desk or on a shelf.

Things are less simple with a laptop. Some models allow you to swap out the original hard disk drive with a larger replacement; transferring the contents from the first drive may require some fancy footwork including providing a temporary enclosure, power source, and data cable. Adding an external drive is as easy as pie, but you may not want to lug around an extra box when you travel.

So before I worry myself with the details of adding more real estate within a laptop, I try to find ways to reduce the ground clutter. A lot of this has to do with the way I use my laptop: It isn't my principal machine. I use my laptop as a traveling extension of my desktop machine, and for that reason I don't need to have every last piece of software nor every data file.

Here's how to put your laptop's hard disk on a diet: Remove any programs you don't need on your travel companion. Many programs offer their own uninstall utility. Look for one as part of the application's listing on All Programs.

The Uninstall feature of Windows also offers a Change or Repair function for many programs. This allows you to add or remove specific components or repair a problem by resetting the installation to its original condition. You have no choice here — some manufacturers allow these advanced facilities, while others give you only the chance to remove their product.

Under Windows Vista, you can uninstall many programs with this method:

*1.* **Go to the Control Panel.**

*2.* **Click the Programs and Features icon.**

3. **Highlight a program.**

4. **Take one of these steps:**

   • **Double-click the filename.**

   • **Click the Uninstall/Change option on the page.**

   The display includes the size of each program; you may be amazed at the bloated amount of space demanded by some little programs. See Figure 3-17.

Windows Vista users aren't allowed to manually remove individual components of the operating system. Some third-party utilities promise to do this for you, but be very wary of using them. Microsoft *may* add a component uninstall feature in future Service Pack updates to Vista.

A very similar facility is offered to users of Windows XP. The icon on the Control Panel in that operating system is called Add or Remove Programs. One advantage of Windows XP: There's a command to Add/Remove Windows Components. You can take away any program or utility that is part of Windows that you don't require; if you change your mind later on, you can add it back on.

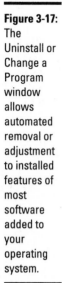

**Figure 3-17:**
The Uninstall or Change a Program window allows automated removal or adjustment to installed features of most software added to your operating system.

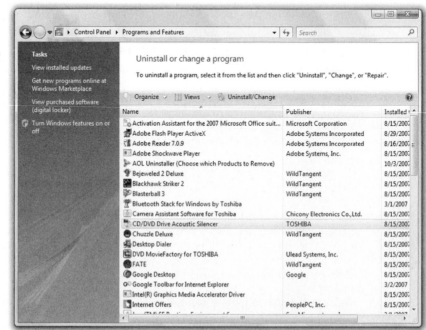

Make sure you have a legal CD or DVD copy of Windows XP before you remove any Windows component; you may need to install the disc in your laptop to add or replace a piece of software you chose to remove.

Once you have slimmed down your machine's programs, do these things:

+ Look for any data files that you can take off the hard disk. I keep my archival copies of files on my desktop machine as well as on external disk drives and DVDs attached to it.

+ Clean off any old files that have moved to your desktop machine.

+ Look for any automatic backup copies of work in progress stored to your disk by word processors and certain other programs; these are to help you recover from a system crash or power outage and serve no purpose once the completed file has been moved to your permanent storage device and archived from there.

## Using Third-Party Maintenance Programs

There's Microsoft, there's you and me, and then there are the third parties: companies like Symantec, Diskeeper, McAfee, and others.

For the vast majority of the readers of this book (and for the author) our computing world begins with Microsoft; although there are a handful of alternatives including various flavors of Linux and even the latest Apple Macintosh operating system. You might assume you're using a current version of Microsoft Windows.

But thanks to a combination of the free marketplace and a boost from the U.S. Department of Justice, Microsoft's operating system was pried open so that a wide variety of utilities and extensions can be installed within or alongside. Some of the utilities — including advanced maintenance programs, defragmenters, and security suites — are better than those included in Microsoft Windows and some are just different.

# Chapter 4: Honk, Honk! Windows Backup and Restore Utilities

## In This Chapter

↳ **Automating the backup process**

↳ **Restoring files from a backup source**

↳ **Using System Restore as a magic bullet (if you're lucky)**

*W*ait! Before you start your day's work, make sure that yesterday's efforts are safely secured.

Centering your business and personal life around your computer is a high-tech good news/bad news story. On the plus side you benefit from the impressive capabilities of word processors, spreadsheets, the Internet, and e-mail that permit you to perform almost all your tasks with ease. The hard disk drive or other digital storage is where you keep your stuff — not in a shoebox under the bed or stacked in a drawer — and you can use your laptop's brain to search for and display anything you've placed in electronic storage.

Data centralization is at the heart of the bad news. What would you do if you pressed the power switch on your laptop and nothing happened? What would you do if the laptop came to life but the hard disk drive had somehow been erased? What would you do if your computer were infected with a virus? And of particular concern to laptop users: What would you do if your laptop were stolen from your office, a hotel room, or an airport?

The answer to the bad news is relatively simple, although it requires a bit of planning and time investment: Make backups and keep them in a secure place. If you're lucky you'll never have to use them; if not, you'll be very pleased with yourself when you can reach onto the shelf to solve the problem of a missing or corrupted file.

## Backing Up Before You Go Go

A *backup* is an extra copy of a file or a full folder of files that you keep in a different location than the original. (There's not a lot of value in making backups and keeping them on the same hard disk drive as the original, and for that matter, it also doesn't make a lot of sense to back up on a storage medium like a CD, DVD, or flash memory key and keep them in your laptop computer travel bag; if the bag and computer are stolen, your backups will go along with them.)

Some programs, including word processors, let you create version backups (which aren't the same as backups) to guard against loss of data. A *version backup* is a copy of whatever file you're currently working on before you began changing the current version. This valuable tool is for when you change your mind and want to go back in time to that earlier version, but in most cases the version backup is stored on the same hard disk drive as the original.

## Choosing files for backup

What type of files should be backed up? The short answer is: anything of value to you that would be difficult or important to replace.

Definitely make backups of the following:

+ Any word-processing files for projects in progress
+ Anything that records important personal information, financial or legal records, and receipts
+ Music
+ Photos
+ Video
+ Important correspondence that arrives (or departs) via your e-mail program

What *doesn't* need to be backed up? The operating system or programs installed on your machine. Instead, keep the original installation discs and product keys or serial numbers so you can reinstall them in case of disaster.

## Choosing frequencies for backup

The amount of time you let go by between data backups should be directly related to your personal and professional threshold of pain. If you lost all the work you've done today, would that be the end of the world, or merely require you to spend a few hours re-creating the files and other documents while they're still somewhat fresh in that other computer — the one between your ears?

If you lost all the work you did today as well as yesterday, that might be more than you're willing or able to stand. And if you were to lose the work of a week or a month or a year . . . please stay away from open windows, railroad crossings, and tax collectors.

Because I spend nearly my entire business day parked in front of my laptop keyboard, I consider it essential to back up all my work daily. I use a combination of temporary backups to devices like flash memory keys, and more permanent weekly or monthly backups to removable media including DVDs and external hard disk drives. And most recently I've begun using the services of automated online backup facilities that promise to keep me protected all the time, nearly up to the minute.

## Backing up manually

You can take charge of your own backup process quite easily. But you have to promise me (and yourself) that you will be 1) diligent, and 2) organized.

Here is the manual backup protocol (a word that was in the jargon of computer geeks for years before the writers of the TV show *24* decided to use it in every other sentence of their scripts) that I follow:

### Daily or anytime I worry

Daily, or anytime I worry that I've just completed something that would pain me to have to redo, I copy the specific files or folders I've been using.

I used to do this on a CD-R disc, which has about 700MB and, bought in bulk, costs as little as ten cents. Burning a CD requires about five minutes, and when it is done I used a felt-tip pen and marked the date and a description of its contents on the disc's front (label side). I stored my CDs in a plastic case on the bookshelf. If I was traveling with my laptop, I brought a box of blank CDs and made copies that I stored somewhere other than my laptop carrying case.

Nowadays, though, I back up using a flash memory key. These little sticks of memory are examples of the inverse pricing model of modern technology: They keep getting larger in capacity and cheaper in price. As this book goes to press, you can buy a 4GB memory key for about $25 and use it over and over again.

I plug a memory key into a USB port on my laptop as I work, and every few hours — or anytime I'm about to leave the room when I travel — I move a copy of all of today's work onto the key. Then I remove the little device and pop it in my pocket or in the hotel safe or amongst my dirty socks in my suitcase.

### Once a week or anytime I'm leaving on an extended trip

Once a week, or anytime I'm about to go on an extended trip, I make an *incremental backup* of all files that have changed in the past week. If I'm working from my office, I make a *double backup:* one set of files is copied to an external hard disk drive and another set is burned to a DVD disc. The external hard disk protects against a failure within my laptop; the DVD goes into a storage container or a safe in my office and stays behind when I travel.

Book III
Chapter 4

Honk, Honk!
Windows Backup
and Restore Utilities

Today's basic recordable DVDs have a capacity of about 4.7GB and don't cost much more than CD-Rs. Dual-layer drives offer as much as 9.4GB. And on the horizon: Blu-ray discs with 25GB single-layer and 50GB dual-layer media.

Most modern laptops come with DVD recorders, although some machines may be one step (or a few dollars) behind the time and offer a CD recorder and a DVD player. You can burn a CD in a DVD recorder but can't create a DVD in a CD recorder.

### Once a month or anytime I finish a major project

Once a month, or any time I finish a major project — like the gigantic book you're holding in your hands — I make a full backup of my laptop's hard disk drive. I already have DVDs with the most recent data, but for this project I make a *mirror* copy on an external hard disk drive.

# Using an Automated Windows XP Backup Program

Instead of doing it yourself, you can use the computer to take care of its own backup processes. It seems only fair, don't you think?

Windows XP and Windows Vista include their own utilities that let you command your laptop to copy all its files, entire folders of files, or individual files. You can put the copies on an external hard disk drive or on any other form of removable media, including flash memory keys, DVDs, and CDs. You can also purchase products (from third-party utility makers) that you may find to be easier to use, more automated, or faster than Microsoft's tool.

Windows XP comes equipped with a basic backup program. It's preinstalled as part of Windows XP Professional; if you have Windows XP Home Edition, you can add it to your system with a few extra steps.

### Adding Microsoft's backup to Windows XP Home Edition

For reasons best understood by the marketing people at Microsoft, Windows XP Home Edition comes with Backup on the installation disc but not on pre-configured systems. You can easily remedy that, though.

Some laptop manufacturers have chosen to save a few pennies (or charge a few dollars more) by not including a physical copy of the Windows installation disc with their machines. Instead, they add a compressed copy of the installation code in a hidden partition on your hard disk drive, allowing you to reinstall the operating system from there if necessary. I think that's a terrible idea; what do you do if the hard disk drive fails? I insist on receiving an actual copy of the Windows installation disk with any computer I buy, although sometimes I have to pay a few bucks for something that's already mine.

Insert the Windows XP CD in the optical drive of your laptop. It should auto-start; if it doesn't, follow these steps:

1. **Open My Computer and double-click the CD icon.**

2. **On the Welcome to Microsoft Windows XP screen, click Perform Additional Tasks.**

   See Figure 4-1.

3. **Click Browse This CD.**

   Windows Explorer opens.

4. **Double-click the ValueAdd folder.**

5. **Double-click Msft.**

6. **Double-click Ntbackup.**

7. **Double-click the icon for Backup.**

   The file is called Ntbackup.msi.

8. **Click Accept Instructions to install the program.**

9. **Remove the Windows XP installation disc when the utility is in place.**

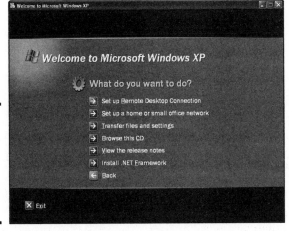

**Figure 4-1:**
Adding
some early,
hidden,
extra
Windows
XP features.

## Running Windows Backup

Once you install the program in either the Home or Professional version of Windows XP, using it is the same. In its standard configuration, the program offers a wizard that offers a streamlined pathway to the most commonly used options for backup.

To open and run the backup program, follow along:

*1.* **Click the Start button.**

*2.* **Click All Programs ⇨ Accessories ⇨ System Tools ⇨ Backup.**

The wizard asks the appropriate question: What do you want to back up? (See Figure 4-2.) You can back up all the contents of your My Documents folder plus favorites and cookies, all information on the computer, or be selective and choose particular files or folders.

This is one reason to use the recommended file folders, including My Documents or Documents; if you use a folder of your own, it may not be automatically backed up or you may have to take a few extra steps to add it to the list of folders for archiving. A distinction exists between working on your documents and settings only, or on those that belong to every user of the computer. (Most laptops are set up with only one user.)

The option to back up all information also creates a system recovery disk that can restore Windows to the condition *as it existed on the day you made the backup* in the event of a catastrophic failure.

The backup process under Windows XP includes an Advanced feature that allows you to set an incremental or differential backup instead of making copies of every file it finds in the specified folders. An *incremental backup* adds only those files you've created since the last time you ran the backup utility; a *differential backup* backs up only the changes to files and folders and settings since the last backup.

The doorway to the Advanced screen is on the last window before the backup process begins; see Figure 4-3. You can back up only files to disks that are current formats, including NTFS, FAT, or UDF.

You must back up files somewhere other than the disk where the files currently are; that makes sense, since the idea is to have a copy to use in the event of the original media's failure or corruption. Under Windows XP, you also can't make backups to a flash memory key or to a tape drive.

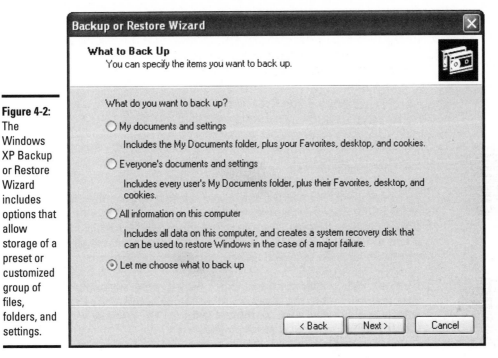

**Figure 4-2:**
The Windows XP Backup or Restore Wizard includes options that allow storage of a preset or customized group of files, folders, and settings.

Once you begin a backup, you can return to other tasks on the computer; the backup goes on in the background. You may notice that your system runs a bit slower than usual, and certain tasks involving opening folders or moving files may take considerably longer (in relative terms) than usual. Any files that you might change or create while the process is under way aren't backed up until the next time you run the utility.

If you make your backups to a recordable CD or DVD, be available to insert and remove discs as needed. You should also have a felt-tip marker to label each disc as it's created; add a numerical or alphabetic sequence so that you know the order of the discs should you ever need to restore data from them.

If you lose one CD or DVD in a sequence of backup discs, you can restore your data — except for the files or folders that were recorded to the missing disc.

Certain technical restrictions also prevent storing backups on a network device in a computer running Windows XP Home Edition. You can, however, save from that machine to a directly attached storage device.

The Backup utility moves most common data and settings file types. The following types of files can't be backed up:

✦ System files (elements of the Windows operating system)

✦ Program files (applications added to the operating system)

✦ Files currently in the Recycle Bin

✦ Temporary files

✦ Files that have been encrypted using Encrypting File System (EFS)

✦ User profile settings

Up to this point, I've written only about backing up your files. The other half of the utility, of course, is restore. To initiate data file restoration, choose the obvious option: Restore. You can return files to their original location or select a new spot; if you're restoring files to a new hard disk drive, you can adjust the location to match its new organizational structure.

Windows Vista comes equipped with a backup program similar in appearance and function to the Windows XP utility, although Vista's runs a bit more quickly and includes a few additional features. The opening screen for Vista's backup program is shown in Figure 4-4.

**Figure 4-3:**
On my fast system it took about two hours to move 100GB of data from an internal hard drive to an external unit.

Backup or Restore Wizard

Completing the Backup or Restore Wizard

You have created the following backup settings:

Name: L:\Backup 120807.bkf

Description: Set created 12/8/2007 at 11:27 AM

Contents: Selected files and folders

Location: File

To close this wizard and start the backup, click Finish.

To specify additional backup options, click Advanced.

Advanced...

< Back     Finish     Cancel

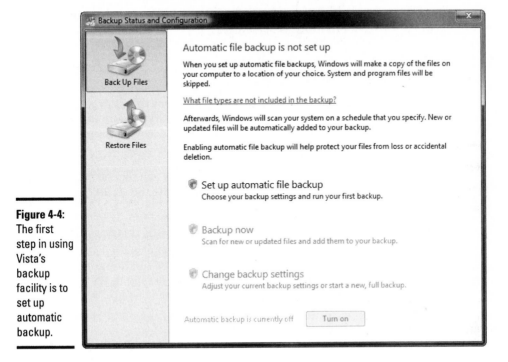

**Book III
Chapter 4**

**Honk, Honk!
Windows Backup
and Restore Utilities**

**Figure 4-4:**
The first
step in using
Vista's
backup
facility is to
set up
automatic
backup.

# Curing Some Evils with System Restore

By now every computer user knows very well that computers aren't infallible. (That doesn't mean that they possess an antigravity force field and are protected against falling off a table; it means that even the most carefully guarded and well-maintained machine occasionally loses its mind or at least stops performing as well as it did yesterday.)

In addition to file and folder backup and restore, Windows offers another backup: System Restore focuses solely on settings and configurations. It doesn't record word-processing, e-mail, or any other data file you create; that's the Backup utility's job.

One of the major causes of meltdowns large and small? Corruption of stored settings, Windows system files, or unintended changes to those same essential elements. How can this happen?

 ✦ **An electrical fault.** If your laptop runs out of power while saving a file or installing a program, or if it somehow receives a power surge or static shock, this can be the result.

 ✦ **A virus or other form of unwanted nasty code.**

✦ **A poorly designed installation program.** Said installation program is one that doesn't follow all of Microsoft's recommendations or does not play well with other applications.

✦ **An incomplete installation.** A power failure or an operating system freeze are two interrupting culprits.

✦ **A rare combination of incompatible software or hardware.** Although software makers spend a great deal of time (some more than others) testing their products, they can't anticipate every possible permutation of code and device.

Never install a program on your laptop when it's running off batteries. If the power runs out before the installation is complete, the result could be damage to the system files.

System Restore won't run on disks smaller than 1GB, which shouldn't be much of a problem for laptop owners; by today's measure that capacity is tiny. In any machine, you need a minimum of 300MB of free space on each hard disk that has System Protection turned on. Similar to the Recycle Bin, as the amount of space dedicated to restore points fills up, the computer deletes older information to make room for new.

## Using System Restore

One solution to a sudden, serious problem with your Windows operating system is go back in time, to a point when it last worked properly. No, this doesn't require use of Doc Brown's plutonium-powered flux capacitor from "Back to the Future." It does, though, require a Windows utility called System Restore . . . and a bit of luck.

System Restore works by taking electronic snapshots (called *restore points*) of your system files and settings at regular intervals and any time you manually instruct it to do so. If you've lived a clean life, helped little old ladies cross the street, and haven't done anything else to bollix up your system, it may allow you to undo damage. A portion of the Windows Vista System Restore screen is shown in Figure 4-5.

The utility records the status system files, programs that have been installed to run under Windows, and the settings in the Windows registry. In certain circumstances it can record changes made to scripts, batch files, and other types of executable files.

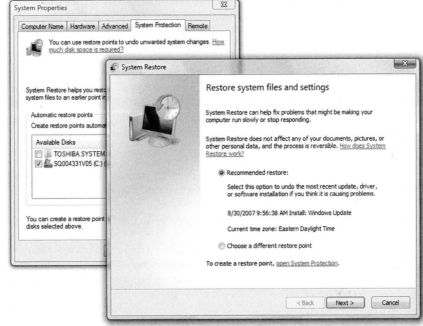

**Figure 4-5:**
When you restore files and settings, you can try the most recently recorded restore point or go onto the utility's calendar to select a specific day.

When it comes to personal files including e-mails, documents, photos, and music, I've both good news and bad. The good news: If they're still on the disk, using System Restore won't touch them. The bad news: If they've been erased or corrupted, you have to try to repair them or unerase them using other methods. (Of course, if you're really a careful user, you've backed up copies of your files on a different drive or on an external medium like a CD or DVD.)

A restore point records only your system files and settings. Choosing a restore point has no effect on any data files you created before or after the snapshot, but software or hardware installed since the restore point won't likely be immediately available to you. Hold off reinstalling anything until you're sure Windows is performing properly.

## Knowing System Restore best practices

You have absolutely no reason *not* to set up your machine to use System Restore. The only minor issue you must decide is how much space to devote to restore points; once you reach the size limit, Windows automatically deletes the oldest restore point to make room for the newest.

When you enable System Restore, it automatically creates a restore point every day, just as a snapshot of your up-and-running machine. It also creates a restore point any time you add a new device driver, receive an automatic update from Microsoft, or install certain new applications.

In my office, I make it a point to manually record a restore point any time I am about to significantly change settings or install a new program. Sometimes this results in a duplicate restore point — my manual point plus the one automatically created in certain circumstances; as far as I'm concerned the duplication is no big deal. I'd rather have a pair of rescue rafts than none.

System Restore works only with NFTS-formatted disks, which is the current drive standard. It doesn't protect drives with FAT32 and earlier FAT file systems.

## When good intentions go bad

This section's main title indicates that System Restore can cure "some" evils. Alas, the utility isn't perfect. System Restore doesn't copy every single system file, and sometimes the one that goes bad isn't included. You can restore all you want and not fix the problem.

Another situation that can arise: Something goes wrong with one or more of your system files while the machine is running, and you keep using it for a while before realizing you need to go back in time. In certain circumstances, your system may endure some additional changes (or even corruption) after the most recent restore point.

How to defend? Backup, backup, and backup. Don't rely on your machine to always be there for you; make copies of essential data files on a regular basis and store them on external drives or disks.

## Restoring your system settings

Follow these steps to use System Restore:

*1.* **Save any open files and close all programs.**

*2.* **Make sure you have current backups of essential data files.**

*3.* **Click the Windows icon.**

*4.* **Choose All Programs ➪ System Tools ➪ System Restore.**

Alternately, you can go to Control Panel, click the System icon, and then choose the System Restore tab.

The utility asks if you want to create a restore point (to set one manually) or if you want to choose a previously recorded snapshot.

5. **Choose one of the following:**

- Create a Restore Point

- Restore My Computer to an Earlier Time

If you want to do a restore, you're shown a calendar; days with one or more restore points are in bold. The Windows Vista version automatically displays data from the past five days; you can click the check box to show restoration points older than that. See Figure 4-6.

6. **Select a restore point just before the day and time you began experiencing problems with your Windows installation.**

7. **Highlight the checkpoint you want to use and click Next.**

The computer chugs along for a few moments preparing the information it needs, and then the system reboots. You've nothing to do but wait. If the restoration is successful, a screen appeared when Windows loads; if the restoration fails, your system restarts in the same condition it was before you attempted a fix. You can try again by selecting a different restore point.

**Book III
Chapter 4**

**Honk, Honk!
Windows Backup
and Restore Utilities**

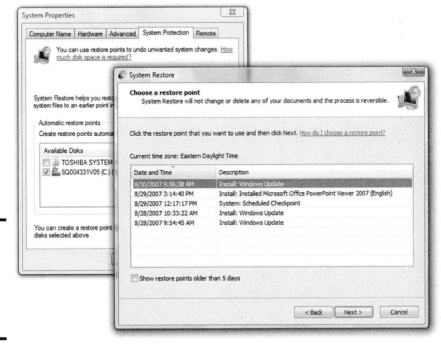

**Figure 4-6:**
A manual selection offers recent restore points.

Try to choose the most recent restoration point when you knew the machine was working properly. Going further back than necessary could result in disabling updates and changes that you'd rather have available.

In normal operations, any time you choose a restore point, System Restore automatically makes a snapshot of the day's files so you can undo any problems you might introduce reaching further back on the calendar. However, if you use System Restore when the computer has been booted in Safe Mode, you can't directly undo the restore. Instead, you have to run System Restore again and choose a specific previous restore point.

# Book IV

# Using Common Applications

The Slide Sorter window in PowerPoint lets
you see dozens of slides in a presentation.

# Contents at a Glance

# Chapter 1: Writing Documents

## In This Chapter

✔ Going from typewriter to typesetter

✔ Formatting, styles, themes, and other flashy stuff

✔ Finding, replacing, and changing text and styles

✔ Discovering new Microsoft Office file formats

*I*'m going to skip right over Neanderthal cave drawings, ancient Egyptian papyrus scrolls, the handwritten Magna Carta of 1215, and the Declaration of Independence of 1776. And I'm not going to discuss the first mechanical typewriters of the 19th century.

All these prior technologies were just variations of a brush and ink or chisel on stone. If you made a mistake you had to go back and redo your work; if you wanted to move a sentence from one place to another you had to cut and paste (with a scissors and glue) or start over from "When in the course of human events . . . "

It was only 40 years or so ago that engineers and programmers began working with the concept of applying computer memory and processing power to the job of creating, correcting, revising, and perfecting an assemblage of characters strung together into groups that had individual and collective meaning: words, sentences, paragraphs, and entire manuscripts.

## Processing Words No Matter the Program

In this book I primarily use examples of office productivity tools from the Microsoft Office suite: Microsoft Word, Microsoft Excel, and Microsoft PowerPoint. I have chosen these because they're the most commonly used applications.

You may have a different set of tools on your machine because you found some special features that suit your needs better, or you prefer a different piece of software because you like the way it's organized. And some users make decisions based on cost; you can find shareware office applications and even free tools offered by major companies like Google.

---

# Get on my cloud

A developing trend in applications — one that may or may not become the way everyone works in coming years — is the use of Web-based applications, also known as *cloud computing*. In this design, the software exists mostly somewhere out there on the Internet while your documents reside on your laptop or sit on a server maintained by the company that offers the software.

---

However, the basic concepts of word processing are the same for all of the various tools. You type, the computer puts the words up on the screen, and together you and the machine make them into pearls of wisdom, beautifully typeset, and safely stored away for the ages.

The most important thing to look for in any word processor is its ability to exchange documents with other applications. You can do your writing and processing in Microsoft Word and send it to someone who works with Corel WordPerfect or Google Docs (one of the cloud computing products that exist on the Web; see this section's sidebar). I'd never recommend using a word processor that can't read files created by any major competitor and can't save a version of its own files in a format that the others can use.

In this chapter I concentrate on some of the less obvious or more useful features that sometimes even the most experienced users overlook.

# Knowing What Elements to Expect

The days of the manual typewriter offered a limited number of choices when it came to the design and appearance of a typed page. You could mechanically adjust the amount of white space on the left and right sides of the page by setting margins, and you could start each page a particular distance down from the top and end at certain height above the bottom.

Everything else — underlines, footnotes, page numbers, chapter and section headings, and the like — were all done by hand and eye. High-school and professional school classes devoted entire semesters to mastering the art of manual formatting. Today, you merely have to choose from an ever-growing menu of options. You can make your documents simple or complex; your choices ensure consistent and neat presentation. Figure 1-1 is a sample page from Microsoft Office Word 2007.

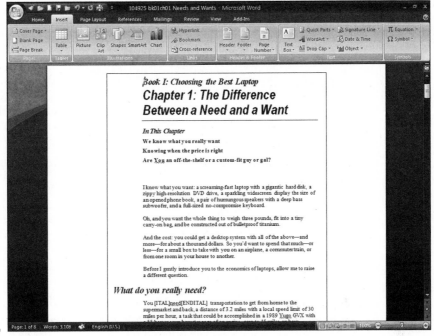

**Figure 1-1:**
A chapter in progress under Word 2007. This new edition added a changing ribbon of options that adjusts to the work being performed.

The elements of a complex document typically include

✦ One or more fonts

✦ Headers and footers (labels that appear at the top or bottom of each page)

✦ Page numbering

✦ Footnotes

✦ Citations

✦ Mathematical equations

✦ Index

✦ A table of contents

✦ A bibliography

To ensure consistency across a project or for all work done in a particular department or an entire organization, you — or a supervisor — can create a document template to apply to any or all files of a particular type.

**Book IV
Chapter 4**

**Writing Documents**

# My back pages

In my first job as a newspaper reporter, I began with a manual typewriter and was thrilled when I was upgraded to an electric version. My typewriter, that is. But here was how my words made it from my hand-scrawled notebook to the front page of the *Gazette:* I pecked away to write sentences on a piece of paper. If I made a mistake, I backspaced and Xed it out — or just reached into the machine with a thick, soft pencil and struck out a word or a sentence. If I wanted to move paragraph five to become paragraph two, I removed the sheet of paper and, with scissors and a role of clear tape, rearranged the paragraphs.

When the article was done, I yelled, "Copy!" and a young kid would dash from one of the corners of the newsroom to grab the sheaf of pages I was holding in my hand. He or she would move over to a shelf along the wall and tape the pages one to another so that they were in a continuous roll. After a copy editor had gone over the story — penciling in corrections and doing some additional cutting and pasting — the entire roll would be placed in a metal cylinder and sent through a whooshing pneumatic tube down two floors to the pressroom.

And there a typesetter (a human, not a machine) would mount my roll of words onto a stand and retype the characters and words into a machine that would set type. There was one last step: A proofreader (a person, drawing a paycheck) read the typeset text and compared it to the typewritten, hand-corrected, cut-and-pasted original.

### The first processed words

As the computer began to become relatively common in offices in the 1960s and 1970s, the first connection between "secretaries" and the machine were introduced. Xerox, IBM, and Wang were among the first companies to offer electric typewriters that had a way of storing words or sentences or even entire documents. The devices began with small blocks of memory in the machine that allowed for corrections, and then we moved onto larger storage devices including paper tape and eventually to magnetic disks.

But it really was not until the late 1970s before workstations connected to a central room-sized computer allowed the first text editors to replace backspacing, pencil marks, scissors, and tape at the keyboard. And then history — at least as it concerns the written word — was changed forever in 1981 when the first IBM PC was introduced.

### Swept aside by technology

The first word-processing software for personal computers (including Multimate, WordPerfect, and WordStar) swept aside almost any reason to hold on to rolls of paper, paste pots, and scissors. Also swept aside: copy boys and copy girls, pneumatic tubes that carry documents, typesetters to retype edited manuscripts, and proofreaders. And in most offices, personal secretaries and entire squadrons of workers in the "typing pool" were let go (which was bad) or given more meaningful and professional job assignments.

Look at this revolution in one other way: With the arrival of the personal computer and its laptop cousin, job descriptions have changed to include a multitude of other tasks. The person at the keyboard no longer merely writes a memo or a letter or a book called *Laptops All-In-One Desk Reference For Dummies.* You're also correcting your own mistakes, editing and revising the structure of your work, and saving a copy for future use. And in the process you're also designing a format, setting the type, and transmitting it to a printer or sending it across the world in a stream of 0s and 1s for reconstruction at the other end.

# Starting a Document

The arrival of Microsoft Office 2007 brought a large, round button in the upper-left corner of the editing screen; the Microsoft Office Button replaces the File menu of previous Office versions, and you can get to many places and do many things from that single button. See Figure 1-2.

Open a blank document and start typing:

*1.* **Click the blank page icon (part of the Office toolbar).**

If you want to get there another way, try one of these methods:

- Press Ctrl + N.
- Click the Microsoft Office Button, and then click New.

A menu appears.

*2.* **Double-click Blank Document.**

*3.* **Click the Microsoft Office Button.**

Choose from a set of options that opens:

✦ **New.** Opens an empty unformatted file.

✦ **Open.** Opens a previously saved file. Windows Explorer opens the folder Word most recently used to store a new or revised file; you can also navigate to any other folder or location on your laptop or on an attached network or Internet location.

✦ **Save.** Saves the currently active and open file in the same location it currently resides.

✦ **Save As.** Allows you to select a specific file format for the current file:

- **Word Document.** This new format is based on the Open XML specification. Files are stored with a .DOCX filename extension and generally require about half the space as previous Word file formats.

- **Word Template.** A special form of file that can apply settings to new or existing documents.

- **Word 97-2003 Document.** A way to save a file created in Microsoft Office 2007 in the older (and larger) file format used by the previous few generations of the program.

- **PDF or XPS.** Lets you save a file created in Word in the Adobe PDF (Portable Document Format) specification, whose files can be viewed or printed on other machines exactly the way you intend. XPS is a similar fixed-layout electronic file format promoted by Microsoft.

Clicking the Microsoft Office Button opens an expanded set of housekeeping functions as well as a list of recently used documents. You can *pin* any of the documents to keep it on the list for easy retrieval; it can be unpinned when you're through using it. (To pin a document . . . wait for it . . . you click the little push-pin icon alongside its name. To unpin, you click the push-pin again. It's an uncommonly logical bit of design.)

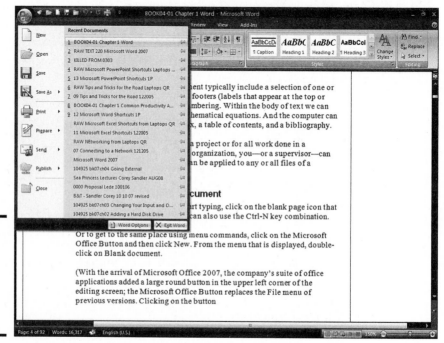

**Figure 1-2:**
An expanded set of house-keeping functions.

## Tapping into templates

A *template* predefines a document's dimensions, fonts, and text style. A template comes in handy when you're working on letterhead, flyers, and other, similar items.

### Creating a template

To create your own template, follow these steps:

*1.* **Start a new document or open an existing one.**

*2.* **Include its basic elements.**

*3.* **Choose File ⇨ Save As ⇨ Template.**

Don't choose one of the document choices.

**4. Decide where to store the template.**

You can put it anywhere you want on your system, but it helps to put it where you can easily find it. When you start a new file and want to base it on a template, browse to its location.

## Opening a new document using a template

Follow these steps to use a template as the basis for a new file:

**1. Click the Microsoft Office Button.**

**2. Click New.**

**3. Under Templates, click Installed Templates.**

**4. Click the template that you want to use.**

The listed templates are on your computer. A new, blank document opens.

You can download a prepared template for documents from Microsoft Office Online; your laptop must have an Internet connection to receive a download. You can go to the Microsoft web site and search for templates; one direct route is to use your Web browser to go to http://office.microsoft.com/en-us/templates/

## Saving a modified template

If you create (or download) and then change a template, you can save it on your laptop for future use. By default, customized templates are automatically saved in the My Templates folder.

As long as you open a template, make changes, and then re-save it as a template, all will be well. If you make the mistake of saving a template as a document, you have to reopen and re-save it as a template for that purpose.

**1. Click the Microsoft Office Button.**

**2. Click Save As.**

The Save As dialog box opens.

**3. Click Trusted Templates.**

The Save as Type list drops down.

**4. Select Word Template.**

**5. Enter a name for the template.**

**6. Click Save.**

# Formatting a Document

Because nearly all current word processors exist in the virtual world that is the memory of a graphical user interface like Windows, they come very close to defying the laws of physics. You can use fonts of nearly any size or design, run text in any direction, and add any color, emphasis, or special effect imaginable.

The only physical constraints placed on a document created in a word processor are those related to your hardware. For example, your printer has limits on the paper size it can handle and some fonts may be too small to be seen or too large to be printed. And you can specify a color that only a bumblebee can see, which is kind of besides the point of word processing for humans.

## Setting margins

Under most versions of Microsoft Word, you can set the margins for the entire document with these steps:

*1.* **Press Ctrl + A.**

This selects all text.

*2.* **Right-click and choose the Paragraph menu.**

*3.* **Enter left or right indentations in inches.**

Microsoft Office 2007 adds another route.

*1.* **Press Ctrl + A.**

This selects the entire document.

*2.* **Click the Page Layout tab.**

*3.* **In the Page Setup group, click Margins.**

You're offered a choice of predetermined margin settings:

- **Normal.**
- **Narrow.**
- **Wide.**
- **Windows 2003 default.**
- **Custom.** You can assign Custom as the new default. The Default setting becomes part of the template on which the current document is based; this permanently changes the template.
- **Office 2007.** Includes left, right, top, and bottom margins.

*4.* **Click your preferred setting.**

## What's your type?

Type sizes use an electronic version of an old printer's scale that uses *points* as a measurement. An inch has 72 points, and so a 36-point font uses characters about ½ tall. (If you think about it, though, you realize that a capital *A* is taller than a lowercase *a,* and letters including *j* and *y* descend below the baseline of other characters. And some fonts get really funky, following rules of their own for some or all of their characters.)

On a computer, point sizes are standardized to mean the full size of the available space for the character: from the top of the highest ascender

to the bottom of the lowest descender. Therefore, a 72-point capital *M* is about ¾ of an inch tall, and two lines of 36-point type without extra spacing between them occupy about the same ¾ inch space.

One other point: In printing terms, a *font* means a particular design for a set of characters, set at a particular size. For example, in an old print shop you'd say that this book is set in a font of 9.5 point Times New Roman. They needed to use that sort of terminology because each font (style and size) was kept in a separate drawer somewhere.

## Choosing point sizes

In electronic typesetting — which is, after all, what you're doing when you use a word processor on a GUI — the term *font* refers only to the type style, such as Times New Roman. The operating system and its hardware determine the type size. Without modification, the standard range of allowable type sizes under Microsoft Word is from 1 point to 1638 points, or about ½₂ of an inch to about 22 inches high.

The size you see on your laptop's screen is related to the LCD's resolution as well as to the zoom setting you chose in the word processor. Only when you print something is a *true* size used, and even then this applies only if you don't shrink or enlarge the printed document. Your printer has its own point size limits.

Set the point size for a block of type (or the entire document) with these steps:

*1.* **Select characters.**

Press Ctrl + A to choose all of the text.

*2.* **Type a value in the Type Size box displayed on the menu bar.**

Choose any value from 1 to 1638, and make adjustments in tenths of a point. For example, you can set type at 9.5 or 9.6, but not 9.55.

Book IV
Chapter 4

Writing Documents

Follow these steps if you're using Microsoft Word 2007:

*1.* **Select any block of type and bring your mouse pointer to it.**

A mini-toolbar appears.

*2.* **Choose one of the following steps:**

- Directly enter a point size in the window.

- Click the icons for Grow Font or Shrink Font. (The icons show a letter *A* with an upward-facing or downward-facing arrow.)

In Word 2007 and previous versions, you can choose a font with the following steps:

*1.* **Highlight a block of text.**

*2.* **Right-click to display the menu.**

*3.* **Click to select Font.**

*4.* **Choose from the window displayed in Figure 1-3.**

**Figure 1-3:**
The full font window includes typefaces, styles, size, colors, and effects. The preview window shows how changes will appear.

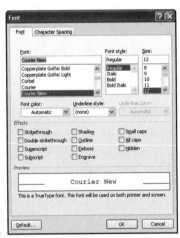

## Assigning line spacing

A *line* on a manual typewriter was a fixed amount of space, related to the unchangeable size and style of the characters it pounded onto a sheet of paper. But a word processor running under a GUI like Windows can choose from an infinite supply of fonts of varying design and then assign a size to the characters ranging from small to huge.

Therefore, when you choose line spacing in a word processor, it assigns a value related to the font and type size you chose:

**1.** **Select the line to which you want to set a particular line spacing.**

Press Ctrl + A to choose all of the text.

**2.** **Right-click and select the Paragraph menu.**

The Paragraph dialog box is shown in Figure 1-4.

**3.** **In the Line Spacing box, make your choice.**

**Figure 1-4:** The Paragraph dialog box includes options for alignment of text, indentation, spacing between paragraphs, and line spacing.

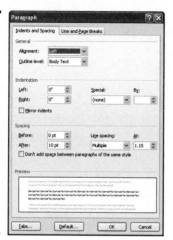

Users of Microsoft Word 2007 have an additional route:

**1.** **On the Home tab, locate the Paragraph group.**

**2.** **Click Line Spacing.**

You can enter a number such as 1.0 for single-spacing, 1.5 for line-and-a-half, or 2.0 for double-spacing.

For a more precise measurement, click Line Spacing Options to display the Paragraph window. Here you can select the particular design you want to use.

These options are available from the Paragraph window:

- **Single**. The computer finds the largest character in a particular line and uses that as the basis for calculating a minimum amount of space to place between lines of type. The amount of space varies depending on the fonts, but usually is just a few points; for example, a 12-point typeface may occupy about 14 points of space.

- **1.5 lines.** The computer performs the same calculations it would for single-line spacing, and then applies 1½ times the amount of space.

- **Double.** The computer allocates twice as much space between lines as it would for single-line spacing.

- **At least.** A more sophisticated setting, this allows the computer to determine the minimum amount of line spacing needed to fit the largest font or graphic on the line.

- **Exactly.** If you have a specific design in mind, choosing this option sets a fixed line spacing that Word won't adjust. For example, the book you're reading is set in 9.5-point text with exactly 11 points of line spacing.

- **Multiple.** This option, added under Microsoft Word 2007, sets the line spacing as a percentage of single line spacing. Entering 1.25 increases the spacing by 25 percent.

## Inserting a symbol

There is no need to be limited by the 52 letters (upper- and lowercase versions) and 40 or so numbers and symbols that appear on a typical laptop keyboard.

A wide range of special symbols are part of the various fonts installed on your machine, as well as half a dozen or so special-purpose fonts that consist entirely of icons, symbols, and special characters. You can find a yen, a pound, or a euro, as well as smiley faces and computer-specific symbols.

*1.* **Click in the text where you want to insert a symbol.**

*2.* **In Word 2007, click the Insert tab and locate the Symbols group.**

*3.* **Click Symbol.**

In previous versions of Word, click the Insert menu and then click Symbol.

A drop-down list appears.

*4.* **Click the symbol you want to insert.**

If the symbol you want isn't in the Symbol drop-down list, click More Symbols. In the Font box, choose a different font and locate the symbol you want to use; highlight it and then click Insert.

Some of the more commonly used fonts in Windows, including Times New Roman and Arial, are considered expanded fonts and include extended characters, including accent marks and special characters for foreign languages. You should also explore the Wingdings and Webdings fonts for unusual symbols.

## Inserting a special character

The difference between a symbol and a special character is a matter of familiarity. To begin with, "special" means characters that aren't on the keyboard. If you're old enough to have used a typewriter, you'll recall that many of them could print a cent sign, like this: ¢.

You can also insert a symbol by clicking the Insert Symbol menu item of Microsoft Office.

*1.* **Click in the text where you want to insert a special character.**

*2.* **In Word 2007, click the Insert tab and locate the Symbols group.**

*3.* **Click Symbol ➪ More Symbols ➪ Special Characters tab.**

   In previous versions of Word, click the Insert menu ➪ Symbol ➪ Special Characters tab.

   A drop-down list appears.

*4.* **Click the character you want to insert.**

## Selecting text in the body of a document

One of a word processor's key tools is the ability to select text or items anywhere in the document. From there you can move, delete, copy, or change their appearance.

You can select specific blocks of text dozens of ways. Table 1-1 shows you the power tools you should know.

| Table 1-1 | Selecting Text |
|---|---|
| *Function* | *Method* |
| Selecting all text | Press Ctrl + A. Under Microsoft Word 2007, you can also click the Home tab and find the Editing group. Click Select ➪ Select All. |
| Selecting a special block of text | Click at the beginning or end of a block of text and hold down the mouse button as you drag the pointer over the text you want to select. |
| Selecting a word | Double-click anywhere within a word. |
| Selecting a sentence | Hold down the Ctrl key and click anywhere in a sentence. |
| Selecting a paragraph | Triple-click anywhere in a paragraph. |

*(continued)*

**Table 1-1** *(continued)*

| Function | Method |
| --- | --- |
| Selecting a large block of text | Click at the start of a block of text. Release the mouse button and scroll to the end of the selection; hold down the Shift key and click the mouse. |
| Selecting a vertical block of text | To choose a block of text that is vertical, without extending to the end of a line, click at one corner of the text and hold down the Alt key while you drag the pointer down. |

## Moving sentences, paragraphs, or graphics

Here's where "cut and paste" loses the scissors, paste pot, or roll of tape. Because characters or pictures on a GUI screen are considered objects by the operating system, you can pick them up and move or otherwise manipulate them with a pointing device.

Follow these steps to move an item:

*1.* **Highlight an item you want to move.**

*2.* **Press Ctrl + X.**

This cuts the object and places it into computer memory.

*3.* **Move the pointer where you want the object.**

*4.* **Press Ctrl + V.**

To copy and paste an item you've selected, follow these steps:

*1.* **Press Ctrl + C.**

This places a copy of the object into computer memory.

*2.* **Move the pointer to the location where you want the object.**

*3.* **Press Ctrl + V.**

The item is pasted where your cursor is.

You don't have to paste an item into the same document. Once you either cut or copy an object, you can switch to another document and move the pointer to a location to paste the object there.

You can also move or copy objects by dragging them:

*1.* **Highlight an item you want to move or copy.**

**2. Keep the left mouse button pressed and drag the highlighted text to where you want it.**

**3. Release the mouse button.**

## Undoing mistakes

If you delete a block of text, change a font, move some copy from one place to another, or perform just about any other action within Microsoft Word, you can change your mind and undo the action. In Microsoft Word 2007, you can undo and redo as many as 100 previous actions.

You can't undo some actions, such as clicking any Microsoft Office Button command (including saving a file).

The most direct way to undo an action is to press Ctrl + Z. In Word 2007, you can also click the Undo icon in the Quick Access Toolbar at the top of the screen. If you change your mind again and want to Redo an action, press Ctrl + Y. In Word 2007, you can also click the Redo icon in the Quick Access Toolbar at the top of the screen.

## Applying styles and themes

Microsoft Word includes a collection of predefined styles for elements of your document: various levels of chapter and section headings and captions, as well as emphasis or color for particular types of content.

**1. Select a block of text.**

Under Microsoft Word 2007, the available set of styles is automatically offered any time you choose a block of text. A mini toolbar appears near the selected text.

**2. Click the Styles icon.**

This icon is a capital letter A with a small artist's pen.

**3. Pick the design you want to use from the Quick Styles.**

An example is shown in Figure 1-5. Before you click a style, you can preview its effect on your text by merely hovering your pointer over one of the offerings.

The Styles list shows only those styles that you already used in the document. If you don't see a particular style listed in the Quick Styles gallery, click Apply Styles or press Ctrl + Shift + S to open the Apply Styles task pane. Then type the style that you want to apply.

**Figure 1-5:**
A set of
Quick Styles
is a shortcut
added to
Microsoft
Word 2007.

## Applying a theme

Themes offer a way to refine or customize the particular Quick Styles set
for a document. You can change styles, fonts, type sizes, and colors. When
you apply a new font theme, the system changes the fonts for all headings
and the body of text for the current document.

### Working with a predefined style

To use a predefined style, apply it to the document you're working on.

1. **In Microsoft Word 2007, click the Home tab and locate the
   Styles group.**

2. **Click Change Styles.**

3. **Choose Fonts.**

4. **Choose the predefined font theme you want.**

### Creating a custom font theme

A custom font theme is created when you define its elements and store it on
your machine under a name or description.

1. **In Microsoft Word 2007, click the Page Layout tab and locate the
   Themes group.**

2. **Click Theme Fonts ⇨ Create New Theme Fonts.**

3. **Select the fonts and sizes you want to use in the Heading Font and
   Body Font lists.**

*4.* **In the Name box, type a name for the new font theme.**

*5.* **Click Save.**

## Creating formatted lists

You can set up Word to automatically create bulleted and numbered lists as you type, or you can add bullets or numbers to existing lines of text.

### Adding a bulleted or numbered list

You haven't reached this point in this book without escaping from the clutches of a bulleted or numbered list. Typographers use the term *bullets* to refer to round, square, or other-shaped symbols that present a list of information with emphasis. A special form is the numbered list, which as you no doubt guessed, means the list uses numbers instead of bullets; the numbered list is useful for presenting instructions in a particular sequence or to rank items by importance.

✦ At the start of a sentence, type an asterisk (*) to start a bulleted list.

✦ To start a numbered list, type **1** at the start of a sentence. Then press the spacebar or the Tab key. When you press the Enter key, the next line begins with 2.

✦ To finish a bullet or numbered list, press Enter twice, or press the Backspace key to delete the last bullet or number in the list.

### Adding bullets or numbers to an existing list

If you didn't add bullets or numbers to a list when first you wrote it, you can add them later:

*1.* **Select the items to which you want to add bullets or numbering.**

*2.* **Under Microsoft Word 2007, click the Home tab and locate the Paragraph group.**

*3.* **Click Bullets or Numbering.**

To see additional bullet styles or numbering formats, click the arrow next to Bullets or Numbering.

### Turning off automatic bullets or numbering

If bullets and numbering begin automatically and you'd rather they not, follow along:

*1.* **Click the Microsoft Office Button.**

*2.* **Click Word Options.**

**3.** **Click Proofing ⇨ Click AutoCorrect Options ⇨ AutoFormat As You Type tab.**

**4.** **Deselect the Automatic Bulleted Lists check box, deselect the Automatic Numbered Lists check box, or deselect both.**

The check boxes are under the Under Apply as You Type section.

In earlier versions of Word, click Tools ⇨ AutoCorrect Options. Make the same changes noted in this section.

## Running a tab

Back in the day of the manual typewriter, tab stops were physical barriers that stopped the carriage (the mechanism that held the paper and the rubber roller behind it) from left to right. These little clips let you set a paragraph indent and manually create columns in a table.

The system worked reasonably well, although users often had to change tab stops for any unusually shaped tables, and fancy formatting like hanging indents or adjustable-width cells were very difficult to accomplish. And advanced styles like decimal stops? Not for the faint of heart.

### Displaying and using the ruler to set stops and indents

The fastest way to set manual tab stops is to display the horizontal ruler across the top of a document and click with your pointer to insert markers on your virtual page.

At the top-left corner of the ruler is a box that shows the currently selected type of tab. Click in the box to cycle through the five available types. When you see the type you want to use, click in the ruler where you want it to be.

The markers for first line indent and hanging indents are already on the ruler. You can click and drag one or the other to where you want them.

This paragraph is set up as a *first line indent.* The second and subsequent lines are set against the left margin. Back in the day of the typewriter, this was the standard design for letters; more modern designs use no indent but add an extra line between paragraphs.

This paragraph is set up as a *hanging indent.* The second and subsequent lines are indented by a specified amount of space. It is a style employed by some designers for emphasis, or for all the text in a document.

You can set a bar tab stop before or after you type your paragraph.

You can bring up the horizontal ruler visible on your screen three ways:

✦ Bring the pointer up to the very top of the page of text, just below the menu ribbon or menu bar. The menu comes down after you hold the pointer there for a second or so.

✦ Click the View tab (in Microsoft Word 2007) or the View menu (in other versions of Word) and enable the Ruler check box. Deselect Ruler to remove the display later.

✦ In Microsoft Word 2007, you can click the View Ruler button that sits at the top of the vertical scroll bar on the right side of the screen.

### Choosing a tab stop or paragraph indent

Word offers five types of tabs, plus two types of paragraph indents, including features that would have made a typist's heart flutter. See Table 1-2 for the available tabs.

| Table 1-2 | | Available Tabs |
|---|---|---|
| *Symbol* | *Function* | *Purpose* |
| **L** | Left tab | Sets the starting position for text that will continue to the right. |
| **⊥** | Center tab | Sets the position for the middle of text. Text will center on this position, adjusting to the left or right as needed. |
| **⅃** | Right tab | Sets the starting position for text that will align to the left of the tab. |
| **⅃.** | Decimal tab | The decimal point will remain in the set position and numbers will align to its left for whole numbe (integers) and to its right for decimal fractions. |
| **❙** | Bar tab | Inserts a vertical bar at the tab position (and isn't the same as your running account at the local tavern). |
| **▽** | First line indent | Choose this indent and then click in the upper half of the horizontal ruler to set the starting position for the first line of each paragraph. |
| **⊔** | Hanging indent | Choose this indent and then click in the lower half of the horizontal ruler where you want all subsequent lines of a paragraph to start. |

An alternate way to place tab stops or indents is to enter the precise location you want in the Tabs dialog box. This box also allows you to insert a specific character as a leader between tab stops; a *tab leader* (often a series of periods) fills blank space between columns of text or numbers.

**Book IV
Chapter 4**

**Writing Documents**

A bar tab is similar to strikethrough formatting on a line of text, but it runs vertically through the selected paragraph or paragraphs at the bar-tab stop.

The easiest way to display the Tabs dialog box is to double-click any tab stop on the ruler. In Microsoft Word 2007, an alternate way to display the same Tabs dialog box is to click the Page Layout tab and then click the small arrow at the bottom right of the tab. In the Paragraph dialog box, click Tabs.

## Finding and replacing text

One of the true power tools of word processing is the ability to find a particular word or phrase and replace or reformat it. (Over the years this has also been called *search and replace.*)

The uses of find-and-replace are myriad. Want to change the name of a character in a novel? How about searching for every instance of the name of a product and changing it to a bold italic font? And how about updating every mention of a particular date?

Microsoft Office Word 2007 can find and replace text, formatting, paragraph breaks, page breaks, and other items. Advanced features allow searching for and changing noun or adjective forms or verb tenses.

### Finding and replacing text

Follow these steps to the most direct route to the Find and Replace dialog box:

*1.* **Press Ctrl + F.**

*2.* **On the Find tab, enter the text you're looking for.**

Microsoft Word 2007 has a menu route to the same place: Click the Home tab and click Find (on the Editing group).

*3.* **Choose depending on your preference:**

- To find each instance of a word or phrase one at a time, click Find Next.

- To find all instances of a specific word or phrase at one time, click Find All ⇨ Main Document.

If the Match Case check box is selected, Word searches only for an exact match; if you're looking for *Red Sox,* that's what you find. Any instance of *red sox* is ignored.

*4.* **Click the Replace tab and type the substitute text.**

Say you're changing every instance of the name *Chuck* with *Charles*. The replacement text uses the same capitalization as the text it replaces unless you select the Match Case check box.

### Finding and highlighting text

Another option available under Word 2007 is to find and highlight every occurrence of a particular word or phrase. This feature is an editing tool; the highlights are gone when you save or print the file.

Why highlight particular words? Any professional writer will tell you that every once in a while a particular word becomes much too easy to use in a document; this is especially a problem if you've started a manuscript on one day, added to it on several subsequent visits to the file, and then finished it weeks later. Want to see how many times you used "manuscript" in a manuscript? Find all instances and highlight them. The system will temporarily encase each instance in a block of color, and the Find and Replace screen will give you an accounting.

Do this to highlight a word or phrase in Word 2007:

**1.** **Click the Home tab and locate the Editing group.**

**2.** **Click Find.**

**3.** **In the Find What box, type the text you want to search for.**

**4.** **Click Reading Highlight ⇨ Highlight All.**

To turn off highlighting onscreen, click Reading Highlight ⇨ Clear Highlighting. Or, just ignore the highlighting; the next time you close the file it fades away to just a memory.

### Finding and changing specific character formatting

Say you began a file about the barely remembered story of the great ship "Titanic." After consideration, you decide that you'll follow a style that places every name of a ship in italics, like this: *Titanic*.

Using Find and Replace, you can search for every use of the name, and restyle it in italics. (Or, you could have made that particular text bold, or changed its color to red, or just about any other combination of emphases.) Going the other way, say you decided every time you boldfaced a word in a document, that you really should have used italics.

Using Find and Replace, you can search for a particular formatting assignment (in this case bold) and change it to italics. You're not looking for a *word* but rather a *typographic style*.

1. **In Word 2007, click the Home tab and locate the Editing group.**

2. **Click Replace and find the Format button.**

   You may have to click More to show additional options.

3. **To search for text with specific formatting, type the text in the Find What box.**

   Skip to Step 6.

   To find formatting no matter what the text, go to Step 4.

4. **Leave the Find What box blank.**

5. **Click Format, and then select the format you want to find and replace.**

6. **Click the Replace With box and click Format.**

7. **Select the replacement format or combination of formats.**

   If you also want to replace the text, type substitute text in the Replace With box.

Finally, you have the choice between a one-click automatic replacement of every instance of the specified formatting (Click Replace All) or stepping through each instance and deciding whether to apply the changes (click Find Next ⇨ Replace or Find Next to move on without making a change).

### Finding and replacing formatting codes

Although you usually can't tell when looking at the screen, your text is sprinkled with special codes that indicate formatting decisions. That's how the word processor knows you want a space between words, a tab at the beginning of a paragraph, a paragraph break at the end, among others.

One common habit that some former typewriter users lapse into is putting double spaces at the end of each sentence. That's easily fixed: Search for all instances of two spaces and replace them with one space.

You might also find that a file uses double paragraph breaks. This might have happened because the original version of the file was created using single spacing and it was later converted to double-spaced text. Again, an easy fix: Search for any pair of paragraph breaks and substitute just a single one.

1. **In Word 2007, click the Home tab and locate the Editing group.**

2. **Click Find.**

3. **Click the Special button.**

If the Find and Replace dialog box displays its smaller version, click More to expand your options.

**4. Click the item you want to search for.**

In Figure 1-6 you can see the available special characters.

**5. To replace the item, click the Replace tab.**

**6. Enter the substitute formatting code (or text) in the Replace With box.**

**7. Click one of the following:**

- Find Next
- Find All
- Replace
- Replace All

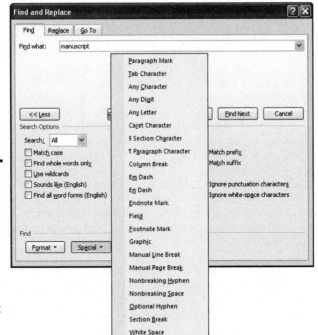

**Figure 1-6:** You can use these special characters as part of a find-and-replace assignment in Microsoft Word.

You also can use keyboard characters instead of selecting from the pull-down menu. For example, you can search for ^p to find a paragraph mark, or ^t for a tab character. Table 1-3 lists a few of the common formatting characters you can use in this way.

| Table 1-3 | Formatting Character Codes |
|---|---|
| *Character or Symbol* | *Formatting Code* |
| Paragraph mark* | ^p |
| Tab character | ^t *or* ^9 |
| Em dash (the longer dash) | ^+ |
| En dash (the shorter normal dash) | ^= |
| Caret | ^^ |
| Manual line break | ^l *or* ^11 |
| Manual page break | ^m |

*Doesn't work if Use Wildcards option is turned on.*

## Characters gone wild (card)

The most commonly used magic characters for wildcard searches are the asterisk (*) and the question mark (?).

✦ * tells the computer to search for any string of characters at the start, end, or in the middle of your query.

✦ ? tells the computer to find any word that has any single character at the location of the question mark in your query.

Say you want to find all versions of the word *dog* in a document. If you search for *dog\**, the computer comes back with all instances of these words: *dogs, doggy, doggies, doggone, dogged, dogfish, doggerel, dogleg* . . . you get the idea.

The one word that wouldn't be found? *Dog.* That's because the asterisk extends the search to forms that include the word *dog.* If you want to limit your search to the set of three-letter words that begin with *do,* you could ask the computer to search for *do?.* It would find *dog* as well as *dot, doc, doe, don, dos, dot,* and *dow.*

Searching with wildcards is very useful, but you must be as specific and limiting as possible. For example, if you throw an asterisk in the middle of a short word, you may find hundreds of responses that don't give you the results you want. For example, searching for *d\*d* comes up with words that meet that criteria but probably have nothing to do with what you're hoping to find: *dad, did, disappointed, departed,* and *doodad* among them.

It would really confuse the computer if you searched for a character that's defined as a wildcard (searching for question marks or asterisks, for example). The way to clear things up: type a backslash before the character. For example, type \? to find a question mark or \* to find an asterisk in your file.

First the basics on using wildcards in a search:

*1.* **In Word 2007, click the Home tab and locate the Editing group.**

*2.* **Click Find or Replace.**

*3.* **Select the Use Wildcards check box.**

If the Find and Replace window displays in its smaller version, click More to expand your options.

*4.* **Follow one of these steps:**

- Choose a wildcard character from a list. Click Special, click a wildcard character, and then type any text in the Find What box.

- Directly type a wildcard character in the Find What box.

*5.* **If you want to replace the item, click the Replace tab and enter the substitute text in the Replace With box.**

*6.* **Click Find Next, Find All, Replace, or Replace All.**

For most users, the asterisk and question mark suffice for quickly locating a particular word in a file. However, if you're searching through a gigantic encyclopedia, spending a few moments to create a more precisely focused query will pay off greatly.

Table 1-4 shows a more complete list of available wildcards for searching in Microsoft Word 2007.

| Table 1-4 | Advanced Wildcards | |
|---|---|---|
| *To Find This* | *Use This* | *For Example* |
| A single character | ? | do? finds dog, don, and dot |
| | | d?g finds dig, dog, and dug |
| A string of characters | * | d*g finds dog, dig, digging, and disappointing |
| The start of a word | < | <(enter) finds entertainment and entering, but not center or centered |
| The end of a word | > | (on)> finds on, upon, and spoon, but not once, onerous, or onomatopoeia |
| One or the other of a set of characters | [ ] | t[ai]n finds tan and tin but not ton |
| A single character in an ascending range | [-] | [l-r]ight finds light, might, night, and right |
| Any single character except for one that falls within the specified range | [!x-z] | shar[!a-l]ck finds shard, share, and shark but not sharp |

Believe it or not, some even more complex wildcard commands are in the word processor's help system. You can also use parentheses to group searches to narrow down the possibilities even more precisely.

## Advancing Your Microsoft Office 2007 Functions

As part of the Microsoft Office 2007 enhancements, several important new features extend across most of the programs in the suite, including Microsoft Word 2007, Microsoft Excel 2007, and Microsoft PowerPoint 2007. I describe them here because most users begin with a word processor, but keep them in mind for all your work if you're lucky enough to run the latest version of Office on your laptop.

✦ **Microsoft Office Diagnostics.** This utility includes diagnostic tests that may help determine why one or more components of Microsoft Office (or other programs running under Windows) are crashing your system or otherwise becoming annoying. For more details, see Book X.

✦ **Program Recovery.** The Office 2007 components are better able to prevent the loss of work when a program closes abnormally (Microsoft happy-talk for "crashes"). The latest version of Office is set up to attempt to recover as many elements of the program's state at the moment of a crash. As an example, if you had several files open when your laptop took an electronic dive, after a reboot Office tries to come back with those same files open.

The first thing you should do when you create any type of file is give it a name and store a copy of it; this allows your software program to store temporary backups of the file as you work on it and makes it much easier to recover from a crash.

✦ **Merging spelling checker.** Several of the spelling checker options for Microsoft Office programs have been made *global.* That means settings or options that you chose in one of the programs applies to all other software in the suite. Examples of this include assignment of a non-standard or foreign-language dictionary for use in all programs. You can also apply an exclusion dictionary across more than one program; *exclusion dictionaries* allow the spelling checker to find words you want to avoid using in your dictionary. Excluded words might be ones you feel are improper or are disallowed in your personal or institutional style guide. The spelling checker has been enhanced to find some (but not all) contextual spelling errors. If you type *Put this book their,* all of those words are spelled correctly but the word you want to use is *there,* not *their.* The latest version of contextual spell checking works with documents written in English, German, and Spanish.

# Formatting Files in Word 2007

Consider new ways the computer can structure the file that contains the document itself. Unfortunately, this is confusingly called a *file format*. Here, *format* refers to the file itself and not its contents.

## Open XML file formats

Microsoft Office 2007 presents a new set of file formats for storing work. In a few words: The new file formats are more compact. (Compared to previous formats, they require less space on a disk — with a potential reduction of as much as 75 percent — to hold the same amount of information.) They also offer some advanced features for power users.

The new file format is called Microsoft Office Open XML, and it was released along with Microsoft Office Word 2007, Microsoft Office Excel 2007, and Microsoft Office PowerPoint 2007. According to Microsoft, the advantages of XML include the following:

✦ **Compactness.** Files are automatically compressed or zipped, made as much as 75 percent smaller in some cases. This saves disk space for storage and reduces the amount of time required to send files by e-mail, over networks, or over the Internet. When you open a file, it automatically unzips; when you re-save a file, it automatically zips again.

✦ **Improved recovery from damage.** Files are structured in a modular design to keep different data components separate from each other in the file. In theory, this means that if one component — a graphic, chart, or table, for example — becomes corrupt, you can open and use the rest of the file.

✦ **Enhanced privacy.** Personal information and business-sensitive information, such as author names, comments, tracked changes, and file paths can be easily identified and removed with a utility called Document Inspector.

✦ **Improved security against macro viruses.** Files saved using the default *x* suffix (such as .docx for Word, .xlsx for Excel, and .pptx for PowerPoint) can't contain Visual Basic for Applications (VBA) macros and XLM macros. Only files whose filename extension ends with an *m* (such as .docm, .xlsm, and .pptm) can contain macros.

That's the good news, and if you're working by yourself or exchanging files with others who use the same new file formats, you've no good reason *not* to use the new technology. The not-quite-so-good news is that if you're sending your files to someone who's using yesterday's formats, you have to convert the files.

**Book IV
Chapter 4**

**Writing Documents**

### Converting Word 2007 files

It's no big deal to get and use the compatibility pack to change over newer files to make them useable on an older machine. Or you can save your files in the older file format before you send them to an old-school user. The only disadvantage is that some advanced features embedded in a file created in the Office 2007 versions of Microsoft programs may not be available to users of earlier software. Office 2007 includes a compatibility checker that examines files saved in an older file format to see if any features are unsupported; you are advised of any potential problems and allowed to remove the advanced features before continuing with a retro-save.

Microsoft offers the free Microsoft Office Compatibility Pack for Word, Excel, and PowerPoint 2007 File Formats. You can install this conversion tool on systems running older versions of Word; it allows them to open and use files saved with the .DOCX filename extension. Go to www.microsoft.com and search for Office Compatibility Pack.

By default, files created in components of Microsoft Office 2007 are saved in XML format with new filename extensions that add an $x$ or $m$ to the extensions. The $x$ signifies an XML file that has no macros, and the $m$ signifies an XML file that does contain macros.

The 2007 version of Office happily accepts documents created with any current version of Word, including Microsoft Office Word 2003, Word 2002, or Word 2000. The program automatically turns on something called Compatibility Mode; you'll see that indicated in the document window's title bar (at the top of the screen).

Compatibility Mode ensures that — until and unless you convert the old format file to a new XML file — no new or enhanced features in Office Word 2007 are available. This ensures that you don't introduce a feature that the original author (or others using older versions of Word) can't use.

## Controlling Microsoft Word from the Keyboard

It's not just that some people learned to use computers in the days before the coming of the mouse (although it's sometimes hard to teach an old cog new tricks). The fact is that the fastest way to accomplish a command is to keep your hands on the keyboard rather than lifting them off and moving a mouse, spinning a trackball, or piddling with a pointing stick.

All the keyboard commands in Tables 1-5 through 1-16 are things you can accomplish by going to one or more menus or windows within Microsoft Word or the Windows operating system. For many users, the best decision is to combine the two routes to success: Memorize a few of the most commonly used keyboard commands and use the mouse for the remainder.

| Table 1-5 | Major Commands Using Function Keys |
|---|---|
| *Function* | *Command* |
| Get Help or go to Microsoft Office online web site | F1 |
| Start context-sensitive Help or Reveal formatting | Shift + F1 |
| Move text or graphics | F2 |
| Copy text | Shift + F2 |
| Print Preview | Ctrl + F2 |
| Insert an AutoText entry after program displays suggestion | F3 |
| Create an AutoText entry | Alt + F3 |
| Change case of letters | Shift + F3 |
| Repeat previous action | F4 |
| Repeat Find or GoTo action | Shift + F4 |
| Display GoTo menu | F5 |
| Move to the last change | Shift + F5 |
| Go to the next pane or frame; Switch between Help pane and Word | F6 |
| Go to the previous pane or frame | Shift + F6 |
| Display Spelling command | F7 |
| Find the next misspelling or grammatical error; Check Spelling as You Type check box must be selected on the Spelling & Grammar tab | Alt + F7 |
| Display Thesaurus command | Shift + F7 |
| Extend a selection | F8 |
| Shrink a selection | Shift + F8 |
| Choose the Size command | Ctrl + F8 |
| Extend a selection or block; follow with arrow key | Ctrl + Shift + F8 |
| Update selected fields | F9 |
| Switch between a field code and its result | Shift + F9 |
| Insert an empty field | Ctrl + F9 |
| Unlink a field | Ctrl + Shift + F9 |
| Switch between all field codes and their results | Alt + F9 |
| Activate the menu bar; move through pull-down menus with Tab | F10 |
| Display a context-sensitive shortcut menu | Shift + F10 |
| Go to the next field | F11 |
| Go to the previous field | Shift + F11 |
| Lock a field | Ctrl + F11 |
| Unlock a field | Ctrl + Shift + F11 |

**Book IV
Chapter 4**

**Writing Documents**

*(continued)*

**Table 1-5** *(continued)*

| Function | Command |
| --- | --- |
| Display Save As command | F12 |
| Choose Save command | Shift + F12 |
| Choose the Open command | Ctrl + F12 |
| Choose the Print command | Ctrl + Shift + F12 |

Note that these shortcuts work with Microsoft Word 2003 and later versions; some earlier versions of the word processor won't support all the shortcuts.

| Table 1-6 | Additional Function Key Commands |
| --- | --- |
| **Function** | **Command** |
| Open command | Ctrl + Alt + F2 |
| Choose Save command | Alt + Shift + F2 |
| Quit Microsoft Word | Alt + F4 |
| Display Microsoft System Information | Ctrl + Alt + F1 |
| Cut to the Spike | Ctrl + F3 |
| Insert contents of the Spike | Ctrl + Shift + F3 |
| Close the window | Ctrl + F4 |
| Restore the document window size | Ctrl + F5 |
| Restore the program window size | Alt + F5 |
| Edit a bookmark | Ctrl + Shift + F5 |
| Go to the next window | Ctrl + F6 |
| Go to the previous window | Ctrl + Shift + F6 |
| Choose the Move command | Ctrl + F7 |
| Update linked information in a source document | Ctrl + Shift + F7 |
| Run a macro | Alt + F8 |
| Maximize the program window | Alt + F10 |
| Display Microsoft Visual Basic code | Alt + F11 |
| Maximize document window | Ctrl + F10 |

| Table 1-7 | Managing Documents and Web Pages |
| --- | --- |
| **Function** | **Command** |
| Create new document of the same type as the current or most recent document | Ctrl + N |
| Open a document | Ctrl + O |

| Function | Command |
| --- | --- |
| Close a document | Ctrl + W |
| Split the document window | Alt + Ctrl + S |
| Remove document window split | Alt + Shift + C |
| Save a document | Ctrl + S |
| Display Open dialog box | Ctrl + F12 |
| Display Save As dialog box | F12 |
| Display shortcut menu for a selected item such as a folder or file. Use Tab to move between options or areas in the dialog box | Shift + F10 |

**Table 1-8**             **Editing and Moving Text and Graphics**

| Function | Command |
| --- | --- |
| Delete one character to the left | Backspace |
| Delete one word to the left | Ctrl + Backspace |
| Delete one character to the right | Delete |
| Delete one word to the right | Ctrl + Delete |
| Cut selected text to the Office Clipboard | Ctrl + X |
| Undo the last action | Ctrl + Z |
| Cut to the Spike to collect a group of items for pasting in one place | Ctrl + F3 |

**Table 1-9**             **Moving the Insertion Point**

| Function | Command |
| --- | --- |
| One character to the left | ← |
| One character to the right | → |
| One word to the left | Ctrl + ← |
| One word to the right | Ctrl + → |
| One paragraph up | Ctrl + ↑ |
| One paragraph down | Ctrl + ↓ |
| One cell to the left (in a table) | Shift + Tab |
| One cell to the right (in a table) | Tab |
| Up one line | ↑ |
| Down one line | ↓ |
| To the end of a line | End |

(continued)

**Book IV
Chapter 4**

**Writing Documents**

**Table 1-9** *(continued)*

| Function | Command |
| --- | --- |
| To the beginning of a line | Home |
| To the top of the window | Alt + Ctrl + Page Up |
| To the end of the window | Alt + Ctrl + Page Down |
| Up one screen (scrolling) | Page Up |
| Down one screen (scrolling) | Page Down |
| To the top of the next page | Ctrl + Page Down |
| To the top of the previous page | Ctrl + Page Up |
| To the end of a document | Ctrl + End |
| To the beginning of a document | Ctrl + Home |
| To a previous revision | Shift + F5 |
| Jump to the location of the insertion point when the document was last closed | Shift + F5 |

**Table 1-10**         **Formatting Characters**

| Function | Command |
| --- | --- |
| Copy formatting from text | Ctrl + Shift + C |
| Apply copied formatting to text | Ctrl + Shift + V |
| Change the font | Ctrl + Shift + F |
| Change the font size | Ctrl + Shift + P |
| Increase the font size | Ctrl + Shift + > |
| Decrease the font size | Ctrl + Shift + < |
| Increase the font size by 1 point | Ctrl + ] |
| Decrease the font size by 1 point | Ctrl + [ |
| Change the formatting of characters (Font command, Format menu) | Ctrl + D |
| Change the case of characters | Shift + F3 |
| Format characters as all uppercase | Ctrl + Shift + A |
| Apply bold formatting | Ctrl + B |
| Apply an underline | Ctrl + U |
| Underline words but not spaces | Ctrl + Shift + W |
| Double-underline text | Ctrl + Shift + D |
| Apply hidden text formatting | Ctrl + Shift + H |
| Apply italic formatting | Ctrl + I |

| Function | Command |
|---|---|
| Format characters as small capitals | Ctrl + Shift + K |
| Apply subscript formatting (automatic spacing) | Ctrl + = |
| Apply superscript formatting (automatic spacing) | Ctrl + Shift + + |
| Change the selection to the Symbol font | Ctrl + Shift + Q |
| Display nonprinting characters | Ctrl + Shift + * |

| Table 1-11 | Formatting Paragraphs |
|---|---|
| **Function** | **Command** |
| Single-space lines | Ctrl + 1 |
| Double-space lines | Ctrl + 2 |
| Set 1.5-line spacing | Ctrl + 5 |
| Add or remove one line space preceding a paragraph | Ctrl + 0 |
| Center a paragraph | Ctrl + E |
| Justify a paragraph | Ctrl + J |
| Left align a paragraph | Ctrl + L |
| Right align a paragraph | Ctrl + R |
| Indent a paragraph from left | Ctrl + M |
| Remove a paragraph indent from left | Ctrl + Shift + M |
| Set a hanging indent | Ctrl + T |
| Reduce a hanging indent | Ctrl + Shift + T |
| Remove paragraph formatting | Ctrl + Q |

| Table 1-12 | Finding, Browsing, and Replacing Text |
|---|---|
| **Function** | **Command** |
| Find text, formatting, and special items | Ctrl + F |
| Repeat find (with Find and Replace window closed) | Alt + Ctrl + Y |
| Replace text, specific formatting, and special items | Ctrl + H |
| Go to a page, bookmark, footnote, table, comment, graphic, or other location | Ctrl + G |
| Switch between documents or sections of a document | Alt + Ctrl + Z |
| Open a list of browse options; use the arrow keys to select an option, and then press Enter to use the selected option | Alt + Ctrl + Home |

**Book IV
Chapter 4**

**Writing Documents**

| Table 1-13 | Performing Actions on Text or Objects |
|---|---|
| *Function* | *Command* |
| Copy the selected text or object | Ctrl + C |
| Cut the selected text or object | Ctrl + X |
| Paste text or an object | Ctrl + V |
| Undo the last action | Ctrl + Z |
| Redo the last action | Ctrl + Y |
| Cancel the last action | Esc |
| Make characters bold | Ctrl + B |
| Make characters italic | Ctrl + I |
| Make characters underlined | Ctrl + U |
| Decrease font size | Ctrl + Shift + < |
| Increase font size | Ctrl + Shift + > |
| Remove paragraph or character formatting | Ctrl + spacebar |
| Insert nonbreaking space | Ctrl + Shift + spacebar |
| Insert nonbreaking hyphen | Ctrl + - |

| Table 1-14 | Changing the View |
|---|---|
| *Function* | *Command* |
| Switch to print layout view | Alt + Ctrl + P |
| Switch to outline view | Alt + Ctrl + O |
| Switch to normal view | Alt + Ctrl + N |
| Switch to Reading View | Alt + R |
| Expand or collapse subdocuments in a master document | Ctrl + \ |

| Table 1-15 | Reviewing Documents |
|---|---|
| *Function* | *Command* |
| Turn Track Changes on or off | Ctrl + Shift + E |
| Insert a comment | Alt + Ctrl + M |
| Close the Reviewing Pane if it is open | Alt + Shift + C |

| Table 1-16 | Previewing and Printing Documents |
|---|---|
| *Function* | *Command* |
| Switch in or out of print preview | Alt + Ctrl + I |
| Move around the preview page when zoomed in | arrow keys |

| Function | Command |
|---|---|
| Move by one preview page when zoomed out | Page Up or Page Down |
| Move to the first preview page when zoomed out | Ctrl + Home |
| Move to the last preview page when zoomed out | Ctrl + End |
| Print a document | Ctrl + P |

## Finding key combos

You can find the key combinations by going back to that Symbol chart. (You can even get to it without using the mouse; try pressing the Alt key, then the I key, then the S key.)

You'll find two pages of information. One presents the full range of available characters for the current font; behind it is a tab for Special Characters. If you see the symbol you want on the special page, look for a simple shortcut key combination like Alt + Ctrl + R for ®. Otherwise, look for the symbol on the full listing; when you find it highlight it and then look the preassigned Shortcut key at the bottom of the table. For example, the keyboard shortcut for the ¼ symbol is Alt + 0188.

The trick here is to use the numeric keypad of your laptop to enter the character. Turn on Num Lock, hold down the Alt key, type the number combination using the numeric keypad, and then release Alt. Voila! You have earned a ¼.

Some characters are more complex to invoke than others. For example, some non-English characters require you to enter a number first and then (without an intervening space) type a key combination like Alt + X. For example, to get this interesting character, ę, I entered 0119 and followed it immediately with Alt + X.

Where's the Num Lock on a laptop? Well, you're going to have to find it for yourself, since the manufacturer could have placed it almost anywhere. On my newest machine, you turn on or off Num Lock by pressing the Fn key and then the F11 key. (An older machine uses F9.) Then use the numeric keypad which is embedded in the keyboard amongst the characters on the right side. (My new machine even has a shortcut to the shortcut; I don't have to turn on and off the Num Lock. All I have to do is press and hold Fn + Alt and then type the numbers on the numeric keypad.)

Tables 1-17 through 1-20 shows some of the more valuable special characters and their standard keyboard shortcuts (which assumes that you have not changed the shortcuts by assigning them to a macro, something else you can do to speed the process). I've ordered them by function.

# The symbolism of the keyboard

How the ♦♥♠P♣±| do you get Microsoft Word to use symbols and special characters that are not on the keyboard? Earlier in this chapter I discussed how to use the Insert Symbols menu items. There are several other ways to use the extended character set of standard fonts or any of the icons or symbols or nonstandard letters that are part of special fonts.

**Using the mouse to insert a ® symbol**

1. At the point where you want to add the symbol, take one of your hands off the keyboard and find the mouse.

2. Click the Insert menu.

3. Click the Symbols tab.

4. Click and hold the slider arrow on the Symbol chart and pull down slowly until you see the (r) symbol.

5. Release the slider arrow and click the ® symbol.

6. Your choice:

    • Double-click the highlighted symbol.

    • Move the mouse and click the Insert button.

7. Close the Symbol chart.

8. Return your hand to the proper position on the keyboard so you can continue typing.

**Using the keyboard to insert a ® symbol**

1. At the point where you want to add the symbol, press Ctrl + Alt + R.

So, now, tell me again how using a mouse is quicker and simpler than using the keyboard? The key, to pardon the pun, is to know the key combinations; they're not secret, but they are hidden.

| Table 1-17 | Monetary Symbols |
|---|---|
| *Symbol* | *Command* |
| € | Alt + 0128 |
| ¢ | Alt + 0162 |
| £ | Alt + 0163 |
| ¥ | Alt + 0165 |

| Table 1-18 | Punctuation and Typesetting Symbols | |
|---|---|---|
| *Symbol* | *Unicode (Hex)* | *ASCII (Decimal)* |
| ¡ | 00A1 followed by Alt + X<br>Alt + Ctrl + ! | Alt + 0161 |
| ¶ | 00B6 followed by Alt + X | Alt + 0182 |

| Symbol | Unicode (Hex) | ASCII (Decimal) |
|---|---|---|
| ¹ | 00B9 followed by Alt + | Alt + 0185 |
| ² | 00B2 followed by Alt + | Alt + 0178 |
| ³ | 00B3 followed by Alt + | Alt + 0179 |

| Table 1-19 | Business and Math Symbols | |
|---|---|---|
| Symbol | Unicode (Hex) | ASCII (Decimal) |
| © | 00A9 followed by Alt + X or Alt + Ctrl + C | Alt + 0169 |
| ® | 00AE followed by Alt + X or Alt + Ctrl + R | Alt + 0174 |
| ™ | 2122 followed by Alt + X or Alt + Ctrl + T | Alt + 0153 |
| ° | 02DA followed by Alt + X | Alt + 0176 |
| ± | 00B1 followed by Alt + X | Alt + 0177 |
| μ | 03BC followed by Alt + X | Alt + 0181 |
| ¼ | 00BC followed by Alt + X | Alt + 0188 |
| ½ | 00BD followed by Alt + X | Alt + 0189 |
| ¾ | 00BE followed by Alt + X | Alt + 0190 |

| Table 1-20 | Accented Characters | |
|---|---|---|
| Symbol | Unicode (Hex) | ASCII (Decimal) |
| À | 00E0 followed by Alt + X | Alt + 0224 |
| Á | 00E1 followed by Alt + X | Alt + 0225 |
| Ç | 00E7 followed by Alt + X | Alt + 0231 |
| È | 00E8 followed by Alt + X | Alt + 0232 |
| É | 00E9 followed by Alt + X | Alt + 0233 |
| Ê | 00EA followed by Alt + X | Alt + 0234 |
| Û | 00FB followed by Alt + X | Alt + 0251 |

## General keyboard shortcuts

Think retro. Almost everything a mouse can do, you can do from the keyboard, including manipulate text. Tables 1-21 through 1-23 show some of the most useful commands.

| Table 1-21 | Selecting, Copying, and Moving Text |
|---|---|
| *Function* | *Command* |
| Select all | Ctrl + A |
| Select range of text in a document. (Press and hold while using any arrow key) | Shift |
| Press and hold with any of the arrow keys to highlight a block of text | Ctrl + Shift |
| Copy selected text or image to the Clipboard | Ctrl + C |
| Cut selected text or image | Ctrl + X |
| Paste selected text or image | Ctrl + V |
| Undo the previous action. Some programs have multiple levels of Undo | Ctrl + Z |
| Delete selected text or image | Delete |
| Delete selected item permanently without placing the item in the Recycle Bin | Shift + Delete |
| Rename the selected filename by typing in a new name from the keyboard | F2 |

| Table 1-22 | Moving the Insertion Point |
|---|---|
| *Function* | *Command* |
| Move the insertion point to the beginning of the next word | Ctrl + → |
| Move the insertion point to the beginning of the previous word | Ctrl + ← |
| Move the insertion point to the beginning of the next paragraph | Ctrl + ↓ |
| Move the insertion point to the beginning of the previous paragraph | Ctrl + ↑ |

| Table 1-23 | Working with Programs in Open Windows |
|---|---|
| *Function* | *Command* |
| Switch between open items | Alt + Tab |
| Switch to the previous open program | Alt + Shift + Tab |
| Cycle through items in the order they had been opened | Alt + Esc |
| Open the shortcut menu for the active window | Alt + spacebar |
| Display the shortcut menu for the selected item | Shift + F10 |
| Display the System menu for the active window | Alt + spacebar |
| Display the Start menu | Ctrl + Esc or ⊞ |

| Function | Command |
|---|---|
| Display the corresponding pull-down menu | Alt + underlined letter |
| Perform a command from an open pull-down menu | Underlined letter of a command name |
| Open the next menu to the right, or open a submenu | → |
| Open the next menu to the left, or close a submenu | ← |

# Chapter 2: Crunching Data with Spreadsheets

## In This Chapter

✔ Going inside a spreadsheet

✔ Operating as if formulas and functions are your friends

✔ Entering data on a worksheet

✔ Making your work fit to be printed

*I*f electronic spreadsheets had been available in the Victorian Era of 150 years ago, one of the first buyers would have been Ebenezer Scrooge. No matter that he would have had to invest in a computer and software: Even the most miserly of bosses can quickly see how valuable a product like Microsoft Excel is.

Way back at the dawn of time — about 1980 — the first spreadsheet (not the first word processor) was the "killer application" that suddenly made buying a personal computer a no-brain decision. The first computer spreadsheet was VisiCalc, which helped move the Apple II from hobbyist's toy to business tool. By the time IBM released the first official PC in 1981, the concept had won the attention of accountants, financial officers, and entrepreneurs: the people with the authority to sign the purchase orders.

Think of an electronic spreadsheet as a *data processor*. Note that I didn't call a spreadsheet a *number processor*. One of the strengths of an electronic spreadsheet is that, right from the start, it went way past the simple accounting books that Bob Cratchit worked with by candlelight in Scrooge's counting house.

## Starting the Incredible What-If Machine

An electronic spreadsheet uses the computer's power to create, organize, and format data: numbers, words, and symbols. Then it adds computerized formulas that you can apply to that data in a multitude of ways. At its most basic level, then, you can look at an electronic spreadsheet as an automated calculating and accounting machine: Enter the number of widgets in one cell, the price in another, the sales tax rate in a third, and look for the sum. See Figure 2-1.

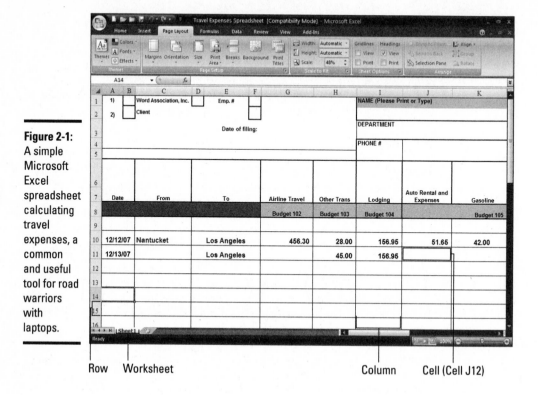

**Figure 2-1:**
A simple
Microsoft
Excel
spreadsheet
calculating
travel
expenses, a
common
and useful
tool for road
warriors
with
laptops.

Row    Worksheet                                    Column    Cell (Cell J12)

But in the hands of a creative user, electronic spreadsheets are a *what-if?* machine. What if you decrease the price by 5 percent but increase shipping costs by 50 cents a unit? Based on your experience over the past 12 years of business, what's the expected effect of increasing the discount rate to your biggest customers while raising prices for small orders? And one other thing: Spreadsheets are marvelous tools for creating lists and tables. They can function as a basic database for information that you can sort, format, search, and change.

I'm a word guy, myself. I leave the accounting to my accountant. But I do use spreadsheets all the time to help keep track of stuff. I have one Excel spreadsheet that I use to track my investments in mutual funds, bonds, and stocks; I feed it numbers once a week so I can watch my progress toward becoming a billionaire. (I'm not quite there yet.)

I also have a spreadsheet that includes the artist name, album title, and inventory number for my substantial collection of music on CDs. The inventory number correlates to the slot number in my automated CD player. I can search for any CD, or sort the list by genre based on the codes I've assigned each disc.

# Spreading out an Excel 2007 Sheet

In this chapter I use Microsoft Excel, in its most current version, as the example of how a spreadsheet works. Excel is by far the market leader in this category, although — just as with other Microsoft Office components — you can find shareware and even free software *(freeware)* that come close in their range of offerings.

## Working the books

A spreadsheet is structured like a huge assemblage of boxes. Here's the organizing principle:

✦ The vertical lines that descend from the top of the page define *columns*. (Think of the columns that support the roof of a great building.) Each column is topped by an identifying letter; the first column is A, the second is B, and so on.

✦ The horizontal lines that move from one side of the page to the other define the *rows*. (Think of rows of books on a shelf.) At the left side of each row is an identifying number, starting with 1 at the top-left corner and increasing in value heading down the page.

✦ The box created by an intersecting column and a row is called a *cell*. Each cell is identified with a label consisting of the column letter and row number. Therefore, the first cell on the page is A1; if you move four rows in and four rows down, you're at cell E5.

In Microsoft's implementation of an electronic spreadsheet, an Excel file is called a *workbook*. Each workbook can then contain one or more *worksheets*. Figure 2-1 shows these elements. It's not quite as confusing as it sounds. The advantage of this design is that you can create multiple spreadsheets on the same subject and switch among them by clicking the tabs at the bottom. You could devote one worksheet to one product, to one customer, or to one employee. They can exist as independent entities, or you can link the contents of one sheet (or one or more cells on one sheet) to a cell on another sheet.

It's the sort of thing that would have given Bob Cratchit — or you or me — a tremendous headache if we had to maintain it in a handwritten book or even on a set of word-processing files. But with a computer and spreadsheet software in charge, it's an organized thing of beauty.

The contents of any cell in a spreadsheet can be one of four types of data:

✦ **Text.** This includes labels for columns or rows, names of individuals or products, or any other characters with no numerical value.

✦ **Values or constants.** Any number with a specific value. This includes prices, costs, and counts, as well as dates and times.

✦ **Logical values.** A determination of whether a particular proposition or calculation is true or false, correct or incorrect, valid or invalid.

✦ **Formulas.** A mathematical calculation or expression that you can apply to a constant to yield a new value, a logical value, or text.

## Counting on simple formulas

The basic mathematical operators (slightly updated from Bob Cratchit's time) are still used in a spreadsheet. All of the symbols are directly available from the computer's keyboard. They include those in Table 2-1.

| Table 2-1 | Mathematical Operators | |
| --- | --- | --- |
| Symbol | Function | Result |
| + | Addition | If you ask the system to work on 2+2, it returns a calculated value of 4. |
| − | Subtraction | The returned value of 63–27 is 36. |
| * | Multiplication | The asterisk is for multiplication; 45*32 returns a value of 1440. |
| / | Division | The slash symbol is for division; 1440/32 yields a value of 45. |

 You must take one extra step, though: You must indicate to Excel (or any other spreadsheet program) that what you entered is a mathematical formula and not just some text. In Excel, you do this by preceding the entry with an equal sign, as in =2+4.

You can apply the same formulas to the contents of a cell. Say you want to apply a 75 percent markup to the wholesale price of the product included in Cell F26. The formula would be F26*1.5 or 1.5*F26. (Again, though, you need to precede the formula by an equal sign, as in =F26*1.5.)

## Showing compunction with functions

How about instructing the system to calculate the sum of all the values in cells from A10 through A25? What if you want to sum A10 through A22 and add that value to the sum of cells B36 through B72? Perhaps instead of the sum, you'd rather average all the values?

### The sum and average of all fears

For many users, the most commonly used function is SUM, which adds the values of specified cells or a range of cells. The basic syntax is thus:

=SUM(*first value, second value*)

In a SUM function, blank cells return a value of 0. If you include a text cell in a SUM function, the spreadsheet refuses to go along and proclaims an ERROR.

The values can be a constant, an individual cell, or a range of cells. You can sum up a range of cells these ways, among others:

✦ =sum(B1:B20). Adds the sum of all cells from B1 through B20.

✦ =sum(B1:B20, C5). Adds the sum of cells from B1 through B20 plus the value of C5.

✦ =sum(B1:B20, C4:C16, 1250). Sums the range of cells from B1 to B20, plus the range of cells from C4 to C16, and adds 1,250 to the total.

Excel's Average function works in the same way. A formula that averages a range of cells sums them all up and then divides the total by the number of cells.

The function follows:

=Average(*first value, second value*)

✦ The Max function examines a range of cells and returns the largest (maximum) value it finds.

✦ The Min function locates the smallest (minimum) value in the range.

✦ The Count function reports the number of cells that contain numerical data in a specified range of cells. Blank cells or text aren't included in the result.

### Weird science (and math and logical functions)

You could let the computer apply complex functions built into its library. Here's a random sampling of some financial functions:

✦ **ACCRINT.** Accrued interest for a security that pays periodic interest.

✦ **DB.** Depreciation of an asset for a specified period using the fixed-declining balance method.

✦ **YIELDMAT.** The annual yield of a security that pays interest at maturity.

**Book IV
Chapter 2**

**Crunching Data
with Spreadsheets**

You can directly enter a financial function like one of those just listed. If you're a pro, you could rattle this one off in your sleep: =YIELD-MAT(1012008,1012009,12152007,7.5,95,2).

However, for the rest of us, help is available just a few clicks away. In previous versions of Excel, you could go to the Help system to see available functions with instructions on using them. With the arrival of Excel 2007, a Function Library has been installed in the ribbon bar at the top of the screen.

*1.* **To use the library, click the Formulas tab.**

*2.* **Locate the Function Library.**

See Figure 2-2.

*3.* **Click the pull-down button to display installed functions.**

*4.* **Choose from the following options:**

- **Financial.** Banking, loans, investments, amortization, and similar functions.

- **Math and Trig.** Mathematical and trigonometric calculations.

- **Statistical.** Average, median, percentile, and correlation calculations.

- **Engineering.** Binary, decimal, and octal conversions as well as specialized features.

**Figure 2-2:** The statistical functions pull-down menu of the Functions Library is one of the key improvements in Microsoft Excel 2007.

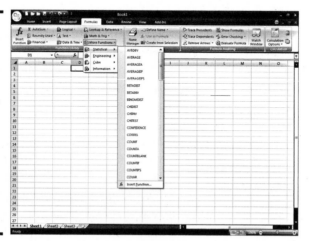

On the logical side you can also choose from functions for AND, OR, IF, TRUE, FALSE, and others. Date and time functions calculate the number of days between dates, to insert the current or a future date, and even to calculate hours, minutes, and seconds between specified moments in time.

### Entering data in a cell

To directly enter numbers, text, or a formula into a cell use the pointer to click on a location. Type the numbers of text and then press Enter (to enter the text and move down a cell in the same column) or Tab (to enter the text and move one column over to the right).

To enter more text data on a new line within the same cell, enter a line break by pressing the key combination Alt-Enter.

To enter dates in a cell, use the pointer to click a location. To enter a date, use a slash or a hyphen to separate the parts of a date. For example, type 8/19/1946 or 19-August-1946.

To enter times, follow along:

✦ Type a time in the form of *hours:minutes* or *hours:minutes:seconds* as in 9:23 or 9:23:03.

✦ To distinguish between a.m. or p.m., type an *a* or *p* after the time, as in 10:23 a to display 10:23 AM.

To enter the current date and time, type Ctrl + Shift + ; (semicolon). To enter a date or time that updates and stays current when you reopen a worksheet, use the TODAY and NOW functions.

## Printing Excel Spreadsheets

If you need to print an Excel spreadsheet, a few moments spent choosing an efficient and attractive design go a long way. The key to getting the best output is to click Print Preview before printing. Then click Page Setup to make custom choices.

From the Sheet tab of Page Setup you can instruct Excel to print gridlines to outline cells and make other choices. The Page tab includes the ability to set Scaling, which can adjust a larger page to fit a smaller-size page. See Figure 2-3.

**Book IV
Chapter 2**

**Crunching Data
with Spreadsheets**

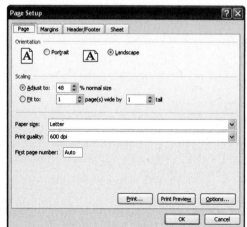

**Figure 2-3:**
Clicking one of the Scaling options on the Page tab of Page Setup allows you to shrink the printable image.

# Introducing New File Formats of Excel 2007

In the previous chapter of this book, I discuss the new file-format options that were introduced with Microsoft Office 2007. The new file formats are more compact (compared to previous formats, they require less space to hold the same amount of information) and they offer some advanced features.

The new Excel 2007 formats follow:

✦ .xlsx. The default filename extension for Excel Workbook is a ZIP compressed archive. It substitutes for the former binary .xls format, although support for Excel macros has been removed for security reasons.

✦ .xlsm. The new filename extension for Excel Workbooks with macros enabled.

✦ .xlsb. A new filename extension and format for Excel workbooks with macros but in binary form, allowing quicker document opening and saving. This format is to be used with very large documents with tens of thousands of rows or several hundred columns, or both.

✦ .xltm. A template document for workbooks, with macro support.

✦ .xlam. Excel add-ins for extra functionality and tools. By its nature, it includes support for macros.

See Book IV, Chapter 1 for information on how to add the ability to interchange Excel files between current and older versions of the spreadsheet program.

# *Taking Excel Shortcuts*

Mice are nice, but not always easy to control . . . especially on a laptop, and especially in the tight confines of a tiny desk in a hotel room. One solution is to use the extensive set of keyboard shortcuts. Tables 2-2 to 2-12 tell the tale.

| Table 2-2 | Navigating within Excel |
|---|---|
| *Function* | *Command* |
| Close the selected workbook window | Ctrl + W<br>or<br>Ctrl + F4 |
| Restore the window size of the selected workbook window | Ctrl + F5 |
| Switch to the next pane in a worksheet that has been split | F6 |
| Switch to the previous pane in a worksheet that has been split | Shift + F6 |
| Switch to the next workbook window when more than one workbook window is open | Ctrl + F6 |
| Switch to the previous workbook window | Ctrl + Shift + F6 |
| Minimize a workbook window to an icon | Ctrl + F9 |
| Maximize or restore the selected workbook window | Ctrl + F10 |
| Copy a picture of the screen to the Clipboard | PrtScr |
| Copy a picture of the selected window to the Clipboard | Alt + PrtScr |

| Table 2-3 | Managing Worksheets |
|---|---|
| *Function* | *Command* |
| Insert new worksheet | Shift + F11<br>or<br>Alt + Shift + F1 |
| Move to next sheet in workbook | Ctrl + Page Down |
| Move to previous sheet in workbook | Ctrl + Page Up |
| Select current and next sheet | Shift + Ctrl + Page Down |
| Select current and previous sheet | Shift + Ctrl + Page Up |

**Table 2-4**            **Moving within Worksheets**

| Function | Command |
| --- | --- |
| Move one cell up, down, left, or right | arrow keys |
| Move to edge of the current data region | Ctrl + arrow key |
| Move to beginning of row | Home |
| Move to beginning of the worksheet | Ctrl + Home |
| Move to last cell on the worksheet, in the bottom-most used row of the rightmost used column | Ctrl + End |
| Move down one screen | Page Down |
| Move up one screen | Page Up |
| Move one screen to right | Alt + Page Down |
| Move one screen to left | Alt + Page Up |
| Display the Go To dialog box | F5 |
| Display the Find dialog box | Shift + F5 |
| Repeat last Find action (same as Find Next) | Shift + F4 |
| Move between unlocked cells on a protected worksheet | Tab |

**Table 2-5**      **Entering, Formatting, and Calculating Data**

| Function | Command |
| --- | --- |
| Complete a cell entry and select the cell below | Enter |
| Start a new line in the same cell | Alt + Enter |
| Fill the selected cell range with the current entry | Ctrl + Enter |
| Complete a cell entry and select the previous cell above | Shift + Enter |
| Complete a cell entry and select the next cell to the right | Tab |
| Complete a cell entry and select the previous cell to the left | Shift + Tab |
| Cancel a cell entry | Esc |
| Move one character up, down, left, or right | arrow keys |
| Move to beginning of the line | Home |
| Repeat last action | F4 or Ctrl + Y |
| Create names from row and column labels | Ctrl + Shift + F3 |
| Fill down | Ctrl + D |
| Fill to the right | Ctrl + R |
| Define a name | Ctrl + F3 |
| Insert a hyperlink | Ctrl + K |

| Function | Command |
|---|---|
| Enter the date | Ctrl + ; |
| Enter the time | Ctrl + Shift + : |
| Display a drop-down list of the values in the current column of a list | Alt + ↓ |
| Undo the last action | Ctrl + Z |

**Table 2-6** **Editing Data**

| Function | Command |
|---|---|
| Edit the active cell and position the insertion point at the end of the cell contents | F2 |
| Start a new line in the same cell | Alt + Enter |
| Edit the active cell and then clear it, or delete the preceding character in the active cell as you edit cell contents | Backspace |
| Delete the character to the right of the insertion point, or delete the selection | Delete |
| Delete text to the end of the line | Ctrl + Delete |
| Display the Spelling dialog box | F7 |
| Edit a cell comment | Shift + F2 |
| Complete a cell entry and select the next cell below | Enter |
| Undo the last action | Ctrl + Z |
| Cancel a cell entry | Esc |
| Undo or redo the last automatic correction (when AutoCorrect Smart Tags is displayed) | Ctrl + Shift + Z |

**Table 2-7** **Inserting, Deleting, and Copying Cells**

| Function | Command |
|---|---|
| Copy selected cells | Ctrl + C |
| Display the Microsoft Office Clipboard for multiple copy and paste actions | Ctrl + C, Ctrl + C (Same command, twice in quick succession) |
| Cut selected cells | Ctrl + X |
| Paste copied cells | Ctrl + V |
| Clear contents of the selected cells | Delete |
| Delete selected cells | Ctrl + - |
| Insert blank cells | Ctrl + Shift + + |

**Book IV
Chapter 2**

**Crunching Data
with Spreadsheets**

**Table 2-8**                                    **Formatting Data**

| Function | Command |
|---|---|
| Display the Style dialog box | Alt + ' |
| Apply the General number format | Ctrl + Shift + ~ |
| Apply the Currency format with two decimal places (negative numbers in parentheses) | Ctrl + Shift + $ |
| Apply the Percentage format with no decimal places | Ctrl + Shift + % |
| Apply the Exponential number format with two decimal places | Ctrl + Shift + ^ |
| Apply the Date format with the day, month, and year | Ctrl + Shift + # |
| Apply the Time format with the hour and minute, and AM or PM | Ctrl + Shift + @ |
| Apply the Number format with two decimal places, thousands separator, and minus sign (–) for negative values | Ctrl + Shift + ! |
| Apply or remove bold formatting | Ctrl + B |
| Apply or remove italic formatting | Ctrl + I |
| Apply or remove underlining | Ctrl + U |
| Apply or remove strikethrough | Ctrl + 5 |
| Hide the selected rows | Ctrl + 9 |
| Unhide any hidden rows within the selection | Ctrl + Shift + ( |
| Hide the selected columns | Ctrl + 0 |
| Unhide any hidden columns within the selection | Ctrl + Shift + ) |
| Apply the outline border to the selected cells | Ctrl + Shift + & |
| Remove the outline border from the selected cells | Ctrl + Shift + _ |

**Table 2-9**                        **Selecting Data, Cells, Rows, and Columns**

| Function | Command |
|---|---|
| Select entire column | Ctrl + spacebar |
| Select entire row | Shift + spacebar |
| Select entire worksheet | Ctrl + A |
| Select only the active cell (with multiple cells selected) | Shift + Backspace |
| Select all objects on a sheet (with at least one object already selected) | Ctrl + Shift + spacebar |
| Alternate between hiding objects, displaying objects, and displaying placeholders for objects | Ctrl + 6 |

**Table 2-10**                    **Extending a Selection**

| Function | Command |
| --- | --- |
| Turn extend mode on or off. In extend mode, EXT appears in the status line, and the arrow keys extend the selection | F8 |
| Add another range of cells to the selection; or use the arrow keys to move to the start of the range you want to add, and then press F8 and the arrow keys to select the next range | Shift + F8 |
| Extend the selection by one cell | Shift + arrow key |
| Extend the selection to the last nonblank cell in the same column or row as the active cell | Ctrl + Shift + arrow key |
| Extend the selection to the beginning of the row | Shift + Home |
| Extend the selection to the beginning of the worksheet | Ctrl + Shift + Home |
| Extend the selection to the last used cell on the worksheet (lower-right corner) | Ctrl + Shift + End |
| Extend the selection down one screen | Shift + Page Down |
| Extend the selection up one screen | Shift + Page Up |
| Extend the selection to the last nonblank cell in the same column or row as the active cell | End + Shift + arrow key |
| Extend the selection to the last used cell on the worksheet (lower-right corner) | End + Shift + Home |
| Extend the selection to the cell in the upper-left corner of the window | scroll lock + Shift + Home |
| Extend the selection to the cell in the lower-right corner of the window | scroll lock + Shift + End |

**Table 2-11**                    **Setting Up a Chart**

| Function | Command |
| --- | --- |
| Create a chart of the data in the current range | F11 or Alt + F1 |
| Select the next sheet in the workbook; press repeatedly until the chart sheet you want is selected | Ctrl + Page Down |
| Select the previous sheet in the workbook; press again until the chart sheet you want is selected | Ctrl + Page Up |
| Select the previous group of elements in a chart | ↓ |
| Select the next group of elements in a chart | ↑ |
| Select the next element within a group | → |
| Select the previous element within a group | ← |

**Book IV
Chapter 2**

**Crunching Data
with Spreadsheets**

| Table 2-12 | Previewing and Printing |
|---|---|
| *Function* | *Command* |
| Display the Print dialog box | Ctrl + P<br>or<br>Ctrl + Shift + F12 |
| Displays Print Preview screen | Alt + F, V |
| Move around the Print Preview page when zoomed in | arrow keys |
| Move by one page in Print Preview when zoomed out | Page Up<br>or<br>Page Down |
| Move to the first page in Print Preview when zoomed out | Ctrl + ↑<br>or<br>Ctrl + ← |
| Move to the last page in Print Preview when zoomed out | Ctrl + ↓<br>or<br>Ctrl + → |

# Chapter 3: Presenting Yourself with PowerPoint Professionalism

## In This Chapter

✔ **Understanding the point of a presentation program**

✔ **Designing and editing a PowerPoint show**

✔ **How do you get to Carnegie Hall? Rehearse!**

Y ou don't need to study Sigmund Freud to understand one of the most common dreams: You're up on stage before an audience of your peers or your professors or the people you most want to impress . . . and you're naked, undressed, nude: what the Brits call *starkers*.

By most analyses, it indicates a fear of being unprepared. All eyes are upon you and you've got nothing to say or show.

Now if you're a well-trained actor, you've no fear here. I've seen some marvelous one-man or one-woman shows that feature masterful soliloquies that seem to fill an empty stage with spectacular scenery and clothe the actor in the most evocative of costumes.

But for the rest of us, myself included, anytime I go up on stage I want to be fully dressed . . . and fully prepared. Actually, I give lectures pretty often these days: on cruise ships, at libraries and bookstores, and just about anywhere that gives me an invitation (and an LCD projector for my laptop).

Therein lies the not-so-secret path to success for most modern-day, presentation-giving road warriors: Bring your own scenery, costumes, music, special effects, and script. And for many people the best way to do that is to use presentation software; Microsoft PowerPoint is the most commonly used and, by most judgments, the best of breed.

The program is to be viewed on a large screen using an LCD projector or other technology. You can also merely gather a handful of colleagues around your laptop for an up-close and personal presentation.

## Pointing out Your Power Spots

Several work areas open up when you start PowerPoint:

✦ **Normal view** is fittingly named for what is the normal, new, opening PowerPoint presentation screen. It presents a blank canvas, along with a full suite of power tools on standby in the ribbon or menu bar at the top. See Figure 3-1.

Slides tab                                          Main pane

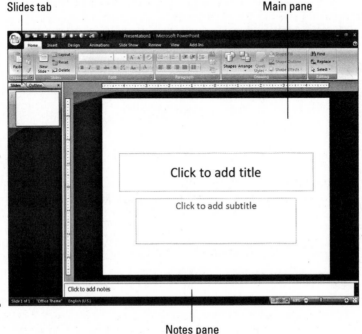

**Figure 3-1:**
An empty
PowerPoint
presenta-
tion, in
the Normal
view of
PowerPoint
2007.

Notes pane

✦ The **main slide pane** (on the right side of the view within the area marked by the horizontal and vertical rulers) is where you create, edit, and refine individual slides. Depending on the style you chose, the main pane may include predefined locations where you can add a title or sub-title or insert a drawing, photograph, or chart.

✦ The **slides tab** (on the left side of the screen) shows a thumbnail minia-ture version of each slide already created. You can see how the current slide relates to those that precede and follow it, and you can also drag thumbnails into a different order or delete them.

✦ The **Notes pane** (at the bottom of the Normal view) is where you enter comments or a script; the information here will not be projected onto the screen at a presentation, but if you work in Presenter view you can see them on the laptop. Notes can also be printed out as handouts for your audience.

When you first start, the Notes pane is just one-line deep. To increase the available space to read notes, point to the pane's top border and wait a moment until the pointer changes into a two-faced arrow; keep the mouse button pressed down and drag the border up. The slide you see on your laptop gets smaller to accommodate the growing Notes pane, but changes you make to the Notes pane size don't affect the size of the slide when it projects.

The best presentations are those that keep the information displayed onscreen to just the essential points, and use the notes for your background information. You can fill the Notes pane with material cut and pasted from a word processor, from slides created in PowerPoint, or just about anywhere else on your system.

# Designing and Refining a PowerPoint Presentation

Presentations have no official prescription, but most experts follow the same structure that speechwriters often do: Tell them what you're going to tell them, tell them, and then tell them what you told them.

## Structuring a presentation

You could try this basic structure:

+ **Main title slide.** You can display a summary title (accompanied by an attractive piece of art, if possible) as attendees arrive for your presentation. It's a good way to be sure the equipment works properly, and it gives you a jumping-off spot for your show.

+ **Introduction.** This slide tells the audience what you're going to tell them: the major points or subjects of your presentation.

+ **Detail slides.** One or more slides expand upon and develop the points you seek to make. The structure should follow basic outlining: major point, minor point, details, and then back to a new major point. Don't bore your audience by leaving one slide on display too long; try to have enough slides to make changes every few minutes during your presentation.

+ **Summary slide.** Here's where you tell them what you told them. This reinforces your message and gives you talking points for your summation.

When you add a slide to your presentation, you can continue with the same slide layout used in the previous slide or you can choose a layout for the new slide. To add a new slide of the same design

## Outlines

A quick aside into how to give the verbal side of a presentation: Write out a speech, break it down into as spare an outline as you can, and then deliver your comments from the outline. It comes out much more naturally and is more interesting than if you read from a script.

*1.* **Click the Home tab.**

*2.* **Locate the Slides section.**

*3.* **Click the small icon of a slide at the left side of the ribbon.**

To add a slide with a different layout, click New Slide. The Slides Gallery appears in a drop-down window. See Figure 3-2. (In older versions of PowerPoint, click File ➪ New Slide.)

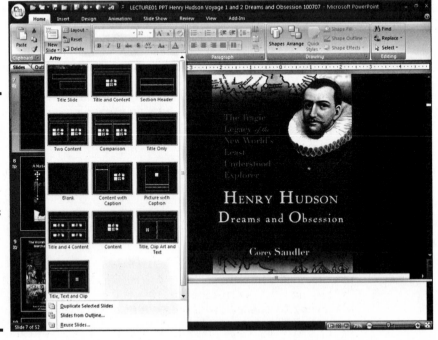

**Figure 3-2:** The display of available layouts in the Slide Gallery is presented in the colors you chose for the general theme for your presentation.

The placeholders shown in each slide can be used for text, or you can click the icons to insert objects including clip art, art from your own collection, and SmartArt graphics generated within the program.

## Adapting the Normal template

The Normal view in PowerPoint 2007 uses a blank presentation template. Nothing fancy, but easy to work with, you can readily customize it.

To create a new presentation based on the Blank Presentation template, follow along:

*1.* **Click the Microsoft Office Button.**

*2.* **Click New ➪ Blank and Recent.**

Blank and Recent is in the Templates section.

*3.* **Double-click Blank Presentation.**

## Copying a slide to use as a template

One of the most efficient ways to plow your way through a complex presentation is to use a successful slide as the model for another; an easy way to build one off the other is to copy a slide and then modify to the second version.

*1.* **In the Slides tab, find a slide you want to duplicate.**

*2.* **Right-click the slide and then click Copy.**

*3.* **Release the mouse button and then use the pointer to go where you want to place the copy.**

*4.* **Right-click and click Paste.**

You can copy a slide into your laptop's memory and then place it in another presentation open within PowerPoint.

## Applying a new layout to an existing slide

You can take one of several tactics:

✦ Concentrate on the layout of slides before entering text and art.

✦ Lay out the basic material and then come back and apply a new layout to a set of existing slides.

✦ Return to a finished presentation months or years after finishing it and refresh it with a new look for a new audience, or give it a new look when presenting it again with new information.

To change the layout of an existing slide, follow these steps:

1. **Open a presentation in PowerPoint.**

2. **In the Slides tab, click the slide whose layout you want to change.**

   The Slides tab is on the left side of the screen.

3. **Click the Home tab ⇨ Slides.**

4. **Click Layout and choose the new layout to apply.**

   In older versions, click the Layout menu item and then choose a new layout.

## Themes like an attractive presentation

Separate and apart from *slide layout* (the location of titles, images, and notes) is your presentation's *design.* Your goal is to create an attractive look (or use a predefined design) that communicates information well. I'm talking about using fonts that are

✦ Easy to read

✦ In colors that viewers can easily see

✦ In combinations that engage the viewer

Office PowerPoint 2007 automatically begins with a basic *design* called the Office theme anytime you begin a project based on the Blank Presentation template. Hover your pointer over an example or click one to see what it looks like to change a theme. As long as you don't save your file, any browsing you do here doesn't make permanent changes.

However, changing the theme is as easy as pointing and clicking:

1. **Click the Design tab ⇨ Themes.**

2. **Click the down arrow at the right side of the first group of themes.**

   The display expands into the full set of built-in designs. See Figure 3-3.

   In older versions of PowerPoint, click the Formatting toolbar, then click Design ⇨ Color Schemes.

 By default, PowerPoint 2007 applies theme changes to all the slides in a presentation. If you want to change the appearance of one slide only, or a selected group of slides, hold down the Ctrl key as you click a slide (in the Slides pane on the left side of the page); continue holding Ctrl as you select other slides. When you have finish choosing slides, right-click the theme you want to apply, and then click Apply to Selected Slides.

**Figure 3-3:**
You can experiment with changing any of the built-in themes (called Color Schemes in previous versions of Power-Point).

## Rearranging slides

You have two ways to change slides around in a presentation. The most direct way — but not always the easiest — is to click a slide in the Slides pane and hold the mouse button while you drag it within the pane to a new location. This works well when you want to move a slide a few positions in the presentation structure.

A much better tool for dealing with large and complex presentations is to open the Slide Sorter window. This button is available from the ribbon bar of PowerPoint 2007 or as a menu item in earlier versions. (See Figure 3-4.) You can click any slide and drag it to a new spot or delete it from the show. Using either method, you can select multiple slides to move, delete, or copy by pressing and holding the Ctrl key while clicking slides.

## Adding and formatting text

Bulleting or numbering your text can help make it much more readable.

✦ Prepare your text in a word processor or other program, copy it to computer memory, and then paste it into place.

✦ To add text to any slide, click the placeholder where you want to add text; type or paste text.

✦ To switch between a bulleted list and unbulleted text, select the text and click the Bullets text or icon.

✦ To change the bullet characters, click the arrow next to Bullets, and then choose the style you want.

✦ From the ribbon bar in the Home tab of PowerPoint 2007 (or the Layout menu of previous versions), you can change fonts, type sizes, type styles, colors, and other attributes.

**Figure 3-4:**
The Slide Sorter window allows a global view of dozens of slides in a presentation (in this case a photo travel essay).

## Checking spelling

By default, PowerPoint checks the spelling of all text you enter onto slides. Look for words underlined with a squiggly red line; that indicates that the system hasn't found the word in the spelling dictionary. Make any necessary changes as you create the slides. If you prepare your text in a word processor or other program, you can spell-check it there before copying and pasting it into place in PowerPoint.

Once you complete the presentation, have PowerPoint go back and re-examine the entire presentation. Not only does this help you check one more time for spelling errors, but it also helps you discover inconsistencies: Did you spell *labor* in the American style in some places and use the English spelling *labour* elsewhere?

To initiate a spell-check on a document, follow these steps:

*1.* **Press Ctrl + Home.**

You're taken to the first slide in your presentation.

*2.* **Click the Review tab and locate the Proofing group.**

*3.* **Click Spelling.**

If the program discovers any words it believes are misspelled, PowerPoint displays a dialog box with the word indicated. As a component of Microsoft Office, the spell-checking process uses the same engine (and the same dictionary) used in Microsoft Word and other elements of the suite.

*4.* **Choose one of the following:**

- **Ignore All instances of the particular word (thereby declaring it to correct).**

- **Add the word to the built-in dictionary so that it isn't flagged as incorrect again**

- **Change the spelling of the word**

If you change the word, select from one of the selected spellings shown in the box or enter your own fix. (If you choose Change All, the program alters all instances of the word it finds in the current presentation.)

## Adding clip art to a slide

Why do PowerPoint presenters insist on including a Halloween goblin, a Thanksgiving turkey, a Christmas tree, or Uncle Sam in a top hat? The answer, I'm afraid, speaks to the power of symbols — no matter how overused or cheesy.

When you use a very familiar icon, you receive quick recognition and little chance of misunderstanding. On the other hand, you're not demonstrating a great deal of creativity. Does it sound as if I'm not a big fan of clip art? (Cue the picture of exploding fireworks, accompanied by a sound effect of an audience delivering an ovation. You know exactly what I mean, because you've seen the combination a thousand times.)

PowerPoint, as well as other components of Microsoft Office and certain other applications come equipped with a collection of colorful, familiar, and easily recognized clip art drawings. You can add clip art you've purchased from commercial collections, downloaded from free sources, or drawn by yourself.

Here's how to insert clip art:

*1.* **Click a slide.**

If the slide has a placeholder for clip art, click there; otherwise the image is inserted in the center of the slide.

**2.** **Click the Insert tab and locate the Illustrations group.**

**3.** **Click Clip Art.**

The Clip Art task pane opens.

**4.** **Locate the drawing you want to insert.**

You can

- Move through the collection by pulling down on the scroll bar on the right side of the pane.

- Click an icon that allows you to organize clips on your system. (See Figure 3-5.)

- Connect to the Internet to search for clip art in Office Online.

**5.** Once you've found the clip art you want to use, click on it to insert it into your slide.

Once it is in place, it can be stretched to resize it and it can be rotated. You can also add text to help make your point even more obvious.

Clip Art task pane

**Figure 3-5:**
The Clip Art task pane is shown at the right; the Microsoft Clip Organizer in the middle of the screen searches art by category or location.

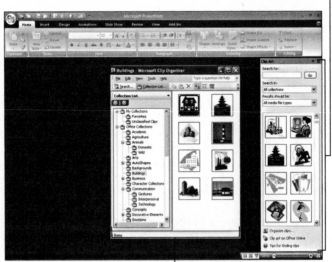

Microsoft Clip Organizer

## Adding SmartArt graphics

SmartArt is art that is, well, a heck of a lot smarter than mere clip art. Do you want to illustrate the fact that the company's revenues are falling off the cliff? You could show picture of a cliff . . . or you could present real numbers from your presentation tumbling down a slope. (The numbers are tumbling, that is; you're not tumbling while presenting.)

PowerPoint includes layouts in the SmartArt catalog. To convert existing text to a SmartArt graphic, you can either enter text and apply a graphic to it, or choose a graphic and enter text that fills it out.

To convert text to a SmartGraphic in PowerPoint 2007, do these steps:

*1.* **Click the placeholder.**

*2.* **On the Home tab, locate the Paragraph group.**

*3.* **Click Convert to SmartArt Graphic.**

You can experiment with any of the SmartArt graphics by hovering your pointer over the thumbnails. The initial set shows layouts intended to spruce up bulleted lists; to see the entire set, click More SmartArt Graphics.

*4.* **Complete the customization.**

Edit the text or add new material, resize it, rotate it, or apply a different Quick Style to set its color palette.

Figure 3-6 shows a simple SmartArt graphic I created to explain the manufacture cost of our company's best widget.

To insert a piece of SmartArt to a blank slide, follow these steps:

*1.* **Click the Insert tab and locate the Illustrations group.**

*2.* **Click SmartArt.**

The Choose a SmartArt Graphic dialog box appears on the left side of the PowerPoint frame.

*3.* **Click the type of SmartArt graphic you want to use.**

If you hover your pointer over a graphic, it displays a preview.

**Book IV
Chapter 3**

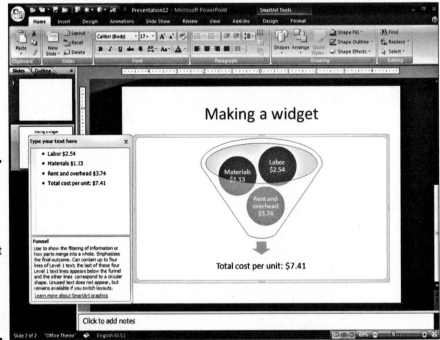

## Setting smooth (or flashy) transitions

One of the arts that make watching a movie enjoyable comes in the form of editing between scenes. Very rarely do you see a "jump cut" that switches from one location to another, one actor to another, or one annoying product placement to the next. Instead, editors employ devices including fades, wipes, and dissolves; these make one scene morph smoothly into the next. When done well, viewers barely notice they're happening.

You can apply the same sort of effects between slides in a PowerPoint presentation. One slide can fade out while a new one fades in. That often is the best way to move from slide to slide in a professional boardroom presentation.

If you're making a sales presentation or entertaining an audience, you can choose flashier transitions — effects impossible to miss. These include starbursts, animated wipes from corner to corner, and other attention-demanding devices. In addition to the transition type, you can set the speed at which it unfolds as well as the *trigger* (keyboard, mouse click, or a particular period of time) that sets it in motion.

You can apply a transition to a slide as you create it, or you can go back and edit slides in a completed presentation. You can also apply the same transition to all the slides in a show.

1. **Click the Animations tab and locate the Transitions to the Slide group.**

2. **Click the transition you want to use.**

   An example appears in Figure 3-7. As with most other effects, you can see a preview by hovering the pointer over the transition's icon.

**Figure 3-7:**
A sampling of available basic fades and dissolves as well as more complex wipes that you can apply to a PowerPoint slide.

## Going out on the Web from PowerPoint

We live in a connected society, and increasingly, a wireless world. So why not reach out from your laptop to the Internet for a live link that pops up in the middle of your presentation? You can if you embed a hyperlink in your show.

Think about something like this: You're lecturing about investment strategies and, with a click of a button on a PowerPoint slide, you go to an up-to-the-moment report on the Dow Jones Industrials or an individual equity. Or perhaps you have an extended video stored on a server back in your office that someone else is updating for you; a link to the office network could bring it to PowerPoint. And if you want to get really fancy, you could add a link to a video feed from the CEO's desktop.

As you're sitting at your desk, doing these things and more is quite easy. Just connect your laptop to your network or the Internet via a wired or wireless link.

Beware: If you're taking your show on the road, some serious headaches could easily ruin it. Are you certain the conference room or stage has a high-speed Internet connection? Are there firewalls or other security measures that could block access to live feeds? This is the sort of presentation I give only after testing it *in the place where it is to be delivered.* And I'm in the room an hour before the scheduled presentation time to test everything, and am prepared to switch to an alternate show that doesn't depend on going out on the Web.

Hyperlinks can take you

✦ From one slide to another (allowing a sort of freeform jump that you can adjust based on changing conditions as you give your presentation)

✦ To a network, an Internet location, or another PowerPoint presentation on your computer

✦ To another program and file on your laptop, such as a spreadsheet or graphics program

Follow along to add a hyperlink:

*1.* **Select the item that you want to enable as a hyperlink.**

The item can be text or another object, such as a graphic.

*2.* **Click the Insert tab and locate the Links group.**

*3.* **Click Hyperlink.**

The Insert Hyperlink dialog box appears.

*4.* **Click the button in the My Places box that identifies the link target.**

The choices include

• Existing File or Web Page

• Place in This Document

• Create New Document

• E-mail Address

## Naming and saving a presentation

Files created in this format can only be opened in Office PowerPoint 2007 or a current version of the PowerPoint Viewer.

Take these steps to save your presentation in PowerPoint 2007:

*1.* **Click the Microsoft Office Button and point to Save As.**

*2.* **Choose one of the following:**

- **PowerPoint Presentation:** To save the file in the most current, most efficient file format.

- **PowerPoint 97-2003 Presentation:** To save a copy of the presentation in a format that can open in either PowerPoint 2007 or earlier versions. If you save your file in the older format, you lose any special features accessible only in PowerPoint 2007; this affects features only, not the content of your show.

   In earlier versions of the program, click File ⇨ Save As. You can save files in the default format called PowerPoint 97-2003.

Your other options for saving files from PowerPoint 2007, shown in Figure 3-8, include:

- ✦ **PowerPoint Show.** Files saved in this format always open within PowerPoint in Slide Show view, ready for projection. In other words, choosing this option launches directly into presentation mode, as opposed to editing mode. That doesn't mean you can't switch to editing; it's just a question of how the program starts.

- ✦ **PDF or XPS.** You can save your file as a PDF or XPS presentation for use on any machine that has permitting software; this is a good way to send someone a copy of your presentation for easy viewing and difficulty changing.

- ✦ **Other Formats.** You can modify PowerPoint 2007 with add-ins so you can save files in other file formats.

Name your presentation and save it as soon as you begin working on it; this helps you recover work in case the software, the operating system, or the hardware freezes or crashes. What? You thought Windows Vista was crash proof? Please contact me for details of the bridge I am selling in Brooklyn.

Once you give a file a name and type, you can quickly save versions as you work on them by clicking the Microsoft Office Button and then clicking Save (or, in older versions, by clicking the File menu and then Save). Users of any version can press Ctrl + S.

**Book IV
Chapter 3**

**Presenting Yourself
with PowerPoint
Professionalism**

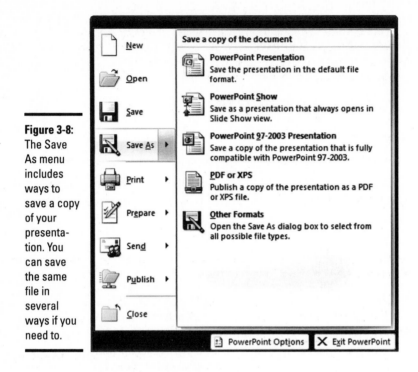

**Figure 3-8:**
The Save As menu includes ways to save a copy of your presentation. You can save the same file in several ways if you need to.

## Putting on at the Ritz

You can do hundreds of things to create and format content in your presentation; I've touched on just a few dozen. But eventually it's showtime.

But wait: Before you take your presentation up on stage or into the boardroom, perform a full set of tests, tryouts, practice sessions, and rehearsals. In other words, don't let the first time you make your presentation be the first time PowerPoint has operated outside of editing mode.

### Testing in Slide Show view

Slide Show view displays your presentation as closely as possible to the way it will appear when your audience sees it. Editing features are turned off, notes are hidden away, and all that appears is the show itself.

Why do I say "as closely as possible"? Because many modern laptops offer widescreen LCDs that don't match precisely the image that you see if you use an LCD projector or a large-screen projection television for your PowerPoint presentation. Many widescreen laptops tend to show ovals (wider than they are tall) on built-in screens, but the image is correct when projected on an external screen.

You're also going to want to check that all the transitions between slides are working properly and that slides advance when you want them to change — on a mouse click or a keyboard command. If you're going to work with a wireless remote control — a nifty addition to any speaker's toolkit — you should test that out in Slide Show view as well.

To turn on the view in PowerPoint 2007, follow these steps:

*1.* **Click the Slide Show tab and locate the Start Slide Show group.**

*2.* **Click one of the following:**

- **From Beginning:** To start with the first slide of the presentation.

- **From Current Slide:** To start with the slide currently highlighted in the Slide pane.

   The presentation opens in Slide Show view.

*3.* **Click the mouse or keyboard or use your remote control to advance to the next slide.**

   To return to Normal view at any time, press the Escape key.

## *Preparing for external projectors or screens*

Assume nothing. Here's a checklist of questions you need to have answered before you send your PowerPoint presentation out on the road:

✦ Will the presentation be delivered from the laptop computer you used to create it, or do you need to use another computer at your destination?

✦ Where will the presentation be stored:

- On the laptop you bring with you?

- On an external storage device such as a flash memory key, a CD, or DVD?

- On an external hard disk drive?

   Will it be made available over the Internet or an office network?

✦ Will you, the person who developed the presentation and knows it inside and out, deliver the presentation? Or will someone else run the laptop and speak to the audience? Will the presentation be designed to run itself?

The answers to each of these questions can send you off in a different direction or require a different type of preparation.

## Handouts and notes

You can use speaker's notes as a script for your presentation, and you can consider using them as leave-behinds for audience members. The notes display one slide at the top of each printed page; at the bottom is any text in the Notes pane.

Handouts don't include the contents of the Notes pane. You can print one, two, three, four, six, or nine slides per page. The three-slides-per-page handout includes a section of ruled space for handwritten notes.

## *Rehearsing the show*

The first level of rehearsal should take place at your own desk.

+ Close the door, shut off your phone, start a clock or timer, and then present the show.

Most people have a different speaking voice and can project more energy when standing up; perform at least one of your rehearsals in a position close to the one you'll use when delivering the presentation to a live audience.

+ Keep a notepad on your desk to jot down comments about things that need fixing or changing. Look for slides that seem out of place or unnecessary.

+ After completing the first run-through, check the clock to see how closely your presentation fits your allotted time. Make sure you leave some extra time for questions.

+ Make one of your final run-throughs using equipment identical to (or at least similar to) the hardware you'll use when making your actual presentation. Make sure you know how to turn on the external video output from your laptop, and test that it works with an LCD projector.

## *Packaging for distribution*

If you're preparing your presentation to send to another location, one excellent solution is to "package" the show. This brings together the presentation in finished form, along with any files linked to it (such as videos or sound effects), as well as a copy of Microsoft Office PowerPoint Viewer 2007.

About the Viewer: This software is available free through the Microsoft web site and, as part of most Microsoft Office packages, allows you to view, read, and print PowerPoint presentations but not to edit or change them.

I always include in my traveling case a copy of the PowerPoint Viewer on CD, along with a current copy of my various lectures and presentations, just in case my laptop goes bad or goes missing. It's never happened on the road, but just in case, I'm ready to make my presentation on whatever I could beg, borrow, or buy at my destination.

You can record a packaged presentation on

✦ CD

✦ DVD

✦ Flash memory key

You can send it

✦ Via e-mail

✦ Directly over the Internet

## Presenting New PowerPoint 2007 Features

As with the other components of Microsoft Office 2007, the latest version of PowerPoint can store and use files that employ an improved, compressed file format. The Open XML Format takes up less space, and components are segmented within the file so corruption of one part doesn't render the entire file unusable.

I've found the new XML file format results in a reduction of about 50 percent when you compare the same PowerPoint presentation saved in the current or a previous file format.

Other elements new to PowerPoint 2007 include

✦ The ribbon menu, which brings together features and commands under categorized tabs and related groups.

✦ A larger collection of predefined QuickStyles, layouts, table formats, and effects that can begin a presentation creation or that you can apply to a completed one.

✦ Custom layouts that contain as many placeholders as you want. These markers are for inserting charts, tables, videos, graphics, SmartArt graphics, and clip art. You can save your custom layouts for future presentations as well.

✦ Text controls, including the most advanced font designs, including small caps, strikethrough or double strikethrough, and double or color underlines. You can also add fills, lines, shadows, glow, *kerning* (tightening of spacing between letters), and 3D effects to text.

## Amping Presenter view

Office PowerPoint 2007 improves on Presenter view. Now you can

✦ Run your presentation with notes and thumbnails of later slides from one monitor — at a podium, for example — while the audience views the show on a second monitor (or on a screen with an image from an LCD projector).

✦ Preview text that shows the effect of the next click before: Will it move to the next slide, will it add a graphic or text element, will it begin an animation?

✦ Black out the screen during a presentation and then resume where it was halted; this tool might be appropriate during a question-and-answer period or if you schedule a break in the middle of a presentation.

## Pumping up security

If you give copies of your presentation on disc or send it over the Internet, you might struggle with maintaining the integrity of your work. Also, you need to prevent unauthorized persons from learning information about you or your company without your permission.

With PowerPoint 2007, you can do all the following:

✦ Hide the author's name

✦ Delete all comments made in the course of its design

✦ Restrict attempts to change a finished file

### Making a presentation read-only

Using the Mark As Final command on a PowerPoint file allows other users to read and present it, but blocks attempts to edit or change it. Editing commands, proofing marks, and typing are disabled.

However, the solution isn't permanent: A user can open your PowerPoint file, turn off the Mark As Final setting, and change it at will.

To mark a file as final, follow these steps:

*1.* **Open the document.**

*2.* **Click the Microsoft Office Button.**

*3.* **Choose Prepare ➪ Mark as Final.**

### Removing metadata and personal information

The Document Inspector, a component of Office 2007 programs, checks files for hidden *metadata* (info about your info), personal information, and content stored in your presentation. The inspector finds these kinds of things: comments, document properties (including creation dates and the author name), document management server information, invisible objects, off-slide content, presentation notes, and custom XML data.

You can customize the Document Inspector to add checks for additional types of hidden content. For more information, please read *PowerPoint 2007 For Dummies* (Wiley).

## Taking PowerPoint Shortcuts

As with other power tools for the road warrior, Microsoft PowerPoint can work in a parallel universe: a full set of commands you can execute from the keyboard, as well as with a mouse or other pointing device. That's a very good thing, because it allows you, the presenter, to concentrate on the show — not the machine. See Tables 3-1 through 3-22.

| Table 3-1 | General Commands: Function Keys |
|---|---|
| *Action* | *Keyboard* |
| Display Help; display the Office Assistant | F1 |
| Start context-sensitive Help | Shift + F1 |
| Select the text box (with text or an object selected inside the text box); select text within a text box (with the text box selected) | F2 |
| Save As command | Alt + F2 or F12 |
| Save command | Alt + Shift + F2 or Shift + F12 |
| Change the case of letters | Shift + F3 |
| Repeat the last action | F4 |
| Repeat the last Find (Find Next) | Shift + F4 |
| Close the window | Ctrl + F4 |
| Quit PowerPoint | Alt + F4 |
| Quit PowerPoint | Alt + Shift + F4 |
| Slide Show command (View menu) | F5 |
| Restore the presentation window size | Ctrl + F5 |
| Move to the previous pane | Shift + F6 |

**Book IV Chapter 3**

Presenting Yourself with PowerPoint Professionalism

*(continued)*

**Table 3-1** *(continued)*

| Action | Keyboard |
|--------|----------|
| Restore the program window size | Alt + F5 |
| Move to the next pane | F6 |
| Move to the next presentation window | Ctrl + F6 |
| Move to the previous presentation window | Ctrl + Shift + F6 |
| Spelling command (Tools menu) | F7 |
| Move command (presentation Control menu) | Ctrl + F7 |
| Find next misspelling (If Automatic Spell Checking enabled) | Alt + F7 |
| Size command (presentation Control menu) | Ctrl + F8 |
| Activate the menu bar | F10 |
| Display a shortcut menu | Shift + F10 |
| Maximize the presentation window | Ctrl + F10 |
| Maximize the program window | Alt + F10 |
| Activate the menu bar | Ctrl + Shift + F10 |
| Display Visual Basic code | Alt + F11 |
| Open command (File menu) | Ctrl + F12 |
| Print command (File menu) | Ctrl + Shift + F12 |

**Table 3-2**  **Controlling a Slide Show**[*]

| Action | Keyboard |
|--------|----------|
| Perform the next animation or advance to the next slide (same as if the mouse button had been clicked) | Any of the following:<br>Enter Page Down<br>$\rightarrow$<br>$\downarrow$<br>spacebar |
| Perform the previous animation or return to the previous slide | Any of the following:<br>P<br>Page Up<br>$\leftarrow$<br>$\uparrow$<br>Backspace |
| Go to slide <number> | *number* + Enter |
| Display a black screen, or return to the slide show from a black screen | B<br>or<br>. (period) |
| Display a white screen, or return to the slide show from a white screen | W<br>or<br>, (comma) |

**Table 3-8** **Applying Character Formats**

| Action | Keyboard |
| --- | --- |
| Change formatting of characters (Font command, Format menu) | Ctrl + T |
| Change case of letters | Shift + F3 |
| Apply bold formatting | Ctrl + B |
| Apply underline | Ctrl + U |
| Apply italic formatting | Ctrl + I |
| Apply subscript formatting (automatic spacing) | Ctrl + = |
| Apply superscript formatting (automatic spacing) | Ctrl + Shift + + |
| Remove manual character formatting | Ctrl + spacebar |

**Table 3-9** **Copying Text Formats**

| Action | Keyboard |
| --- | --- |
| Copy formats | Ctrl + Shift + C |
| Paste formats | Ctrl + Shift + V |

**Table 3-10** **Aligning Paragraphs and Indents**

| Action | Keyboard |
| --- | --- |
| Center a paragraph | Ctrl + E |
| Justify a paragraph | Ctrl + J |
| Left-align a paragraph | Ctrl + L |
| Right-align a paragraph | Ctrl + R |

**Table 3-11** **Working in an Outline or Slide Pane**

| Action | Keyboard |
| --- | --- |
| Promote a paragraph | Alt + Shift + ← |
| Demote a paragraph | Alt + Shift + → |
| Move selected paragraphs up | Alt + Shift + ↑ |
| Move selected paragraphs down | Alt + Shift + ↓ |
| Show heading level 1 | Alt + Shift + 1 |
| Expand text below a heading | Alt + Shift + + |
| Collapse text below a heading | Alt + Shift + - |
| Show all text or headings | Alt + Shift + A |
| Turn character formatting on or off | / |

| Action | Keyboard |
| --- | --- |
| Stop or restart an automatic slide show | S or + (plus sign) |
| End a slide show | Any of the following: Esc Ctrl + Break - (hyphen) |
| Erase on-screen annotations | E |
| Go to next hidden slide | H |
| Set new timings while rehearsing | T |
| Use original timings while rehearsing | O |
| Use mouse-click to advance while rehearsing | M |
| Return to the first slide | Both mouse buttons for 2 seconds |
| Redisplay hidden pointer and/or change the pointer to a pen | Ctrl + P |
| Redisplay hidden pointer and/or change the pointer to an arrow | Ctrl + A |
| Hide the pointer and button immediately | Ctrl + H |
| Hide the pointer and button in 15 seconds | Ctrl + U |
| Display the shortcut menu | Shift + F10 or right-click |
| Go to the first or next hyperlink on a slide | Tab |
| Go to the last or previous hyperlink on a slide | Shift + Tab |
| Perform the mouse-click behavior of the selected hyperlink | Enter while a hyperlink is selected |
| Perform the mouse-over behavior of the selected hyperlink | Shift + Enter while a hyperlink is selected |

*These keyboard shortcuts work while a PowerPoint slide show is being presented in full-screen mode. You can press F1 during a slide show to see a list of controls.*

**Table 3-3** **Creating and Editing Presentations**

| Action | Keyboard |
| --- | --- |
| Create a new presentation | Ctrl + N |
| Insert a new slide | Ctrl + M |
| Make a copy of the selected slide | Ctrl + D |
| Open a presentation | Ctrl + O |
| Save a presentation | Ctrl + S |

*(continued)*

**Table 3-3** *(continued)*

| Action | Keyboard |
| --- | --- |
| Close a presentation | Ctrl + W |
| Print a presentation | Ctrl + P |
| Run a presentation | F5 |
| Quit PowerPoint | Alt + F4 |
| Find text, formatting, and special items | Ctrl + F |
| Replace text, specific formatting, and special items | Ctrl + H |
| Insert a hyperlink | Ctrl + K |
| Check spelling | F7 |
| Cancel an action | Esc |
| Undo an action | Ctrl + Z |
| Redo or repeat an action | Ctrl + Y |
| Switch to the next pane (clockwise) | F6 |
| Switch to the previous pane (counterclockwise) | Shift + F6 |

**Table 3-4**      **Deleting and Copying Text and Objects**

| Action | Keyboard |
| --- | --- |
| Delete one character to the left | Backspace |
| Delete one word to the left | Ctrl + Backspace |
| Delete one character to the right | Delete |
| Delete one word to the right | Ctrl + Delete |
| Cut selected object | Ctrl + X |
| Copy selected object | Ctrl + C |
| Paste cut or copied object | Ctrl + V |
| Undo the last action | Ctrl + Z |

**Table 3-5**      **Moving around in Text**

| Action | Keyboard |
| --- | --- |
| Move one character to the left | ← |
| Move one character to the right | → |
| Move one line up | ↑ |
| Move one line down | ↓ |
| Move one word to the left | Ctrl + ← |
| Move one word to the right | Ctrl + → |

| Action | Keyboard |
| --- | --- |
| Move to end of a line | End |
| Move to beginning of a line | Home |
| Move up one paragraph | Ctrl + ↑ |
| Move down one paragraph | Ctrl + ↓ |
| Move to end of a text box | Ctrl + End |
| Move to beginning of a text box | Ctrl + Home |
| Move to the next title or body text placeholder* | Ctrl + Enter |
| Repeat the last Find action | Shift + F4 |

*\* When the last placeholder on a slide is selected, press Ctrl + Enter to insert a new slide in the presentatio*

**Table 3-6**      **Selecting Text and Objects**

| Action | Keyboard |
| --- | --- |
| Select one character to the right | Shift + → |
| Select one character to the left | Shift + ← |
| Select to the end of a word | Ctrl + Shift + → |
| Select to the beginning of a word | Ctrl + Shift + ← |
| Select one line up | Shift + ↑ |
| Select one line down | Shift + ↓ |
| Select an object (with text selected inside the object) | Esc |
| Select an object (with an object selected) | Tab or Shift + Tab until the ob want is selected |
| Select text within an object | Enter |
| Select all objects in the slide pane | Ctrl + A |
| Select all slides in the slide sorter view | Ctrl + A |
| Select all text in the outline pane | Ctrl + A |

**Table 3-7**      **Changing or Resizing the Font**

| Action | Keyboard |
| --- | --- |
| Change font | Ctrl + Shift + F |
| Change font size | Ctrl + Shift + P |
| Increase font size | Ctrl + Shift + > |
| Decrease font size | Ctrl + Shift + < |

**Table 3-12**             **Working in Windows Boxes**

| Action | Keyboard |
|---|---|
| Switch to the next program in the window | Alt + Tab |
| Switch to the previous program in the window | Alt + Shift + Tab |
| Display the Windows Start menu | Ctrl + Esc |
| Close the active presentation window | Ctrl + W |
| Restore the active presentation window | Ctrl + F5 |
| Switch to the next presentation window | Ctrl + F6 |
| Switch to the previous presentation window | Ctrl + Shift + F6 |
| Switch to the next window pane in the clockwise direction | F6 |
| Switch to the next window pane in the counterclockwise direction | Shift + F6 |
| Move the window pane split in a maximized presentation window | Alt, ←, ↓, P to select the splits, arrow keys to position the split, then Enter |
| Move the window pane split in a presentation window that is not maximized | Alt, -, P to select the splits, arrow keys to position the split, then Enter |
| Carry out the Move command (Presentation icon menu, menu bar) | Ctrl + F7 |
| Carry out the Size command (Presentation icon menu, menu bar) | Ctrl + F8 |
| Minimize the presentation window | Ctrl + F9 |
| Maximize the presentation window | Ctrl + F10 |
| Select a toolbar button in the Open or Save As dialog box (File menu) | Alt + number (1 for the leftmost button, 2 for the next, and so on) |
| Update the files visible in the Open or Save As dialog box (File menu) | F5 |

**Table 3-13**             **Working in Dialog Boxes**

| Action | Keyboard |
|---|---|
| Switch to next tab in dialog box | Ctrl + Tab |
| Switch to previous tab in dialog box | Ctrl + Shift + Tab |
| Move to next option or option group | Tab |
| Move to previous option or option group | Shift + Tab |
| Move between options in selected drop-down list box or between some options in a group of options | arrow keys |

**Book IV
Chapter 3**

**Presenting Yourself
with PowerPoint
Professionalism**

*(continued)*

**Table 3-13** *(continued)*

| Action | Keyboard |
| --- | --- |
| Perform action assigned to selected button; select or clear the check box | spacebar |
| Move to option in a selected drop-down list box | first letter of the option name |
| Select option; select or clear a check box | Alt + letter underlined in the option name |
| Open selected drop-down list box | Alt + ↓ |
| Close selected drop-down list box; cancel command and close dialog box | Esc |
| Perform action assigned to default button in dialog box | Enter |

**Table 3-14**                   **Working in Text Boxes**

| Action | Keyboard |
| --- | --- |
| Move to beginning of the entry | Home |
| Move to end of the entry | End |
| Move one character to the left | ← |
| Move one character to the right | → |
| Move one word to the left | Ctrl + ← |
| Move one word to the right | Ctrl + → |
| Select from insertion point to the beginning of the entry | Shift + Home |
| Select from insertion point to the end of the entry | Shift + End |
| Select or cancel the selection one character to the left | Shift + ← |
| Select or cancel the selection one character to the right | Shift + → |
| Select or cancel the selection one word to the left | Ctrl + Shift + ← |
| Select or cancel the selection one word to the right | Ctrl + Shift + → |

**Table 3-15**         **Using the Open and Save As Dialog Boxes**

| Action | Keyboard |
| --- | --- |
| Go to previous folder | Alt + 1 |
| Open the folder up one level from the open folder | Alt + 2 |
| Open Web search page | Alt + 3 |
| Delete selected folder or file | Alt + 4 |
| Create new subfolder in the open folder | Alt + 5 |
| Switch between List, Details, Properties, and Preview views | Alt + 6 |
| Show the Tools menu | Alt + 7 |

| Table 3-16 | Working with Menus* |
|---|---|
| *Action* | *Keyboard* |
| Display a shortcut menu that shows a list of commands relevant to the selected object | Shift + F10 |
| Display the program Control menu | Alt + spacebar |
| Select the next or previous menu command | ↓ or ↑ |
| Select the menu to the left or right, or switch between a submenu and its main menu | ← or → |

*To choose any menu command from the keyboard, press Alt followed by the letter underlined in the menu name to display the menu. Then press the letter underlined in the command name. As an example, to check spelling, press Alt + T to open the Tools menu, and then press S.*

| Table 3-17 | Working with Toolbars |
|---|---|
| *Action* | *Keyboard* |
| Make the menu bar active | F10 |
| Select the next toolbar | Ctrl + Tab |
| Select the previous toolbar | Ctrl + Shift + Tab |
| Select the next or previous button or menu on the active toolbar | Tab or Shift + Tab |
| As appropriate: Open the selected menu; Perform the action assigned to the selected button; Select an option in a list box or on a menu; Enter text in the selected text box. | Enter |
| Move through options in a list box or on a menu | arrow keys |

| Table 3-18 | Browsing Web Presentations* |
|---|---|
| *Action* | *Keyboard* |
| Move forward through the hyperlinks in a Web presentation, the address bar, and the links bar | Tab |
| Move back through the hyperlinks in a Web presentation, the Address bar, and the Links bar | Shift + Tab |
| Perform the assigned "mouse click" behavior of the selected hyperlink | Enter |
| Go to the next slide | spacebar |
| Go to the previous slide | Backspace |

*These keyboard shortcuts can be used to view a Web presentation using Microsoft Internet Explorer 4.0 or later.*

**Table 3-19**            **Browsing Hyperlinks in a Slide Show**

| *Action* | *Keyboard* |
|---|---|
| Go to the first or next hyperlink | Tab |
| Go to the last or previous hyperlink | Shift + Tab |
| Perform the mouse-click behavior of the selected hyperlink | Enter while a hyperlink is selected |
| Perform the mouse-over behavior of the selected hyperlink | Shift + Enter while a hyperlink is selected |

**Table 3-20**            **E-mail Messages***

| *Action* | *Keyboard* |
|---|---|
| Send current presentation as an e-mail message | Alt + S |
| Open the Address Book | Ctrl + Shift + B |
| Check names on the To, Cc, and Bcc lines against the Address Book | Alt + K |
| Select the next box in the e-mail header or the body of the message | Tab |
| Select the previous field or button in the e-mail header | Shift + Tab |

*To send the presentation as the body of a message, activate the E-mail header by pressing Shift + Tab as many times as necessary. If text within a text box is selected, press F2 to select the text box before pressing Shift + Tab.

**Table 3-21**            **Getting to Help**

| *Action* | *Keyboard* |
|---|---|
| Move between the navigation pane and topic pane | F6 |
| Display the Options menu in Help | Alt + O |
| Display the program control menu | Alt + spacebar |
| In navigation pane, switch to the next tab | Ctrl + Tab |
| In navigation pane, switch to the Contents tab | Alt + C |
| In navigation pane, switch to the Answer Wizard tab | Alt + A |
| In navigation pane, switch to the Index tab | Alt + I |
| In navigation pane, open a selected book or Help topic | Enter |
| In navigation pane, select the next book or Help topic | ↓ |
| In navigation pane, select the previous book or Help topic | ↑ |
| In the topic pane, go to the next Help topic | Alt + → |
| In the topic pane, go to the previous Help topic | Alt + ← |
| In the topic pane, go to the first or next hyperlink | Tab |
| In the topic pane, go to the last or previous hyperlink | Shift + Tab |

| Action | Keyboard |
|---|---|
| In the topic pane, follow a selected hyperlink | Enter |
| In the topic pane, display a topic from a thumbnail | F6, Tab, Enter |
| In the topic pane, scroll toward the beginning of a Help topic | ↑ |
| In the topic pane, scroll toward the end of a Help topic | ↓ |
| In the topic pane, scroll toward the beginning of a Help topic in larger increments | Page Up |
| In the topic pane, scroll toward the end of a Help topic in larger increments | Page Down |
| In the topic pane, go to the beginning of a Help topic | Home |
| In the topic pane, go to the end of a Help topic | End |
| In the topic pane, print the current Help topic | Ctrl + P |
| In the topic pane, select the entire Help topic | Ctrl + A |
| In the topic pane, copy the selected items to the Clipboard | Ctrl + C |

| Table 3-22 | Using the Office Assistant* |
|---|---|
| **Action** | **Keyboard** |
| Display the Assistant balloon | F1, if the Assistant balloon is showing |
| Select a Help topic from the list the Assistant displays | Alt + *number* (Alt + 1 is the first topic, Alt + 2 is the second, and so on) |
| See more Help topics | Alt + ↓ |
| See previous Help topics | Alt + ↑ |
| Close an Assistant message | Esc |
| Get Help from the Assistant | F1 (Assistant must be turned on) |
| Close a tip | Esc |
| Show the Assistant in a wizard, or turn off Help with the wizard | Tab, spacebar |

*To perform most of these actions, the Office Assistant must be turned on and visible. To turn on the Assistant at any time, click Show the Office Assistant on the Help menu. To temporarily hide the tool, go to the Help menu and click the Hide the Office Assistant. Note: Not all wizards have Help provided by the Assistant.

**Book IV
Chapter 3**

**Presenting Yourself
with PowerPoint
Professionalism**

# Chapter 4: Checking Your Calendar

## In This Chapter

✔ Keeping a calendar

✔ Contacting others

✔ Filing data into your address book

hird-party software companies used to offer a number of calendar products, as well as components that come with hardware (like smart cell phones and *personal data assistants [PDAs]*). Microsoft offered calendar features as part of free MSN or Hotmail accounts. And Microsoft's Outlook program has included a calendar function for many years, although it has mostly been used in office settings, not by individual users.

With each new version of Windows and Office, Microsoft has expanded its offerings with creativity and adaptation. So it is with the Calendar function, a software feature that's floated around for a long time but only just arrived as a full-fledged, official component of the operating system with the introduction of Windows Vista.

## Picking a Calendar

Which calendar to use? If your office or organization employs Microsoft Outlook (which isn't the same as Outlook Express), then you may have that calendar system set up and running on your machine.

✦ Enable Outlook, although some of its features are rather heavy-duty tools — kind of like using a backhoe to excavate a flower pot.

✦ Buy and install a third-party calendar program.

✦ Employ the facilities of Hotmail, Yahoo, Google, or other online services.

✦ Use Microsoft's Windows Calendar. This came about with the introduction of the Windows Vista operating system.

## Windows Calendar

The Windows Calendar has several components:

✦ An **electronic appointment scheduler** is the program's heart. Once you enter an event, the system can alert you however many days, hours, or minutes ahead of time. You can also set up recurring appointments: weekly meetings, or rent or mortgage payment dates, and the like.

✦ **Reminders** can pop up on your laptop, or you can integrate your calendar with your lists of contacts so e-mail messages go to invitees or confirmed meeting participants. See Figure 4-1.

✦ Another core component is the **personal task list**. With this you can create a list of things to do, along with deadlines for accomplishing each task, and priority rankings for each event. The to-do list is integrated with your calendar, and it can send you reminders. When you finish a task, you can check it off as completed.

✦ You can set up **multiple calendars** for everyone who uses your laptop — family members or workgroup members. Users of the same computer can coordinate their personal schedules with anyone else who grants them permission to see their calendar.

**Figure 4-1:** The main screen of Windows Calendar stores events, appointments, reminders, and a connection to the Windows Contacts utility.

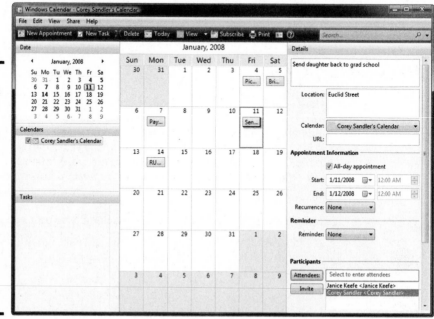

Consider a set of family calendars stored on the same machine. Mom or dad can check out the kids' schedules (at least the information the kids are willing for share with parents) and can add events to their own or to their children's calendar. Appointments from each calendar are color coded so you can easily see who "owns" an event.

As you move deeper into the bells and whistles, it is important to understand that Microsoft has made Windows Calendar fully compatible with the industry-standard iCalendar format, which a number of other hardware and software makers, including Apple, also support. This allows you to easily exchange information from your personal calendar with other Windows Calendar users or with people who use a piece of software compatible with iCalendar data.

You can also subscribe to free or fee-based web sites that accept data in the iCalendar format. However, just because an application accepts data in the iCalendar format doesn't mean it uses all the data you collected or that the information is presented the way you intend. Proceed carefully.

Here are some of the ways iCalendar sharing can work:

✦ Two or more individuals, or an entire group, can publish their personal calendars to an online site that merges the information into a single calendar.

✦ Someone can download another person's information (with permission) so their events and data can be displayed alongside your own in your Windows Calendar on your laptop.

✦ You can set up a shared calendar for a group such as a fundraising committee, a soccer league, a poker club, or a carpool. Publish to the Web and others can see.

✦ You can merge commercially prepared event information into your own Web-based or laptop-based calendar. For example, you could download the Boston Red Sox season schedule so every game appears on your personal calendar, along with less-important events like dental appointments, meetings at work, and mortgage payment due dates.

Calendar information published online can be made open to anyone, or you can grant permission to anyone (or only to those with a password) to read or make changes. Be sure you understand the security process for published calendars before putting any sensitive information online.

From the View menu, you can examine your calendar by day, entire week, work week, or month. From the same menu, click the Details Pane to see all the information you entered; click again to minimize the clutter.

**Book IV
Chapter 4**

**Checking Your
Calendar**

TECHNICAL STUFF

# Knowing where the time goes

I remember being in Taiwan in the early 1980s and observing how much of the nation was gearing up to build its economy around building for the world market their own versions of computer monitors, keyboards, motherboards, and other technological essentials. They said it was an honor to make an improvement to someone else's product.

To Microsoft's credit . . . or to its detriment, depending on how you choose to view the software giant . . . the company has a long history of watching the marketplace and bringing into its own products the best of Other People's Inventions. The time-honored practice didn't start there; think of the automobile industry. Within days after the first car hit the road, hundreds of companies were coming up with their own version of the same thing: faster, better, cheaper, or flashier. You can't copyright or patent an idea (the car, the computer, the electronic calendar); all you can attempt to protect is your own particular expression of that idea.

Microsoft's very first product, MS-DOS, was an adaptation of another company's operating system. Windows was produced in admiration of Apple's Macintosh operating system, which itself came from an idea that came out of a Xerox lab.

For many people, calendars came to the computer by way of PDA (personal data assistant) like the original Palm Pilot and its more sophisticated cousins, BlackBerry and Apple's iPhone. (I long ago gave up using my Palm Pilot but still use its PC-based calendar function on my laptop and desktop.)

The calendar has evolved thusly:

- The original product was an electronic version of a wall calendar. You could enter appointments on particular dates and at specific times and the computer kept track of all of your appointments in a database; you could also print out a schedule for the day or for a week or month. I can still go back at least ten years in my Palm calendar to find out much of the details of my life — at least those I recorded on the calendar. See the accompanying figure.

- The next step was a relatively minor one that rang a bell with many users: adding an alarm clock. If you had an appointment for a phone conference on January 7 at 10:30 a.m., you could assign your calendar to remind you a day before, an hour before, or as a fancy French cook might say, "à la minute," which means at the exact moment you need it.

- From there, telephone began integrating with the calendar. Before the advent of *VoIP (voice over Internet protocol)* telephony, some makers began connecting a calendar to an advanced dial-up modem that could call over the *POTS (plain old telephone system)* wires. That particular feature wasn't much used.

- The fourth generation of calendars, now current on most laptops, includes integration with your office network as well as Internet services. When you start planning a meeting, you can check the calendars of all of the people you want to invite (assuming they've granted you permission to do so), and you can place an appointment on their calendar. Further, the software can send out reminders by e-mail, instant message, or by cell phone text message.

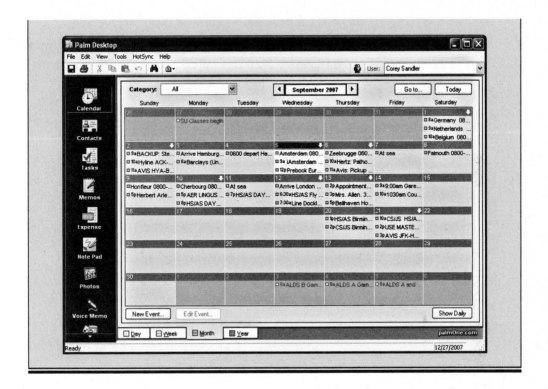

To create an entry, follow along:

*1.* **Click the New Appointment item.**

A mini window opens.

*2.* **Enter a description of the event.**

You can also enter a location. Any information you add here can be searched for from within the program; it's a great way to jump to an old calendar entry or on the schedule for an upcoming date.

*3.* **Set a starting and ending time for an event.**

On the other hand, an event can occupy the entire day.

*4.* **Enter a potential attendee's e-mail address in the Attendees list.**

This invites someone to attend the event.

*5.* **Click Invite.**

## Microsoft Office Outlook 2007 Calendar

Microsoft Outlook may not work so well for individuals and small groups. I don't mean to scare you away, but in my opinion, of all the programs in the Microsoft Office suites, Outlook is one of the least user-friendly software applications.

The Microsoft Office Outlook 2007 Calendar connects just about everything in the Microsoft suite to each other. The calendar is integrated with

✦ Your address book (also called Contacts in Windows Vista)

✦ E-mail settings

✦ The Internet

✦ Most applications (including word processors, spreadsheets, graphics programs, and databases)

You can

✦ Customize the calendar a number of ways with color coding

✦ Select a time slot on the calendar

✦ Determine participant availability based on their calendars (with automatic warnings of conflicts)

✦ Create a meeting description

✦ Send invitations

Invitation recipients can accept, tentatively accept, or decline your invitation online, and you can track responses.

You can share and merge Outlook calendars on a Windows SharePoint Services 3.0 site, a facility used by some large businesses and institutions. Changes you make on your laptop are automatically synchronized with the online calendar the next time you connect to the Internet.

# Making Contact

Does your personal address book have contact names, or does your contact list constitute your address book? This question has no right or wrong answer, although Microsoft introduced a change in terminology with the arrival of Windows Vista.

In previous editions of Windows, the e-mail client (either Outlook Express or Outlook) maintained a database that was called the Address Book. With

Windows Vista, a very similar — but not identical — utility is now called Windows Contacts.

As a user, the changeover doesn't much matter to you. If you upgraded your system from Windows XP to Windows Vista, your address book automatically became a contacts list in the process. You can export the contacts list to a previous version of Windows or other programs that are set up to work with Microsoft's earlier utility.

Do these steps to export Windows Contacts to a version that an earlier Microsoft Address Book utility or another program:

*1.* **Click Export in the Contacts taskbar.**

*2.* **Choose between formats:**

- **CSV (comma separated values)**

- **vCards**

Use CSV for Address Book in Windows XP.

*3.* **From the program where you want to use the file, click Import and specify the data location.**

See Figure 4-2.

In addition to being a simple database for information about your friends and business acquaintances, the Contacts folder functions as the address book for Windows Mail — Outlook Express's successor. In the process of creating an e-mail message in Windows Mail, you can select a recipient from the list maintained by Windows Contacts.

**Figure 4-2:**
The Family tab allows you to track important dates and names of family members or friends and business acquaintances.

**Book IV
Chapter 4**

**Checking Your
Calendar**

**Figure 4-3:** The main tab can hold professional and personal information; you can also upload a photo to remind you of the face behind the e-mail address.

Here are the items of information that each Contacts page can store:

✦ The contact's full name, along with a job or professional title and a nickname. See Figure 4-3.

✦ One or more e-mail addresses. You can store as many e-mail addresses as you want for a contact; one as the default e-mail address, which your program uses unless you tell it otherwise.

✦ A photo, uploaded from your system.

✦ Home address, wired and cell phone numbers, and personal or business web sites.

✦ Work address, phone numbers, web sites, and job-related information such as job title, department, and office location.

✦ Family information (including a helpful reminder of an acquaintance's gender — Is D.J. a him or a her?), plus birthdays and anniversaries. (As the saying goes: One of the keys to success in life is sincerity. Once you can fake that, you've got it made.)

✦ A blank Notes page for any information that helps you conduct business or personal affairs with your contact.

✦ Digital IDs. You can add the equivalent of a signature to messages to "sign" a document for legal or business purposes. A digital ID can also encrypt messages.

## Importing contacts into your Windows Contacts

Windows Contacts can accept data saved in these formats:

✦ .wab

✦ LDIF (LDAP Data Interchange Format)

✦ VCF (vCard)

✦ CSV (comma-separated values)

To bring contacts into Windows Contacts, follow these steps:

**1. Click the Windows button and type** Windows Contacts **in the Search box.**

This is the easiest way in Windows Vista to open Windows Contacts.

**2. Click the Import button.**

The button's at the top of the Contacts window. See Figure 4-4.

**3. Select the type of file you want to import.**

**4. Go to the file and click Import.**

Note that any existing .wab files on your machine are automatically converted to Windows Contacts format if you upgrade from Windows XP to Windows Vista.

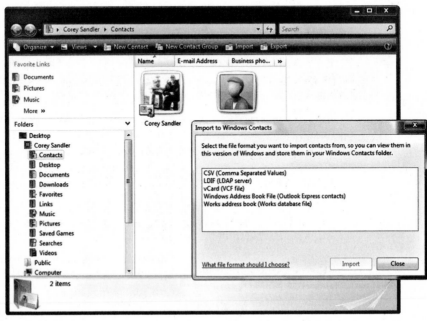

**Figure 4-4:** The Import and Export functions of Windows Contacts are available as buttons directly located on the main screen of the program.

## *Exporting address information from Windows Contacts*

To export addresses from Windows Contacts, click the Export button from the program's main screen. This saves information in either CSV or vCard format. (Note that no built-in function directly saves Contacts files in Windows Address Book format; you have to export in one of the supported formats and use the conversion function available as part of Windows XP.)

Some third-party programs — commercial as well as freeware — promise to convert files of one type to another. Some programs can import an Excel file.

# *Going Old School with Address Book*

If you're still working with Windows XP or earlier editions of the Windows operating system, you will find the similar Address Book available — although hidden a bit deeper.

You can open the Windows Address Book several ways, including going to the command line prompt and entering WAB.EXE. For most users, though, an easier route is this:

*1.* **Open Outlook Express.**

*2.* **Click Tools ⇨ Address Book.**

Windows Address Book is delivered as a companion piece to Internet Explorer; Windows Contacts comes as part of the Windows Vista operating system. Either way, Windows users are likely to find one or the other on their machine.

The Windows Address Book is similar to the newer Windows Contacts utility, although it hues much closer to the concept of a just-the-address book. It lacks some of the features available to Windows Vista users, including recording digital IDs, notes, birthdays, and photo posting.

You can add names to the address book manually, or you can automatically record the address of someone who sends you an e-mail. Here's how to simplify that process:

*1.* **Open an e-mail message from someone you want to add to the Address Book.**

*2.* **Right-click the user's name.**

*3.* **Click Add to Address Book.**

If you have more than one e-mail address for a single individual or organization, you have to identify one as the default address; unless you instruct the e-mail client to use one of the alternate addresses, all outgoing mail goes to the default address.

4. **With the book open, click the Name tab.**

5. **Add any information you choose.**

You can tell the system to automatically add an e-mail address to your Address Book anytime you reply to a message. This assumes that you consider the person or organization worthy of inclusion in your book:

1. **Click the Tools menu in Windows.**

2. **Click Options.**

3. **Click the Send tab.**

4. **Select Automatically Put People I Reply to in My Address Book.**

To send a message to someone in your address book, you have two options:

✦ Start typing in the first few characters of the person's name. The system attempts to fill in the rest of the address from the book. The more characters you enter, the more specific your instruction can be.

✦ Open Outlook Express (or another e-mail client that works in a similar manner) and, in the To field, click the small icon that looks like an open book. You also can get to addresses for the Cc: and Bcc: fields.

## Importing contacts into your Windows XP Address Book

The standard format for data stored in a Windows Address Book (WAB) is a .wab file. You can export a WAB's contents on one machine as a .wab file and import it into a WAB on another machine. It's as easy as it sounds . . . right?

You also can bring in data from other programs that use data storage formats that Windows Address Book can convert:

✦ Netscape Communicator

✦ Microsoft Exchange Personal Address Book

✦ Eudora Pro

✦ Eudora Light Address Book (through version 3.0)

✦ LDIF-LDAP data interchange format

✦ Any text file saved as a .csv (comma-separated values) file or other similar format

Going the other way, if you're using a third-party address book program, see if it can export its information to a .wab or .csv format. If so, perform that step, save the file in a particular location, and then import the file into the Windows Address Book.

Once Windows Address Book is open, here's how to import a file:

1. **Click File ⇨ Import.**
2. **Click Address Book (WAB) option.**

   This brings in a file saved in that format.

   Or, click Other Address Book to display a list of alternate formats.
3. **Click the name of the address book format you want to import.**
4. **Click Open.**

## Exporting contacts from your Windows XP Address Book

To output a file that can be used by other Windows Address Book programs or by third-party software that can accept data from it, do the following:

1. **Open Windows Address Book.**
2. **Click File ⇨ Export.**
3. **Click Address Book (WAB) option.**

   This saves a copy of a file saved in the .wab format.

   Or, click Other Address Book to save a copy in either the Microsoft Exchange Personal Address Book format or as a .csv text file.
4. **Select where you want to store the file.**
5. **Click Save.**

# Watching It Fly

Your laptop's clock function is one of those things you can pretty much count on working all by itself; it doesn't need winding, automatically corrects for Daylight Savings Time, and can even be instructed to check its time against the mothership at Microsoft.

When you install Windows, or when you configure a new laptop fresh from the store, one of the important questions that even a computer can't figure out is this: What time zone is it in? (Yes, I'm certain the next generation of laptops will include built-in GPS functions, but for the moment you've got to tell the machine where you've brought it for activation.)

However, once you turn your machine on and install and activate Windows Vista (or Windows XP), it is pretty capable of keeping time. Microsoft has included a function that automatically adjusts for leap year and Daylight Saving Time when appropriate, and if you enable it, your machine can go out onto the Internet and synchronize its clock with a highly accurate reading at a Microsoft facility or an official time-keeping laboratory (such as the National Institute of Standards and Technology).

With the introduction of Windows Vista, Microsoft added the ability to have as many as three clocks available for display in the taskbar; configure them by double-clicking the clock in the taskbar and selecting settings for one, two, or three displays. One can be the "normal" time where you laptop usually resides, while a second can be the current time at a branch office anywhere in the world, and the third can be set to be the local time where you are anytime you travel. See Figure 4-5.

**Figure 4-5:**
The clock function in Windows Vista has been expanded to permit the display of as many as three different times of day in different parts of the world.

# Book V

# Playing with Multimedia

The 5th Wave          By Rich Tennant

ADVANCED COMMUNICATIONS IN THE LUPINE COMMUNITY

"Woo!"

# Contents at a Glance

# Chapter 1: Walking Through Windows Media Player

## In This Chapter

✔ **The master of all media**

✔ **Playing a CD or DVD**

✔ **Ripping music from a disc**

✔ **Managing digital rights**

The first personal computer, and the first laptop computers, were about as communicative (to humans) as the beeps and squawks uttered by the famed "Star Wars" robot hero R2D2. My first IBM PC was capable of little more than monotone beeps: You had your short beep, your long beep, and your combination short-long or long-short beeps.

The original IBM PC of 1981 was intended as a tool for small business, and the idea of a computer as a musical instrument, a music player, a video recorder, or a video player wasn't even a pipe dream. The purpose of the tiny speaker in the computer was primarily to give audio cues during the system boot and to provide a few beeps for the primitive early games.

Remember (if you can) that even the VCR was a hot new product at the time; Sony first came to market with its Betamax system in 1975 and the competing (and ultimately triumphant) VHS format arrived a year later. It took until about 1988 before computer manufacturers began to consider giving the PC a voice. Early companies in the field included Creative Labs, which continues as a premier device maker; it was only within the past few years that motherboard manufacturers began adding sound circuitry as a basic component.

Today nearly every laptop computer comes with a set of chips that can reproduce music, voices, and effects in a range of quality that runs from mediocre to superb. Laptops suffer one significant disadvantage in comparison to desktop computers: There is little room to install decent-quality speakers in a system where engineers have worked for years to trim every possible inch and ounce out of the box.

## CDs and DVDs to PCs

Compact disc technology was introduced a few years after the first PC and it took a while before the technology was adapted to deliver data in a computer. The first DVDs (an acronym for one of two almost-forgotten names: *digital video disc* or *digital versatile disc*) were delivered to home market in the late 1990s, moving over to computers a few years later.

Modern laptops have moved past the beeps and boops. Computers can talk to you, reading text or delivering messages. They can play music from a CD. As noted, most laptops today include built-in circuitry to add sound features to the motherboard. A relatively small number of machines have a sound adapter card slot, and there are options for external sound adapters that attach to a USB port or plug into a PC Card or Express Card slot.

I discuss a few hardware options later in the chapter, but first I deal with the software side of the equation. And let me begin by introducing an all-encompassing word adopted by Microsoft that seems to apply to all things that aren't numbers or words: They call it *media* and it's the centerpiece of the Windows Media Player.

What is *media?* Today's definition includes music, sounds, digital images, digital video, and *streaming* (imported) versions of sound, music, and video that arrive in your laptop over the Internet or through an external device (such as an electronic musical instrument, a video or audio player, a camera, or a microphone).

Windows Media Player (WMP) has plenty of alternatives, including Apple's QuickTime and Real Network's RealPlayer. All of them work well, and more or less in the same way. In this chapter, I concentrate on Microsoft's WMP since that software is delivered as a component of Windows XP or Windows Vista.

## Sounding Out Windows Media Player

The essence of Windows Media Player is an electronic control panel to organize and play digital media files. Beyond that it lets you

✦ **Burn** CDs with copies of music stored on your laptop

✦ **Rip** music from a CD to store the files on your machine

✦ **Sync** (pronounced *sink*) your digital media files from your laptop to a portable music player like an iPod

And you can spend money within the program with a link to online stores. There you can buy digital media content and download it to your laptop.

## Playing an audio or video file

Windows Media Player can play any digital media file stored in one of its accepted file formats; the media can be located in your Player library, elsewhere on your computer, in a folder on a machine on a local area network, on a folder on a machine accessible over the Internet.

Is your audio or video file too fast, too slow, or distorted? The first step in troubleshooting quality problems in files processed by Windows Media Player is to determine if your system is using the most appropriate, current drivers for its sound card or sound chips. See the manufacturer's web site or check for driver updates on the Windows Update web site (www.windows update.microsoft.com).

### Playing a file from your Library

Follow these steps to play a file stored in your WMP Library:

1. **Click an icon in the upper-left corner of the WMP window.**

   This chooses a media category. When you click, the icon changes to indicate your selection:

   • A pair of musical eighth notes for music

   • A tiny framed image for pictures

   • A frame of film for video

   • A small television for recorded TV

   • A combination of a musical note and a small picture to indicate other media

   WMP keeps your last selection the next time you return to the program.

2. **Click the Library tab at the top of the window.**

3. **Browse or search for the item you want to play.**

4. **Click + drag the item(s) to the List pane.**

   You can drag

   • Individual items (a song, a sound, a video clip)

- A group of items (gathered by clicking with the pointer on multiple items while holding down the Ctrl key)

- Collections of items (items sorted into categories such as albums, artists, genres, and other information or ratings)

If the List pane isn't visible, click the Show List Pane button (a large blue arrow). The button is to the right of the WMP search box. If the arrow points to the left, the pane isn't displayed; if it points to the right, clicking the arrow removes the List pane.

If the List pane already contains items, you can remove all of them at once by clicking the Clear List Pane button (a stylized red X at the top of the playlist).

5. **Double-click an item to begin playing it.**

If you selected a group or collection, all the items play; to select a single item only, drag the item to the List pane instead.

Right-clicking a track opens the way to a Properties window with details about the bit rate and other details of the recording, in this case a subpar 128 Kbps disc.

Some audio or video files contain *markers,* which are like tracks on a CD or chapters on a DVD. If the file you selected has markers, you can jump to any section by selecting a marker, and play audio or video from that point:

*1.* **Click the View menu (part of the Classics Menu).**

*2.* **Point to File Markers.**

*3.* **Click the marker you want.**

The WMP includes electronic versions of the familiar VCR control buttons. The large right-facing triangle starts the selected item; once a piece of music or video is playing, that icon changes to a pair of vertical bars that function as a pause button. On either side of the play/pause button you find a button that returns to the start or end of a file. And finally, all the way to the left is a square box that stops things. See Figure 1-1.

If you're playing a recorded video, an added control sits just above the VCR-like buttons. You can grab the Seek slider with the onscreen pointer and move it left to back up to an earlier part of the video; move the slider right to advance to a later section. You may find it difficult, if not impossible, to grab hold of the little blue Seek button as it moves; click the pause button to freeze the image and then move the slider.

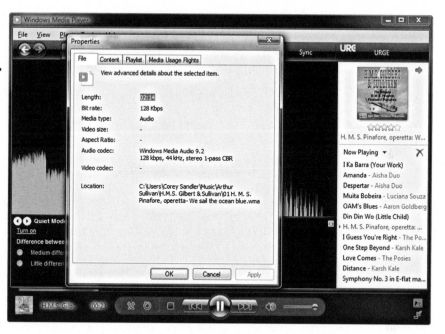

**Figure 1-1:**
Windows
Media
Player has
identified a
CD inserted
into the
drive on my
laptop (a
relatively
antique and
certainly
obscure mix
of operettas)
and is ready
to play it.

## Playing a file from outside your Library

To go directly to a collection or an individual media file somewhere on your
laptop, the easiest method is to instruct WMP to show the Classics Menu.
The menu bar gives you quick and easy access to most WMP options,
including ones not shown in the player's standard buttons.

*1.* **Press Ctrl + M key.**

If it's not already, the Classics Menu view turns on and the menu bar
appears.

*2.* **Click File ➪ Open.**

*3.* **Highlight the file you want to play.**

*4.* **Click Open.**

## Playing a file from a web page or at a network location

Windows Media Player can control a file that lives on a web page, at a
location on the Internet, or on a local network.

To play a file on a web page, click the link on the web page.

To play a file on the Internet by entering the *URL* (its Web address) to the file, follow along:

*1.* **Press Ctrl + M.**

*2.* **Click File ⇨ Open URL.**

*3.* **Type the file's URL.**

*4.* **Click OK.**

## Rocking the CD or DVD hardware

Way back in the days of old, you needed a separate CD player to play a music disc. And for you really old folk, there was this thing called a *record player* that used vinyl platters and a tone arm with a diamond-tipped needle the converted little squiggles on the platter into sound waves, at least until the needle finally wore a hole in the platter. And you also used to need a DVD player to produce a movie's video and audio. Before then there was the suitcase-sized VCR, and before that? Well, you had to watch a television set or actually leave your house to go to a movie theater.

But I digress: Today's modern laptop computers are pretty close to being the master of all media. A built-in optical drive can play high-quality music or display high-resolution images from a nearly indestructible disc (because its digital information is read by pulses of laser light).

As delivered, Windows Media Player can play audio CDs or data CDs that contain music or video files. It can also display files written to *video CDs (VCDs)*. VCDs are similar to DVDs, although the images' quality and size aren't as large and the disc capacity is about ⅛ that of a DVD.

To play a DVD in your laptop, you need a DVD drive and the appropriate DVD decoder software installed in your system. Some decoders are set to work only with their own DVD player software, while others work also within Windows Media Player.

You can — within the range of capabilities of your tiny laptop speakers — adjust some of the music's tonal qualities and range by using the graphic equalizer that is part of WMP. See Figure 1-2. The graphic equalizer adjusts the relative strength of the audio signal across its range from bass (in this case, 31 Hz) to high treble (16 KHz). You can also choose various effects that make your music visual, in the case of Figure 1-2, a fountain-like display that would be right at home out front of a Las Vegas casino.

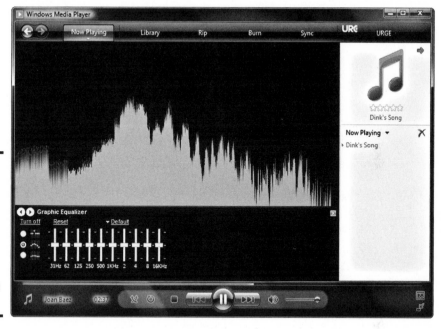

**Figure 1-2:**
Adjusting the relative strength of the audio signal across its range from bass to high treble.

## Controlling a CD with WMP

Start the player first, and then insert a CD into the laptop's optical drive. In most situations, your system is set up to start playing within WMP when it automatically recognizes the presence of a disc.

If the disc doesn't automatically *load* (start), or if you installed the disc into the drive before you started WMP, follow these steps:

*1.* **Click the arrow below the Now Playing tab.**

*2.* **Click the letter or name of the drive that contains the disc.**

The CD starts playing from the beginning. However, if you'd like to skip one or more tracks on a CD, follow these steps:

*3.* **Click the Now Playing tab.**

*4.* **Click the Next button.**

The icon shows two right-facing arrows and a single bar — the designer's way of indicating fast-forward to the next section.

If you change your mind and want to hear a song you skipped, double-click the song in the playlist. It plays immediately.

5. **When you're done, find the disc's name in the Navigation pane.**

6. **Right-click its name.**

7. **Click Eject.**

   This stops the disc and ejects it from the drive.

## Controlling a DVD with WMP

Start the player and put a DVD into the drive. Your system is probably set up to start playing within WMP when it reads the disc.

### Playing chapters

You can play video on WMP with these steps:

1. **Start the player.**

2. **Insert a DVD into the laptop's optical drive.**

   If the disc starts automatically, skip to Step 5.

   If the disc doesn't automatically *load* (start), or if you installed the disc into the drive before you started WMP, follow Steps 3 and 4.

3. **Click the arrow below the Now Playing tab.**

4. **Click the letter or name of the drive that contains the disc.**

   The video starts playing from the beginning. However, you don't have to be a slave to the order. Skip to different parts with these steps:

   • To choose individual sections of DVD, click a DVD title or chapter name in the List pane.

   • To choose a specific part of a VCD, double-click a VCD segment in the List pane.

5. **Right-click the disc's name in the Navigation pane.**

6. **Click Eject.**

   This stops the disc and ejects it from the drive.

### Playing special features

DVD creators can add from a palette of special features; Windows Media Player supports most of them. Among them you may find are playing special features on a DVD such as foreign language dubbing, subtitles, "director's commentaries" that substitute for or augment the actors' words, and parental controls.

To play special features on a DVD, follow along:

*1.* **Click the DVD button.**

*2.* **Click Root Menu.**

The Root Menu is called Title Menu on some systems.

*3.* **Click the Now Playing tab.**

*4.* **Click the links to any available special features.**

*5.* **Click the DVD button and then click Close Menu.**

This starts or resumes playback.

On some DVDs you can simulate a camera-angle adjustment. (Actually, it's more of a viewing angle if you think about it, but they didn't ask me when they named the feature.)

Click the DVD button.

Select Camera Angle if it's available.

Choose the viewing angle you want to use.

Follow these steps to use parental controls for DVDs:

*1.* **Sign in as the administrator for your laptop.**

*2.* **Create a Limited or Restricted user account for each person who'll use the laptop with parental control settings applied.**

If you don't set up your computer with Windows user accounts and passwords, you're double-locking the front door while leaving the back door wide open.

*3.* **Start Windows Media Player.**

*4.* **Click the arrow below the Now Playing tab.**

*5.* **Click More Options ➪ DVD tab ➪ Change Settings.**

*6.* **In Select a Rating, select the highest Motion Picture Association of America (MPAA) rating that you want users with Limited/Restricted accounts to watch.**

As an example, if you select PG, the user with that account can't watch a DVD with a more restrictive rating, such as PG-13 or R.

## Standard file types for WMP

Windows Media Player plays back files recorded in many — but not all — of the most common formats for audio, video, and images. You can add supported file types by installing their codecs as supplied by third-party companies or by Microsoft.

A *codec* is a piece of software that compresses or decompresses (co-dec) a digital media file.

If you're looking for additional codecs, Microsoft recommends visiting www.WMPlugins.com to search for officially endorsed system expansions; they warn that installing codecs from other sources may cause incompatibilities, file corruption, and dandruff. Okay, I made up that last serious medical issue, but the other two problems are the sort of thing you want to avoid.

Table 1-1 shows the standard file types that Windows Media Player works with.

| Table 1-1 | Windows Media Player Files | |
|---|---|---|
| *File* | *Abbreviation* | *File Format* |
| Audio CD | cda | Audio |
| Windows Media audio | asx, .wm, .wma, .wmx | Audio |
| Windows audio | .wav | Audio |
| MP3 Audio | .MP3, .m3u | Audio |
| Windows Media | .wm, .asf | Video |
| Windows Media video | .wmv | Video |
| Windows video | .avi | Video |
| Microsoft Recorded TV file | .dvr-ms | Video |
| Movie file | .mpeg, .mpg, .mpe, .mlv, .mp2, mpv2 | Video |
| Compressed image files | .jpg, .jpeg, gif | Picture |
| Tagged Image File | .tif, .tiff | Picture |
| Bitmap | .bmp | Picture |
| Windows Metafile | .wmf | Picture |
| Portable Network Graphics | .png | Picture |

What important file types are missing from this list? If your digital camera stores images in a RAW format, files of that sort aren't supported by WMP; you should be able to change the camera settings to TIFF or JPG or use a different graphics program to process them. Also not supported: animated GIF files, which you can view only as still images.

## Setting Windows Media Player as default program

As a multipurpose "player," you can set up WMP as the default program for specific media types or for all its supported file formats. You can also make an AutoPlay setting so WMP is automatically used to playback CDs or DVDs that you put into your laptop's optical drive.

To assign WMP as the default player for a particular type of file, do the following:

*1.* **Open a folder that contains a file of the type you want to change.**

*2.* **Right-click the file you want to change, and then click Open With.**

*3.* **Click the name of the program you want to use to open this file automatically.**

*4.* **Select the Always Use the Selected Program to Open This Kind of File check box.**

If you'd rather not have WMP as the default, deselect the check box.

*5.* **Click OK.**

## Menus, tabs, and classical music

Microsoft's engineers spent years trying to make every Windows application and utility look and act more or less the same; with the arrival of Office 2007 and Windows Vista they began to get jiggy with it. Windows Media Player is one of the products that has group-related tasks under tabs or in ribbons that mutate based on the tasks you're currently performing . . . or on the system's guess about what you're about to do next.

In WMP, the old menu bar is still available even though Microsoft no longer wants to use that name; they call it the Classics Menu. The quickest way to show Classic Menus is to open Windows Media Player and press the Ctrl + M key combination. Press the same keys to go back to the future.

If you want to get to the same place by a slightly more complex route, do this:

*1.* **Right-click an empty area of the taskbar.**

*2.* **Click Show Classic Menus from the popup mini-window.**

Good empty places include just to the left of the Now Playing tab or a blank space to the left or right of the playback controls. To hide the menu bar, reverse the steps and remove the check mark next to Show Classic Menus.

WMP tabs are displayed even if you also turn on the Classics Menu bar. You can base your commands on the method that works best for you. In my experience, the tabs work best for preset commands, while the menu bar is the most efficient way to get into the program to make changes to settings or configuration.

The standard tabs follow:

✦ **Now Playing.** Here you can initiate the play of a CD or DVD, choose a *visualization* (you might call it a picture or an abstract image that pulses in time with the music), shuffle items on your play list, repeat songs on the list when all have been played, change volume and other audio settings, or switch to full-screen mode.

✦ **Library.** This section provides access to your digital media collection and offers tools to organize them. Click one of the items in the address bar (on the left side of the window) to choose among music, pictures, or video. You can also create, edit, or delete *playlists* (collections of music sorted in any manner you choose).

✦ **Rip.** Here's the doorway to taking digital files from a CD and making a copy on your hard disc for other purposes. You change settings, including the file format and the *bit rate* (the amount of information collected per millisecond of audio).

✦ **Burn.** Once you create a playlist, you can burn it to an audio CD for replay in a home or car stereo system or other device. This tab also includes adjustments to settings for the quality of the CD (including some basic audio-editing features such as making the volume of all songs equal across the entire disc).

✦ **Sync.** Here you can bring songs back and forth between devices you might attach to you laptop, including portable music players and memory devices.

✦ **Media Guide.** This gateway goes to an expanding number of online stores that are ready, willing, and happy to sell you their services, including individual song tracks, entire albums, or online streaming services including satellite radio (converted to an Internet stream).

# *Rip It Good*

*Ripping* is the process of copying music from an audio CD to a computer. If you use WMP to rip music, it reads the digital information on the disc and stores a copy on your hard disk as a WMA (Windows Media Audio) or MP3 file. Both of these file formats use compression to reduce the size of the files; in doing so, some of the original CD's quality is lost, although not all listeners can tell the difference between an original and the copy.

Once you rip a file, you can play it directly from its storage place on the hard disk or download it to a portable music player (like an Apple iPod or a Microsoft Zune). You also can burn the files to a CD as a personal mix or as a copy of the original CD.

Be aware that most music, video, and other *intellectual property* is copyrighted and may be sold with a license that limits its use. For example, the book you're holding in your hand is copyrighted by the publisher, who has purchased that right from the author. You have the right to read the book, give it to someone else, or resell it, but in general you don't have the right to photocopy its contents or scan it into digital form and store it away from the book itself.

In general, it's considered acceptable to rip a disc that you own but not so legal to make a copy of someone else's music.

The verb *rip* word contains a hint of its probable origin: "ripping off" something that doesn't belong to you. That may or may not be the case in your own system. The thinking behind the legal hair-splitting is this: If you're making a copy of something you own and don't sell or give away the original, you still are only able to play the music on one device at a time. But if you copy a disc and give it to someone else or share the digital file over the Internet, two or tens of thousands of people could play the music at the same time, and that wasn't expected by the music owner when it was sold in the first place.

Windows Media Player 11 doesn't support copying the contents of copy-protected video DVDs.

Ripping a file is as easy as a click:

*1.* **Place a CD in your laptop drive.**

WMP may immediately start playing the first song on the disc.

You can rip a file while it plays, or you can stop playback and individually select the tracks on the CD that you want to copy to the laptop.

*2.* **To stop playback, click the Now Playing button**

*3.* **Click the VCR-like square box.**

*4.* **To rip a file, click the Rip button.**

The software lists all the tracks on an audio CD; for nearly all CDs, the program can communicate with a Microsoft or third-party server for information about the disc including, in many cases, an image of the cover art. See Figure 1-3.

Windows Media Player adds ripped files to your Player Library. During Windows installation, by default that location is set as \MUSIC under the user name currently signed in (for example, C:\Users\Corey Sandler\Music). You can change the storage place for ripped files by displaying the Options dialog box. (Display the Classic Menu toolbar, click Tools ⇨ Options ⇨ Rip Music tab.) See Figure 1-4.

**Figure 1-3:**
To rip a file in Windows Media Player, click the Start Rip button at lower right; you can select individual tracks or copy the entire disc.

If you change the storage folder for ripped files, WPM can apply those changes — as well as a change to the naming style — to any files already in place.

To change previously ripped files, follow along:

1. **Display the Classic Menu toolbar.**

2. **Click Tools ⇨ Options ⇨ Rip Music tab.**

   The Options dialog box appears.

3. **Click the Library Tab.**

4. **Select the following check boxes:**

   • Rename Music Files Using Rip Music Settings

   • Rearrange Music in Rip Music Folder, Using Rip Music Settings

Once you rip a file, you can't use Windows Media Player to change the file format between .wma and .MP3, or make an alteration to the bit rate. You must instead either rip the file again or use an audio-editing program.

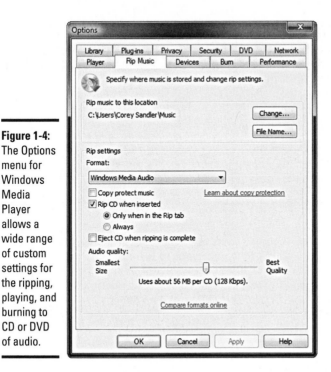

**Figure 1-4:**
The Options menu for Windows Media Player allows a wide range of custom settings for the ripping, playing, and burning to CD or DVD of audio.

# Managing Rights

When you buy an operating system or a program or a piece of music, you're purchasing the right to use the product. In most cases, squadrons of lawyers stand at the ready to come after you waving lawsuits if you try to use the digital information in ways not intended by the seller (such as making unauthorized copies or incorporating part or all the information in a product of your own).

Some companies don't even sell you the product. Instead, you're licensed to use the product in certain specific applications but aren't given ownership.

## Microsoft Digital Rights Management

Microsoft, which is also in the business of selling intellectual property in the form of software, has included Microsoft *Digital Rights Management (DRM)* technology in WMP version 11. The protection rights are for content owners; if DRM is applied to a track on a CD or on a file you downloaded from an online store or other source, you must have media usage rights to play, burn, or sync the music. This area is in the process of being defined. If this particular form of licensing takes hold, sellers of music or video may sell unlimited or limited usage rights along with the files.

### IP

*Intellectual property (IP)* is a product of the mind. For example, the book you're reading was concocted by your humble author and the copyright on that intellectual property is held by the publishing company. When you buy this book you're paying a small amount of money for the paper and ink, but the largest portion of the expense goes to pay the author, the editors, the designers, and the publishers for their creative efforts. As a buyer you own the paper and the ink; you can recycle it as papier mache if you like. But you don't own the ideas and research within.

If Windows Media Player tries to use a protected file that's missing rights, or if the rights have expired, WMP will attempt to acquire the rights by communicating with the seller online. If you tell WMP not to automatically check for content rights, the program will stop and ask you to obtain them anytime it doesn't find permission to play or repurpose a media file.

Follow these steps to turn off automatic rights acquisition:

*1.* **Click the arrow below the Now Playing tab.**

*2.* **Click More Options ⇨ Privacy tab.**

*3.* **Clear the Automatically Check If Protected Files Need to Be Refreshed check box.**

## Rights management for downloaded content

Online music sellers, an industry that seems on the path to replacing most, if not all, traditional CD sales, have also experimented with various DRM technologies. Some sellers have added DRM, then taken off the restrictions; a few have experimented with selling songs with and without the limitations at differing prices.

As a user, be sure you understand what rights you're buying, and be aware that (at least in theory) it may be possible for a copyright holder to track down the source of pirated music all the way to the first violator.

WMP also works with a Microsoft service intended to assist users who purchase media usage rights for files licensed to one computer or device that the owner wants to *migrate* to a different computer. The program communicates with a Microsoft server that, in effect, unregisters the link to the original computer and reregisters it on another machine. The DRM seller can limit the number of migrations; in some designs, the user may enable a file on more than one machine, provided only one copy is in use at one time.

# Chapter 2: Feeling the Music, Seeing the Stream

## In This Chapter

✔ **Bringing music into your laptop**

✔ **Upgrading your laptop to work around audio limitations**

✔ **Plugging into external headphones and speakers**

✔ **Streaming some media**

Current laptop computers are extremely capable multimedia devices: They can play CD audio, DVD movies. They include inputs for external audio sources and outputs that send signals to stereo systems and other devices. That's the good news. The not-quite-so-good news, as noted in Book I, Chapter 1, is that a laptop's small boxes don't have a whole lot of real estate.

Designers have managed to squeeze an amazing amount of hardware onto a laptop motherboard, including integrated sound-adapter circuitry that generates a broad range of audio signals. The quality of a typical laptop's audio signal is generally equal to that generated by a desktop machine with a sound card.

A few shortcomings exist:

✦ Even the most high-end laptops don't have enough room for a decent set of speakers. The Toshiba Satellite P205 demonstration machine used as this book's example includes an above-average system: a pair of recessed speakers labeled Harmon/Kardon, a brand name that should impress many audiophiles. The speakers themselves, about the width of a quarter, are pretty impressive but no one's going to confuse their sound with a decent desktop speaker system, especially one with a subwoofer unit that sits on the floor.

✦ A motherboard with built-in audio circuitry performs well in playback but is extremely limited — or utterly incapable — when capturing certain incoming audio sources (as it is for many desktop computers as well). For example, on most systems, you can't capture streaming audio or video and in some configurations you're also limited to capture sound coming into your laptop from a line source (such as an external CD player or stereo).

# What You See Is What You've Got

On modern laptops, the trend is to offer more and more all-purpose inputs and outputs — primarily USB but also FireWire ports — while minimizing the number of dedicated connectors such as serial, parallel, and media input and output ports.

The advantages of all-purpose ports are many:

✦ The port functions at higher speeds than older connections.

✦ You only have to worry about one type of connector.

✦ The wiring supplies power as well as data interchange.

The Toshiba Satellite P205, an example of a very well equipped, middle-of-the-pack laptop, comes with just two audio jacks:

✦ A headphone output, which can power headphones and earbuds as well as external speakers that have their own power source to amplify the sound.

✦ A microphone input, which can accept input from a compatible external microphone. And in certain designs (including Toshiba's), the mike input also works with most line inputs, including the low-level amplified output of an external CD player, a tape recorder, a television set, and the line output of a stereo system.

A *line input* is a constant-level signal provided by an amplifier that the laptop can adjust. This is different, for example, from a microphone input, which accepts a signal that varies in strength based on loudness or other characteristics.

Don't send a high-wattage, amplified signal into your laptop. (A stereo system, for example, usually offers both an amplified and a line output; use the line option.) Although laptop designers claim to the computers can accept most audio signals, you don't want to damage your machine by testing just how strong a signal is too strong. When in doubt, get an external sound card with a line input.

# Working Around Audio Insufficiencies

What do you do if your laptop falls short when it comes to audio features?

## Get back jack

Some older laptops (and a handful of current machines specifically intended as multimedia processors) include a dedicated line input to allow you to bring all sorts of audio input into the machine. Some of these laptops also had old-style red, green, and yellow circular RCA jacks — like the ones on the back of a VCR — that let the computer output a signal directly to a stereo system or a television set. (Red and green were left and right audio signals, and yellow was the composite video signal.)

The first thing is remember that with a laptop — any laptop — comes a compromise: You're buying a lightweight, portable, and *highly integrated device*. That means designers have squeezed a whole lot of stuff into a very small space, and usually little — if any — provision is made for internal electronics modifications. By contrast, most desktop machines are much more versatile. They're designed to be taken apart, and they include extra expansion slots for devices — like a high-end sound adapter — that you can plug directly into the system bus.

But workarounds solve many problems.

Any of the following solutions adds line input and output plugs, bringing in sound from other electronic devices or sending output to them. Some of the expansion devices add bells and whistles, like support for 5.1 channel surround-sound speaker systems.

### Rounding out with a sound card

You can purchase and install a sound card that plugs into the PC Card or Express Card slot on your laptop to replace the limited sound circuitry on the motherboard. Sound cards add features, quality, connectors for different types of devices, and enhanced software to capture sound. (This home-theater specification places speakers at left and right front, left and right behind the playback device, one center channel speaker at front, and a separate nondirectional subwoofer speaker for bass effects.)

As an example, the SoundBlaster X-Fi notebook adapter plugs into an Express Card slot and brings a full blast of features. A slightly less capable sound card that uses a PC Card is the SoundBlaster Audigy 2 ZS.

### Speaking of a USB sound device

This solution isn't quite as elegant because the device is external, but it's every bit as effective. The USB sound adapter, about the size of a deck of cards, draws its power from the laptop and exchanges data over the USB cable to the laptop.

If you install a sound-card upgrade to an Express Card, PC Card, or USB slot, you may have to disable the built-in sound circuitry on your laptop's motherboard; this avoids conflicts between resources and software. In most cases you can disable the built-in circuitry through the setup screen for the system BIOS. (Check the instruction manual for your laptop or watch for a brief message on its screen as it boots to learn the key to press to display the BIOS setup. Common choices include F10, F2, or the Esc key.)

## Adding Capture Software

Most laptops with audio circuitry built into the motherboard are deficient in one important area: Music-capture programs often can't grab the audio stream. There's no particular technological reason for this; I've owned laptops with no such restriction. However, modern laptop marketers have sought to come up with a reason for buyers to pay several hundred dollars (or even a few thousand dollars) extra for a premium machine. One of the things they've done is place artificial limitations on some built-in facilities.

Solutions exist:

✦ If you're adventurous you may find software or hardware drivers that unlock the capabilities of built-in hardware. Take care before experimenting with any such unauthorized alteration to your system; set a System Restore point for the operating system and keep notes about any changes you make so you can undo them if your efforts make things worse than they were.

✦ If you're not as adventurous, buy an add-on sound adapter that includes its own software suite. These adapters may install in a PC Card or ExpressCard slot or attach to the laptop by cable to a USB port. As an example, most sound hardware from Creative Labs includes utilities that capture any sound passing through the adapter. (Creative calls this setting the "What U Hear" option.) Other software elements include a *wave* editor that lets you enhance, edit, or sample portions of any recording stored in one of the recognized sound formats, including .wav files. See Figure 2-1.

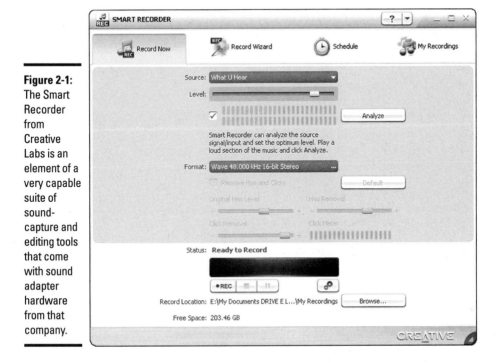

**Figure 2-1:**
The Smart
Recorder
from
Creative
Labs is an
element of a
very capable
suite of
sound-
capture and
editing tools
that come
with sound
adapter
hardware
from that
company.

# Plugging into External Speakers and Headphones

If you've listened to an Apple iPod pumping music through a tiny set of ear-buds, you realize the incredible power and clarity that can be delivered to your ears when they're nearly in direct contact with a set of headphones. No distortions are caused by the shape of the room, furniture, or the television playing in the next room; you also can't hear the horn of an oncoming car . . . which is one really good reason not to use headphones of any kind while driving.

You can purchase just about any set of headphones that matches the plug size. (Typically laptops have a 3.5mm mini-phone stereo jack; 3.5mm is also sometimes described in English measurement as ⅛ inch and the two specifications are interchangeable.) And more and more headphones have USB port connections, which allow them to draw a bit of electrical power along with the audio signal; you will likely have to install a device driver to instruct your laptop to send music or sound through the USB channel instead of to the headphone jack.

Any well-stocked electronics store (Radio Shack, Best Buy, and Circuit City amongst them) should be able to sell you a converter that allows you to insert plugs of one size or shape into a port of another design. Among the common converters are ¼-inch to ⅛-inch (3.5mm) plugs. You can also purchase extension cords that allow headphones to operate at a distance from the source of music.

Old-style studio headphones with earmuff-sized cans on each ear generally require larger connectors and require more power to operate; in any case, you'll have a hard time finding these old-school devices at your basic home electronic shop.

If you've got the space in your carrying case, or if you use your laptop at your desktop when you're off the road, the best solution may be to purchase a set of external speakers. These plug into the headphone port on your laptop or into the USB port. External speakers require electrical power to amplify the audio signal to an acceptable level. The more sophisticated the speaker system, the more power they generally require.

External speakers can get power three ways:

+ Through the USB port. This delivers a maximum of about 5 volts and as much as ½ an amp of power, although all devices sharing the USB chain also share the power. And even more significantly, this draws power (and shortens run time between recharges) any time the computer is running off its battery.

+ From built-in replaceable or rechargeable batteries. External speakers can be powered by their own batteries, which typically deliver a few hours of use.

+ From power supplied by a separate AC adapter. If you're using external speakers at your desktop or on the road, the best solution is to use speakers that draw power from their own AC adapter. These speakers can be larger, louder, and offer better sound quality.

# Poring Over Streaming Media

*Streaming audio* or *video* is a signal that comes over the Internet or other network on request; for example, you can listen to a radio station by connecting to a streaming site. This is different from downloading a package of music or video, sent to you as a file, that you store on your laptop and then play. You can subscribe to streaming video of baseball games, audio of radio stations from around the world, or listen to Internet-only music stations.

## Pointing to 'casting

Streaming media uses the still-evolving and still-expanding Internet to let you use all three means of transmission. (See this section's "Radio days" sidebar.)

✦ Point-to-point

✦ Narrowcasting

✦ Broadcasting

Instant messaging is an example of point-to-point, and video conferences are available from laptop to laptop (through the services of companies like AOL as well as specialized business service companies). Web sites like YouTube let you request a point-to-point feed of a video (produced by an amateur or professional or even a commercial or political organization seeking to sell a product, candidate, or idea).

Subscription services sold over the Internet are an example of narrowcasting. For example, you can purchase a subscription to listen to "radio" coverage or watch video coverage of Major League Baseball games, or you can subscribe to music services like XM Satellite Radio, which comes down off the satellite, onto the Internet, and into your laptop.

And broadcasting is becoming more and more popular on the Internet. Most of the major television and cable networks now let you watch their productions on their laptops. Some of these shows are offered *on demand,* meaning a signal is being sent from point to point; other shows are simply made available to any computer user who does the Internet equivalent of tuning into a live feed of a news or entertainment feed.

Radio stations also put their broadcasts on the Internet — a great way to keep up with events in your old hometown or to monitor the local coverage of a major event from far away. And we've begun seeing a number of customizable radio stations that allow you to select particular artists or genres and receive a stream of music to your laptop. One example is Pandora, which delivers free music accompanied by onscreen ads; another example is AOL Music, which delivers music occasionally interrupted by commercials.

## Knowing the nuts and volts of streaming

Here's what you need to receive, listen to, or view an Internet stream:

✦ A modern laptop computer running

- A current version of a media-capable operating system, such as Windows Vista or Windows XP.

- A fully updated Web browser such as Microsoft's Internet Explorer, Mozilla's Firefox, or other software.

# Radio days

Think way back to the early days of radio, like the 1880s when German physicist Heinrich Hertz performed his research on electromagnetic radiation (called at the time *aetheric waves* or *Hertzian waves,* and now more commonly known as *radio waves*). Jump forward a few decades and consider the practical implementation of many of those ideas by Italian-American inventor and businessman Guglielmo Marconi, who began his experiments in Europe and then crossed the channel to Canada and then America.

By 1904, Marconi had a small commercial service that communicated with ships at sea, and in 1912 the *S.S. Titanic* had company-trained telegraphers aboard the ship on its maiden (and only) voyage. One of Marconi's employees — involved with monitoring the rescue efforts for the *Titanic* — was a young man named David Sarnoff, who went on to pioneer commercial radio at the Radio Corporation of America (RCA), the forerunner of today's NBC network.

What's the thread here? Hertz was sending a signal from a single transmitter to a single receiver; even though the process is a lot more complex today, essentially that happens when you communicate by Instant Message (IM) from one computer to another — the information isn't meant to be shared with others.

Marconi began his work with sending a signal to and from an identified group of clients — ships at sea and land-based stations. That's similar to what you might call *narrowcasting.* The information is out there and available, but not intended for the public at large.

And then Sarnoff helped launch what you now know as the broadcast industry. From one source — a network at first — a signal is sent into the ether for anyone and everyone to receive and use. From NBC came "Fibber McGee and Molly" and "Burns and Allen" and other early megahits of radio.

Regularly update your Web browser with current versions of video enhancements such as Java. Some web sites warn you if the necessary software isn't found on your machine, and then direct you to install it.

✦ A broadband Internet connection, such as one received via a cable modem, fiber-optic signal, or DSL connection; your computer may be directly connected to the incoming feed with an Ethernet cable or may be indirectly connected — at a slightly slower speed — through a WiFi wireless link. (Dial-up telephone connections are no longer worth considering when it comes to working with Internet media.)

✦ A sound card or built-in sound processing circuitry on your laptop's motherboard.

✦ A decent set of speakers, either built-in or external.

✦ A video adapter, video memory, *and* a video processor capable of generating a high-resolution moving image.

✦ A high-resolution LCD to show the image.

✦ A full-strength, up-to-date firewall and antivirus program (discussed in detail in Book IX). Anytime you open a door between your computer and the outside world (especially if you leave it open for an extended period, as when you're accepting a continuous stream of information) you expose your machine to infiltration attempts by mischief makers and evildoers.

# Chapter 3: Hamming It Up for the Webcam

## In This Chapter

✔ Broadcasting from your rec room

✔ Looking at webcam's hardware and software sides

✔ Adding an external webcam to a laptop

*A*rtist Andy Warhol entered the book of famous quotations in the 1960s when he somehow looked into the 21st century and said, "In the future everyone will be famous for fifteen minutes."

How in the world did he imagine YouTube, streaming video feeds from network television, and the fact that I can sit here at my laptop and smile for the webcam built into frame above the LCD and narrowcast myself from here on my little island to anywhere in the world capable of receiving a broadband Internet signal? I can be famous for fifteen minutes . . . or all the time.

Other than self-aggrandizement and inflation of my ego, what purpose does a *web camera (webcam)* serve?

✦ Recording an audio and video e-mail to send to family. (Remember how Dr. Heywood Floyd kept in touch with his wife and daughter back home on earth in the classic film, *2001: A Space Odyssey?* Just like that. Only from your den to your mother's kitchen.)

✦ Producing your own sales pitch, instructional video, or personalized message for a business client or prospect. (Here, let me show you how great our pearl-inlay sushi knife cuts through the Buffalo phone book in one slice.)

✦ Starring in your own entertainment/political manifesto/ego trip of a video to post on a website that tells all sorts of unimaginably personal details available to anyone and everyone in the world to see.

✦ Posting your own travelogue based on videos and still pictures taken with your camera, cell phone, or even the laptop itself.

✦ Peeking into your home or office while you're somewhere else in the world. Is the dog on the sofa again?

# Casting about for Hardware

You must have three essentials before you can send video from your laptop:

✦ **A webcam.** It can be built into the computer itself, as is the case with this book's demonstration machine, the Toshiba Satellite P205, which has a 1.3 megapixel camera installed in the LCD's upper frame. See Figure 3-1. Or you can purchase a separate camera that attaches to your laptop through the USB port; you may set up the camera to clip on to the top or side of the LCD or you may sit it by itself on your desktop.

✦ **A broadband Internet connection.** Video, whether streamed live or transmitted as a file, demands a great deal of space on the hard disk or on the Internet connection.

✦ **Software to control the camera.** Sophisticated applications adjust the brightness and contrast, sharpen the image, perfect the colors, and package up the results for streaming to the World Wide Web or attaching to an e-mail.

If you really want to get fancy about it, you can also add a video-editing suite that lets you carve up video shots with your webcam — or from any other video source — and edit it into a mini movie.

## Camera Assistant Software

In this chapter I use as an example product called Camera Assistant Software (CAS), which is a capable generic program supplied by Toshiba to support the built-in webcam (made by Chicony) in many of its current laptops. Other camera and software combinations work in a similar fashion.

You can launch the CAS toolbar from the taskbar, or (in its default configuration) have it lurk just off the left side of the LCD; just hover your onscreen pointer in its home area and it appears, ready to open the camera lens and apply other controls to its use.

You can drag the toolbar to another location onscreen or assign menu options to a specific location at top, left, or right. Right-click the toolbar to display an Auto Hide option to keep the controls out of the way anytime you aren't using them.

The following CAS options appear similarly in most other basic camera-control programs.

### Preview

Start Camera turns on the video system; you see a preview image on your screen. The video isn't being recorded or streamed at this point.

TECHNICAL STUFF

## Zoom a zoom zoom

Four-hundred percent (4X) zoom is called a *digital zoom* and is made by cropping a section of the image sensor and electronically enlarging the picture — it's not as sharp or clear as the result you get from an optical zoom that uses an adjustable lens, but then again, you're working with a tiny camera-on-a-chip not much bigger than a pinhead.

## Effects

Apply some special pictures and icons to your video with Effects. Want to include a Valentine's heart, a bouquet of roses, or a big red set of lips? Like to add a filigreed or flowery frame to the image? These effects and others are offered here.

## Properties

In CAS, you can adjust the lens zoom between normal, or 100 percent, and 400 percent (4X).

In Figure 3-1 you see the lens as the tiny bright spot at the top of the LCD frame. On the laptop screen you can see me poking my digital camera through the light tent in my studio to photograph the computer photographing me.

**Figure 3-1:** I turned on the built-in webcam in the Toshiba Satellite P205 laptop.

Other options include the ability to horizontally flip an image — removing the mirror effect you see when you look at a screen that shows the image through the camera lens. You can also flip an image vertically; somewhere out there is a problem for which that's the solution.

You can compensate for flicker in an image caused by slight differences in electrical systems around the world. In North America and most of the rest of the world, power alternates 60 times per second, also called 60 hertz or 60 Hz; if you're in one of the few places that use 50 Hz, you might experiment with changing this setting.

Adjusting the flicker setting compensates for the changes in lighting caused by light bulbs running on alternating current (AC), including fluorescent bulbs; the laptop itself is running on direct current (DC) power provided by its adapter.

Some camera software programs can *pan* the image slightly to the left or right or up or down. You can, of course, accomplish pretty much the same thing by moving the laptop on your desk or adjusting the angle of the LCD screen with a built-in camera.

CAS also includes a night mode that boosts the exposure levels for dim lighting (although the pictures are of lower quality) and a backlight compensation setting.

## Settings

CA's advanced options let you adjust the quality of digital snapshots, video, and audio captured through built-in or attached devices. See Figure 3-2. In general, you want to use the highest resolution for pictures, the fastest frame rate for video, and the highest sampling rate for audio. However, you must consider several issues:

✦ You can't capture images or audio at qualities greater than the CA hardware's capabilities. Cameras are limited by the resolution and sensitivity of the image sensor, as well as the quality of the tiny lens, while you can't compare the quality of the small microphone to a sophisticated studio recording device.

✦ The frame rate for video and the compression rate for audio or video is related to the speed of the laptop's microprocessor and available RAM.

✦ The type of file formats supported are set by the designers of the control software.

✦ Files created using the highest resolution, frame rate, or sampling rate *and* a file format that doesn't compress are going to be significantly larger, compared to lower-quality selections.

**Figure 3-2:**
The Options tab of the CAS Properties window allows you to adjust zoom, flip the image horizontally or vertically, and compensate for flicker caused by differing AC electrical cycle rates.

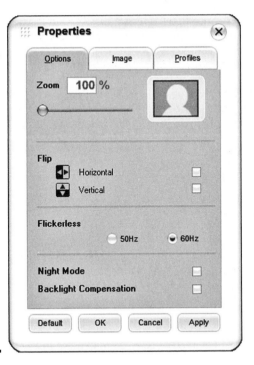

As an example, the CAS program on this book's sample Toshiba laptop allows picture capture at a resolution as high as 1280 × 1024 — equivalent to about 1.3 megapixels of information. At the low end, you can capture images at a setting of 160 × 120, which may only be appropriate for uses such as a background image for a cell phone. CAS permits storage of still photos as compressed JPEG files, PNG files (which use a lossless compression scheme), as well as uncompressed BMP bitmaps.

A *lossless* compression scheme promises to reduce the size of the file without causing any degradation in the quality of the image; compare this to a *lossy* compression which may result in some loss of quality. If you save a file in a lossy compression style, such as JPEG, and then reopen the file for further editing, the quality will continue to degrade each time you save the file.

A high frame rate for a video capture smoothes the image flow onscreen. The traditional frame rate for motion pictures is 24 frames per second (fps), and most television broadcasting uses technologies that emulate the same sort of capture rate. At 24 fps and higher, the human eye doesn't notice the flicker of the spaces between the frames; at lower rates, movement appears choppy or streaky.

A slow frame rate of 1 fps makes no attempt to offer the illusion of smooth movement, but could be useful in monitoring a scene over a long period of time: spying on your cat over an eight-hour day . . . or even more sneaky endeavors. (Don't break any laws, please; personal privacy laws are increasingly strict.)

## Upgrading Your Laptop to Add a Webcam

While many current laptops come equipped with a tiny webcam and microphone, you can easily add external hardware to a modern machine. External webcams and microphones often deliver higher-quality images and add flexibility: You can place the camera far from the laptop or hold it in your hand to use it like a movie camera.

Among uses of external webcams: capturing high-quality images of people for use in creating ID cards or an online database of faces. This sort of arrangement is now commonly used for checkpoints at entrances to buildings or events, and many hotels and cruise lines capture an image of the faces of their guests to help with security.

Standard external webcams plug into a USB port on a laptop. You can also purchase devices that communicate wirelessly using a WiFi network.

Consider, for example, Microsoft's LifeCam Web Camera. The golf ball–sized unit captures video at as much as 1.3MP resolution (1280 × 1024) at 30 fps; you can set still-image resolution as high as 5MP (2560 × 2048), equal to most consumer-grade digital cameras. The camera automatically adjusts for low-light conditions and also offers pan and tilt options.

The Linksys Wireless-G Pan/Tilt/Zoom Video Camera sends live video to a WiFi system and from there to a local network or out onto the Internet. See Figure 3-3. It includes advanced MPEG-4 video compression to produce a high-quality video stream at a high frame rate and resolution of as much as 640 × 480. Video features include an *infrared (IR)* filter cut, which allows you to capture images in low light when using an IR lamp. You can take and save snapshots (in JPEG format) of the image. A security mode can instruct the camera to send an e-mail message with an attached short video whenever motion is detected in the field of view.

**Figure 3-3:**
You can
control the
Linksys
WCV200
wireless
camera
from afar
over the
Internet.

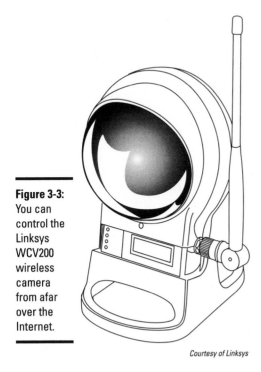

*Courtesy of Linksys*

# Chapter 4: Gaming with a Laptop

## In This Chapter

✔ **Gaming to the outer fringes**

✔ **Tricking out a laptop for gaming**

✔ **Extreme processors and laptops**

*L*et us together agree on two very important and quite disconnected facts:

✦ The first computers were designed for very mundane tasks like totaling up the profits at an ancient Babylonian tag sale or mechanizing the manufacture of a knitting mill.

✦ Given the chance, nearly every man and woman will attempt to turn even the most sophisticated of tools into a toy.

Therefore, it comes as absolutely no surprise that as soon as the first personal computers began arriving in homes and offices, games began to arrive on computers. Among the first: simple card games like solitaire, basic shoot-em-ups, and simple adventure games that used keyboard commands and the player's imagination to conjure up an imaginary world of twisty, turny passages and bizarre underworld creatures.

And then, it should be even less a surprise that when the first laptop computers arrived in the marketplace, the push was on make them available as portable gaming machines (in addition to managing huge product databases, human resources files, and e-mail on the road).

## Stuffing a Wild Laptop

In many ways, a modern laptop computer is a mini-me version of a desktop computer: It can do (or be adapted to do) anything a full-sized computer can. The solution isn't always neat and elegant, though. The original concept for a laptop was to bring together all the disparate pieces of a desktop machine — keyboard, mouse, monitor, and speakers among them — into a single, small, two-part box.

Today a laptop lets you play most any game available on a desktop. The trick, though, is this: finding a way to play the game at a speed, volume, and clarity that equals or surpasses the capabilities of a desktop machine fully tricked out with upgrade, accessories, and doodads.

The good news: It's possible. The bad news: You need to start with an absolutely top-of-the-line laptop, and you're going to have to spend a lot of money to buy it and upgrade it. If your idea of computer gaming is Solitaire, you don't need to read any further in this chapter. If you're looking for 3D, multiplayer, fully immersive games with surround sound, get out your checkbook.

Basically, you need a laptop with no compromises. Most laptops are designed to be lightweights: small, simplified components that sip very shallowly from the supply of electrical power stored in their battery. None of these are concerns for desktop makers, and most game designers don't give much (if any) thought to the amount of power and real estate their games demand. They want to astound users with graphics and sound and action . . . not portability.

For instance, some people are perfectly happy with a little car with two seats and a tiny trunk, powered by a hamster cage of an engine that runs for hundreds of miles on a few gallons of gasoline; that pretty perfect specification is for a vehicle that's for point-to-point commuting and it makes eminent economic and ecological sense. But then there are people who, for reasons that vary from real necessity to issues of ego and irrational competitive urges, must own either a street-legal race car that guzzles gas like a drunken sailor or a monster truck capable of carrying a herd of cattle. You clearly don't need a cattle truck to drive from your home to the convenience store to pick up a bag of chips, and a race car looks cool — but very silly — caught up in bumper-to-bumper traffic at rush hour.

But back to gaming: If you want to use your laptop to play Halo 2 or Madden NFL Football or to take part in a massive nationally networked role-playing game, you just might need a laptop that looks like a Hummer with the horsepower of a Ferrari under the hood.

Here's your Top Ten shopping list for a laptop that you use for some serious gaming:

+ **The fastest and most powerful microprocessor you can find.** You don't want to compromise on a processor whose primary selling feature is the fact that it draws less power, generates less heat, or costs less money.

+ **Lots of RAM.** The more the merrier, up to the maximum supported by the motherboard, the processor, and the operating system. On many modern laptops that means 2GB to 4GB. Oh, and be sure to use the fastest design of memory supported by your system.

+ **A high-speed advanced graphics card.** The basic built-in graphics chips offered on most laptop computers just doesn't cut it when the future of the entire human race is threatened by an incoming Argrulikan Triple-Twisted Death Ray Beam. For the best performance, you want a laptop that comes with a built-in graphics card with its own video memory; a tiny handful of specialized laptops even allow the manufacturer to customize the system with the card of your choice (provided a shrunken version installs within your laptop's case).

✦ **A full-featured sound card.** This is more a want than a need, but if you're serious about gaming you're not going to want to settle for the basic facilities of sound chips on the laptop's motherboard; you're going to want SoundBlaster or similar circuitry added to the system. Advanced audio features include *spatial imaging,* which is a bit of electronic magic that can make sounds seem to move from place to place or to originate from behind.

✦ **An amplified, external set of speakers.** Although some laptops now offer sorta-kinda acceptable speakers in the case, they can't come anywhere close to the strength, volume, and clarity of a large set of external speakers with their own powered amplifiers. If you're going to use your laptop at home or another fixed location — or if you don't mind carrying a suitcase packed with a set of speakers — you can attach external speakers, including 2.1 systems (left, right, and subwoofer), 3.1 (left, right, center, and subwoofer), or 5.1 (left, right, center, rear left, rear right, and subwoofer). Another alternative: a high-quality set of headphones that bring the hiss and rumble of the death ray directly into the recesses of your ear canals.

✦ **A gaming controller.** Most action games need this, because a touchpad just isn't sufficient when it comes to saving the world from demons.

✦ **A large, fast, hard drive.** Modern games can occupy tens of gigabytes of storage space, so you need the room. And they go back to the hard drive regularly to load more scenes and characters, so you want a drive with a fast transfer speed. Today's fastest hard drives spin faster (7,200 or 10,000 rpm) and use advanced protocols like serial ATA (SATA) to move data. On the horizon (and in a few early systems already) are solid-state "drives" that store information in non-moving flash memory; they're not quite as fast as a hard drive in certain circumstances but they hold promise for the future.

✦ **A speedy, fat pipe of a network.** You can enjoy many modern games as multiplayer contests with participants all over the world. Another class of games resides on a central server, with players signing on to look in and join from wherever they are. And finally, many games offer regular updates delivered to players over the Internet. In each of these cases, you need a fast broadband connection like those delivered by a cable modem, DSL modem, or fiber-optic system. An old-fashioned, dial-up telephone connection just won't cut the mustard . . . or stop that death ray.

✦ **A large, colorful, and quick-reacting high-resolution display.** The high end of the laptop market offers LCDs that are taller and wider with each generation. (At the same time, the serious road warrior continues to look for smaller and lighter machines; after a week on the road, every ounce of plastic and silicone feels like it weighs two pounds.) But, again, you can plug an external big-screen LCD or monitor into your laptop; heck, you can even attach your laptop to a big-screen HDTV or projection TV.

✦ **An appropriate cooling system.** All of this power — the fast processor, the large memory block, the extra graphics and audio cards, the fast-spinning hard disk — generates a great deal of heat within the laptop case. To protect the electronics, the system needs fans, passive heat-transfer devices and other technologies to keep the innards cool . . . or at least not melt-down hot.

✦ **Sufficient power.** If you run all of the preceding devices (including cooling fans) from your laptop's built-in battery, you can't expect to run very long without a recharge. Plan on getting a second battery or a source of AC power to run your machine when you sit down to play games.

## Extreme processors for laptops

The first few generations of laptops were basically shrunken versions of desktops: smaller motherboards, tightly packed with components, and space for an off-the-shelf microprocessor.

As users began to make a pair of contradictory demands — more speed and longer running time from battery power — engineers had to scramble. The two leading processor makers, Intel and AMD, began introducing versions of their CPUs specifically aimed at laptop designers' needs, including low power draw and reduced heat production. Among the tricks they employed were processors that adjusted their speed to match the particular task they were performing.

And, of course, when it comes to laptops designed for advanced gaming, engineers faced extreme challenges. Running games requires a tremendous amount of horsepower, a huge block of RAM, and a high-performance video and audio subsystem.

### Intel's Extreme Edition processors

Among Intel's latest offerings specifically aimed at gaming laptops are chips in the Intel Core 2 Duo Extreme Edition series. As an example, the X7800 is a CPU based on the Merom processor design. Officially rated at a processing speed of 2.6 GHz, the X7800 is delivered *unlocked,* meaning that designers (and techie users) can *overclock* the chip to higher speeds.

The real restriction on speed of an unlocked processor is the system's ability to cool off the chip and the laptop's interior.

### AMD Turion 64 X2 processors

AMD's equivalent to Intel's work is the AMD Turion 64 X2 dual-core family, mobile versions of the desktop AMD64 processor line. AMD emphasizes the processor's ability to work with multiple threads of information simultaneously; different programs or different elements of the same software can access specialized elements of the two cores of the processor at the same time.

The process for manufacturing AMD Turion 64 mobile technology emphasizes thermally efficient processor operation, enabling reduced power consumption during various system performance states and sleep states. And there is an additional C3 Deeper Sleep state to improve performance, reliability, and security of existing and future virtualization environments. What, you might ask, is a virtualization environment? It's a current technical buzzword for systems that make groups of computers, storage devices, or other hardware act as if they were merely one.

## An extreme gaming laptop

If you've got the money, someone out there will have the product of your dreams. You may find what you're looking for at the high end of the line for a major laptop maker — like Dell's XPS brand or certain models in Toshiba's Satellite series — or you may need to buy from a specialty computer maker like Alienware. See Figure 4-1.

Alienware began as a "boutique" maker of ultra-high-end laptops and desktops for gamers. In 2006, the company was purchased by Dell Computer with promises that it would continue to operate on its own, with its own product line and out-of-this-world designs and engineering. Thus far the promise has been kept.

One example of one of the most advanced laptops for gaming enthusiasts, as this book goes to press, is the Alienware Area 51 m9750. The system is powered by an Intel Core 2 Duo T7600 processor running at 2.33 GHz with 4MB of cache. The primary differences between an Alienware laptop and a machine meant for the mass market are two:

✦ The machine is capable of including some very advanced components including multiple graphics cards.

✦ You can easily customize the machine before or after purchase.

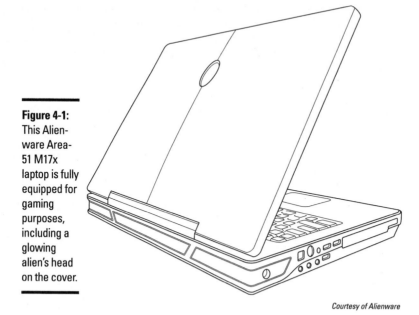

**Figure 4-1:**
This Alien-
ware Area-
51 M17x
laptop is fully
equipped for
gaming
purposes,
including a
glowing
alien's head
on the cover.

I constructed a gaming laptop of my dreams based on available components from Alienware. In addition to the processor, here's the machine I configured:

✦ Video cards: Dual NVIDIA GeForce 8700M GT adapters, each with 512MB of dedicated video memory.

✦ Memory: 4GB Dual Channel DDR2 SO-DIMM RAM.

✦ Display: 17-inch WideUXGA 1920 x 1200 LCD with Clearview Technology.

✦ Operating system: Windows Vista Home Premium.

✦ Hard drive: 200GB drive running at 7,200 rpm.

✦ Optical drive: 2X Blu-ray writer/DVD±RW burner.

✦ Wireless Network Card: Internal Intel PRO Wireless 3945 a/b/g mini-card.

✦ Sound card: Creative SoundBlaster X-Fi Xtreme Audio.

✦ Media center: Remote control and ATSC TV tuner.

✦ Mouse: Logitech V450 laser cordless mouse for notebooks.

✦ Game Controller: Alienware Dual Compatible Gaming Pad.

✦ External speakers: Logitech Z-5300e 5.1 280-watt speakers.

Oh, and it comes in a "stealth black" case that looks like a flattened version of Darth Vader's helmet and they throw in a free Alienware baseball cap and mousepad. The price for this ultimate toy, in early 2008, was $4,998 . . . more than three times the price for a typical high-end business machine, but this isn't a typical business machine.

At the same time Alienware offers a version of the same machine with a 64GB solid-state drive, a block of flash memory with no moving parts. Figure 4-2 shows the bottom of the Alienware Area-51 M17x. Two graphics adapters are at top left, two RAM module slots are centered, and a pair of hard disk drives are at lower right. The large open compartment at bottom left is ready for insertion of a high-capacity battery.

**Figure 4-2:**
Under the
access
panels at
the bottom
of the
Alienware
Area-51
M17x.

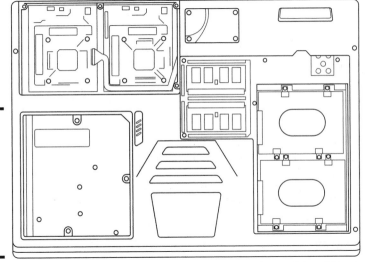

*Courtesy of Alienware*

# Book VI

# Managing Your Power Supply

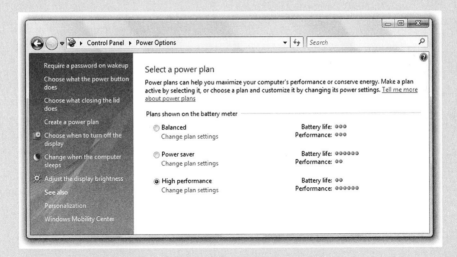

The Windows Vista Power Options window lets
you choose from three laptop power plans.

# Contents at a Glance

# Chapter 1: Using Your Power for Good Purposes

## In This Chapter

✔ Learning your ACs and DCs

✔ Adopting an adapter

✔ Keeping your battery in tip-top shape

*Y*ou know that the biggest difference between a laptop and a desktop computer is that one's designed to be moved from place to place and the other is pretty much consigned to staying put. It's like the difference between a bicycle and a lounge chair. (You can sit on both. . . .)

The other difference — and this is more important to some users than others — is that a laptop is for using when you're away from a standard electrical wall outlet. Some users transport their laptops from a desk in one office to a desk in another (even if it involves eight hours of flying) and never use the machine in between. All they need is an AC adapter and a wall outlet with juice.

But the rest of us live the mobile life. When I leave my desk, I usually continue my work on the ferryboat (island life is such a bother), then fire up the laptop once again on an airplane, and finish my day in a hotel room checking e-mails and baseball box scores. And sometimes I run my laptop in the rental car to look up driving instructions or to make a change to a presentation.

Here's how your laptop can get its power in any one day:

✦ AC outlet. Overnight, I top off the charge in the built-in batteries using wall current. And when I'm at the gate in the airport, the second thing I look for (after I find out just how far behind my schedule my plane will be) is a wall outlet to restore as much power as possible before squeezing into seat 36B.

Some airports are more accommodating to laptop-toting customers than others, offering special areas with desks and a whole row of AC outlets. Other places, though, make wall outlets as easy to find as a free meal in coach class. Carry a small, lightweight multi-outlet power strip in your laptop bag. If you find only a single AC outlet, and some punk is powering up his iPod, politely request he allow you to install the power strip and share. It's a nice way to meet tech-savvy people, too.

✦ Battery power. Between AC outlets, the laptop runs on its rechargeable batteries. Depending on the model, the type of battery, and the tasks you perform, most machines can run from two to four hours.

✦ Airline power sources. Some airlines offer either DC or AC outlets at some seats.

✦ Automobile power sources. Many laptops can draw DC power from outlets within cars. You can purchase a DC inverter to produce AC power for your adapter. And finally, some new cars now offer a built-in 110-volt AC outlet.

# Adapting to AC

The purpose of an AC adapter is to change the current that runs your lightbulbs, television set, and the air pump for your inflatable holiday tableau of a life-size Santa Claus and eight reindeer (plus Rudolph) into a different kind of power for your laptop.

The current that comes from your wall outlet is relatively high-voltage AC current. The internal circuitry of your laptop requires low-voltage DC current to do its thing. Your laptop can run off the AC adapter's power when you have it plugged in at your desk. Or it can get its juice from a battery that you can recharge by the very same AC adapter.

What's inside the AC adapter? It's actually a relatively simple device, if you've got a basic understanding of electricity, electronics, and physics. Right . . . you don't really care, do you? All you want is the juice to power up your laptop.

Here are the basics: An AC adapter consists of three parts.

## Electrical cord

A standard electrical cord attaches to an AC outlet at one end and the laptop's AC adapter at the other. (See Figure 1-1.) Depending on where in the world you live, the end of the cord that attaches to the power source can be any of more than a dozen different designs.

✦ In the United States, Canada, Japan, much of the Caribbean and Central America, and scattered other places around the world the plug has two flat blades (like the one in Figure 1-2). Sometimes a third round grounding connector is there. This design is for use with current ranging from 100 to 120 volts.

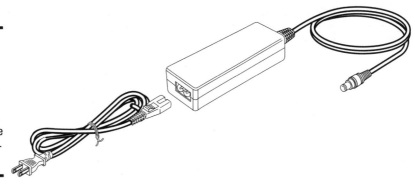

**Book VI**
**Chapter 1**

Using Your Power
for Good Purposes

**Figure 1-1:**
The incoming power to an AC adapter comes in on a detachable and replaceable cord.

✦ In most of the rest of the world, wall current ranges between 220 and 240 volts, and different types of plugs are used. Some have round pins arranged in a triangular pattern, some have round mail power pins and circular female grounding points, and a large number of plugs (throughout the United Kingdom and countries influenced by the Brits over the last century) use two horizontal and one vertical blade.

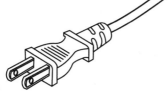

**Figure 1-2:**
A two-blade AC plug.

*Courtesy of Toshiba America, Inc.*

## Permanently attached cord

At the other end of the adapter, in most designs, you'll find a permanently attached cord. This delivers the reduced-voltage, rectified current (more about these terms in a moment) from the adapter to the laptop computer itself.

The plug at the end of this cord matches the attachment point within the laptop. (See Figure 1-3.) Not all plugs are the same; partly this avoids unfortunate accidents where a user might try to use an improper adapter with a particular laptop. (The wrong adapter could deliver too much or too little DC voltage, or could deliver the voltage with its polarity in the wrong place. If you look very closely at the specifications on the back of any AC adapter, you see a little diagram that shows whether the positive side of the current flow comes from the core of the connector or from its outer shield.)

**Figure 1-3:**
The DC end of the adapter is usually designed to make it difficult (but not impossible) to use the wrong power supply with a particular laptop.

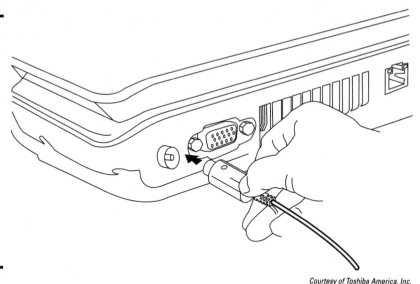

*Courtesy of Toshiba America, Inc.*

Always use the AC adapter designed for your laptop's particular brand and model, or a third-party adapter from a reputable company that specifically recommends its device for your computer. Don't assume that two adapters that look similar will deliver the same voltage to your laptop.

## Adapter proper

In the middle is the adapter itself. For reasons lost to the winds of time, it's called an AC adapter; I guess it got that name because it *adapts* alternating current to direct current. It would have been just as understandable to me if it were called a DC adapter, since it outputs direct current to the laptop. Or you could (as some manufacturers do) call it an AC/DC adapter. In any case, this black box sits between an incoming AC power cord and an outgoing DC power cable.

Inside the box are two main components:

✦ A device that *transforms,* or switches, the voltage. As I noted, AC wall current is generally either about 110 or 220 volts, and most laptops are looking for about 15 to 20 volts.

✦ A *rectifier* that changes AC to DC.

Modern laptops generally use sophisticated switching power supplies that are capable of accepting AC power anywhere in the range of about 100 to 240 volts and outputting a stable and clean voltage that meets the needs of the laptop internal battery charger and the circuitry of the computer itself. They generate little heat and usually function without problem for many years. The only downside: They're usually relatively large — about the size of a flashlight.

Cheap little adapters like those you might use with a cordless telephone or an inexpensive radio may use old technology that involves spools of different lengths of copper wire that induce a reduction in voltage as they move from one to the other. They also burn off a great deal of the voltage in the form of heat. In general, they're inefficient, bad for the planet, and present a real (although very rare) risk of causing a fire.

Voltage conversion is just half of the adapter's job. The other assignment is to rectify and filter the voltage.

Think of AC current as a continuous series of rising and falling waves; the rectifier's job is to square these up into a continuous one-way flow. The most common design uses an electronic device called a *diode* that squares up the power. The final step is to filter the DC current to remove any remaining fluctuations or wobbles related to its AC origins. Most designs employ a capacitor for this purpose. Think of it as a can of electrons; it allows power to settle in for a few tiny fractions of a second and then lets the calmed power flow out the other end.

## Depending on a Battery

A battery is, by its very nature, a dynamic device. (That's a hoot-and-holler pun for engineers; if you get the joke you just might be a geek.)

What I mean is that a battery is changeable and volatile. It can accept an electrical charge and hold it for a while, and then discharge it as needed. How much of a charge? How long will it hold it without dissipating? And how long can its parcel out its electrons before it goes flat?

The answer to all of these questions: It depends.

✦ **On the battery's design and size.** Today's most common design uses a technology based on Lithium Ion chemistry, sometimes called LIon. These batteries can pack a lot of power in a small, relatively lightweight cell. And then the designers can choose to use 4, 6, 9, or however many cells they feel is powerful enough but not too heavy as to turn a laptop from a lightweight contender to a heavyweight champion.

✦ **On how many batteries are in your laptop.** Some cases are designed to accept one battery plugged into a compartment on the underside, with a second battery installed in a multipurpose bay on the side. (The same bay can also be used for a plug-in hard drive or for a CD or DVD drive.) Once again, multiple batteries add more productive time . . . and weight.

✦ **On the size and efficiency of your laptop's major components.** For example, a 17-inch, high-resolution LCD draws more power than a 12-inch, medium-resolution display; the brightness setting you choose for the LCD also affects the amount of power. The microprocessor's type and speed also make a difference; some processors are designed to *slow reduce* their draw (and operate a bit slower) when the laptop is on batteries. In other designs the microprocessor adjusts its speed to match the tasks. Another big draw: RAM.

✦ **On the tasks you're performing.** Anything the requires the spinning of a motor—like a CD, DVD, or hard disk drive—can draw down a battery fairly quickly. Playing a movie from a DVD is just about the most draining assignment you can give your laptop: it uses the drive, the LCD, and the audio subsystem.

✦ **On the instructions you have given the laptop's built-in battery-management system.** If you make the proper adjustments—best suited to the particular way you use your machine—the laptop will know when it is proper to temporarily shut down the hard drive, turn off the LCD, or even go into hibernation.

✦ **On how well you've treated your battery.** Have you pampered it, kept it well fed when needed, and put it on a diet when needed? And have you kept track of its birthdays?

Do you need an *uninterruptible power supply (UPS)* or a surge protector between your AC adapter and the wall? Well, no . . . and yes. You've no need for a UPS because your laptop is already running on a battery. But as far as protection from a power surge or spike: The AC adapter includes electronics that convert AC to DC and also step down the voltage from 110 to 240 volts at the wall to about 20 volts (depending on the model) at the laptop; that process puts a bit of buffering in the circuit that may protect your computer.

A serious surge could fry the adapter. I recommend using a surge protector for all electronic devices.

The last two of these concepts are the ones over which you have the most control.

## Taking it easy on your battery

Two users with the identical laptop computers, the same batteries, the same operating systems, and the same set of software can vary greatly the number of hours they can use their machine away from an AC wall outlet. One might find the battery good for only a 90-minute railroad commute from Stamford, while the other may peck away for six hours between takeoff from Boston and landing in London.

The key to getting the most out of your battery is to sip most gently from its cup:

◆ **If you're not using a device, turn it off.** For example, switch off the WiFi transceiver when you don't need to communicate wirelessly. (Anytime the WiFi is on, it searches for a connection, and if it finds one, uses power to negotiate an agreement to communicate.)

◆ **Avoid unnecessarily using the hard drive.** If your word processor is set to autosave your work every 5 minutes, consider changing that to every 10 or 15 minutes.

◆ **Resist the temptation to play a music CD while you work.** And understand that watching a movie on your laptop can burn through a battery before you get to the end of said movie. A CD or DVD drive spins constantly when in use and eats up a lot of power. A better solution: Convert some songs to MP3s or WAV files and store them on your hard drive; playing music from that source is much less demanding on the battery than from a CD. Even better: Get a separate music player like an iPod and leave your laptop for work.

Book VI
Chapter 1

Using Your Power
for Good Purposes

◆ **Don't use external devices that draw power from the laptop battery.** These include desktop mice and memory card readers. Some users have devices that allow them to charge an iPod or a cell phone from the computer battery; that's okay, but you don't get power for free. The power goes from the laptop to the other device.

◆ **Find a comfortable environment.** Extreme heat (over 80 degrees) makes your battery discharge more quickly than usual and could, in the worst case, result in a meltdown; cold temperatures make batteries sluggish, which may affect your laptop's ability to do those wonderful things you expect it to do.

◆ **Make sure the cooling vents aren't blocked by dirt or by objects.** This includes seatback tray tables or stray pieces of paper. The fans within laptops are critical to your system's health, but they don't need to spin all the time. Most machines use a temperature sensor that switches the fan on when needed and off when the interior has cooled down.

◆ **Turn down the light.** The LCD uses a fair amount of power for its ordinary functions, and it also uses a backlight (essentially, a tiny fluorescent-like bulb that illuminates the screen from behind). Most laptop power-control utilities automatically reduce backlighting when the machine runs on batteries. See if you're comfortable manually reducing the screen brightness yourself; most machines use a function key command from the keyboard for this purpose. If you're on an airplane, try turning down the screen brightness and switching on the overhead reading light; try not to accidentally hit the flight-attendant call button — they're pretty cranky these days.

◆ **Reduce the load on your microprocessor.** Unless you really need to run multiple programs at the same time, avoid multitasking. Close any applications (including utilities that automatically load with your machine) that you don't need open. These steps allow some processors to slow down and use less power, and may also reduce the draw by the RAM.

✦ **Be aware of the varying demands of different software.** Most basic office programs, including Microsoft Word and Microsoft Excel, are reasonably good at loading quickly and efficiently using memory. Other programs, including digital image editors like Adobe Photoshop and some music players and editors, demand a lot of memory and processor effort.

✦ **Understand the difference between Hibernate and Standby (or Suspend).** Hibernation saves an image of your desktop, including all open files and documents, and then turns off the power to your computer. When you return and restore power, it loads everything the way it was without having to load the operating system and applications. By comparison, Standby or Suspend shuts down some of the machine's components, including the LCD and sometimes the hard disk drive, but provides power to RAM so your work isn't lost and you can quickly bring the machine back to operating status. In general, Standby is a good solution for a quick timeout — going down the aisle from seat 34C to the restroom and back — but not best if you won't be using your machine for 20 minutes or more. Consult the maker of your machine for advice on the particular technology employed.

## Charging it up

Happy birthday to you, happy birthday to you. You've been charged and recharged 400 times, and now you are through.

Did you ever imagine you would read such deathless prose in a book about laptops? I could go on and on . . . but I'll be kind and stop right now. But the point is: Batteries have a finite life. They can be recharged only a certain number of times before they die. And death can be sudden, or it can be an annoying, drawn-out process.

## Battery up

The original design for rechargeable batteries used lead compounds; these had a number of disadvantages: Lead is heavy, it is dangerous to human health, and they weren't the best at holding and maintaining a charge for a long period of time.

The next major improvement was nickel compounds, including nickel cadmium (often referred to as *NiCad*) batteries. A similar, newer design is *nickel metal hydride (NiMH)*, which holds a charge a bit longer. The principal disadvantage of nickel-based batteries is something called the *memory effect.* Over time, if a battery is regularly partially discharged and then recharged, the full capacity is reduced.

Nearly all current laptops use *lithium ion (LiOn)* technology. These batteries have a very high energy-to-weight ratio (meaning they pack more power into a lighter package than most other technologies). An unplugged laptop holds on to its charge for a longer time, and these batteries don't suffer from memory effect (explained in this section's sidebar).

In 2007, several laptop makers were forced to recall the LiOn batteries in their machines because of a mildly annoying problem: Some were bursting into flame or at least overheating and damaging the case and its internals. That's not good. The total number of batteries involved was quite small, but the recall was (appropriately) huge. Always register your laptop with the maker so they can contact you in case of a recall or upgrade.

According to manufacturers, a lithium-ion battery should be good for between 300 and 500 discharge and recharge cycles. And you don't need to — and shouldn't — drain the battery all the way to zero every time; that actually shortens its life. Top off this type of battery regularly and fully discharge it about once every 25 or so uses; the value of this sort of cycle is that it helps the laptop's built-in battery voltage "fuel gauge" properly monitor its condition.

When I talk about keeping track of birthdays or the number of charges/discharge cycles, I'm really not asking you to keep count on your desktop or the wall of your cell (or office). Just keep in mind that nothing lasts forever; if you use your laptop on batteries twice a week, that means you subject it to about 100 cycles per year. On that kind of schedule, a battery should last about three to four years.

You may notice that the battery no longer delivers three or four hours of power, and that its usable time continues to shorten. Or one day, its get-up-and-go has completely gotten-up-and-went. Why? Because over time, *oxidation* (a change in the properties of internal metal; on a piece of iron you call it rust) increases resistance within the battery and eventually it can no longer reliably deliver its charge.

## Treating your battery kindly

Like Queen Latifah would have sung in the movie "Chicago," if she was talking about laptops instead of the inmates on murderesses row in the Cook County Jail: When you're good to your battery, your battery's good to you.

You can do these important things:

✦ **Keep your cool.** A LiOn battery holds its charge best when the temperature is between 32 degrees and 77 degrees Fahrenheit (about 0 to 25 degrees Celsius). It slows down if it gets much colder, and it loses its ability to hold a charge if it gets much hotter. Does this mean that keeping your laptop in the trunk of your car on a hot summer day isn't a good idea? Yup.

✦ **Remove the battery.** If you're going to use your laptop for an extended time while connected to an AC power source, turn off the machine and remove the battery. A LiOn battery generates heat (and shortens its life) if you charge it while the computer is in use with AC power.

When you remove the battery from your laptop and run the machine on AC power, you're adding one risk: If the power fails, you won't have the battery ready to take over immediately and thus you will lose any unsaved work. If you're at your desktop, consider adding an uninterruptible power supply.

✦ **Avoid running your battery down to zero.** It's okay to do this from time to time, but don't make it a regular habit. With a modern LiOn battery, it is better to have many partial discharges and recharges instead of constantly running it down to empty. (Older nickel cadmium batteries were just the opposite—they preferred full discharges and recharges.)

✦ **Put a charge on.** If you remove your battery to store it for a while, give it at least a 40 to 50 percent charge; certain types of laptop batteries can fail if they discharge all the way to zero. Check the charge level at the power utility on your taskbar. (When they're in your machine, the built-in software monitor should give you enough warning to allow you to shut down with at least a bit of power still in the cell.)

✦ **Don't stock up.** I stock our pantry with several dozen of each anytime the supermarket has a sale on canned soup and breakfast cereal, but the same doesn't apply when it comes to laptop batteries. You're better off buying fresh batteries from a reliable source just before you need them; ask about the manufacturing date before buying.

If you have a spare LiOn battery, keep the extra one (with about a 40-percent charge) in a cool place. You can wrap it carefully in plastic (not aluminum foil, which could short it out) and place it in the refrigerator or another cool place. Give the battery a few hours to gradually warm to room temperature before attempting to use it or recharge it.

# Finding Hidden Batteries

Most laptops have, in addition to the main battery, two other much smaller batteries buried deep within the box.

## Real-time clock

The *RTC,* or *real-time clock,* is to maintain the internal clock . . . in real time. That is how the laptop knows the time as well as the date whenever you turn on the machine. It also has another purpose: to provide a trickle of power to the computer's setup information, which is recorded in a special form of memory called CMOS (non-volatile) memory. The little RTC battery is recharged from the main battery and should keep time and hold power for at least a month all by itself (without power from the AC adapter or from the main battery).

For that reason, if your laptop is going to sit unused for an extended period of time (several months or more) you should top off the main battery every month or so. Or you can keep the laptop plugged into an AC source while it is on the shelf.

An RTC battery should last three to five years or more; that's the good news. The bad news is that on nearly every modern laptop, the RTC isn't something a user can replace. If the battery fails (you may see an error message at startup, or find that the clock or the setup configuration becomes flaky, corrupted, or otherwise odd), you have to arrange for factory service.

## Backup battery

This rechargeable battery, common on many but not all laptop designs, provides enough power to keep the computer's volatile memory (RAM) alive when the computer is in Standby mode.

Also charged by the main battery or the AC adapter, the backup battery usually holds data and settings in computer memory for several days (to a week or so) after the main battery has been fully discharged. Like the RTC battery, the backup battery should be good for three to five years or more, and mere mortals aren't to replace it. The laptop has to go to the repair shop if it fails.

You can use a laptop without a functioning backup battery — you just won't be able to use Standby mode once the main battery has given all it has to give.

# Chapter 2: Replacing or Upgrading Your Power Source

## In This Chapter

↝ **Power trips and tips**

↝ **Replacing or upgrading a battery**

↝ **Alternate sources of power for the road warrior**

*W*elcome, cellmates. Our power to travel cordlessly is linked to the output of your laptop's rechargeable battery. The following are the facts of life, at least as it relates to batteries:

✦ Some batteries are more powerful than others.

✦ Some batteries can hold a charge longer than others without being attached to wall current.

✦ Some batteries can better withstand repeated charges and discharges than others.

✦ All batteries will die. Some will stop suddenly and some will fail over time.

The good news is that batteries are a portable device all by themselves. You can replace them when the fail, and depending on your laptop model, you may be able to upgrade them or install a second battery.

## Measuring Battery Capacity and Power

Without getting too deep into the details of electricity you can measure these things:

✦ **Voltage.** One *volt* is defined as the amount of pressure required to push one *amp* of current against one *ohm* of resistance. In electrical terms, this is the *amperage*.

✦ **Wattage.** This number tells you the total amount of work you can do with the battery. Multiplying voltage times amperage calculates wattage.

In your home or office, your electric company calculates your bill on the basis of kilowatts per hour, which is a measurement roughly equivalent to using 1,000 watts of power for an hour. (For example, a 100-watt light bulb burning for 10 hours consumes 1 kilowatt.) Laptop computers use power in smaller quantities, typically demanding somewhere between 35 and 75 watts of peak draw. (*Peak draw* might occur in this situation: The LCD is fully lit, the graphics adapter is drawing constantly changing, complex images derived from a DVD, a whole bunch of RAM is being powered, the hard disk drive is spinning, and the WiFi adapter is switched on.)

## Battery wattage or amperage

When it comes to the bucket of power called a battery, we're not quite at the point where a small, lightweight laptop can have access to a kilowatt or more of stored power. Instead, we talk about watt hours or sometimes amp hours.

One *watt hour (WHr)* is the amount of electric energy required to power a 1-watt load for an hour. A laptop that draws an average of 20 watts per hour runs for about two hours on a fully charged battery rated at 40 WHr.

Another way to rate a battery is to express its capacity in *amp hours (AH)*. Amp hours are like the explosive potential of a tank of gas, while watt hours represent the distance that power can drive the car.

To convert watts to amps, use this formula:

watts / volts = amps

You may see amp hours expressed like this: 4.4 AH. Or some techie may prefer to rate the same battery as 4400 mAH. (An mAH is a milli-amp hour, and 4,400 milli-amp is the same as 4.4 AH.)

Batteries offered today usually range in capacity from about 25 WHr to as much as 96 WHr. An ordinary range of amp hours for laptop batteries is from about 4 to 8. When it comes to choosing a battery, watt hours or amp hours are really the only number (other than the weight) to which you need to pay attention. A larger capacity is better than a smaller bucket of juice . . . and heavier.

## Battery weight

The more watt hours a battery produces or amp hours it contains, the longer the laptop can operate. You'd think, then, that the solution was oh-so-simple: Get as many as you can. The problem is that batteries require metals and chemicals to hold a charge, and the greater the capacity, the heavier the device.

## Breeding hybrids

Scientists are hard at work developing new hybrid metals and *electrolytes* (literally, the juice within the battery) that can hold more power without turning into an electronic cinder block. The current champion—at least for consumer-grade products—is Lithium Ion (LiOn) technology. Other designs in the labs include polymer-based alkaline, lithium nickel manganese oxide, lithium cobalt oxide, and Spam in a Can. Okay, I made that last one up, although it probably could generate gas one way or another.

**Book VI
Chapter 2**

Replacing or
Upgrading Your
Power Source

The manufacturer may tell you that a battery has four cells, six cells, nine cells, or almost any number of cells. The more cells of a particular technology, the more space for stored energy, but the news you can use is the WHr or the AH rating.

## *Replacing the Battery*

For many users, the laptop becomes technologically outdated or starts to have other problems after about four years. If the battery fails or no longer holds a sufficient charge, you can easily replace it.

Even if you can no longer use an older laptop, try to remember others: A school or individual might find your outdated machine very useful.

Prices for laptop batteries usually range from $50 to $150.

✦ Start with your laptop manufacturer's web site or telephone sales department. Get a price for a replacement, and make sure you find all the warranty details.

✦ Check the Internet for third-party battery suppliers. You may find the identical name-brand battery for less. And you may also be offered Brand X replacements at a significantly lower price; some of the third-party batteries even promise to hold a larger charge. Personally, I've had no problems using generic batteries. However, I would pay close attention to the warranty; what happens in the one-in-a-million-or-so situation where a battery overheats or otherwise damages your laptop?

Here's how to replace the battery:

**1.** **Turn off your laptop and disconnect the AC adapter.**

**2.** **Release the latch or other attachment devices that hold your battery in place.**

See Figure 2-1.

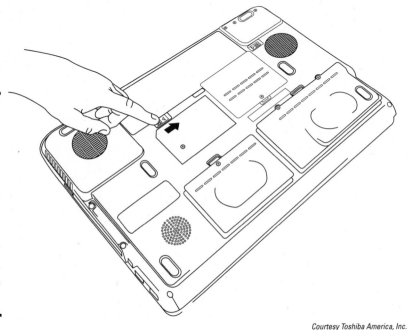

**Figure 2-1:** Many laptops include a latch that locks the battery into place; this safeguards against it being accidentally dislodged or left behind.

*Courtesy Toshiba America, Inc.*

**3.** **Slide the old battery out of its compartment or storage bay.**

See Figure 2-2.

Avoid touching the contacts on the battery itself or inside the bay; the oils on your fingertips could reduce the conductivity of the battery.

**4.** **Take the replacement battery out of the box.**

**5.** **Slide it into the notch or bay.**

See Figure 2-3.

**6.** **Close the safety latch to lock it into place.**

**7.** **Reconnect the AC adapter and give the battery a full charge.**

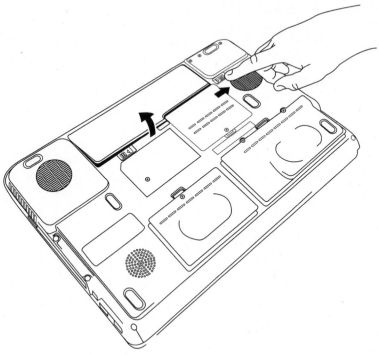

**Figure 2-2:**
Press the
release
button if
there is one
and carefully
lift the
battery out
of its com-
partment.

*Courtesy Toshiba America, Inc.*

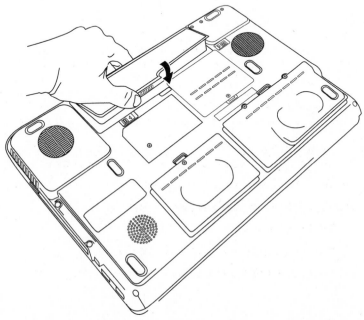

**Figure 2-3:**
Installing a
new battery.

*Courtesy Toshiba America, Inc.*

That's about as simple a repair as you're going to find on a laptop. You need to know these things when replacing a battery:

+ **Meet the specifications.** You can't squeeze a 3-inch battery made for a Dell laptop into the 2-inch slot on a Toshiba. It's physically impossible, and even if you *could* squeeze it in, the electrical connectors probably wouldn't line up.

+ **Match the voltage.** If your original battery was rated at 14.8 volts, that's the ticket for the replacement model. Don't go over or under the specified power.

+ **Consider going high capacity.** Within the manufacturer's specifications, you may be able to replace your original battery with one with a higher watt hour or amp hour rating. This allows you to work longer and harder . . . and give your muscles a bit of extra exercise when you lug the laptop.

+ **Get fresh.** You've no good reason to buy a used battery (or an unused model that has been collecting dust on a shelf somewhere). Check the date of manufacture; I consider anything older than about 18 months to be suspect. (It's like the unidentified frozen meat that's been in the back of the freezer for longer than you can remember; it may be fine, it may have lost its ability to please, or it may make you sick. Don't take the chance.)

# Mining Other Sources of Power

Someday we'll be able to deliver power to our laptops with tiny fuel cells or magic pills. A global effort exists to provide simple little machines to third-world children (the One Laptop Per Child initiative, at http://laptop.org) that you can power up by a hand crank or foot pedal. But most of you are tied to an electrical outlet at one point or another: either to run your laptop in the office, or to recharge the internal battery for use on the road (or in the air or in the park).

A few alternates can bring power from sources other than a wall outlet and I'm going to avoid the subject of personal windmills, sewing machine treadles, and pocket-sized nuclear reactors.

## Adding a second internal battery

Certain laptop models — generally larger and more sophisticated systems — offer a multipurpose bay on one side or the other of the bottom box to hold a secondary rechargeable battery (or an extra hard disk drive or CD/DVD drive or other device).

This second battery is usually smaller than the main battery, which means that it holds less energy. Depending on the model, though, it should add from one to three hours of extra life . . . and close to a pound of weight.

### Adding an external battery

It's not the most elegant— kind of the computer equivalent of adding a side-car to a motorcycle or training wheels to a bicycle — but another solution is to purchase and use an external, or *auxiliary,* battery.

This device is commonly a small, pizza-box-like unit that sits beneath your laptop and connects to its standard power port. A second device is like a brick that sits alongside your laptop or on the floor. These batteries come in a range of capacities, including models that meet or exceed the stored power of the main battery. Most include an electronic circuit that automatically adjusts the output voltage to your machine's needs and a set of converter tips that allow them to mate with laptops of differing designs. You may also find external batteries specifically designed to work with your particular model.

These external batteries typically cost a bit more than a standard main battery because they include their own charger and because they may hold a higher capacity. And they add between 1 and 2 pounds to your load and take up almost as much space in your carry-on bag as the laptop itself.

## Adapting to Plane and Car

As a modern road warrior, if I'm not at my desk, in a hotel, or on a cruise ship, I'm probably in a car or on an airplane. The laptop's internal batteries come in handy at these places . . . for as long as they last. You have several ways to operate your computer or recharge batteries (or both) while in a car or airplane.

### Powering up in the air

Some airlines, on some planes, offer power to the people at some seats. If this sounds a bit iffy, that's because it is; you can't predict with any certainty whether a particular plane will offer this feature. A few airlines promote this service on certain long-distance flights that cater to businesspeople.

The most common design is a system called EmPower, which delivers DC current; you need a special adapter (available from either your laptop manufacturer or from a third party) to connect to your machine. Some airlines offer DC power through circular outlets just like the ones you find in automobiles. And a handful of planes come equipped with 110 volts of AC power to some or all seats. (Some commuter and long-distance trains offer AC outlets.)

## *Powering up down on the ground*

We used to call a car's power outlet a "cigarette lighter," back when they held circular devices that glowed red hot after a few moments of power, long enough to light a tube of tobacco that the user then inhaled. It all sounds so barbaric, doesn't it? Today, many cars come with several outlets for use with adapters to power or charge cell phones, music players, GPS receivers, and laptops.

Like an airline DC source, an automobile DC power outlet can generally deliver enough juice to run an electrical device like a laptop, but takes a long time to recharge batteries. And there is a chance of overloading the car system if you try to draw too much power; the vehicle's electrical system is protected by fuses that can shut off the charger (or the engine, if you really overdo it).

One other option is an *AC power inverter,* which converts the DC power from your car into 100 volts of AC, which can provide voltage to an AC adapter for your laptop (which then reconverts the power to DC). If that sounds like a fair amount of wasted power and possible danger from overheating, that's because all of that is true. For most laptop users, a better solution is to use a direct DC connection.

# Chapter 3: Power-Management Utilities

## In This Chapter

✔ **Turning down the power**

✔ **Making a power plan and checking it twice**

✔ **Customizing your personal battery demands**

**C**ar makers have faced a perplexing contradiction for many years: People want big, fast, and feature-filled vehicles . . . but they also want their vehicles to sip very daintily from the gas tank. It's the same thing with laptop computers: You want large screens, fast microprocessors, and all sorts of doodads including DVD drives, WiFi communication, and much more . . . and you want your batteries to last for weeks between recharges.

The answer, and I'm back to laptops now, is in two parts: proper hardware design (to minimize battery power demands) and software that manages the system intelligently. On modern laptops, the software is usually a combination of specific tools offered by the manufacturer plus more general management as part of Windows XP or Windows Vista.

## Using Power-Management Utilities

On my current Toshiba Satellite, the hardware interacts with the Windows Vista operating system to offer three preconfigured *power plans.* (In Windows XP these were called *power schemes,* which sounds a bit sinister, but means the very same thing.) You can also customize the settings; see Figure 3-1. The standard choices follow:

✦ **Balanced.** This setting tries to make everyone happy. It provides full performance when you need it and reduces power draw during inactivity. Microsoft rates it like this: Battery life ***, Performance ***.

✦ **Power saver.** If you really need to squeeze the most out of your battery (say you're on a long airplane trip), this setting reduces power usage by slowing down system performance. In addition to adjusting hardware, power saver may also turn off some power-grabbing features of Windows Vista such as the flashy Aero interface. Battery life *****, Performance **.

✦ **High performance.** This plan maximizes system performance and responsiveness and has no conscience when it comes to devouring electricity. If you've got important work to do in a short period of time, this is your sprinter. Battery life **, Performance ******.

**Figure 3-1:**
The Power Options window on the Windows Vista Control Panel includes a choice among three laptop power plans. Some manufacturers offer their own versions of this utility.

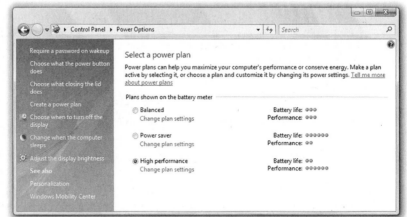

You can also customize the settings within each plan or scheme, and you can create your own group of settings. See Figure 3-2.

**Figure 3-2:**
Customize each power setting to meet your needs; make the biggest impact by adjusting display brightness and length of time before the display turns off during inactivity.

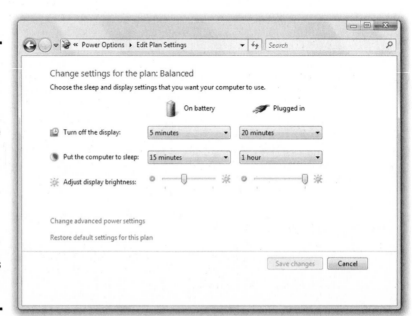

# Charging up Your Battery Options

The most current CPUs and associated chipsets include advanced features that minimize the power draw when your machine is running on batteries. Some directly reduce the draw by shutting down or slowing components, while others indirectly save power by doing things like reducing the amount of generated heat.

Available options include

+ Setting the computer to go to **sleep** after a particular period of inactivity.

+ **Customizing** the laptop's reactions to presses of the power or sleep buttons, or what happens if you close the running machine's lid. Among the options are automatic sleep or hibernation modes or a shutdown of the system.

+ Adjusting the **LCD brightness.** Bright screens burn more power; you may get by with a dimmer display, especially if you're on an airplane and can use the overhead lamp to deliver some reflective light.

+ **Turning off** the LCD after a period of inactivity. The system can sense that the keyboard or mouse or other devices have not been used and shut off the display; flicking a finger at the touchpad or the keyboard will bring it back to life.

+ **Shutting down** the hard disk drive when you're not using it. If you're reading a screen or working on a document that is loaded from RAM instead of the hard drive, the system may be able to turn off the hard disk drive motor to save power. When you need it again, it may take a second or two to spin back to full speed.

Be sure to consult your laptop's instruction manual or onscreen help screens for advice on the best way to use your machine's power-saving features.

If you choose to switch between available power plans, try to think ahead. For example, change over from High Performance to Power Saver while the machine is running on AC power in your office, hotel, or the airport lounge. That way you lose less power in booting up on the plane or elsewhere away from wall current.

# Advanced Power Settings

Many major laptop manufacturers offer an amazing *panoply* (that means a whole bunch) of customizations for your computer's power demands. These advanced settings are available:

+ From a separate Control Panel item

✦ A specialized utility program on the taskbar

✦ As an additional window added to the Edit Plan Settings window shown in Figure 3-2

On the Toshiba Satellite P205 I use as a sample machine, Toshiba allows me to choose between high-performance or more modest (and less power-draining) battery-optimized settings for components (including the cooling system, the hard disk drive, the WiFi adapter, selective shutdown of inactive USB ports, display brightness, and half a dozen other options). See Figure 3-3.

On the computing side, you can instruct the computer not to waste power performing automatic disk indexing while the laptop is running on batteries (a good idea). And you can even turn down the standard speed for your laptop's CPU when it needn't rev at full speed.

**Figure 3-3:**
On the
Toshiba
Satellite
P205 sample
machine, the
manufac-
turer has
included
advanced
power saver
settings for
many
individual
components.

If you're sharing a laptop with someone else, or if the IT department set things up, you may need to get administrator rights to make changes to preconfigured plans.

# Book VII

# Upgrading Your Laptop

The 5th Wave — By Rich Tennant

"Okay, enlarge the chicken bone by 900 percent and attach it to an e-mail to the museum saying, "Getting close...send more money.""

# Contents at a Glance

# Chapter 1: Adding RAM

## In This Chapter

✔ Tagging memory to GUI

✔ Purchasing more memory power

✔ Preparing for ReadyBoost

*1*t's time for analogy-orama. If the microprocessor is management and the hard disk is the warehouse, then memory is the receiving, sorting, and shipping department.

I use this particular analogy because I want you to think of *Random Access Memory (RAM)* as the place where work actually gets done and where activity ceases when the lights are turned out. And I also want you to consider this: Once you have a laptop with a reasonably fast and capable microprocessor, the best way to get the most out of your machine is to give it a large amount of memory.

I used to say that all memory was erased when the power was turned off . . . and that remains true for most RAM . . . but a few new technological wrinkles are in the area, which I get to later in this chapter.

Let me put this another way: If you have a choice between a laptop with an adequate microprocessor and a full load of memory, or a machine with a supercharged CPU and insufficient RAM, go for more memory. (And, as I discuss in this chapter, if your machine is under-equipped in the memory department, you can almost always fix that if you spend some money on the problem.)

## Knowing How Much Is Enough

Why do today's laptops require so much memory? The answer is a GUI one. My original PC used only text and commands; today's machines are almost entirely based on graphics and commands initiated through the graphical user interface most people call Windows. The price for that convenience is the need for lots of money; the good news is that the price of memory has plummeted over the years to a tiny fraction of what it once was.

## Memory for money

I've bragged (or complained) about my personal history with the personal computer. But here is a point of reference: The first IBM PC, introduced in 1981, had a basic model that included just 16K of RAM. That was barely enough to hold the original Disk Operating System (DOS) and a few pages of text or numbers. I was among the first to buy one of the machines, and I was smart enough to shell out a whole bunch more money to equip my machine with a whopping 256K. (My cost? About $5,000.)

More memory is better than less memory . . . up to a point. Giving your machine more work space means speeding up all the applications running on it, and making it easier to have more than one program open at a time.

However, the sky isn't the limit: Each motherboard and chipset design has an *optimum,* or maximum. If you exceed that amount of RAM, you could actually end up slowing down your laptop: The processor may have too many places to manage data efficiently. Another downside to excess memory: It draws power from the battery and generates heat, which also uses power because it makes internal fans run longer and harder.

Today, the recommended minimum amount of memory for a Windows Vista–based machine is 1GB of RAM (about 60,000 times more working space than the original PC), and I think that is insufficient by half: Go with 2GB. (If you're running a laptop with Windows XP, the realistic minimum is 512MB, but I recommend 1GB or 2GB.)

### Defining your terms

Let me define a few critical terms in the context of this book:

+ **Memory:** A chip or other form of hardware that can hold information.

+ **Random access memory (RAM):** A form of that device that allows the processor to jump directly to a particular bit of data.

A brand new, unshuffled deck of playing cards is arranged in a specific order: ace, two, three, four, and so on up to jack, king, and queen in each of four suits. In this new, unshuffled deck, if you wanted to get to the three of hearts, you would probably have to make your way through the 13 cards in the clubs suit, then the 13 in the diamonds suit, and then past the ace and deuce of hearts. Depending on the data's complexity, it can take a long time to get past all the wrong data before getting to what you want.

Now consider opening that same deck of cards and laying them out face up on a desk. You could see at a glance where the three of hearts was sitting and you could reach right in and grab it without having to move past all the other cards. This is a form of random access memory.

✦ **Storage:** On your laptop, storage includes your hard disk drive; you might also store files on an external hard disk drive, on a recordable CD or DVD, or even on a flash memory key.

Then imagine stuffing the deck of cards in a file cabinet along with ten other, older, shuffled decks as well as copies of every electricity, water, and cable bill you've ever received. In computer terms that is storage.

Most storage, including standard hard disk drives and CD or DVD discs, isn't as quickly accessible as RAM because a disk drive's read/write head must wait for the sector on the spinning disk to move into position. And if the queen of hearts is located just past the three of clubs, the drive has to make one complete revolution to allow the system to pick them up in that particular order.

✦ **Volatile:** Retained only for as long as the memory chips receive regular supplies of electricity. When the power is turned off, the memory disappears.

✦ **Non-volatile:** Whatever is written to a hard disk, a CD or DVD, or other similar forms of storage is more or less permanent. It will stay there even when the power is turned off. (Why do I say "more or less permanent"? If the disk is purposely or accidentally erased, or damaged, the data can go away.)

Finally, think of memory as temporary or transitory. Those face-up cards could be blown away by a gust of wind. More to the point, the standard form of laptop RAM is volatile. By contrast, storage is non-volatile.

I talk about storage on hard disk drives, optical drives including CDs and DVDs, and other devices in Book VII, Chapter 3 of this book.

## The odd numbers of computer math

A majority of people are lucky enough to have been born with an evenly divided set of ten fingers, and for that reason ancient mathematicians developed a counting system based on tens. You call that the decimal system, from the Latin decimal meaning one-tenth.

Quickly, class: 10 times 10 is 100, and 10 times 100 is 1,000. Easily done, right?

Now the Greeks also worked with groups of ten in their math, but their language is Greek to them . . . not Latin. The Greek word (or prefix) *kilo*, abbreviated as K, stands for 1,000; the word *mega* stands for 1 million; *giga* stands for 1 billion. So far, I'm speaking a familiar language: If I say I was paid two megadollars for my most recent bathing-suit modeling session, you should reasonably understand that to mean $2 million. (And I'm worth every drachma.)

But as I explain in Book I, Chapter 3, computers use an entirely different form of math. To begin with, they don't have ten fingers. But more to the point, a modern computer accomplishes its magic by applying brute force to just two numbers: 0 or 1. It's called *binary math*. (Yes, I know 0 isn't a number; it's the absence of a value. But that's human thinking, not computer thought.)

The money in our wallets—leather or virtual—is mostly measured in parts of ten. Inside a computer, it's all parts of two. To be more precise, binary math is applied to computer "words" made up of 8 or 16 or 32 digits. An 8-digit word made up of either 0s or 1s can range in size from 0 (00000000) to 255 (11111111); to the computer that means 256 possible values.

String together two of those words, and you've got 512 possible values; a group of four offers 1,024 variations. When you referring to computer words, also known as *bytes,* you call that last value a *kilobyte.*

Do you see the problem yet? A kilobyte would seem to mean a thousand bytes, but it's actually 1,024. When you talk about small numbers, it's an error (or at least a misunderstanding) of only about 2 percent. But consider the difference between a decimal understanding of a gigabyte of $1,000^3$ (1,000,000,000 bytes) and a binary accounting of $1,024^3$ (1,073,741,824 bytes). Up there amongst the gigabytes, the difference is more like 7.5 percent.

So, when you buy a gigabyte of RAM, are you getting 1,000,000,000 bytes or 1,073,741,824 bytes? Well, when you're dealing with RAM, the answer is neither. The raw capacity is actually $1,024^3$, although perhaps 10 percent of the RAM is taken up with overhead, including indexing and error checking; however, when you buy 1GB of memory, you're really getting that number of memory locations in true binary math — 73.7 million more than a mere billion.

But things get squirrelly in hard disk drive measurements. Here the marketing department gets involved. Sometimes a drive is measured in decimal math and sometimes in binary math, and always in terms of what sounds like a larger and more saleable product.

In Table 7-1 you can see a table that translates common binary math terms. I present both bytes and bits; a computer byte or word is made up of eight bits.

| Table 1-1 | | Binary Math |
|---|---|---|
| *Abbreviation* | *Meaning* | *Value* |
| Kb | Kilobit | 1,024 bits |
| KB | Kilobyte | 1,024 bytes |

| Abbreviation | Meaning | Value |
|---|---|---|
| Mb | Megabit | 1,048,576 bits |
| MB | Megabyte | 1,048,576 bytes |
| Gb | Gigabit | 1,073,741,824 bits |
| GB | Gigabyte | 1,073,741,824 bytes |
| Tb | Terabit | 1,099,511,627,776 bits |
| TB | Terabyte | 1,099,511,627,776 bytes |
| Pb | Petabit | 1,125,899,906,842,624 bits |
| PB | Petabyte | 1,125,899,906,842,624 bytes |
| Eb | Exabit | 1,152,921,504,606,846,976 bits |
| EB | Exabyte | 1,152,921,504,606,846,976 bytes |
| Zb | Zettabit | 1,180,591,620,717,411,303,424 bits |
| ZB | Zettabyte | 1,180,591,620,717,411,303,424 bytes |
| Yb | Yottabit | 1,208,925,819,614,629,174,706,176 bits |
| YB | Yottabyte | 1,208,925,819,614,629,174,706,176 bytes |

Don't throw away excess memory that you remove from a laptop as part of an upgrade project. Give it to a school or a community organization. If you must, sell it through an online auction site. Someone, somewhere can use it.

## Using Your Brain When Buying Memory

You must take four critical first steps before buying memory for a laptop computer:

1. **Determine the memory type and kind of module or holder it's mounted on.**

2. **Find out the maximum amount of memory your machine is capable of managing.**

3. **Know the total number of sockets available for module installation.**

4. **Find out how much memory is already installed in the machine and what configuration is used.**

   Is all the memory on one module? Are two modules of equal size already installed? Are two unequal modules in place?

Most of today's current machines use tiny postage stamp-sized modules called SODIMMs (Small Outline Dual In-line Memory Modules). That means small pieces of memory on a stick with a tiny set of 200 connectors at the bottom that plug into a matching socket.

You must match the exact type of memory and module to your machine's needs. You can find the necessary details by consulting the instruction manual for your machine or by visiting a number of online web sites for memory vendors; the best of them allow you to enter the model number or part number of your laptop (you find both on a label on the underside of your machine) and receive a report about compatible devices.

For this book's sample Toshiba Satellite P205, the proper memory is a DDR2 SDRAM (double data rate 2 synchronous dynamic random access memory) module. You don't really have to know exactly what all of the jargon means; in almost every machine you just need to match the description and specification exactly; you can't upgrade or change the memory module design for a laptop motherboard.

In general, memory modules are marked with a MHz (megahertz) speed or with a PC rating such as PC133. The higher the speed rating, the faster the chip or module can operate. I'm talking about tiny incremental differences, and once again, you have little or no choice: You have to match the specifications of your laptop's motherboard.

(In a few cases you may be able to install modules of a faster speed than your laptop can handle, or a second module that's faster than the first one already in place. Either way, the machine will operate no faster than the slowest component or specification.) Do so only if you have no other option; mixing and *not* matching is a potential headache.

As delivered from the factory, this particular model can ship with as little as 256MB, which is way too little to run current versions of Windows. A bit of research into the machine's specs tells me two sockets are available for memory; I could have also opened the hatch on the bottom of the box to see for myself. (You may also be able to use an online scanning tool offered by your laptop maker, or by memory vendors like Crucial through their web site www.crucial.com.)

The only reason to buy the machine with the minimum amount of RAM is if you can save a lot of money by removing the memory already in place and install modules you purchase on your own. That used to be a reasonable strategy, but today the prices of RAM have declined so much, often it's less expensive to buy a new laptop fully fitted out with the amount of memory you want to have, hold, and use.

Here's the problem: You buy a machine with 1GB of RAM installed and you want to run the laptop with 2GB of memory. If the machine, as delivered, has two 512MB modules in place, you're going to have to remove and replace one or both. You could install a single 2GB module, two 1GB modules, or keep one of the 512MB modules and install a 2GB stick in the other slot for a total of 2.5GB.

## Knowing where to go

Sometimes the best price comes if you purchase your laptop fully equipped with the amount of memory you want. Laptop makers buy memory in huge quantities, and their prices are sometimes reasonable. And be sure to calculate the lost value of any memory modules you may have to remove if you upgrade by yourself.

To buy from third-party sources, shop at places that treat memory as a commodity: online stores, catalog marketers, and computer superstores.

In the early days of computerdom, it generally made sense to spread out your memory across several modules to reduce the chances of failure. Current memory modules, though, are pretty well tested and reliable. The chips themselves are less likely to fail than the module that holds them, the socket on the motherboard, or the wiring to that socket. Today, go large.

Memory makers use an unpleasant but accurate term about the function of modules: *infant mortality*. If a stick is going to fail, most likely it's either dead on arrival — very rare since factories test them — or fail within a few hours or days of installation (after going through a few cold-to-hot-to-cold cycles).

Pay attention to the price variations caused by supply and demand. A 2GB module should, in theory, cost a bit less than two 1GB modules because it requires only one circuit board, connector, and packaging. Sometimes, though, a particular size of memory module may be out of whack because of shortages or high demand.

## Checking up on your memory

If you watch very, very carefully you may be able to watch the numbers fly by onscreen as your laptop boots up. This is one way — not a very accurate or easy one — to see how much memory is recognized for use by your machine. There are better ways.

This is an easier way to obtain a report on installed (and useable) memory:

1. **Go to the System Properties report within Windows.**

2. **Click the Start button and then choose Control Panel.**

3. **Double-click the System icon.**

   Under Windows Vista you see a declaration of the amount of RAM in the system section. Under Windows XP you see the complete System Properties report.

4. **Click the General tab.**

   Now you can see the amount of installed memory recognized by the system.

Another, more involved and more accurate way to examine the memory in your machine is to run a test on the system. Most laptop makers provide at least a basic test utility. Toshiba's PC Diagnostic offers a report on components, as seen in Figure 1-1. One step beyond, you can ask the system to test any selected pieces of hardware; this particular utility gives you only a Pass-Fail report, which is okay if you receive all passing grades; if problems crop up, you need additional tools. A report on a properly functioning machine is shown in Figure 1-2.

**Figure 1-1:**
A diagnostic program, in this case provided by Toshiba to laptop customers, offers a detailed report on installed hardware, including installed memory.

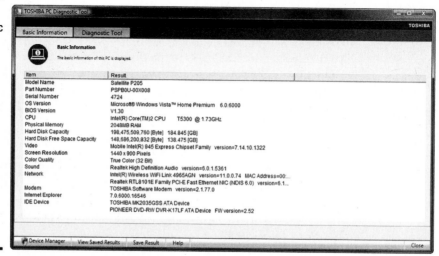

**Figure 1-2:**
A diagnostic test puts all a laptop's major components through a series of basic tests that can reassure you (or start you on a bug hunt).

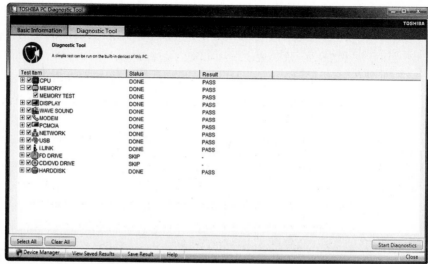

# Cramming Some RAM in a Laptop

The general process of installing memory modules in a laptop is very similar from one brand to another; today, nearly every laptop design places an access panel on the bottom of the machine and uses similarly latching sockets. The description I use here is from the sample Toshiba Satellite P205 laptop.

You want to make sure that the machine has no electrical power and is cool and stable. Take these preliminary steps:

*1.* **Turn off the computer using the Windows shut-down process.**

You lose stored data if you use Sleep or Hibernation mode.

*2.* **Unplug the AC adapter cable that runs to the laptop.**

Why remove the AC adapter and the battery before installing memory modules? First of all, plugging them in while power is on could result in damage to the RAM. Secondly, doing any work on a laptop while power is applied could result in a damaging spark.

*3.* **Remove the battery.**

*4.* **Disconnect any other cabling to the laptop, including an Ethernet cable or a telephone modem wire.**

If the machine has been running recently, allow it to cool for about 15 minutes; memory modules can become quite hot when they are in use.

*5.* **Locate a small Phillips-head screwdriver.**

A screwdriver with an X-shaped head; make sure it's in good condition and not chewed up or misshapen.

*6.* **Place a soft cloth or other protective mat on a desktop.**

*7.* **Turn the laptop over so that its bottom is facing up.**

*8.* **Locate the memory module slot cover.**

For an example of a typical arrangement, see Figure 1-3.

*9.* **Carefully remove the screw that holds the cover over the memory compartment.**

Hold the screwdriver at a right angle to the bottom of the laptop and turn the screw carefully; it shouldn't require a lot of force to remove. Once the screw is removed, put it in a safe place. Use a piece of clear tape to attach it to the desktop or the side of the computer.

*10.* **Ground yourself before touching the memory module.**

Touch any grounded metal surface, like a light stand, or touch the center screw on an electrical outlet.

**Book VII**
**Chapter 1**

**Adding RAM**

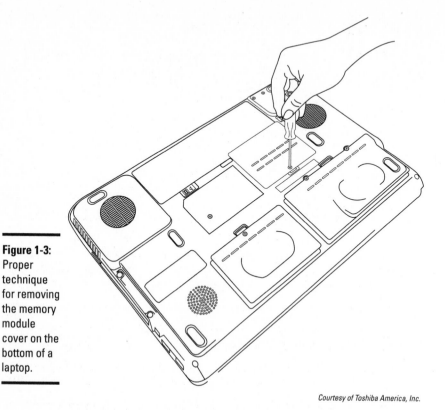

*Courtesy of Toshiba America, Inc.*

**Figure 1-3:**
Proper
technique
for removing
the memory
module
cover on the
bottom of a
laptop.

## Removing a memory module

Here are the steps for removing a memory module:

1. **Carefully release the latches on the side of the module holder.**

2. **Lift it to an approximately 30-degree angle from the bottom surface of the laptop.**

3. **Gently slide the module out of its connector and out of the slot.**

   This step is shown in Figure 1-4.

## Installing a module into an empty socket

These steps help you install a module into an empty socket:

1. **Carefully remove a new memory module from its packaging.**

   Avoid touching the connectors; doing so can reduce conductivity because of oils on your finger.

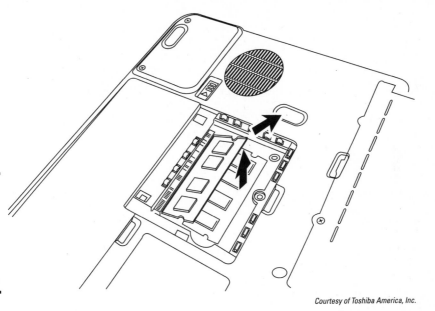

**Figure 1-4:**
Lifting up a
memory
module
holder and
removing
the memory.

**2. Locate an empty module slot.**

If two sockets are in the compartment and the top one is filled and the bottom is empty, remove the top module first.

**3. Pick up the memory module by its sides and aim its connectors toward the socket.**

Be sure to align the notch in the connector with the matching key in the socket. See Figure 1-5.

**4. Slide the module into place.**

Most sockets align at about a 30-degree angle.

**5. Once the module is fully inserted into the socket, press down on the top edge of the device to latch it into place.**

This way it's flat to the laptop's bottom. The carrier should snap into place with latches. See Figure 1-6.

**6. Replace the memory compartment cover and lock it down with the screw.**

Don't overtighten the screw.

**Figure 1-5:**
Align the notch in the connector of the memory module with the corresponding key in the socket.

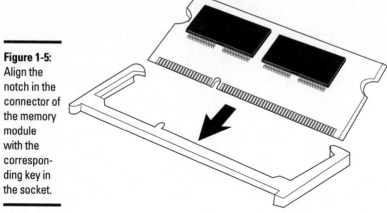

*Courtesy of Toshiba America, Inc.*

**Figure 1-6:**
Gently push the module, in its carrier, back to a flat position on the bottom of the laptop. It should gently latch into place.

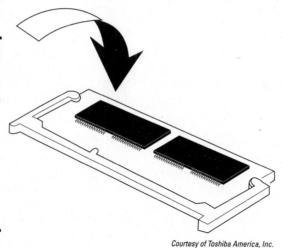

*Courtesy of Toshiba America, Inc.*

## Going post-installation

Here's what you do after installing memory:

*1.* **Reinstall the main battery.**

*2.* **Turn the laptop right-side up.**

*3.* **Reattach the AC adapter cable and other connections.**

*4.* **Restart the computer.**

# Flashing for ReadyBoost Memory

With the arrival of Windows Vista — and a particular design of motherboard and chipsets — Microsoft introduced a new way to add a block of memory to your system by plugging in an external flash memory key (or even a memory card or stick like the ones used in digital cameras and audio players).

It's called Windows ReadyBoost, and it uses flash memory — a form of non-volatile memory — as a place to temporarily hold some of the information retrieved from disk reads. The data on the external block of memory is recorded in a special format that, to the system, is easier to access than if it were kept on the internal hard disk drive.

As part of ReadyBoost technology, the Vista operating system offers redundant protection: At the same time the information contained in disk reads is recorded to attached flash memory, it's also written to a reserved segment of your hard disk drive. In technical terms this is known as a *write-through cache.* This protects against information loss if the flash memory key is removed from the system.

Now if you think about it, recording data to an easily removable piece of hardware like a flash memory key represents a pretty serious threat to data security. If the external memory were stolen or lost, an unauthorized person might be able to read its contents. To guard against this, Vista automatically applies encryption to the data on the key, making it difficult, if not impossible, for it to be misused.

Some other fancy tricks are applied to the process. Because it's non-volatile, flash memory is a bit slower than ordinary RAM when it comes to writing data. And in some circumstances it responds more slowly than a hard disk drive.

But in actual use, the relatively slow ReadyBoost memory response is mostly a factor when it comes to reading lengthy, sequential files such as music or streaming video. To deal with this, Windows Vista takes a quick look at the size and nature of files, and ReadyBoost technology automatically diverts Vista's attention from the flash memory to the hard drive if it's called upon to work with oversized files.

Looked at the other way, ReadyBoost is at its best when it comes to working with small blocks of information. As a RAM device, even a relatively slow flash memory key still delivers information faster in most cases than a hard disk drive (which has to wait while its read/write heads are moved to a particular location and then wait again for the spinning platter to bring the needed data into view).

Finally, you've got to have the right type of flash memory key to enable ReadyBoost. When you plug an external memory block into a laptop running Windows Vista, the operating system runs a quick performance test; if the memory is too slow, a message informs you that it can only be used for data storage, and not as an extension of system memory. See Figure 1-7. It's likely that ReadyBoost won't accept older flash memory keys you already own. When you go shopping, look for devices labeled as "Vista Ready" or "ReadyBoost Ready."

**Figure 1-7:**
My new laptop and my new flash memory key work well together, but the operating system determined that the memory was not fast enough to be used with ReadyBoost technology.

# Using ReadyBoost

Vista notices anytime you plug a flash memory key into a laptop, and the operating system asks if you want to speed up your system using the memory or use the memory as a place to hold files. If you choose to speed up the system with ReadyBoost, the system displays a Properties screen for the memory and a new tab that supports ReadyBoost. Here you can adjust the amount of space you want to allow the system to use for cache; you can devote all the memory to that purpose or divide the memory between cache and file storage.

The minimum amount of flash memory for ReadyBoost purposes is 256MB, and any amount beyond that offers improvements in performance. The maximum is 4GB.

When this new technology was introduced, Microsoft recommended that the way to get the best ReadyBoost performance was to match the capacity of the flash memory device to the amount of installed system memory. Thus, if you have 2GB of RAM in the machine, you would get the best performance by installing 2GB of ReadyBoost-compatible flash memory. This may change with future updates and Service Packs for Windows Vista; keep posted on changes by visiting the Microsoft web site and searching for ReadyBoost.

To be recognized as a ReadyBoost device, the flash memory has to be all in one device; if you install two flash memory keys in two different USB ports, Vista recognizes only one of them (the device with the earlier alphabetic drive identification) as available for ReadyBoost.

**Book VII
Chapter 1**

**Adding RAM**

# Chapter 2: Adding or Replacing a Drive: Internal, External, CD, or DVD

## In This Chapter

✔ **Reading the spinning library within your laptop**

✔ **Downsizing a drive, affecting design**

✔ **Protecting a drive from traveling insults**

✔ **Installing a replacement drive**

✔ **Going external for storage**

✔ **Changing optical specs: CD and DVD upgrades**

*A* hard disk drive or a CD or DVD drive is basically very large, very fast, revolving filing cabinets. Oh, and they're served by an extremely efficient and quick librarian who knows where everything is at all times, can go and get your information in the blink of an eye, and never takes a coffee break.

Disk drives record information by placing tiny electrical charges on a magnetized surface. CD or DVD drives use optical recording methods, burning teensy pits or making dark marks on a reflective disc. Either way, your computer is recording the 0s and 1s of binary data on a circular medium. In general, the absence of a magnetic or optical mark at a particular location indicates a 0, and the presence of a mark is interpreted as 1.

A magnetic hard disk drive uses a platter that is spelled with a *k*, a *disk*. A CD drive, which is a computer adaptation of a music-playing device developed in Europe, uses a platter that is spelled with a *c*, a *disc*. DVD drives were developed simultaneously for computers and home-theater systems, and for my purpose I use the disc spelling. Do any of these distinctions really matter? Only to copy editors and others (like me) who are paid to obsess over tiny details . . . and get them right.

Inside a hard disk drive one or more platters spin at a constant speed, while one or more heads move in from the outside (or back from the center) of the disk to read information recorded at a particular location or write new data. (That's why we call them *read/write heads*.)

Don't do this (open your laptop, that is) at home; allow me to do it for you. In Figure 2-1 you can see the guts of a laptop from my collection.

**Figure 2-1:** Its protective cover removed, here is the interior of a basic hard disk drive. This model, from a desktop computer, has three platters and six read-write heads that move in from the outside to the core.

Depending on the hard disk drive's *density* (how closely data is packed together) and the drive's overall capacity, it may have only one platter or two or more platters. Most hard disk drives also record information on both top and bottom of each platter. To go along with the multiple platters, the drive has an equivalent number of read/write heads — one for each side of the platter.

The drives spin at a very high rate of speed; a typical laptop hard drive rotates at least 4,200 times per second and, at today's high end, as much as 7,200 or 10,000 revolutions per second. (Old-fashioned floppy disk drives, no longer common, spun at just 300 revolutions per minute in their final versions.)

And finally, unlike floppy disk drives or optical drives (CDs and DVDs), hard disk drives are sealed units, with their platters and read/write heads protected from damage by dirt, dust, and sticky substances that could make them literally grind to a halt.

## Going Tiny, Laptop Style

While the basic design of a laptop's hard disk drive is similar to a drive in a desktop PC, some very important differences exist. A laptop drive has to be

✦ **Much smaller and much lighter** (because you'll be stowing and carrying it)

✦ **Much less demanding of electrical power** (since it often runs on battery power)

✦ **Built and installed to resist damage** to its platters or to the information recorded on them (because a laptop is specifically intended to be moved around from one place to another)

## Making 'em small

Drives intended for a laptop have to be miniaturized, of course, because they need to fit within a notebook case; PC designers can use hard drives of almost any shape or weight. The standard PC drive is 3.5 inches wide, and about 1 inch thick.

For a current laptop, a typical hard disk drive is about the size and weight of a pack of playing cards. Most laptops use drives that are 2½ inches wide and a bit more than ⅓ inch thick (9.5mm); today's tiniest are just 8.5mm thick, which is almost exactly ⅓ inch.

The next step down is a 1.8-inch-wide device you can install within the laptop or as a plug-in PC Card or Express Card. And now you see tiny drives half again as wide, popping up at 0.85 inches: That's less than an inch square. Smaller than a postage stamp. These tiny drives are in cell phones, digital audio players, PDAs, and digital cameras, but laptops are next.

And we've begun seeing the first solid-state hard disk drives for laptops — essentially, permanently installed flash memory. They're relatively fast and have no moving parts, which is a good thing. On the downside, they're (currently) very expensive when compared to "old-fashioned" mechanical hard disk drives, and for that reason the first models have relatively small capacities of 64GB.

The other part of the miniaturization equation is the push for a reduction in weight. To some designers and laptop users, weight is the equivalent of racing decals on a sports car; they want to brag about how their new laptop weighs just 27 ounces. (To others, the issue is more about practicality. A 5-pound laptop case can begin to feel like a 50-pound iron anvil at the end of a day of traveling from home to airport to hotel.)

A typical modern 2½-inch notebook hard drive weighs somewhere near 100 grams, or about 3½ ounces, an amazing feat of productive shrinkage. And the newest 1.8-inch-wide drives are as light as 62 grams, or just over 2 ounces.

# Downsizing and data transfer

Although high-end laptops are now available with drives that spin at the same high speeds as the best desktop devices, most laptop hard drives spin slower to reduce power demands. One effect of a slower speed is a potential reduction in the data transfer rate. It's simply a matter of physics: The read/write head waits for a particular spot on the disk to come beneath it. If one drive spins twice as fast as another, there could be a delay of as much as nearly 100 percent between grabbing bits of separated data.

A second factor is that data transfer is fastest at a drive's outer tracks — tracks with the largest circumference. More circumference means the capacity for more data in a particular track. (*Circumference* is the actual distance around the circle.) At the same rotational speed, more data in a track means faster throughput. If you're working with smaller platters on a laptop's drive, the outer circumference is going to be less. A 3-inch circle has a circumference of about 9.4 inches, while a 2-inch circle is a mere 6.3 inches. In addition to possible differences in the rotation speed, the larger drive in this example has a circumference about 50 percent larger.

Other components that affect the speed of transfer of data include the motherboard design and the chipset used. If you purchase a current machine, it most likely uses a SATA (serial ATA) hard drive and disk controller hardware, which is as fast as a consumer-grade machine is going to function. Older laptops use PATA (parallel ATA, also called IDE) drives and standards, which are slightly slower in certain circumstances.

## Making 'em efficient

Reducing the drives' power demands means longer batteries use while you travel. Two factors are at work here:

✦ Reduced draw of current with ultra-efficient motors and low-friction bearings.

✦ Lower power draw usually generates less heat within the closed case of a laptop and therefore requires less power demands by cooling fans.

## Making 'em sturdy

Although I've been known to occasionally gently kick the PC that sits beneath my desk when its internal fans start to vibrate like a 747 preparing for takeoff, in general a hard drive in a full-sized PC lives a pretty sheltered life. It doesn't get moved very often, isn't likely to fall, isn't in a spilled coffee's pathway, and it doesn't have to go through X-ray machines. (And I also protect it against electrical surges or brownouts by plugging the machine into a capable uninterruptible power supply.)

Alas, a laptop is nowhere nearly as pampered. It faces a hundred threats in the office and on the road. It can fall off the airport X-ray machine, be dropped off a desktop, suffer a sudden soaking, or even pick up a bit of sand or dirt.

And so engineers have devoted themselves to building stronger and better protected disk drives for laptops. The first step: guarding against damage from a fall. Engineers have two ways to accomplish that:

✦ Passive design safeguards. These elements include cushioning the hard drive against damage — things that include stronger materials, tiny springs or rubber mounting, and the like.

✦ Active safeguards. A few companies make these, including Lenovo (successor to IBM) with its Active Protection System for some of its ThinkPad laptops. Like the sensor in a car airbag, the disk drive watches for sudden changes in motion that include acceleration (as a laptop tumbles off a desk) or deceleration (as it hits the floor). It reacts within half a second to park the drive's read/write heads in a place where they won't crash into the platters and then it stops the drive's spin.

## *Hiring, Firing, and Wiring*

Engineers have gone back to the wiring past. New technologies allow serial communication to operate at extremely fast speeds, without any of the complexities of parallelism.

*Serial ATA (SATA)* requires only four thin wires in a casing similar to a telephone cable. The first specification for SATA requires only four 500 millivolt (½ volt) signals; future versions are expected to allow signal voltages half again as strong at 250 millivolts, or 1/4 volt.

And within the next few years, SATA will break out of the box to offer something quite logically called *external SATA (eSATA)*. This allows high-speed communication with new drives and other devices. Think of it as USB on speed.

## *Replacing a Laptop Hard Drive*

The first few generations of laptops came with hard disk drives deeply embedded within their sealed cases. Removing one to replace or upgrade it was a difficult, time-consuming, and expensive process that generally required the involvement of a professional repair shop.

## From serial to parallel and back

Serial wiring is the original design for most communication within and outside a PC. This was the best engineers could come up with at the time: the eight bits of a computer byte (or word) were strung, one behind the other, and sent down a pair of wires, one in each direction. (Other wires were in the cable for special signaling.)

Serial communication works, although at first it was slow. First of all, each byte had to be separated by code to show where it began and ended. And many designs also added error-checking or error-correcting codes that allowed the computer to figure out if all the received information was accurate. Finally, serial communication was simply slow because it was the equivalent of a two-lane highway; every bit had to follow one behind the other and there was no passing lane.

The next development in personal computers was parallel communication. In this design, all eight bits of a computer word were sent at the same time along an 8-wire cable or a 16-wire cable for bidirectional exchange. This was adopted for most uses that required bunches of information transmission: Printers were among the first places these cables went.

Parallel communication was also adopted for the transfer of data within a computer — from the microprocessor to the hard disk drive and back, as one example. Inside a computer—desktop or laptop—the motherboard and the drive had to be connected by an unwieldy 40- or 80-wire cable and a 40-pin connector. And 26 of the wires had to carry 5-volt signals.

That worked for more than a decade as engineers pushed the speed of communication across the parallel superhighway faster and faster. But eventually they ran into problems of physics: minor imperfections in cables or the tiniest of variation in length might mean that one of the eight bits might arrive a millisecond before or after the others. The result: a traffic jam.

An *R* word is missing from this chapter. I speak only of *replacing* a hard disk drive, not *repairing* it. The fact is that a hardware failure (a crashed head, a damaged motor or platter) or a fried electronic circuit is almost never worth repairing. The only exception: for a price (a large one), some specialty labs can recover essential and irreplaceable data from some failed drives. Maintaining regular data backups is a lot less expensive.

Today, nearly all current laptops have made the hard disk drive modular; the drive either slides into a bay on the side or latches into a compartment on the bottom. The drive is held in a special carrier that matches the laptop case, and exposed is a set of small connectors that deliver power to the device and send and receive data. In this design, you unplug an original drive and install a new one: plug and play.

## Installing a plug-in drive

The best of the systems make changing a hard drive as easy as swapping a battery. In Figure 2-2 you can see one example of a laptop hard disk in a carrier and the empty bay awaiting its installation.

**Figure 2-2:** Turned on its back, you can see how this particular hard disk carrier design holds a drive in a cage; the data and power connectors plug into mating ports in the laptop.

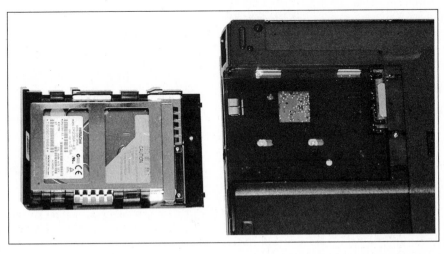

A reminder: Always remove both the AC adapter and the laptop's battery before handling any of the machine's internal parts. Don't take the chance of having any electrical power in the laptop that could be shorted out by a tool, screw, or other conducting material.

Follow these basic steps for working with a drive that's already installed in a carrier designed for your laptop:

*1.* **Turn off the laptop.**

*2.* **Unplug the AC adapter.**

*3.* **Prepare your work area.**

You want a clean, well-lit, and stable surface. Place a soft cloth or other cushioning material to protect the top of the laptop; you can use almost anything that isn't metallic or packing an electric charge.

*4.* **Remove the battery.**

*5.* **Ground yourself before touching the old drive, and again before opening the bag or box that holds the new drive.**

Ground yourself by touching the middle screw on an electrical wall outlet, or by touching a metal pipe.

6. **Locate the hard disk drive compartment or bay.**

Your laptop instruction manual should include a chart showing its position.

7. **Unscrew any locking screws that may be holding the drive in place, or unlatch any catches.**

Set aside the screws in a safe place; make notes on any unusual steps you had to take.

8. **Slide or lift the hard drive out of its bay or compartment.**

9. **Reverse the steps to install, latch, and power up the new drive.**

## Using a generic drive

Depending on your laptop's design or market popularity, you may be able to purchase a "bare" mobile hard disk drive from a computer parts supplier and make it work. A *bare drive* is sold as a simple spare part, without all the fancy packaging and extra cost of an item sold in a retail store. You may install the new drive into the original carrier by carefully disassembling it, or you may purchase a carrier from another source. (It may come indirectly from the same source as the one your laptop maker used, or it may be a concoction from a third party.)

### Installing a new drive in the original carrier

Follow along to reinstall a new drive:

1. **Turn off the laptop.**

2. **Unplug the AC adapter.**

3. **Prepare your work area.**

You want a clean, well-lit, and stable surface. Place a soft cloth or other cushioning material to protect the top of the laptop; you can use almost anything that isn't metallic or packing an electric charge.

4. **Remove the battery.**

5. **Ground yourself before touching the old drive, and again before opening the bag or box that holds the new drive.**

You can ground yourself by touching the middle screw on an electrical wall outlet, or by touching a metal pipe.

6. **Locate the hard disk drive compartment or bay.**

Your laptop instruction manual should include a chart showing its position.

7. **Unscrew any locking screws that may be holding the drive in place, or unlatch any catches.**

    Set aside the screws in a safe place; make notes on any unusual steps you had to take.

8. **Carefully open the carrier that holds the drive and disconnect the mechanism.**

    You need to remove some screws or other holding devices; place the screws in a safe place and make notes about anything unusual you have to do on the reinstallation.

9. **Take the old drive out of the carrier and set it aside on a non-static surface.**

    Handle both the old and the new drive with care, holding them only by their sides. Don't touch the circuit board, and be careful not to damage the connectors for data and power at the back. Avoid putting weight on the top or bottom of the drive. And finally, make sure that you don't cover the drive's vent or "breather" hole with tape, a cable, or plastic parts.

10. **Unplug internal connectors that run from the drive to the external connectors on the outside of the carrier.**

11. **Install the new drive in the carrier.**

    The new drive has to match the original in size and location of attachment points and connectors.

### Installing a new drive in a new carrier

If your machine and particular model is from a major manufacturer, third-party computer-parts suppliers may offer conversion kits that let you put together your own carrier and drive. If you're lucky, the company that sells the carrier may provide a good set of instructions. If you buy both the carrier and the new drive, it may provide very specific instructions . . . or even do the assembly for you. If you're not lucky, you'll have to figure it out for yourself . . . or spend a few hours on the phone with a support technician in a place far, far away.

## Taking a quick leap into jumpers

Today's current laptops are most likely to use internal SATA controllers and drives. Each SATA drive is a system unto itself, and there's no need to identify it to the computer — the cabling does that. If you're working on a SATA drive (check your laptop's specs) you can skip to the next section of this chapter.

Okay, the rest of you must have an older machine that uses a laptop version of a standard ATA/IDE drive. In that situation, each drive must be identified to the computer as either the *master* or *slave* drive on a particular cable and controller. In most setups, the drives are identified when you place a *jumper* (a little plastic-cased metal clip) across a specific set of pins. The jumper serves the same purpose as a switch; when it connects two pins, that particular circuit is completed and a particular message is sent to the computer.

 Now, all that said: Very few laptops have more than one internal hard drive and the drive bays are directly connected to the motherboard's hard drive controller by a cable that makes no provision for a second device on the same link. Most hard drive manufacturers ship their equipment with a default setting as the master device. But spend a moment looking at the drive and any instruction manual that comes with it to see if you need to make any changes to jumpers.

## Configuring the BIOS and the Drive

Depending on your laptop and the hard disk drive you install, putting a new drive into place may be as easy as plug and play: The laptop discovers the new drive and automatically changes its BIOS setup menu — the built-in circuitry that sets up the computer *before* Windows or any other operating system is loaded, and then serves as an intermediary for all actions from then on.

However, and though less common with modern machines, in some situations, you might have to perform more feats of strength:

✦ Install a special utility, provided by the hard drive maker, to instruct the BIOS.

✦ Manually make settings before the drive is recognized. Read carefully the instructions that come with the drive.

✦ *Partition* the drive (divide it into a boot sector and one or more data sectors). This may happen if you're putting into place a completely empty hard drive. Again, follow any instructions provided by the drive maker.

And finally, you have to install Windows or another operating system on the drive to allow it to boot the computer. Follow the instructions provided with the operating system to install it from the machine's DVD or CD drive.

# Super-sizing Simply with External Drives

For most users, a laptop is an extension of the desktop computer at home or in the office. You should keep your archives (every word-processing file you've written), your full collection of photo and music files, or your extra software (you may not need to travel with advanced graphics and audio-editing software) on your desktop. Prune away anything that needn't occupy space on your laptop's hard drive and keep it on your desktop.

What if your laptop's internal hard drive is working properly and is packed with just the essential software and data, but you're still running short on space?

One solution that doesn't require changing the internal hard drive: adding a small, light external drive. Several years ago, external hard drives were about the size and weight of the book you're reading and cost several hundred dollars. Today, you can buy a new device not much bigger than a deck of cards at a cost that provides change from a hundred-dollar bill.

You buy a drive in a box and then connect the data cable to the laptop. The upgrade is as easy as you could want.

Every modern laptop today includes at least two (and often four or more) USB ports that deliver both data and power connections. And the most advanced of today's machines and those on the drawing boards have at least two *External SATA (eSATA)* ports, which are similar but faster ways to communicate with devices.

Using an external hard disk drive has a few disadvantages, though:

✦ They draw power from the laptop and thus reduce battery life when the computer is away from an AC outlet.

You can also purchase an external drive that takes its own power from an AC adapter rather than from the laptop. That's fine if you're working at a desk in a hotel room or an office; it's not a good solution if you're computing at 35,000 feet above Omaha.

✦ They add about half a pound to the amount of weight you need to drag around with you and also take a bit of space in your laptop bag or on your seatback tray table.

The two fastest data-exchange standards for most laptops are USB 2.0 or eSATA. If your older laptop is capable only of working at USB 1.1 speeds, you can purchase a PC Card or Express Card adapter that upgrades its speed. You also need to be running a current version of Windows to use USB 2.0: Windows Vista, Windows XP, or Windows 98SE.

---

## Coming attraction: Drive-sized flash memory

As this book goes to press, the largest flash memory keys available at reasonable prices have a capacity of 16GB. You can add a bit of extra storage this way; in fact, you could plug two or perhaps four keys into your machine. The laptop treats each as a separate "drive."

However, Samsung has already introduced the first "solid state" hard drive for laptops. The initial device has 64GB of storage. Larger drives from Samsung and other manufacturers are sure to be on the way.

---

## Giving Your Optical Drive a New Look

This section is short and simple.

Repairing or replacing a built-in CD or DVD drive on *most* current laptops isn't a project I recommend to most end users. Heck, even for guys like me who have taken apart (and put back together) nearly every piece of mechanical or electronic equipment in my home and office, this job isn't undertaken easily.

✦ The main reason I hesitate to advise you to undertake this sort of job is that it, first of all, generally requires you to open your laptop's sealed case. It often also demands removing a number of other parts that get in the way. If you send your laptop to a repair shop, they can do this sort of work for you, but expect that the labor cost (not the part itself) may leave you stunned.

✦ The second reason: Purchasing an external CD or DVD drive that attaches to your laptop through its USB port is easy and inexpensive. (Future models will connect to an eSATA port.)

# Chapter 3: Changing Your Input and Output Options

## In This Chapter

✔ Getting USB out of an old machine

✔ Boosting the speed of an older USB port

✔ Bringing back the missing serial or parallel port

✔ Breaking SATA out of the box and onto your desk

*F*or much of America's economic history — especially the automobile industry — the working philosophy for design and marketing was "bigger, better, faster." Think tail fins, lots of chrome, and gas-guzzling, turbo-charged engines.

When it came to computers, though, the mantra was downsized: It became "smaller, better, faster." That was the thinking that led to the evolution from the first room-sized computers to the personal computer, and then once again when the personal computer became portable.

Today, laptops are better and faster . . . and getting smaller in most components. (One exception to the trend: widescreen laptops, which are lighter and faster than ever before but growing wider and taller as people use them as multimedia powerhouses. They're still pretty small, though.)

## Survival of the Fittest: USB Adaptations

You can add more than one high-tech adjective to the mix: adaptable. One of the beauties of a modern laptop is the pathways that allow them to be upgraded to the latest and greatest — the best and the fastest.

Got an old machine that still uses serial and parallel ports? Or a machine with USB ports but a printer that needs an old-style parallel connection? Have a machine with an original USB 1.1 port? How about a current machine with USB 2.0 but no FireWire outlets? Does your laptop offer no PS/2 ports for an old-school external mouse or keyboard?

You can solve all of these problems, and others, with one or another form of *adaptation*. You need a way into your laptop's internal bus (its data highway), and often you can easily accomplish that.

## Adding USB 2.0 ports

Older-model laptops without USB ports can usually sprout them almost instantly if you install an adapter in a PC Card or Express Card slot. PC Card technology was common in laptops from about 1990 until 2006; a smaller, faster, and better technology called Express Card was introduced in 2005 and is present on most current machines.

PC Card to USB adapters are plug-and-play solutions. They tap into the laptop's data bus and power supply at one end and offer at least two USB 2.0 ports at the other. (One word of caution: The USB ports are often rather dangerously exposed to damage. Take care not to snap them off when you place your laptop in its case, or anytime you move the laptop around on a desktop.)

On the software side, you must be running a current or very recent version of Windows that supports USB. These include Windows Vista, Windows XP, Windows 2000, and Windows 98SE. In some situations you will need to add a driver, supplied by the adapter maker or already present within Windows.

If your machine is so old that it doesn't have a PC Card slot, you're out of luck when it comes to quick-and-easy solutions. You've no other access to the bus of the laptop's motherboard and no way to convert a standard serial port to USB. However, try taking your serial printer or modem and attaching it to a more-adaptable machine that can communicate with your older laptop over a network.

## Changing a USB 1.0 port to 2.0

To be accurate about it, you don't really upgrade a USB 1.0 or USB 1.1 port to a better and faster USB 2.0 port. Instead, you work around the older technology (barely adequate for use with hard drives and probably unacceptable with CD and DVD drives) by installing a newer set of ports.

The solution is to use a PC Card or Express Card adapter.

Devices designed for USB 2.0 are downwardly compatible with the earlier USB 1.1 specification, working at the slower speed. Cables designed for USB 1.1 should perform at USB 2.0 speeds with an advanced port; however, you need a USB 2.0 hub to extend high-speed communication.

## Adding a USB hub

When I write about adding a USB hub, I'm not suggesting you put your laptop on wheels . . . although way back in the early days of personal computing there was a class of suitcase-sized "transportable" machines that had rollers beneath their 50-pound cases.

A hub is a way to extend and expand your USB circuit to allow a single laptop to work with dozens of peripherals. The *hub* splits the data signal and also divides the power that comes from the laptop to run many external devices.

All the elements of a USB chain have to adhere to the same standard to receive high-speed performance. If you have a USB 2.0 port and USB 2.0 devices, a hub that you install to stand between them must also meet USB 2.0 specifications. If you use a hub that meets only the 1.1 specification, devices attached to that hub operate at the original standard's slower speed.

Hubs are available in two types:

✦ **Unpowered.** Merely splits the signals and power. For laptop users, an unpowered hub works fine for low-draw devices like an external mouse or a simple webcam. But you may find that using an unpowered hub for a network adapter or a hard disk drive may result in poor performance, or may draw too much power from your laptop's battery.

✦ **Powered.** Connects to an electrical outlet and boosts the current available to devices. Hubs without their own power source, or those with insufficient power, can restrict the number of peripherals you can use on a USB channel or can cause intermittent failures.

The halfway solution is to carry a powered hub in your suitcase or computer bag and use it whenever an AC outlet is available — in a hotel or office or an Internet café — and avoid using high-demand peripherals when your machine is running on its own batteries.

## Converting from one USB to serial or parallel

Say that your laptop is thoroughly modern but some of your peripherals aren't. For example, I still have a few special-purpose devices, including a perfectly capable laser printer that accepts only an old-fashioned parallel connection.

The solution is to purchase a USB converter. You can find devices that plug into a USB port on your laptop and provide either an old-fashioned serial port or an old-school parallel port . . . or both.

At my office, I use a two-in-one converter from Keyspan that works flawlessly in the background; my desktop computer and my laptop computer (when it is attached to the office network by wire or by a WiFi connection) can use the laser printer without problem, despite the fact that none of my current computers have a parallel port any more.

## Cutting the cord to USB

Sometime in the next few years you should be seeing the next step in the evolution of the Universal Serial Bus: Wireless USB. The wireless system is expected to allow communication between a PC and a device at 480 Mbps at a distance of 3 meters (just under 10 feet) and 110 Mbps at 10 meters (about 32 feet). And, of course, you can purchase an adapter that plugs into a standard USB port to broadcast wirelessly.

### Using older mice and keyboards

The oldest of mice and keyboards were built to connect to serial ports on early computers. If you're still using one of these as a peripheral to your laptop, you need a USB-to-serial converter; see the preceding section in this chapter.

The second generation of external mice and keyboards adopted a standard developed by IBM for a particular line of personal computers; the hardware used a small round connector called a PS/2 port. If your peripheral is looking for that kind of link, the solution is to buy a small conversion plug that accepts the cable from the mouse or keyboard at one end and plugs into a standard USB connector at the other.

Similarly, if you have an older laptop that actually does have a PS/2 port and you need to use a current keyboard that expects to find a USB connector, the cable can be adapted from one standard and shape to another with a simple converter.

## Playing with FireWire

USB is still the most common high-speed flexible communications standard for laptops, although some machines also offer a competitive technology called IEEE 1394, which is also known as FireWire on Apple products and i.Link on some Sony video products. If you're deeply involved with video products, you may consider a FireWire connection a necessity instead of a luxury.

IEEE 1394's speed is very close to USB 2.0, delivering 400 Mbps; an advanced specification called 1394b moves data at twice that speed. Future plans call for optical fiber versions at 1,600 and 3,200 Mbps.

This specification uses a six-wire cable for computer devices: a pair of wires for data, a second pair for clock signals, and a third pair delivering electrical power. A four-wire version of the cable is for self-powered devices such as camcorders.

You can buy a laptop (including all Apple models) with FireWire built in, or you can add IEEE 1394 to a Windows machine by plugging in a PC Card or Express Card that adds a pair of ports. As with USB, you must be running Windows 98SE or later versions (Windows 2000, ME, XP, or Vista).

## Pushing SATA out of the Box

Within most current laptops, the connection between the motherboard and disk drives and CD or DVD drives has switched over from IDE (now renamed Parallel ATA) to the extremely flexible *Serial ATA (SATA)* specification. This specification replaces a cumbersome 40- or 80-wire ribbon with a two-wire cable. The next step, soon to arrive on laptops and desktops, is *External SATA (eSATA)*.

In theory, eSATA is much faster than USB 2.0 and IEEE 1394b (FireWire) and can work with a slightly longer external cable (as much as 6 meters [+19 feet] in length). As with the other standards, devices are *hot swappable,* meaning you can install, turn on, turn off, or disconnect them while the machine is running.

New laptops will have a set of eSATA ports as well as USB ports. But in the meantime, manufacturers are already offering converters. You guessed it: a device that plugs into a USB port to convert it to work with eSATA devices.

Book VII
Chapter 3

Changing Your Input
and Output Options

# Chapter 4: Going External with Printer, Network, and Special Peripherals

## In This Chapter

✔ Going from dots on screen to ink on paper

✔ Scanning the horizon for words and images

✔ Adding a facsimile of a fax machine

✔ Mousing, trackballing, and keyboarding outside the box

✔ Adding or fixing wireless insufficiencies

**M**uch of this book extols the virtues of the laptop computer as an all-in-one wonder device. It has a microprocessor, a motherboard, a keyboard, a pointing device, and a screen all in a single two-piece box. Its wireless communication system allows you to connect to the Internet to send and receive e-mail and files.

For many users, a laptop has all you need. You pick up your files at your desk and take it with you on commuter trains, airplanes, and to offices, libraries, schools, and anywhere else you do your work. The only external device you need is the AC adapter to recharge the laptop's batteries between excursions.

However, some functions that you occasionally perform with your laptop aren't yet incorporated into standard machines. Here are a few:

✦ Printing hard copies of files or e-mails

✦ Scanning documents as images or for optical character-recognition conversion to text files

✦ Using full-sized special-purpose pointing and input devices, including drawing tablets, keypads, and card readers

✦ Projecting presentations, photos, or other files onto large screens

These examples aren't part of "standard" portable computers. Today you can go into a restaurant and find the server with a handheld special-purpose computer that reads your credit card and prints a charge slip; or return a rental car and watch the attendant scan a bar code on the vehicle to produce a printed receipt. I don't need an LCD projector built into my laptop, because I know that anywhere I go to give a presentation will have facilities that plug directly into my machine.

## Connecting to a Printer

You can produce a hard copy of a file on your laptop at least seven ways:

✦ Take your laptop to an office or a service bureau where you can directly connect a cable from the computer to a printer. The most common such connection uses a USB port on the laptop, like the one shown in Figure 4-1. If this is the first time you've used this particular laptop with a particular printer, you may be prompted to install a device driver; follow the onscreen instructions to do so. When you're ready to print, be sure to select the printer you want to use.

✦ Some printers can communicate with laptops that have Bluetooth or infrared broadcasting systems. Bring your laptop within range of such a printer and follow onscreen instructions to make a connection. Again, you may need to install a device driver if this is the first time a particular combination of laptop and printers talk to each other.

✦ Connect your laptop to a *local area network (LAN)* in an office or service bureau (you may need a login and password to do so) and then use any printer available on the network. The connection can be wired (using an Ethernet cable) or you can use a WiFi wireless link. You may need to install a printer driver.

✦ Output a copy of the file you want to print to a form of removable media: The easiest and quickest solution here is a flash memory key. You could spend a few minutes burning a recordable CD or DVD. Then take the media to a computer in an office or service bureau and install it in a directly attached (or network) computer to a printer. (Don't forget to retrieve your memory key or disc after the print job is complete; at the least you're leaving behind your property and at worst you could be exposing personal or business information to persons who have no need to see it.)

✦ Connect to the Internet by wired or wireless means and send your file to a service bureau for printing. For example, you can send files to chain stores like Staples, FedEx Kinko's, The UPS Store, or OfficeMax or to a local equivalent and drop by to pick up black-and-white or color printouts, announcements, business cards, brochures, collated and bound catalogs — just about anything you can design on your laptop.

✦ E-mail a file (as an attachment) over the Internet to a colleague or friend who can accept it and print it for you on his system. You can e-mail across the country, ahead to the next stop on your road trip, or to a machine in the next cubicle over.

✦ Wait until you get back to your home or office and print it there on an attached or networked printer.

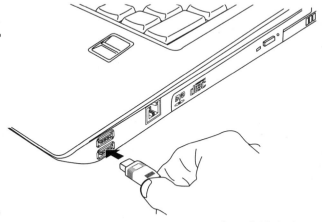

**Figure 4-1:**
Just about any current external device with a wired connection uses a USB 2.0 port, like the one shown here.

*Courtesy Toshiba America, Inc.*

## Connecting to a Scanner

A desktop scanner is a great way to capture a picture of a drawing, create a shareable document, or grab hold of a printed document and run its image through optical character-recognition software.

A *PDF* is a portable document format developed by Adobe Systems that converts text or graphics into a format for display on any current laptop or desktop without regard to machine features such as display resolution or processor design. In other words, it allows you to create and send a file to someone else and expect that what they see on their screen or in a hard copy printout is identical (or nearly so) to what you see. PDFs can be created with Adobe software as well as from within many modern office tools, including the latest versions of Microsoft Office.

Scanners range from remote control-sized devices that can read the bar code on an inventory tag to desktop units that look at entire letter- or legal-sized pages. In between, you find handheld pen scanners that pick up a line or a paragraph of text at a time.

The most common connection between a current-generation laptop and a scanner is a USB cable. However, wireless units can transmit information by WiFi, Bluetooth, or infrared signals. And you could connect (by wire or wirelessly) to a LAN and use a scanner available to that system's users.

# Faxing from Your Lap

Remember fax machines? For some people they were essential tools in the office — it was the way to send contracts, grainy product images, and written confirmation of trip details, deals, or other arrangements. Today, e-mail does much of the work formerly done with fax machines. You can send documents, pictures, and any other type of file as an attachment. And if the user must "see" an image of a document, you can scan it (see the previous section) as a PDF or as an image file and transmit it from place to place.

But if you still must send or receive a fax, you have many ways to use your laptop instead of a standalone facsimile machine. Let me start with the most direct: using your laptop's built-in facilities.

Many laptops still ship with a built-in dial-up modem, and the majority of those units throw in facsimile emulation software. What do I mean by *emulation?* This class of software sends and receives the same sort of line-by-line scan that a fax machine uses, but instead of working from or printing to a piece of paper, the image exists as a bitmap in computer memory. I could, for example, send an image of the page I'm writing at this very moment from my laptop to a fax machine, or from my laptop to another laptop that has facsimile emulation software installed.

The process is relatively straightforward, although the details of using various fax software programs differ from one machine to another; read the instructions displayed onscreen for details. The biggest downside: You'll be using a dial-up connection at dial-up speeds. For those who are used to working with high-speed broadband Internet connections, this is an unpleasant — or at least annoying — reminder of Ye Olden Days of Computing. Figure on speeds of 30 to 60 seconds to transmit or receive each page; even if your laptop is especially fast, it's limited by the telephone connection and the fax machine or computer at the other end of the wire.

You can send and receive faxes other ways as well:

✦ Connect your laptop to a LAN in an office or service bureau (you may need a login and password to do so) and then use any fax machine available to you on the network. The connection can be wired (using an Ethernet cable) or you can use a WiFi wireless link. You may need to install a special driver or a fax software program.

✦ Output a copy of the file you want to fax to a form of removable media. Again, the easiest and quickest solution here is a flash memory key but you could also spend a few minutes burning a recordable CD or DVD. Then take the media to a computer in an office or service bureau and install it in a computer attached directly (or over a network) to a fax machine. (And to repeat my earlier warning, don't forget to retrieve your memory key or disc after the fax job is completed.)

✦ Connect to the Internet by wired or wireless means and send your file (a word-processing document, a PDF, an image file, or other information) to an Internet-based fax service. A number of such companies are available — use your Internet search engine to find one. Some services are free, sending your fax with an advertising page attached; other services charge a few dollars for receiving your electronic file and re-sending it to a fax machine.

✦ Connect your laptop to a printer (directly or indirectly through a network or service bureau) and create a hard copy of what you need to send. Then find a traditional dial-up fax machine and send it out the old-fashioned way.

# Adding an External Mouse or Keyboard

I like my collection of laptop computers very well, thank you. But when I'm at my desk, none of them can quite compare to the ease of use I get from my desktop PC. I'm not complaining, just explaining. I have large hands and a heavy touch, and I can really fly along on a full-sized keyboard — especially one with keys that move down to a solid bottom with a satisfying click. I'm always on the lookout for the best keyboards — ones that most remind me of the old-style IBM Selectric design.

It's the same thing with pointing devices. My large hands (and a bit of shoulder pain) make it much easier for me to work with an oversized trackball that sits next to the keyboard, rather than having to reach out onto the desk to grab a mouse.

I make do the best I can when I'm traveling with my laptop. But I know that my typing speed on a shrunken keyboard with a reduced-depth click is less than my speed on a desktop keyboard. And as far as using the high-tech touchpad on my laptop, well . . . I'll just say I miss my trackball.

But when I know I'm going to be working for an extended period away from home — a few weeks in a villa in Tuscany, perhaps, or an extended world cruise, or even just a week in a hotel on a consulting job — I often pack a full-sized trackball or mouse in my suitcase and sometimes even throw in a keyboard. Together they weigh about a pound.

Modern versions of external input devices like a mouse, trackball, drawing tablet, or keyboard simply plug into an available USB port. These devices require very little electrical power (and most only draw current when you push a button or spin a wheel).

If you have an older input device, it might be expecting to find a PS/2 port like those offered on older laptops and desktops; you can purchase an adapter that sits between its plug and the USB port on your machine. Similarly, if you

**Book VII
Chapter 4**

Going External with
Printer, Network, and
Special Peripherals

have an older laptop that actually has a PS/2 port, you can buy a little gizmo that converts a USB plug into a PS/2 plug.

You're not required to, but if you use an external input device you might want to disable the built-in touch pad or stick to avoid confusion. Check the instruction manual for your machine to see if you can disable the pointing device from the keyboard, from a setting made to its Mouse Properties screen, or from the BIOS setup screen.

Check out the Mouse Properties page, part of the Control Panel, to find out about available customization for the pointing device in your laptop or installed as an external device. An example is shown in Figure 4-2.

**Figure 4-2:**
The Mouse Properties screen for the built-in touchpad on a Toshiba Satellite laptop. A similar screen is added to your system as part of the device driver software for an external mouse or trackball.

 Most Mouse Properties screens include advanced features such as delegation of specific tasks to the left or right buttons. Another valuable option is to enable Snap To functionality. With this feature turned on, the pointer automatically appears in the default button of any dialog box you come to. This allows quick navigation through common tasks with a series of clicks or taps.

## Knowing Which Network You're With

Today nearly every modern laptop comes equipped with an Ethernet port for wired connection; an Ethernet system is the most commonly used office networking design. You also find a built-in WiFi adapter that cuts the cord between the machine and a nearby access point for a wired network.

Beyond these two basics, some laptops add one or both of a pair of specialty wireless communication protocols: Bluetooth or infrared. I talk more about these two means of communication in Book VIII, but for the moment let me explain that these last two methods are well suited for closely located devices.

You can work with a printer across the room or exchange data between your cell phone and your laptop using Bluetooth, for example. What do you do if

✦ Your machine isn't equipped with the wireless networking device you want to use?

✦ Its built-in WiFi system is outmoded by faster and better communications standards?

✦ The built-in system fails?

The answer to all three questions: Work around the problem by buying and using an external adapter. The solution here is to use a PC Card, Express Card, or USB adapter to communicate with the laptop's internal data bus. (Coming devices will likely use the developing eSATA specification as well.)

Of the three options, the most likely problem to be solved is number two: technological obsolescence. The most common set of specifications for wireless communication fall in the IEEE 802.11 series, which begins at 802.11b and (as this book goes to press) has gone through commercial release of faster or more capable 11a and 11g variants with two more versions (11n and 11y) ready to arrive soon.

If you don't have a problem with what you've got installed in your machine, you don't have a need for a change. But if you have an older system built with 802.11a technology, you might want to upgrade so you can work at greater speeds or at greater distances from an access point.

If you add a new WiFi adapter to a machine with existing built-in circuitry, turn off the prior system. This prevents conflicts within the computer and reduces the electrical draw that would occur with two transmitters and receivers in the same box. Consult your laptop's instruction manual or support desk for advice on disabling an unused WiFi system.

The third situation, a failure of the circuitry, is relatively rare. If your machine suffers a major electrical failure because of overvoltage, overheating, or an excess of gravitational forces (as in a fall from the table to the floor), it's likely that your problems will be greater than just the WiFi module.

# Book VIII

# Networking and Linking to the Internet

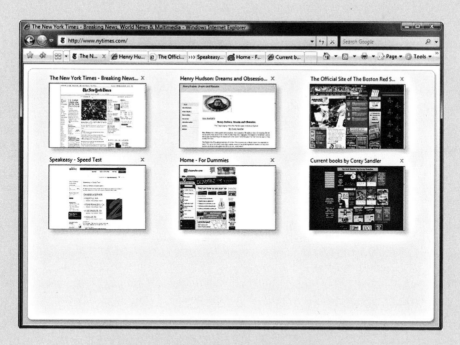

Click the Quick Tabs icon to see thumbnails of
all open Internet pages at the same time.

# Contents at a Glance

# Chapter 1: Networking with Other Machines

**M**ainframe and then desktop computers were at first isolated boxes of processors and data. Then they became linked to each other through a *local area network (LAN)* and to the rest of the world through the Internet.

When the first laptop computers became popular, they followed pretty much the same path. At first, the idea was that a laptop was something that could be used between offices. I worked with some of the very first portable PCs, lugging them onto commuter trains and airplanes and then using a serial cable to connect to a desktop machine or copying my completed work onto floppy disks to transfer the data.

It wasn't long, though, before desktops and laptops turned to the telephone to make the connection. Specialized mail services like MCI Mail allowed you to send messages or files to a central computer where they waited for the recipient to sign on and retrieve them . . . over a painfully slow dial-up connection where speeds were sometimes measured in minutes per page.

For years, laptops worked with external dial-up modems the size of a paperback book; eventually designers found a way to shrink the components of the modem so they could be integrated into the case. A little further along in the development process of the laptop, designers added a *network interface card (NIC),* which brought the Ethernet into the machine.

In this chapter I examine the hardware and software components necessary to allow a laptop to join a LAN. You stick to wired technology here; in Book VIII, Chapter 3, I discuss the next step in network evolution, wireless communication.

# Dissecting Network Components

A laptop that lives all by itself is, at heart, no different than a machine that is connected to a network. Within its case is a microprocessor, memory, storage, and input and output components including a keyboard, a pointing device, a display, and connections for use with printers and other external hardware.

Now, to become part of a network you must add three more essential elements:

✦ **A network interface card (NIC).** Greatly simplified in its modern incarnation, this is a small set of chips that manages the bundling of packets of data or commands to be sent out on the network and the reception and unbundling of packets addressed to it from other devices.

Nearly all current laptops now come equipped with an Ethernet port that serves this purpose; it accepts a cable with an oversized version of the familiar telephone connector. If your laptop does not have an Ethernet port, or if the built-in circuitry is outdated or fails, it can be replaced by a NIC that plugs into a PC Card or ExpressCard slot, or attaches to the laptop through a USB port.

✦ **A set of wires that links two or more computers and other devices together.** In nearly all designs for LANs, the wires don't go directly from one computer to another, but instead go through a device located (in logical terms) as if it were the hub of a wheel. This *router* accepts incoming data from any device linked to it and then re-routes it to the proper destination — another computer, a printer, a shared modem, or other devices.

In a wireless or WiFi system, the laptop broadcasts its signal to a wireless router that retransmits the information to the proper destination. The principles are the same as for a wired system . . . except for the lack of wires.

✦ **A software protocol and network management system.** Today, networking is built into all current versions of the Windows operating system.

## Taking a quick trip into the ether (net)

The vast majority of LANs are today based around the Ethernet specification; you're not required to use it, but you'd have to go well out of your way to set up a network that employs different conventions. (You can also buy a keyboard that doesn't have QWERTYUIOP as its top row of characters, and you can use Linux instead of Windows.) But for most of us, there is no need to buck a well-proven trend. Ethernet performs pretty well and our goal is get our work accomplished, not to prove a point by being the odd one out.

The core of Ethernet is a set of definitions of hardware and software protocols that encase chunks of data within a packet that includes the sender's and receiver's address, as well as other necessary information for communication between machines that aren't directly connected to each other.

Today, laptop users typically use one of three Ethernet flavors which differ principally in their velocity.

✦ 1000BASE-T also known as Gigabit Ethernet. The current speed champion gives you the basic information you seek right in its name: it's theoretically capable of moving as much as a gigabit, or 1,000 megabits of data per second.

✦ 100BASE-TX. Also in common use and runs at speeds as fast as 100 Mbps.

✦ 10BASE-T. Older systems may offer this, which operates no faster than 10 Mbps.

Note that an Ethernet is only capable of working at the speed of the slowest component in a particular connection. For example, if you have 1000Base-T NICs but a 100Base-TX router or hub, the network will move data no faster than 100 Mbps. If you have a 100Base-TX router that connects to a 10Base-T NIC in a computer on the network, you're limited to that slower speed.

The cable that runs between the Ethernet port on your laptop and a router or other device is a heavy-duty, higher-capacity version of a telephone wire. As various versions of the standard have been introduced, the cable has gotten a bit more robust; today the best cables are called Category 5e, which is a slight improvement over (and in most cases interchangeable with) Category 5. At each end of the cable is something called by designers an *8P8C modular connector;* the name means "eight position, eight connector." (The connector is also commonly but incorrectly referred to as an RJ45 plug; a distinction without a difference for most users.)

Thus far I've written only about how an Ethernet is wired. Now consider — briefly and simply — how it works.

The first thing to understand is that data isn't sent as a continuous stream from one location to another; if the system worked that way, in one example it would require opening a channel between my office and Paris anytime I wanted to send an order for fresh brioche. Instead, data is cut up into little snippets that are like envelopes with a sender's address and a recipient's address on each end.

The hardware side of the Ethernet interface inserts each packet into the extremely fast stream of data that moves by on the electronic superhighway; the computer watches the traffic and looks for a gap large enough to merge into traffic. If somehow two or more devices try to fill the same gap, there will be a collision, but the computer senses this and simply re-sends the data.

At the router, the electronics in that box scan the intended address for each packet and checks it against a list it maintains for every attached computer on the network. When it finds something intended for one of its clients, it redirects the packet to its destination.

### Something about spokes

Early in this book I explain that a computer accomplishes its magic not because it's smart, but because it's extremely fast. The same applies to the physical design (the *topology*) of a network. It doesn't really matter if the cable connecting the laptop that sits on the left wing of my desk to the desktop on right side goes 6 feet in a straight line or if it goes down through the floor to a router in the basement and comes up in a hole on the other side of the room and passes through three other machines before arriving at its destination. Unless you're talking about links that travel hundreds of miles, delays caused by cable length are measured in fractions of thousandths of a second.

Most simple networks — including virtually every wired and wireless system in the home and small office — use a design called *hub-and-spoke,* also known as a *star topology.* This sort of network is centered around a hub, switch, router, or (in a very large or complex system) server. The path from one computer to another passes through the central device.

This sort of design offers advantages:

✦ Some protection. The failure of any spoke — whether it's a NIC in a computer, the computer itself, or a networked device such as a printer or broadband modem — doesn't bring down the entire network.

✦ Some workaround. And if the hub — a router, switch, or server — fails, the network goes down, the individual computers can continue to do their work albeit without connection to each other.

### A bit about buses

A less commonly used form of network uses a *bus topology:* Each machine is connected to a *peer* machine to its (logically speaking) left or right. At each end of the bus, a *terminator* loops the signal back the other direction.

The bus must remain unbroken from one end to the other (with all the machines turned on and NICs performing properly); the network won't work if

✦ The cable is damaged

✦ A connector comes undone

✦ A network interface fails

## Broadening your horizons

What do I mean by *broadband?* In technical terms it means that the delivery mechanism can bring a wide frequency of signals. Wider or broader is better than narrower (like dial-up over an old-style phone system). If it helps you to visualize, think of broadband as a big, fat pipe full of many different varieties of *stuff* moving at high speed; that's got to be better than a thin straw that takes a long time to transport a small amount of just one flavor.

### Running in rings

A *ring topology* is a closed system; all the members of a network are arranged in something approximating a circle and the wiring goes from one machine to the next, all the way around, until it completes the circuit.

All the components — cables, connectors, and interfaces — must be working properly for the network to operate. (You may be old enough to remember Christmas tree light sets that were electrified with serial wiring; the failure of one lamp shut down the entire string.)

## Hubs, switches, and routers

A hub doesn't have to sit at the exact center of a circle, like a real hub on a bicycle wheel. But it's situated that way in logical terms.

Let me explain that by painting a word picture of my real office:

✦ At the moment, I'm sitting at the keyboard of my main production computer.

✦ A short Ethernet cable runs from that computer, along the floor, to an eight-port router on a shelf in the corner.

✦ The eighth port on the router goes to a two-foot Ethernet wire that connects to a broadband cable modem that allows every machine in my network to connect to the Internet at high speed.

✦ To my left are two laptops; one connects by a short Ethernet cable to the hub and the other uses its built-in WiFi circuitry to make a wireless connection to the network.

✦ Around to my right is another desk with a computer, and that machine plugs into a wall jack that connects about 15 feet down into the basement and back up again out through an outlet and from there into the same eight-port hub.

## Smarter than a hub

The original design for a hub was for a dumb device that merely brought everything together and then allowed signals to pass back out to every attached device on the network; if the packet wasn't intended for a particular computer, it ignored the information. We've gone way past that concept by now.

Hubs were first replaced by intelligent switches, and now switches have been mostly supplanted by routers.

A *switch* improved on a hub by adding some intelligence to read the address of an incoming packet and then selecting a path to send it directly to the intended recipient. Going directly allows every machine that is part of the network to use the full bandwidth of the network and also improved its efficiency by reducing the opportunity for collisions between packets.

A *router,* also called a *gateway,* adds one more very important element to the network switch: the ability to allow an entire network to also share a single broadband modem for Internet access. (The delivery system for the modem can be cable, DSL, fiber optics, or a dedicated high-speed telephone connection.)

Another way to look at a router is to think of it as a device that serves as a LAN hub at the same time it connects to the outside world (or to another network) through a gateway.

✦ All the way over on the opposite end of the office is another computer that I use to manage an archive of photos and old files; it connects by cabling that goes down into the basement and over to the hub, traveling about 30 feet.

✦ Another cable coming out of the hub connects through the wall to my left.

✦ In the room there, the cable goes into a WiFi router that broadcasts a signal throughout my home and office, allowing me to take a laptop out on the deck on a sunny day or into the family room if I want to play some streaming video or audio there.

✦ Finally, the WiFi router has four wired ports of its own, one of which is connected to a cable that stretches about 15 feet to a machine in the study.

✦ The eighth port on the router goes to a tw2-foot Ethernet wire that connects to a broadband cable modem that allows any and every machine in my network to connect to the Internet at high speed.

In no way does this design resemble a circle. And none of the cables are the same length, so the spokes are all irregular. But if I wiped clean the image of this complex network and just think in terms of how all the devices (including a few I left out in an attempt to make this a bit easier to visualize) connect to each other through the router, what you've got here is a hub-and-spoke network.

# Hello, Operator? Modem Madness

The purpose of a modem is to translate the digital 0s and 1s that exist within a laptop into an analog electrical wave that can travel over a telephone wire. The word modem is a concatenation of modulator-demodulator.

Today very few of us still use a standard telephone modem, but the same principle applies to users of much faster DSL and cable modems. And the concept of a modem has been applied to other forms of communications we now commonly use: wireless networks, cell phones, and fiber-optic networks.

## Types of modems

In this section I talk about the four most common direct-connection modems:

✦ Dial-up telephone modems

✦ Cable modems

✦ DSL phone line modems

✦ Fiber-optic translators

Today, cable and DSL modems are the most commonly used in homes and office. Fiber-optic system (including Verizon's proprietary FIOS service) use is growing in regions where they're offered, while old-style dial-up telephone modems are fading away rapidly.

---

## Smooth modulater

In most of the modern world, the telephone wires that come into your home and office are little different from the system designed by Bell in the 1870s. They're a simple pair of copper wires — one (usually covered in green insulation) is an electrical *common* or *ground,* and the other (usually red) carries 6 to 12 volts of DC power.

When you speak into the microphone end of a telephone, your voice *modulates* the current into a varying wave. At the other end of a simple point-to-point circuit, a telephone receives that modulated signal and uses it to make sounds in a speaker held up to a human ear.

The wave is called an *analog* signal. Think of it as an analogy of the sound: The pitch and volume of the human voice are represented by the peaks and valleys, and the distance between them by an electrical wave.

As I discuss in Book VIII, Chapter 6 about *Voice over Internet Protocol (VoIP),* the basic telephone systems become much more complex once they include the ability to call any phone anywhere rather than just connect directly between two points. But for your purposes here, imagine all connections are direct.

---

### Dial-up telephone modems

The first modem I worked with, in a wire service newsroom, was a box of wires and flashing lights that could move the news to a teletype machine at about 75 bits per second (bps); that's the rough equivalent of about 8 characters per second or 100 words per minute. Transmitting just the words (without the photographs, illustrations, and clever cartoons) in the book you're holding in your hands might take nearly 20 hours.

Things were looking a bit more promising when the first telephone modems for personal computer were introduced, quadrupling the speed all the way up to 300 bps.

To send identifiable characters, one behind the other, over a serial communication cable like a telephone wire, the computer has to add coding to mark the beginning and end of 8-bit computer words or bytes. It also inserts other data to help with error checking or error correction. Therefore, the net throughput of a 300 bps modem might be equivalent to about 27 bytes per second. If modems hadn't advanced beyond that point, the World Wide Web would never have been possible.

Now, the big question: Why am I bothering to discuss this ancient and slow technology? Good question; if you have a choice of any of the other, faster means of communication, use them.

The first few generations of laptop computers didn't come with an internal modem. There were two good reasons for this:

+ Not everyone wanted one.

+ The pace of change in modems was so great that it made little sense to put one inside the box. It made more sense to ask users to buy the latest portable modem and attach it to a serial port or later to a USB port.

And then in recent years, modems became so small that they were built into the motherboard of nearly all laptops. Many users may not even know they have one inside the box; look for a port on the side of the box for connecting a telephone cable. The connector for a telephone wire looks very similar to the one for an Ethernet cable, except the phone device is smaller.

Don't try to force the wrong connector into the improper port; it's hard to do, but some people try. See Figure 1-1.

The best speed you can realistically expect with a dial-up modem is somewhere in the range of about 42K; there are simply too many places where a good signal can go bad on the old telephone system.

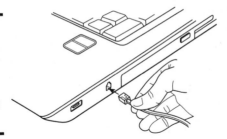

**Figure 1-1:**
A port for a
built-in dial-
up modem
on the side
of a current
laptop.

The only real advantage to holding on to this old technology is that maybe somewhere, someplace you bring your laptop is beyond the reach of broadband or wireless communication.

But almost everywhere you'll find a telephone. For that reason I maintain an account with AOL, one of the last of the remaining *Internet service providers (ISPs)* that maintains dial-up modem service in locations across the United States and in many nations around the world. (AOL also allows for near-instant connection over a broadband link.)

## Cable modems

From the same people who bring you "The Three Stooges" marathons and reality shows even sillier and less believable than Moe, Larry, and Curly comes the high-speed, generally reliable cable modem link.

*Cable modems* use the same large coaxial wiring that brings television into your home or office; the cable is broad enough to carry hundreds of video signals as well as Internet. It does this by sending multiple signals at different frequencies on the same wire; the Internet is given a chunk of the spectrum for downloading to your computer and uploading from it.

In most cable Internet systems, the signals travel as an analog wave. The cable modem modulates the digital information in your computer to send it upstream, or demodulates an incoming analog wave to convert it to digital for use in your computer. An example of a current cable modem is in Figure 1-2.

Cable upsides:

✦ The Internet is constantly available to your computer (as with other broadband technologies such as DSL and fiber-optic systems). You don't have to dial a number; it's like electricity in your wall outlet, ready when you need it.

✦ You can easily add a router or gateway between the cable modem and your computer to link several laptops or desktops to the same Internet connection (as this chapter explores earlier).

**Book VIII
Chapter 1**

Networking with
Other Machines

✦ You can also add a WiFi wireless router to spread a signal throughout your home or office, allowing you to bring your laptop from room to room.

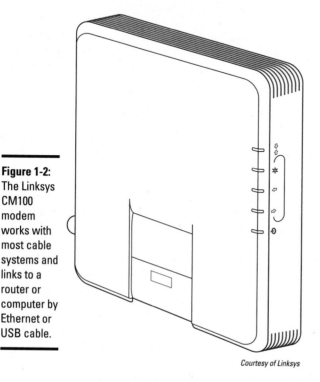

**Figure 1-2:**
The Linksys CM100 modem works with most cable systems and links to a router or computer by Ethernet or USB cable.

*Courtesy of Linksys*

Even though a router subdivides access to a single connection, the chances are you may never notice an impact. The incoming signal is very fast, and the chances that any two machines will make a major demand on the system at the exact millisecond is very unlikely.

Before you add cable Internet service to your home or office, make sure you're getting a high-quality cable television signal. You're going to be using the same incoming cable you already use; if it's less than acceptable for Moe, Larry, and Curly, it's not going to be very good for YouTube. Insist that the cable television connection be brought up to specifications; the company may have to add an amplifier at the street or in your home to improve a weak signal.

### The downside of cable modems

Most cable Internet offerings are *unbalanced,* meaning that the download stream of web pages, audio, video, and e-mail is given a bigger piece of the "pipe" than the upstream signal (which might include a request for a website, an order for a pizza, or a transfer of funds in your banking account).

This generally makes sense, although if you intend to send large amounts of graphics or video, you may want to look for a broadband service that gives you more speed for uploading. For most users, much more data comes downstream to your laptop than goes upstream.

Here in my office, I use a cable modem for the Internet. I typically receive a download signal that ranges from about 5 to 7 Mbps (more than 100 times faster than a dial-up modem) and an upload speed that ranges between about 280KB and 1.8 Mbps. Why do I report a range of speeds for downloading and uploading? Because the speed of travel is affected by the traffic on the road, or in this case, the traffic in the pipe.

The cable between your home or office and the central office of the cable company is shared by all users along the way; it doesn't matter what televisions shows they're watching, but if you happen to share a cable with one or more neighbors who are heavy downloaders of Internet graphics, it could slow down response. The same applies when it comes to uploading; if someone on your cable is running a 24-hour webcam pointed at his goldfish bowl, it just might slow down your ability to upload your own files.

In truth, though, cable companies generally do a pretty good job of balancing out the loads. They may add extra cables in areas with lots of customers or otherwise adjust their service, such as replacing older copper-based coaxial cables with fiber-optic links.

Consider carefully whether you want to give over your Internet connection to the cable company if

+ Your cable television system is prone to regular outages.

+ You've had other problems with them.

The only way to find out the quality of service you'll receive may be to try it out; if you find that the useable speed is too slow for your needs, ask the cable company to make it better or consider changing to a different provider.

### What's up, DOCSIS?

When cable Internet service was introduced, a number of technical designs *(protocols)* were put forth for the modem's design. Today, though, nearly all devices adhere to a standard called *DOCSIS (Data Over Cable Service Interface Specification)*.

Your modem must meet the requirements of your particular cable company; once you're connected to the Internet it doesn't matter what type of modem is used by the person or web site at the other end.

You can get a cable modem a number of ways:

✦ Some cable companies provide a free modem with their service.

✦ Some cable companies require you to purchase or rent one.

✦ You can buy your own cable modem, although the cable company might not provide support for something they didn't install.

### DSL modems

Sometimes speed limits are made to be broken, and that's what technology allowed designers to do in the 1990s: They found a way to push past what had been considered the physical limits of the original telephone system.

*Digital Subscriber Line (DSL)* service manages to deliver Internet downloads at speeds of as much as 1.5 mps, about 30 to 40 times as fast as a standard dial-up telephone modem could deliver. DSL takes advantage of the fact that standard voice telephone service uses only a small segment of the available frequency range of copper wiring, sending analog voice signals in the range from 0 KHz to 4 KHz; that narrow band works well over long distances.

The now mostly outmoded dial-up modem modulates its signal into the same 4 KHz-wide band; generally you can't use the same standard telephone line for both voice and data at the same time. The engineers who developed DSL set their sights higher: A DSL modem sends its signals in the frequency range between 25 KHz and 1 MHz, much higher and wider on the wire. And they left in place the 0 to 4 Hz channel, meaning that users can retain their voice telephone service on the same phone line if they choose.

DSL upsides:

✦ DSL is much faster than dial-up.

✦ The DSL line from your home or office to the phone company's switching center isn't shared with other users. You don't have to worry about how much the bandwidth your neighbor is grabbing.

DSL downsides:

✦ It can only deliver a fraction of the speed brought by cable or fiber-optic systems.

✦ DSL is only available where the plain old telephone system isn't very, very old and decrepit and places that aren't too far from the phone company's central office. Generally, the service is available to homes or offices no farther than 2 or perhaps 3 miles from a central switch where the signal can be moved onto newer, higher-capacity technology.

At first, DSL was offered only as an upgrade to existing voice telephone customers. But today, as more and more people use cell phones or VoIP technologies, the phone companies have begun to offer *naked* or *dry-loop* DSL service. That may sound either enticing or uncomfortable, but all that means is that the system only delivers the high-frequency bandwidth between 25 KHz and 1 MHz and not offer a voice-service dial tone lower on the radio-frequency spectrum.

As I warn about cable modem providers, make sure you receive a good, quality voice telephone service before committing to using DSL; if they can't give you a signal clear enough to speak with your friends and family, how can they bring an Internet channel good enough to surf the Web?

### Fiber-optic systems

A developing wave in technology, led in the United States by Verizon Communications, is fiber-optic service. Verizon cleverly calls its offering FiOS, which stands for . . . fiber-optic service. Another name for this type of service is *Fiber to the Premises (FTTP)*.

Fiber optics to the home is a 21st-century design. Today, its slowest offering starts about where cable Internet begins, at 5 Mbps downloading and goes on from there to speeds of as much as 30 and even 50 Mbps.

Fiber-optic upsides:

✦ The biggest advantage is that it's the newest technology available to consumers. The telephone system dates back to about 1875, cable television was introduced in the 1950s, and DSL is a retrofit to Alexander Graham Bell's original concept.

✦ Uploading is much faster, starting at about 2 Mbps and currently topping out at about 20 Mbps.

✦ Fiber-optic service providers offer various levels of service; obviously the faster the speed, the higher the price.

As with other types of Internet service, your results may vary because of the condition of wiring at your home or office, the quality of the cable in your neighborhood, and Internet and network congestion. Fiber-optic service and other types of Internet carriers (including cable, DSL, and dial-up telephone) have two significant differences:

✦ Fiber-optic cables carry signals in the form of laser-generated pulses.

✦ The signal is digital from your computer to the fiber-optic system.

Instead of a modem, a fiber-optic system uses a device, called an *Optical Network Terminal (ONT),* that converts incoming pulses of light to an electrical signal that travels over an Ethernet cable to your computer; going the other direction, the ONT converts an Ethernet signal back to pulses of light.

Because fiber optics is the new kid on your block, it holds the promise of many future enhancements. You can expect services like

+ Virtually unlimited movies on demand

+ Video conferencing

+ Burglar alarm monitoring

+ Automated meter reading

## Testing your speed

You know what the seller has promised you. But how fast is your Internet connection really performing?

+ Check with your ISP for any utilities or notices of problems (or upgrades); go to the Web page for your provider and look for a support page.

+ Test your Internet connection. Many independent and free services report on your upload and download speeds as well as any quality issues it can detect. Some services allow you to check your results against those reported by neighbors using the same company for Internet, or to see how your results stack up against those who use a competitor's service.

I make it a habit to check in on the system's quality of service every few weeks to see if there's been any significant change in one way or another; I also go to one or the other web site (in the following list) anytime I suspect there may be a problem with my service.

I regularly use these two very reliable test pages:

+ **www.speakeasy.net/speedtest** A site run by a company that resells Internet services to small businesses. Their site offers the ability to communicate with servers spread around the United States; I usually test a nearby site and a distant one. An example of a test is shown in Figure 1-3.

+ **http://miranda.ctd.anl.gov:7123** A test site at the Argonne National Laboratory in Argonne, Illinois. You receive an upload and download speed report, as well as details that may help you, or a technician, troubleshoot a slowdown in your Internet service.

**Figure 1-3:**
A Speak-easy speed test of a broadband Internet connection, showing a healthy download speed of 7,165 kbps (7.2 Mbps) and an upload speed of 1,845 kbps.

# Chapter 2: Managing a Windows Network

## In This Chapter

✔ The software side of networking

✔ Clicking, pointing, and configuring your way to connectivity

✔ Naming machines and workgroups

✔ Sharing folders, files, and printers

✔ Sharing an Internet connection

*S*o you have this wonderfully equipped, extremely capable portable computer that allows you to do all of your computing tasks — from business to entertainment — anywhere in the world. Why would we possibly want to hook it up to other computers in a local network or over the Internet?

It's not a trick question. For many of us, our laptop is the be-all and end-all . . . up to a point. The fact is that, like humans, eventually even a computer needs to have a bit of discourse and interchange with others.

What's the latest news? Who has sent us mail? What is the balance in our checking account? Has the home office changed the prices on Model 6SJ7 widgets, and how many are in stock in the warehouse? The answers to each of these questions lie somewhere else: on another computer that may be across the room, across the country, or somewhere in that cloud of information we call the Internet.

And there are other reasons. Can I get a printout of my order? Can I synchronize my calendar with the other members of my workgroup? Can I back up my irreplaceable files on a remote server?

## Speaking of Networking

In the early days of computing, setting up a network was a black art requiring squads of specialists, companies of electricians, and platoons of technicians to oversee the installation of cabling, *network interface cards (NIC)*, and modifications to operating systems that were not intended to play well with others.

We're past all that: Today all current versions of Windows come equipped with fully capable networking software and nearly every laptop is good to go with a built-in NIC for wired networking and a WiFi module for high-speed wireless communication.

A few definitions are in order:

✦ A *NIC* is an adapter that controls the flow of information to and from a laptop when the machine is connected using an Ethernet cable. It's called a *card* because in its original form it was an adapter that plugged into the bus of a desktop PC. Today, network interface circuitry is built into nearly all computer motherboards.

✦ Networking *protocols* are collections of software that work with the operating system to manage the incoming and outgoing flow of data.

✦ A *WiFi adapter* is a transmitter/receiver for wireless communication between a laptop or desktop and a base station or other device.

The NIC has a connector, which looks like a slightly oversized telephone jack, that attaches to an Ethernet cable; today's most commonly used cables are called Category 5 or Category 5e; they differ slightly in the *stringency of their specifications.* That's a fancy way of saying that 5e (as in *enhanced*) is theoretically capable of delivering a higher quality of communication. Both 5 and 5e work with networks that deliver data at speeds of as much as 100 Mbps.

If you're buying new cable, use 5e. And if you're taking the next step up, to Gigabit Ethernet, use Category 6 cabling, designed specifically for that speed.

Whatever cable you use, one end attaches to the NIC and the other to a router, switch, hub, or (in some arrangements) directly to another laptop or PC.

If your laptop doesn't have a NIC or WiFi module, or if you need to work around an outdated or failed piece of hardware, you can install hardware for one or both functions in a PC Card or ExpressCard slot, or as an external device that attaches to a USB port. You need a port that delivers USB 2.0 speed for Gigabit Ethernet; the older USB 1.1 specification supports 10 or 100 Mbps Ethernet communications.

## Networking Soft (ware)ly

On the software side, you need a driver to connect your NIC to the operating system, and your operating system needs to supply network protocols that are compatible with the network to which you seek a connection. Windows can support multiple protocols on the same system.

To see the networking connection properties of your machine, do the following:

Under Windows Vista, do this:

*1.* **Click Start ➪ Control Panel.**

*2.* **Click the Networking and Sharing Center.**

*3.* **Click View Status for the Connection.**

*4.* **Go to the Status page.**

*5.* **Click the Properties button.**

See Figure 2-1 for an example of a Vista report.

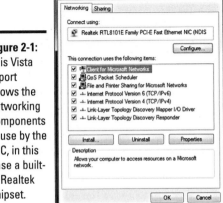

**Figure 2-1:**
This Vista report shows the networking components in use by the NIC, in this case a built-in Realtek chipset.

For Windows XP users, follow here:

*1.* **Click Start ➪ Control Panel ➪ Network Connections.**

*2.* **Double-click the network.**

The Local Area Connection Status screen appears.

*3.* **Click the Properties button.**

A list of protocols in use appears.

Current operating systems typically include some or all of these built-in network protocols:

✦ **Client for Microsoft Networks.** This is the essential piece of software for standard Windows-based networks; it is needed in order to be able to remotely access folders, files, printers, and other shared resources. It is only required in Microsoft-to-Microsoft networks; if your office or organization uses a different protocol it is necessary only if you travel with your laptop to a location set up differently.

And it has nothing to do with the Internet; for that reason, some security experts caution that you pay special attention to any file-sharing settings you make on a system that uses the Client for Microsoft Networks as well as an Internet protocol.

✦ **Internet Protocol or Microsoft TCP/IP (TCP/IPv4 or TCP/IPv6).** The Transmission Protocol Control (TCP) and the Internet Control (IP) are the basic building blocks for networking as well as the Internet; the IP part of the equation draws its roots all the way back to the first version of the Internet as a government-military-academic network. IPv6 is the latest extension to the code, put in place to deal with the incredible and unanticipated growth in the number of Internet addresses. Nearly all machines will require one or both of these sets of code; IPv6 was introduced as an element of Windows Vista.

✦ **QoS Packet Scheduler.** Introduced with Windows 2000 and Windows XP, this is a protocol that works to set priorities for the most efficient ordering of packets sent across a network.

✦ **Microsoft NetBEUI or NetBIOS.** This is an older networking protocol used in versions of Microsoft's operating system through Windows 98; it has been replaced on modern machines by the Client for Microsoft Networking. It may be necessary if you have a mix of machines that includes some running older versions of Windows or employing older hardware designed for outmoded protocols.

✦ **Microsoft IPX/SPX.** Also less commonly used, this Microsoft protocol is compatible with most existing Novell NetWare networks such as might be found in large businesses or organizations. Novell also offers its own version of the protocol that may offer some advantages to users.

Depending on your laptop's particular hardware components, or the demands of certain routers, switches, or other components, the installation process may automatically add other pieces of software to the networking suite; in some situations you may need to manually install networking components or configure them.

# Identifying Computers to Each Other

Once the hardware is configured you have to give each computer the equivalent of a little tag that says, "Hello. My Name is . . . " and then you have to

✦ Grant permission if any folders or files are to be shared

✦ Specifically permit the sharing of attached peripherals such as a printer

The first step is to assign all the computers in a particular network to a common workgroup name. As indicated in Table 8-1, the default name for workgroups changed between Windows XP and Vista.

TIP

I recommend that you use a name of your own design: This helps avoid confusion if you end up dealing with multiple workgroups and it adds a small extra measure of protection against unauthorized outsiders who might try to gain access.

## Setting or changing a workgroup name under Windows XP

To find or change the workgroup name on a computer running Windows XP, do this:

*1.* **Click Start.**

*2.* **Right-click My Computer.**

*3.* **Click Properties.**

*4.* **In System Properties, click the Computer Name tab.**

You see the workgroup name.

*5.* **Click Change.**

If you want to change the name, that is.

*6.* **Type the new name in the Computer Name box.**

*7.* **Click OK.**

The Computer Name tab is shown in Figure 2-2.

**Figure 2-2:**
To rename a computer or to join a workgroup in Windows XP, click the Change button in the Computer Name tab.

**Book VIII
Chapter 2**

Managing a
Windows Network

## Setting or changing a workgroup name under Windows Vista

To find or change the workgroup name on a computer running Windows Vista, do this:

*1.* **Click Start ➪ Control Panel.**

*2.* **Act based on your setup:**

- You're using the simplified Control Panel menu: Click System and Maintenance ➪ System.

- You're using the Classics view: Click System.

The System page, shown in Figure 2-3, is displayed. This page includes details about your computer including its

- Manufacturer

- Model

- Processor

- Amount of RAM

- Windows Experience Index for the machine

**Figure 2-3:**
The System page of Windows Vista brings together many of the details of your machine, including a section where you can change the network workgroup and the computer name.

You find the workgroup name is in the section Computer Name, Domain, and Workgroup Settings section.

3. **Click the Change Settings button.**

4. **Type the name of a workgroup.**

5. **Click OK.**

You're asked to restart your computer so the changes take effect.

# *Visiting Windows Vista Network Center*

Center is apt, because many new and improved network functionalities appear in Vista:

+ Network Center
+ Network Map
+ Network Explorer
+ Network Awareness

**Network Center** includes reports on how your machine is functioning as a member of a *local area network (LAN)*.

**Network Map** displays the various links graphically, and if one of the PCs in your LAN loses its link, you can see the problem and use Network Diagnostics in search of a solution.

The center is also the entryway to adding connections to other available networks or the creation of a new one. The Network Setup Wizard allows you to set up wired or wireless networks by identifying unconfigured network devices and adding them to the network. Also included are features to lock down some of the network settings to protect against intrusion and damage.

Under Windows Vista, network settings can be saved to a USB flash drive to allow quick and easy configuration of additional PCs not yet connected. Windows Vista automatically tunes itself to receive more data at any given time by detecting your Internet connection speed and the amount of bandwidth available to you.

**Network Explorer** simplifies the process of sharing files and peripherals, presenting a view of all PCs and devices (including printers and modems) on the network; it replaces My Network Places from Windows XP. Among its advances: the ability to directly interact with certain devices. For example, you may be able to adjust settings or control music playback of current hardware.

**Book VIII
Chapter 2**

**Managing a
Windows Network**

**Network Awareness** can adjust applications based on changing network elements. Among uses of this technology are a home office machine that switches between personal use and connection to a corporate network; the Network Awareness utility recognizes the change and can adjust firewall settings to open or close ports as needed for IT management tools.

And Microsoft promises to keep data more secure with enhanced support for the latest wireless security protocols, including WPA2. Safeguards in the operating system help users stay away from fraudulent wireless networks that appear to be legitimate wireless hotspots but are instead intended to capture keystrokes or steal personal information.

## Ch . . . ch . . . changes in Windows Vista

Windows Vista brought a number of improvements in the process of setting up a network, along with a few changes that may affect some users who have mixes of Windows operating systems on the various machines that are linked. See Table 2-1 for a description of the differences introduced with the new operating system.

| Table 2-1 | Default Network Settings in Windows Vista and Windows XP | |
|---|---|---|
| *Feature* | *Windows XP* | *Windows Vista* |
| Default workgroup name | MSHOME (Windows XP Home Edition) | |
| WORKGROUP (All other Windows XP editions) | WORKGROUP (all editions) | |
| Shared folder name | Shared Documents | Public |
| Simple file sharing | Enabled by default | Not enabled by default; to permit access to shared folders a user name and password must be assigned and used |
| Detection and access to computers on the network | Detects and accesses computers in the same workgroup | Detects and accesses all computers on the network, regardless of which operating system they're running or which workgroup they're included in |
| Place to change settings and preferences | My Network Places | Network folder |
| Network controls | Located in various utilities of the operating system | Mostly located in the Network and Sharing Center |

## Setting the network location type

Under Windows Vista, you can assign a *network location type* that automatically applies a group of security (and other) settings appropriate for the type of network in use.

There are three network location types:

+ **Private.** This computer is part of a network that has some degree of protection from intrusion by strangers; this may include a router or hardware firewall or software protection. Most home and small business networks are this type.

+ **Public.** This computer is connected to a network available for public use. Examples include networks in hotels, restaurants, airports, libraries, and other purposely open system.

+ **Domain.** This form of private computer is connected to a network that contains an Active Directory domain controller. Many actively controlled workplace networks are configured this way.

To check the network location type or to make changes, do the following:

*1.* **Click Start button ➪ Control Panel.**

*2.* **Click Network and Internet ➪ Network and Sharing Center.**

If you use the Classics menu, click directly on Network and Sharing Center.

The network location type is displayed in parentheses next to the network name; see Figure 2-4.

*3.* **Click the Customize button.**

This option is to the right of the network name.

*4.* **In Set Network Location, click one:**

- **Private**
- **Public**
- **Domain**

*5.* **Click Next ➪ Close.**

## Changing file and printer sharing options

Under Windows Vista, when you set or change your network location type to Private, network discovery is automatically turned on. This setting affects whether your computer can find other computers and networks and whether those other devices and networks can see your computer.

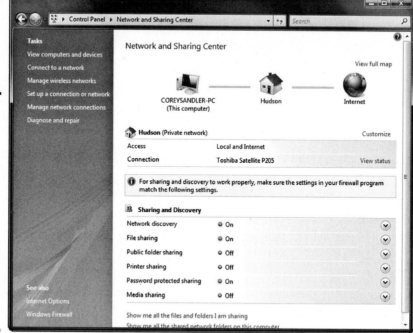

**Figure 2-4:**
The
Network
and Sharing
Center of
Windows
Vista shows
that this
particular
laptop is
part of a
Private
network
named
Hudson.

There are three network discovery states:

✦ **On.** Your computer can see other network computers and devices and other network computers can see your computer. This makes it easier to share files and printers.

✦ **Off.** Your computer can't see other network computers and devices and can't be seen by other network computers.

✦ **Custom.** The user or a system administrator can select certain specific settings. Nontechnical users should tread carefully here; an incorrect setting could make your computer invisible to other machines or open it up to unwanted intruders.

The Network and Sharing Center is also the place where you can make custom choices for sharing. In general, if your machine is otherwise protected by a firewall program — either from Microsoft or a third party — you should consider turning on

✦ File sharing

✦ Public folder sharing

✦ Printer sharing

For the most secure level of protection for your networked machine, you can turn on password-protected sharing. When this option is enabled, only persons who have a user account and password on the machine you're configuring are allowed to access shared files, the Public folder, or any printers or other shared devices.

When file sharing is on, files and printers that are opened for sharing on your laptop can be accessed by other machines on the network. Printer sharing (for devices attached to the machine you are configuring) can be turned on or off.

Public folder sharing can be set up in one of three conditions:

+ Anyone with network access can open files.

+ Anyone with network access can open, change, or create files in the folder.

+ Sharing is turned off; only persons logged on to the local computer can access the folder.

You can turn on media sharing to allow people and machines on the network to access music, images, and videos on the computer you're configuring, and this computer can also find the same types of shared files on other machines on the network.

# Joining a Workgroup

The basic Windows network is a *peer-to-peer* system; this means that all laptops as well as desktop computers in the network are considered the equal of each other; no central computer is in charge and any computer can communicate directly with another.

At the core of a Windows peer-to-peer network is a *workgroup*. You can set up your network with just one workgroup, or there can be subdivisions with multiple workgroups of machines that can see and work with each other.

**Book VIII
Chapter 2**

When you first configure a new laptop under Windows Vista or Windows XP, somewhere between much and all the work of setting up the Workgroup is done for you. You can also use automated utilities to transfer settings from one machine in an existing workgroup to a new machine.

To see a display of all of the computers that are members of a particular workgroup under Windows XP, do this:

*1.* **Open My Network Places.**

*2.* **Choose View Workgroup Computers.**

**Managing a
Windows Network**

This option is in the pane on the left. The display shows any member of the workgroup that's turned on and connected to the network; any machine that is offline or turned off isn't listed.

**3. Press the up arrow.**

All workgroups registered on the network appear.

## Your Laptop's Name and Address, Mac

From the start of human history, we have applied names to the places we live. That's how his buddies could tell Joe's Cave from Mary's Pile of Twigs Near the Creek. Eventually (and actually, relatively recently in some parts of the world, including rural America) it became necessary to add numbers to addresses. Oh, and then we get into ZIP codes.

If it makes sense for a slow, human-directed operation like the U.S. Postal Service or your local police or fire department to require that locations have numbers and street names, it's even more obvious that a high-speed, high-volume machine like a personal computer needs a similar kind of addressing scheme. In many ways, the biggest assignment given to laptops and PCs is the establishment and maintenance of a huge and expanding database that keeps track of where each and every one of millions and billions of bits of information are stored; the same applies for the components of a network.

All networks — wired or wireless, local or wide area, and the Internet — work by assigning a unique name or number to the sender and to the receiver and then encapsulating that information in all of the small packets of data it transmits. The intended recipient looks for packets with its address, snags them from the passing stream, and then reassembles the pieces into a complete file.

Every laptop connected to a network has the following identifiers:

✦ **An IP (Internet Protocol) address.** Within a network, each IP address is unique; some IP addresses are intended to be globally unique, meaning there is only one such address anywhere on the Internet. Any device — a computer, network equipment (like routers and switches), or peripherals (like printers) — can be assigned an IP address. In some network setups an IP address is established only for a current session, while in more common small networks it is applied permanently.

✦ **A MAC or Physical Address.** A Media Access Control (MAC) address is a unique code physically encoded within most network interface cards (NICs) or their equivalents in a computer. The MAC acts like a name for the device; it is a required element of networking but especially useful in situations where pieces of hardware may have only temporary IP addresses for each session. Together the IP and MAC help the network be precise in identifying and locating a NIC.

✦ **A local "name" on the network.** For the purposes of the user, devices are also given a name that presumably is easier to remember than a complex MAC or IP address. You can call your computer just about anything; I call mine all sorts of names depending on how they're treating me today.

The Windows operating system also allows users to append notes to the name of devices. For example, I may give my machines names based on their particular user or use (Janice's PC, or Deep Archive Server) and I might add notes identifying that a particular machine is a Core 2 Duo laptop while another is an antique Pentium 4 used as a storage device.

The importance of the name is that it serves as a bridge between the computer (which "thinks" only in terms of numbers) and its human users (who relate much more comfortably to names and descriptive words). A computer can very easily figure out that Janice's computer is called 192.185.1.232, but I find it a lot easier to think of the resources on her computer as residing on Paul.

## Naming computers in Windows Vista

There are at least three quick and relatively easy ways to change the name of a laptop if you're running Windows Vista.

Way 1:

1. **Click Start.**

2. **Right-click Computer.**

3. **Click Properties.**

   The System window appears.

4. **Click the Change button.**

   The button is in the Computer Name, Domain, and Workgroup Settings section.

Way 2:

1. **Click Start ➪ Control Panel ➪ System and Maintenance ➪ System.**

2. **Click the Change button.**

   The button is in the Computer Name, Domain, and Workgroup Settings section.

Way 3:

1. **Click Start.**

2. **Type** sysdm.cpl **into the Search box.**

*3.* **Press Enter.**

The System Properties window appears.

*4.* **Click Change.**

Now you can alter the computer name or workgroup. See Figure 2-5.

**Figure 2-5:**
The direct way to changing a computer's or workgroup's name under Windows Vista is displayed by entering a command in the Start menu search box.

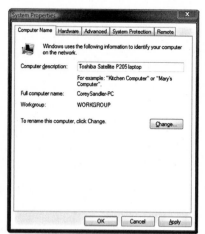

## Naming computers in Windows XP

You can learn the name of your laptop on the network, or make changes, in this way:

*1.* **Click Start ➪ Control Panel.**

*2.* **Click the System icon.**

*3.* **Click the Computer Name tab.**

*4.* **Type text into the Computer text box.**

You directly add or change the name this way. No requirement says a computer must have a description.

*5.* **Click the Change button.**

Now you can make changes to the full computer name, or to the workgroup name.

Each computer name on a network must be unique, and there can be no spaces in the name. But when it comes to workgroup names, they need to be the same on each machine that claims membership; any differences will cause the operating system to consider the two groups to be separate.

## Finding your laptop's IP address in Windows Vista

Here is one way to learn the IP address (and much more) for a computer successfully connected to a network, under Windows Vista:

*1.* **Click Start.**

*2.* **Right-click the Network button.**

*3.* **Select Properties.**

*4.* **Click View Status for the computer you want to check.**

The Local Area Connection Status window opens.

*5.* **Click Details.**

Here you find technical details of the connection including the IP Address, the Subnet Mask, and Default Gateway. See Figure 2-6 for an example. There's no need to understand the gruesome details of these technicalities, but they may be needed in troubleshooting or configuration of advanced devices and may be requested by a support technician.

Included in the displayed information is the MAC address, although just to make things confusing, it is called instead the Physical Address.

**Figure 2-6:**
The Network Connection Details for a laptop running under Windows Vista. For the protection of my system I have edited out some of the details a hacker might be happy to see printed in this book.

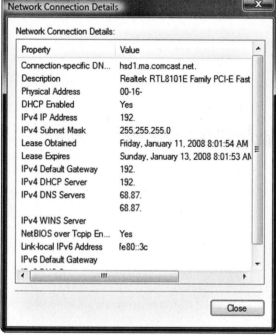

Network Connection Details:

| Property | Value |
|---|---|
| Connection-specific DN... | hsd1.ma.comcast.net. |
| Description | Realtek RTL8101E Family PCI-E Fast |
| Physical Address | 00-16- |
| DHCP Enabled | Yes |
| IPv4 IP Address | 192. |
| IPv4 Subnet Mask | 255.255.255.0 |
| Lease Obtained | Friday, January 11, 2008 8:01:54 AM |
| Lease Expires | Sunday, January 13, 2008 8:01:53 AM |
| IPv4 Default Gateway | 192. |
| IPv4 DHCP Server | 192. |
| IPv4 DNS Servers | 68.87. |
| | 68.87. |
| IPv4 WINS Server | |
| NetBIOS over Tcpip En... | Yes |
| Link-local IPv6 Address | fe80::3c |
| IPv6 Default Gateway | |

Close

### Finding your laptop's IP address in Windows XP

Here is one way to learn the IP address (and much more) for a computer successfully connected to a network, under Windows XP:

**1. From Windows Desktop, click the My Network Places icon.**

**2. Locate View Network Connections.**

It's on the left pane.

**3. Double-click your network connection.**

Note that your laptop may include several connections, including a

- Wireless network
- 1394 or FireWire connection
- Local Area Network

**4. Choose the Local Area Network.**

The first window you see is the Local Area Connection Status on the General tab. Here you can see the status of the connection, the amount of time (duration) it has been active, and the current speed.

**5. Click the Support tab.**

## Playing Nice, Sharing a Folder

To make a folder on a desktop or laptop available to other authorized computers in the same Local Area Network, it needs to be shared. The folder can be shared with only those users with accounts on the laptop you are configuring, you can open it up for access by anyone on the network, or you can give permission only to specific users.

When you share a folder you are making available all of its contents, including those of subfolders held within. Individual files can't be shared; they must be placed within a shared folder to be accessible.

In most cases, you don't want to share the root folder (the topmost folder of a disk drive) or any of the system folders that hold Windows and its settings. Keep this unavailable to avoid intentional or unintentional damage to your essential system files.

### Sharing a folder under Windows Vista

Windows Vista allows sharing of files from any folder where permission is granted, or from the Public folder. A shared folder and the files within can be accessed by anyone logged onto your computer or by someone on another computer on the network.

If you share files from their current location without copying them to another location or to the Public folder, you can specify which users or machines can have access. To do this, follow these steps:

*1.* **Locate the folder with the files you want to share.**

*2.* **Click one or more files or folders.**

*3.* **On the toolbar, click Share.**

   The File Sharing dialog box opens.

*4.* **Click the text box's drop-down arrow.**

*5.* **Click the name of a person previously identified to the network.**

*6.* **Click Add.**

   You can also type the name of the person you want to share files with, and then click Add.

   If you don't see the name of the person with whom you want to share files, click the text box's drop-down arrow and then click Create a New User.

If password protection is turned on for your computer, the person you're sharing with must have a user account and password on your computer in order to access the files and folders you're sharing. You can turn password protection on or off in the Network and Sharing Center.

Once you add a name to the list of people who can share a particular folder, you can also set permissions for users. See Figure 2-7.

*1.* **Click the drop-down arrow under Permission Level for each name.**

*2.* **Select one of these options for each name:**

   • **Reader.** This gives read-only permission to another user; that person can view shared files but cannot edit or delete them.

   • **Contributor.** Users with this level of permission can view or add shared files, but can only edit or delete files they have contributed. Contributor status is only available when folders are shared; individual files can't be given this permission level.

   • **Co-owner.** These users can view, add, edit, or delete any shared file.

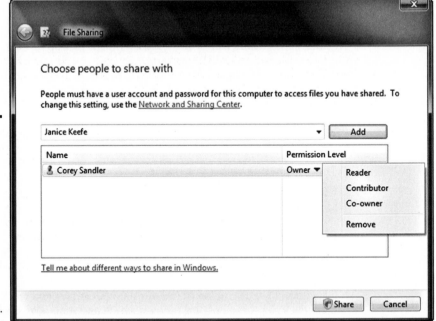

**Figure 2-7:**
When you choose people to share network access in Windows Vista, you can assign three levels of permissions.

## Notifying other users of changes to sharing settings

Once you have completed setting sharing for a folder or file you will receive confirmation from the system. You may want to notify other uses that a folder has been shared or permissions otherwise changed. Windows Vista helps notify:

✦ Click E-mail to open a Windows Mail e-mail message containing a link to your shared files; enter the e-mail addresses for the proper recipients.

✦ Click Copy to automatically copy the displayed link to the Windows Clipboard. You can then open an e-mail program or *instant message (IM)* program and paste the link into the message.

If you change the name of a file or folder after you it has been shared, any link you sent to other users will no longer work; you must send them a new link or otherwise notify them of the change.

## Sharing files in Windows Vista with the Public folder

To share files from the Public folder, copy or move files to the Public folder or one of its subfolders, such as Public Documents or Public Music. Anyone with a user account on a particular computer can access the Public folder on that machine; in addition, you can decide whether to extend that folder on the network.

Anything in the Public Folder is open to viewers with permission to access it; individual files and folders located there can't be restricted.

By default, network access to the Public folder is turned off; you have to turn it on if you want to enable sharing. You can also turn on password-protected sharing to limit network access to the Public folder to only those with a user account and password on your computer.

## Assigning permission levels to users

You can set specific permissions for individual folders or groups of folders. You also can set varying levels of general permission for users.

The right to assign permission levels to users is given only to system administrators and users with administrator accounts; if you are the only user on your laptop, you're likely to be the administrator unless you're working with an organization that configures and manages laptops for users.

Available permission for users follow:

- ✦ **Full control.** Users can see the contents of a file or folder and make changes to existing files and folders as well as create new files and folders. They can also run programs from a folder.

- ✦ **Modify.** Users are permitted to make changes to existing files and folders but cannot create new ones.

- ✦ **Read & execute.** Users can see the contents of existing files and folders but cannot make changes to them or delete them. They can also run programs from a folder.

- ✦ **Read.** Users have read-only access to folders and the files within them.

- ✦ **Write.** Users can create new files and folders and make changes to existing files and folders.

## Sharing a folder under Windows XP

Here's how to share a folder in Windows XP:

1. **Go to My Computer.**

   Any other Windows Explorer display (including My Documents, My Music, and My Pictures) will do, too.

2. **Click the folder.**

   The folder's highlighted.

*3.* **Do one of the following:**

- **Right-click and choose Sharing and Security.**

- **Choose File ⇨ Sharing and Security.**

A Properties dialog box appears.

*4.* **Locate the Share This Folder on the Network check box.**

It's in the Network Sharing and Security pane.

*5.* **Choose one:**

- To share the folder: Add a check mark to the Share This Folder on the Network check box.

- To remove sharing permission: Click an existing check mark in the Share This Folder on the Network check box.

You can't share the folder if it's marked Private in the Local Sharing and Security pane on the same dialog box.

*6.* **Enter a Share Name text box.**

A *share name* is a nickname that appears on the screens of other users in the network. You can use this to make the folder name more descriptive of its contents.

*7.* **If you think it's safe, you may enable the Allow Network Users to Change My Files check box.**

Stop and think before permitting others to alter your files. It is one thing to allow others to retrieve information from your computer and something completely different to allow them to change your data.

On the other hand, if you're setting up a network for your own benefit — for example, preparing your laptop and desktop to exchange files for your Road Warrior travels — this facility allows that process to be done easily.

When you're finished making settings regarding sharing, the folder's icon changes to show an outstretched hand beneath its picture.

# Accessing Another Computer on a Local Network

Once you set up your computer's networking facilities, you can see any shared folders or resources offered by computers on the network. Windows XP and Windows Vista operate in a similar fashion.

## Viewing a Windows Vista network

Check out a Vista network this way:

*1.* **Click the Start button.**

*2.* **Click the Network button.**

*3.* **Double-click the workgroup name.**

Its shared resources are displayed. See Figure 2-8.

You can double-click any folder or device to open and examine its contents or properties.

## Viewing a Windows XP network

Check out an XP network this way:

*1.* **Click the Start button.**

*2.* **Click the My Network Places icon.**

The My Network Places icon may be directly on the Windows Desktop.

*3.* **Click the View Workgroup Computers button.**

*4.* **Double-click the icon for a listed computer**

Now you can view a list of shared resources on that machine.

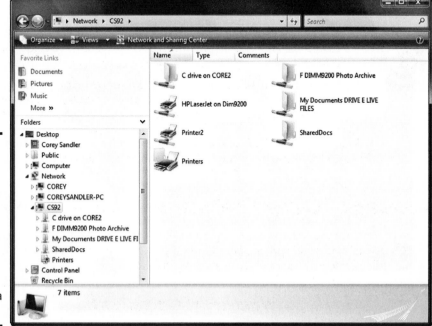

**Figure 2-8:** The Network and Sharing Center of Windows Vista shows icons for shared folders and devices on a network.

# Mapping a Folder

You can instruct Windows to *map* a shared folder on another computer to a virtual disk drive letter on your own machine. When you perform any Open or Save command on your laptop, the shared folder looks as if it's in your machine. The mapped folder also appears in Computer (in Windows Vista) or My Computer (in Windows XP).

Folders have to be already listed as shared before you can map them.

## Mapping in Windows Vista

To map a folder on a network in Windows Vista

**1. Click Start ➪ Computer.**

**2. Click Map Network Drive.**

This option is on the toolbar at the top of the window.

You see a window that asks, "What network folder would you like to map?" (See Figure 2-9.)

**3. Choose a drive letter from A to Z.**

Choose any except those already in use; most modern laptops have a hard drive at C, and a CD or DVD drive at D, and may not be using other letters.

You can use any system here that works for you; some people like to work backwards from Z, while others search for letters that have some meaning, like L for letters.

**4. Click the folder you want to map.**

To find it, you may have to browse through shared network resources.

**5. Click Finish.**

Remove the mapping of a network drive this way:

**1. Open the Computer window.**

**2. Choose Tools ➪ Disconnect Network Drive.**

If you don't see the Tools menu, press the Alt key to display the Classics menu toolbar.

**3. Select the icon for the mapped drive you want to disconnect.**

**4. Click OK.**

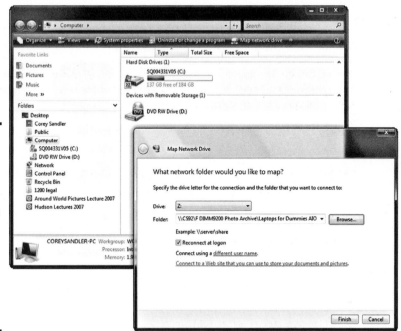

**Figure 2-9:**
Mapping a
network
drive under
Windows
Vista begins
with a
command
from the
toolbar
of the
Computer
window.

## Mapping in Windows XP

To map a folder on a network in Windows XP, do this:

*1.* **Go to any Windows Explorer window.**

This includes My Network Places, My Computer, My Documents, My Music, and My Pictures.

*2.* **Choose Tools ⇨ Map Network Drive.**

The Map Network Drive dialog box opens.

*3.* **Choose a drive letter from the drop-down list.**

You can use any unassigned letter, but you might want to choose an unusual letter that will help remind you of the contents and location of the drive.

*4.* **Click the Browse button.**

*5.* **Select the folder or subfolder.**

The folder's network name, which Windows expresses using the computer's name, appears in the Folder box.

*6.* **Click the Reconnect at Logon check box.**

This instructs the computer to search for this folder each time it is turned on.

**7. Click Finish.**

Some security firewall software or hardware may be set up to automatically block access to shared folders; Windows Vista may stop to ask your permission before making a connection. Read and understand the instructions for any firewall or other security software to learn how to use it properly.

Do this to remove the mapping of a network drive:

*1.* **Open any Windows Explorer window.**

*2.* **Choose Tools ⇨ Disconnect Network Drive.**

*3.* **Select the icon for the mapped drive you want to disconnect.**

*4.* **Click OK.**

# Sharing Devices and Internet Connections

Devices on LANs can be shared in one of two ways:

✦ If they're equipped with their own NIC, they can be directly addressed by laptops and desktops.

✦ If they're directly attached to a computer on the network, they can be shared by other computers that have been given proper permission.

In many offices, this means a workgroup or several workgroups can share a single printer or connect to the broadband connection from a modem attached to a network router or other similar hardware.

## Sharing a printer

A printer with its own Ethernet interface attaches to your network hub or router and can get instructions and data from any computer on the network. As long as the printer and the router are powered, any laptop or desktop computer with proper access can sign on to the network and use it.

Because a network printer is meant to exist independently (unassigned to a particular computer), it may be configured by using your browser to go to a Web-like page located within the machine, or it may have a control panel located on the printer itself.

There is no operational difference between a wired and a wireless network in the office. A network can be one or the other, or use a mix of both means of communication. And devices, from computers to printers or modems, can "attach" to the network physically or over radio waves.

If you attach a printer directly to a computer with a USB or other type of cable, you can make that printer available to other computers on the network anytime the computer is turned on, Windows is running, and the printer is on.

### Enabling a printer for sharing under Windows Vista

Do this to share a printer attached to your computer:

*1.* **Click Start ⇨ Control Panel ⇨ Network and Internet ⇨ Network and Sharing Center.**

See Figure 2-10.

*2.* **Click the Printer Sharing drop-down arrow.**

The section expands.

*3.* **Click Turn on Printer Sharing.**

*4.* **Click Apply.**

*5.* **Go to the Control Panel.**

*6.* **Click Printers.**

There you see the names or icons for any attached printers.

*7.* **Right-click a device.**

*8.* **Select Sharing.**

The Properties dialog box opens.

*9.* **Click Share This Printer.**

Now the printer's available on the network.

**Figure 2-10:**
Windows
Vista's
Network
and Sharing
Center
opens the
door to
printer
sharing.

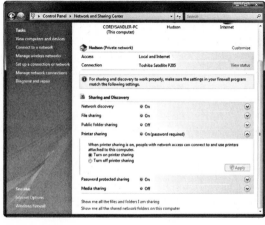

### Enabling a printer for sharing under Windows XP

Do this to share a printer attached to your computer:

1. **Go to the Control Panel on the computer with an attached printer.**

2. **Click the Printers and Faxes icon.**

3. **Click to select the printer you want to share.**

4. **Right-click.**

   A pop-up menu appears.

5. **Choose Sharing.**

   Alternately, you can choose File ⇨ Sharing.

   The Properties dialog box opens.

6. **Choose depending on your needs:**

   • To enable sharing: Click to put a check mark in the Share This Printer check box.

   • To disable sharing: Remove the check mark from the Share This Printer check box.

   If you choose, you can give the printer a name.

7. **Click OK.**

   A shared printer's icon changes to show an outstretched hand beneath its picture.

## Sharing an Internet connection

You have two ways to share a broadband Internet connection: one involves hardware and the other, Windows facilities that simulate the hardware with software.

### Using a hardware router

For superior performance and ease of use, purchase a router that sits between the cable modem or DSL modem and the computers on your network. The *router* can communicate with computers in the network by an Ethernet cable or wirelessly.

Today's routers have many upsides:

✦ They are relatively inexpensive — generally in the range of $50 to $100 — and quickly pay for themselves by sharing the cost of an Internet connection.

✦ They are also relatively easy to configure.

✦ Once set up, they shouldn't need any further attention until time comes to replace them with the latest, greatest, next new thing.

✦ Once enabled and connected to the Internet, the router can operate independently; any computer on the network can use it, regardless of whether any other machine is powered on or signed onto the network. This is the most significant advantage of using a hardware router.

In theory, each additional machine that shares an Internet connection is taking a slice of the incoming flow of data on the pipe. Depending on the pipe capacity, a finite amount of information can flow in each direction at any one moment in time; if that amount is $X$ and eight machines share the pipe, the possible result could be a reduction to $X / 8$.

However, in practice, it's relatively rare for two or more machines to make a demand on the incoming or outgoing pipe at the same moment. Most users send out a request to view a Web page and then sit and read the screen; it takes only a few fractions of a second to download a page full of information.

The most likely situation where a shared network connection can slow down: when two or more systems are using streaming audio or video. But with a fast cable or fiber-optic connection, enough stuff is moving through the pipe to support several concurrent streams, as well as many additional occasional demands.

If overall Internet performance slows down to an unacceptable level, you may be able to upgrade the speed of the connection (for a price); contact the provider to see if they offer a faster service. Or you could install additional incoming connections.

### Using software to share an Internet connection

Windows Vista and Windows XP offer a software-based means of sharing an Internet. Although you save the cost of a hardware router, this solution has several disadvantages:

✦ The computer running the sharing utility will need to be powered up and running to allow it (and other computers on the network) to use the Internet.

✦ Activities on the computer itself may slow down the process of sharing the Internet feed to the network.

With Windows Internet sharing, any computer on the network can locate and use an Internet connection through its Network Connections window.

Here's how to enable Internet sharing under Windows Vista:

**Book VIII
Chapter 2**

**Managing a
Windows Network**

*1.* **Click Start.**

*2.* **Right-click Network.**

The Network and Sharing Center opens.

*3.* **Click Manage Network Connections.**

The Network Connections window appears.

*4.* **Right-click a listed Internet connection.**

*5.* **Click Properties.**

The Properties dialog box for the selected networking scheme opens.

*6.* **Click the Sharing tab.**

See Figure 2-11.

*7.* **Choose based on your needs:**

- To enable sharing: Enable the Allow Other Network Users to Connect Through This Computer's Internet Connection check box.

- To disable sharing: Disable the Allow Other Network Users to Connect Through This Computer's Internet Connection check box.

*8.* **Click OK.**

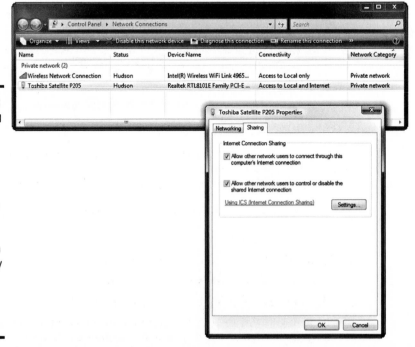

**Figure 2-11:** The Sharing tab allows enabling and disabling Internet Connection Sharing. Consult the help screen to make any needed changes to network properties.

To use software-based Internet Connection Sharing, most systems need to enable Internet Protocol Version 4 or 6 (TCP/IPv4 or TCP/IPv6) for each computer on the system to obtain its own IP address automatically. Follow the instructions displayed on the Sharing tab.

Here's how to enable this software solution under Windows XP:

*1.* **Click Start ➪ Control Panel.**

*2.* **Click the Network Connections icon.**

*3.* **Click one of these icons:**

- **Internet connection**

- **Modem**

- **ISP**

*4.* **Right-click.**

A pop-up menu appears.

*5.* **Choose Properties.**

Or choose File ➪ Properties.

The Properties dialog box opens.

*6.* **Click the Advanced tab.**

*7.* **Choose based on your needs:**

- To enable sharing: Enable the Allow Other Network Users to Connect Through This Computer's Internet Connection check box.

- To disable sharing: Disable the Allow Other Network Users to Connect Through This Computer's Internet Connection check box.

*8.* **Click OK.**

## Automated Network Diagnostics

Windows Vista introduced a set of advanced automatic diagnostics and troubleshooting tools that should help *most* users determine the cause of *most* problems with network connectivity.

If a computer on the network loses Internet connectivity, do this:

*1.* **Go to the Control Panel.**

*2.* **Choose the Network and Sharing Center.**

A display indicates which connection is down.

*3.* **Click the task pane on the left side of the windows.**

Diagnose and Repair tries to determine the cause of the problem and find possible solutions for automatic or manual repair.

# Chapter 3: Going Wireless

## In This Chapter

- ✔ Cutting the cord to local networks and the Internet
- ✔ What's to do with a WiFi connection?
- ✔ Understanding WiFi technology
- ✔ Equipping your laptop for wireless communication
- ✔ Configuring a WiFi network
- ✔ Cellular, Bluetooth, and infrared networks

*W*hen the personal computer arrived, one of the biggest complications was the thicket of wires and cables and protocols you had to manage to get your machine to communicate with a printer, a modem, or to another computer.

Sometimes the incompatibility was physical: 9-pin serial, 9-pin CGA video, 15-pin VGA video, 25-pin parallel, 25-pin serial, 36-pin Centronics parallel printer, 50-pin SCSI, 50-socket disk drive, 68-pin advanced SCSI . . . I could go on and on with a nearly endless list of different designs for the wiring and the hardware at each end.

And sometimes the incompatibility was electrical: A cable might plug perfectly into a receptacle of a matching shape, but in the early days of computing there was no guarantee that a specific pin in the computer would deliver a particular signal. There were entire books written about plugs and cables and there were pieces of hardware that could convert one type of plug to another, one type of cable to another, and the vaguely threatening class of devices nicknamed "gender benders" that could change a male plug (pins out) to a female receptacle, or the other way around.

These were the facts of personal computing life that began with desktop machines and continued on through the first few generations of laptops, too. I have in my closet an early portable computer that came equipped with a parallel port, a serial port, an output for video on an external monitor, a mouse port, a modem port, and a set of three audio inputs and outputs.

Today the primary means of wired communication for a modern machine is the *USB port,* a nearly universal means of connecting most computer-related devices to each other. The USB has replaced standard serial and parallel ports for printers, scanners, memory card readers, and all manner of devices.

In theory, a USB port could be used for just about anything. They're not on the market yet, but designers have come up with LCDs and monitors, sound cards, and networking devices that can do their thing with the serial string of 0s and 1s sent their way from a USB port.

# Doing What with a Wireless Network?

In many ways, laptops and WiFi were made for each other. Here are three ways laptop users have cut the cord . . . and lived to brag about the productivity it has brought them.

## Expanding your home or office facilities

It's no secret: I do the bulk of my work on a conventional desktop machine that is connected to the Internet and to other machines in my office by a wired network.

I also own and use several laptops, and they're not just for travel.

✦ I can take a laptop anywhere in my office or anywhere in my home and continue my work without benefit of wires. If I want to go over my investments with my financial advisor, we can meet at the dining room table or out back on the deck and bring a full-speed network connection to my laptop.

✦ When a carpenter comes over to the house to discuss remodeling our kitchen and bathroom, we can sign onto the Internet from the worksite and look at sinks and vanities and appliances.

✦ I've entertained guests throughout the house with a laptop that streams Internet music or a changing display of digital photographs from the collection on one of my desktop hard drives.

One of the advantages of a wireless network in a home or office is that they often do not require any substantial changes to the structure; you don't need to drill holes in walls or floors to string cables. That can be messy, and in some situations expensive if you need to bring in an electrician or a carpenter.

## Becoming a road warrior

My various laptops have allowed me to wirelessly connect to the Internet from the North Pole, Cape Horn, Australia, the South Pacific, all through Europe, and just about anywhere in between. I've used the facilities of Internet cafés, public access sites in libraries and public buildings, and latched onto a signal offered as a courtesy by businesses and government agencies.

A few years ago, wireless *hotspots* were rare and exciting; you could find designated areas where users could latch onto a signal in airports, hotels, coffee shops, and many other public and private places. Today they're pretty common, almost to the point where users complain to eateries, hotels, and businesses when they can't find them. Some hotspots are free and open to the public while others require payment of a daily or monthly subscription fee.

When I am on the road, I read my e-mail (including audio attachments of voicemail from my telephone), upload files to my clients, send messages to my family, use voice over Internet telephone services to place calls, and consult essential web sites including banking (where I can pay bills and monitor deposits).

I'm also able to use the Internet to check on my home alarm system and to read critically important news, including the Boston Red Sox standings.

## Visiting business clients

One of the problems business and personal laptop users have when they arrive at a client's office or a friend's home is finding a way to use their machine without having to make changes to their own system or their host's equipment to deal with security issues and compatibility.

Plugging into a wired network is often difficult to accomplish. The wired router may not be easily accessible, it may be fully in use without any available ports, or the system administrator may have set up firewalls or other blockades to prevent unauthorized users from signing on.

By contrast, most wireless networks are designed to be readily available to outsiders. In a business setting, it is very likely that the administrator has enabled security settings but as a guest it should be easy for you to obtain permission to sign on; you need to be given the network SSID (its name) as well as a user ID and a password.

Once you're on the network, your privileges may be unlimited or you may be restricted only to access to the Internet which may be all that you need. If you need to read or write files or folders on the network, you need to be given access to them; similarly if you want to use a printer or other piece of hardware it will have to be shared with you.

Sharing files, folders, and equipment like a printer on a wireless network is done in the same way these are made available on a wired network. See Book VIII, Chapters 1 and 2 for details.

Book VIII
Chapter 3

Going Wireless

## Seeing Hot Spots

It used to be that the business and tourist traveler expected a hotel to deliver a clean place to sleep, a vending machine in the hallway, and a television to keep us amused. I still appreciate a comfortable bed, but today many travelers have a new requirement in second place on their list: WiFi.

Hotels have come to realize that for a relatively small investment they can install wireless access points in their buildings to make happy those of you — the readers of this book — who travel with a laptop as a constant companion. In many places, this access is free — part of the cost of the room, just like the basic cable service to the television. Some hotels charge a fee for access, although that may put them at a competitive disadvantage if the place across the street provides WiFi for free.

A similar trend has developed at many coffee shops and other casual eateries; they have come to realize that they can differentiate themselves from their competitors by enabling a WiFi network along with their double cinnamon dolce lattes. (Among eateries offering free service is Panera Bread Company.)

You'll also find free Internet access at many public libraries and in some public buildings.

There are also services that offer hourly, daily, or monthly subscriptions to WiFi access. In most such setups you can turn on or off your account any time you need to do so. Companies like T-Mobile, a major cell phone service provider, offer subscription plans to WiFi at many Starbucks, Borders Books, FedEx-Kinko's, and other locations.

You can also visit national web sites that allow you to search by airport or ZIP code; most of these will give you the locations for paid commercial access. One such web site is www.jiwire.com.

Think of the things we take for granted today: cell phones, Web-connected personal data assistants, and Internet cafes. Although early mobile and cell phones started out using analog signals, by now nearly all the people walking around talking into their hands are exchanging digital information.

Most modern cell phone systems are now digital. Many cable television services transmit programming digitally. And within the next decade, most of the "old" analog broadcasts will convert to digital radio and digital television. (Unless there's a last-minute reprieve, analog television broadcasts come to an end in February of 2009.)

# Allow me to give you an analogy

It took almost 20 years before computer designers updated an older wonder technology for use in the modern world: it's called radio. The first use of radio waves to transmit information was more than a century ago: 1887, to be precise, when the first experiments in transmission of what came to be known as Morse Code were sent from one spot to another without wires.

Interestingly, Morse code was essentially a binary code: it had only two characters, a short click or tone and a long click or tone. These dots or dashes symbolized letters which could then be strung together to form words and sentences. The letter *S* was dot, dot, dot; the letter *O* was dash, dash, dash.

However, from more than a century, these codes and then the audible words and music of broadcast radio and eventually television were created through the use of an analog signal transmitted as electrical waves. In one form the waves conveyed information by variance in height or size; this was AM or amplitude modulation radio. In another form the signal delivered sound or pictures by varying the frequency or length of the waves; this was FM or frequency modulation. Either way, radio was analog, as in an analogy of the information. Think of this: a high tone or a loud sound was represented by its analog in the form of a high wave in an AM signal.

The first computers (and some current computers) still used analog signals. For you youngsters out there: We used to communicate over the telephone using a modem that warbled out an annoying chatter or varying tones. Our computers, which worked internally by manipulating digital information, would send data to a modem (a modulator-demodulator) that would convert the digital information into an analog signal that would travel like an electronic voice over the telephone to another modem that could convert the warbles back into 0s and 1s.

This worked reasonable well because telephone technology was designed to carry sounds. "Hello, Joe's Pizzeria" is a sound, just as the individual warbles that represented 0s or 1s of binary codes were sounds.

But modern technology finally caught up. If, in commercial radio's Golden Age in 1947 we lived in a cloud of signals, by 2007 we were in a dense fog of radio waves getting thicker minute by minute.

The acceleration of radio use has come about with a switchover from analog waves to digital signals.

Which brings you to laptops and what has become generically known as *WiFi*. The term itself is a geeky play on words, meaning Wireless Fidelity. Way back in the early days of recorded music on large, heavy platters we passed through a period where the quality advanced to High Fidelity, or HiFi. I'm telling you this because I like to explore the derivation of words and terms, but trust me: call it WiFi (pronounced why-fie) and keep it to yourself how you ever knew how it came to bear that name. Even the geekiest of geeks would look at you oddly if you were to ask for the location of the nearest Wireless Fidelity hotspot. One common industry icon for WiFi technology is shown in Figure 3-1.

**Figure 3-1:**
The computer industry's symbol for WiFi can be found on laptop hardware and networking devices as well as in some onscreen utilities.

*Courtesy Toshiba America, Inc.*

The correct name for the technology that underlies WiFi is (for the moment, and for most systems) one of several variations of 802.11. The *Institute of Electrical and Electronic Engineers (IEEE)* helps simplify (Ha! You say?) technology by setting up committees to determine standards that various companies can then adopt for their products. They use numbers for their standards, and the ones that apply to WiFi are in the group called 802.11. At this time there are four flavors of 802.11 in common use, and they are demarked as subsets of that numeric name: a, b, g, and n.

As this book goes to press, 802.11n is the next new thing, supplanting 802.11g, 802.11a, and the comparatively ancient 802.11b. Each standard is *downwardly compatible* with earlier sets of code. Here's what that means:

## Back to analog

Musical purists and old-school photographers bemoan the very subtle subtleties they claim to be able to detect between an analog record and a digital CD or between a film and photographic paper print and a digital image. They are probably correct, because in theory there can be an infinite range of differences between a particular note or color in an analog world while the distinction between tone or color number 23643 and 23644 is forever fixed. However, there is little likelihood we will revert from digital to analog in most applications . . . and I'm not convinced that most mere mortals can see or hear colors or tones that lie between finite digital values.

802.11g also works with machines that support 802.11b or 802.11a; going the other direction, though, an 802.11a transceiver in a laptop or a router for such a system will only operate at that slower, weaker technology and isn't downwardly compatible with anything else.

Digital communication has a number of advantages over analog:

✦ **Precision.** If computer designers agree that the code 83 (or 1010011 in binary) stands for "S" or that a color made up of Red 242, Green 30, and Blue 70 represents a rich but not gaudy shade of red we have a very high probability that a properly set up electronic device will reproduce exactly that letter or color.

✦ **Accuracy.** When we speak words to each other there is a great possibility we may misunderstand what we hear; it is much less likely that a computer system will misread a 0 for a 1, and the computer "words" can include error-checking algorithms that correct for errors or request a retransmission.

✦ **Economy.** Digital signals, because they consist of just 0s and 1s, require a much narrower "band" in the radio frequency. This allows more and more signals to squeeze into the spectrum without interfering with each other.

✦ **Speed.** With the advance of technology and the increasing demands of the marketplace, engineers have found better and better ways to pump more and more digital data at higher and higher speeds across radio signals.

✦ **Locality.** Carefully designed hardware, coupled with advanced security features, allow millions of WiFi systems to coexist in a community or a region or a state without interfering with each other even if they use the same radio frequency. When I turn on my laptop in my office I usually can see at least three other wireless local area networks in my very rural neighborhood; the password protection on my router keeps outsiders from getting into my system and keeps me out of my neighbor's networks.

# *Working a WiFi Network*

Nearly everyone has greatly enjoyed the experience of flying the friendly skies from one place to another. In general, that means we get to use a *hub-and-spoke scheme:* To get from Boston to San Diego, for example, you might fly from Boston to Dallas and then meet up with people from all over the country who get off their incoming planes to join you on a flight from Dallas to San Diego.

In the airline example, the hub (Dallas, in this case) receives incoming passengers, gathers them together in groups, and then transmits them to their destination. Coming back, the same process occurs in the other direction.

## Inside a WiFi network

A WiFi communications system is similar to other radio technologies including walkie-talkies and cell phones. However, 802.11 devices are designed for relatively short-distance, higher-speed work.

One important difference: WiFi operates in a high-frequency band of 2.4 GHz or 5 GHz. Compare that to AM radio which is relegated to the radio space between 530 and 1710 KHz in North America, and FM which operates between 87.5 and 108 MHz. K stands for a thousand, M for a million, and B for a billion. And Hz: That means the number of cycles per second, measured in Hertz and named after German physicist Heinrich Hertz who made some important discoveries and demonstrations of radio waves in the 1880s.

Enough about airlines; I love flying and hate airports. But the same general principle applies to a WiFi network.

The signals from your laptop (or from a desktop or other electronic device with wireless capabilities) are transmitted in a more or less circular pattern throughout your home or office or other workplace. Somewhere within the reception range of the signal, a wireless router serves as a hub for those signals.

The router can serve several purposes:

✦ It can be the gateway to a broadband Internet connection, allowing one or more wireless devices to send signals and receive responses for that purpose.

✦ It can be the access point to a single desktop computer, allowing interchange in both directions with the wireless computer.

✦ It can accept signals from a wireless device and move them along to a printer.

✦ It can be the hub that allows interchange of data between and among a large number of wireless devices. You can connect one laptop to another, or a laptop to a desktop, or establish a wireless network that serves an office full of electronics.

### What's the frequency?

A higher frequency generally travels a shorter distance, which makes it a good choice for local area networks; at the same time it can carry more data than a signal sent at a lower frequency.

Devices that operate in the 2.4 GHz band may suffer from interference caused by common office and household appliances including cordless telephones, microwave ovens, and wireless baby monitors. Engineers attempt to compensate for this by designing WiFi systems to work on any of three frequency bands within their allocated range, and they can also *frequency hop* rapidly between the different bands to deal with interference and permit multiple devices to use the same wireless connection simultaneously.

Bluetooth wireless devices, used by some laptops, cell phones, and personal digital assistants, also operate in the same 2.4 GHz range but are less likely to cause or suffer from interference because they use a scheme called *frequency hopping spread spectrum signaling.* As the name implies, this spreads a signal across multiple frequencies.

802.11a and the developing 802.11n specifications use the 5 GHz band, which is less crowded with household appliances and also offers eight nonoverlapping channels as opposed to the three in the 2.4 GHz frequency band.

### WiFi by the 802 numbers

Never mind the alphabet, 802.11b was the first technology in this series to reach the market. The *a* specification came a bit later.

✦ **802.11b** is the slowest of the modern standards but when it was first introduced it was the least expensive and easiest to implement. Systems of this type transmit in the 2.4 GHz frequency band. They are capable of moving as much as 11 Mbps of data.

✦ **802.11a,** the out-of-alphabetic order standard, transmits data within the 5 GHz band and can move up to 54 Mbps of data. Although it is fast, the use of the higher-frequency band slightly reduces the overall range of devices because these signals are more likely to be absorbed or deflected by walls or other solid objects between the transmitter and receiver.

✦ **802.11g** devices also transmit signals in the 2.4 GHz band, but they are much faster than 802.11b. WiFi equipment based on this specification can move as much as 54 Mbps of data. Much of the gain is the result of using a more efficient coding technique. (If you must know, 802.11g introduced orthogonal frequency-division multiplexing, a step up from complementary code keying. I could explain the difference to you, but we'd both require a padded room before, during, and afterwards.)

✦ **802.11n** isn't yet an official standard, although that has not prevented a number of manufacturers from offering devices that seem to fit the still-developing specification. It's a pretty safe bet that 802.11n, when final, will encompass the unofficial versions. These devices operate at 5GHz and 2.4GHz, as needed, to deliver the best signal, and can deliver about 74 Mbps of data. These devices also add multiple-input multiple-output (MIMO) technology; it's pronounced *mee-moh* by those in the know, and it permits the use of multiple antennas at both the transmitter and receiver to improve performance. As such it is less affected by certain types of interference, and antennas do not have to be "aimed" to deal with walls and corners. See Figure 3-2.

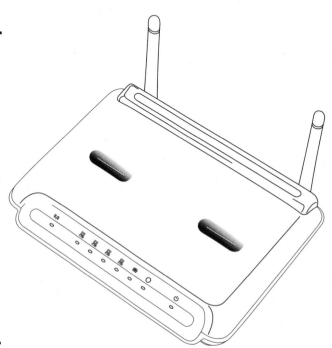

**Figure 3-2:** A Belkin WiFi router in the unofficial "Super G" class that combines the 802.11g specification with MIMO antennas that can be used independently or together to improve the reach of the radio signal.

Each successive specification is *downwardly compatible* with previous designs, which means that an 802.11n device also works with the earlier a, b, and g protocols.

Avoid placing a wireless router in direct proximity to a 2.4 GHz cordless phone or a microwave oven. In addition, if your home or office has both a 2.4 GHz router and telephone system, use the configuration panel on the router and any switches on the phone to assign them to widely separated channels.

As an example, Belkin recommends setting its router at 11 and any phone at 1. You may need to experiment with various channel pairs to avoid interference, especially if you have neighbors with their own systems.

In Table 3-1 I present a summary of three official WiFi specifications, along with two others that appear near to finalization and manufacture. The 802.11y specification is expected to be administered in the United States under license by the Federal Communication Commission for use by commercial ISPs.

Don't expect the ranges listed here to necessarily match what you actually get; all sorts of things (walls, metal, interference, and even atmospheric conditions) can have an effect. In other words, your mileage may differ.

| Table 3-1 | | WiFi Standards | | | |
|-----------|--------------|---------------------|------------------------------|------------------|-----------------------|
| *Protocol* | *Release Date* | *Radio Frequency* | *Maximum Data Rate* | *Indoor Range* | *Outdoor Range* |
| 802.11a | 1999 | 5 GHz | 54 Mbps | About 114 feet | About 390 feet |
| 802.11b | 1999 | 2.4 GHz | 11 Mbps | About 120 feet | About 450 feet |
| 802.11g | 2003 | 2.4 GHz | 54 Mbps | About 120 feet | About 450 feet |
| 802.11n | 2009 (est.) | 2.4 GHz or 5 GHz | 248 Mbps (2 data streams) | About 225 feet | About 800 feet |
| 802.11y | 2008 to 2009 (est.) | 3.7 GHz | 54 Mbps | About 160 feet | As much as 3 miles |

# Does Your Laptop Do WiFi?

Here's the easy part: Nearly all current laptops come equipped with built-in facilities for WiFi communication. Models arriving in the stores as this book goes to press will most likely offer 802.11n; older machines may have come with 802.11g, 802.11b, or 802.11a.

So, if your laptop has one of the latest standards built in, you're all set — at least when it comes to the hardware side of the equation. I discuss configuring your operating system for wireless communication later in this chapter.

But if your laptop doesn't have built-in WiFi, if the included version is outdated, or if the wireless hardware breaks, you have several good solutions:

✦ **Install a WiFi adapter in a PC Card or Express Card slot.** If you go this route, you'll have to learn to take care not to damage the small nub of an antenna that extends from the end of the adapter; it is easy to break off and destroy the card or even damage the slot of the laptop. It's also important to turn off the power to the card when it is not in use. You'll also be dedicating one of a limited number of slots on your laptop to a single purpose.

Attention passengers: Airlines prohibit the use of radio transmitters (including WiFi systems, cell phones, and remote control devices) while in flight. You need to turn off the power to your wireless system or remove it from a PC Card or ExpressCard to comply.

✦ **Replace the built-in adapter with a new unit certified by the original equipment manufacturer.** If you replace the built-in hardware (only a relatively few laptop manufacturers design their machines in a way that allows end users to get at the adapter without disassembling the entire case) you will have to carefully follow instructions mandated by the Federal Communications Commission (in the United States) or the equivalent in other countries; they do this to avoid the possibility of interference with other radio systems.

✦ **Add an external WiFi adapter that connects to your laptop through the USB port.** You may have problems with this solution if your laptop has USB 1.0 or 1.1 ports instead of the more advanced and speedier USB 2.0 design. This solution has two designs:

- A simple device, about the size of a pack of gum, that plugs into the port and extends out to the side; the antenna is built into the case. Again, the device presents a bit of a threat to the health of your machine because it sticks out a few inches; a glancing blow or a careless return of the laptop to its carrying case with the adapter in place could damage it or the USB port.

- A small external WiFi transceiver that attaches to the laptop with a USB cable. Although this is an extra piece of hardware to drag around, it is much less likely to become damaged while in use.

## Disabling the Original WiFi Adapter

If your laptop has built-in WiFi but you add a new adapter that connects through the PC Card adapter or a USB port, you will need to remove or disable Windows drivers for the original unit. You should also make sure that you turn off the switch for the built-in unit to save battery power and to avoid the possibility of interference.

To disable the drivers, do this:

*1.* **Go to the Windows Control Panel.**

*2.* **Double-click System.**

The System Properties panel appears.

*3.* **Choose the Hardware tab.**

*4.* **Choose Device Manager.**

*5.* **Click that the + next to Network Adapters.**

The hardware managed there appears in a list.

*6.* **Double-click the wireless component.**

Its properties are displayed.

**7. Click the Device Usage drop-down arrow.**

**8. Select Do Not Use This Device (Disable).**

This instructs Windows not to use the drivers associated with it.

# Building a Wireless Network

The process of putting together a wireless network is mostly a matter of configuring devices. There are, by definition, no wires that need to be strung along the floor or through the walls; in many systems the only wires are a connection to a network router or a broadband modem, and a source of power.

✦ If you already have a wired network in place, all you may need to add is a *wireless access point.* This box connects at one end to an existing Ethernet hub and terminates at the other end with an antenna that broadcasts and receives signals.

✦ If you don't have a wired network, or if you want to extend and expand an existing one, the hardware you need is a *wireless router.* This box contains a port that connects to your broadband modem or to a port on an existing wired router and also includes its own router and Ethernet hub as well as an antenna to send and receive WiFi signals.

Depending on the design of your home or office, you may be able to install a single WiFi access point or wireless router and reach everywhere you want to send the signal. Or you may have to find a way to extend the reach of your wireless signal by bringing an Ethernet cable to another part of the structure and installing the wireless router there or by adding a WiFi range extender or repeater. A repeater does exactly what its name suggests: it receives wireless signals (incoming or outgoing) and then rebroadcasts them in an amplified form.

## Setting up a WiFi router

The first wireless routers were built by . . . and for . . . highly technical users. The instructions were written for an audience of programmers and engineers and not necessarily in English. There were switches to be set and in some cases there were requirements to modify the operating system.

Happily, nearly all of that confusion is in the past. Today many routers come with self-installation CDs or with telephone support desks that can quickly walk you through the process.

If you want to get a sense of the task that lies ahead of you, visit the web site of a router manufacturer before buying and reading the instruction manual. If you find insufficient assistance on the web site (or over the phone), I suggest buying a product from a different company.

In general, the process of installing a WiFi device begins by connecting the router to the same computer that is attached to your broadband modem; this allows automated configuration software to obtain the information it needs without any intermediary devices along the way.

### Initial setup for a wireless router

Here is a typical setup:

1. **Turn off the power to your broadband modem.**

   If there isn't an on/off switch, remove the power supply to the device.

2. **Connect the power adapter to the back panel of the wireless router.**

3. **Plug the adapter into an AC outlet.**

   Check that the power LED illuminates.

4. **Connect an Ethernet cable to the broadband modem.**

5. **Restore the power to the modem.**

6. **Insert the other end of the Ethernet cable into the WAN (wide area network) port on the back panel of the wireless router.**

   The WAN light should illuminate.

7. **Insert another Ethernet cable between LAN Port 1 (on the back panel of the wireless router) and any available Ethernet port on the NIC (network interface card) of the computer you're going to use to configure the WiFi system.**

8. **Shut down.**

9. **Restart the computer connected to the WiFi router.**

   Let Windows fully load.

10. **Open your Web browser.**

    Internet Explorer or Mozilla Firefox are examples.

11. **In the address bar of the browser, type the URL for the built-in setup screen of the wireless router.**

    For example, type http://192.168.0.1 for most D-Link routers.

12. **Press the Enter key.**

    To see a list of the standard addresses for setup screens as well as default usernames and passwords from several major makers, see Table 3-2.

    Depending on your device maker, you may have to enter a user name such as **admin** (for administrator), and you may have to enter a password.

    Consult the instructions for details. Once you log in, the home screen of the built-in setup system appears. See Figure 3-3.

| Table 3-2 | Router Setup Screen Addresses | | |
|---|---|---|---|
| *Router Manufacturer* | *URL* | *Default User Name* | *Default Password* |
| 3com | http://192.168.1.1 | admin | admin |
| D-Link | http://192.168.0.1 | admin | |
| Linksys | http://192.168.1.1 | admin | admin |
| Microsoft | http://192.168.2.1 | admin | admin |
| Netgear | http://192.168.0.1 | admin | password |

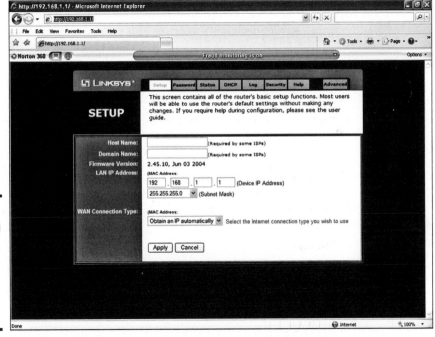

**Figure 3-3:**
The opening screen of the setup utility for a Linksys wired router.

**Book VIII**
**Chapter 3**

**Going Wireless**

A typical automated process *(wizard)* includes the option to establish a password for control of your router. I strongly suggest you do so.

Choose a password that isn't related to anything in your personal or business life and throw in some numbers and special characters. This password is just to control settings made for the router; whatever strange password I come up with I usually write on an index card and place within the box for the router which then goes into my Closet of Old Boxes for Devices Attached to My Computers.

Any properly designed piece of network equipment should be compatible with similar or complementary devices made by other manufacturers. In my primary system, I have a Motorola cable modem feeding through a D-Link telephone adapter to a Linksys router; elsewhere in the building a Belkin wireless router broadcasts WiFi signals. That said, configuring devices sometimes is easier when all of your devices wear the same badge. Be prepared to push technical support for assistance if you find yourself facing an irrational incompatibility.

From this point on, the automated wizard should determine most of your settings by electronically interrogating your broadband modem. Among the information it needs to know is if your Internet provider uses a dynamic IP address (the most common configuration for cable modems) or a PPPoE connection (more commonly used by DSL providers). Other options include a static IP address.

- ✦ A **dynamic IP address** is one that is automatically assigned to a computer (or a networking device) by a remote server at the Internet provider; this is part of what is called a Dynamic Host Configuration Protocol. A dynamic IP address may change at any time if the ISP needs to reconfigure its system.

- ✦ A **static IP address** is one that is manually assigned to a computer or network device by an administrator or ISP. If the static address is later changed by the provider, equipment settings must be updated.

- ✦ A **PPPoE (Point-to-Point Protocol over Ethernet)** is used by some DSL providers to provide a connection that creates a virtual link between two ends of a connection even though the actual data is still encapsulated in packets of digital information.

If the system is unable to determine your settings, you will have to instruct it yourself. You should be able to find out what sort of configuration you need by calling your Internet provider or consulting its Web page.

If you have selected Dynamic IP Address, you should be offered the option to Clone MAC Address (to automatically copy the MAC address of the network adapter in your computer). You can also type in the MAC address.

You can find the MAC address by consulting the Properties page for your NIC.

On the other hand, if you need to enter a static IP address, a different screen requests full information including the assigned IP Address, subnet mask, and DNS addresses. You should get that information from your ISP to enter the details on this screen.

If your ISP uses PPPoE you will need to enter a user name and password for your particular service; again, this should be made available to you by your Internet provider.

Once the details of the address have been settled, you will need to set — or approve the default for — the SSID and Channel.

*SSID (Service Set Identifier)* is the name of the network. Why not call it "network name" instead of a forgettable acronym? Ask the engineers.

I strongly recommend that you change the name of the SSID. Many routers will be called "default" or be given the moniker of the router manufacturer: D-Link or Linksys, for example. Just think about it: there are a few dozen router makers, with three or four of them owning a major share of the market; the chances of your wireless or wired router being within range of another device of the same is pretty high.

The important thing here is not security but identity; you want to be able to quickly recognize your network. Give it a name that is recognizable to you but that doesn't reveal any information you don't want outsiders to see.

Routers have a number of channels they can use, slight variations on their assigned radio frequency. Most come delivered to use channel 6 and that may work just fine for you. However, if there is more than one WiFi network in your home or office, or you run into interference from a neighbor's system or other wireless devices in your home or office such as wireless telephones, experiment with changing the channel setting for the router here.

### Securing your wireless network

Now comes the question of security. Do you want to allow anyone within reach of your wireless signal to be able to use the network, or worse, eavesdrop on the electronic information that passes between devices? Even worse: If you've enabled "sharing" of files or folders, an outsider who gets through the electronic front door may be able to get into the data on the disks of any machine on the network.

The only good reason to operate your network wide open is if you're intentionally setting up a public hotspot. In that case, disable file and folder sharing.

The most commonly offered security options follow:

✦ **Wired Equivalency Privacy (WEP).** To sign on to a network that uses WEP, you need to know the WEP *key,* usually a numerical password. Most routers offer a choice between 64-bit and 128-bit encryption, with 128-bit encryption much more difficult for a hacker to crack.

WEP 64-bit codes are ten digits or letters in length, which happens to coincide with the size of an American or Canadian telephone number (without the preceding 1). More secure 128-bit numbers require 26 digits, which may require a bit more planning on your part. See if you can come up with a quotation or a name (not yours) that happens to be that length. Follow the instructions offered by the router maker to enter and verify a key.

One common type of key or password is a telephone number. That's fine, but don't use your own number or one associated with you. On my systems, I use as keys old phone numbers of friends and relatives. There is no way anyone could guess that I'm using the phone number for the Chinese takeout restaurant that was down the block from my office 20 years ago; why do I still remember that number?

✦ **WiFi Protected Access (WPA).** A newer and more robust form of security, WPA is considered by many experts to be an improvement on WEP. WPA2, the latest implementation, is included with Windows Vista and Windows XP with Service Pack 2 installed; if your copy of Windows XP has not been updated you should do so for this reason and many others.

✦ **Media Access Control (MAC).** This system functions as if you were issuing keys only to a specified and pre-identified group of users. A router based on MAC does not use a password to authenticate users but instead compares the address it finds within each computer's network interface card to see if it is on the authorized list of users for your network. If you add a new machine or want to grant a visitor access to your network you will have to sign on to the configuration screen of your router and add a new MAC address to the list.

All the instructions I've given generally work with a widely varying mix of machines. The extra wrinkles come if your system (like mine) has extra devices like a telephone adapter and a wired router.

The key here is to configure the newest piece of equipment — the wireless router in this instance — with a direct connection from it to your computer and the incoming feed of your broadband modem. Once the device has been configured, you can shut down your network and rewire the connections to enable the other devices.

In my system, the wiring goes like this: cable modem to telephone adapter to wired router to directly connected computers. The wireless router plugs into one of the ports on the wired router, and my laptop machines communicate with that device and from there onto the wired network.

## Improving the range of your WiFi network

In the best of circumstances, a WiFi system should operate at speeds approaching that of a wired network, and there should be a perfect circle of reception surrounding the antenna of your wireless router.

In the real world . . . things are rarely that perfect. All radio signals are subject to these things:

✦ **Attenuation.** Loss of strength over distance or because of atmospheric conditions.

✦ **Interference.** Corruption caused by another signal on the same or nearby frequency.

✦ **Blockage.** The inability of a signal to pass through certain materials.

Some walls reduce or even block transmission of radio waves (especially in old offices and some houses that used metal lath to hold plaster). Also capable of blocking signals:

✦ File cabinets

✦ Refrigerators

✦ Other substantial and dense objects

✦ Interference from other wireless devices

I've already mentioned cordless phones, microwaves, and baby monitors; you could also run into problems from your neighbor's wireless network.

Another possible element of the system that can affect the quality and reach of a signal is the antenna design. Many routers can transmit and receive signals that move on a flat plane, like all the points of a compass laid flat on a table. But the same router may not be as efficient when directing a signal upward and through the ceiling, or downward and through the floor.

### Adjustments to positioning and settings

Here are some things you can do to enhance the reach of a basic wireless network:

✦ Find the best location for the router. In some situations this may be the center of your home or office, but in others the best location might be in a corner that has a relatively unobstructed "view" of the computers that will seek to use its signal. In my setup, my home office is located at one end of our large multistory house; I ran a cable from my office into a room in the center of the house and placed a wireless access point high up on a shelf there to broadcast everywhere I wanted the signal to go.

✦ Make sure your wireless router is not near large metal objects and other obstructions.

✦ Keep wireless routers away from transceivers for cordless telephones that use the same 2.4 GHz frequency range. You might want to experiment with different cordless phone systems, including those that operate in the higher 5.8 GHz or the lower 900 MHz range to see if this reduces or eliminates interference.

**Book VIII Chapter 3**

**Going Wireless**

✦ Consider placing a WiFi transmitter high up on a shelf to extend coverage over obstructions and into upper floors.

✦ Experiment with alternate channel settings for the router. Most WiFi equipment comes preset to use a particular channel, but this may be the same one used by other routers or by other wireless equipment. Try making adjustments to the channel through its configuration screen.

✦ Keep your wireless router current by downloading and installing any updated firmware for your router; check the web site for the manufacturer of your device every six months or so. You should also make sure you are using the most current device driver for Windows to enhance your computer's ability to control networks.

### Updating and enhancing your wireless hardware

Here are some things you can purchase to boost your wireless network to the next level.

Upgrade your wireless hardware so that it matches the capabilities of your newest and most advanced laptop. (Remember that a laptop with the latest and greatest WiFi equipment will communicate no faster or better than the router or wireless access point's top speed.) Current laptops come equipped with 802.11g or 802.11n WiFi circuitry; if your router is an 802.11b device, that is the speed you'll get. The good news: prices for wireless equipment, like most technology, continue to go down even as capabilities improve.

Upgrade the standard antenna on your router from the omnidirectional design provided by most manufacturers. An omni antenna is meant to send the signal in all directions; a directional signal allows you to aim the signal where you need it. Check with the maker of your router, or electronics suppliers, for information about purchasing a replacement antenna.

Boost the capabilities of an older laptop's wireless hardware by disabling its built-in WiFi circuit and antenna and installing an external adapter that uses the latest technology and has a larger antenna. External WiFi devices may plug directly into your laptop's USB port or attach to it by cable. You can also purchase adapters that plug into a PC Card or ExpressCard slot.

Repeat or expand your signal. You can add a wireless amplifier (called a repeater or a range expander) that picks up the signal from your router and then retransmits it. The best use of this sort of device is to place it somewhere near the edge of your existing signal; it then rebroadcasts the signal to cover more territory. See Figure 3-4.

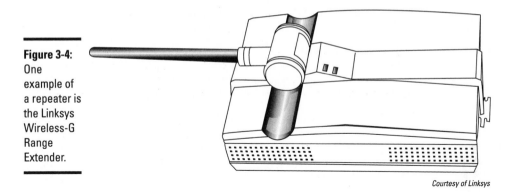

*Courtesy of Linksys*

**Figure 3-4:**
One
example of
a repeater is
the Linksys
Wireless-G
Range
Extender.

# Setting up a Wireless Network in Windows

To this point this chapter focuses entirely on the hardware side of the equation: the WiFi transceiver in your laptop and the wireless router or access point in your home or office network. The third leg of the stool is the configuration of your laptop to communicate with a wireless network.

Once again, this is an area that has gone from almost hopelessly complex back in the day before networking was a part of Windows to almost ridiculously easy now that wired and wireless communication has been totally integrated into the operating system. For users of Windows XP and Windows Vista, once the hardware has been properly set up you're just a few clicks (and a power switch) away from getting online or on the network without benefit of wires.

With the arrival of Windows XP Service Pack 2 and later, Windows Vista, Microsoft has put forth a set of technologies under the umbrella name of Windows Rally. Included amongst them is Windows Connect Now (WCN), a specification and design intended to automate the configuration of devices in a wireless network.

Microsoft envisioned that manufacturers of wireless equipment, including routers, access points, and attached devices would fully implement this standard but as of 2008 the embrace has been less than complete. In theory, the technology is built around the transfer of settings from device to device on a flash memory card — routers and other devices would have a USB port for that purpose. Once elements of the network have received their instructions, the flash memory card would be removed and wireless communication would proceed. Windows Connect Now is a fine idea, and its time may come.

But for most users the best advice is this: Buy good quality equipment from a manufacturer that provides a reasonable level of customer support and plan on following the instructions for your particular device carefully . . . and calling for help if you need it.

**Book VIII
Chapter 3**

**Going Wireless**

## On/Off

There are several reasons your laptop has one or more ways to turn off the power to built-in WiFi circuitry. One is to save battery power when it is not needed. A second reason is to allow you to comply with instructions from airlines and certain highly secretive and demanding government agencies that may not want you to be able to communicate in places they control. That said, it is often difficult to find the on/off switch on many laptops; I will be the first to admit that I once suffered through an hour of waiting on the telephone to speak with a support technician in a far-off land in order to learn that the reason my new laptop was not working with the wireless network was that the switch — mentioned in the manual but not shown on any diagrams — was turned off.

And so, the critical advice: Find the switch and learn how to use it.

In the following sections I concentrate on the utilities provided by Microsoft as part of current versions of Windows. At the end of this chapter I will give you a glimpse at one of the highly capable automated wireless configuration tools offered by a laptop maker for its own line of machines.

### Windows Vista wireless wizardry

Under Windows Vista, once the hardware is *in place and powered up,* here's how to set up the software side of wireless networking.

*1.* **Turn on the power switch for the built-in WiFi circuitry of your laptop.**

For setup purposes only, you may have to reroute Ethernet wiring so your laptop (or the desktop that controls the network) is directly linked to the wireless router. That way it can make settings on the device's configuration screen. Consult the instructions that come with the WiFi device for details.

*2.* **Run the Set up a Wireless Router or Access Point wizard on the computer attached to the router.**

*3.* **Click Start** ⇨ **Control Panel** ⇨ Network and Internet ⇨ Network and Sharing Center.

*4.* **In the left pane, click Set Up a Connection or Network.**

*5.* **Click Set Up a Wireless Router or Access Point.**

The wizard walks you through the steps.

If you want to share files and printers that are in computers or attached to your network, set your network location type to Private and turn on network discovery, file sharing, and printer sharing.

### Testing the network

You should test the setup for the network on each computer that is authorized to communicate with it.

Do this on each machine: Click Start ➪ Network. A window opens and you should see icons for the computer you're testing, as well as those for each of the other computers and devices that you have added to the network.

Any time you have a mix of versions of Windows on your network, it may take a period of time — as much as several minutes — for some machines running different versions to show up on particular network display.

If the computer you are checking has an attached printer, the icon for that device may not be shown on other computers until you have enabled printer sharing for the network and have shared that specific printer. (Printer sharing is available in all versions of Windows Vista except for the most basic, uncommon version: Windows Vista Starter.)

### Automatically adding a device to an existing network

A very easy way to automatically configure a laptop to work with a network is to use the facilities of Windows Vista to copy the necessary settings to a flash drive.

Here's how to do this under Windows Vista:

1. **Turn on a computer that is successfully communicating with a network.**

2. **Plug a flash memory drive into a USB port on the computer.**

   The AutoPlay dialog box appears onscreen.

3. **Click Wireless Network Setup Wizard.**

4. **Follow the onscreen directions to copy settings to the flash memory.**

5. **When the task is completed, remove the flash memory from the computer.**

6. **On the laptop you want to add to the wireless network, click Start ➪ Control Panel.**

7. **Click Network and Internet.**

8. **In the Network and Sharing Center, click Add a Device to the Network.**

9. **Follow the instructions in the wizard.**

### Manually adding a computer running Windows Vista

To do the work of configuration of your laptop yourself you'll need the details of any security measures put into effect in the setup of the router.

*1.* **Turn on the laptop and start Windows Vista.**

*2.* **Click Start ➪ Connect To.**

You see a display of any wireless networks detected by your laptop. (See Figure 3-5.) If you hover your onscreen pointer on or near one of the names you can learn some of the details of the network, including the strength of the signal and whether the system is protected by password security.

*3.* **Click the network you want to use.**

*4.* **Click Connect.**

If the network requires validation, enter the network security key or passphrase.

*5.* **Click OK.**

If you have successfully made the connection, you get a confirmation message. You can also check for yourself; click Start ➪ Network. You should see icons for the computer you just added, as well as for other computers and devices that are part of the network.

**Figure 3-5:**
The Connect to a network screen of Windows Vista shows any wireless systems within the reach of your laptop's built-in antenna.

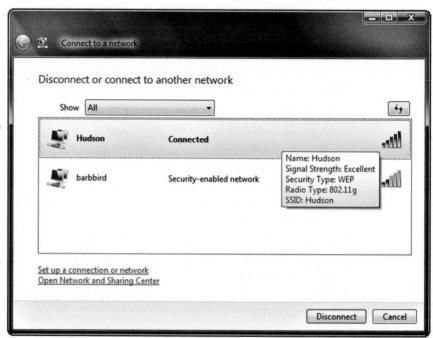

## Windows XP wireless wizardry

The Wireless Network Setup Wizard for Windows XP arrived with Service Pack 2 of that operating system. If you're running XP and haven't installed Microsoft's improved version: Stop whatever you're doing (I guess that would be reading this book) and go forth and update.

There are no good reasons not to install major updates like Service Packs for your Windows operating system except 1) if you do not have a legal license for the version you are running, or 2) you do not have enough space on the hard drive in your laptop.

In the first instance . . . well, I'm not going to endorse innocent or willful piracy; bite the bullet and buy a real copy of Windows — you'll sleep better at night and your system will run smoother and with less risk of security breaches with all updates applied. In the second situation, if your hard disk drive is that close to being full it is time to add more storage by either replacing the internal drive with a larger one or adding an external drive (and moving some data off the internal drive to make space for Windows and programs).

The wizard of Windows XP SP2 provides the same two pathways to creating a wireless network that are offered in the newer Windows Vista: an automated process that is based around settings transferred from machine to machine on a USB flash drive, and a manual process.

### Automated network setup under Windows XP

To set up a new laptop to work with an existing wireless network, begin by turning on the machine and its WiFi circuitry.

*1.* **Load Windows XP.**

*2.* **Click Start ⇨ Control Panel.**

*3.* **Choose a step depending on what Control Panel view you have:**

- If you are using the Classic view of Control Panel, click directly on Wireless Network Setup Wizard.

- If you are using the Category view of Control Panel, click first on Network and Internet Connections and then click Wireless Network Setup Wizard.

*4.* **Follow the step-by-step instructions presented by the wizard.**

*5.* **For use with a Windows Connect Now device, insert a USB flash drive into your laptop.**

*6.* **Tell the wizard to save your wireless network configuration settings to the flash drive.**

7. **Bring the flash drive from one machine or device to each other.**

8. **Installing it in a USB port to provide wireless communication settings.**

### Manual configuration of a WiFi network under Windows XP

If you have the necessary details for an existing network, it is pretty easy to do the configuration manually. (I keep notes on all details of my networks in an old-fashioned notebook I keep on the shelf in my office; I also keep the same information on an index card that I place within the box or instruction manual for any piece of networking equipment I add to my system.)

Here are the basic steps; your experience may differ slightly based on the particular mix of hardware in your laptop and out amongst the components of the network.

1. **Click Start ➪ Control Panel.**

2. **Double-click Network Connections.**

3. **Click the wireless network connection icon.**

4. **Under Network Tasks, click View Available Wireless Networks.**

   A list of wireless networks appears. You may see only the one in your home or office or you may see others from neighbors or nearby offices.

5. **Choose the wireless network you want to use.**

6. **Click Connect.**

In some situations, the list of available wireless networks may not be complete; some public networks may have multiple names or otherwise be hidden. To show all wireless networks, click Show Wireless Access Point Names.

If you are attempting to work with a public wireless network or a managed network in a large organization, you may be asked to download additional files that will allow your computer to connect to the network. You should only allow a network to download files onto your machine if you trust its provider . . . and if your machine is properly protected; when in doubt, try to find a network that does not seek to alter your laptop in any way and merely opens itself up to visitors.

Connecting to a new wireless network is just one of many tasks where the importance of having a capable — and completely updated — antivirus and firewall program is essential. That is, unless you have complete faith that no one has attempted to include anything malicious, mischievous, or merely annoying in a publicly accessible network. And if you believe that to be the case everywhere you go . . . well, let's just say you and your laptop are cruising for a bruising.

If the network you choose has one or more elements of a security system enabled, you will have to obtain and enter the proper network key.

### Adding a device to an existing network

A very easy way to automatically configure a laptop to work with a network is to use the facilities of Windows XP to copy the necessary settings to a flash drive.

Here's how to do this under Windows XP:

1. **Turn on a computer that is successfully communicating with a network.**

2. **Plug a flash memory drive into a USB port on the computer.**

3. **In the USB flash drive dialog box, click Wireless Network Setup Wizard.**

4. **Follow the onscreen directions to copy settings to the flash memory.**

5. **When the task is completed, remove the flash memory from the computer.**

6. **On the laptop you want to add to the wireless network, click on the Start button and then click on Control Panel.**

7. **Click Network and Internet.**

8. **In the Network and Sharing Center, click Add a Device to the Network.**

9. **Follow the instructions in the wizard.**

### Adding wireless devices to a network

A still-developing area of networking is the introduction and use of devices like printers and hard disk drives that can communicate wirelessly with machines on the network. The simplest solution here is to find a device that embraces Microsoft's Windows Connect Now; these allow automatic configuration with the temporary installation of a flash memory card into a USB port on the device.

As an example of products in this category, D-Link offers wireless routers, access points, and "central home drives" that can be placed anywhere within the cloud of WiFi signals in your home or office.

## Using proprietary wireless configuration tools

Most of the major laptop manufacturers now offer their own suite of utilities intended to make it easy for users to connect their new machines to an existing wired or wireless network. The basic concepts are the same, although specific details will vary from manufacturer.

I will use as an example the Toshiba Assist program that is part of the sample Toshiba Satellite P205 laptop referenced in this book. This utility comes preinstalled as a shortcut on the desktop and is also available from within a Toshiba utilities folder.

Begin by making sure that the WiFi power switch is turned on. Loading the program brings the home page, as shown in Figure 3-6.

The task panel on the left side of the screen offers four options:

✦ **Connect.** The utilities here include the ConfigFree Connectivity Doctor, which assists in setting up or troubleshooting a wireless connection, as well as utilities for use with Bluetooth networks.

When the doctor is called upon, it will analyze your network connections and provide detailed information about network settings including the status of the connection, the type of protocol in use (802.11g, for example), and the communication speed currently available. See Figure 3-7. Another interesting element of the tool is the Radar report which scans in all directions from your laptop to show you a representation of the relative location and distance of any WiFi systems; see Figure 3-8.

**Figure 3-6:**
The home page of Toshiba Assist offers access to the ConfigFree utility for setting up a link to a wireless network. On this model, the utility offers utilities to enable and configure Bluetooth networks.

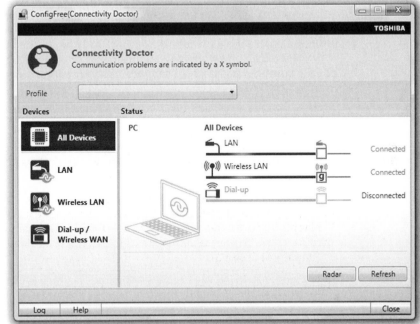

**Figure 3-7:**
The Connectivity Doctor of Toshiba's ConfigFree utility shows the status of all communication networks currently available on your laptop.

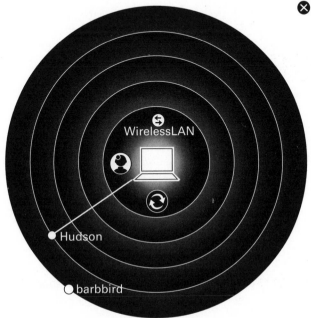

**Figure 3-8:**
Toshiba's WiFi Radar shows that my laptop is nearest the WiFi router I call Hudson, about 30 feet from my office. It also detects my neighbor's network about 100 feet away.

A very useful feature of the tool is access to Profile Settings, which allows you to save differing details for various networks you may use on a regular basis. For example, you could have a profile for your home or office network, one for a public network, and one for the secured network you occasionally use at a client's office or a friend's home. The following settings can be saved (or automatically captured) in a profile:

- **Internet settings.** LAN settings, including proxy server settings, and the address of a home page that will open automatically with your Web browser.

- **Devices.** Software-based enabling or disabling of wired and wireless network devices. On a Bluetooth system, the profile includes the power status for that network's antennas.

- **TCP/IP settings.** The nitty-gritty of the network configuration, including DHCP, IP address, subnet mask, default gateway, DNS server, and more; these are the details that are often automatically set but sometimes require manual adjustment unless you are using a tool like Toshiba's utility.

- **Personal firewall setting.** Any adjustments you have made to the Windows-based firewall aimed at a particular network are saved in the profile.

To create a profile, click the networked computer icon in the notification area of ConfigFree. Choose Profile ➪ Open Settings ➪ Add to Create and Save a Profile.

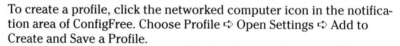

✦ **Secure.** Access to screens to set a supervisor or user password. When you set a supervisor password you can choose to allow or block users from changing the hardware configuration for the laptop. Enabling a user password makes it necessary that any user must enter a password at the time the laptop is powered on.

✦ **Protect & Fix.** This is the portal to a proprietary Toshiba PC Diagnostic Tool that tests most of the hardware components of the laptop along with many of its essential software tools.

✦ **Optimize.** In the Toshiba utility, this option allows quick access to a suite of proprietary tools including adjustments and settings for a CD/DVD acoustic silencer, a mouse setup screen, and other specialized functions.

## Cutting the Wires Other Ways

Although the vast majority of wireless communication for laptops involves one or another form of WiFi radio, there are several other ways to get on line without running a long, long cord to your beach chair. Some systems are close cousins to WiFi (like Bluetooth), some are older and less capable

## Be prepared

First a confession: Years ago I once cobbled together my own unofficial wireless/dial-up/cell phone hybrid connection when I was literally in the middle of nowhere and I needed to check e-mail no matter how sketchy and slow the connection.

Here's what I did: I had purchased from my cell phone manufacturer a cable that connects to a laptop through a USB port and allows for a number of functions including uploading and downloading photos from the phone's camera, uploading snippets of music to be used as ringtones, and . . . I discovered, a way to use the cell phone as a data modem. I was intrigued, especially since the cell phone service provider was not offering Internet access.

So here we were cruising on a slow barge through one of the most remote places in the lower 48 states: a bayou in Louisiana with more alligators than people. There were no settlements for miles but every few minutes I would notice a blip on my cell phone as a signal

somehow managed to make its way to the river. I configured my laptop to call an AOL dial-up number and waited for a bar or two to appear on the cell phone; I clicked Dial and watched the phone make a painfully slow connection.

For about three minutes, I had one of the most obscure (and slowest) connections to the Web in the history of the Internet but it did work and I was able to check my mail before the signal faded and we were back in the technological dark ages. And, of course, you will need a cellular modem. It is now possible to officially do what I unofficially did in that Louisiana bayou: connect your cell phone to your laptop via a USB cable and use its circuitry and antenna to connect to the Internet. A more elegant, and usually faster, alternative is to use a specialized cellular modem that installs in a PC Card or Express Card slot in your laptop. And a few laptop manufacturers have begun to offer machines with this sort of specialized wireless receiver and transmitter built into the case.

special-purpose connections (like infrared), and some are adaptations of existing communications networks for other purposes (like Internet over cellular phone networks).

## Linking to the Web with a cell phone modem

Most major cell phone providers have upgraded their systems to offer broadband Internet access to laptop users who are within reach of their cell towers. A few caveats:

✦ Internet service is not available everywhere, even if phone service is offered. Many companies offer very good service in large cities but very limited coverage in rural areas.

✦ The speed of connection is faster than dial-up, but much slower than DSL or cable service. A typical speed is about 200 Kbps, about four times as fast as dial-up but nowhere near the 3 to 7 Mbps offered by true broadband providers. And some locations — and some cell phone providers — offer very slow speeds.

✦ You need to subscribe to the cell phone company at some level; some providers separate the Internet service from the voice service while others require you to have an agreement that covers both.

✦ Available Internet services are based on *EDGE (Enhanced Data rates for GSM Evolution)* for cell companies using *GSM (Global System for Mobile Communications)* technology. Typical speeds for this sort of system are about 200 Kbps in areas with full coverage.

✦ A more advanced service is *EV-DO (Evolution-Data Optimized)* for use with phones and cell services using *CDMA (Code Division Multiple Access)* technology. Today these systems are capable of download speeds of twice to three times the speed of EDGE.

Some companies offer multiprotocol plans. For example, T-Mobile's cellular Internet plans (in 2008) allow users to switch over to conventional WiFi and use their laptops to connect at higher speeds at any of the company's Hot Spots in coffee shops and other locations at no extra charge.

Contact cell phone providers and ask the following:

✦ What technology do you use for laptop to cellular Internet services?

✦ What speed can I expect in locations where you will travel?

✦ What is the cost for use of the service?

  • Are charges based on minutes of connection or megabytes of data?

  • Am I committed to a monthly contract or can I purchase connectivity when I need it?

  • Am I required to sign up for a one- or two-year contract, which is the model for voice service on cell phones?

✦ How long is the trial period for the service. It might be worthwhile to give cellular Internet service a test before you commit to a long-term contract.

## Bluetooth wireless communication

Believe it or not, not every technological advancement in computing and communications is Made in America. They're not even all Made in China or Japan.

As just one example, consider the Bluetooth wireless standard which was put forth as an alternative to 802.11 protocols by Ericsson in Sweden, where researchers were working on new cell phone technologies including ways for devices to communicate with each other locally. An Intel technician and amateur historian dubbed the standard in honor of Harald Bluetooth, a Scandinavian king who brought together the two warring communities of Denmark and Norway in the tenth century.

Bluetooth operates in the same 2.4 GHz band used by 802.11b and 802.11g but requires considerably less power than its WiFi equivalents. In the marketplace, Bluetooth lost out to 802.11 standards for computer communication, but it has been adopted by a number of pocket-sized electronic devices including cell phones, personal data assistants, cordless headsets, and other equipment.

One of the advantages of Bluetooth technology is that the hardware does all the work; when any two compatible devices find each other they negotiate between them the technical details of communication: elements like exchanging electronic addresses and selecting the best protocol for data. As part of the conversation, the devices determine if one device needs something from the other, or if one unit needs to control the other. Once they've negotiated all they need — techies call this a *handshake* — the devices set up a temporary, highly local personal-area network, also called a *piconet*.

One way Bluetooth devices avoid interference from and with other radio frequency devices is by working at a very low power level. Transmissions are made at 1 milliwatt, which is one thousandth of a watt; by comparison, a typical cell phone uses 1 to 3 watts (one thousand to three thousand as much power) to communicate with the nearest tower.

The devices in a piconet make use of spread-spectrum frequency hopping to help avoid interference. The devices continually change the exact frequency they are using to any of 79 tiny slices of the radio pie, hopping randomly 1,600 times per second. This makes extremely unlikely that there will be any sustained amongst a room full of Bluetooth devices. Even if two units end up on the same frequency for a fraction of a second they will bounce to a different randomly selected setting almost immediately. Bluetooth will reject or ask for a re-send of the data any time it senses corruption in one of the tiny packets of data it receives.

For a period of time, a number of laptop makers offered both Bluetooth and WiFi adapters in their machines, but today's models have mostly dispensed with old Harald's method. However, it is easy to add Bluetooth to a laptop through use of a PC Card or ExpressCard adapter or a USB device.

## Older tech: Infrared systems

One technology that has come . . . and may have gone . . . is the infrared device. We all use these systems every time we change the channel on our television with a remote control; at one time it was envisioned that infrared (IR) would be used to transmit data between a computer and a printer or other peripheral across the room.

IR is radiation of a frequency lower than visible light (below red) but higher than microwaves. The technology has one big disadvantage in comparison to WiFi and Bluetooth: Devices have to be able to "see" each other across the room. Signals might be able to bounce around a desk or off the ceiling but not through a door or wall.

For computers, infrared communication is an adaptation of the 802.11 standard, with a top speed of about 1.6 Mbps, but only if there is nothing in the way and if the angle of communication is head-on or no more than about 15 degrees off center.

Many laptops two or three generations old (perhaps three to six years old) came with infrared circuitry and a small red-filtered window for use in communication. The IR port is a specialized version of a standard serial port.

Windows, from Windows 98 and later, include built-in support for IR ports, often using an industry standard name of IrDA. An Infrared Wizard configures the IR serial port and troubleshoots communication between devices. There are a handful of cordless mice and keyboards available for use with IR systems; if you're buying a new system there is little reason not to use WiFi instead.

## On the horizon: Wireless USB

Within the next few years, many laptops will come equipped with an extension of the already ubiquitous USB port. *Wireless USB (WUSB)* devices are expected to include hard disk drives, CD/DVD drives, modems, printers, digital cameras, LCD projectors, and things we haven't even thought of yet.

In its initial version, USB can communicate between devices at speeds of about 480 Mbps, which is comparable to real-world throughput on a wired USB 2.0 circuit. Designs are already in the works to double WUSB to at least 1 Gbps by about 2010.

Although it technically isn't a network — it's a means of communication between disparate devices — it shares many of the same attributes as WiFi and Bluetooth. WUSB uses a technology called Ultra Wideband radio, allowing devices to communicate at distances of about 10 meters (39 feet) within a home or office.

A WUSB system will be logically organized as a hub-and-spoke topology with devices communicating through a central host. Just as with wired USB, the host will have the capability of working with as many as 127 devices. Unlike a wired USB system, though, since the devices will not be physically connected to a computer or a USB hub, each piece of equipment must have its own source of power either from batteries or an AC adapter.

# Chapter 4: Spinning the Web

## In This Chapter

✔ Seeing what's to do on the Internet

✔ Getting online

✔ Choosing and using a Web browser

✔ Using Favorites, tabs, and other zippy Web tools

**W**hat a tangled Web we receive, when first we practice to retrieve. (First of all, apologies to Sir Walter Scott, who is the author of the original quote: "What a tangled web we weave, when first we practice to deceive." Second of all . . . I fact-checked the quote on the Internet where I confirmed that it was Scott, not William Shakespeare, who gave first warning about modern online research.)

In any case, by this time nearly everyone has used the Internet in one form or another. But what exactly is it?

The *Internet* is, at its core, a huge network of networks. Any person or country (at least those in places where repressive governments haven't intruded) can open up the contents of computer-based data (words, images, numbers, and music included) and send to anyone else who has access to the system.

Components of the Internet include the World Wide Web, usually called the Web, which is a more or less organized (but essentially unsupervised) system of web sites. Also on the Internet are services including e-mail, news groups, and point-to-point file sharing. Included in the mix are streaming media including music and video, as well as digitized telephone service called *Voice over Internet Protocol (VoIP)* which I discuss in Book VIII, Chapter 6.

## Cruising the Web

I could just as reasonably asked the question in the negative: Is there anything left to do or see that *isn't* on the Internet?

On a typical day, my wife and I perform the following essential tasks with a few clicks of the mouse:

✦ Download, read, and respond to dozens of pieces of mail sent to us by business associates, friends, and family. (We also throw away dozens of pieces of electronic junk offering to sell us watches, pharmaceuticals, and access to millions of dollars in secret Nigerian bank accounts or Italian lottery winnings.)

✦ Communicate by *instant message (IM)* between laptops and desktops (and cell phones and PDAs) anywhere in the world within reach of the Internet or a cell phone signal.

✦ Make all our phone calls without any connection to the plain old telephone system. In and around our office and home, all calls travel wirelessly to a base station and from there by wire to a telephone adapter that communicates over the Internet. When we travel, we use a cell phone (with a link to the Internet) and a softphone that allows a WiFi-enabled laptop to place and receive phone calls anywhere we can latch onto an Internet connection.

✦ Shop for home improvements, clothing, books, music, and just about anything else. In recent years, we've purchased four new cars for ourselves and our children in negotiations that began and ended without having to set foot in an automobile dealership until the moment came to pick up the keys.

✦ Conduct nearly all our banking through secure online web sites. We can see the balances in our accounts and pay bills without need for exchanges or papers . . . or stamps.

Speaking for myself, there remain just two occasional reasons to actually visit a bank (or more commonly, an ATM): to obtain cash for the increasingly rare instances where we have to pay for something without flashing a credit or debit card or arranging for electronic transfer of funds, and to make a deposit of checks that arrive in the mail. And I don't expect to need to visit the bank for deposits much longer; there already exists a system that allows you to scan a check and send its image to the bank for deposit.

✦ Research the contents of any one of those billions of Web pages through the use of increasingly sophisticated *search engines,* including Google. Efforts like Project Gutenberg are in the process of scanning or manually entering the text of tens of thousands of books no longer under copyright and making them searchable and readable online.

✦ Upload and download files with my clients, including publishers and business partners.

✦ Listen to music provided for free by sites like www.pandora.com or purchase music through Apple's iTunes or similar commercial enterprises like Amazon.

✦ Catch up on episodes of commercial television or watch video news reports.

✦ Map the quickest and most efficient route between any two places on the map, and zoom in from space to look at satellite images of almost any place on the planet.

✦ Go on location to check the weather and traffic conditions through any of thousands of web cameras. (Attention grandparents and parents: You, too, can add to your daily worries by seeing if there is snow or rain or other problems for your family.)

# Discerning the Good, the Bad, and the Ugly Internet

One of the beauties of the Internet is that it is essentially unmonitored or controlled. There is no systematic before-publication censorship, no after-the-fact policing of political opinion (in most of the world, although some countries including China and certain nations in the Middle East attempt to control the spread of independent or outside ideas, with limited success), and no borders.

These are, alas, also the weaknesses of the Internet. There are no editors and although the government of one nation may object to the content of a web site (or even attempt to block access to it), there is basically nothing that a government can do unilaterally about activities that are rooted somewhere out there in cyberspace.

What is *cyberspace?* The best definition I know of actually reaches back to old technology: the telephone. If you and I were to speak on the phone, where is that conversation taking place? It isn't in my office, and it isn't at your location. It is somewhere in between, an unmapped meeting of the electrons: cyberspace.

Just because you find some information posted on the Internet doesn't make it necessarily true or accurate or up-to-date.

For centuries, readers and scholars have relied upon professional editors and journalists to separate the wheat from the chaff; sometimes it seems as if since 1990, the Internet has existed as a place to publish the chaff.

Although there will always be someone who feels that an established old-line publication like *The New York Times* or *The Wall Street Journal* may have a political or economic or cultural bias, there is at least some reason to believe in the benefit of a professional check-and-balance and accountability. That is not so when it comes to the proliferation of *web logs (blogs)* on the Internet, however interesting some of them are; they represent unverified (and sometimes unverifiable) opinion and sometimes fiction masquerading as fact.

And then there are the pirates of the Caribbean and all of the other oceans and land masses of the world: It is very easy to hide behind a Web domain or an e-mail address for reasons ranging from a desire for privacy to outright criminality. Like it or not, the Internet is also the home of more than a few people out to steal our money . . . and much worse.

In Book IX, I tell you about steps you can take to erect security firewalls, antivirus and antispam utilities, and ways to protect your identity and personal information from the would-be electronic evildoers.

## Getting on the Internet

The process of using the Internet is not quite as mysterious as it might appear to a complete neophyte. Think of it in terms more familiar: How do you go about watching television in your home?

To watch television you need the following: a television, an account with an electricity utility for power (delivered from the power plant to your home), and finally, a way to tune into one or hundreds of data signals floating out there in the ether.

Okay, back to the computer. Let me translate the television example into Internet terms and services. Here's what you need to use the Internet:

✦ A computer with sufficient horsepower and graphics capability to handle the stream of data that comes its way and convert the information into words, images, and sound. (That's the television part of the metaphor, right?)

✦ Electricity from an AC outlet or a built-in rechargeable battery to energize your laptop.

✦ A way to connect to the Internet. That connection could be delivered by an account you have with an Internet service provider that feeds data over a cable television circuit, a DSL telephone wire line, a fiber-optic cable, Internet from a satellite, or even a poky dial-up link over the plain old telephone system. And the connection could come via a wireless link between your laptop and a local or regional transmitter or receiver.

✦ A way to tune in the data. On a television set that is handled by a piece of electronics called, appropriately enough, a *tuner;* for many of us, the tuning is handled by a converter box provided to us by a cable television company. On a computer, though, the tuning is performed by a piece of software called a browser; the most common one for Windows users is supplied by Microsoft and called Internet Explorer. The browser communicates with other computers somewhere out there in cyberspace and delivers to your laptop the page or stream or nugget of information you're looking for.

*Broadband* is a fat pipe that gushes more data per millisecond than is possible for a human (and most machines) to absorb, while not-broadband is a narrow straw of a connection that is slow and limited. Forget about what anyone else tells you about life in other contexts: When it comes to Internet connections, fat is good. In Book VIII, Chapter 1, I discuss the difference between broadband and standard connections to the Internet.

## Choosing a browser

Back in the early days of office automation (back when the very idea of a "personal" computer would have gotten you laughed out of the board room) there was a maxim that held a great deal of sway in business: "Nobody ever got fired for buying IBM." What they meant by that was: Why take chances with Brand X — even if we think it is better or cheaper or faster — when we know that there's no risk in going along with the choice that almost everyone else is making?

### Internet Explorer

In many ways, that's the message of Microsoft in selling the Windows operating system and its Office suite of programs. And from the start, Microsoft's Windows Internet Explorer has been included as a "free" component of Windows. (For a short period of time, Microsoft offered a version of IE that could run on a Macintosh operating system but current editions of the browser are exclusively for Windows. Today, Apple Safari browser can run on both Mac and Windows-based machines.)

Internet Explorer is a very impressive product and has over time held on to a market share near 90 percent; today it runs on more than 80 percent of all personal computers of all brands and types. It may not be the flashiest or the easiest to use, and many technical types strongly contend that it continues to have many serious flaws when it comes to protecting the security of data on machines on which it runs. (It's a bit of an open question, though: Do the majority of virus and spam authors target machines running Internet Explorer because it is easy to do so, or because it is by far the most commonly used browser?)

In any case, no one is likely to be fired because they use Windows Internet Explorer on their Windows-based machine. It's the official browser of Microsoft, after all.

### Mozilla Firefox and Opera

On Windows machines, in distant second place, is a browser with the geeky name of Mozilla Firefox which may be used by as many as 15 percent of machines.

**Book VIII
Chapter 4**

**Spinning the Web**

## It's a jungle out there

The product began as Phoenix, which was later translated to a more contemporary Firebird and then changed to Firefox after a dispute with the backers of another product called Firebird. A creature in China is called a *firefox* — a species of Panda, apparently — but that may be just coincidental.

And Mozilla? That name came from its long-ago origin as a group trying to compete with one of the first (pre-Microsoft) browsers, a product called Mosaic. Mozilla was a contraction of Mosaic-killer. Do you see why corporate types were more readily attracted to a company called Microsoft offering a product with the straightforward name Internet Explorer?

Whatever the name, Firefox is a fully capable browser with a fair number of fans who prefer its style. And though it isn't immune to security assaults, the number of viruses aimed at Firefox is much less than those directed at Internet Explorer.

In even-more-distant third place for Windows users is the Opera browser, which has its roots in a Norwegian telecommunications company. The browser also runs on Apple's Mac OS X, Linux, and some other operating systems.

### Choosing the browser for you

I've used all major browsers for Windows and found things to like in each of them. But like the old-timers in 1981, my job — as an explainer of technology — demands a concentration on Windows Internet Explorer. No one is going to lose their job by staying with the product that has an 80 percent market share; if that number ever drops to a minority, I'll lead the charge to a new browser.

The fact is that all the browsers operate in a similar manner. Some have a few extra features that may be obvious to the user or may be hidden in the code and delivered in the form of enhanced security or efficiency.

And, by the way, why not have two or more different browsers loaded on your system? You can even run several browsers at the same time, although this does open the door to resource conflicts.

In this chapter, I concentrate on Windows Internet Explorer. I also present some keyboard shortcuts for both IE and Firefox.

For details about how to inform Windows about the particulars of the hardware and the networking protocols of your system, see Book VIII, Chapter 2.

## Netscape Navigator loses its way

Netscape Navigator, the first commercial Web browser, officially reached the end of its life in February of 2008 when its current owner, AOL, announced it would end further development and technical support. Netscape's market share had all but disappeared, replaced by its open-source cousin, Firefox.

Users will still be able to download and use Netscape, but AOL will not longer offer security

and compatibility updates. I recommend that any remaining Netscape users — you probably both know each other personally — change over to Firefox or Windows Internet Explorer.

Netscape was introduced in late 1994 as a commercial product, but Internet Explorer followed and (leaving out some serious legal wrangling with Microsoft over the years) the company was purchased by AOL in 1999.

Most browsers, including Windows Internet Explorer, install a shortcut on your machine's desktop and may also insinuate themselves onto the taskbar. And just for good measure most also pin themselves to the Start menu of Windows. Clicking the icons or shortcuts automatically starts the browser. Clicking a link in a document also generally launches the page within your default browser.

## Finding Your Way on the Web

When you first start a browser it will display the *home page*. Many browser makers, including Microsoft, deliver their product with a particular home page preset as the default page; some laptop makers install Windows and a browser with the home page set to their product support page. And if you configure your system with the assistance of your ISP (a cable television company or a DSL provider, for example), they may put their own page in place.

Be on the lookout for web sites that helpfully offer to "make this page your home page." Sometimes it's easy to miss this sort of electronic land grab. Many current security software programs will detect and block any attempt to change your home page without your permission.

None of this means that you have to use someone else's suggestion (or demand) for your home page. You can set a news site like the online edition of *The New York Times* or your favorite sports team or the main page for your preferred search engine.

To get back to your home page at any time, click the Home button on the toolbar. If you're so unlucky as to be still using a dial-up modem, you can get to the Internet faster by setting a blank screen as your home page. That way you won't have to wait for graphics and text to download before you trudge to the page you really want to visit.

## Can I have your address?

Although the World Wide Web exists only in cyberspace, there has to be a way for visitors to find their way to the front doors of each of its sites. Behind the scenes, a collection of huge databases keeps track of where every Web page is located through the use of a Web address.

In technical terms, the address is called a *Uniform Resource Locator (URL)*.

A few examples of URLs:

✦ www.microsoft.com is the front door to the company that makes and sells Windows, Internet Explorer, Microsoft Office, and many of the other tools you likely use on your laptop. In current browsers, you don't have to type the three *w*s; they're assumed.

✦ www.dummies.com is the place to learn about the latest, greatest, and smartest additions to the best-selling *For Dummies* books.

✦ www.econoguide.com is one of the web sites I maintain to promote my books and to receive messages from (mostly) satisfied readers.

The basic elements of a URL are these:

**http://**    Addresses are preceded by either http:// or https:// to indicate the use of the Hypertext Transfer Protocol in its basic or "secured" form. HTTP is used in most intranets and the World Wide Web. In fact, it is so ubiquitous that for an address on Web you don't even need to fill it in; the browser will do the work for you if you begin the URL with www.

**www**    An indication that the web site is part of the World Wide Web. There are other corners of the Internet and the intranet available to some or all visitors but stored and indexed in facilities that aren't considered part of the Web.

**domain**    This is the heart of the address, a word or phrase that is relatively easy for humans to remember. The domain name is used by the browser to locate a page, but once computers are speaking to computers the domain name is replaced by a more complex series of numbers that help find the page and direct the components of the Internet to deliver it to your laptop.

**.com**    A domain type, also called a *top-level domain*. In its original design, .com was envisioned as a subdivision devoted exclusively to commercial enterprises; today it is more of a "common" name. Other top-level domains include the following:

- .edu for educational institutions
- .gov for government agencies
- .mil for military functions
- .org for organizations

Some nations have second-level domains, such as .com.ar for commercial enterprises in Argentina or .co.uk for companies in the United Kingdom.

Later in this chapter I give you a list of useful keyboard shortcuts for use with Internet Explorer. Here's a sample: If you want to go to a location that is named in the most common fashion (like www.dummies.com) you can just enter the domain (dummies) and then press Ctrl + Enter from the keyboard to convert it to the proper URL.

## Links and recent pages

Today we mostly think in terms of links. You'll find them almost anywhere on the Internet. You'll see a word in a color (often, but not always, blue) and usually underlined; click that link and it will take you somewhere else — to a different page on the same web site or to a completely different web site. Links can also be tied into a picture or image; click the HDTV set to go to a page that tells you all of the specs and the ordering information for that product.

To test whether an item on a Web page is a link, bring your onscreen pointer to hover over it. If it is a link, you should see both of the following things on your screen:

✦ The mouse pointer changed to a hand with a pointing finger.

✦ A URL in the status bar at the bottom of Internet Explorer. This shows the web site that the browser goes to if you click the link. (Try to get in the habit of looking at the proposed address before clicking on a link; that is one way to involve your own judgment in the process of securing your machine against visits to unwanted or dangerous web sites.)

Links are an essential element of the Internet. They are what makes the Web tick. When you use a search site like Google, the results you get are in the form of links you can click to jump to a new page. When you're shopping for books or a pair of fleece-lined bunny slippers on Amazon, you get to check out the available products by clicking a link.

Another important element of the Web is the ability to go backward or forward in your history of jumps from page to page. To go back to the previous page from the one you've linked to, click the Back button. You can go back several pages, and then you can use the Forward button to move ahead to where you started.

**Book VIII
Chapter 4**

**Spinning the Web**

# Hyper indeed

One of the original concepts for what we now call the Internet was something called *hypertext,* which was a way to think of data in three dimensions. A reference to something you found on a page did not exist in a vacuum; clicking it would link to a definition or to a page with a great deal of detail about the subject. In 1987, Apple introduced a version of this precursor to the Internet with its "HyperCard" application for early versions of the Macintosh computer.

Another way to revisit a page you've looked at in your *current session* is to use the Recent Pages menu. In Internet Explorer 7, you find it in the Favorites Center section of the browser; it uses a yellow five-pointed star as an icon. You can also jump directly to the Favorites Center by typing the key combination of Ctrl + H.

At the Favorites Center, click the down arrow in the History section and then select a page from the list. You can look by

- ✦ Date
- ✦ Site
- ✦ Most visited
- ✦ In order for visits made today

See Figure 4-1.

## Setting or changing your Internet Explorer home page

To set a particular web site as your home page in any current version of Windows Internet Explorer, do the following:

*1.* **Click Tools ⇨ Internet Options.**

*2.* **Click the General tab.**

See Figure 4-2.

*3.* **In the Home page section, do one of the following:**

- • Type the web address for the page you want to set
- • Copy and paste the address from an online source.
- • Click Use Current to assign the Web page you're currently viewing.

- Click Use Default to reset the home page to the one recommended by your browser or laptop maker or whichever group of programmers has inserted its preference into the coding for the browser.

- Click Use Blank to open your browser with a clean, meaningless white page. This allows the browser to load slightly faster, but some users get the added advantage of being able to instantly blank the screen if someone approaches the workstation unexpectedly; then again, you could also quickly jump back to *The New York Times* if you don't want someone to see your real interests.

Note that in Windows Internet Explorer 7 (and later editions to follow) you can create more than one home page, with each one assigned to its own *tab* on the browser screen. To do so,

*1.* **Type each address on its own line.**

When you open IE, each web site you listed as a home page is available on its own tab

*2.* **Click between them.**

You can close any of the tabs without affecting its assignment as one of your regular home pages.

**Figure 4-1:** The History submenu of IE7 allows you to pick from recently visited sites to jump directly to them.

Book VIII
Chapter 4

Spinning the Web

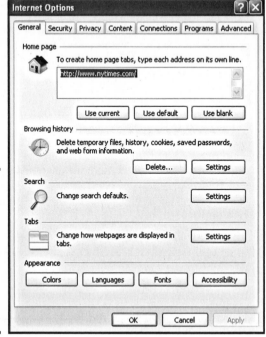

**Figure 4-2:**
You can set
the home
page for
Internet
Explorer on
the General
tab of
Internet
Options.

## Problems with home pages

You turn on your browser, expecting to see on your home page all the latest news and stats for the Boston Red Sox but instead there is something quite unpleasant and unwanted; it could be the New York Yankees home page or it could be something even more unwanted. What has happened?

✦ Your system may have a virus.

✦ Some web site you visited may have changed your home page without your permission.

✦ Someone else might have been using your machine and made a change without checking with you first.

The first step to try is to reset the home page to the one you want.

*1.* **Navigate to that page.**

Or follow the instructions in the previous section, and select Use Current.

*2.* **Go to the Internet Options page.**

*3.* **Type the Web address for the site you want.**

*4.* **Close Internet Explorer and reload it.**

If it now goes to the home page you have specified, the problem may be fixed.

If that doesn't work — or if the problem recurs later on — your computer's software may have been changed without your permission. Here's how to deal with the situation: Install and run a capable antivirus program. (Make sure you keep it up to date; most such programs download the latest alerts and repairs daily, anytime you are connected to the Internet.)

According to Microsoft, a number of viruses include, as one of their annoyances, a change to your home page.

Another possibility is that third-party software (that is, software that does not come from the Microsoft mother ship) might have taken over control of your browser. Programs that may do this, according to Microsoft, follow:

✦ Xupiter toolbar from Xupiter.com

✦ SecondPower Multimedia Speedbar from SecondPower.com

✦ GoHip! Web browser enhancement from GoHip.com

An antivirus program should remove malicious code. Run a full scan of your system and follow instructions for cleaning and removing any viruses it finds.

If you installed one of the browser "enhancements," you should be able to remove them with this:

*1.* **Go to the Windows Control Panel.**

*2.* **Select the icon in your operating system:**

   • **Windows XP and earlier:** Add or Remove Programs icon

   • **Windows Vista:** Programs and Features icon

If you are running an older version of Internet Explorer (version 6 or older) consider updating your system to the latest edition of the browser (version 7 as this book goes to press, with version 8 expected to be released soon).

Don't perform an update before you've checked for viruses.

Internet Explorer 7 for Windows XP and Windows Internet Explorer 7 for Windows Vista include some security improvements that Microsoft says make them less susceptible to spyware and to malware. They also include a feature to allow quick reset of browser settings (to get past changes made without your knowledge or permission).

To use reset Windows Internet Explorer 7, do the following:

*1.* **Click Tools ➪ Internet Options.**

2. **Click the Advanced tab.**

3. **Click Reset.**

   The Reset Internet Explorer Settings dialog box opens.

4. **Click Reset.**

   Let Internet Explorer 7 finish restoring the default settings

5. **Click Close.**

6. **Click OK, OK.**

   You exit the configuration screen.

7. **Close Internet Explorer 7.**

8. **Reload Internet Explorer 7.**

   The changes take effect.

If the problem with your Internet Explorer 7 browser is so severe that you can't start the program, try resetting:

1. **Go to the Windows Control Panel.**

2. **Select Internet Options.**

3. **Click the Advanced tab.**

4. **Click Reset.**

   This option's in the section of the window called Reset Internet Explorer Settings.

## Searching the web

Imagine if the billions of Web pages and hundreds of billions of words and images on those pages were just scattered about . . . like the pages on the real wood desktop in my office. That's a frightening thought . . . and more to the point . . . it would be a useless pile of stuff.

The utility that makes the Web work for us is the *search engine,* a form of software robot that searches through all of the material on the Internet to construct a giant index of subjects and content. If you want to find out whether there ever was a left-handed catcher in Major League Baseball (a very rare athlete) all you have to do is to go to a search engine and type in something like **left-handed catcher.**

Click . . . and you get a list of hundreds of web sites and individual pages about the subject. I learned that in the course of baseball history there have been only five lefties who caught at least 100 games, led by Jack Clements who was behind the plate for the Philadelphia Phillies for most of his career from 1884 to 1900. Who knew?

## Choosing a search engine

Dozens of companies and organizations offer search engines that promise to uncover the hidden, obscure, and distant corners of cyberspace. That's both the good news and the bad news.

Think about it: If a search engine were perfect, you'd need only one. The facts are that different search engines use differing methods and produce varying results.

There are three basic ways search engines work:

✦ A *crawler* system with robotic *spider*s or other computer-based methods

✦ A library-like system based on squadrons of humans who hunt for data

✦ Hybrid systems that augment the computer's findings with human editing

In my experience, I can find just about anything on the Internet through any of the major search engines; it's more a matter of learning how to use each of them in the best way.

Microsoft is pushing to make its Live Search a major competitor to Google. (That system began as MSN Search, but was renamed as part of the company's major shift to the Live brand and package of services.) See Figure 4-3.

**Figure 4-3:** Microsoft's Live Search is based on a computer-driven crawl of the Internet. As with Google and others, you can search for data, images, video, maps, and other specific types of content.

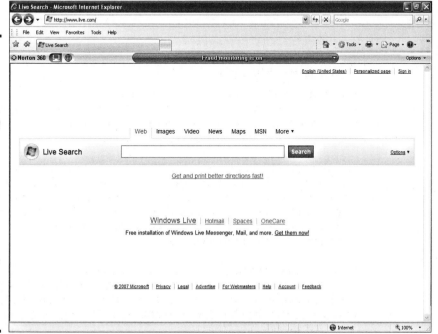

For most people, the best-known search engine is Google, which uses spiders that crawl through the Internet constantly in search of new or changed information or web sites. The company's work has become so popular that its name has become an informal verb: "I Googled your name before I went out with you on a date. What was it like to be the son of a famous embezzler?"

In the end, I suspect that most users will follow the same sort of pattern that I do: I have one favorite search engine (it happens to be Google) that I consult first and I usually find what I am looking for there. But if the results I get aren't good enough, or if I want to see if another utility comes up with some alternate suggestions, I move on to a second (and sometimes a third) search engine. Here are some places to try:

✦ **Altavista.** Born at Digital Equipment Corporation, the Altavista search engine was adopted by Yahoo for its offering; after DEC was sold to (and consumed by) Compaq and that company's eventual merger partner Hewlett-Packard the search engine continued as an independent offering. Today it uses technology from Yahoo. www.altavista.com

✦ **A9.** A search engine offered by the Internet shopping site Amazon, it is a combination of a traditional search engine with product links. www.A9.com

✦ **Dogpile.** A self-described metasearch engine, Dogpile checks the results from a number of other search engines in responding to your request. www.dogpile.com

✦ **Google.** The hugely successful and very useful search engine from Google is now the tip of the sword of the offerings of that company; Google is hoping to grow even larger with offerings including "cloud" computing (Web-based applications). www.google.com

✦ **Live Search.** Microsoft's search engine is growing and improving as the company pours resources into its Live brand. Like Google, Microsoft hopes to offer a suite of applications and utilities that build on the search engine. www.live.com

✦ **Lycos.** One of the original search engines, it has made forays into services including Web portals and provision of other services. http://search.lycos.com

✦ **Yahoo!** Another "old" company in the search engine field, Yahoo also offers mail, news, and applications. http://search.yahoo.com

### Using a search engine

At its most basic level, using a search engine is as easy as apple pie. As a matter of fact, I just typed the words "apple pie" into Google and in one-tenth of a second my screen was filled with the first 10 of approximately 4,720,000 different web sites or references to that particular dessert.

And just as I should have expected, most of the initial listings were recipes for pies made with apples. But there is no way that I have the time to go through all 4.7 million of the listings — at least not today.

One other thing: In general, a search for apple pie gives you all web sites in which both the word *apple* and *pie* appear. This includes recipes for apple pie as well as an article about using an Apple computer to create a pie chart.

 To search for the exact phrase in Google (and most other engines), put it in quotes. For example, "apple pie" only returns pages that have those two words next to each other and in that order. That reduced the number of pages by a few hundred thousand.

If I wanted to be more specific (say I'm looking for French apple pie), I could put those words in quotes. I just did, and by gosh, there were only about 18,800 pages to look at.

Consult the help pages for whichever search engine you use. You'll find many ways to be more specific in your searching, including the use of exclusionary symbols. (You could search for pie recipes but not those with apple in their name.) There are ways to add operators including "or" and "not" to a search.

 And some web sites, including Google, allow you to search by filling in a form that permits all sorts of specificity. A few seconds spent using Google's Advanced Search page may save you minutes or hours in reviewing the results of a query. See Figure 4-4.

### About search results

How does a particular result rise to the number one position in a search results screen? In a truly honest world, that would be because it is the best possible answer to your question.

If you have been very specific in your request that may be true. However, more often a particular web site is at the top because its designers have worked hard to include various tags and codes that increase the chances for a high "ranking" in a search. And because of the unregulated and unedited nature of the Web, there is also the chance that a search will turn up a page with phony tags and headlines masking content unrelated to your search; that's where the human librarians at some search companies are supposed to exercise judgment.

And finally, most search engines also sell advertising to pay for their expensive operations. Google, for example, sells "sponsored links" that run down the side of the page with your search results. You can ignore them; I know that I do.

**Figure 4-4:**
The
Advanced
Search page
of Google
allows you
to make very
specific
requests of
the index of
web sites.

Beware, though, of some search engines that might not be quite as forthright in their labeling of paid advertising.

### Exploring with the Instant Search Box and more

Windows Internet Explorer includes an Instant Search box alongside the Web address box at the top of the browser screen.

*1.* **Type a keyword or phrase.**

*2.* **Press Enter.**

> The engine searches for results and displays them on the current page of the browser. To display the search results on a new tab in the browser, enter the terms, and press Alt + Enter.

You can jump from anywhere on a browser page directly to the IE search page by pressing the Ctrl + E key combination.

Microsoft, as you might expect, would hope that all users employ the Live Search engine (or its MSN Search predecessor) and Internet Explorer as delivered will have Live Search designated as the default place for searches. You can, though, change which search engine to use as the default utility by clicking the down arrow alongside the search box.

You can also perform certain types of searches directly from the Internet Explorer address bar. To do so, follow along:

*1.* **Type one of the following in the address bar:**

- **Find**

- **Go**

- **?**

*2.* **Also in the address bar, type a search term or web site name.**

*3.* **Press Enter.**

To have the results shown in a new tab in IE7, press Alt + Enter.

## Dealing with pesky pop-ups

Somewhere, someone out there is perfectly happy with *pop-ups* — small special windows, usually selling something or otherwise seeking to distract you from whatever it is you're trying to accomplish — that appear on top of or within Web pages.

Internet Explorer 7 and later editions include a utility that will block *most* pop-ups. Why only "most" of them? Because advertisers are constantly looking for new ways to get around attempts to stifle their attempts to divert your attention from whatever it was you really wanted to see on a Web page. If Microsoft (or one of a number of third-party software utility makers) comes up with a mechanism that blocks pop-ups that try to insinuate themselves onto an Internet page the cat-and-mouse game is under way; sometimes the loophole exists for just a few days before an update is sent to Windows users and sometimes it takes longer.

In general, you shouldn't run two or more pop-up blockers on a single computer. That's an open invitation for conflicts and crashes. Choose either the built-in facilities of Windows Internet Explorer 7 or those from a third-party company (including standalone products and those that are part of a security suite).

### Using Internet Explorer's pop-up blocker

To enable or disable the built-in pop-up blocker of Windows Internet Explorer 7, do this:

*1.* **Click Tools.**

*2.* **Hover your pointer over the Pop-up Blocker menu item.**

A window opens. See Figure 4-5.

**Book VIII
Chapter 4**

**Spinning the Web**

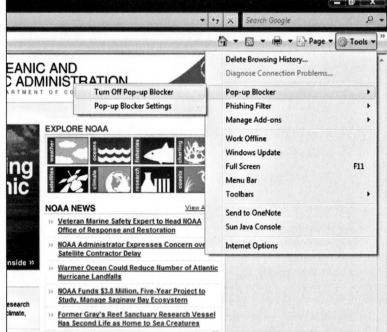

**Figure 4-5:**
You can turn the pop-up blocker on or off with a setting from the Tools menu; Internet Explorer 7 is delivered by Microsoft with the blocker enabled.

*3.* **Choose an option:**

- **Turn On Pop-up Blocker**
- **Turn Off Pop-up Blocker.**

If it's on, you'll turn it off . . . or the other way around.

### Configuring the IE7 Pop-up Blocker

Windows Internet Explorer includes several options for how its built-in pop-up blocker works. To make settings, do this:

*1.* **Click the Tools menu.**

*2.* **Hover your pointer over the Pop-up Blocker menu item.**

A window opens.

*3.* **Select Pop-up Blocker Settings.**

See Figure 4-6.

**Figure 4-6:**
Settings for
the built-in
Pop-up
Blocker
allow you to
permit
certain sites
to avoid the
rules.

4. **If you choose, type a URL in the Address of Website to Allow text box.**

   When you visit one of these sites, the blocker is automatically turned off. Why would you do this? Some sites are designed to display essential information such as prices or product explanations as pop-ups, rather than by taking you to a different page.

5. **If you choose, enable the Play a Sound When a Pop-Up Is Blocked check box.**

6. **If you choose, enable the Information Bar When a pop-up Is Blocked check box.**

   This way you're notified when something is blocked.

7. **Click the Filter Level drop-down arrow.**

8. **Choose an option:**

   • **Low** allows all pop-ups from secure sites.

   • **Medium** blocks most automatic pop-ups.

   • **High** is supposed to bar the door to all pop-ups.

**Book VIII
Chapter 4**

**Spinning the Web**

## My favorite back pages

Do you remember the time you found that absolutely wonderful page about the best travel sights in Longyearbyen on the Svalbard archipelago near the North Pole? Could you help me out with the URL? I can't find my notes where I wrote down the address.

Actually there's a much better way to remember web sites to which you may one day want to return. What you need to do is to save the address as a *Favorite*. Once that is done, you can quickly go to your Favorites list and click a listing to return.

### Saving a Web page as a favorite

With Internet Explorer running, do this:

*1.* **Go to the Web page you want to save as a favorite.**

*2.* **Click the Add to Favorites button.**

It's at the upper-left corner of the browser; its icon is a plus mark on top of a star.

*3.* **Click Add to Favorites.**

Or press Ctrl + D.

The Name box fills with a name for the Web page based on the preassigned title for the site; you can change that name by typing in text of your own.

*4.* **Choose a folder in which to store the favorite.**

You can use the preassigned folders of the Favorites list or add ones of your own.

*5.* **Click Add.**

See Figure 4-7.

### Opening a Web page from the Favorites list

To return to a Web page you have saved as a favorite, do this:

*1.* **Open Internet Explorer.**

*2.* **Click the Favorites Center button.**

It's marked in IE7 with a five-pointed star icon.

*3.* **Locate the Favorites Center window.**

The Center has three options: Favorites, Feeds, and History.

*4.* **Click Favorites if it isn't already selected.**

Your Favorites are listed.

*5.* **Click the Web page you want to open.**

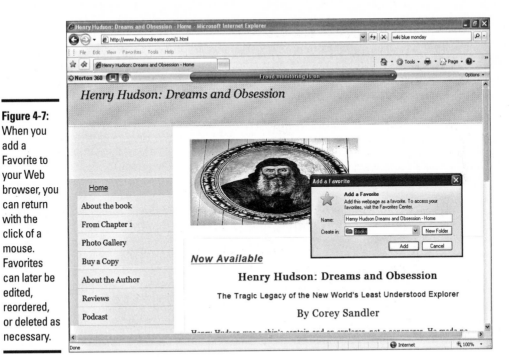

**Figure 4-7:**
When you add a Favorite to your Web browser, you can return with the click of a mouse. Favorites can later be edited, reordered, or deleted as necessary.

## Organizing your favorites

Too much of a good thing, of course, can lead to a messy and disorganized list of favorites, which defeats the whole purpose of having the list. The good news is that you can use the Windows structure of folders and subfolders to organize your Favorites by subject, project, date, or any other structure you want to apply.

To organize your favorites, do this:

*1.* **Click the star-shaped Favorites Center icon.**

*2.* **Locate the three tabs: Favorites, RSS, and History.**

*3.* **Click Favorites.**

Your Favorites are listed.

*4.* **Right-click anywhere in the Favorites Center**

*5.* **Click Create New Folder.**

*6.* **Click + drag the Favorite to the folder of your choice.**

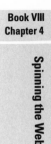

**Book VIII
Chapter 4**

**Spinning the Web**

## Keeping tab of multiple Web pages

The first versions of Web browsers were only capable of displaying one page at a time. If you clicked on a link that was designed to open up without closing the current page, your computer would be instructed to load a second copy of the browser . . . or a third or a fourth.

Although modern machines and current versions of Windows can have more than one instance of a browser (and many other programs) running, that generally isn't an efficient way to use your laptop's memory and other resources. Your system will slow down and may eventually crash.

With the arrival IE7 (preceded by Mozilla Firefox, which introduced the concept to Windows-based system) users can now open multiple tabs to hold many pages. Only one copy of the Web browser needs to be running, and you can click the various tabs to quickly switch your view from one page to another.

✦ To open a Web page on a new tab, click the New Tab button (an empty tab to the right of the last currently running tab).

✦ To close a tab, click the small X button on the right side of the tab.

✦ Click the Quick Tabs icon to see smaller versions of all open pages at the same time. The icon shows four stacked boxes to the left of the tabs. See Figure 4-8.

**Figure 4-8:** You can jump from one tab to another in IE7 by clicking its tab or by clicking the down arrow to the left of the tabs. To view all current tabs, click the Quick Tabs icon.

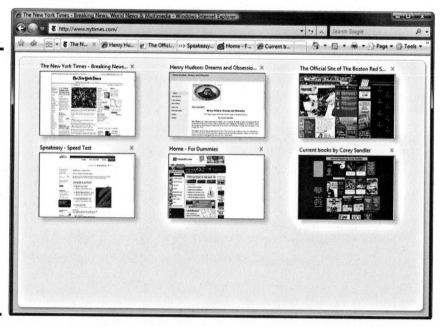

### Saving a group of tabs

Say that you've developed your own group of Web pages that cover all of your basic interests: news, sports, a stock ticker, and an online auction site for used baseball gloves. Or perhaps you like to check six newspapers every morning.

IE7 allows you to save a group of tabs as a single Favorite:

*1.* **Open Internet Explorer.**

*2.* **Open multiple web sites on tabs.**

*3.* **Click the Add to Favorites button.**

*4.* **Click Add Tab Group to Favorites.**

*5.* **Type a folder name.**

*6.* **Click Add.**

To open the saved group, follow along:

*1.* **Open Internet Explorer.**

*2.* **Click the Favorites Center button.**

*3.* **Click the folder you want to open.**

*4.* **Click the folder's drop-down arrow.**

All the Web pages in the group open on separate pages.

### Returning to the same set of tabs without saving them

One way to temporarily save a collection of tabs is to tell the browser as much when you close Internet Explorer. If you click the red X to close IE7 (or if you use the Alt + F4 key combination for the same purpose) the browser displays a small window asking: Do You Want to Close All Tabs?

To instruct the browser to start with all of the current wWeb pages running on tabs the next time you run it, enable the Open These the Next Time I Use Internet Explorer check box. (If you don't see that check box, click the Show Options arrow to expand choices.)

### Turning off tabs

Although tabbed browsing is a nice addition to Internet Explorer, you can choose to turn off that feature:

*1.* **Open Internet Explorer 7 (or later).**

*2.* **Click Tools ➪ Internet Options.**

3. **Choose the General tab.**

4. **In the Tabs section, click Settings.**

5. **Click the Enable Tabbed Browsing checkbox to clear it.**

6. **Click OK twice.**

7. **Close Internet Explorer.**

8. **Reopen Internet Explorer.**

The change is enabled.

### Feeding your browser

A *feed* or *syndicated content* is a form of information that can be automatically delivered to your browser. It's a way to track news or changes to a web site or a blog without having to load the page.

Two common types of feeds are

✦ **RSS.** Really Simple Syndication is a type of Web feed that can deliver news headlines and alerts, updates to blogs, podcasts, and other information. The document can contain the entire document or merely a summary of changes. Users can read RSS content with a specialized RSS reader or through the built-in facilities of IE7.

✦ **XML.** The Extensible Markup Language is a way for authors to format their content so that it can be displayed on a variety of devices and using a number of different operating systems. RSS is a form of XML, and IE7 can work with feeds sent using either specification.

When you visit a web site that offers this sort of content, the Feeds button on the toolbar lights up. (The button is an orange icon that looks like it is radiating out a message from an antenna.) Click the button to display the feed or to subscribe to it.

## Taking Internet Explorer 7 Shortcuts

Tables 4-1 through 4-9 help you on your way.

| Table 4-1 | General IE Shortcuts |
|---|---|
| *Task* | *Shortcut* |
| Full Screen Mode on or off | F11 |
| Cycle through: Address Bar, Refresh button, Search Box, and items on a Web page | Tab |

| Task | Shortcut |
|------|----------|
| Open the current Web page in a new window | Ctrl + F |
| Print the current page | Ctrl + P |
| Select all items on the current page | Ctrl + A |
| Zoom in | Ctrl + + |
| Zoom out | Ctrl + - |
| Zoom to 100 percent | Ctrl + 0 |

| Table 4-2 | Navigation |
|-----------|------------|
| *Task* | *Shortcut* |
| Go to home page | Alt + Home |
| Go backward | Alt + Left |
| Go forward | Alt + Right |
| Refresh page | F5 |
| Refresh page and the browser cache | Ctrl + F5 |
| Stop downloading page | Esc |

| Table 4-3 | Favorites Center Shortcuts |
|-----------|----------------------------|
| *Task* | *Shortcut* |
| Open Favorites | Ctrl + I |
| Open Favorites in pinned mode | Ctrl + Shift + I |
| Organize Favorites | Ctrl + B |
| Add current page to Favorites | Ctrl + D |
| Open Feeds | Ctrl + J |
| Open Feeds in pinned mode | Ctrl + Shift + J |
| Open History | Ctrl + H |
| Open History in pinned mode | Ctrl + Shift + H |

*In Pinned Mode, the Favorites window doesn't close after clicking a link.*

| Table 4-4 | Tab Shortcuts (IE7 and Later) |
|-----------|-------------------------------|
| *Task* | *Shortcut* |
| Open link in new background tab | Ctrl + left mouse button |
| Open link in new foreground tab | Ctrl + Shift + left mouse button |

*(continued)*

**Table 4-4** *(continued)*

| Task | Shortcut |
| --- | --- |
| Open Quick Tab view | Ctrl + Q |
| Close tab (If only one tab is open, closes window) | Ctrl + W |
| Open new tab in the foreground | Ctrl + T<br>or<br>Double-click an empty space on the tab row |
| Open new tab in the foreground, from the Address bar | Alt + Enter |
| View list of open tabs | Ctrl + Shift + Q |
| Switch to next tab | Ctrl + Tab |
| Switch to previous tab | Ctrl + Shift + Tab |
| Switch to a specific tab number | Ctrl + number (any number between 1 and 8) |

| **Table 4-5** | **Address Bar Shortcuts** |
| --- | --- |
| Task | Shortcut |
| Select the Address Bar | Alt + D |
| Automatically add http://www. to the beginning, and .com to the end of text entered in the Address Bar | Ctrl + Enter |
| Automatically add http://www. to the beginning, and the domain suffix you have specified to the end of text entered in the Address Bar | Ctrl + Shift + Enter |
| Specify the default domain suffix for automatic insertion in the Address Bar | Tools ⇨ Internet Options ⇨ Languages |
| Open in a new tab the web site address that has been entered in the Address Bar | Alt + Enter |
| View list of previously typed Web addresses | F4 |

| **Table 4-6** | **Instant Search Box** |
| --- | --- |
| Task | Shortcut |
| Select the Instant Search Box | Ctrl + E |
| View list of search providers | Ctrl + ↓ |
| Open search results in a new tab | Alt + Enter |

| Table 4-7 | Advanced Tasks |
|-----------|----------------|
| *Task* | *Shortcut* |
| Open the Windows Run box to launch a program, folder, document, or Internet resource | ⊞ + R |
| Disable all add-ons to Internet Explorer (Using the Windows Run box) | ⊞ + R, then enter **iexplore.exe – extoff** |
| Find and install add-ons to Internet Explorer | Tools ⇨ Manage Add-ons ⇨ Find More Add-ons |
| Turn on AutoComplete to instruct Internet Explorer to automatically fill in web site addresses based on your previous history | Tools ⇨ Internet Options ⇨ Advanced ⇨ Use inline AutoComplete |
| Temporarily display the Menu Bar at the top of the screen | Alt |
| Permanently display the Menu Bar at the top of the screen | Tools ⇨ Menu Bar |
| Change how tabs work in Internet Explorer | Tools ⇨ Internet Options. On the General tab, locate the Tabs section, then click Settings |
| Delete cookies, passwords, form data, history, and temporary Internet files | Tools ⇨ Delete Browsing History |
| Print current page | Ctrl + P |
| Print part of the current page | Use the onscreen pointer to select part of the page, press Ctrl + P, click Selection ⇨ click Print |

| Table 4-8 | Basic Commands in Firefox and Internet Explorer | |
|-----------|---------------------------|----------------|
| *Task* | *Microsoft Internet Explorer* | *Mozilla Firefox* |
| Add Bookmark | Ctrl + D | Ctrl + D |
| Back | Backspace or Alt + ← | Backspace or Alt + ← |
| Bookmarks | Ctrl + I | Ctrl + B Ctrl + I |
| Caret Browsing | N/A | F7 |
| Close Tab | Ctrl + W | Ctrl + W Ctrl + F4 |
| Close Window | Ctrl + W Alt + F4 | Ctrl + Shift + W Alt + F4 |
| Complete .com Address 2 | Ctrl + Enter | Ctrl + Enter |
| Complete .net Address 2 | N/A | Shift + Enter |

*(continued)*

Book VIII
Chapter 4

Spinning the Web

**Table 4-8 *(continued)***

| Task | Microsoft Internet Explorer | Mozilla Firefox |
|------|------------------------------|-----------------|
| Complete .org Address 2 | N/A | Ctrl + Shift + Enter |
| Copy | Ctrl + C | Ctrl + C |
| Cut | Ctrl + X | Ctrl + X |
| Decrease Text Size | Ctrl + - | Ctrl + - |
| Delete | Del | Del |
| DOM Inspector | N/A | Ctrl + Shift + I |
| Downloads | N/A | Ctrl + J |
| Find Again | N/A | Ctrl + G<br>F3 |
| Find As You Type Link | N/A | ' |
| Find As You Type Text | N/A | / |
| Find Previous | N/A | Ctrl + Shift + G<br>Shift + F3 |
| Find in This Page | Ctrl + F | Ctrl + F |
| Forward | Shift + Backspace<br>Alt + → | Shift + Backspace<br>Alt + → |
| Go Down One Line | Down | Down |
| Go Up One Line | Up | Up |
| Go Down One Page | PageDown | PageDown |
| Go Up One Page | PageUp | PageUp |
| Go to Bottom of Page | End | End |
| Go to Top of Page | Home | Home |
| Full Screen | F11 | F11 |
| Help | F1 | F1 |
| History | Ctrl + H | Ctrl + H |
| Home Page | Alt + Home | Alt + Home |
| Increase Text Size | Ctrl + + | Ctrl + + |
| Move to Next Frame | N/A | F6 |
| Move to Previous Frame | N/A | Shift + F6 |
| New Mail Message 3 | N/A | Ctrl + M |
| New Tab | Ctrl + T | Ctrl + T |
| Next Tab | Ctrl + Tab | Ctrl + Tab |
| New Window | Ctrl + N | Ctrl + N |
| Open File | Ctrl + O | Ctrl + O |
| Open Link | Enter | Enter |
| Open Link in New Tab | Ctrl + Enter | Ctrl + Enter |

| Task | Microsoft Internet Explorer | Mozilla Firefox |
| --- | --- | --- |
| Open Link in New Window | Shift + Enter | Shift + Enter |
| Open Address in New Tab 2 | Alt + Enter | Alt + Enter |
| Page Source | Ctrl + F3 | Ctrl + U |
| Paste | Ctrl + V | Ctrl + V |
| Previous Tab | Ctrl + Shift + Tab | Ctrl + Shift + Tab<br>Ctrl + PageUp |
| Print | Ctrl + P | Ctrl + P |
| Redo | Ctrl + Y | Ctrl + Shift + Z<br>Ctrl + Y |
| Reload | F5<br>Ctrl + R | F5<br>Ctrl + R |
| Reload (override cache) | Ctrl + F5 | Ctrl + F5<br>Ctrl + Shift + R |
| Restore Text Size | Ctrl + 0 | Ctrl + 0 |
| Save Page As | | Ctrl + S |
| Save Link Target As | | Alt + Enter |
| Select All | Ctrl + A | Ctrl + A |
| Select Location Bar | Alt + D<br>F4<br>Ctrl + Tab | Ctrl + L<br>Alt + D |
| Select Next Auto-Complete entry in text field | | Down |
| Select Previous Auto-Complete entry in text field | | Up |
| Select Next Search Engine in Search Bar | | Ctrl + Down |
| Select Previous Search Engine in Search Bar | | Ctrl + Up |
| Select Tab [1 to 9] | Ctrl + [1 to 9] | Ctrl + [1 to 9] |
| Stop | Esc | Esc |
| Toggle Check box | spacebar | spacebar |
| Undo | Ctrl + Z | Ctrl + Z |
| Web Search | Ctrl + E | Ctrl + K |

**Book VIII
Chapter 4**

**Spinning the Web**

| Table 4-9 | Mouse Shortcuts in Internet Explorer and Firefox | |
|---|---|---|
| *Task* | *Microsoft Internet Explorer* | *Mozilla Firefox* |
| Back | Shift + Scroll down | Shift + Scroll down |
| Close Tab | N/A | Middle-click Tab 1 |
| Decrease Text Size | Ctrl + Scroll up | Ctrl + Scroll up |
| Forward | Shift + Scroll up | Shift + Scroll up |
| Increase Text Size | Ctrl + Scroll down | Ctrl + Scroll down |
| New Tab | N/A | Double-click Tab Bar |
| Open in Background Tab | N/A | Ctrl + click 2<br>Middle-click |
| Open in Foreground Tab | N/A | Ctrl + Shift + click 2<br>Shift + middle-click 2 |
| Open in New Window | Shift + click | Shift + click |
| Paste URL and Go | N/A | Middle-click Tab 1 |
| Save Page As | N/A | Alt + click |
| Scroll line by line | N/A | Alt + Scroll |

# Chapter 5: Exchanging E-mail, IMs, and Newsgroups

## In This Chapter

✔ Getting onboard for e-mail

✔ Using Outlook Express and Microsoft Mail

✔ Using enhanced Microsoft Live Mail features

✔ Keeping e-mail safer

✔ Using instant messaging — right now

*F*or many people, most important communication now arrives in electronic form: letters, notices, invoices, greeting cards, bank statements, and even junk mail. The Postal Service and competitors like FedEx, UPS, and DHL are mostly relegated to delivering packages ordered over the Internet and some of the remaining forms of media still holding on to print and paper: magazines, books, and a diminishing number of catalogs.

In more recent times, we have seen the rise of an even-more-urgent form of communication: *instant messaging (IM)*. This system opens a virtual channel between two (or more) computers, and once you establish a link it allows you to send quick notes. IM services have expanded to allow file attachment and many permit streaming video or audio connections. The principal difference between IM communication and e-mail is that IM parties have to be online at the same time, just as they would be in a telephone call.

Yet another form of electronic communication is the *newsgroup,* which actually draws its roots from before the rise of the Internet. Today, privately operated bulletin boards are mostly obsolete, but they're very common on commercial sites. If you visit Microsoft in search of help with Windows, you're likely to be directed to their "knowledge base" of information; some of the material may be provided by the manufacturer and some may come from users.

## That's BBS

Soon after the arrival of computers in academia, homes, and offices came *bulletin board services (BBS)* which were, as the name suggests, forms of one-way-at-a-time communication. You could dial up a BBS anywhere in the world and post a question or read an answer or even download a file or program. BBS operators monitored the boards from time to time, mostly to enforce whatever rules of propriety or security the owner chose to put into effect.

## *Fielding Microsoft's Triple Play*

With the arrival of Windows Vista, Microsoft introduced a new e-mail and newsgroup client with the wonderfully clever name of Windows Mail. It succeeds a program with a confusing and vague name, Outlook Express. And within a few months after Windows Vista was released, Microsoft came out with yet another program, Windows Live Mail.

Allow me to attempt to untangle these threads:

✦ **Outlook Express** is a basic e-mail client that has been a part of Internet Explorer since Version 4 was released in 1997. (The current version of Internet Explorer is Version 7, with a newer edition expected in 2008 or 2009.) Just to make things confusing, Microsoft offered a more fully featured e-mail and calendar program called Microsoft Outlook or Microsoft Office Outlook as part of certain of its Office suites. Outlook and Outlook Express are distantly related; despite its name, Outlook Express isn't a stripped-down version.

✦ **Windows Mail** was launched as a part of Windows Vista in early 2007. The program was an upgrade and replacement for Outlook Express but only for Vista users. And in a move that probably made sense to the marketing department (or the legal department), Windows Mail is considered part of the Vista operating system and not part of Internet Explorer.

✦ **Windows Live Mail** arrived in late 2007 as a replacement for both Windows Mail and Outlook Express. You can install it on any system running Windows Vista or Windows XP with Service Pack 2. This version of an e-mail client includes the features of Windows Mail as well as some visual enhancements that make it fit into Microsoft's plans for its Windows Live Web-based product line, as well as some technical improvements. Windows Live Mail is a free download for registered users.

TECHNICAL STUFF

---

# Why I don't live at the PO

Although it's electronic in nature, e-mail's basic structure is a system more like the old Post Office than the new Internet. You can send someone an e-mail any time and the recipient can read and receive it whenever she chooses to (providing her laptop or desktop is turned on). When the first e-mail services were launched, they were called "store and forward" systems; your message was received by an intermediary computer and held there until the recipient picked up messages. Today, that structure still is in place. Although most of us now have always-on Internet connections (broadband modems, WiFi, or cellular signals) and mail pops up in our inbox whenever we're on our computers.

---

Should you upgrade your e-mail client from Windows Mail to Windows Live Mail, or from Outlook Express to Windows Live Mail? In my opinion, the answer is yes . . . but there's no reason to rush to action.

TIP

If e-mail is critical to your personal or business life, I suggest waiting a while before taking the plunge. Let others be the guinea pigs, testing out the new software. Check the message boards at the support departments of Microsoft and read the web sites of computer reviews and wait for the electrons (and the inevitable glitches of a new program) to settle.

Of course, if your machine is running Windows Vista, you have no choice in the matter. The operating system automatically includes Windows Mail, and Microsoft has declared its intention to persuade users to download Windows Live Mail, although it isn't yet required.

## Bypassing Microsoft

Though Microsoft might want you to think otherwise, other companies sell e-mail clients and some organizations even give them away.

+ **Eudora.** Distributed by Qualcomm (and named, in a nice touch, after the short-story author Eudora Welty). In 2007, Qualcomm ended active development on the software.

+ **Mozilla Thunderbird.** What Qualcomm endorsed after ending Eudora development. You can get this free application (as well as the free Mozilla Firefox Internet browser) at www.mozilla.com.

## Getting ready for e-mail

To use e-mail on a laptop, you need the following:

✦ **Internet access.** For a direct connection to an e-mail server you need an account with an *Internet service provider (ISP)*. If you'll use your laptop on the road through an Internet café (or as an add-on to an existing shared network), you can access most e-mail services through whatever service they provide.

✦ **An e-mail program or Web-based service.** As noted, these include Windows Mail, Windows Live Mail, Outlook Express, Microsoft Office Outlook, Eudora, and Thunderbird. You can also connect to e-mail servers through Web-based portals that reach into the proprietary systems of ISPs, or are free standalone services open to any Internet user; these include Google's Gmail, Microsoft's Hotmail, and Yahoo! Mail.

✦ **An e-mail address.** Provided by an ISP or Web-based e-mail service, or created when you register for your own domain. An e-mail address consists of

   • A user name

   • An @ sign (pronounced *at*)

   • Domain name

The user name can be your real name, your nickname, or anything else you want as an identifier. The domain name consists of a label registered for a company or individual, followed by a domain name type such as

   • .com (for commercial)

   • .org (for organization)

   • .edu (for an educational institution)

   • .gov (for a government agency)

For example, a proper e-mail address might be someguy@someplace.com.

To use the e-mail client, in addition to your e-mail address at an ISP, you need to know a few technical details such as names of the incoming and outgoing e-mail servers, and the type of system. When you sign up for an e-mail account, your ISP should present this information to you; many services offer to automatically configure your e-mail client, filling in the details. Here is a guide to the essential elements:

✦ **Server information.** The two most common types of mail servers use either the *Post Office Protocol (POP)* or *Internet Message Access Protocol (IMAP)*. Some providers offer a choice of either. Once you instruct your e-mail client which protocol to use, you must enter the appropriate information for an incoming and outgoing server.

An example of a set of POP servers might be as follows:

   Incoming mail (POP): pop.mymailserver.com

Outgoing mail (SMTP): smtp.mymailserver.com

An IMAP setup is very similar, except for the incoming details:

Incoming mail (IMAP): imap.adifferentserver.com

Outgoing mail (SMTP): smtp.adifferentserver.com

✦ **Incoming mail server information.** Enter your full account name (usually your e-mail address) and the password for that address. If you're going to be the only user, or if you protect the machine with a password at bootup — a good practice for laptop users — you can tell Windows to remember your password so you don't need to enter it each time you check your mail.

✦ **Other details.** Some e-mail providers may ask you to specify a nonstandard *port* for your computer to use for incoming or outgoing messages or other changes.

TECHNICAL STUFF

# E-mail acronyms and you

POP servers are the most common design for e-mail. Also referred as POP3 (the most current specification for the protocol), these systems transfer incoming messages to files that are stored on your computer. Once they have been downloaded, they are usually deleted from the server.

IMAP servers, most of which now use the IMAP4 specification, don't automatically download messages to your computer. Instead, you see the header, which includes the sender's name, the subject, and the date and time the message was sent. Some systems also display just the first few lines of the message on your screen again, without downloading it to your computer. You can delete messages without reading them or you can open the mail from the server — again, without downloading it to your machine. Copies are stored on the server until you delete them or make local copies on your computer.

If you use an IMAP server, you can check your mail on several different machines over the course of time; POP messages live on the machine that first downloaded them. Another advantage is that IMAP systems keep your system at a considerable distance from potentially harmful e-mails; you can delete them without them ever residing on your computer.

HTML e-mail is a form of message based on a version of the same markup language used to create Web pages. It can be flashy, animated, and colorful, which is why advertisers (junk and otherwise) often use this style. The fact that it can include active links and mini-applications also makes it attractive to some virus or spyware authors. Most e-mail clients, including Outlook Express, Windows Mail, and Windows Live Mail can accept HTML mail. Security settings permit users to block images and other external content in HTML-based messages; the two versions of Windows Mail permit an exception to that block for messages from people or organizations added to a user's Safe Senders list.

*Simple Mail Transfer Protocol (SMTP)* servers do just what their name suggests. Working with either a POP or IMAP incoming e-mail server, SMTP sends e-mail messages to the Internet.

# Using Windows Mail or Outlook Express

In this section I discuss some of the basics and important customization features of Outlook Express and its Windows Vista replacement Windows Mail. Later in this chapter I expand coverage to include Windows Live Mail, Microsoft's announced replacement for both products.

If you're an Outlook Express veteran, the newer Windows Mail will appear and perform quite similarly.

✦ Some of the toolbar icons have been changed to make them fit better with the spiffed-up Windows Vista interface.

✦ Some new features allow more customization of how you see your mail (including the location of the Reading pane). See Figure 5-1.

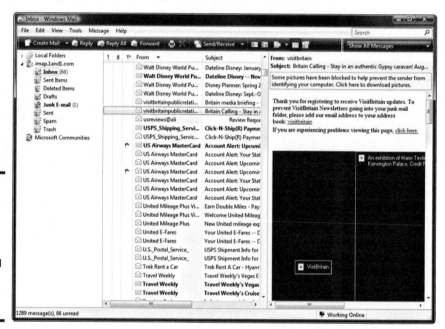

**Figure 5-1:**
The main screen of Windows Mail, with the Reading pane to the right of the messages.

But the most important changes are on the safety and security side.

✦ Messages are stored in smaller individual files or groups of files. A separate index database speeds searching through mail messages and, because the index is separate from mail files, a corrupted or accidentally erased index can be rebuilt.

One of the long-time landmines within Outlook Express was its single database file for all stored mail messages; the file could get quite large, which could slow down operations, and more importantly, if the file became corrupted, you could lose years' worth of messages.

In recent years Microsoft and some third parties have offered utilities that can repair certain problems with Outlook Express database files. Some types of corruption are easier to repair than others, though.

✦ Account setup information is stored in the folder that holds Windows Mail. This makes it much easier and safer for users to copy or move a Windows Mail configuration and all the stored messages to another machine.

✦ Windows Mail includes a basic junk mail filter (a so-called Bayesian filter that examines mail and looks for words commonly found in unwanted messages; the filter also can automatically add or subtract from its list based on your handling of messages). Other features include the ability to block certain e-mail senders based on your experience with them.

✦ Now you can stop attempts to *phish* your private information including passwords, account names, and banking or credit card details. A phishing filter alerts you to e-mail of this sort, or that shares some of the characteristics of this sort.

✦ One element of e-mail clients that's often overlooked by current users is the ability to read or subscribe to newsgroups. In addition to allowing access to the unmonitored (and sometimes dangerous) world of public newsgroups, Windows Mail automatically offers you access to a full set of Microsoft Help Groups that may bail you out of difficult computer- or software-related problems.

Windows Mail is part of any standard installation of Windows Vista.

## Adding an account in Windows Mail or Outlook Express

To manually add an e-mail account, follow these steps:

*1.* **Gather the necessary information.**

*2.* **Open the program.**

*3.* **Click Start ➪ All Programs ➪ Windows Mail or Outlook Express.**

If you have a mail shortcut on your desktop or toolbar, you can click that as a quick way into the program.

*4.* **Choose Tools ➪ Accounts ➪ Add ➪ E-mail Account.**

*5.* **Follow the screen-by-screen instructions and enter the details.**

Among the questions you'll answer is the choice of a display name; this is the name that recipients of your mail see on their own e-mail client. It isn't the same as your e-mail address, but if someone hits the Reply button, their software program will recognize and use your address from the details included in the message. See Figure 5-2.

To remove an e-mail account, follow along:

*1.* **Open the e-mail client.**

*2.* **Click Tools ⇨ Accounts.**

*3.* **Highlight the account you want out of the program.**

*4.* **Click the Remove button.**

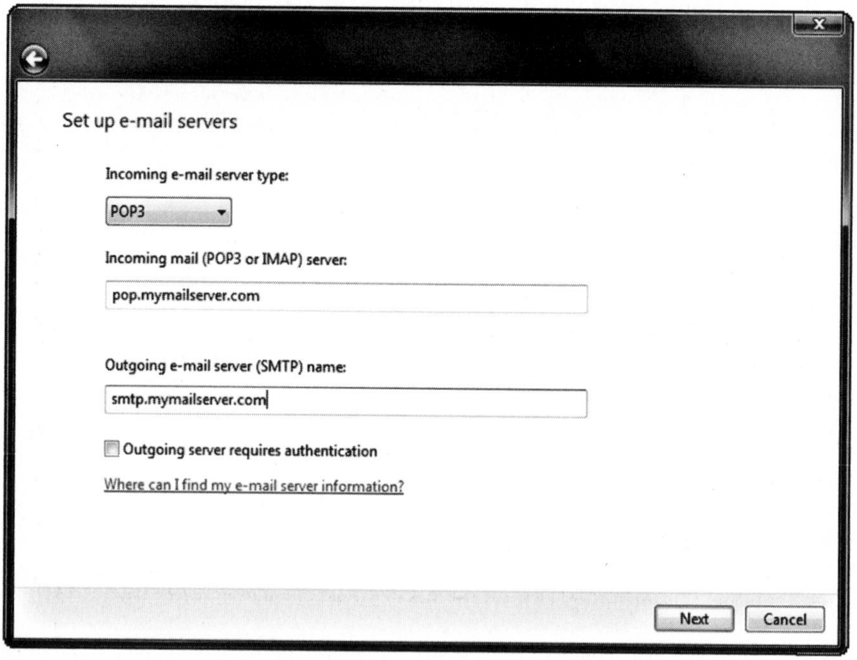

**Figure 5-2:**
Your e-mail provider should offer a listing (or phone support) to help fill out the forms of the Windows Mail e-mail account setup wizard (and the similar screens of Outlook Express).

Set up e-mail servers

Incoming e-mail server type:

POP3

Incoming mail (POP3 or IMAP) server:

pop.mymailserver.com

Outgoing e-mail server (SMTP) name:

smtp.mymailserver.com

☐ Outgoing server requires authentication

Where can I find my e-mail server information?

Next    Cancel

## *Reading e-mail messages and replying*

When you first open Windows Mail or Outlook Express, the program checks for any received mail and sends any messages it finds waiting to go out. After then it's set up to automatically jingle your mailbox every 30 minutes; you can issue a right-now command by clicking the Send/Receive button in the toolbar.

You can change the default interval with these steps:

*1.* **Click Tools ⇨ Options.**

*2.* **Go to the General tab.**

*3.* **Set the time between automatic searches.**

The time can be any number of minutes from 1 to 480.

In the same section (see Figure 5-3) you can instruct the system to play a sound anytime new messages arrive; depending on your work habits, that can be very helpful or very annoying.

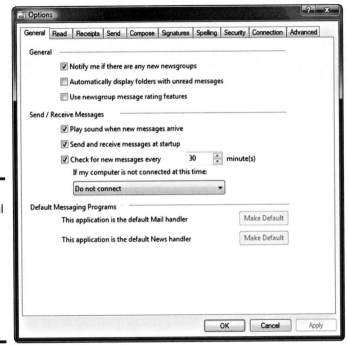

**Figure 5-3:**
The General tab of the Options window allows customization of alerts for new mail.

Folders abound:

✦ **Inbox.** New mail goes here, on the right side of the panel. Mail remains in the Inbox unless you move it to another folder; the folder name is bold anytime an unread message is within. The system also displays a number next to the Inbox folder name to indicate how many messages you haven't read.

✦ **Junk E-mail or Spam.** For Windows Mail users, depending on your settings, some messages may go directly into this folder.

✦ **Deleted Items.** Messages you delete go here. This action is automatic for POP systems but must be enabled under Advanced Options for IMAP systems.

You can take several routes when reading and responding:

✦ To **read a message**, click its header in the message list; as much of its contents as will fit will appear in the preview pane. To read the e-mail in a separate window, double-click its header.

✦ To **reply to a message**, click the Reply button. The program fills in the sender's e-mail address from the information received with the original message.

✦ To **reply to everyone who received a message**, click Reply All. Your response goes to the original sender as well as to anyone listed on the To: or Cc: line of the message.

## Creating and sending e-mail messages

To create a new e-mail, follow these steps:

*1.* **Click the Create Mail button.**

Appropriately named button, no? A blank New Message window opens.

*2.* **Enter at least one e-mail address in the To: box.**

To send to more than one recipient, list a semicolon between addresses. For example, To: somebody@somewhere.com;someone@elsewhere.com

You can enter e-mail addresses you've previously encountered one of two ways:

• The standard setting for most e-mail clients is to maintain a listing of all addresses you use. For example, once you've sent an e-mail to someone@elsewhere.com, the next time you start typing in *someone,* the e-mail client offers you that e-mail address; you can accept the suggestion by pressing the Enter key; keep typing and it goes away.

• Use the records stored in Windows Contacts (in Windows Vista) or the very similar Windows Address Book (in Windows XP and previous editions).

*3.* **If you want to Cc someone, enter that e-mail address in the Cc: box.**

You can send one or more Ccs, or leave that field blank. If Bcc: isn't shown, add it to your options by clicking View ➪ All Headers.

One of the settings in the Send options automatically adds the e-mail address of anyone to whom you send a reply to the Contacts or Address listings. You can manually add listings by clicking Tools ➪ Windows Contacts (or Address Book) and filling out the form that opens.

## Copy that

*Cc:* is a term that has held onto a version of its original meaning even though technology has marched on. The acronym once meant "carbon copy" and indicated to the principal recipient of the message that a copy was sent to someone else as well; carbon paper was placed between sheets of plain paper to make copies of type-written or hand-written characters. The recipient of a message can see the names of persons who receive a carbon copy; to hide the identities of additional recipients of a message, put their name in the Bcc: (Blind Carbon Copy) field.

To adjust how Windows Mail or Outlook Express handles the database of e-mail addresses, go to the program's main screen and click Tools ⇨ Options, and choose from the Send tab.

**4. Enter a subject in the Subject text box.**

You can (and should). Although it isn't required, some e-mail clients (and some e-mail recipients) are very suspicious of messages that come with a blank subject . . . and definitely likely to reject or consign to the Junk E-mail folder any message with a subject that looks like, well, junk.

**5. Enter your message in the blank area of the message window.**

At the top of the text area is a set of buttons similar to those in a word processor. You can choose

- Font
- Size
- Bold
- Italics
- Numbered lists
- Bulleted lists
- Indents
- Justification of the text to the left, right, or center of the message
- Picture insertion

**6. Click the Attach File button (paper clip icon) in the taskbar.**

This enables you to attach a file — text, spreadsheet, database, graphics, music — to an e-mail. Another very valuable e-mail use is sending.

**7. Locate the file and click Open;**

A new box lists attachments below the subject line.

*8.* **Click the Send button in the mail window.**

This puts your message out into the stream of data on the Internet; depending on the message size, the network congestion, and, in some cases, where the message is going, it should arrive somewhere between immediately and very soon.

Some e-mail systems may limit the size of messages, and others may automatically reject mail that includes attachments out of concern that they may contain damaging viruses or spyware. If your mail is rejected or your recipient tells you that your attachment isn't coming through, you may have to

✦ Find an alternate way to send a file; this includes *file transfer protocol (FTP)* sites, which allow direct transfer from one computer to another over the Internet.

✦ Reduce the size of files by splitting them into pieces or reducing the resolution of an image.

## *Requesting a receipt for sent messages*

You press the Send button and watch with a sense of satisfaction as a message disappears from your screen and reappears in the Sent box. All is well. Or is it?

How do you know the person to whom you sent the mail has received the message? Is he away on a six-month expedition to Antarctica? Is her laptop broken? Did you type a mistake in the e-mail address? Is the e-mail address broken? And, maddeningly, did your perfectly legitimate e-mail somehow get diverted into a junk or spam folder or, even worse, was it deleted before the recipient even got to see it?

One way you can get some further satisfaction when you send an e-mail is to request a receipt. When you do this, most recipients see a message on their screen indicating that the sender has requested they send a receipt. (See Figure 5-4.) Notice the word "request." The recipient can oblige you by clicking Yes, or ignore your plea for a receipt by clicking No. And some mail servers automatically strip out requests for receipts.

Therefore, if you get a receipt for a message you've sent, you know it arrived at its destination; if you don't get a receipt, the message may or may not have been delivered. (You can send a second request, or you can use that antique technology called the telephone to place a call and ask if the e-mail was received.)

To request a receipt for a specific message, do these easy steps:

*1.* **Create an e-mail.**

*2.* **Click Tools ➪ Request Read Receipt.**

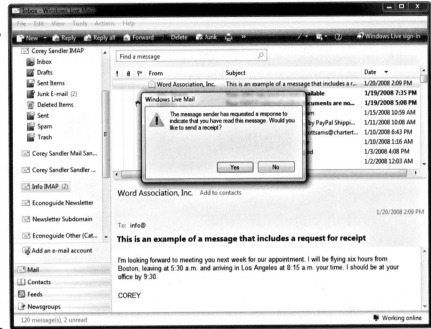

**Figure 5-4:** When you request a receipt for mail a message like this one will usually appear on the screen of the recipient. It's up to them whether to give you the notice you have asked for.

To instruct your e-mail client to automatically request a receipt for all mail you send, do these steps:

*1.* **Click Tools ➪ Options.**

*2.* **Go to the Receipts tab.**

*3.* **Select the Request a Read Receipt for all Sent Messages check box.**

   This check box is in the Requesting Read Receipts section.

## Deleting messages

Deleting messages can be as simple as highlighting a message and then pressing the Delete key . . . except that it doesn't always work that way.

### POP

On a system using a POP server, all incoming mail is delivered to your laptop or desktop and resides in a folder there. If you highlight a file and press Delete, it's removed from the Inbox and moved to a Deleted Files or Trash folder; depending on your settings in the Options window, that mail either

✦ Is permanently deleted the next time you shut down the e-mail program.

**Book VIII
Chapter 5**

Exchanging E-mail,
IMs, and
Newsgroups

✦ Stays in the folder until you go into it and throw away the files.

This is similar to the way the Windows Recycle Bin serves as a temporary stopgap to give you a second chance to "undelete" a file you accidentally removed or to rescue you from a change of mind.

### IMAP

Things are different with an IMAP-based system where users have several options. From the Options window you can choose to do the following:

✦ Permanently (and irretrievably) throw away a message when you move to another folder or close down the e-mail client. When you delete a message from an IMAP folder, you see a strikethrough (like `this`) applied to the header. This indicates the message is marked for deletion from the central server.

✦ Immediately remove mail marked for deletion by clicking the Purge Deleted Messages button.

✦ Instruct Windows Mail or Windows Live Mail to move deleted messages on an IMAP system from the Inbox to a Deleted Message folder; the message is still on the remote server but isn't permanently thrown away until you clear out the folder.

## Setting other special IMAP features

Because IMAP accounts store messages on a central server and not on your laptop, you can, to a great degree, customize the way your e-mail client works on your machine. You can have all messages, only new messages, or only message headers downloaded to your machine.

I use IMAP for my e-mail, and I prefer that Windows Mail download only message headers to any machine I use to check mail. This protects from inadvertent downloading of malicious mail and also keeps my mail organized; over the course of a week I might check for messages from my desktop machine, from one of my laptops, from a cell phone, or from a machine I borrow at a client's office or at an Internet café. From any location, I can read mail, delete junk, reply to messages, and move messages to special folders and always see the same results at any machine I use to sign on.

Although you can create message rules for POP mail accounts to search for specific words or phrases to identify junk mail, Microsoft (and, in fairness, most other companies offering software to consumers) hasn't yet extended this feature to IMAP accounts. The principle problem here is the same thing that makes IMAP so attractive: The mail doesn't live on your machine until you download it.

If you use an IMAP service, see if the provider offers a junk mail or spam filter that they apply to messages on their server. Several of the companies I deal with apply a vacuum to messages; messages are either diverted into a junk folder or are marked JUNK or SPAM before they go to my system.

## Junk and other modern annoyances

Permit me to step up onto my soapbox for a moment: Democracy is a great thing, but one of its shortcomings is that it leaves open the door for people who charge full-speed right up to the limits of the law and sometimes way past the line. That's why the Web is home to (highly profitable) pornography sites and ridiculous or dangerous political and social opinion or phony news sites, and that's why my daily e-mail harvest typically includes a few dozen annoying solicitations for things I don't want to buy.

Call it junk, call it spam, call it annoying when it starts to overwhelm your inbox, costing you time and money. You can easily understand why people send this stuff out: It's essentially free to send out millions of messages if you've got the addresses. (And even if they don't have actual e-mail addresses, some spammers just blast their junk out to millions of made-up names with the hope that a small percentage of them are real.)

The good news is that lots of smart people at Microsoft and other companies have devoted a great deal of effort to find ways to enlist computers in the fight to identify junk mail and malicious mail. The bad news is that, like real diseases, the bad guys are just as busy looking for ways to find ways to defeat the defenses.

Users of Outlook Express have to look elsewhere for assistance in hunting down junk and spam; you can

✦ Purchase filter programs from companies such as Symantec.

✦ Subscribe to online services from other sources that add on to that e-mail client and attempt to be of assistance.

With the introduction of Windows Mail (and the enhanced Windows Live Mail), though, Microsoft has delivered a capable junk e-mail filter that analyzes messages and moves suspect mail to a special folder in the e-mail client. Users can view the junk mail folder and delete any messages, or instruct the program that individual messages are ones you consider legitimate.

If you instruct Windows Mail or Windows Live Mail that a particular message is legitimate, it knows that another message from that address should go to your regular Inbox. On the other hand, if junk slips by the filter and arrives in your Inbox, you can instruct the e-mail client to be on the lookout for future mail of that type or from that source and provide instructions to either place it in the Junk E-mail folder or completely block it from arriving in your system. See Figure 5-5.

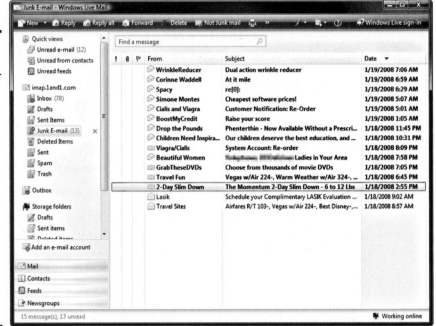

**Figure 5-5:**
The Junk
E-mail folder
of Windows
Mail or
Windows
Live Mail is
the
automatic
destination
of
messages
the e-mail
client
believes to
be
unwanted
communi-
cation.

### Lowering your exposure to junk

The only way to eliminate the risk of receiving junk is to never sign up for an e-mail address. Other than that, you need to know how to keep a low profile in cyberspace.

✦ Avoid giving your e-mail address to people who don't need to have it. Don't publish it on web sites or newsgroups.

✦ If a web site asks for your e-mail address, consider whether it's in your best interest to give it to them. Can you opt out of promotional mailings? Can you limit what the web site will do with your address? For example, you might find it acceptable for a particular store to send you the occasional bulletin about a sale, but you might not want that company to share your address with other vendors.

✦ If you receive junk mail, your best bet is delete it. If you reply to it, the sender will know it has reached a real address; asking to be removed from a mailing list sometimes has the effect of putting you on hundreds more.

### Setting up a Trojan Horse

One strategy to limit the amount of junk mail you receive is to create several e-mail addresses:

✦ Use one or two as your principal "official" address and be very careful who you give it to; use it for banks, government agencies, employers, and others who have a legitimate reason to reach you.

✦ Create one or more additional addresses through one of the free e-mail services offered by companies including Microsoft, Google, and Yahoo. Use that address when you're shopping or visiting sites where you're uncertain of the sponsor's intentions.

I have a few such Trojan Horse addresses and they regularly fill up with all sorts of junk . . . but I only visit them from time to time and quickly spin through them to see if anything of value has somehow ended up in the manure pile.

## Adding a newsgroup account

Newsgroups are the modern vestiges of the old bulletin board systems that preceded the Internet. There are newsgroups that are maintained by major companies like Microsoft, others monitored by organizations including professional associations, and then there are those that are the technological equivalent of the Wild, Wild West.

Your Internet service provider may offer you access to the full panoply of newsgroups available on the Internet or may offer a "cleaned-up" set that attempts to eliminate obvious pornography sites and others that may be considered offensive. You can also obtain unfiltered access to newsgroups by subscribing to newsgroup services you can search for and find on the Web.

Take special care if you venture into newsgroups other than those from established groups. Make sure you have a current antivirus program and a capable firewall installed. And even then, be very cautious about revealing anything to newsgroup members: This is a great place to use a Trojan Horse e-mail address rather than your primary one.

To add a newsgroup account in Outlook Express:

*1.* **Click Tools ➪ Accounts.**

*2.* **Switch to the News tab.**

*3.* **Click the Add button.**

To add a newsgroup account in Windows Mail or Windows Live Mail:

*1.* **Click Newsgroups**.

The option is in the left pane of the screen.

*2.* **Click Add a Newsgroup Account.**

3. **Type a name in the Add a Newsgroup Account text box.**

   This is the name you use when you post messages. Pseudonyms are acceptable in most, but not all, newsgroups.

4. **If required, enter an e-mail address.**

   This allows other newsgroup readers to contact you. Tread carefully here — leave it blank if you can or use an address other than the one you use for business.

5. **Enter the name of the news server you want to connect to.**

   Your ISP can provide this. Among Microsoft's servers is news.microsoft.com.

6. **If the server requires a login and password, click the check box that indicates this requirement.**

7. **Click Next.**

8. **Enter the necessary information.**

# Feeling Safe with Windows Mail and Windows Live Security

Why do bad things happen to good programs? Just as the Web has been infected by ugly people and ugly places, e-mail has been adopted by many companies and individuals as a way to distribute junk . . . and worse.

In this section I discuss ways to deal with junk and phishing e-mails. In Book 9 I examine antivirus and specialty security software in more detail.

## Setting the junk e-mail filter

The more aggressive you are setting the bar for junk mail, the more likely that "good" mail is sent into improper isolation. On the other hand, being too loose with your setting is going to let a lot of garbage into your Inbox.

Whichever starting point you choose, you should be very dedicated to examining the contents of your Inbox and your Junk E-mail folder for the first few months after setting up a Windows Mail or Windows Live Mail system. The more time you spend identifying junk that sneaks through (or legitimate mail that ends up in the junk drawer), the better the program is at separating the wheat from the chaff.

To set the level of junk e-mail filtering, follow along:

*1.* **Click Tools ⇨ Safety Options.**

If you can't see the menu bar, click the Show Menu icon on the toolbar and then click Show All Menus. This displays the Classics Menu options.

*2.* **Go to the Options tab.**

*3.* **Assign the level of junk e-mail protection from available choices:**

- **No Automatic Filtering.** All e-mail, except for messages from blocked senders, is sent to your Inbox. If you're using a POP-based server, only mail from blocked senders is treated as junk mail.

- **Low.** Only obvious junk e-mail is sent to the Junk E-mail folder. You can expect a fair amount of clever garbage to get through to your inbox.

- **High.** Obvious junk mail, as well as messages considered unwanted, are sent to the Junk E-mail folder. All other e-mail is sent to your Inbox.

- **Safe List Only.** The most restrictive setting, this option only sends to your Inbox messages from people or organizations that you've identified to the program as safe senders. (A *safe sender* is someone you recognize or otherwise have reason to trust. You're in charge here.) All other e-mail messages are sent directly to your Junk E-Mail folder.

One other option is to automatically delete all suspected junk e-mail instead of sending it to the Junk E-mail folder.

To add a sender (or the sender's domain) to the safe sender's list, or to add a sender (or the sender's domain) to the blocked senders list highlight the message and then click on the Actions menu item. Then click on the Junk e-mail item and choose an action.

## Fighting phishing

Yet another subcategory of computer subspecies are scammers who send *phishing* e-mails. These messages use false pretenses to entice users to reveal private information such as bank accounts, passwords, and other details. The messages may try to impersonate a well-known real web site such as eBay or your own bank.

Windows Mail and Windows Live Mail include a filter that examines incoming mail to try to identify phishing. It might uncover the fact that the sender is different from the one claimed in an e-mail, for example. And Microsoft, in cooperation with other companies and organizations, maintains lists of known phishing messages. See Figure 5-6.

**Book VIII
Chapter 5**

**Exchanging E-mail,
IMs, and
Newsgroups**

**Figure 5-6:**
A warning message says a downloaded message or header (on an IMAP-based server) appears to be either junk or an attempt at phishing.

**Windows Mail**

Windows Mail has downloaded a message that appears to be junk or phishing e-mail. Junk e-mail messages are automatically moved to the Junk E-mail folder for your safety.

You should check the Junk E-mail folder regularly to ensure that you don't miss e-mail that you wish to receive.

What is phishing?

☐ Please do not show me this dialog again

[ Open Junk E-mail Folder ]   [ Junk E-mail Options... ]   [ Close ]

Always be suspicious of an e-mail that appears to

✦ Come from a bank or other business with whom you do business if it asks you for information that organization already has. Why would a bank contact you and ask that you "reconfirm" your login name and password, or for your account number? You should also be wary of messages that ask you click on a link that might attempt to download malicious software to your computer.

Look at the status line at the bottom of the browser when you're hovering your mouse pointer over a link; if they seem to be going in different directions, that's a pretty good indication that something is awry. For example, Bank of America is probably not sending e-mail from ripoff@deweycheatemandhow.com.

✦ Be from someone you know. Wait, let me rephrase that because most messages I get from friends and family are a bit odd: Watch out for messages asking for personal or financial information.

When in doubt about a message, use your own address book and call the person or organization who appears to have sent it to you; don't use any phone number or e-mail address in the message — that could be phony, too.

To change phishing settings, follow these steps:

*1.* **Click Tools ➪ Safety Options.**

*2.* **Go to the Phishing tab.**

*3.* **Select the options you want.**

   **Options include the following:**

- No Automatic Filtering

- Low (which moves only the most obvious messages to the junk folder)

- High (which catches most junk as well as quite a few that are not junk)

- Safe List Only (which only allows mail if it comes from someone you identified as a safe sender)

I suggest starting with Low and seeing how that works for you; make adjustments as needed.

*4.* **Click OK.**

Guard your personal information with these tips:

✦ **Keep it to yourself.** Don't give information to people or organizations who have no right to ask for it.

✦ **Check up.** Read your bills and financial statements each month and contact the bank or creditor if you have questions about activity.

✦ **Read your history.** Review your credit history at least once a year to see if someone has done something in your name without your permission; contact credit agencies immediately if you're certain of illegal activity. Ask that a fraud alert be placed on your credit report to advise banks and lenders of problems not of your own doing.

✦ **Keep up to date.** Regularly update Microsoft Windows and Internet Explorer to make sure you have the latest security enhancements.

✦ Change the passwords or PINs on all online accounts every few months, and change them immediately anytime you suspect a problem. See Book IX, Chapter 1 for how to make strong passwords.

## Setting security zones

Windows Mail and Windows Live Mail let you set *security zones* that determine whether to allow *active* content, such as ActiveX controls and scripts, to run from inside HTML e-mail messages. Some hackers have used scripts to inject viruses into computers. A moderate security level allows most active content to run, or you can choose a more restrictive security level.

To set your security zone, follow these steps:

*1.* **Choose Tools ➪ Safety options.**

*2.* **Go to the Security tab.**

*3.* **Select a Windows Internet Explorer security zone.**

In the Virus Protection section, you see these options:

**Book VIII
Chapter 5**

Exchanging E-mail,
IMs, and
Newsgroups

- **Internet zone** is a balance between security and utility and is appropriate for most users.

- **Restricted sites zone** works within a more secure but restrictive environment. Microsoft has its own list of sites that are flagged as potentially dangerous if you receive mail from that domain.

## Blocking unwanted messages: POP accounts

If you determine that a particular sender (someone@someplace.com) or an entire Internet domain (someplace.com) is sending mail that you don't ever want sullying your Inbox, you may be able to block messages. This feature is only available for POP-based mail (systems that download all incoming messages to your computer). It isn't available to IMAP or HTTP mail accounts.

If you receive mail from a POP server, mail received from any blocked sender is automatically marked as junk and sent directly into the Junk E-mail folder.

Similarly, you can specify individual addresses or entire domains as safe senders, which ensures that mail from that particular source gets through to your Inbox without being diverted.

To block or allow messages from a particular sender, follow these steps:

*1.* **Highlight a message.**

*2.* **Click the Actions menu.**

If you can't see the menu bar, click the Show Menu icon on the toolbar and then click Show All Menus. This displays the Classics Menu options.

*3.* **Choose Junk E-mail.**

Options appear. See Figure 5-7.

*4.* **Click one of the following:**

- **Add sender to blocked senders list**

- **Add sender to safe senders list**

*5.* **To block an entire domain, click one:**

- **Add sender's domain to blocked senders list**

- **Add sender's domain to safe senders list**

You can manually add a particular individual or domain:

*1.* **Click Tools ⇨ Safety Options.**

*2.* **Choose the Blocked Senders tab.**

*3.* **Click Add.**

*4.* **Type the e-mail address or domain you want to block.**

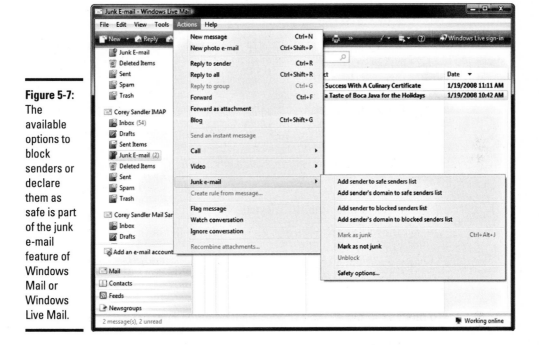

**Figure 5-7:**
The available options to block senders or declare them as safe is part of the junk e-mail feature of Windows Mail or Windows Live Mail.

To enable mail from a particular source, follow these steps:

1. **Click Tools ⇨ Safety Options.**

2. **Choose the Safe Senders tab.**

3. **Click Add.**

4. **Type an acceptable e-mail address or domain.**

# Windows Mail and Windows Live Enhancements

**Book VIII
Chapter 5**

Windows Mail comes as part of Windows Vista and isn't available to users of previous operating systems, including Windows XP. The newest e-mail client, Windows Live Mail, is expected to replace both Windows Mail and Outlook Express.

I talk first about Windows Live — available to all Windows users — and then discuss Windows Live Mail.

**Exchanging E-mail, IMs, and Newsgroups**

## Using Windows Live

Windows Live is a collection of Web-based utilities, services, and programs. At its inception, all the services are free to Windows users; someday, somehow, I expect Microsoft will seek to gain some income from Windows Live either through the collection of fees or the sale of advertising or both.

Windows users aren't (yet) required to establish an account with Windows Live. And you can run Windows Live Mail with or without a connection to its namesake home base.

However, if you do sign in to Windows Live (see Figure 5-8), you can use services like these:

✦ **Photo E-mails.** I discuss these in the next section of this chapter.

✦ **Windows Live Messenger.** This is the latest incarnation of Microsoft's instant messaging service.

✦ **Windows Live Call.** A component of Windows Live Messenger, this permits free "phone" or video calls from PC to PC. Both ends of the conversation need to have Messenger installed and running; you can use your laptop's built-in microphone and webcam (if they're installed) or you can add equipment that attaches to your laptop through audio and video inputs or through a USB port.

✦ **Windows Live Contacts.** When you establish a Windows Live account, your laptop's address book or contacts (as they're called in Windows Vista) can be shared amongst Windows Live Hotmail, Messenger, and other products that use Windows Live Contacts. This allows you to sign on from any machine and easily send messages to your regular correspondents.

✦ **Blogs.** The Windows Live Spaces feature allows users to create and maintain personal *web logs (blogs)* about any topic that makes you happy . . . or sad or mad. You can make your material available to anyone or to specified readers, and you can use *RSS (Really Simple Syndication),* a way to automatically feed content from your blog to subscribers who ask to be updated.

You can get a Windows Live account several ways:

✦ Go to http://get.live.com/ and follow the instructions.

✦ Go to Windows Live via the wondrously simple web site www.live.com and sign in from there.

✦ Sign in from within Windows Mail Live.

✦ Click the Windows Live sign-in button (in the upper-right corner) or click Get a Windows Live ID. Follow the onscreen instructions.

**Figure 5-8:**
The Windows Live installer is the gateway to most of the free services offered at Microsoft's site. You can customize the options and add elements later.

To change which Windows Live ID you sign in with, or to stop automatic sign-in from within Windows Live Mail, follow these steps:

*1.* **Choose Tools ⇨ Options.**

*2.* **Go to the Connections tab.**

*3.* **Choose an option:**

- **Sign In with another ID**
- **Stop Signing In**

Your Windows Live ID employs the same user name and password for any Windows Live, MSN, or Office Live sites and services. If you have a Passport Network, Hotmail, or Messenger account, you can use also use it as your Windows Live ID.

## Sending photo e-mails

No matter what Microsoft e-mail client you use, you can send photos as part of your messages. Simply attach a graphics file or embed a picture in the body of the message (called an *inline* image). Either way, senders (and recipients) have to be concerned about the size of the resulting message; a large color photo saved at a high resolution and at a large size can run to several megabytes to tens of megabytes.

With the arrival of Windows Live Mail, Microsoft introduced a new means of sending photos between users called *photo e-mail.* This feature uses a central server managed by Microsoft to hold high-resolution images you upload to it; your e-mail recipients see small versions *(thumbnails)* of the picture that they can click to view larger and sharper.

To create a photo e-mail you must sign in to Microsoft's Windows Live service. A link from Windows Live Mail lets you do this; see Figure 5-9. Other advantages of using Windows Live include access to a Web-based collection of your Contacts, which makes it easier for you to send messages when you're away from your own computer.

Unless your laptop is well protected behind a good sign-on password, though, using Windows Live to store your Contacts and other information makes it possible for others who might use (or steal) your laptop to see your Contacts and other information stored at the Microsoft server.

**Figure 5-9:**
The Windows Live sign-in allows you to have your laptop remember your password, which automates the process.

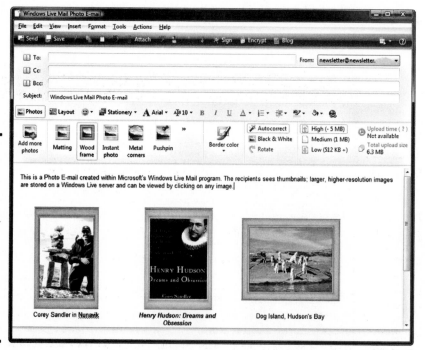

Once you sign in, your e-mail client expects you to link with Windows Live each time you turn it on; to change that, follow along:

*1.* **Choose Tools ⇨ Options.**

*2.* **Go to the Connection tab.**

*3.* **Click the Stop Signing In button**

The button is in the Windows Live services section.

As part of the free Windows Live service, you can

✦ Send as many as 500 images in photo e-mails per month.

✦ Upload as much as 500MB of images to the Microsoft server in each photo e-mail.

✦ Arrange the images in your e-mail to one of several formats.

✦ Adjust size.

✦ Make simple enhancements to contrast and brightness.

✦ Add frames or borders.

✦ Insert captions.

See Figure 5-10.

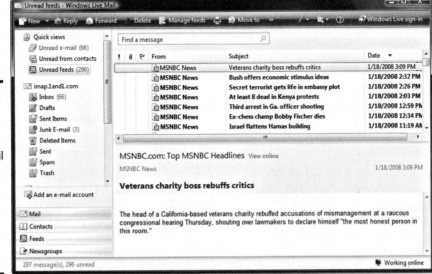

**Figure 5-10:** This Windows Mail Live Photo E-mail includes three thumbnails of images I uploaded from my laptop.

**Book VIII
Chapter 5**

**Exchanging E-mail, IMs, and Newsgroups**

You also can download the image files to your computer; depending on your Internet connection speed, this could take a few minutes to much longer. Photos stay on the Microsoft server for 30 days.

To create a photo e-mail with Windows Live Mail, do one of the following:

*1.* **Click New.**

A new e-mail message is created.

*2.* **Click where in the message body you want to insert photos.**

*3.* **In the message window, click Add Photos.**

Or follow these steps:

*1.* **Click Insert ⇨ Image ⇨ Photo E-mail.**

*2.* **Select the photo file you want to insert.**

To select multiple photos, hold down the Ctrl key as you click each of the photos.

*3.* **Click Add.**

*4.* **Click Done.**

## Adding RSS feeds to your Inbox

Windows Mail and Windows Live Mail include an easy-to-configure *RSS feed* to add updates from any web site or blog that supports feeds.

To add feeds, follow these steps:

*1.* **Click the Feeds button.**

The button is in the panel on the left side of the screen.

*2.* **Click Add a Feed.**

The e-mail clients come with a set of feeds from Microsoft and some of its associated companies, such as MSNBC. See Figure 5-11.

*3.* **Enter the URL for the feed.**

You also can subscribe to a feed directly from a Web site. The process varies slightly from site to site or feed type to type, but it all begins by clicking a button that reads something like Subscribe.

The e-mail clients come with a set of feeds from Microsoft and some of its associated companies, such as MSNBC. See Figure 5-11. To rid yourself of this burden, follow along:

*1.* **Right-click a feed in the left panel.**

*2.* **Select Delete.**

**Figure 5-11:**
As delivered, Windows Live Mail comes set up to monitor RSS feeds from Microsoft, MSN, and MSNBC.

## *Adding a signature to messages*

A nice finishing touch for outgoing messages is to include a formatted signature. This can include your name, address, and phone number, an advertising message, or a message from your legal department. (For example: This e-mail may contain confidential or privileged information. If you think you have received this e-mail in error, please advise the sender by reply e-mail and then delete this e-mail immediately.)

Some users have their antivirus program insert a message indicating that the outgoing information has been scanned for viruses. That seems reassuring, although such a message can also be faked by evildoers.

This feature is available in all three of Microsoft's mail programs. With the arrival of Windows Mail and Windows Live Mail you can create several signatures if you have multiple e-mail accounts and assign an individualized signature to any or all of them.

**Book VIII
Chapter 5**

**Exchanging E-mail,
IMs, and
Newsgroups**

To create a signature, follow these steps:

*1.* **Open your e-mail client.**

*2.* **Choose Tools ⇨ Options.**

*3.* **Choose the Signatures tab.**

*4.* **Click New and type your signature.**

> This option is in the Signatures area. See Figure 5-12.

**Figure 5-12:**
The Options
Signatures
tab is
home to
signatures
you created
as text or
have stored
as a
formatted
HTML file.

To edit an existing signature, do this:

*1.* **Click the signature you want to edit.**

*2.* **In the Edit Signature box, type changes to your signature.**

To use a file you created in a text editor, word processor, or HTML (Web page design) program, do these steps:

*1.* **Click File.**

*2.* **Click the signature you want to use.**

3. **Choose an option based on your needs:**

   - **Apply the signature to every message you send.** Click the Add Signatures to all Outgoing Messages check box. This option is in the Signature Settings section.

   - **Remove the automatic insertion of a signature.** Select the signature, and then click Remove.

   - **Rename a signature.** Select the signature, click Rename, and type a new name.

### Using different signatures for different accounts

If you're using Windows Mail or Windows Live Mail, you can assign specific signatures to different mail accounts.

1. **Click Tools ⇨ Options.**

2. **Click the Signatures tab.**

3. **Choose a signature from the Signatures section.**

4. **Click Advanced.**

5. **Select the account you want to use the signature with.**

6. **Click OK.**

### Using a signature only for selected messages

Follow these steps to assign any predefined signature to a specific message:

1. **Create the signatures.**

2. **Save them as a file on your disk.**

3. **Click the Signatures tab.**

4. **Locate the Signature Settings section.**

5. **Make sure the Add Signatures to all Outgoing Messages check box is clear.**

   If it's been previously enabled, click it again.

6. **Type your message.**

7. **Click Insert ⇨ Signature.**

   The Insert menu appears only while you're composing a message.

8. **Click the signature you want to use.**

9. **Click Send.**

Windows Mail Live works with systems running Microsoft Windows XP SP2 or later and with Windows Vista. Windows XP Professional x64 Edition isn't supported.

## Minding Your E-mail Manners

An e-mail isn't the same as a letter (remember those?) and not the same as a conversation (face-to-face or telephone). Although e-mails can be very casual and are a great way to communicate information quickly, they can also at times seem abrupt, cold, and even rude . . . or way too familiar in situations where they should be businesslike.

These suggestions come from Microsoft and other sources about proper e-mail etiquette (sometimes called *netiquette*):

✦ **Be cool.** Stop and think before sending an angry message. Like lawyers sometimes say, "You can't unring a bell." A message once sent is impossible to recall; sometimes the best message is the one you don't send.

✦ **Mind your Ps and Qs.** Take the time to proofread your message before you send it, and use the spelling checker. There's little excuse for an error in an e-mail, and many recipients will judge you harshly for mistakes that should have been fixed before the Send button was pressed.

✦ **Curb the funnies.** Be careful with your use of humor in any message, and especially in business situations. Your true meaning may be misconstrued, or it may completely overwhelm the substance of your e-mail.

✦ **Offer a topic.** Use an appropriate subject line. You need to grab the attention of the recipient, and you also want to try to avoid antispam and junk-mail filters that look for certain words or topics in a subject line.

✦ **Don't assume that an e-mail is confidential.** The message could be accidentally misdirected, or the receiver could forward it to someone you don't want to correspond with. And if the recipient prints out your e-mail, whatever electronic safeguards you may have placed on it are useless.

Tables 5-1 through 5-3 give you shortcuts to use in various Microsoft e-mail clients.

| Table 5-1 | Windows Mail and Outlook Express Keyboard Shortcuts |
|---|---|
| *Task* | *Shortcut* |
| Go to your Inbox | Ctrl + I |
| Go to next message in the list | Ctrl + > <br> Ctrl + Shift + > |

| Task | Shortcut |
|---|---|
| Go to previous message in the list | Ctrl + < <br> Ctrl + Shift + < |
| Go to next unread mail message | Ctrl + U |
| Go to next unread folder | Ctrl + J |
| Move between the message list, folder list (if on), and Preview pane | Tab |
| Go to Windows Calendar (Windows Mail) | Ctrl + Shift + L |
| Show/hide folder list | Ctrl + L |
| View properties of a selected message | Alt + Enter |
| View message in HTML | Alt + Shift + H |
| Create new mail | Ctrl + N |
| Open selected message | Ctrl + O <br> Enter |
| Close selected message | Esc |
| Forward a message | Ctrl + F |
| Delete a mail message | Ctrl + D <br> Delete |
| Select all messages, or select all text within a message | Ctrl + A |
| Print selected message | Ctrl + P |
| Mark message as read | Ctrl + Q <br> Ctrl + Enter |
| Reply to message author | Ctrl + R |
| Reply to all | Ctrl + Shift R |
| Send a message | Alt + S <br> Ctrl + Enter |
| Send and receive mail | Ctrl + M <br> F5 |
| Insert signature | Ctrl + Shift S |
| Help topics | F1 |
| Find text | F3 |
| Find text (advanced) | Ctrl + Shift + F |
| Check spelling | F7 |
| Check names | Alt + K <br> Ctrl + K |
| Open Address Book (Outlook Express) | Ctrl + Shift + B |
| Open Contacts (Windows Mail) | Ctrl + Shift + C |

**Book VIII
Chapter 5**

**Exchanging E-mail, IMs, and Newsgroups**

| Table 5-2 | Shortcuts to Windows Live Mail Enhancements |
|---|---|
| *Task* | *Shortcut* |
| View blocked images | F9 |
| New photo e-mail | Ctrl + Shift + P |
| Blog | Ctrl + Shift + G |
| Mark as junk mail | Ctrl + Alt + J |

| Table 5-3 | Newsgroup Shortcuts |
|---|---|
| *Task* | *Shortcut* |
| Download news for offline reading | Ctrl + Shift + M |
| Go to next unread news thread | Ctrl + Shift + U |
| Refresh news messages and headers | F5 |
| Expand a news thread (show all responses) | + (plus) <br> ← |
| Collapse a news thread (hide messages) | - (minus) <br> → |
| Mark all news messages as read | Ctrl + Shift + A |
| Mark a thread as read | Ctrl + T |
| Post a message | Alt + S <br> Ctrl + Enter |
| Reply to all | Ctrl + G |
| Go to next unread newsgroup | Ctrl + J |
| Go to a newsgroup | Ctrl + W |

# Snagging Web-based E-mail Programs

To this point, this chapter deals with e-mail systems primarily delivered by ISPs meant to be managed by client software on your laptop: programs like Outlook Express, Outlook, Windows Mail, Windows Live Mail, Eudora, and Thunderbird.

Another class of e-mail services that perform in a different manner — in some ways better and others less attractively than the way ISPs work. Web-based e-mail, sometimes called *webmail,* was designed primarily for access through a Web browser.

In its purest form, messages are sent and received entirely through the web site and e-mails don't live on your laptop.

✦ The advantage: You can easily move from machine to machine — yours or someone else's — and leave the storage and safekeeping of your mail to the Web provider.

✦ The downside: You don't have access to your older mail when your machine is *offline* (not connected to the Internet).

However, over time, just as standard ISP-based e-mail are allowing travelers to check e-mail from any machine without using an e-mail client, so, too, have webmail providers found ways to let you download some or all of your messages to folders on your laptop.

To some users, one of the real advantages webmail is the relative level of anonymity it affords users. In most cases you can open a Web-based account and create a user name, password, and e-mail address without having to provide a verified true identity. For honest users this allows an alternate address they can use for special purposes without having to worry about unwanted disclosure of personal details. For dishonest users, a webmail account may afford some protection from law-enforcement agencies.

Even if you don't list your real name and address, a Web-based e-mail company may be able to determine the IP address for the machine you use to sign on from. This may or may not be enough to provide a trail to you, but it is one detail over which you have little control.

Among Web-based e-mail services are

✦ Windows Live Hotmail

✦ Gmail from Google

✦ Yahoo! Mail

You can access some of the services, including Hotmail, from within an e-mail client like Windows Live Mail.

# Letting Your Fingers Do IMing

Want to see me send a message? Want to see me do it again? Like a variation on an old, not-very-funny joke about a quick-draw gunfighter, that's the sort of exercise many people go through when they first use an instant messaging service.

*Instant messaging,* universally called *IMing* (pronounced *eye-emming*) or sending an *IM (eye-emm),* is somewhat like the text equivalent of making a telephone call. You type your message — a sentence, a phrase, an *emoticon* that, like a smiley face, is supposed to convey emotion — and you press Enter or click the Send button onscreen. In an instant (more or less) the message appears on the screen of the person you're IMing.

Unlike an e-mail, using an IM service requires some sort of Internet connection at the time the conversation is going on. However, that doesn't mean the person you're sending a message to has to be at his keyboard the moment your message is sent; it appears onscreen and waits to be read. (Think of leaving a voicemail at a telephone answering machine.)

For many people, using an IM is the least formal form of communication and also one that lends itself very well to our attention-deficit multitasking way of life. You can send snippets back and forth in a close approximation of a conversation: Q: "Has it started snowing there yet?" A: "We're getting buried. Six inches since noon." And meanwhile you're typing away on your keyboard for the sales report due in an hour.

The IM process has been appropriated by many commercial enterprises who offer to let visitors into a website "chat" with a salesperson or a support engineer. For the user, this offers a bit of a shield between actually having to speak with a live human being; for the company or organization it offers a way for one agent to serve several people at the same time — switching from one window to another — as well as giving the ability to push Web links and images as part of the IM connection.

To use instant messaging on your laptop you need these things:

✦ A wired or wireless Internet connection

✦ An account to use it

✦ An IM program (like those listed in "Instant messaging programs" later in this chapter)

That's it. You don't need an e-mail account, and once you load an IM program onto your laptop in most cases you don't even need to be running a Web browser; most IM clients operate as standalone mini-applications.

## The eyes of a nation are upon you

Make sure you're running a capable and fully updated antivirus program before loading and running an IM program. Like most everything else that connects to the mostly unregulated Web, most IM programs are attractive targets by Internet pirates.

Hackers may successfully deliver virus and spyware code within an infected file that might be sent from one user to another during an IM session, as well through *poison URL* links that lead to web sites that try to download malicious code.

Another concern for some businesses and government agencies is the fact that some IM sessions manage to get around their monitoring of e-mail communication. Like it or not, various laws require records be kept of all communication that could possibly be used in commission of crimes or illegalities including the delivery of insider information about stock and other financial instruments.

## Instant messaging programs

There are more than a dozen major providers of instant messaging to the public; a number of other companies offer chat functions to businesses and organizations. If you subscribe to AOL, that company's IM is part of the package. Similarly, if you join Microsoft's Windows Live service, you have to go out of your way to *not* end up with an account and access to Windows Live Messenger.

Here are some of the top IM client providers:

✦ **AOL Instant Messenger.** Available as part of an AOL membership or free as a standalone application. See Figure 5-13. To obtain a copy of the program, visit www.aim.com.

✦ **eBuddy.** A Dutch-owned company, its service supports various instant messaging services including AIM, Google Talk, MySpace IM, Windows Live Messenger, and Yahoo! To download, visit www.ebuddy.com.

✦ **IBM Lotus Sametime.** This instant messaging and web conferencing application is sold by IBM though its Lotus Software division. For information, see www-306.ibm.com/software/lotus/sametime.

✦ **ICQ.** This program, whose name is meant to be pronounced *I seek you* was developed in Israel and is now owned by AOL. To download, visit www.icq.com.

✦ **Jabber.** A popular open-source product that is meant to be adopted and adapted by various users and companies. To obtain a copy, visit www.jabber.org.

✦ **Skype.** Headquartered in Luxembourg with its routes in Sweden and Denmark, it is today owned by eBay. For information visit www.skype.com.

✦ **Windows Live Messenger.** Free from Microsoft it runs under all current versions of Windows as well as through the Windows Live web site; a Windows Live user name can be used for this and other services. To subscribe, visit http://get.live.com/messenger.

✦ **Yahoo! Messenger.** You can download this advertisement-supported client and use it with a generic Yahoo! ID. This allows you access to other Yahoo! Services. To obtain a copy, visit http://messenger.yahoo.com.

**Book VIII
Chapter 5**

Exchanging E-mail,
IMs, and
Newsgroups

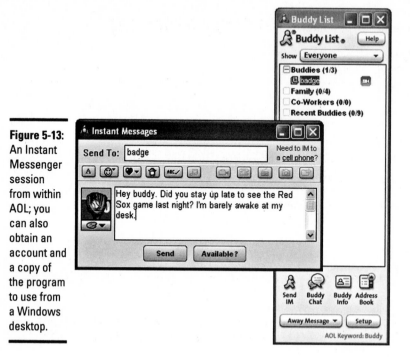

**Figure 5-13:**
An Instant
Messenger
session
from within
AOL; you
can also
obtain an
account and
a copy of
the program
to use from
a Windows
desktop.

# Chapter 6: Communicating with VoIP

## In This Chapter

✔ Making phone calls without the phone company

✔ Getting a good VoIP when you need one

✔ Testing the quality of an Internet phone call

✔ Making beautiful music: VoIP and laptops

*W*hen the Internet began to take hold in the 1990s, it didn't take long for engineers to realize two important things about the *plain old telephone system (POTS):*

✦ Although some small, incremental improvements could be made to the system, it was no longer practical to use the original phone system for Internet communication.

✦ The new high-speed, high-capacity means of communication — including broadband connections like cable, DSL, and fiber-optic links — could be used for much more than merely transmitting data.

Like what? Video, audio . . . and telephone service.

*Voice over IP (VoIP)* comes in on the considerably more modern and capable coaxial cable strung by what used to be called the *cable television company.* VoIP networks are much more efficient than the old-style telephone network.

✦ They don't need to open and maintain a sustained connection between the caller and the recipient; any two points on the Internet are never really connected, but instead are basically tuned into the data stream looking for packets addressed their way.

✦ Because a call is broken into millions of little packets, the network can easily share cables and wireless transmission media amongst thousands of users at the same time.

✦ Because the packets are digital, computers can squeeze all the air (and silence) out of a signal and send only the information that matters. By some estimates, a VoIP call that takes five minutes from beginning to end might occupy the equivalent amount of bandwidth required for about one minute of POTS.

## Pa Bell

In the beginning, there was the telephone. Well, not quite the beginning: more like in the 1870s when Alexander Graham Bell . . . and four or five other inventors who were chasing after the same ring . . . created the first working telephone system.

The system: a voice-actuated transmitter in the mouthpiece connected by a pair of copper wires to a tiny electrically driven loudspeaker in a device at the other end of the circuit. The signal traveled as an analog wave along the wire. This simple technology worked in 1876 when Bell summoned his assistant: "Mr. Watson. Come here. I want to see you." And it still works more or less the same way today.

Why do I say the original telephone works more or less the same way it did when Bell and others laid out its design? The technology is little changed, but the success of the system led to complexity and distance.

Where pairs of wires ran directly from one building to another, the next step was to run the pairs of wires to a central switchboard where a human operator connected the incoming pair to an outgoing line to complete a circuit between two specific points.

And then when neighborhoods and then cities and, finally, countries and continents became interconnected, there needed to be multiple switchboards (or mechanical switches) to connect local loops to long-distance trunks. And as the distance increased, amplifiers were needed to boost power.

But the basic idea of the plain old telephone system, a pair of copper wires connecting Point A to Point B, still applies for standard telephone calls. Switching from one set of wires to another is handled automatically, and many calls change back and forth between analog and digital signals along the way. Some signals are bounced up to a satellite in space to be redirected down to an Earth station, and other calls moved as flashes of light along a fiber-optic cable. But with a little explanation, Bell would have easily recognized his invention in its modern form.

## Rocking the Laptop Telephony

Here's how laptops can take advantage of Internet telephony:

✦ Making and receiving telephone calls through your laptop anywhere in the world where you can connect to the Internet. While the same may be possible with a cell phone, consider the fact that international calls on a VoIP system may cost only pennies per minute, while cell-roaming charges can easily run several dollars per minute.

Some Internet cafés, including many on cruise ships, attempt to block use of VoIP, claiming that users are consuming too much of their bandwidth. In many cases the real reason is they don't want to lose the revenue they otherwise receive by charging exorbitant rates for cell phone or satellite telephone communication. As a user, you should complain

about any café that blocks VoIP and you should seek alternatives: other
cafés, and other, unblocked Internet telephone providers.

✦ Most VoIP systems allow video conferencing as well as phone calls,
again at very low rates. You can use the built-in webcam on many laptops or add a clip-on camera.

✦ You can use your laptop to listen to voicemail left for you on your home
or office phone. You may sign into a web site that stores your voicemail,
or you may have all voicemail sent to your e-mail address and get messages by downloading your mail.

## Cutting the Cord

Several years ago, I gave Mr. Bell and Mr. Watson their walking papers. I literally cut the connection between my home and office and the copper wires
that ran to the phone company's central office about a mile away. On the
island of Nantucket where I live and work, the first local service was introduced in 1887 and some of the infrastructure is still in use.

I replaced the creaky (and more expensive) phone service with a VoIP telephone service. Same phone number, same phones within my home and
office, and (nearly) the same quality of voice communication.

It works this way:

✦ A coaxial cable comes into my office. It's the same cable that brings
"American Idol" and other drivel (sorry, I mean "entertainment"); a
splitter sends one signal to the numerous TV sets scattered about and
another signal goes to a cable modem.

✦ The cable modem output goes (via a standard Ethernet cable) to a VoIP
gateway. This device, sometimes called an *Internet telephone adapter,* is
similar to a modem in that it converts an analog signal from regular telephone devices to a digital signal that can go out over the Internet. It also
compresses outgoing signals and decompresses incoming calls.

In most setups, the VoIP gateway passes the Internet signal through to your
computer or to a router that allows multiple laptops or computers to share
the signal. Some VoIP providers offer a device that combines a router and
telephone gateway in one box.

A VoIP gateway is sometimes also called an *analog telephone adapter (ATA).*
Within the box, an incoming analog wave from a standard telephone is electronically sampled so it can be broken into small packets of digital information
that travel over the Internet. Other functions provided by a VoIP gateway
include call routing and signaling over the remnants of Bell's public switched
telephone network; this gives a dial tone at your end and rings the telephone

# The digital revolution dials a phone call

Computers manipulate digital information. A character onscreen is represented by a number (or set of numbers). So, too, a sound's volume or pitch of a sound or whether it is a high treble or a low bass tone is made digital. There are many advantages to converting Alexander Graham Bell's analog waves to digital numbers:

✔ They can be made more precise.

✔ They can be amplified and sent great distances without fear of garbling.

✔ They can be protected from corruption.

And perhaps most importantly in this era of *local area networks (LANs), wide area networks (WANs),* and the global Internet, digital information doesn't need to be transmitted or received in a continuous and orderly stream. It can instead be broken up into pieces and reassembled at the other end.

On the Internet, for example, a message from Point A to Point B that reads, "The check has been received" might (in logical terms) be divided into five pieces, each within a digital packet that includes the identity of the sender, the identity of the receiver, and a sequential number. The packets are cast out onto the Internet like marbles in a pinball machine and

eventually reach their destination, where they quite possibly arrive like this:

check [word 2]

been [word 4]

The [word 1]

has [word 3]

received. [word 5]

The machine at the other end gathers all the pieces and reorders them into a sentence. If for some reason it finds a word missing from the sequence, it can request that it be re-sent. All of this happens within tiny fractions of a second, whether the two computers are across the room from each other and connected by wire, across the office from each other and communicating by WiFi connection, or on the other side of the world from each other and linked by dozens of different pathways including fiber-optic links, microwave transmission, and satellite uplinks and downlinks.

A working VoIP system at a fixed location like your home or office doesn't need a computer to operate. However, you get a number of advantages when setting up a traveling VoIP system. See the "Rocking the Laptop Telephony" section in this chapter for more information.

at the number you've dialed. (Dialed? That's a word that has lost its original meaning; yes, kiddies, us old folks used to use a rotary switch to "dial" a number.)

The packets include data like your phone number, the number you're calling, and the IP address of your connection to the Internet. Also in the packet are instructions to a VoIP gateway somewhere else in the world that converts the digital pieces back into an analog signal if the number you called is a traditional telephone; you can also communicate from VoIP gateway to VoIP gateway and stay in digital mode all the way.

In most cases, a telephone conversation initiated by someone with a VoIP system will travel most of the way to its destination using the Internet — a system that begins with the local cable to your home or office and then usually moves across major cables or satellite connections before it gets near your call destination. And then the "last mile" may travel to the person you're calling over a pair of copper wires that Bell would recognize.

If both ends of a conversation are using VoIP, the entire interchange may travel over Internet facilities, coming in and going out over cable coaxial or DSL lines.

I could have set up a very similar system using a DSL Internet service instead of a cable modem.

## Deciding POTS is the pits

Here are some of the advantages of VoIP:

✦ VoIP service generally costs less than an old-fashioned POTS if you include long-distance call packages. Nearly all VoIP providers have completely eliminated the distinction between local and long-distance calls and have also turned off the meter that charged for length of calls. You can make a phone call across the street or across the nation without regard to distance or time; just like the Internet, your telephone service is available to you all the time for a flat fee. (Some providers include "free" service to Canada in their package.)

✦ Calls to international destinations are generally very inexpensive.

✦ VoIP providers include a package of advanced telephone services including

• Call forwarding

• Call waiting

• Caller ID

• "Do-not-disturb" schedules

• Speed dialing

• Conference calling

Most systems allow you to set up an address book on your computer or on a web site that helps you keep track of phone numbers and also integrates with the caller ID system; when someone whose name is in my address book calls me, my telephones display their name whether their number is public or its identity blocked.

✦ All providers also include voicemail; one especially interesting feature offered by some providers sends an e-mail with an attachment that includes your voicemail. I regularly use that feature to listen to my voicemails using my laptop from anywhere in the world.

VoIP has some disadvantages, although technology is dealing with most of them:

✦ Because the calls are broken into packets, sometimes a slight delay (called *latency*) is built into the communication. You may have to teach yourself to wait a half-second before responding to someone who's talking to you; I sometimes apologize in advance to callers, explaining that I'm on an Internet phone line and I don't want them to think I'm being rude if I occasionally seem to interrupt them. (It's a good conversation starter, too; it shows others how technically advanced you are.)

✦ Some systems may deliver voice quality that is slightly less *full* than a standard telephone call. Your voice may sound tinny.

✦ When a VoIP call is in progress, the telephone gateway may grab a large portion of the available bandwidth which may slow down other tasks on the Internet. The faster your connection, the less likely you are to notice this effect. And you can also contact your VoIP provider and ask about available settings (downloaded over the Internet by a technician) that can adjust how much of the bandwidth can be claimed by the phone system.

Your VoIP provider needn't be affiliated in any way with your *Internet service provider (ISP)*. The phone is just another device using the Internet. You can use an Internet service offered by your ISP or you can mix and match.

✦ If you use different providers for Internet and VoIP services, you may run into a "blame-the-other-guy" response if you have technical problems. The VoIP company may say their service is working fine and that the cable or DSL company is delivering an inferior connection; the ISP may claim that their signal is just fine and that the phone provider is offering subpar service. In my experience, I can push the phone provider a bit harder since they know I can easily change services; remind them of that and make them prove they've done everything possible to give you the highest-quality VoIP service.

✦ Your phone service won't function if your home or office loses electrical power. Some providers, though, offer an adapter that comes with a built-in rechargeable battery backup that keeps the connection alive for several hours; you can also purchase your own *uninterruptible power supply (UPS)* and plug the phone adapter and modem into that device. If your Internet service goes down, though, your VoIP service won't work even if the power is on.

Be sure you understand how your VoIP provider handles 911 calls. Dialing that number still gets you to an emergency response agency, but unless you've registered an address with your provider — and you're at that location — the information they receive may not automatically provide them with your address.

Many VoIP providers automatically require you to confirm your phone location any time they detect that their telephone adapter has been unplugged or has lost power (a possible indication that the phone has moved). This sort of safeguard doesn't work with pure Internet services that don't use a telephone adapter, such as Skype.

A valuable feature offered by many VOIP providers is an automatic re-routing of calls to another number in the event your service isn't working properly (because of a power outage or an Internet outage, for example). My VoIP provider automatically sends incoming calls to my cell phone if necessary.

## Finding VoIP services

Dozens of companies, small and large, offer VoIP services. Some are divisions of major telecommunications companies that are trying to hold on to customers in one way or another:

+ AT&T (CallVantage)
+ Comcast
+ Verizon

Others are new technology companies that have little or no infrastructure of their own (other than computers) to manage routing and accounting for calls; these include companies like

+ Skype
+ Vonage
+ Magic Jack

In my experience, the old-line telecommunications companies generally offer a better product, although they may not be the least expensive services.

# Getting to VoIP at Home or Work

Here's what you need to use VoIP at a fixed location like your home or office:

+ A broadband Internet service. This can come from a cable modem provider, a DSL service from a phone company or independent provider, or a fiber-optics service.
+ A VoIP *gateway* (telephone adapter) and a broadband modem. Some VoIP providers offer both devices in one box.

Because VoIP systems use the Internet instead of telephone wires, you're required to notify the Internet phone provider of your address so 911 and other emergency services can function properly. Anytime your phone adapter is turned off or loses power, you have to re-register your address.

✦ An account with a VoIP provider. These companies provide a telephone number or (in most cases) transfer an existing standard telephone number or cell phone number to their service.

✦ A laptop or desktop computer for system configuration and to manage the special features. You don't actually need a computer to use a functioning VoIP system, and your computer doesn't need to be powered on or running any software for the phone adapter and cable modem to provide service.

✦ One or more telephones. In the simplest setup, you can merely plug a wired telephone into the standard telephone jack on the back of the phone adapter. But it's also very easy to extend telephone service throughout your home or office. Here are two ways to do that:

*1.* **Attach a multiphone wireless telephone base station to the back of the phone adapter.**

*2.* **Place additional phones anywhere they can receive a strong signal.**

And this way:

*1.* **Disconnect your existing telephone system.**

*2.* **Go to the Network Interface.**

The old copper wires had come into your home or office here.

*3.* **Unplug the incoming wires.**

*4.* **Change the wiring at the box.**

You should have a closed loop of a system.

*5.* **Plug a telephone cable from your VoIP gateway into a phone outlet.**

You can then plug ordinary telephones into any outlet that formerly used the old phone company wiring.

If the rewiring scheme sounds vague or frightening, it's only because I want you to follow the recommendations of your VoIP provider. Ask them for technical assistance in reusing your existing "inside" wiring. (Don't be frightened — the electrical power in a phone line isn't dangerous — but you do need to do the job properly, and some VoIP companies have differing recommendations based on their equipment.)

# Getting Quality VoIP

For a VoIP system to work well, you need

✦ A high-speed Internet connection

✦ A clean, well-performing network

## Troubleshooting

Network congestion, poor-quality connections (wired or wireless), and atmospheric conditions can conspire to make your telephone conversation sound like it's coming from the bottom of a deep well . . . in a hurricane . . . with six simultaneous conversations working their way into and out of the call at the same time. It shouldn't be like that.

Before you call your VoIP service support desk, do a bit of troubleshooting on your own:

✦ Does the signal seem to degrade under certain conditions — whenever you run streaming video from YouTube, for example?

✦ Does the signal seem fine in the morning but fall apart at 3 p.m. — just about the time the neighbors' kids get home from school and start trolling the Web?

✦ Has your voice connection gotten worse since you moved your wireless telephone from one spot to another — such as the other side of the house?

Each of these conditions, and others, has a different troubleshooting path to follow:

✦ Your telephone adapter may need to be re-set by your service provider to grab hold of more of the Internet bandwidth.

✦ You may need to upgrade your connection speed.

✦ You may need to fix or replace your plain old telephone system.

## TestMyVoip

A number of online web sites can test your Internet connection with a special emphasis on technical problems that can affect the sound quality. Among my favorites is www.testmyvoip.com, which is offered by Brix Networks, a supplier of services and software tools to Internet providers.

The basic TestMyVoip report, shown in Figure 6-1, allows you to bounce a simulated call from your location to places like Boston, Montreal, London, San Jose, and Sydney. An overall score compares your VoIP score against the Pony Express, tin cans and string, a crummy cell phone call, a decent cell phone call, and the best telephone-like service you could hope for.

**Figure 6-1:** My VoIP system test shows it currently performs about as well as I could hope for, a condition that in my rural location is better than I got from the old telephone company.

The Brix scale runs from 1.0 to 5.0 but the best most users can hope for on a VoIP system is a score of about 4.4. If your score is significantly below that level, click Detailed Results to learn an amazing array of information about your signal, including

✦ The percentage of discarded digital packets

✦ The average and maximum amount of loss of continuous signal

✦ The amount of time it took to set up and dial your call

What can you do about problems pointed out by tests like those provided by Brix? Nothing, by yourself. However, when you call your VoIP support desk and ask them to run tests on your line, you'll be well-armed to rebut their claims that "everything looks good." I've found that just mentioning that I know of the existence of www.testmyvoip.com is enough to get my complaint escalated from someone whose job it is to make customers go away to someone whose job it is to actually fix a problem.

# Equipping a Laptop for VoIP

You can connect your laptop to a VoIP service three ways.

## Traveling with a telephone adapter

Bring your VoIP phone adapter with you, which also moves your telephone number. For example, if you have VoIP service in Boston, with a 617 or 781 area code, you can travel anywhere in the world and connect to the Internet to make and receive phone calls at that number. Your neighbor across the street can make a local call to you, and it will ring your laptop in Norway (or leave a voicemail you can pick up).

## Setting up a softphone on your laptop

A *softphone* uses software to emulate the hardware of a telephone adapter. In most cases this requires a separate telephone number; you can, though, request a number almost anywhere in the world that makes sense to you. The number could, for example, appear to be in the Boston area if that makes it easier for people to reach you. Or you could receive a softphone number in London or Paris or almost anywhere in the world, which might be more cost-efficient if you need to make calls from that location; callers from back in Boston or Biloxi, though, have to make an international call to reach you.

Softphones are available from companies that also operate hardware-based VoIP systems; companies include AT&T (CallVantage) and Vonage. They provide a software application that you install on your laptop that integrates with your permanent account at your home or office.

Companies like Skype are entirely based on softphone technology. See Figure 6-2. These ad hoc services use the same conversion from voice to digital packets that a VoIP telephone adapter or a softphone employs. However, you can purchase a telephone that has the Skype software embedded, instead of being resident on the laptop computer; either way you need to get out onto the Internet to communicate.

Many softphone programs are designed to look like a telephone keypad, adding easy-click access to advanced features. If your laptop has a built-in microphone, you can use that together with the machine's speakers to function as a speakerphone, although for privacy (and clarity) you should instead purchase and use a headset and microphone that attach to your machine's built-in sound adapter.

**Book VIII
Chapter 6**

**Communicating
with VoIP**

**Figure 6-2:**
The Skype
softphone
software
running on
my laptop
allows me
to enter a
number for
almost
anyplace
on earth.

## Softphone (IP) telephone

These devices attach to your laptop through a USB port or an Ethernet cable
and integrate with the softphone software; these handsets automatically
load your VoIP software on your laptop and include a keypad, speaker, and
microphone.

You can also purchase a WiFi phone that communicates with most WiFi
hotspots in Internet cafés, offices, and some homes to directly connect
without attaching to a computer:

✦ If the wireless network is open and unsecured, you should be able to get
   onto the Internet and make calls.

✦ If the network is secured, you need to login and enter a password to gain
   access (if the network owner permits this).

# Book IX

# Protecting Your Laptop

## The 5th Wave

By Rich Tennant

"Needlepoint my foot! These are Word fonts.
What I can't figure out is how you got the
pillow cases into your printer."

# Contents at a Glance

# Chapter 1: Traveling with a Laptop

## In This Chapter

✔ **Giving it away isn't good**

✔ **Carrying a laptop in style and safety**

✔ **Locking the hardware**

✔ **Dealing with disaster**

*1* travel nearly half the year to all the distant corners of the world, and I can no longer conceive of going out the door without my laptop. I've transferred funds to pay my children's college tuition from Ua Pou in the Marquesas Islands of the South Pacific. I've exchanged e-mails with my investment advisor from Cape Horn at the tip of South America. I've sent IMs and video mail from Svalbard near the North Pole.

If my laptop computer had ever 1) been stolen or left behind, 2) dropped from an outrigger canoe into the Great Barrier Reef, or 3) fallen to the floor whilst computing from Chile, I could well have suffered an almost incalculable loss far beyond the value of plastic, silicon, and metal.

The laptop-equipped road warrior fields three major threats:

✦ Losing a machine worth hundreds or thousands of dollars.

✦ Losing the contents of the hard disk drive (or other storage medium). What value to a dishonest person is personal information, financial data, and business data stored in a laptop that goes missing or is stolen?

✦ Electronic theft of data sent from or to your machine: the sneakiest form of cyber crime. A moderately clever crook can send spyware over the Internet or even pluck data out of the wireless signals that engulf us at home, at work, and on the road.

Be careful out there. In this chapter, I offer some tips about how to be a smart road warrior.

# *Keeping It to Yourself*

My dear, sweet, and very bright wife stepped onto a crowded subway train in Rome a few years ago; she stepped off minus her wallet. Maybe it was the city map she held, or perhaps her very stylish but obviously foreign clothing. Whatever it was, she was a very attractive mark for a team of pickpockets who moved quickly past her and off the train.

Any experienced traveler, and that includes most road warriors, knows that he should limit the amount of cash he carries, keeping his wallet deeply buried or even hidden away inside his clothing. Try to blend in and keep a low profile.

But all that's mere window dressing if you're walking around town, riding in cabs, and passing through airports with a rectangular cloth or leather satchel about $12 \times 16$ inches. The first laptop computer bag I owned had a great big label on it advertising the brand of the machine inside; today's bags are generally less conspicuous but it doesn't really matter: You might as well be strolling the streets yelling, "I've got a $1,500 laptop computer in this bag! And it's got all of my bank and credit card account numbers and login information listed in a file called Passwords."

And it's not just thieves you have to worry about. Every year tens of thousands of computer bags are left behind in hotels, restaurants, taxicabs, rental cars, at airline security checks, in overhead baggage compartments, and sitting on the corner.

It's not the subject of this book but still worth pointing out: The convergence of cell phones and banking and computing functions means that a great deal of personal information is now being carried around in much smaller and much easier-to-lose electronic devices. Think twice and then again before storing any personal or financial information on a cell phone.

## *Carrying a laptop the smarter way*

Engineers haven't yet developed an invisible laptop (how could you find it once you put it down?), but you can do some things to lessen the likelihood that your computer is stolen or lost — and to reduce the effects if a laptop nevertheless goes missing.

I start with physical protection. Software security comes later.

✦ **Get strong coverage.** Buy a sturdy bag to hold your computer and make sure it has sturdy zippers and clasps. I prefer a case that also includes an internal strap with a Velcro closure that holds the laptop within a cushioned chamber; the strap helps protect against the machine tumbling out of a case when the zippers and clasps open, and it also makes it more difficult for a thief to reach in and grab the machine while you've got the bag over your shoulder.

✦ **Shun labels.** Make sure the bag doesn't advertise for the computer manufacturer. Remove labels or cover them if you must.

✦ **ID yourself.** Place several ID tags on hooks and straps of the bag and make use of any internal compartments for additional identifying information. Put your name, phone number, and e-mail address on the tags; that is sufficient for an honest person (or a lost-and-found department) to contact you. Most experts recommend against adding your address or your company name; that might give a dishonest person enough details to at least attempt to get into your financial and personal accounts.

✦ **Keep keys separate.** Don't keep your car and house keys in the pocket of your laptop case; in addition, make sure your car and house keys don't have your home address and auto license number on them; a smart crook might be able to figure out your address from documents in the bag or on the hard drive, but don't make it easy for him. If you lose your keys and your identity can't be traced from them, all you have to do is replace the keys; if your name and address are on the keys, you probably should call a locksmith and change all the hardware.

✦ **Reward returners.** Add the phrase "Reward for Return" to the ID tags. This might improve the chances that a finder will contact you.

✦ **Play tag.** Several companies offer anonymous tracking tags to apply to your laptop (and any other valuable) in hopes that a finder will do the right thing. These tags include a code number, a telephone number, and an e-mail address. If someone finds your machine and contacts the ID company, they serve as an intermediary to arrange the return without revealing your name and address. Companies with this sort of service include

- ArmorTag at www.armortag.com
- BoomerangIt at www.boomerangit.com
- StuffBak at www.stuffbak.com
- TrackItBack at www.trackitback.com
- YouGetItBack.com at www.yougetitback.com
- zReturn at www.zreturn.com

In most services, you purchase a subscription to cover your equipment for particular period of time; annual charges are generally less than $25.

✦ **Keep passwords elsewhere.** Don't include in your laptop case a notebook with all of your user IDs, passwords, account numbers, Social Security number, and the combination for your locker at the health club. I advise against making such a list at all, but if you *must,* I offer some suggestions about ways to encode them in a moment; put any such list in a separate bag — stuck in with your dirty socks or under the lining of your suitcase.

✦ **Strategize for separation.** Think about your strategies for times you and your laptop case may be briefly separated. I recommend holding onto your laptop anytime you use a taxi; don't put it in the trunk. If you're traveling on an airline, the safest place for your laptop and its case is on the floor under the seat in front of you; if you must put it in an overhead compartment, put it somewhere you can watch during the flight and get to it quickly during the mad scramble to get off the plane at the end of the flight.

✦ **Hide it.** Never leave a laptop in plain sight in a car. Move it to the trunk — if you're sure no one's watching you — or hide it beneath a seat.

✦ **Vault it.** In a hotel, see if the in-room safe is large enough to hold your laptop. You may also be able to leave your machine in the vault at the front desk of one of the better hotels; I wouldn't try this at the No-tell Motel out on the shopping strip.

✦ **Keep your eye on the X-ray.** One of the most challenging places for a road warrior is airport security (and some government and private buildings) where bags must go through an X-ray machine. In theory, a properly designed and maintained X-ray machine won't damage your laptop, but here's something that might: a fall from the conveyer belt or rollers. Another concern is that someone on the "safe" side of the X-ray machine might take your laptop bag (on purpose or by accident) and head off for a flight to Keokuk (or just turn around and exit the airport with a free laptop).

  • My best solution for security lines is to travel with a wing man (or wing woman). Let your confederate go through the metal detector ahead of you and wait for valuables to arrive.

  • If I'm traveling alone, here's my procedure. First of all, I put my wallet, cell phone, keys, and other valuables in zipper pockets of my jacket. Then I send items through the X-ray machine in reverse order of their value: shoes, books and papers, the laptop-less case, then my jacket, and finally my laptop. Once I see the laptop go through the scanner, I proceed through the metal detector.

## Locking the hardware

A delivery courier strolls out the door with a stack of boxes; does the security guard at the door open up each one to look for a laptop snatched off a desktop? The pizza delivery guy walks through the hallway of a dorm; are you certain there's not a $2,000 portable between the pepperoni and the Hawaiian special? Does your company's recycling program include a check of waste bins to see if an organized theft ring is trying to sneak a fully functioning Dell into the dumpster?

All of these scenarios, and more, are real. Just imagine that a thief has come into your home or office. What are the most valuable small items he can grab? In my house, this includes the Crown Jewels of Freedonia in the living room . . . and several laptop computers. Everything else is either in a safe or too bulky.

A laptop by definition is supposed to be easy to take and run. So how do you lock one down? Here are a few suggestions:

✦ **Get cable.** Nearly all current laptop include a hardened slot at the back to work with special cables and locks that you can attach to a desk, pipe, or other fixed object. Cables won't stop a truly dedicated thief (especially one who comes with a chain cutter or a Ginsu knife), but will slow down a casual rip-off artiste. If someone intends to resell something they've stolen, they don't want to damage the case by breaking off the lock.

- One example is the MicroSaver Portable Notebook Combination Lock from Kensington; the device, about the size of a desktop mouse, includes a retractable 4' aircraft-grade steel cable; the end that plugs into the security slot of the laptop includes a three-tumbler combination lock.

- If you want to really raise a ruckus, products like the MicroSaver Alarmed Computer Lock, also from Kensington, include a loud, battery-powered alarm that sounds if someone tampers with the lock.

✦ **Enforce house arrest.** It's not hardware, but it might help you enlist the police in retrieving a stolen laptop: A company's software installs on the laptop's hard drive and keeps in occasional contact with the company's monitoring center over the Internet. If your machine is stolen or goes missing, you can contact the company and put it on alert. From that point on, the service waits to find someone using your laptop with a connection to the Internet and can, in many cases, pinpoint its location through its IP address on the Web.

The system isn't perfect — some IP addresses aren't tied to a particular location, and thieves might use temporary WiFi connections — but it's a step in the direction of remotely tracking your equipment. CompuTrace claims that its code can survive a disk drive reformatting, and some laptop companies have announced plans to embed tiny LoJack or similar chips inside the cases of their machines where they can't be disabled without damaging the system. Service is by annual subscription; as this book goes to press, the service costs less than $50 per year.

Manufacturers include

- CompuTrace LoJack at www.lojackforlaptops.com
- Brigadoon's PC PhoneHome at www.pcphonehome.com
- Inspice's Inspice Trace at www.inspice.com
- XTool's Laptop Tracker at www.xtool.com
- zTrace Technologies' zTrace Gold at www.ztrace.com

## Beefing up your password

Sorry to have to tell you this, but using the name of your pet parrot (dead or alive) as a password is pretty lame. So, too, is using your birthday or your wife's middle name.

The problem is that a dedicated hacker could probably find any of these details with a bit of searching on the Internet. Don't use your birthday, birth year, your partner's name, your children's names, or anything else that a determined hacker might be able to glean from public records. An automated assault could try every possible pet name — trust me, there aren't all that many — to get into your system.

✦ **Go alpha and numeric.** The best way to create a strong password is to use a combination of words and numbers that have meaning to you but aren't traceable to you. Do you remember an old friend's phone number (not their current number)? Did that friend have a strange nickname? And was there a particularly unusual food that you — or your friend — enjoyed or despised? Using that formula, I might construct a password like this: ReverendKL5-1243TofuPie

No way could someone guess that password or could a computer randomly figure it out. (Note that not all operating systems or web sites distinguish between upper- and lowercase, but it can't hurt to include them.) And I could even make a great big note on my desktop that reminds me of the password but would be of no help to anyone else. The hint might say: Fran's nickname, phone, yucky soy dessert.

✦ **Make it meaningful.** A totally random password like J8kl)$32H*/xc is a very strong defense, but is also very difficult to remember, and in some cases a password-cracking program may determine the method used by your software's random-password generator.

✦ **Be unpredictable.** If you want to include the word Spoon in your password, try replacing one or both of the letters *o* with a zero. Or even better, try something odd like a pair of parentheses to represent the *o*. One example: sP()()n

✦ **Be fickle.** Change your passwords every few months. I know that's easier said than done, but it's good practice in case someone has picked up some of your personal information and is poised to attack. One way to avoid having to come up with a completely new password is to create a replaceable component. For example, if your current password is ReverendKL5-1243TofuPie, you could change the food every few months. Make it ReverendKL5-1243Curds&Whey for a while, and then change it to Tapenade.

## *Locking the software*

If a thief is after your machine, she doesn't want to damage it; that would reduce its value. But if a laptop's real worth is the information on the hard drive, a bit of broken plastic won't stand in the way of a theft. Or the crook might even remove the hard drive — smaller than a paperback book — and leave the computer.

The most important strategy is this: Always act as if the information in your laptop is about to disappear. It (along with the machine that holds it) could be stolen or lost or corrupted or made unreadable. Therefore, please remember **Sandler's Top Three Rules of Laptop Data Security**:

*1.* **Back up your data to a form of removable media.**

*2.* **Keep the backup in a safe place, separate and apart from the laptop.**

*3.* **See Rules 1 and 2.**

Keep all sensitive information off the hard disk drive:

✦ If your office is set up with a secure web site, keep data there and sign in over the Internet.

✦ Store all sensitive information on removable media. Consider these possibilities:

  • A password-protected USB flash disk. Corsair's Flash Padlock is a block of flash memory that you can access only after you enter a numerical password of as many as 10 numbers, which, not coincidentally, is the same length as a phone number. (I suggest using a phone number of a friend or relative with a different last name.) Once the Corsair is unlocked, it appears just like any other storage device on your machine; it automatically locks when you remove it from your laptop. The product is available at retail stores and web vendors.

  • A fingerprint reader. These block access to the hard disk by anyone other than the person attached to the proper finger. IBM (and its successor owner of the laptop line, Lenovo) has offered this technology. A small reading pad, on the wrist rest below the arrow keys, verifies a user's identity when he swipes a finger across a tiny sensor. Once identity is established, users are automatically logged on. The solution blocks most casual attempts at unauthorized use, but probably wouldn't keep someone from removing the hard disk drive and offloading its information to another drive.

  • A CD-R, CD-RW, or recordable DVD that you can mix in with your music disks and store away from the computer.

✦ Store the removable media in a different suitcase or in your pocket.

### Requiring a password to log on to Windows

When you install or activate Windows, you're offered the opportunity to add a system password that must be entered each time the machine is turned on; on advanced versions of the operating system a distinction is made between the Administrator (who can change the system's configuration and settings) and a User (who can sign on and use the system but can't change the way it operates).

Enable and set a Windows logon password. Although this isn't a very strong defense against a determined hacker, it should protect against unwanted access by an amateur. Passwords are usually set at the time Windows is installed or first activated; you can also add a password to a system already configured if you have Administrator access.

To enable or change password on a Windows XP or Windows Vista machine, follow these steps:

*1.* **Click Start ⇨ Control Panel ⇨ User Accounts.**

*2.* **Click an option based on your needs:**

- **Choose an Existing Account** (Go to Step 3.)

- **Add a New User** (Go to Step 4.)

*3.* **Choose Add or Change a Password.**

*4.* **Establish a password.**

The logon screen appears. It includes a password hint to help you remember a forgotten code; be as vague but meaningful as possible in creating a hint.

Adding a password won't prevent someone from stealing your laptop, and some programs allow hackers to break most codes. In addition, putting a password on a drive does not prevent someone from reformatting the drive or replacing it with a new one, although your data may be protected from misuse.

If you created a system or startup password, you can later change or remove it once you properly sign on to the system. Under Windows XP or Vista, do this:

*1.* **Go to the Control Panel.**

*2.* **Click the User Accounts icon.**

*3.* **Click one of the following:**

- Create a password for your account

- Change your password

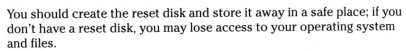
*4.* **Type the password in the New Password box.**

*5.* **Type the password in Confirm New Password box.**

If you forget your password, you can use a password reset disk to create a new one; the "disk" can be a USB flash drive or CD. To create the disk, follow along:

*1.* **Open the Control Panel.**

*2.* **Click the User Accounts icon.**

*3.* **Click Create a Password Reset Disk.**

You should create the reset disk and store it away in a safe place; if you don't have a reset disk, you may lose access to your operating system and files.

Some third-party and free sources offer tools that allow you to get past a forgotten or corrupted system password; that fact should give you pause. Microsoft itself warns that this is not an industrial-strength lockdown of your data but merely part of a comprehensive security plan.

## Password protecting and encrypting a file

Most current software programs (including the Microsoft Office 2007 suite and later editions) let you encrypt and add password protection to an individual file. The lockdown can prevent someone from opening, deleting, or changing a file. Again, the level of security isn't anywhere near that used by spy agencies, but it should deter the casual finder or keeper of your laptop.

Microsoft doesn't offer any assistance in recovering a lost password; if you lose the password, you won't be able to open the file.

If you must write down the code for a file, do so in a notebook that isn't stored with your laptop, and use some coding to hide it. If the password is the phone number of an old friend plus the year your cat was born, make a note like this: Chuck#+catyr.

To encrypt and set a password to open a document, do the following:

*1.* **Open the Microsoft Office 2007 program and file you want to protect.**

*2.* **Click the Microsoft Office Button.**

It's at the top-left corner of the screen.

*3.* **Choose Prepare ⇨ Encrypt Document.**

The Encrypt Document dialog box opens. See Figure 1-1.

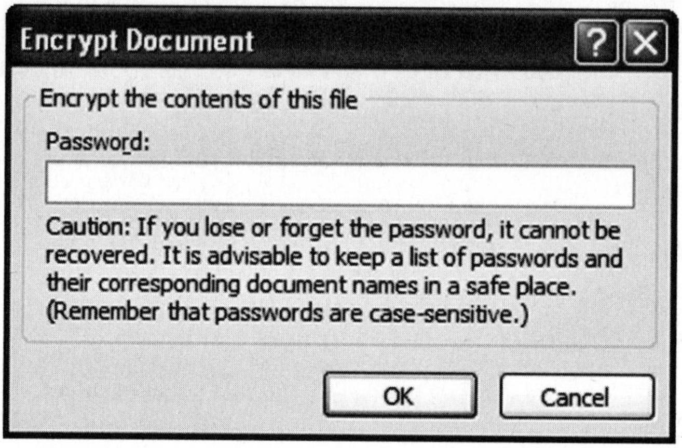

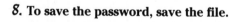

**Encrypt Document**

Encrypt the contents of this file

Password:

Caution: If you lose or forget the password, it cannot be recovered. It is advisable to keep a list of passwords and their corresponding document names in a safe place. (Remember that passwords are case-sensitive.)

OK          Cancel

**Figure 1-1:**
Microsoft Office 2007 can encrypt individual files created under any of its components.

4. **Enter a password in the Password text box.**

   It can be as many as 255 characters.

5. **Click OK.**

   The Confirm Password dialog box appears.

6. **Type the password in the Reenter Password text box.**

7. **Click OK.**

8. **To save the password, save the file.**

A strong password

- ✦ Is longer than a short password (at least 10 to 14 characters).

- ✦ Combines uppercase and lowercase letters, numbers, and symbols. For example, here's one: 25yorBit!78.

Use a phone number of someone who isn't easy to link to you, and mix in a strange word; WA7202903gruyere. (And no, I don't use either of those passwords in my system or with any banks.) Or you can use an obscure quotation or phrase; don't use something guessable like "The quick brown fox jumps over the lazy dog."

### Setting a password to restrict others

You can assign two passwords, and they must be different:

- ✦ One to access the file

- ✦ One to provide specific reviewers with permission to modify its content

To prevent unauthorized viewers from seeing or changing a file you created in Microsoft Office 2007, do the following:

*1.* **Open the file.**

*2.* **Click the Microsoft Office Button.**

It's in the upper-left corner of the screen.

*3.* **Click Save As.**

The Save As screen appears.

*4.* **Click Tools ⇨ General Options.**

The Tools menu is in the lower-left corner. See Figure 1-2.

*5.* **Type a password in the Password to Open text box.**

This password requires that users enter a password before they can view the document. Under this less-secure system, the password can't be longer than 15 characters.

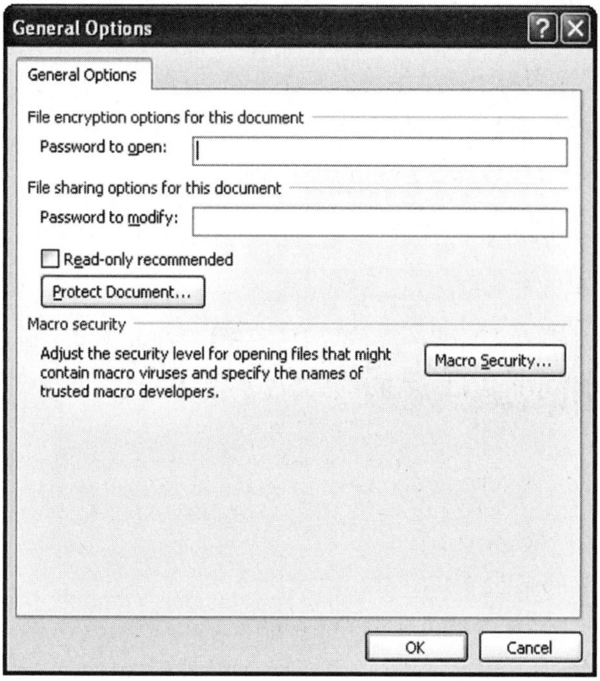

**Figure 1-2:** Microsoft Office 2007 offers encryption of individual files, file-sharing limitations, and read-only recommendations.

6. **Type a password in the Password to Modify text box.**

   This allows viewers to read a document but requires a password before they can save changes. This feature doesn't use encryption; it helps you control the pool of reviewers who can change a file.

7. **Select the Read-Only Recommended check box.**

   This restricts viewers so they can only read a document, not save it with changes. When the reviewers open the file, they're asked if they want to open the file as read-only. The huge loophole to this method is this: A viewer can open a file and use the Save As function to copy the file under a different name for modification.

## Changing a file's password

To change a previously assigned password, follow these steps:

1. **Open the Office program.**

2. **Open the file using the password.**

3. **Click the Microsoft Office Button.**

   The button's in the upper-left corner of the screen.

4. **Click Save As.**

   The Save As dialog box opens.

5. **Click Tools ⇨ General Options.**

   Since you signed in with the password, it appears on the screen.

6. **Select the existing password.**

7. **Type a new password.**

8. **Click OK.**

   You're prompted for the password again.

9. **Retype the new password.**

10. **Click OK.**

11. **Click Save.**

    If prompted, click Yes to replace the existing file.

## Removing a file's password

To remove a password from an Office file and allow free access to it, follow along:

*1.* **Open the file using the assigned password.**

*2.* **Click the Microsoft Office Button.**

It's in the upper-left corner of the screen.

*3.* **Click Save As.**

*4.* **Click Tools ⇨ General Options.**

Since you signed in using the password, you can see the password on the screen.

*5.* **Select the password.**

*6.* **Press Delete.**

*7.* **Click OK ⇨ Save.**

If prompted, click Yes to replace the existing file.

# Encrypting the Disk

For a deeper shade of security — in most situations and against most evildoers — the solution may lie in whole disk encryption. Again, a caveat: the National Security Agency (the domestic spies), the Central Intelligence Agency (our crack international somewhat-secret agents), and the staffs of dozens of other government entities, as well as private snoops, can break just about any code they put their collective minds and banks of computers to.

But if you're talking about whether your average street thief can steal your laptop and then break encryption . . . that's rather unlikely. The same loophole exists here as with many other systems: A casual thief is more liable to try to erase or remove the disk and replace it before reselling it.

The idea of whole-disk encryption is that the process is independent of the operating system; it blocks access to Windows, makes all files on the drive unreadable, or both. Among sources of this technology are PGP Whole Disk Encryption and TrueCrypt. And the hard disk maker Seagate is leading the way from the hardware side with its Momentus drives that include built-in encryption chips.

## Microsoft's built-in encryption utilities

The Encrypting File System (EFS) permits users to encrypt files so that only a person who properly logged onto an account can access them. Users with the following platforms can use EFS:

+ Windows XP Professional
+ Windows XP Media Center
+ Windows Vista Business
+ Windows Vista Ultimate

Its primary advantage may also be its disadvantage: No additional password is needed beyond the one required to log onto an account. Once someone is through that door, there's no further protection.

To use EFS, follow this brief set of instructions:

*1.* **Right-click the file or folder you want to protect.**

*2.* **Select Properties.**

*3.* **Click the Advanced button.**

*4.* **Click the Encrypt Contents to Secure Data check box.**

When you initially encrypt a folder, the system may require some time to create a new folder and encrypt its contents; once the folder is marked encrypted, any file saved or copied to it later is automatically encrypted as it's recorded, with little impact on performance.

The downsides of EFS:

+ If you're logged into your machine when it's stolen or lost, the door is wide open (at least until someone turns it off or it runs out of battery power).

+ You may lose file access if Windows itself suffers corruption and must be reinstalled or substantially repaired.

+ Hacking tools to get past EFS barriers are widely available.

Microsoft added a stronger and thus far more secure version of encryption as part of Windows Vista in its Ultimate edition. Bitlocker prevents Windows from booting without the proper password (before login), protecting both the operating system and its files. However, it is subject to the first two shortcomings of EFS outlined before: Once the door is open, all is revealed, and a corruption of Windows itself could make everything on the disk unreadable.

For more information on EFS or Bitlocker, consult the Microsoft web site at www.microsoft.com.

## Software-based encryption programs

Software encryption is the next level up in security planning from scrambling the data on the disk and requiring a password before they can be read. However, like a password that exists in the BIOS, software encryption uses a decoding key located somewhere on the drive, and a determined (or professional) crook should eventually figure out how to break the code.

No matter what form of software-based encryption you use, keep your Windows operating system up-to-date and regularly consult your encryption software maker's web site for updates. Hackers will always try to prove their worth by breaking the supposedly unbreakable; if and when that happens, Microsoft and other makers usually come up with a fix and the game continues.

Another shortcoming of software-based encryption programs is that they function as an element of Windows or other operating systems. And in most cases, for technical reasons they can't encrypt the operating system files themselves; they only encrypt data and settings. However, the loophole here is that most applications store temporary and backup versions of files, as well as fragments of files, in various places on the disk. These may exist outside of the encrypted "bubble" around your critical files.

Examples of industry-standard technology follow:

✦ **PGP Whole Disk Encryption** offers a platform that lets you use that company's file and e-mail encryption products, as well as those offered by other companies, spread across a managed network. See www.pgp.com/products/wholediskencryption for more details.

✦ **TrueCrypt** is an open-source (read: free) disk encryption program. The software creates a virtual encrypted disk within a file and mounts it as a real disk. You can use it to encrypt an entire hard-disk partition or a storage device such as USB flash drive. The process is automatic and conducted in real time (as data is recorded and without significant reduction in speed). In theory, a TrueCrypt volume can't be identified or distinguished from random data.

It's impossible to beat the price on TrueCrypt, since it's offered for free. However, as an open-source product (meaning that anyone can read and modify its coding), there's always the possibility that someone might succeed in cracking its system or corrupting it. Use the Internet and user groups to check on the current status of the product. Consult www.truecrypt.org for more information.

✦ **Cryptainer** is available in a free basic version called Cryptainer LE and a more fully featured commercial edition. Cryptainer Mobile edition encrypts any data on any media including USB flash drives, CD or DVD discs, and external drives. See Figure 1-3. The LE version creates multiple 25MB encrypted containers on your hard disk that you can load and unload as needed. You can view, modify, and hide all types of files with a single password. The product works with all current versions of Windows (including 95 and 98 as well as XP and Vista). Consult www. cypherix.com/cryptainerle for more information about the free version.

## Hardware-based disk encryption

Most laptops include in their setup BIOS a means to set a password before you can access an installed hard drive; however, a number of hacker tools allow someone to determine this password and once someone has bypassed it, she can read everything on the drive.

### Full disk encryption

Seagate's Full Disk Encryption (FDE) system (introduced to consumers with its Momentus line of hard disks) and similar concepts are different in that the *encryption key* (the code that decrypts the data) isn't stored on the drive or in the BIOS. No amount of physical attack on the machine by a hacker is going to locate a decryption key because it isn't on the laptop.

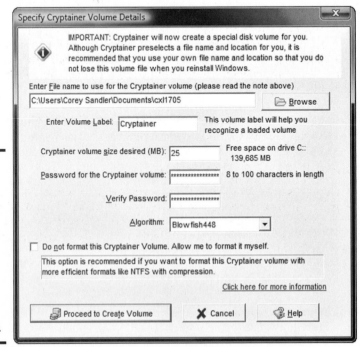

**Figure 1-3:**
The Cryptainer control window allows creation of hidden volumes with complex passwords.

Under FDE, you've no need to initialize a new disk or to encrypt the full contents of a large drive when the software is added to an existing disk. All data is encrypted as it records, and according to Seagate the process occurs at full interface speed. In other words, no overhead is involved.

Under software encryption schemes, if the key to the encryption software is compromised, you must change it. This usually involves completely decrypting and re-encrypting the entire drive. Since the key to an FDE drive is locked into the hardware, it can't be corrupted.

### Removable flash memory key

Another option is to use a removable flash memory key that holds the decoding key for an encrypted disk. One such product is the PCKey from Kensington. The system combines an access key that plugs into the laptop's USB port and holds the complex decoding key; you must enter a password into an onscreen form. Both are required before any user is permitted to use the machine and any network to which it connects.

All data on the hard drive is encrypted by the PCKey system; when an application requests it, the encoded data passes through the PCKey filter and is decrypted for storage in the computer's system memory for the application's use. It's re-encrypted when written back to the hard drive.

The encryption algorithm for PCKey is quite strong and difficult to break; the loophole with this system appears if the laptop is up and running with the key in place and the password entered. In that situation, a thief could access all the data on the machine until turning it off. The solution: Remove the key and take it with you any time you walk away from your laptop.

If you forget your password or lose the key, contact Kensington and answer a set of questions to obtain a replacement code.

## Adding the Sys Key utility

You can add yet another layer of Microsoft-brand protection to your passwords by adding the Sys Key utility to your Windows XP or Windows Vista laptop. Sys Key encrypts copies of user passwords stored on your hard drive and adds a more complex encryption scheme to basic passwords. See Figure 1-4.

**Figure 1-4:**
The Sys Key
utility of
Windows XP
or Windows
Vista adds
extra layers
of security
to encrypted
files and
settings.

To Configure Windows System Key Protection, do the following:

*1.* **Click Start ⇨ Run.**

Run is a way to issue a command directly from a program that exists outside the operating system.

*2.* **Type** syskey **in the Run text box.**

*3.* **Press Enter.**

*4.* **Select the Encryption Enabled check box.**

The check box is in the Securing the Windows Account Database section. Enabling this option encrypts the password database and is the recommended setting.

*5.* **Click Update.**

*6.* **Click Password Startup.**

This requires that a strong password start Windows.

*7.* **Enter a complex password.**

The password should include a combination of upper- and lowercase letters, numbers, and symbols; the code should be at least 12 characters long, with a maximum of 128 characters.

# *Keeping Panic in Check (list)*

What to do if, despite all your best efforts, your laptop really goes missing or your software becomes corrupted? Don't spend too much time cursing, screaming, or crying; as good as it might feel, that won't help, and time is a-wasting.

Follow these steps:

✦ **Call the boss.** If the machine or software is owned by or related to a business, government agency, or any other organization, immediately notify your employer or legal department. They should have a plan to deal with the loss of confidential or other important information.

✦ **List your data.** Make notes about any data files you know are on your machine's hard disk. Don't forget:

- Files you may have deleted but are still in the recycle bin

- Backup copies of earlier editions of your documents (Many applications, such as word processors, make these copies)

- The contents of your e-mail folder

✦ **Get the cops.** Contact the local police or other law enforcement agency where the laptop was stolen or lost. File a complete report as soon as possible. Include a description of the brand and model as well as its serial number and other information.

✦ **Jog your memory.** Get your most recent set of backup files for the machine. (You've been making backups on a regular basis, right?) Use a borrowed or rented machine — if you're sure that machine is secure — and refresh your memory about any confidential data that may have been on your laptop's hard drive.

✦ **Call all accounts.** Contact your bank, credit card companies, and any other institution with which you have financial or personal accounts. They may put a notation on your account to be on the watch for fraud; they may close existing accounts; or they may disable your current user ID and password and ask that you create new ones.

✦ **Write to your dear diary.** Maintain a journal with model numbers, serial numbers, and an inventory of components and add-ons that you travel with. I have one copy of this list in my wallet and another copy with important papers in my office. Don't bother to keep the list in the laptop's carrying case; that probably won't help at all.

✦ **Admit to the admin.** If you use your laptop with any networks that use password protection, notify the administrator; you may have to change user IDs and passwords. If you run your own wireless network in your home or office, make the changes yourself.

## Have you taken out the recycling?

One way to slightly reduce the risk of damage caused by a lost laptop: Get in the habit of clearing out the Recycle Bin each time you shut down the machine. That setting is available in the operating system. You can also use an IMAP mail server instead of a POP3 mail server so your e-mails aren't stored locally on your laptop (but are instead kept on a central server). And you can also have applications like word processors not automatically create backups of files in progress. Each of these policies has disadvantages, but they're the safest way to treat data stored in a moveable (and losable) laptop.

✦ **Be fickle. Again.** Change any user ID and passwords for e-mail and other applications that are automatically filled in by Windows or a built-in utility on your laptop; if you manually enter user IDs and passwords you can decide for yourself whether or not to make changes.

✦ **Stake your claim.** Notify your insurance company (or the administrator of your company or organization's insurance) to file a claim for the loss of the laptop. Some policies include coverage for software application loss; most policies, though, don't cover data loss.

# Chapter 2: Guarding Against Intruders

## In This Chapter

✔ **Locking the doors against electronic burglars**

✔ **Setting up and using a firewall**

✔ **Going with antivirus, antispam, and antispyware**

✔ **Getting a security suite**

✔ **Cleaning up after yourself**

*H*ere at the Department of Laptop Security, we're very concerned that all road warriors understand and follow all our rules, regulations, suggestions, pleas, wishes, and hopes regarding one very important little detail: keeping the front and back doors closed and locked.

That's really what it comes down to. Although it seems so silly to some people, the fact is that an entire subspecies of humans devotes its every waking hour to (electronically) turning the door knobs and rattling the screen doors of laptop and desktop computers all over the world. Some do it for the sport, the computer equivalent of graffiti artists who get their jollies by defacing other people's property. Some of them are in it for the money, looking to steal your bank account information and whatever other personal data you may have stored within your machine.

In the previous chapter I discuss ways to hold onto your machine and protect the contents of your hard drive in case the laptop is stolen or lost at sea (or from a car, or a plane, or a train, or otherwise misplaced). In this chapter, you explore ways to keep people from breaking into your machine from afar.

## Breaking and Entry, Laptop-Style

Let me get one thing out of the way right at the start: If you bought a new laptop from a major manufacturer and ran it, unaltered, right out of the box, without ever connecting to the Internet, you'd have a very good — but not perfect — chance of never having to worry about computer viruses. And you'd have no reason to fear spam, malware, adware, spyware, or phishing. (I define each of these terms in a moment.)

# Whoops

Back in the early days of personal computing... and the early days of computer viruses ... I received a new version of a personal finance program from a major software vendor, sent to me for review in *PC Magazine,* where I was executive editor. I installed the program on a machine and all of a sudden the machine began behaving strangely. I assumed it was a flaw with the new program itself until I rebooted the machine and an early antivirus program flashed a warning on my screen: My PC was infected. To make a long, sad story short: The financial software company had hired a service bureau to duplicate its product onto floppy disks (the medium of the time) and unbeknownst to all, their computers were infected. Today that's pretty unlikely to reoccur... but not impossible.

In theory, a brand-new laptop from the factory comes equipped with Windows or another operating system and a basic set of applications that have been verified, scanned, checked, and otherwise given a close look-see by the manufacturer. It's highly unlikely that the machine will arrive infected.

As long as you use your machine in its unaltered state and completely avoid connecting to another computer, the Internet, or e-mail, your laptop is like the boy in the bubble: safe from infection . . . but also unable to fully experience life.

Table 2-1 reveals the ways a virgin machine can become sullied by disease and distress. I ranked threats in relative order of likelihood from very rare to very common. I awarded one star to the least likely culprits and as many as five to the biggest threats.

| Table 2-1 | Threats to a New Machine |
|---|---|
| *Your Action* | *How Likely It Is to Happen** |
| Through the installation of an infected program supplied on a CD, DVD, or other media. As noted (see sidebar), this is rather unlikely; software makers are under orders from their lawyers and marketing departments to double- and triple-check for rogue code. | ★ |
| A virus or other form of malware on a bootable disk installed in a floppy disk drive or other device. Relatively few current laptops have a floppy disk drive, and your system BIOS has to be set to boot from the drive to load the nasty code. | ★ |

| Your Action | How Likely It Is to Happen* |
|---|---|
| Accepting a bootleg copy of a program or a shareware utility given you on a floppy disk, flash memory key, CD, or DVD. | ★★ |
| Installing onto your machine a data file that includes macros (like those available in word processors and spreadsheets) that include malware. | ★★★ |
| By connecting to the Internet by a wired or wireless connection and downloading drivers, utilities, icons, and programs from sources you don't know and trust. | ★★★ |
| Downloading any active content (programs, utilities, animated icons, music, and more) through an instant messenger (IM) program. | ★★★ |
| Accepting an offer from a pop-up screen on the Internet that offers a free program or utility that you didn't request. | ★★★★ |
| Opening and running an attachment on an e-mail that you didn't request or that comes from an unknown source. | ★★★★ |
| Clicking a link in an unsolicited e-mail. | ★★★★ |
| Opening your folders and files to others on a local area network or on a public network (like you might find at an Internet café). | ★★★★ |
| Not installing and enabling a capable firewall utility (or using the one built into current versions of Windows) and going online or onto a network. | ★★★★ |
| Though it isn't a *cause* of infection, I reserve a special set of stars for anyone who operates a laptop without a capable and fully updated antivirus program in place. If you had a proper antivirus in place, chances are very good that it would prevent all the preceding infections. | ★★★★★ |

*One star is the least likely to happen; five stars means it's one of the biggest threats.

# Being Neighborly with a Firewall

Good fences, as Robert Frost observed, make good neighbors. In the case of computers, good fences help you distinguish between good neighbors and nasty intruders.

The Internet is a fast-moving stream of billions of snippets of information called *packets*. The situation is made better (or much worse, depending on how you look at it) by bringing high-speed broadband connections to homes and offices on cable, DSL, and fiber-optic systems. In addition to the danger posed by the huge volume of data that moves on a broadband circuit, there's also the fact that these connections are always on: Your machine is hooked up to the Internet all the time. A connected PC sticks an electronic toe into the stream looking for packets addressed to your address. And when you click an Internet link or send an e-mail, your machine is creating a packet with your return address.

Hackers create viruses and other malware that fly around on the Internet, jiggling the doors of tens of millions of PCs until they find one they can open. The odds of breaking in are low, but even a tiny percentage of success can make these miserable louts very happy.

One of your laptop's most important security program components is the enabling and use of a good *firewall*.

The original term comes out of construction and automobile manufacturing: a solid physical barrier intended to stop the spread of a fire. In the world of computing, a firewall is a piece of hardware or software that stands guard between your laptop and the outside world. Its role is to inspect all network traffic that passes through it and decide whether to

✦ Block the data

✦ Allow it through based on a set of rules

✦ Halt data and display a message asking you to decide whether to proceed

A firewall erects a defensive ring for your computer. It stands physically or logically at the point where data comes into an individual machine or an entire network; its primary purpose is to prevent unauthorized access to your machine. It can't, however, protect against an assault that doesn't *go* through the firewall. For example, if you load software from a CD or DVD, you're inside the hardware fence.

Several kinds of firewalls exist:

✦ **Application gateway firewall** (also known as a *proxy*), are the most common type of device. You can have the firewall check packets against a particular list of addresses or limit the actions of particular applications. For example, the proxy could block downloads or prevent a packet from initiating a file deletion or change.

✦ **Packet filters** allow entrance only to packets from specified addresses.

✦ **Circuit-level firewalls** only permit communication with specific computers and Internet service providers.

✦ **Stateful inspection firewalls** are the newest and most advanced design. These devices actually read the contents of packets and block those that are determined to be harmful or an unauthorized threat to privacy.

Why do you need both a firewall and an antivirus program? If you want to think in law enforcement terms, the firewall keeps any potential evildoers away from a place where they might try to commit a crime. An antivirus system stops a criminal act by someone who's gotten past the wall with a weapon.

## Hardware firewalls

Hardware firewalls are very effective because they literally are separated from the computer or network they protect. The incoming signals from a broadband modem connected to the Internet or from a local area network have to be approved by the firewall "appliance" before they get to a computer. You find hardware firewalls in many large companies and organizations that can afford the cost of the device (from several hundred to several thousand dollars for a basic unit, rising from there based on the amount of traffic and number of machines protected) as well as the cost in payroll for a trained professional to manage the network.

One intermediate step is to use a wired router that includes a basic firewall. These systems, though not quite as full-featured as a dedicated hardware firewall, add another fence where a network of computers link to each other and to a broadband modem.

Router firewalls only provide protection from computers on the Internet, not from computers on the other side of the router: your local network. If a machine on the network becomes infected, it can easily spread a *worm* (a self-replicating piece of unwanted code that sends copies of itself to as many places as it can before it's squashed) to other machines on the network. For that reason, you should also enable a software firewall on each machine.

## Software firewalls

As a laptop user, a hardware firewall may protect you when you connect your portable computer (either by wire to an office network or wirelessly to a WiFi system). But most of the time you won't have the hardware between you and the wild, wild Internet; instead you'll use a piece of software intended to stand between your computer's essential files and the outside world.

*Software firewalls* (also called *personal firewalls*) can

✦ Be written as utilities within the operating system

✦ Be a package that sits in front of or behind the operating system to protect the data on the machine

✦ Block incoming traffic based on a set of rules and exceptions you establish

✦ Detect and alert you to unusual outbound traffic, which can indicate that your laptop has become infected by spyware

To allow a particular program to send information back and forth through the firewall (also called *unblocking a program*), tell the utility to establish an exception. You can also allow a program through the firewall by opening one or more ports.

## Explaining how firewalls work

The best firewalls use a combination of techniques to protect your computer in hopes that one or more of them are capable enough to find something worth blocking (or at least worth notifying you about). Here are some of the ways firewalls check data packets:

✦ **Packet filter.** A basic set of rules that specifies which Web addresses are permitted to communicate with a network, or which types of applications are allowed to send data.

✦ **Stateful inspection.** A more advanced form of filtering in which the firewall attempts to determine if you requested incoming packets; traffic that comes to the door without a good reason to be there is considered suspect.

✦ **Network Address Translation (NAT).** This allows a router or hardware firewall to show just a single IP address, preventing the outside world from knowing about any and all computers connected on the protected side of the network. NAT is included in nearly all current routers as a basic protection; don't buy a router that doesn't provide it.

Firewalls can't block viruses attached to e-mail messages because firewalls don't examine message content; that's why you need an antivirus program. Similarly, a firewall can't tell that an e-mail is an attempt at phishing, unless the message comes from an IP you identified as one you want to block. (Phishing is explained in this chapter's "Field guide to computer diseases" section.)

## Windows Firewall

Current versions of Microsoft Windows (all editions of XP with Service Pack 2 installed, plus all editions of Vista) come with Windows Firewall. When you install or activate the operating system, the firewall is automatically turned on. See Figure 2-1.

If you install a third-party firewall like ones offered by McAfee or Symantec, they turn off the Windows firewall to prevent conflicts and confusion.

**Figure 2-1:**
The Windows Firewall on my Toshiba Satellite P205 laptop is in place and ready to help (but I turned it off because the machine runs a security suite from McAfee).

To use the Windows Firewall, the utility must be turned on. In this setting (the default when Windows is installed or activated) most programs are blocked from communicating through the firewall. To unblock a program, you can add it to the Exceptions list (on the Exceptions tab).

In addition, Microsoft recommends the following settings:

✦ All network connections (home or work, public place, or domain) should be protected.

✦ The firewall should be turned on for all network connections.

✦ The firewall should be set to block any inbound connection that doesn't match an exception.

To view or edit Windows Firewall settings, click the Windows Firewall icon in the Control Panel. There you can

✦ Turn the utility on or off

✦ Click Change Settings to make adjustments

✦ When you turn on Windows Firewall, click the Block all Incoming Connections check box (see Figure 2-2)

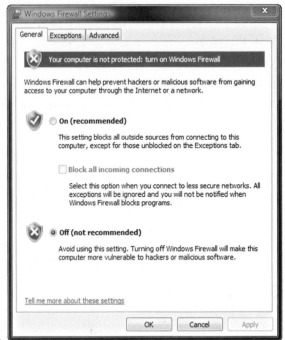

**Figure 2-2:**
When
Windows
Firewall is
turned on,
you can
block all
incoming
connections
by clicking
the check
box in the
settings box.

Block all Incoming Connections rebuffs all unsolicited attempts to connect to your computer; it provides a high level of security for your laptop — especially when you're using a public network at an Internet café or in a hotel or coffee shop.

When you enable this setting, the following is true:

✦ You aren't notified when Windows Firewall blocks programs.

✦ Programs on the Exceptions list are ignored.

✦ You can view most Web pages, send and receive e-mail, and send and receive instant messages.

### Unblocking a program in Windows Firewall

By its design, Windows Firewall and other software firewalls want to block all programs. The key is to teach the utility which ones you want to allow through.

To unblock a specific program, follow these steps:

*1.* **Open the firewall utility.**

*2.* **Click Allow a Program Through Windows Firewall.**

This option is in the left pane.

*3.* **Select the check box next to the program you want to allow.**

*4.* **Click OK.**

### Adding a port in Windows Firewall

If the program you want to unblock isn't on the Exceptions tab, you may need to open or add a port. (This is often required to enable multiplayer games conducted over the Internet, for example.)

A firewall exception is only open while needed. By contrast, an open port stays open until you close it; this could put your machine at risk. Close any ports for programs that aren't in constant use.

To add a port, follow along:

*1.* **Click the firewall icon in the Control Panel.**

The firewall program opens.

*2.* **Click Change Settings.**

*3.* **Choose the Exceptions tab.**

*4.* **Click Add Port.**

*5.* **In the Name text box, type a name.**

The name should help you remember the purpose of the open port.

*6.* **Type the port number in the Port Number text box.**

*7.* **Click TCP or UDP, depending on the protocol.**

Most programs communicate using TCP; if the setting doesn't work, try UDP.

## Enabling a third-party firewall

A number of capable software firewalls are available from companies whose name does not begin with *Micro* and end with *soft*. Some are integrated into a complete suite of utilities, and others offer advanced features.

Since Windows XP and Windows Vista come with a firewall as part of the operating system, you may receive a warning message from the Windows Security Center if

✦ You turn off the official Windows Firewall and enable no replacement

✦ It doesn't recognize the replacement you installed

✦ The third-party firewall doesn't report its status to Windows

To instruct Windows that all is well, do the following:

*1.* **Click Start ➪ Control Panel ➪ Security Center.**

You get a glance your firewall status, automatic updating, malware protection, and other security settings. See Figure 2-3.

*2.* **Click I Have a Firewall Solution That I'll Monitor Myself.**

Choose this only if Windows doesn't recognize your third-party firewall.

Security Center displays your firewall settings as Not Monitored, and you no longer receive notifications about your firewall.

*3.* **Track the status of your unsupported firewall.**

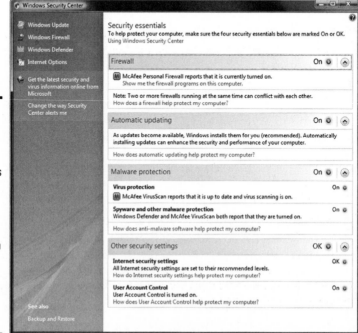

**Figure 2-3:**
The Windows Security Center gives you a quick report on various protective utilities from Microsoft, as well as most major third-party sources.

When Windows XP with Service Pack 2 and Windows Vista first came out, sometimes the operating system didn't recognize well-known third-party firewalls, including McAfee and Symantec. That's since been fixed. If Windows doesn't recognize your firewall, consult the support page for the maker of your security software for updates.

Many alternative personal firewall products are available as add-ons to Windows and other operating systems. The following are among the better-known products:

✦ CA Personal Firewall at http://shop.ca.com

✦ McAfee Personal Firewall Plus at http://us.mcafee.com

✦ ZoneAlarm at www.zonealarm.com

All are capable products, but in my opinion they offer only slight improvements over the built-in firewall included with Windows Vista and Windows XP with SP2.

I recommend you consider buying and using a full security suite that includes antivirus, antispam, and an enhanced firewall product.

# Getting Your Antivirus Vaccine

There's a reason many types of computer malware are called viruses: They follow many of the same models and methods as the nasties that cause disease in humans. Viruses can

✦ Spread

✦ Replicate themselves

✦ Mutate from one form to another

And just as with human diseases

✦ Sometimes there's a cure

✦ Sometimes you can only treat the symptoms

✦ Sometimes the only effective response is to try to block the infection in the first place

Antivirus software works in two basic ways; most programs include both methods in their arsenal. See Figure 2-4.

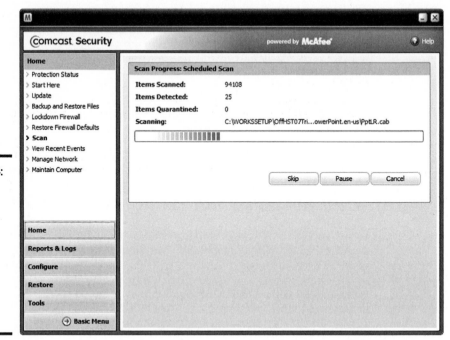

**Figure 2-4:**
Antivirus programs examine your machine when it boots as well as while it runs.

## Field guide to computer diseases

What exactly are viruses and all those other nasties? In the broadest of terms, they're all considered *malware* in that their purpose is to do evil (or at least annoying) things when they arrive in a computer.

You can visit the Symantec web site at www.symantec.com and click the ThreatCon button to see a regularly updated report on the latest threats, risks, and vulnerabilities that are circulating on the wild, wild Internet. See Figure 2-5.

✦ **Virus.** A piece of code, usually embedded within a program, utility, or other software, intended to make your computer do something without your permission. Some viruses are self-replicating, meaning that once they're on a machine they copy themselves and look for ways to spread to other computers. Some viruses are harmless pranks that display messages or change settings, while others are aimed at corrupting your software or erasing the data on your storage devices.

✦ **Worm.** A particular type of virus designed to get into a machine and then spread itself to other machines through network connections, the Internet, and e-mail.

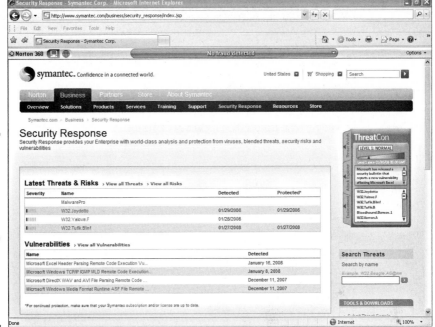

**Figure 2-5:**
The Internet
weather
report for
this
morning,
according to
Symantec,
shows an
ordinary
Level 1
threat.

✦ **Spyware.** Designed to insinuate itself onto your computer and then collect personal and financial information, which it sends to another person or group. They're not doing this out of mere curiosity; the purpose is to steal from you or your organization.

✦ **Phishing.** A nasty form of spyware that arrives as an e-mail or an unsolicited pop-up message on a web site. One example: You receive an e-mail with the logos and colors of a familiar bank or credit card company. For some reason they're asking for information they already have: Why would a credit card company ask you to confirm your credit card number, for example? The thieves behind these efforts are impersonating real organizations and hoping to trick you into revealing information.

Never respond to a request for financial or other personal information unless you're certain of the validity of the message; call your bank or credit card company or other organization using a telephone number you find on the card itself or on a legitimate bill; never reply to a suspicious e-mail or call any phone numbers on the message — they may well be phony, too.

✦ **Adware.** Code placed by businesses seeking to learn about your shopping and buying habits or to place ads on your Internet pages based on what they find out about you. Some adware is obvious, such as certain *cookies* left behind on your machine after you visit particular web sites to track your preferences; other adware is more insidious, sneaking onto your machine and into elements of the operating system or other software.

✦ **Spam.** Unsolicited e-mail advertising. You're one rare bird if your e-mail inbox doesn't fill up each day with ads for fake Rolexes, bogus handbags, and a full assortment of pharmaceuticals from "enhancement" products to happy pills and sleeping potions. If you get advertisement e-mails that you don't want, it's spam. The best solution: Use a spam filter that detects junk and either deletes it or puts it in a separate folder.

Don't reply to spam or ask to be taken off a mailing list; that only encourages them.

## Typing your antivirus

My doctor friend loves antibiotics; come in with a hangnail and he'll offer you the latest cure in a pill. My mother, who wanted me to be a doctor, recommends vitamins; she's got one for hangnails, too. And my wife, who plays doctor with me, believes that coffee (sometimes with Irish whiskey) will fix whatever ails you.

It's kind of the same way with antivirus programs. They're each trying to prevent or cure a disease, but each takes a different approach than the others. Although in the end I recommend using a program that includes a mix of every possible defense mechanism, it helps to understand the various approaches that are available.

### Dictionary-based antivirus searching

This mechanism examines files and programs for known virus code (called *signatures*). These programs consult a database collected by the antivirus maker and updated regularly.

Antivirus programs that use a dictionary examine the system from the moment the operating system is booted and continue to be on the lookout anytime you

✦ Upload or download a file

✦ Send or receive an e-mail

✦ Change the system files

In addition, the program can conduct scheduled or on-demand full system scans that examine every file in your computer.

Virus authors have tried to get past dictionary-based hunters by creating *polymorphic* code that changes form or disguises itself. They hope to spread their wares before the dictionary is updated.

### Heuristic analysis

This technology looks for suspicious or downright unacceptable behavior by any program or piece of code. They can catch many polymorphic viruses that aren't in a dictionary and new code that isn't yet listed. For example, a heuristic analyzer might spot a piece of code attempting to change an executable program; the antivirus program stops the effort permanently or asks you for advice.

On the downside, this type of antivirus program can flag some legitimate code as malware.

### Taking out the garbage

If an antivirus program finds some troublesome code, it can

✦ Delete the file

✦ Remove all traces of it from the machine

✦ Put the file into a quarantine folder, placing it out of reach and unable to spread

✦ Attempt a repair by removing just the virus code from an otherwise normal file

## Enjoying a Visit from Antispam and Antispyware

Spam and spyware can be either merely annoying or seriously upsetting and dangerous to your personal finances, credit score, and privacy. Alas, it's very difficult to completely avoid being targeted. You can take steps to reduce your profile or deal with assaults when they come.

Pop-up advertising on your computer, software that collects and relays your personal information or changes your computer configuration without your permission are forms of spyware. Spyware is, by design, made to be difficult to detect or remove; in general, you need to use a specialized antispyware program to dislodge this sort of unwanted code from your machine.

Microsoft has included Windows Defender as part of Windows Vista; Windows XP users can download a free version of the utility to add into their system. Search for the program at www.microsoft.com.

Other antispyware programs are sold by third-party companies or included as part of security suites.

The antispyware programs block attempts to install unwanted code on your machine, scan for spyware, and remove the programs.

## Winning at spy versus spyware

The best way to defend against spyware is to be very careful in the first place:

✦ Install a capable antispyware program and keep it current.

✦ Never click a link in an e-mail that comes from a source you don't know and trust. You shouldn't consider buying pharmaceuticals from some-one who contacts you with an unsolicited e-mail; you certainly shouldn't go to their site.

✦ If you must visit web sites left of the mainstream (pirated software ven-dors, pornography, or illegal offerings), don't download anything. Better yet, don't go there at all.

## Canning spam

Anytime you give anyone your e-mail address, you run the risk that it will be given or sold to someone else. In this day of electronic avarice and fraud, an e-mail is a product that has value to sellers of just about any product (as well as thieves of almost any sort).

Take these steps to deal with spam:

✦ Use a current e-mail client (including Windows Live Mail) that has built-in spam filters. The filters catch and segregate a large percentage of junk mail. These programs may also report spam so the central server can spot later assaults from the same sender.

✦ Don't respond to spam you receive, even if the sender offers an "unsub-scribe" option. If you respond, you're confirming that they reached a real address; they're just as likely to redouble their efforts or sell your address as they are to remove your address from their list.

✦ If you receive mail from a source that has a legitimate reason to contact you — a site where you previously made a purchase — you can request to be removed from their list. They already know you exist because they've conducted business with you.

✦ Disable HTML e-mail messages (or don't allow them to open with images). Most e-mail clients allow incoming messages created using HTML (coding that displays pictures and formatting on Web pages), but won't display the images. HTML messages can contain code that can confirm your identity or even redirect your system to display a new Web page, which could download spyware or viruses.

✦ Set up multiple e-mail addresses. I have several addresses that I use only when I'm pretty certain a transaction is going to attract spam. If the mailbox starts to fill up with junk, I just close that account. Some people call these *disposable e-mail addresses.*

## Security? Suite!

Many laptop users make use of two high-risk communication strategies:

✦ High-speed broadband connections when they're at home or in an office

✦ A mix of ad hoc WiFi networks in Internet cafés, hotels, and other locations while they're on the road.

This potentially dangerous combination calls for a belt-and-suspenders solution.

I recommend all laptop users install an integrated security suite that includes

✦ A firewall

✦ Antivirus

✦ Antispam

✦ Antiphishing

✦ Anti-everything-else-that-you-know-of-and-imagine-that-can-cause-you-electronic-grief

✦ System maintenance

Two of the best suppliers of this sort of comprehensive package are Symantec Corporation and McAfee Inc.

### everNorton

Peter Norton was one of the pioneers of the PC industry, launching his fame (and fortune) in the 1980s with the introduction of the Norton Utilities which permitted "unerasing" deleted files and a few other basic tasks that weren't yet part of the Microsoft operating system. He wrote a column for *PC Magazine* while I was executive editor of that august publication and later. a series of books for early techies. He sold his company to Symantec in 1990 but his name lives on in many of their products.

## Symantec and Norton products

Symantec has a full line of security and maintenance programs. Its flagship product is Norton Antivirus, which runs from your machine; it regularly contacts the company to download new signature files for its dictionary and updates for its antivirus engine.

Another product from Symantec is Norton 360, an all-in-one security and maintenance product that uses tools on your machine, as well as online at the company. It also includes a Web-based backup site for your most critical files. See Figure 2-6.

Key Norton 360 features include the following:

✦ **Antivirus and Antispyware Protection.** Protection against known and emerging threats at the deepest level within the operating system with integrated antivirus and antispyware scans.

✦ **Rootkit Remediation.** Heuristic protection against kernel mode rootkits that have dropped a driver onto the system.

✦ **Behavioral Malware Detection (SONAR).** Behavior-based malware detection that identifies new threats in real time based on application behavior.

**Figure 2-6:**
The Norton 360 PC Security screen shows the status of all of the components of the package, including the firewall and antivirus utilities.

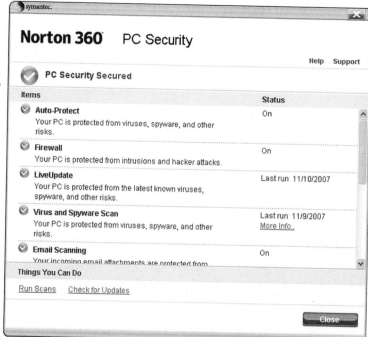

✦ **Smart Firewall.** Automatically configures itself to allow good applications and block spyware, worms, viruses, crimeware, and hackers from stealing sensitive information.

✦ **Intrusion Prevention.** Detects and blocks known and unknown intrusion threats (such as drive-by downloads) from getting onto a computer via system vulnerabilities. A single intrusion signature can protect against thousands of variants.

✦ **Vulnerability Assessment.** Automatic checks for security vulnerabilities including browser weaknesses, weak passwords, and web site redirection, providing a deeper level of protection against common exploits.

✦ **Network Detection.** Optimizes firewall protection using different security settings when connecting to various types of networks. Automatically blocks unknown computers from connecting to your computer while on wireless public networks.

✦ **Phishing Protection.** Identifies and blocks fraudulent web sites attempting to steal personal information. Utilizes black list and heuristic techniques to recognize known and unknown phishing sites. Dangerous sites are clearly marked.

✦ **Web Site Authentication.** Verifies authenticity of trusted brands that are commonly phished, such as financial services and e-commerce sites.

Among new directions taken by Norton 360 is *transaction security* that aims to help protect online shoppers from problems caused by hijacked or phony web sites and phishing expeditions. See Figure 2-7.

**Figure 2-7:**
You can still visit a site that Norton 360 determines is unsafe or unverifiable, but the program displays a message warning that your machine's safety might be compromised.

## McAfee Total Protection

Another capable and broad set of tools is offered by McAfee, Inc. A number of hardware makers and Internet service providers offer the full product or many of its components as part of their service. See Figure 2-8.

The most comprehensive of McAfee's offerings is Total Protection. Included in that package are integrated antivirus, antispyware, firewall, antispam, antiphishing, and backup technologies. In addition, some of the product's other features include:

+ **Do Not Disturb Mode.** Maybe you want to watch movies, listen to streaming audio, or play games. Whatever the case, you don't want the processor interrupted by security checks. This mode defers tasks, updates, alerts when your machine is in full-screen mode.

+ **Backup & Restore.** This utility saves copies of your most valuable files wherever you want, encrypting and compressing your files on a CD/DVD, or USB, external, or network drive.

+ **Image Analysis.** Part of optional family safeguard tools, this utility examines web sites and images for potentially offensive content to block or display a warning.

+ **SystemGuards.** A heuristic analyzer that watches your computer for specific behaviors that may signal virus, spyware, or hacker activity.

+ **X-Ray for Windows.** A utility that detects and kills rootkits and other malicious applications that hide from Windows and other antivirus programs.

+ **Network Manager.** This component monitors PCs across your network for security weaknesses, allowing you to fix security issues from one centralized network map.

+ **EasyNetwork.** A utility to provide automatic printer sharing and drag-and-drop file sharing across trusted computers on your home network.

+ **Shredder.** A tool that digitally "shreds" confidential files, effectively removing all traces of them from your computer.

## Windows Live OneCare

As part of its developing Live collection of tools and utilities, Microsoft has launched its own Web-based antivirus and security service. Consult http://onecare.live.com/ for information on a subscription.

Microsoft, like many other companies offering security services, offers a free PC safety scan that can check for and remove viruses and junk from your hard disk; it's not the same as full-time monitoring, but it may help in an emergency (or at least provide a quick assessment of your system's security).

**Figure 2-8:**
The McAfee
Security-
Center
screen for
a Toshiba
machine
reports
the state
of its com-
ponents.

My little laptop, used almost exclusively as an extra machine for word processing, e-mail, and Internet access when I'm on the road, has in excess of
100,000 files on its hard drive. The vast majority of those are elements of the
operating system and applications that run under it. Every time I turn on the
machine, a significant number of those files are opened, moved, changed, or
updated. And every time I upload a photo from my digital camera or visit a
web site, a big chunk of space on the hard drive is temporarily assigned to
storing a file.

The bottom line: The hard disk drive in your laptop isn't a stable and
unchangeable document, like a printed page in a book. It constantly changes
and is reorganized. And as you explore in Book III, your hard disk drive can
very quickly become a very messy place . . . and in the process end up slowing down your laptop.

# System Maintenance Suites

I suggest buying and installing a maintenance suite. The best bang for the
buck, and the greatest level of efficiency, probably comes with an all-in-one
product that combines maintenance tools with security features like those
discussed earlier in this chapter.

The best are listed here:

✦ Norton 360 from Symantec (a local and Web-based service)

✦ Norton SystemWorks from Symantec (a package that works from your machine)

✦ McAfee Security Center

See Figure 2-9.

We're all honest and upright citizens here, but that doesn't mean we shouldn't do everything we can to cover our tracks at all times. The fact is that your computer is constantly making little notes about web sites you've visited, files you've opened, and even the files you've changed.

Are you comfortable with the possibility that an outsider might be able to read all of that material? Do you want your boss, spouse, or anyone else to be able to reconstruct your day — no matter whether it's innocuously off-topic or more seriously inappropriate?

**Figure 2-9:**
A QuickClean session under way as part of the maintenance facilities of McAfee Security.

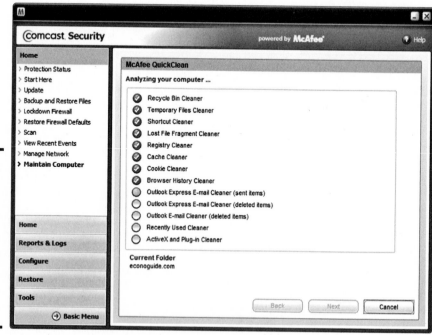

A word of caution to laptop users working in a business: Anything you do on company time using company equipment is subject to monitoring and oversight. You have no right of privacy when it comes to e-mail or web sites. Many heavy-duty laws come into play to make certain investigators can track any possible hint of illegality in the area of insider trading or disclosure of financial information. Don't assume that any of the advice in this chapter applies to you; consult with your supervisor about all applicable policies and laws that affect your job.

# Book X

# Troubleshooting Common Problems

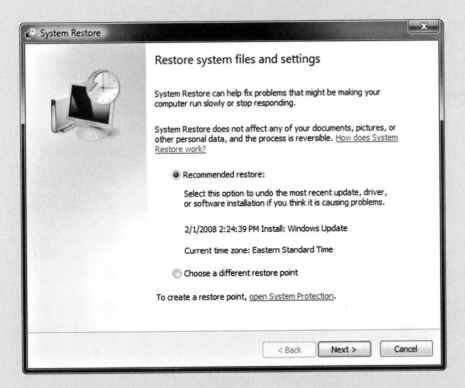

System Restore lets you choose from restore points on your drive.

# Contents at a Glance

# Chapter 1: Sweating the Hard (ware) Stuff

## In This Chapter

✔ Putting your laptop on the doctor's couch

✔ Mastering Device Manager

✔ Working with device drivers

✔ Running a diagnostics program on the hardware

*I*t was working just fine yesterday. The screen was bright and shiny, the hard disk purred like a happy kitten, and the WiFi was wide and fine. But now your laptop is doing an imitation of a black plastic box. Nothing works, and neither do you. Before you take drastic action (throwing a fit, throwing a screwdriver, or throwing it away) read this chapter and the next to see if a solution will bring your plastic box back to life.

You should ask one question first. Not, "What's the meaning of life?" The ultimate question is this: What's changed since the last time your laptop worked properly?

Before you do anything else, try shutting down your machine. Count to five and then turn it back on. If you're lucky, a simple reboot will get you past an occasional situation where an extremely uncommon combination of events results in a problem. If the problem comes back immediately, or comes back on a regular basis, proceed to look for a cure.

✦ Was your laptop struck by lightning?

✦ Did it tumble to the floor from the top of a 12-foot staircase?

✦ Was there a splashdown into a pool of water?

✦ Was it abducted by aliens and inspected with strange probes?

✦ Did your 6-year-old try to insert a peanut butter sandwich into the CD drive?

If Yes is the answer to one of these catastrophic questions, then you have a pretty good idea of where to look for a solution: What got fried, broken, soaked, or gummed up? A professional has to deal with many of these sorts of problems; some may not be fixable — although the data on the hard disk drive may be recoverable.

The first place to look: Did you recently add or change any components (memory, hard disk drive, CD/DVD drive) or plug or unplug any external devices into a slot, port, or other connector on the machine? Retrace your steps to make sure you did the job properly. Check that all cables are plugged in properly, and look for crimps, cuts, or chews in the wiring.

The basic point is this: Begin your quest by trying to going back to the past. In Chapter 2 of this book I discuss the details of System Restore, which automates time travel when it comes to the software side of the equation.

## Giving Your Laptop a Physical

Let's play doctor. A trio of complex tools helps with diagnosis: your eyes, hands, and the highly sophisticated computer between your ears. If your machine has stopped working properly after you changed the hardware, the obvious first step is to see if you made a mistake or if the component has failed.

1. **Prepare a clean, stable, and well-lighted examination table.**

2. **Put a clean piece of cardboard or cloth on a sturdy table and place your laptop on it.**

3. **Unplug the AC adapter from the laptop and set it aside.**

4. **Remove the rechargeable battery from the laptop.**

5. **Ground yourself.**

   Do this by touching a metal pipe or the center screw on the exterior of an electrical outlet.

6. **Examine the computer's top, bottom, and four sides.**

   Look for any obvious signs of damage. Is there a crack in the case? Is coffee oozing out of the USB port? Can you smell peanut butter in the CD drawer? If yes, go to Step 7.

7. **Get thee to a laptop repair shop.**

   If you have a no-questions-asked accidental damage warranty, you may be in luck. If not, get an estimate for the cost of the repair before giving the go-ahead; it might make more sense to buy a new machine.

### Memory modules

If you opened up the hatch on the bottom of the laptop to add or change a memory module, go back to the compartment.

✦ Make sure that the memory modules you added are the proper type for your machine.

✦ Did you install them correctly?

✦ Are the modules latched into place?

If the only change you have made is to add memory and the system refuses to boot after you tried to reinstall the chips:

*1.* **Remove all the new modules.**

*2.* **Restore the original block of memory.**

*3.* **Close the hatch.**

*4.* **Restart the computer.**

If the machine now works properly, consider two possibilities:

• You have the wrong type of memory module.

• The memory is defective.

*5.* **Consult with the memory seller for help.**

## Power problems

If you disconnected the rechargeable battery, or removed and then reattached the hard disk drive, make sure you properly reinstalled the battery. In most laptop designs, the battery clicks into place and then is secured with a latch.

✦ Is the battery correctly installed? Installing a battery upside down is almost impossible, but I've seen people try. And it's rare for a modern battery to short out suddenly while installed in a machine; they more commonly fade over time.

✦ Did your battery take a hit outside the machine? If the battery fell and was damaged while it was out of the machine, or if something metallic managed to short out the connections while it was out of the compartment, a good battery could go bad.

✦ Is something keeping the connectors covered? I've seen a piece of paper or a sticky label cover the connectors on the battery (or inside the battery compartment) preventing the flow of power.

✦ Did your machine work properly until the last time you unplugged the AC adapter? Make sure you properly reinstall the power cable in the three places where it detaches:

• Computer

• Adapter

• Wall outlet

✦ Does the outlet have power? One of the most common causes for laptop "failure" is plugging the AC adapter into an electrical outlet that's off; the outlet may be designed for use with a lamp controlled by a wall switch.

In Europe and many other parts of the world, electrical wall outlets may have a small on/off switch next to the socket. You can test any socket by plugging a lamp or radio into it.

## When an LCD won't display

Modern laptop displays are wonders of color, brightness, and resolution. (That means the pictures are pretty and the words are easy to read.) The machines are surprisingly durable, unless you manage to drop your laptop to the floor with its lid open, or if you back up your car and pass over the computer you left in the driveway.

However, an LCD can fail, and in most situations I don't recommend the average user attempt this repair. The parts are tiny and delicate and the working space inside a laptop would give an ant a cramp.

If your LCD suddenly stops working, take these steps:

*1.* **Reboot the machine.**

See if this was a momentary failure.

If you see the ordinary startup text on the screen (the name of your computer maker and some details about the model), go to the next step.

*2.* **Try to get to the BIOS setup screen.**

The text should tell you how. On many laptops you press one of the F keys or the Escape key during the bootup.

*3.* **Check the LCD settings.**

*4.* **Reset the BIOS to its default configuration.**

Find the option that instructs the system to do that and hope the problem is fixed. Electrical surges, certain software conflicts, and some viruses can cause unwanted changes to the BIOS screen.

*5.* **Go to the step that suits your circumstances:**

• Step 6 if your machine restarts and the screen works properly

• Step 7 if all you see is a black hole, a bright line, or distorted bands of color or gray

*6.* **Run a full antivirus scan.**

*7.* **Consider sending the machine to the repair shop.**

### External devices causing internal problems

Did you install a new external device like a USB hard drive or a keyboard? Here you cross over into a hybrid between hardware and software.

Although these new devices aren't *inside* the sealed box, anytime you add a new piece of hardware to a laptop, Windows looks for and enables a piece of software called a *device driver.* It may change the Windows Registry, a database of nearly every component of your machine.

## Devising a Solution with Device Manager

All the problems discussed previously in this chapter are ones that prevent you from using your laptop. Other types of problems occur once a machine is up and running:

+ A hardware component (like the pointing device, the sound system, or the WiFi transceiver) stops working.

+ External devices connected to a USB, FireWire, eSATA, ExpressCard, or PC Card stop doing their thing.

The first step here is to consult the Device Manager, a component of all versions of Windows. Here you find a list of all the hardware parts the computer has found in its self-checkup. And most importantly, the machine can tell you when it detects a conflict between devices or an outright failure. See Figure 1-1.

Device Manager can do the following:

+ Determine, at a glance, whether the hardware on your computer is working properly.

+ Expand the report for each device to learn details about problems found by the computer. Examine each listing for full details or scan the report for an exclamation point warning or a red X declaration of failure to launch.

If your laptop uses a dual core, quad-core, or (someday an octo-core or a google-core) processor, the Windows Device Manager and other system tools may detect what it thinks are 2, 4, 8, or a google CPUs within your machine. It's still just one microprocessor, but each core is treated as if it stands alone.

+ Change hardware configuration settings or change advanced settings and properties for devices.

+ Identify and learn the details of device drivers loaded for each system component.

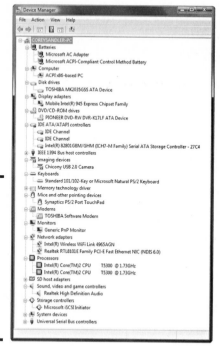

**Figure 1-1:**
The
Windows
Device
Manager
shows all
the laptop's
hardware
com-
ponents.

✦ Install updated device drivers or roll back to the previous version of a driver.

✦ Enable, disable, and uninstall devices.

✦ View devices based on their type, their computer connection, or the resources they use.

✦ Show hidden devices to determine information that might help during advanced troubleshooting.

Current versions of Windows, including XP and Vista, automatically allocate resource settings (including memory locations and *interrupts* — special signals sent by a device to the processor requesting its attention).

In some cases, a hardware manufacturer's support department may tell you to make specific assignments; note any changes you make so that they can be undone in case they cause new problems.

## Opening Device Manager

Device Manager is a standard Windows component. If you've chosen the Classic look for Windows Vista, follow along to get there:

*1.* **Click the Start button.**

*2.* **Go to the Control Panel.**

*3.* **Click a Device Manager icon.**

If you're using the new Vista style, do these steps:

*1.* **Click the Start button.**

*2.* **Go to the Control Panel.**

*3.* **Click Hardware and Sound ⇨ Device Manager.**

In Windows XP, do these steps:

*1.* **Click the Start button.**

*2.* **Go to the Control Panel.**

*3.* **Choose the System icon.**

The System Properties window appears.

*4.* **Choose the Hardware tab.**

*5.* **Click the Device Manager button.**

## Viewing the status of a device

A *status report* tells you

✦ Whether a device has drivers installed

✦ Where it is on the computer's internal bus

✦ Whether Windows considers it to be working properly

To display a report, do these short steps:

*1.* **Double-click a component listed in the Device Manager.**

The Properties screen appears.

*2.* **Select the General tab.**

See Figure 1-2.

If the operating system can't talk with the device, or finds it functioning improperly, a message appears in the Device status window. Follow these steps loosely:

*1.* **Note the problem code.**

*2.* **Try the suggested solution.**

The report may include a suggested solution.

**3. Enter the code into a search engine on the Internet.**

You may also be able to find a solution there.

**4. Call the support department for your laptop or component maker.**

**5. Click the Check for Solutions button if provided.**

Some devices have the button, which lets you submit a Windows Error Report to Microsoft.

## Sorting the display of devices

In the standard or default view presented by Device Manager, components are displayed in groups sorted by type. However, with a click you can re-sort them based on how they connect to the computer (such as the bus or port they use) or on the resources they use.

The value of these alternate views is that they may help diagnose a problem caused by one of the laptop's systems — its USB or ATA bus, for example — rather than failure of a device connected to it.

**Figure 1-2:**
The status report shows the manu-facturer, model number, location, and whether Windows can talk with it in the expected manner.

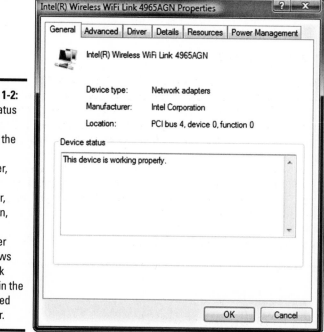

To change the sorting of device, do the following:

*1.* **Open the Device Manager.**

*2.* **Click View.**

*3.* **Select an option:**

- **Devices by Type.** Shows components grouped by type, such as batteries, DVD/CD-ROM drives, or imaging devices.

- **Devices by Connection.** Shows components grouped by how they connect to the computer. Laptops, because their motherboards are much more tightly integrated than those in many desktops, may use only a few types of connections.

- **Resources by Type.** Shows all allocated resources in the laptop and the devices using those resources. The report includes direct memory access (DMA) channels, input/output (I/O) ports, interrupt request (IRQ) levels, and memory addresses.

- **Resources by Connection.** Shows all allocated resources sorted by the type of connection.

- **View Hidden Devices.** *Hidden devices* include those for which a driver is installed but the component is currently unattached; this might include an external hard drive, for example.

# Driver: Follow That Laptop

*Drivers* are the link between hardware and the operating system. The driver translates commands from Windows into instructions that a specific piece of hardware can follow; going the other way, a piece of hardware can communicate with the driver which passes along instructions to Windows. Drivers allow hardware makers to add uncommon features to its equipment.

When a piece of hardware stops working without apparent physical damage, the problem is often due to a corrupted or missing device driver. Device Manager should inform you if the driver has a problem, but you may need an updated version, especially if

✦ You change to a new version of Windows

✦ Windows itself receives a major update from Microsoft while on your laptop

## Repairing or updating a driver

Windows Update, a component of the operating system's current versions, lets you

✦ Check for updates to specific devices

✦ Set the utility to automatically check for new versions of drivers

To update drivers using Windows Update, follow along:

*1.* **Choose Start ➪ Windows Update.**

*2.* **Click Check for Updates.**

This option is in the left pane. See Figure 1-3.

*3.* **If updates are available, click the driver you want to put in place.**

*4.* **Click Install.**

To set Windows to automatically check for recommended updates, follow these steps:

*1.* **Open Windows Update.**

*2.* **Click Change Settings from the options in the left pane.**

*3.* **Choose Install Updates Automatically.**

This is the recommended option. You can instruct the system to install new updates every day at a particular time, or select a specific day of the week. You might want to tell the system to do so every day during your lunch hour or at 4:30 on Friday afternoon, when you anticipate not being at your desk.

Sub-options here include:

• Downloading updates but waiting for the user to choose whether to install them.

• Checking for updates but allowing the user to choose whether to download and install them.

• Never check for updates. This is the officially not-recommended sub-option. This makes your machine more vulnerable to security problems, and you may also miss all kinds of nifty improvements to the system.

If you chose to update automatically, go to Step 4.

The recommended setting is Install Updates Automatically.

*4.* **Choose a time to install any downloaded updates.**

## Manually updating drivers

The automatic process works well for most users and most equipment combinations. However, some especially obscure pieces of hardware (or obscure uses for that hardware) may require you to seek out and install a device driver on your own; you might also be told to do so by a technical support department.

**Figure 1-3:**
When
Windows
Update
appears,
click View
Available
Updates to
see if
updated
drivers for
the devices
in your
machine are
available.
This is the
Windows
Vista
version of
the facility.

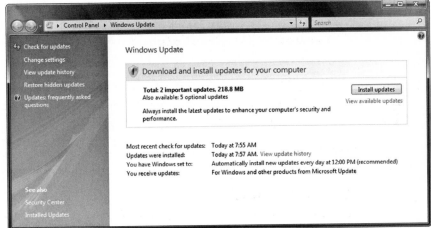

To manually install a driver, follow along:

*1.* **Open Device Manager.**

*2.* **Double-click the device name you want to update.**

*3.* **Click the Driver tab.**

*4.* **Click Update Driver.**

*5.* **Follow the instructions.**

See Figure 1-4.

Printers are treated differently than other devices internal or external to a laptop. To find out the status of printer drivers or to change printer settings, go to the Control Panel and click the Printers icon.

## Restoring a driver to a previous version

Oops. The new driver stopped a device from working. Windows offers a quick way to *roll back* a driver to its previous version:

*1.* **Open Device Manager.**

*2.* **Double-click the category that includes the device to be fixed.**

*3.* **Double-click the name of the device.**

4. **Click the Driver tab.**

5. **Click Roll Back Driver.**

This solution only works if a previous version of the driver is stored within Windows. If you haven't previously updated the driver, or if (for some reason) the earlier driver has been deleted, the Roll Back Driver button isn't available.

## Running a diagnostics program

Laptop: Heal thyself. If Dr. "Bones" McCoy could diagnose and cure most ailments with a wave of his sensor probe, why can't you do the same with laptops? Okay, okay. *Star Trek* was fiction, and we live in the real world or something like that. We haven't quite reached the point where humans or machines can be healed with the wave of a tricorder, but diagnostic tools have made tremendous advances. Physicians can peer into the body with CAT scans and MRIs. And from the very first days of computers, we've been able to examine the function of many technical components by running sophisticated diagnostic programs.

One big caveat here: You can't run a diagnostic program on a laptop that won't boot up and show at least minimal signs of life. The program needs to use the processor and the system's basic pathways to explore the hardware.

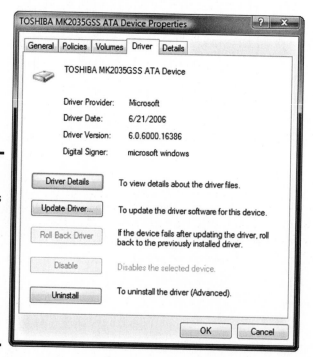

**Figure 1-4:**
The Driver tab includes a button to update the driver manually. You're asked for the new driver's location.

Many laptop manufacturers provide diagnostics programs as part of the basic software that comes with the machine. This helps both the user and the company, because it pinpoints problems with the hope that at least some can be fixed without sending the machine back to its maker.

For example, current models of Toshiba laptops come with a utility creatively named Toshiba PC Diagnostic Tool. The first part consists of a basic information window that displays hardware details, including the model, its serial number, the version of the operating system detected, and major hardware components. See Figure 1-5.

The second part of the utility delivers the tricorder. The Diagnostic Tool tests all of the components installed within the machine; its tests stop at the ports. You can choose to run all tests or concentrate on specific suspects. See Figure 1-6.

**Figure 1-5:**
The Toshiba diagnostics information screen offers a quick inventory of the essential parts of your machine.

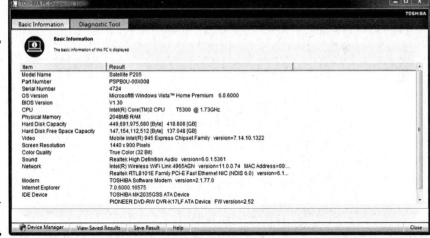

If your laptop doesn't come with a diagnostic program, or if you want to add software that includes more detailed or more rigorous testing, you can purchase utilities from other sources. Some programs let you *loop* a particular test over and over again, which is one way to find an intermittent failure. One product that does a good job is CheckIt diagnostics from Smith Micro Software, Inc. See Figure 1-7.

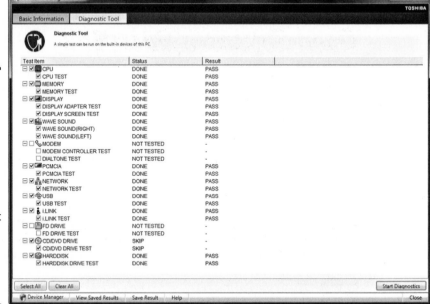

**Figure 1-6:**
Testing this
Toshiba
laptop
model, I
excluded
the dial-up
modem and
told the
software not
to bother
testing the
floppy disk
because it's
not there.

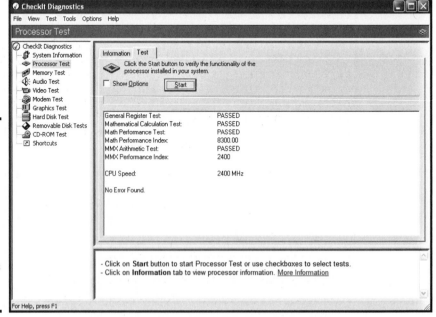

**Figure 1-7:**
Advanced
diagnostics
tests
include
detailed
exercises
and reports
on all of the
components
of your
computer.

# Chapter 2: Knowing When Good Software Goes Bad

## In This Chapter

✔ **Identifying possible problems**

✔ **Getting help from Remote Assistance**

✔ **Using Microsoft Office Diagnostics**

**D**on't go lookin' for trouble; trouble will find you. That's the sentiment of a modern blues song by Steve Goodman; I don't think he was referring to laptops, but maybe he was.

I do know that I once had a few extra minutes while sailing on a ship up at the top of the world, about a hundred miles from the North Pole, and I chose that moment to make an adjustment to Windows I'd never tried before: I changed the LCD screen resolution. Click . . . and there I was, 1,500 miles from the nearest computer technician with a laptop as frozen as the icebergs bobbing all around. Quite an image, eh? And quite true.

Now if I were just an ordinary computer user and not the well-traveled, highly experienced expert who gets to write books about laptops, I might have been up the North Pole without a laptop. But not me: I had in my laptop bag a backup copy of Windows along with a set of standard display drivers and some data recovery utilities. What can I say? I don't travel light. After a few minutes of tinkering, I restored my laptop to the condition it was in before I screwed it up. I tell you this story to bring the basic Boy Scout motto into the computer age: Be Prepared.

What's changed since the last time the laptop worked properly?

If your answer includes any of these, this chapter is for you:

+ I installed new software.

+ I installed new or updated device drivers.

+ I changed the operating system's configuration.

+ I deleted or changed one of the system files of Windows or a program component of an application on my machine.

# Bringing Big Problems via Tiny Changes

You know your laptop's not infallible, and you know that doesn't mean it has an antigravity force field that keeps it from falling off a table. Even the most carefully guarded and well-maintained machine occasionally loses its mind.

A major meltdown cause is corruption of stored settings or Windows system files or unintended changes to those same essential elements. How can this happen?

✦ An electrical fault. If your laptop runs out of power while it is in the process of saving a file or installing a program, or if it somehow receives a power surge or static shock, this can be the result.

✦ A virus or other form of unwanted nasty code.

✦ A poorly designed installation program — one that doesn't follow all of Microsoft's recommendations or doesn't play well with other applications.

✦ An incomplete installation, interrupted by a power failure or by an operating system freeze.

✦ A rare combination of incompatible software or hardware. Although software makers spend a great deal of time testing their products, they can't anticipate every possible permutation of code and device.

Never install a program on your laptop while it runs off its batteries. If the power runs out before the installation completes, the result could be damage to the system files.

## Taking your first tack: Undo changes

If you can identify the changes you made to a configuration setting in Windows, do this:

*1.* **Undo the changes.**

*2.* **Reboot the system.**

Is all well?

I always keep a notebook in front of me on my desk. Each morning I start by marking down the date and a list of to-dos. I also use the page to jot down any changes I make to configurations and settings. That way if something goes wrong, I know where to start my troubleshooting.

The same applies if you just installed software and you're experiencing new problems instead of new solutions: Use the software's uninstall function or follow these steps:

*1.* **Go to the Control Panel.**

*2.* **Click the appropriate icon:**

- Windows XP: Add or Remove Programs icon
- Vista: Programs and Features icon

The software is removed.

*3.* **Reboot.**

See Figure 2-1.

**Figure 2-1:**
You can uninstall or change the components of most Windows programs by using the Programs and Features utility of Windows Vista or the similar Add or Remove Programs utility of XP.

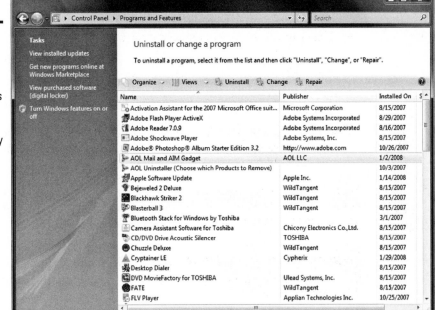

## *Taking your second tack: System Restore*

If manually changing settings or uninstalling a problematic new program doesn't provide the cure, you may have a suffered (or enabled) a sudden, serious problem with your Windows operating system. Microsoft offers a utility that — when it works — is like a silver bullet.

System Restore offers a chance to go back in time when your laptop last worked properly. No, this doesn't require a date with Doc Brown; it does require a Windows utility called System Restore and a bit of luck. System Restore takes snapshots (called *restore points*) of your system files and settings at regular intervals and anytime you manually instruct it to do so. If you've lived a clean life, helped little old ladies cross the street, and haven't done anything else to bollix up your system, it may allow you to undo damage. For further information on System Restore, see Book III, Chapter 4.

If undoing your changes doesn't work and you're thinking of heading over to System Restore, keep these points in mind:

+ **Go early.** System Restore is most likely to work if you go to it immediately after your machine shows problems. The more time that elapses, the more likely you'll make changes to your system; a restoration isn't as likely to fix them.

+ **Personal files are exceptions.** When it comes to personal files including e-mails, documents, photos, and music, there's both good news and bad news. The good news: If they're still on the disk, using System Restore won't help. The bad news: If they've been erased or corrupted, you have to try to repair or unerase them with another method.

Of course, if you're really a careful user, you made backup copies of your files on a different drive or on an external medium like a CD or DVD.

+ **Don't go too far.** Try restore points created just before problems started. If the first restore doesn't work, go further back in time.

Going further back than necessary could result in disabling updates and changes that you'd rather have available. See Figure 2-2.

**Figure 2-2:**
In System Restore, you can choose from a list of all automatically or manually created restore points on your drive.

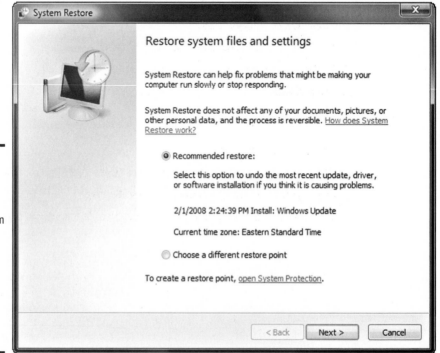

### Opening System Restore

A nearly identical utility exists in both Windows XP and Windows Vista, but the path to it has changed slightly.

To open System Restore in Windows XP, follow along:

*1.* **Click Start ⇨ All Programs.**

*2.* **Highlight the Accessories group.**

*3.* **Click System Restore.**

The standard System Restore configuration has it creating restore points every day, and also just before significant system events are begun; these include a program or device driver installation. You can also create a restore point manually by following Step 5.

*4.* **Click Create a Restore Point.**

Windows automatically adds the date and time, but you can include a short note: "Before changing mouse device driver," for example.

TIP

You can use System Restore only if you've previously turned it on. There's really no reason *not* to use this utility, and it's enabled as part of a standard Windows installation.

In Windows Vista, take this quick route:

*1.* **Click the Windows icon.**

The icon's at the lower-left corner of the screen.

*2.* **Type** System Restore **in the search box.**

*3.* **Press Enter.**

Or this one:

*1.* **Open the Control Panel.**

*2.* **Double-click the Backup and Restore icon.**

*3.* **Click Repair Windows Using System Restore.**

The option is in the panel on the left side of the window. See Figure 2-3.

# Working System Restore

System Restore requires the most current file system, NFTS. It won't protect FAT32 and other FAT disks because these older schemes don't allow shadow copies — the mechanism System Restore uses to hold information about changes to documents and system files.

System Restore won't run on hard disks smaller than 1GB in capacity and under Windows Vista requires that at least 300MB of space be left

available for its use. As the available space becomes populated with restore points, System Restore deletes older ones to make room for new ones.

When you load System Restore and ask it to make a repair, it automatically recommends the most recent restore point. You can also choose from a list of restore points.

**Figure 2-3:**
System Restore will fix many problems caused by unwanted or unexpected changes to the components or configuration of Windows.

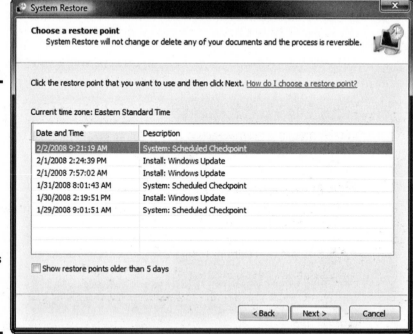

### Undoing a System Restore

System Restore even protects you when you use it to make a restoration; anytime you ask the utility to revert to an earlier restore point, it creates a *new* restore point before proceeding. This way you can undo the changes if they don't fix your problem.

To undo System Restore changes, follow along:

*1.* **Open System Restore.**

*2.* **Click Undo System Restore ⇨ Next.**

# Calling for Help with Remote Assistance

Windows XP and Windows Vista offer the ultimate in loss of control: If you enable Remote Assistance on your machine, another user — a technical support technician, your company's information technology department, or a knowledgeable friend — can connect to your laptop over a broadband Internet connection and see the same things you do . . . and make changes, including adjust settings or download and install drivers or utilities.

The Windows XP and Vista versions of Remote Assistance operate in a similar fashion, although the newer Vista utility has better capability and efficiency.

 Windows Remote Assistance creates an encrypted connection between the two computers over the Internet or a local area network used by both computers. Also, it's possible to control a Windows XP machine from a Windows Vista device, but not the other way around.

### Powering up on your platform

In Windows XP, Remote Assistance is of the Help and Support Center. To open it, follow these steps:

*1.* **Click Start ⇨ Help and Support.**

*2.* **Click Remote Assistance.**

This option appears under Ask for Assistance. See Figure 2-4.

In Vista, Remote Assistance stands alone. The fastest way to it is this:

*1.* **Click the Windows button.**

*2.* **Type** Remote Assistance **in the search window.**

*3.* **Press Enter.**

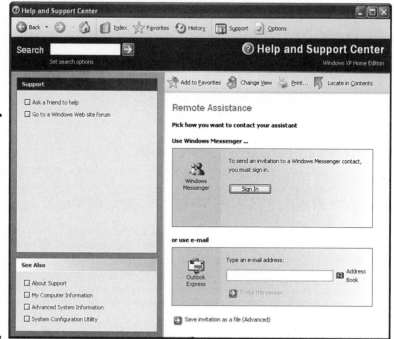

**Figure 2-4:**
Using
Remote
Assistance
you can
invite an
expert to
take control
of your
machine to
diagnose
problems
or make
changes.

The utility sends an invitation to another person to take control. For your protection you can, and should, place a time limit on the session *and* add a password that the other person must enter to gain access to your machine. You can communicate that password by telephone or in a separate e-mail from the invitation.

Remote Assistance requires a great deal of information be passed back and forth between the two machines, and the speed is just barely adequate on a broadband connection (cable modem or DSL). Although it can be accomplished over a telephone dial-up connection, I can't recommend it as a fun activity.

You're granting full access to your computer to someone else; that includes any passwords and personal information on your machine. For that reason, only allow remote access to someone you know or trust, and keep a close eye on what they're doing while in control of your machine. If the other user seems to be heading for an area that isn't appropriate for the repair, cancel the session instantly by pressing the Escape key.

## Sending a Remote Assistance invitation

To request assistance, follow these instructions:

1. **Close any open programs or documents that you don't want your helper to see.**

   Once the Remote Assistance session is under way, the other user can see your screen and open any file or issue any command as if he were sitting in front of your laptop.

2. **Open the Remote Assistance utility.**

3. **Click Invite a Friend to Connect to Your Computer with Remote Assistance.**

   The option's under Ask for Assistance. The Remote Assistance page appears.

4. **Click Invite Someone to Help You.**

   For identification purposes, Microsoft refers to the person requesting help as the *novice* and the person taking control as the *expert*.

5. **Choose which way you'd like to send the invitation:**

   - **E-mail**
   - **Windows Messenger**
   - **Save as Invitation**

   With the e-mail or Save as Invitation methods, you can set a password and a time limit.

6. **Wait for a response from the expert.**

   When the expert receives the invitation, the message asks for the password (if you've set one). The session begins after the invitee enters it. If the invitation is still open and the password is correct, you receive a notification that the expert wants to begin a remote session.

7. **Click the message that instructs both ends of the connection that you're ready to begin a remote-control session.**

When everyone has agreed to communicate, the Remote Assistance Novice chat dialog box opens on your computer, and the Remote Assistance Expert console opens on the expert's computer. At this point, the expert can see everything on your computer but can't take any actions.

The expert can request to take control of your laptop by clicking the Take Control button on the expert console. A message appears on your computer. It's up to you; if you don't give over control, the person at the other end of the line can see what's on your machine but you're still in control. See Figure 2-5.

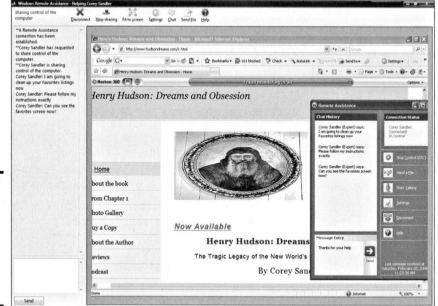

**Figure 2-5:**
A Remote
Assistance
session as
seen on the
screen of
the expert's
computer.

Once you grant an expert permission to work on your machine, don't use the pointing device, mouse, or keyboard. If both ends of the connection attempt to use your machine, the session can become confusing to monitor or could crash. The one exception: You can press Escape or click the Stop button onscreen to end the remote assistance.

# Playing Doctor with Microsoft Office Diagnostics

The current edition of Microsoft's productivity suite, Office 2007, includes its own set of diagnostic tests that may be able to pinpoint problems with one of the programs or a shared component of the suite. The utility also performs a basic check on the laptop's memory, hard disk, and other components. See Figure 2-6.

Do these steps to run the diagnostics:

*1.* **Open any Microsoft Office 2007 program.**

*2.* **Click the Office button.**

*3.* **Click Options for the running program.**

*4.* **Click Resources.**

**5.** **Click Diagnose ➪ Continue.**

The Diagnostics screen appears.

**6.** **Click Start Diagnostics.**

**Figure 2-6:**
The
Microsoft
Office
Diagnostics
checks for
problems
with your
laptop and
with suite
components
and certain
other
productivity
programs.

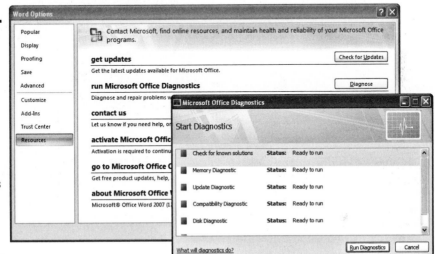

If you can't open Microsoft Office, you can launch the same diagnostics program from the Windows Start menu:

**1.** **Click Start.**

**2.** **Choose All Programs ➪ Microsoft Office ➪ Microsoft Office Diagnostics.**

Microsoft Office Diagnostics replaces similar but less-capable features in Microsoft Office 2003: Detect and Repair and Microsoft Office Application Recovery.

# Searching for Meaning in Software Error Codes

Way back in the day, computer error codes used to be

✦ Very common

✦ Totally meaningless to mere mortals

Today, most programs at least attempt to write words and sentences instead of hexadecimal code numbers.

**TIP**

However, in some situations Windows or an application running within it may present an error message consisting of numbers. Visit these web sites to search for the meaning of your laptop's travail:

✦ Windows Online Assistance at http://windowshelp.microsoft.com/Windows/en-US

✦ Microsoft Events and Errors Message Center at www.microsoft.com/technet/support/ee/ee_advanced.aspx

Another option for Windows Vista users is to search your computer's event logs for information:

*1.* **Click the Windows button.**

*2.* **Enter** Event Viewer **in the search box.**

*3.* **Press Enter.**

*4.* **Double-click Applications and Services Logs.**

This option's in the left pane,

*5.* **Locate the program that had an error.**

You may have to expand a group by clicking the down arrow.

*6.* **Review any error events for that program.**

*7.* **Double-click an event to view a description and links to more information.**

See Figure 2-7.

**Figure 2-7:**
The Event Viewer is an advanced tool for Windows Vista users that displays logs of significant software and hardware events.

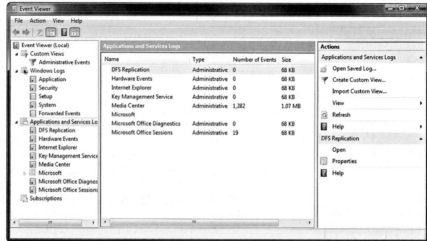

# Index

## Symbols and Numerics

802.11a WiFi specification, 529

802.11b WiFi specification, 529

802.11g WiFi specification, 529

802.11n WiFi specification, 529

8P8C modular connector, 477

* (asterisk) wildcard search character, 282–283

< (greater than) wildcard search character, 283

< (less than) wildcard search character, 283

? (question mark) wildcard search character, 282–283

[] (square brackets) wildcard search character, 283

## A

A9 search engine, 570

AC
  adapter components, 406–409
  outlet, 405
  power inverter, 424

acceleration of radio use, 525

accented characters, 295

accounts
  adding in Outlook Express, 593–594
  removing in Outlook Express, 594
  user, 114–115, 128

ACCRINT function, 303

adding
  accounts in Outlook Express, 593–594
  capture software, 380–381
  clip art in PowerPoint, 321–322
  desktop icons, 162
  desktop shortcuts, 163
  email signatures, 615–618
  external battery, 423
  external WiFi adapters, 532
  gadgets, 118–119, 181
  Microsoft backup to Windows XP Home Edition, 246–247
  newsgroups in Outlook Express, 603
  newsgroups in Windows Live Mail, 603–604
  programs to Quick Launch area, 172
  RSS feeds in Windows Live Mail, 614–615
  second internal battery, 422–423
  shortcuts to desktop, 163
  signatures in Windows Live Mail, 615–618
  SmartArt graphics in PowerPoint, 323–324
  text in PowerPoint, 319–320
  toolbars to taskbar, 168
  USB ports/hubs, 460–461
  webcams, 392–393
  WiFi to laptop, 531–532

address
  disposable email, 675
  dynamic IP, 536
  email, 590
  static IP, 536

address bar shortcut, 582

Address Book
  defined, 132
  exporting, 132–133
  overview, 354
  recording addresses from emails, 354–355

Adobe Photoshop, 197

Adobe Updater, 212–213

adware, 671–672

airline travel
  airplane power sources, 406, 423
  concerning laptops, 19

Alienware, 399–401

all-purpose ports, 378

Alt key, 23

Altavista search engine, 570

AMD
  CPU design, 42–44
  models, 44
  Turion 64 X2 processor, 399

amp hours (AH), 418

analog
  overview, 526
  telephone adapter (ATA), 36, 627

antivirus program
  dictionary-based, 672–673
  heuristic analysis, 673
  repair capabilities, 673
  screen, 670

AOL
  dial-up modem, 483
  Instant Messenger, 623

Apple widgets, 178

Application gateway firewall, 662

applications, maintaining, 212–213

## *X*

## BUSINESS, CAREERS & PERSONAL FINANCE

0-7645-9847-3

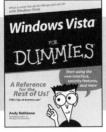

0-7645-2431-3

**Also available:**
- Business Plans Kit For Dummies
  0-7645-9794-9
- Economics For Dummies
  0-7645-5726-2
- Grant Writing For Dummies
  0-7645-8416-2
- Home Buying For Dummies
  0-7645-5331-3
- Managing For Dummies
  0-7645-1771-6
- Marketing For Dummies
  0-7645-5600-2

- Personal Finance For Dummies
  0-7645-2590-5*
- Resumes For Dummies
  0-7645-5471-9
- Selling For Dummies
  0-7645-5363-1
- Six Sigma For Dummies
  0-7645-6798-5
- Small Business Kit For Dummies
  0-7645-5984-2
- Starting an eBay Business For Dummies
  0-7645-6924-4
- Your Dream Career For Dummies
  0-7645-9795-7

## HOME & BUSINESS COMPUTER BASICS

0-470-05432-8

0-471-75421-8

**Also available:**
- Cleaning Windows Vista For Dummies
  0-471-78293-9
- Excel 2007 For Dummies
  0-470-03737-7
- Mac OS X Tiger For Dummies
  0-7645-7675-5
- MacBook For Dummies
  0-470-04859-X
- Macs For Dummies
  0-470-04849-2
- Office 2007 For Dummies
  0-470-00923-3

- Outlook 2007 For Dummies
  0-470-03830-6
- PCs For Dummies
  0-7645-8958-X
- Salesforce.com For Dummies
  0-470-04893-X
- Upgrading & Fixing Laptops For Dummies
  0-7645-8959-8
- Word 2007 For Dummies
  0-470-03658-3
- Quicken 2007 For Dummies
  0-470-04600-7

## FOOD, HOME, GARDEN, HOBBIES, MUSIC & PETS

0-7645-8404-9

0-7645-9904-6

**Also available:**
- Candy Making For Dummies
  0-7645-9734-5
- Card Games For Dummies
  0-7645-9910-0
- Crocheting For Dummies
  0-7645-4151-X
- Dog Training For Dummies
  0-7645-8418-9
- Healthy Carb Cookbook For Dummies
  0-7645-8476-6
- Home Maintenance For Dummies
  0-7645-5215-5

- Horses For Dummies
  0-7645-9797-3
- Jewelry Making & Beading For Dummies
  0-7645-2571-9
- Orchids For Dummies
  0-7645-6759-4
- Puppies For Dummies
  0-7645-5255-4
- Rock Guitar For Dummies
  0-7645-5356-9
- Sewing For Dummies
  0-7645-6847-7
- Singing For Dummies
  0-7645-2475-5

## INTERNET & DIGITAL MEDIA

0-470-04529-9

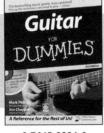

0-470-04894-8

**Also available:**
- Blogging For Dummies
  0-471-77084-1
- Digital Photography For Dummies
  0-7645-9802-3
- Digital Photography All-in-One Desk Reference For Dummies
  0-470-03743-1
- Digital SLR Cameras and Photography For Dummies
  0-7645-9803-1
- eBay Business All-in-One Desk Reference For Dummies
  0-7645-8438-3
- HDTV For Dummies
  0-470-09673-X

- Home Entertainment PCs For Dummies
  0-470-05523-5
- MySpace For Dummies
  0-470-09529-6
- Search Engine Optimization For Dummies
  0-471-97998-8
- Skype For Dummies
  0-470-04891-3
- The Internet For Dummies
  0-7645-8996-2
- Wiring Your Digital Home For Dummies
  0-471-91830-X

**\* Separate Canadian edition also available**
**† Separate U.K. edition also available**

## SPORTS, FITNESS, PARENTING, RELIGION & SPIRITUALITY

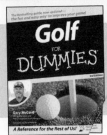

0-471-76871-

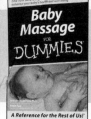

0-7645-7841-3

**Also available:**
- Catholicism For Dummies
  0-7645-5391-7
- Exercise Balls For Dummies
  0-7645-5623-1
- Fitness For Dummies
  0-7645-7851-0
- Football For Dummies
  0-7645-3936-1
- Judaism For Dummies
  0-7645-5299-6
- Potty Training For Dummies
  0-7645-5417-4
- Buddhism For Dummies
  0-7645-5359-3

- Pregnancy For Dummies
  0-7645-4483-7 †
- Ten Minute Tone-Ups For Dummies
  0-7645-7207-5
- NASCAR For Dummies
  0-7645-7681-X
- Religion For Dummies
  0-7645-5264-3
- Soccer For Dummies
  0-7645-5229-5
- Women in the Bible For Dummies
  0-7645-8475-8

## TRAVEL

0-7645-7749-2

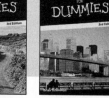

0-7645-6945-7

**Also available:**
- Alaska For Dummies
  0-7645-7746-8
- Cruise Vacations For Dummies
  0-7645-6941-4
- England For Dummies
  0-7645-4276-1
- Europe For Dummies
  0-7645-7529-5
- Germany For Dummies
  0-7645-7823-5
- Hawaii For Dummies
  0-7645-7402-7

- Italy For Dummies
  0-7645-7386-1
- Las Vegas For Dummies
  0-7645-7382-9
- London For Dummies
  0-7645-4277-X
- Paris For Dummies
  0-7645-7630-5
- RV Vacations For Dummies
  0-7645-4442-X
- Walt Disney World & Orlando
  For Dummies
  0-7645-9660-8

## GRAPHICS, DESIGN & WEB DEVELOPMENT

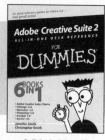

0-7645-8815-X

0-7645-9571-7

**Also available:**
- 3D Game Animation For Dummies
  0-7645-8789-7
- AutoCAD 2006 For Dummies
  0-7645-8925-3
- Building a Web Site For Dummies
  0-7645-7144-3
- Creating Web Pages For Dummies
  0-470-08030-2
- Creating Web Pages All-in-One Desk
  Reference For Dummies
  0-7645-4345-8
- Dreamweaver 8 For Dummies
  0-7645-9649-7

- InDesign CS2 For Dummies
  0-7645-9572-5
- Macromedia Flash 8 For Dummies
  0-7645-9691-8
- Photoshop CS2 and Digital
  Photography For Dummies
  0-7645-9580-6
- Photoshop Elements 4 For Dummies
  0-471-77483-9
- Syndicating Web Sites with RSS Feeds
  For Dummies
  0-7645-8848-6
- Yahoo! SiteBuilder For Dummies
  0-7645-9800-7

## NETWORKING, SECURITY, PROGRAMMING & DATABASES

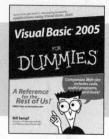

0-7645-7728-X

0-471-74940-0

**Also available:**
- Access 2007 For Dummies
  0-470-04612-0
- ASP.NET 2 For Dummies
  0-7645-7907-X
- C# 2005 For Dummies
  0-7645-9704-3
- Hacking For Dummies
  0-470-05235-X
- Hacking Wireless Networks
  For Dummies
  0-7645-9730-2
- Java For Dummies
  0-470-08716-1

- Microsoft SQL Server 2005 For Dummies
  0-7645-7755-7
- Networking All-in-One Desk Reference
  For Dummies
  0-7645-9939-9
- Preventing Identity Theft For Dummies
  0-7645-7336-5
- Telecom For Dummies
  0-471-77085-X
- Visual Studio 2005 All-in-One Desk
  Reference For Dummies
  0-7645-9775-2
- XML For Dummies
  0-7645-8845-1

## HEALTH & SELF-HELP

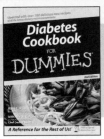

0-7645-8450-2

0-7645-4149-8

**Also available:**

- Bipolar Disorder For Dummies
  0-7645-8451-0
- Chemotherapy and Radiation
  For Dummies
  0-7645-7832-4
- Controlling Cholesterol For Dummies
  0-7645-5440-9
- Diabetes For Dummies
  0-7645-6820-5* †
- Divorce For Dummies
  0-7645-8417-0 †

- Fibromyalgia For Dummies
  0-7645-5441-7
- Low-Calorie Dieting For Dummies
  0-7645-9905-4
- Meditation For Dummies
  0-471-77774-9
- Osteoporosis For Dummies
  0-7645-7621-6
- Overcoming Anxiety For Dummies
  0-7645-5447-6
- Reiki For Dummies
  0-7645-9907-0
- Stress Management For Dummies
  0-7645-5144-2

## EDUCATION, HISTORY, REFERENCE & TEST PREPARATION

0-7645-8381-6

0-7645-9554-7

**Also available:**

- The ACT For Dummies
  0-7645-9652-7
- Algebra For Dummies
  0-7645-5325-9
- Algebra Workbook For Dummies
  0-7645-8467-7
- Astronomy For Dummies
  0-7645-8465-0
- Calculus For Dummies
  0-7645-2498-4
- Chemistry For Dummies
  0-7645-5430-1
- Forensics For Dummies
  0-7645-5580-4

- Freemasons For Dummies
  0-7645-9796-5
- French For Dummies
  0-7645-5193-0
- Geometry For Dummies
  0-7645-5324-0
- Organic Chemistry I For Dummies
  0-7645-6902-3
- The SAT I For Dummies
  0-7645-7193-1
- Spanish For Dummies
  0-7645-5194-9
- Statistics For Dummies
  0-7645-5423-9

# Get smart @ dummies.com®

- **Find a full list of Dummies titles**
- **Look into loads of FREE on-site articles**
- **Sign up for FREE eTips e-mailed to you weekly**
- **See what other products carry the Dummies name**
- **Shop directly from the Dummies bookstore**
- **Enter to win new prizes every month!**

**\* Separate Canadian edition also available**
**† Separate U.K. edition also available**

Available wherever books are sold. For more information or to order direct: U.S. customers visit www.dummies.com or call 1-877-762-2974.
U.K. customers visit www.wileyeurope.com or call 0800 243407. Canadian customers visit www.wiley.ca or call 1-800-567-4797.

| Action | Keyboard |
|---|---|
| Stop or restart an automatic slide show | S<br>or<br>+ (plus sign) |
| End a slide show | Any of the following:<br>Esc<br>Ctrl + Break<br>- (hyphen) |
| Erase on-screen annotations | E |
| Go to next hidden slide | H |
| Set new timings while rehearsing | T |
| Use original timings while rehearsing | O |
| Use mouse-click to advance while rehearsing | M |
| Return to the first slide | Both mouse buttons for 2 seconds |
| Redisplay hidden pointer and/or change the pointer to a pen | Ctrl + P |
| Redisplay hidden pointer and/or change the pointer to an arrow | Ctrl + A |
| Hide the pointer and button immediately | Ctrl + H |
| Hide the pointer and button in 15 seconds | Ctrl + U |
| Display the shortcut menu | Shift + F10<br>or<br>right-click |
| Go to the first or next hyperlink on a slide | Tab |
| Go to the last or previous hyperlink on a slide | Shift + Tab |
| Perform the mouse-click behavior of the selected hyperlink | Enter while a hyperlink is selected |
| Perform the mouse-over behavior of the selected hyperlink | Shift + Enter while a hyperlink is selected |

*These keyboard shortcuts work while a PowerPoint slide show is being presented in full-screen mode. You can press F1 during a slide show to see a list of controls.*

| Table 3-3 | Creating and Editing Presentations |
|---|---|
| **Action** | *Keyboard* |
| Create a new presentation | Ctrl + N |
| Insert a new slide | Ctrl + M |
| Make a copy of the selected slide | Ctrl + D |
| Open a presentation | Ctrl + O |
| Save a presentation | Ctrl + S |

*(continued)*

**Table 3-3** *(continued)*

| Action | Keyboard |
| --- | --- |
| Close a presentation | Ctrl + W |
| Print a presentation | Ctrl + P |
| Run a presentation | F5 |
| Quit PowerPoint | Alt + F4 |
| Find text, formatting, and special items | Ctrl + F |
| Replace text, specific formatting, and special items | Ctrl + H |
| Insert a hyperlink | Ctrl + K |
| Check spelling | F7 |
| Cancel an action | Esc |
| Undo an action | Ctrl + Z |
| Redo or repeat an action | Ctrl + Y |
| Switch to the next pane (clockwise) | F6 |
| Switch to the previous pane (counterclockwise) | Shift + F6 |

**Table 3-4**      **Deleting and Copying Text and Objects**

| Action | Keyboard |
| --- | --- |
| Delete one character to the left | Backspace |
| Delete one word to the left | Ctrl + Backspace |
| Delete one character to the right | Delete |
| Delete one word to the right | Ctrl + Delete |
| Cut selected object | Ctrl + X |
| Copy selected object | Ctrl + C |
| Paste cut or copied object | Ctrl + V |
| Undo the last action | Ctrl + Z |

**Table 3-5**      **Moving around in Text**

| Action | Keyboard |
| --- | --- |
| Move one character to the left | ← |
| Move one character to the right | → |
| Move one line up | ↑ |
| Move one line down | ↓ |
| Move one word to the left | Ctrl + ← |
| Move one word to the right | Ctrl + → |

| Action | Keyboard |
|---|---|
| Move to end of a line | End |
| Move to beginning of a line | Home |
| Move up one paragraph | Ctrl + ↑ |
| Move down one paragraph | Ctrl + ↓ |
| Move to end of a text box | Ctrl + End |
| Move to beginning of a text box | Ctrl + Home |
| Move to the next title or body text placeholder* | Ctrl + Enter |
| Repeat the last Find action | Shift + F4 |

\* When the last placeholder on a slide is selected, press Ctrl + Enter to insert a new slide in the presentation.

| Table 3-6 | Selecting Text and Objects |
|---|---|
| **Action** | **Keyboard** |
| Select one character to the right | Shift + → |
| Select one character to the left | Shift + ← |
| Select to the end of a word | Ctrl + Shift + → |
| Select to the beginning of a word | Ctrl + Shift + ← |
| Select one line up | Shift + ↑ |
| Select one line down | Shift + ↓ |
| Select an object (with text selected inside the object) | Esc |
| Select an object (with an object selected) | Tab or Shift + Tab until the object you want is selected |
| Select text within an object | Enter |
| Select all objects in the slide pane | Ctrl + A |
| Select all slides in the slide sorter view | Ctrl + A |
| Select all text in the outline pane | Ctrl + A |

| Table 3-7 | Changing or Resizing the Font |
|---|---|
| **Action** | **Keyboard** |
| Change font | Ctrl + Shift + F |
| Change font size | Ctrl + Shift + P |
| Increase font size | Ctrl + Shift + > |
| Decrease font size | Ctrl + Shift + < |

| Table 3-8 | Applying Character Formats |
|---|---|
| *Action* | *Keyboard* |
| Change formatting of characters (Font command, Format menu) | Ctrl + T |
| Change case of letters | Shift + F3 |
| Apply bold formatting | Ctrl + B |
| Apply underline | Ctrl + U |
| Apply italic formatting | Ctrl + I |
| Apply subscript formatting (automatic spacing) | Ctrl + = |
| Apply superscript formatting (automatic spacing) | Ctrl + Shift + + |
| Remove manual character formatting | Ctrl + spacebar |

| Table 3-9 | Copying Text Formats |
|---|---|
| *Action* | *Keyboard* |
| Copy formats | Ctrl + Shift + C |
| Paste formats | Ctrl + Shift + V |

| Table 3-10 | Aligning Paragraphs and Indents |
|---|---|
| *Action* | *Keyboard* |
| Center a paragraph | Ctrl + E |
| Justify a paragraph | Ctrl + J |
| Left-align a paragraph | Ctrl + L |
| Right-align a paragraph | Ctrl + R |

| Table 3-11 | Working in an Outline or Slide Pane |
|---|---|
| *Action* | *Keyboard* |
| Promote a paragraph | Alt + Shift + ← |
| Demote a paragraph | Alt + Shift + → |
| Move selected paragraphs up | Alt + Shift + ↑ |
| Move selected paragraphs down | Alt + Shift + ↓ |
| Show heading level 1 | Alt + Shift + 1 |
| Expand text below a heading | Alt + Shift + + |
| Collapse text below a heading | Alt + Shift + - |
| Show all text or headings | Alt + Shift + A |
| Turn character formatting on or off | / |